Praise for *Cinema and th*

"There are few books in film and media studies that can match the scope, erudition, explanatory ambition, and polemical edge of Lee Grieveson's invaluable history of how corporations and government agencies deployed and fundamentally shaped cinema (and other media) as an engine for and emblem of advanced liberal capitalism."

GREGORY A. WALLER, Provost Professor in the Media School, Indiana University

"Grieveson presents the definitive account of media's primacy to our modern world's corporatized and imperiled commons. This is paradigm-shifting work that lays bare for the first time—with lucidity, breadth of vision, and unparalleled detail—the logic of liberal capitalism underwriting film's and radio's infrastructural history in Britain and the United States."

PRIYA JAIKUMAR, Associate Professor, Department of Cinema and Media Studies, University of Southern California

"Lee Grieveson's cultural-materialist tour de force ruthlessly examines the global history of movies and money, detailing the sordid global backstory behind the uncertain and unequal balance between art and commerce. This rigorously researched and deeply felt radical media study evinces a perceptive and thoroughgoing analysis of a medium that has from its outset served an exploitative political economy."

JON LEWIS, author of *Hard-Boiled Hollywood: Crime and Punishment in Postwar Los Angeles*

"This book is a brilliant synthesis of biopolitical theory and concrete historical research. Grieveson shows us how the imperial ambitions of the United States materialize in the content and infrastructure of American media industries. His lucid and persuasive prose dramatizes the centrality of media systems in evolving conceptions of global governance and state power."

ANNA MCCARTHY, Professor of Cinema Studies, New York University

"The interpenetration of the state, finance capitalism, and film is central to this formidable book. I am awed by the volume of scholarship, the force of the analysis, and the style of the narrative. This is a book that will open up a significant subfield in film studies."

COLIN MACCABE, Distinguished Professor of English and Film, University of Pittsburgh

Cinema and the Wealth of Nations

The publisher gratefully acknowledges the generous support of the Ahmanson Foundation Humanities Endowment Fund of the University of California Press Foundation.

Cinema and the Wealth of Nations

Media, Capital, and the Liberal World System

Lee Grieveson

UNIVERSITY OF CALIFORNIA PRESS

University of California Press, one of the most distinguished university presses in the United States, enriches lives around the world by advancing scholarship in the humanities, social sciences, and natural sciences. Its activities are supported by the UC Press Foundation and by philanthropic contributions from individuals and institutions. For more information, visit www.ucpress.edu.

University of California Press
Oakland, California

© 2018 by The Regents of the University of California

Library of Congress Cataloging-in-Publication Data

Names: Grieveson, Lee, 1969- author.
Title: Cinema and the wealth of nations : media, capital, and the liberal world system / Lee Grieveson.
Description: Oakland, California : University of California Press, [2017] | Includes bibliographical references and index. | Identifiers: LCCN 2017019642 (print) | LCCN 2017022858 (ebook) | ISBN 9780520965348 (ebook) | ISBN 9780520291683 (cloth : alk. paper) | ISBN 9780520291690 (pbk. : alk. paper)
Subjects: LCSH: Motion pictures—Political aspects—United States. | Industrial films—United States. | Motion pictures in propaganda—United States. | Motion pictures and globalization. | Capitalism and mass media.
Classification: LCC PN1995.9.P6 (ebook) | LCC PN1995.9.P6 G75 2017 (print) | DDC 791.43/6581—dc23
LC record available at https://lccn.loc.gov/2017019642

Manufactured in the United States of America

27 26 25 24 23 22 21 20 19 18
10 9 8 7 6 5 4 3 2 1

For Lora, and the future, with love
In memory of Barbara, Campbell, Ken, Moyra, Susan, and Vallie

CONTENTS

ILLUSTRATIONS

ACKNOWLEDGMENTS

I have been researching and writing this book for longer than I care to remember. Or indeed can. I got debts that no honest man can pay . . . I offer here but a small down payment on the interest. But a crucial one, because what I have written about and how I have written about it have been profoundly shaped by a lot of people, some of whom I know personally, and am lucky enough to count as family and friends, and some of whom I know only through reading or watching their work. The book that follows would not have been written without them. Latterly, I have come to think of it as a little like the city I work in: a hub through which people, histories, conversations, ideas, and experiences pass. I shall start with the happiest and most profound of these shaping experiences, my partner, Lora, to whom this book is dedicated with love—not least because it simply would not have happened in the way it did without the conversations we have had and the life we have built and lived, happily, together. I have tried to live up to the challenge and the ideals and ethics that Lora embodies and that emerge from her own experiences and commitment to community, family, and forms of civic service. I am grateful for each day we are together; none of them passes without laughter, fun, and myriad acts of kindness and love. Commitment to kindness, generosity, and forms of communal and civic service are integral to the lives of so many of my extended family, stretching from my mum, Barbara (a nurse); to Vanessa, my friend and generous coparent to our loves, Lauren and Riley (also a nurse); to Vanessa's remarkable mum, Moyra (a former nurse); to Lora's lovely mum, Sarah, and her partner, Kathy (both former school teachers, among other things); and beyond that to Lora's grandmother Vallie. I am blessed to have had the guidance of this long line of smart, tough, kind, generous women and to count them all as family.

Plenty of other people have helped along the way. Peter Kramer read every word of this book. It was characteristically generous of him to do so, and the book is immeasurably better for it. Peter is simply one of the most brilliant people I have ever known. Recently our conversations have circled around questions of the usefulness of scholarship, and by one measure the book that follows is an attempt to think further about that question, often with Peter's voice in my head and his comments on the manuscript as my guide. (The book was also shaped along these lines through conversations with Lora about the usefulness of the work we can do.) Peter is my acid test: if I can partly persuade him, I figure I am somewhat right. I believe I can count some victories in that, if also some losses (yes, I am too top-down, too categorical, and the list goes on); but the victories with Peter are precious because he is properly, *genuinely,* brilliant. Generous with it, too – his is not the scholarship of personal gain, of prestige and ambition, of petty state and institutionally mandated "excellence" but rather of curiosity and the attempt to think about complicated ideas by building on and engaging with the work of others.

If parts of this book were hashed out on the phone with Peter, large parts of it took shape on Kay Dickinson's sofa, in various states. Kay took me to Cairo with her a few years ago. I have learned a great deal about the world outside of texts from Kay, as well as about the necessity and possibility of a politicized media studies. The book that follows was profoundly informed by that learning and injunction. I have some catching up to do, as I always do with Kay, but I am learning from her example. I miss her sofa, and laughter, now located mostly in Canada. Recently I have benefited from time spent on Mark Betz's sofa, and I have rehearsed parts of what follows in dialogue with Mark late into the night. Betz is smart, and trenchant, about a lot of things, and wickedly funny too (author of perhaps the best joke in the book that follows: it is short, and you will have to look for it in an end-note, but it is worth it). Betz, Kay, and Peter all have a radical commitment to pedagogy and to turning knowledge into something that can be useful. I have tried to learn.

Partway through the researching and writing of this book, I became codirector, with Colin MacCabe, of a large Arts and Humanities Research Council Resource Enhancement grant for a project on British colonial cinema. (The principal results can be found at www.colonialfilm.org.) I did so because of my commitment to explicating and making available cinema produced in the service of empire but equally for the opportunity to work again alongside Colin. The experience profoundly shaped my thinking (and this book, which was not "this" book before our collaboration). I still regularly recall one small conversation with Colin that took place on the balcony of an apartment he was staying at in Hyderabad, in which he simply dismissed some of my angst and arguments by explaining that we are trying to get as close to the truth as we can. Colin's generosity was why I was in India at all, another profoundly transformative exchange (after Cairo), and this generosity is one of Colin's defining characteristics. Our project succeeded in large part because of our good fortune in hiring Tom Rice to carry out large parts of the research and organization. Tom was a PhD student of mine but quickly became simply a friend and then a trusted colleague. I learned a great deal about British colonial cinema—which features in this book—from Tom. I have greatly valued his friendship these past years. Crucial to that colonial team also was Francis Gooding, a former student of Colin's and a brilliant thinker. F. G. is now a close friend and coconspirator on various things.

Outside of the (dis-)United Kingdom, my close friend Haidee Wasson has been a regular source of support and inspiration. Haidee and I have edited two books together, and I have learned a great deal from her scholarship and commitment to the highest standards of professionalism. She has also taught me much about building institutions and disciplines that are ethical and useful. Because of Haidee, I have gotten to know Charles Acland better and have learned much about the ethics of scholarship and pedagogy as a result. I owe debts to countless other friends, who have helped in ways large and small: David Rodowick for myriad acts of kindness, advice, support; to Jon Lewis for our developing email dialogue and friendship, which switches from football to cinema to life to politics easily (plus Jon's brilliant wife, Martha, who so generously stepped in at the last minute to help with the artwork for this book); Gregory Waller not only for the considerable example of his scholarship but for his generosity and support, which have meant a lot to me over the years; Laura Mulvey for the fun, friendship, and adventure of coteaching a class together; Rebecca Barden for friendship, laughter, and solidarity; Shelley Stamp for being such a generous friend over the years (on which more below); Priya Jaikumar for the pleasures of becoming her friend and for all that I learn through talking with her; Angelique Richardson for being funny and a good friend; and Noah Angell for (among other things) fun and thought-provoking adventures with the pen. Many other people have asked questions, have made comments, and have kindly invited me to talk and share some of this research. This likely not inclusive list includes, in no particular order, Charlie Musser, Joshua Malitsky, J. D. Connor, Charlie Keil, Marissa Moorman, Peter Stanfield, Madhava Prasad, Brian Larkin, Masha Salazkina, Enrique Fibula, Tom Gunning, Luca Caminati, Eric Smoodin, Ravi Vasudevan, Giorgio Bertellini, Lisa Parks, Eithne Quinn, Anna McCarthy, Martin Lefebvre, Jon Burrows, David Francis Phillips, Connie Balides, S. V. Srinivas, David Trotter, Shakuntala Banaji, Roberta Pearson, Margot Brill, William Uricchio, David Nye, J. E. Smyth, Martin Stollery, Richard Butsch, Lydia Papadimitriou, Scott Anthony, Paul McDonald, Timothy Corrigan, Chris O'Rourke, Jacqueline Maingard, Richard Osborne, David Forgacs, Philip Rosen, Ronald Walter Greene, Zoë Druik, Simon Potter, Vinzenz Hediger, Emma Sandon, Yvonne Zimmermann, Marina Dahlquist, Brian Jacobson, and Pierluigi Ercoli. Stefan Lemasson, Jonathan Brill, and Noah Angell generously helped with the artwork at the last minute. Our competitive environment does not always foster collegiality, but all of these people have been generous and kind.

I am grateful also to audiences at the following institutions: Concordia University; University of Nottingham; Harvard University; University of Essex; University of Stockholm; Indiana University; University College London; University of Sussex; University of Manchester; University of Pennsylvania; Liverpool John Moores University; Birkbeck College, University of London; University of St. Andrews; University of Cork; University of Nottingham in Malaysia; University of Warwick; University of Cambridge; English and Foreign Language University, Hyderabad; University of Kent; University of Bristol; Frankfurt University; and the University of Pittsburgh. I have learned a great deal from many other scholars, whom I have never met, as the notes to this book make clear. I should like to state here that this book simply would not be what it is without the scholarship and thinking of (in no particular order) Noam Chomsky, Stuart Ewen, Robert McChesney, Emily Rosenberg, David Harvey, Michel Foucault, Giovanni Arrighi, Eric Hobsbawm, Janet Wasko, Perry Anderson, C. B. Macpherson, Immanuel Wallerstein, Toby Miller, Abderrahmane Sissako, Howard Zinn, Oliver Zunz, and Adam Curtis, among many others.

I am enormously grateful to the University of California Press for publishing this book at this length. I owe a huge debt of gratitude to Mary Francis for soliciting this book for the press, for sticking with me over the years it took to research and write it, as well as for conversations that helped shape it. Mary solicited two very smart and helpful peer-review reports on the book. One of the readers identified himself as Mark Lynn Anderson, a scholar whose work I have long admired. Mark wrote a wonderfully supportive but rightly challenging review that asked me to think hard about what alliances could be made in the formulation of my ideas. (Echoing also my friend Kay.) It was a very useful lesson, which helped me reframe parts of the book. Mark also kindly shared with me some of his own archival findings, which were important as I researched and wrote the chapter on the Hollywood studio system. Once again this is an example of collegiality and solidarity, for which I am greatly thankful. Raina Polivka came on board after Mary moved on to the University of Michigan Press and has been a calm and greatly supportive editor, as she confidently ushered the book into the final stages of completion and production. Raina sent the very long first draft to Shelley Stamp to read and comment on and help shorten. Shelley has long been a friend and inspiration (she was also a reader on my first book for the press, a fortuitous—for me—circularity). Shelley made it clear that the book needed to be simpler, sharper, and a better guide for the readers of this complex history. Raina echoed this critique, and I returned to the book for the final round of significant revisions with these injunctions in mind. The book has been *immeasurably* improved because of their advice. Put another way: if it seems long and wordy now, you should have read the version

Shelley (and Peter) patiently read and improved. I am grateful also for the help of many others at the press who have worked to produce this book, including in particular Zuha Khan, project editor Francisco Reinking, copy editor Ann Donahue, and indexer Conrad Ryan.

I have institutional debts too. UCL's Centre for Multidisciplinary and Intercultural Inquiry has been a productive and collegial space to work within, and for that thanks are owed in particular to my friends Stephanie Bird and Patrizia Oliver. I also thank colleagues within the centre and at UCL, including Roland Francois-Lack, Florian Mussgnug, Kevin Inston, Andy Leak, Joanna Evans, Jo Wolff, Stephen Hart, Ann Varley, Mark Hewitson, Julia Wagner, Claire Thomson, Keith Wagner, Kate Foster, Matthew Beaumont, Philip Horne, Melvyn Stokes, and Helene Neveu Kringelbach. I also owe a debt of gratitude to the Department of Visual and Environmental Studies at Harvard, where I spent a happy and productive year as a visitor during a crucial juncture in the research and writing of this book (albeit while the global financial system teetered on the verge of collapse). My research and thinking have been greatly helped by the smart students I have taught and learned alongside at Harvard, and especially at UCL—even more particularly in the political media class I have taught at the latter these past few years. I have been blessed that smart young people from around the world have found their way to London and my classes. Our conversations have been transformative, and I am humbled by the work these students have gone on to do.

Researching and writing this book were made possible by fellowships from the Arts and Humanities Research Council and the Leverhulme Trust. I am profoundly grateful to both and to UCL for sabbatical leaves. Research and thinking take time, despite the constant injunction to make them more "efficient" now that market logics suffuse education. Considerable thanks are owed also to many archivists and librarians, who helped me navigate the material that is central to the history that follows, at the following institutions, including the National Archives in Washington, DC; National Archives II at College Park, Maryland; the Library of Congress (particularly Madeline Matz and Rosemary Hanes); the British Film Institute National Archive (especially Patrick Russell); the British Library; the National Archives, London; the Chicago Public Library; the New York Public Library (in particular the Rare Books and Manuscript Division and the Billy Rose Theatre Collection); the Institute of Advanced Legal Studies at the University of London; the Academy of Motion Picture Arts and Sciences, the Margaret Herrick Library in Los Angeles (in particular Kristine Krueger); the Widener library and Baker Library and Special Collections at Harvard University (in particular Jennifer Beauregard); Benson Ford Research Centre in Dearborn, Michigan; the Modern Records Centre, University of Warwick; the Department of Special Collections at the Bodleian Library in Oxford; the League of Nations Archives, Geneva; the Imperial War Museum Film Archive (especially Kay Gladstone); and the UCL and

Senate House Libraries at the University of London. Online archives have also been extremely helpful, including, in particular, the significant Prelinger Archives, the Media History Digital Library at the Internet Archive, the Motion Picture Producers and Distributors of America Digital Archive (housed at Flinders University), and the aforementioned Colonial Film Project hosted by the British Film Institute. I am hopeful that I may never have to go to another archive to search through lots of confusing material. But for the help I received while doing so over these past years: thank you.

Lastly I come to thanking my beloved, adored kids, in order of age: Riley, Lauren, and Cooper. Riley never fails to make me smile and laugh. I treasure the fun and conversations I have had with Lauren as she has grown into a confident, smart, funny young woman. Cooper is impossibly adorable, and these past three years have passed (together with his nearly equally adorable mum) in a whirl of tiredness, laughter, and joy. I am not thanking the three of them for helping me finish this book, in fact quite the reverse: really, it is entirely their fault it has taken so long. *But* I am thanking them for that: for the distractions, for the injunctions to leave the office and live; for the challenges; and for the nonstop, relentless fun and laughter. Debts here become shared gifts. The best parts of the years spent researching and writing this book were spent with them—and I hope for more of those moments in the future.

Lee Grieveson, London, June 2017

The Silver Screen and the Gold Standard

Cinema and the Wealth of Nations explores how media, principally in the form of cinema, was used by elite institutions, such as states, corporations, and investment banks, to establish and facilitate a form of liberal political economy that began in the nineteenth century and spread globally thereafter. Didactic and persuasive cinema, and the organizations formed to produce and circulate it, is an important part of this story. I also explore how in the 1920s a corporate media industry was established, and then synchronized with finance capital and other large technology and telecommunications companies, as part of a new corporate-dominated consumer economy. I explore these twin developments of persuasive and commercial media as a *history,* ultimately, of how media was fashioned to supplement forms of territorial and economic imperialism during the interwar years. During this period, the United States eclipsed a British-dominated liberal world system and inaugurated new forms of economic globalization founded on a compact between state and capital. Media played significant roles in that consequential process.

The subject of this history is the enmeshing of media and liberal political economy at the foundation of the modern world of globalized capital, principally from 1913 to 1939, which marked the slow dissolve from one world system to another. But this is not a distant history. *Cinema and the Wealth of Nations* at its broadest is a genealogy of how media was used to encode liberal political and economic power. I examine a specific and foundational conjuncture—the establishment of media forms and a media system instrumental in, and structural to, the emergence and expansion of a *militantly neo*liberal world system that has been (and continues to be) brutally violent, unequal, and destructive.

But first the history: various powerful organizations began to use cinema in the early twentieth century to shape the attitudes and conduct of people, as well as new political and economic practices. Vast numbers of films were produced by the governments of the United States and Britain; by some of the largest corporations of the modern age, such as Ford Motor Company, US Steel, General Electric (GE), and General Motors; and by associated industrial and lobbying groups like the US Chamber of Commerce, the National Association of Manufacturers, and, in Britain, the Federation of British Industries. Powerful agencies engaged in struggles over modes of production, material resources, and axes of exploitation made and circulated media. Frequently the films were collaborations between state and corporate institutions.

Broadly speaking, these films explicated and extolled the advantages of the new technologies, economic practices, and infrastructural and circulatory networks of the second-stage industrial revolution and the ascendant corporate and monopoly stage of capitalism. How to live and consume in the new eras of mass production and consumption were common subjects. Propaganda institutions were also established by states that both produced and monitored media, and these expanded and "exceptional" governmental practices continued thereafter. New forms of distribution and mobile exhibition created alternative networks for the circulation and display of this persuasive media, placing it in extant civil and industrial spaces, such as schools, universities, prisons, and factories. Novel technologies, including mobile cinema vans, circulated media across remote areas in the US interior or across the sprawling British Empire. Over time these intertwined state and corporate practices produced new and innovative film forms, including in 1920s Britain what came to be called "documentary," which was established to help sustain the political economy of liberal empire. Etched still in the photosensitive, halogen silver salts of celluloid, albeit now at times rerendered as digital data, is a record of the modern world of advanced liberal capitalism as it began to coalesce through the actions of the same powerful state and economic institutions that made and circulated the films.

I argue throughout this book that these films, technologies, networks, and media forms were intentionally integrated to shape the conduct of populations and ultimately to facilitate and supplement the establishment of new forms of liberal political economy across the world. Frequently this media was disseminated through newly created educational networks and used to educate and socialize particular populations in new "productive" practices and identities. The films, and the institutions that produced and circulated them, were part of an expansive liberal praxis, driven by political and economic elites to establish new forms of subjective, economic, and political order fit for the new modality of mass production, consumption, and corporate and monopoly capital. Cameras caught the escalation and proliferation of the second stage of the industrial age: the mechanization of agriculture alongside the expansion of extractive mining of mineral and energy resources and the integration of the rural and imperial periphery into a new urban and industrial order; the emergence and growth of the corporation and new forms of "corporate liberalism," which underscored the expansion of global trade;[1] the construction of new infrastructural networks to facilitate economic circulation (from railways to canals and from roads to communicative networks like the telephone and radio); and new procedures of factory mass production (along with efforts to socialize migrant and subaltern workers in new practices of wage labor). With these was the corresponding growth of a consumer economy, enabled by mass production and new distribution networks, that was integral to the broader "corporate reconstruction" of the economy that took place around the turn of the century.

Very little attention has been paid to the history, institutions, and forms of this elite pedagogic media. But I gamble here on the premise that it is worth looking closely at the films, institutions, and practices established by powerful elite organizations for what they reveal, both about the formation of the political and economic rationalities and practices that created our modern world and specifically about the ways media was used and shaped to elaborate that world.

Also critical to my analysis is an account of the commercial media system that emerged in this period as a significant supplement to new forms of consumer capitalism. The history of radio is extremely significant in this regard: formed from complex geopolitical struggles to control communication infrastructure between the residing (British) and emergent (US) world powers, developed through government mandate by large technology and telecommunications corporations in the United States (principally GE and American Telegraph and Telephone Company [AT&T]), and enshrined in US government policy in the 1927 Radio Act to be a medium financed by advertising and not, say, by state or educational actors.[2] I explore this history in chapter 9, "League of Corporations," drawing on the work of significant media historians. Here it is enough to simply observe that *policy* also frames the usefulness of media for a political and economic system that became tied to the expansion of a consumer economy from this precise point onward.

In 1919, the same year the US government, GE, and AT&T (principally) created the Radio Corporation of America (RCA) as a complex hybrid of government and corporate interests—the largest film studio, in what was starting to be called Hollywood, allied with an influential investment bank to attract pools of capital.[3] Paramount, as the studio came to be called, did so specifically to buy property in the form of cinemas and cinema chains, so as to "vertically integrate" by joining together separate aspects of the production, distribution, and exhibition of film into one corporate entity. It became the first media corporation to exercise significant control over all aspects of production, wholesaling, and retail, part of the broader corporate reconstruction of American capitalism that had begun with the railroads in the 1860s and had gathered pace in the 1890s.[4] Bankers played a significant role in that process, using the capital generated from investment—in Karl

Marx's classic formula, M-C-M′—to merge industrial firms into large corporations and controlled monopolistic or oligopolistic markets.[5] GE was formed in 1892 from a merger of separate electrical firms, brokered and financed by the investment banker J. P. Morgan, who had considerable financial interests in Edison GE.[6] By the early 1920s, cinema as exemplar of an emergent cultural industry peddling newly mechanized forms of transient pleasure in expensive real estate evidently began to seem like a productive site for the investment of finance capital. The "silver screen," said one of the investment bank reports written about cinema in the 1920s, could produce a "golden harvest."[7]

The corporate reconstruction of cinema in alliance with capital was consistent with the broader tendencies and logics of those developments as they accelerated from the latter parts of the nineteenth century. It catalyzed with the emergence of a consumer economy that gathered pace in particular in the 1920s, after the development of the corporation and mass production, that was ever-more predicated on spectacle, display, and, indeed, on the transformation of the commodity from a material object under a regime of use value to its dematerialization in relationships of exchange. New forms of value creation in the elicitation of desire and affect were produced in this process, exemplified by cinema and the expansion of new practices of advertising and "public relations." One of the most significant functions of corporate cinema/media may indeed have been to expand the images and associated values of a corporate-produced commodity culture, first across the "core" economies from which it emerged and quickly thereafter to "peripheral" regions across the world system.[8]

Both radio and cinema in its corporate phase were tied together with finance capital and integrated directly and expansively with the new practices of consumption integral to the dawning era of corporate capitalism. The studios, formed into corporate entities with pools of finance capital, began to control many of the most profitable theaters/properties in urban centers and the circulatory networks of distribution that were integral to the realization of rental value from the dematerialized commodity that was film. The corporate reconstruction of cinema and a broader media system produced by large vertically integrated entities with close ties to banks, and as an adjunct to the generation of capital, significantly shaped the forms and functions of that cinema/media thereafter. I shall lay some of my gambling cards on the table here: I take it as self-evident that the corporate and capital control over media, subsumed under the imperative to generate capital, marked a radical diminution of the possibilities of media culture. This, in turn, produced a media system that is patently antithetical to the communicative requirements of a democratic society.[9] The emergence of media forms that required extensive capitalization, and which were controlled by corporate and financial entities, catalyzed with the corporate reconstruction of capitalism and liberalism to radically limit the public sphere. I explore the history of the corporate (re)construction of media here not as an abstract, "academic" exercise but because that history has been integral to the orchestration of power in the modern world, as well as to the relentless expansion of commodity culture and a capitalist market economy across the global system.

Ties between film corporations and investment banks deepened across the 1920s. From around 1925, additional pools of finance capital flooded into the film industry, much of which was used to facilitate the "transition to sound," which resulted in significant alliances between some of the same large technology and telecommunications corporations involved in radio (and other sonic technologies like the telephone and phonograph) and film studios. The "talkies" were born "convergent," driven by the related goals of banks and corporations with interests in technology, patents and media, and established from the same year—1927—that the Radio Act was passed. It makes sense to view these developments together rather than separately, as is usually done (one example of the doleful consequences of the balkanization of the study of media). The synchronization of media, capital, technology, and telecommunications in this period marked something like a "big bang" for the formation of enduring "convergent" tendencies across these sectors, as well as for the further shaping of media as a commodity synced to the generation of capital. GE, to continue with that organization, both as exemplar and as an entity that is extremely important in and of itself, maintained significant control over RCA and created NBC, the radio network, in 1926 and RKO, the vertically integrated film studio, in 1928. GE and other technology and telecommunications corporations considered media to be significant profit generators across various sectors that included technology and intellectual property, as well as box-office.

The corporate reconstruction of media in the United States was enabled and facilitated by state action.[10] Broad developments such as the redefinition of the corporation itself from public entity to private property in the late nineteenth century, which accorded corporations the kinds of constitutional protections afforded individuals, were significant here, as was the related protection of expansive property rights.[11] Further developments helped the media produced by corporate entities to circulate globally. In the early 1920s, the US Department of Commerce proposed that "trade follows the motion pictures," effectively suggesting that film was a form of advertisement for the objects and lifestyles pictured within it, which thus could generate wealth for the nation.[12] After this, the US State Department began reporting on conditions affecting the circulation of moving pictures abroad in its *Daily Consular and Trade Reports,* putting the information-gathering capacities of its foreign and consular offices to work circulating both the pedagogic films produced by corporate and governmental institutions and commercial films produced by corporate media entities.[13] Quickly thereafter, the lobbying and trade group formed by the corporate film studios to advance their economic interests began pressing for the establishment of a motion picture section within the Bureau of

Foreign and Domestic Commerce. The corporate studios had cannily hired a well-connected former Republican Party national chairman called Will Hays to run its lobbying and public relations organization—an early example of the "revolving door" between political and economic elites that helps entrench policy decisions beneficial to capital.

In 1926, Congress responded positively to the request and appropriated resources to help films produced by corporate film studios circulate across the globe as what the influential commerce secretary (and later president) Herbert Hoover described as "a powerful influence on behalf of American goods."[14] Will Hays told students of the Harvard Business School the following year, "I could spend all of my allotted time telling you how the motion picture is selling goods abroad for every manufacturer . . . 'Trade follows the film.'"[15] (In his memoirs, he described the "foreign department" of the mainstream industry's lobbying and public relations arm as "almost an adjunct of our State Department."[16]) What began to emerge was a theory and practice of media's importance and usefulness for economic globalization that was carried through governmental institutions. These were created from partnerships between corporate media entities and the state that were mediated by a lobbying group managed by a well-remunerated member of the political elite. This was corporate liberalism in action. Movies began to operate as the avant-garde for the spread of US commodity culture and capital across the world system at the dawn of the century that would famously be labeled American.[17]

But the political elite in the residing global power, Britain, viewed this situation with considerable alarm. In 1926, the same year the Motion Picture Section was created, a significant imperial conference in London brought together Britain and the mostly white settler dominions to elaborate a system of economic protection for imperially produced goods to combat the rising economic power of the United States. Gathered around the high table of imperial politics to establish a "commonwealth" economic union, the politicians spent a lot of time talking about film. Some of this talk was prompted by the concerns of the trade and lobbying group the Federation of British Industries, which had also begun to argue that film from the United States was functioning like a shop window for the products of advanced US industry.[18] "It requires little imagination," said Sir Philip Cunliffe-Lister, president of the British Board of Trade, "to picture the effect on tens of millions of people seeing American films, staged in American settings, American clothes, American furniture, American motor cars, American goods of every kind."[19] Debates about film were held in the Houses of Parliament, where Conservative Party prime minister Stanley Baldwin talked of "the danger to which we in this country and our Empire subject ourselves if we allow that method of propaganda to be entirely in the hands of foreign countries."[20] Quickly after the imperial conference, the British state created a new institution, the Empire Marketing Board, to foster intraimperial economic exchange. This body housed a film unit that developed "a method of propaganda," to use Baldwin's term, that came to be called "documentary." The head of that unit, in language that registered the developing import of signification for Britain's economic and geopolitical power, talked of the necessity of developing new practices to "project" state power.[21] Documentary emerged as a form of state-produced pedagogical media in the midst of broader geopolitical and economic struggles, largely between the imperial British state and the ascendant US state, which had helped circulate corporate media as a visible signifier of its growing economic importance in the world system. Documentary was a filmic practice born directly of liberal imperialism and the imperative to maintain imperial order and economic primacy in the global capitalist system.

The production of documentary dovetailed with new practices of regulation. In 1927, after pressure from the Federation of British Industries in particular, a form of tariff protection specifically to curtail the movement of US film through its empire was erected by the British.[22] The protection for film preceded the erection of broader tariff protections elaborated during the Depression in the early 1930s, when the British state undertook a momentous shift away from the liberal free trade policies that were integral to imperialism toward a new protectionist regime.[23] Put more forthrightly, film was privileged in this significant transformation of global economic strategies because of its purported semiotic power, which political elites on both sides of the Atlantic began to read as either a supplement or impediment to the fostering of economic growth taken as integral to the remit of the liberal state. British elites worried also that this semiotic power undermined the fictions of racial hierarchy that were integral to imperialism. "I do not suppose that there is anything which has done so much harm to the prestige and position of Western people and the white race," said the Conservative Party former president of the Board of Trade and chancellor Sir Robert Horne, "as the exhibition of films which have tended to degrade us in the eyes of peoples who have been accustomed to look upon us with admiration and respect."[24] Quite clearly the regulation of media dovetailed with the production of media—the Empire Marketing Board film unit having started in 1927, the same time as the Cinematograph Films Act— and both strategies were tied principally to the imperatives of capital, as well as to related concerns about the "projection" of imperial and geopolitical power under a regime of territorial imperialism.

I come back to this history in chapter 8, "Highways of Empire," but it is worth underscoring here that this dialectic of regulation and production marks a dominant logic attending liberal state engagement with media that tends to be split between the production/use of media (and corresponding design of media policy) and the regulation of media regarded as damaging to political and economic goals. I have written previously about the regulation of cinema as part of the liberal regulation of populations. Here I focus more on the production and circulation of media as supplements to liberal governmental practice and political economy.[25] Both, however, are properly understood as dialectical strategies in the shaping of media to be of use to elite groups. Elsewhere in these pages, a similar dynamic will be visible in, for example, the creation of World War I–era propaganda institutions alongside expansive regulations to limit speech/media and prosecute "sedition."

The British strategy failed. Producing dull movies about imperial produce while regulating the circulation of corporate-produced media that seductively celebrated new forms of commodity culture failed to halt the global forces that were pushing the United States to the center of the world capitalist system. Prevalent among those forces were indeed the large transnational corporations which grew from the second-stage industrial revolution, including the technology, telecommunications, and media corporations that, together with investment banks, spearheaded new forms of economic globalization in dialogue with the state that embodied (in the main) new forms of economic rather than territorial imperialism. "The film is to America what the flag once was to Britain," wrote the London *Morning Post* in the midst of debates surrounding the imperial conference.[26] The global circulation of expensively capitalized corporate media symbolized and participated in the transition from British imperialism formed on the basis of territorial power—flags—to the coming American-dominated era of economic and political power somewhat dislocated from geographical possession and embodied in, and circulated through, media. One empire faded as another emerged for its day in the sun, illuminated and accompanied by the bright lights (and sounds) of new technologies of media (and warfare), which helped usher in a new global system of political and economic liberalism with the United States at its center from around the point—1941—that the century was declared American.

I have so far observed and argued that significant political and economic institutions started to produce media in the early years of the twentieth century, integrating this effort with expansive projects to shape the conduct of particular populations and to foster political power and economic development. I believe this was a "biopolitical" and economic project that used media in varied ways to supplement and facilitate liberal practices of governance and political economy.[27] Elite actors like states, corporations, and lobbying and trade groups began to use media most clearly in the years around World War I, an undertaking that expanded across the interwar years, which are my principal focus. I argue in this book that these practices were integrated with long-standing precepts about the liberal organization of political and economic power, which catalyzed with the specific historic conjuncture of (broadly speaking) the second stage industrial revolution, and the formation of corporate and consumer capitalism. What follows is my exploration of the broad dynamics and specific conjuncture of this fusion of media with liberal

governmental and economic practices. I explore this history because it is imperative to explicate clearly how media has been shaped and used to expand the logics
and practices that now structure much of our world. Even more forthrightly, I do
so because it is impossible to understand the nature of modern power without
exploring the historical shaping of a media system that frames and encodes it and
because that exploration and understanding are part of the broader urgent necessity to transform a global system that is profoundly unequal and damaging to so
many people across the world. I shall reflect further on that position and what it
might mean for scholarly and disciplinary praxis in the conclusion.

Before that, however, it is necessary to explicate the parameters of what I have
thus far been calling "liberal political economy." Quite clearly I use "liberal" not in
the common modern parlance of "progressive" but rather to reference limitations
placed on state actions to break free from feudal power and simultaneously to
enlarge the sphere of the market that began in the eighteenth century.[28] The principles of this logic, and its historical emergence and transformation across the
course of the long nineteenth century, are elaborated in chapter 3, "Empire of Liberty." *Broadly speaking,* the liberal revolution beginning in the latter years of the
eighteenth century privileged the limitation of state intervention into the economy
and society on the assumption that this would enable forms of market and individual "freedom." Liberalism modeled what one of the architects of the liberal US
state, Benjamin Franklin, called "frugal government."[29] The theoretical and practical elaboration of liberalism as limited government marked a break with absolutist
forms of monarchical "police" power and the economic system of mercantilism
that militarily exploited resources and markets principally to buttress royal dominance.[30] The political economy of mercantilism was challenged during the course
of the first industrial revolution in Britain, which created economic interests
among manufacturers and applied pressure to limit state intervention.

Adam Smith's arguments are often taken as the archetype of the core principles
of liberal political economy. *The Wealth of Nations,* published in that auspicious
year of 1776, proposed that maximizing private profit and protecting property
rights was the purpose of government policy. Efforts by states to intervene in
industry or the circulation of capital tended, Smith argued, to retard the generation of wealth and interfere with the public good. Smith argued for the removal of
"systems of preference or restraint" to enable "the obvious and simple system of
natural liberty [to] establish itself of its own accord," simultaneously enriching
"both the people and the sovereign."[31] I take these imperatives to be at the core of
liberal political economy: the state's principal remit is to enable economic growth,
and it should do this by protecting property rights while removing regulatory
restraint. The principles of this can be simply glimpsed in, for example, the US
Bureau of Foreign and Domestic Commerce's support for the global property
rights of corporate film studios.

Quite clearly, then, liberal political-economic theory and practice were constitutively shaped by capitalist logics, as Marx observed in his critique of classical
political economy and as others have forcefully argued subsequently.[32] Smith proposed that individuals seek to maximize their self-interest and that their efforts
should be mostly unfettered by state regulation. The liberal revolution thus broke
with hitherto largely dominant traditions in thought and practice that viewed
people as fundamentally social beings, instead defining "man" as an autonomous
being whose own selfhood was a form of property. (The male pronoun is indicative
of the inherently gendered conception of the individual within liberalism.) What
political scientist C.B. Macpherson has called "possessive individualism" was at
the core of liberalism and was premised on assumptions about the workings and
legitimation of a capitalist market society.[33] The concept of the individual in the
political theory of possessive individualism was formed, Macpherson argues, from
capitalist conceptions of property as private and exclusive, according to which
ownership was effectively imagined as constitutive of individuality.[34] John Locke,
for example, another significant early liberal philosopher, used the metaphor of
property for all rights, and both Locke and Smith proposed that the principal role
of the state was enforcing contracts and protecting property rights.[35] Even further,
this emergent liberal praxis imagined property rights as the freedom to *exclude*
others and the power of unlimited appropriation, thereby clearly registering the
formative impact of capitalist logics on liberal conceptions and practices of government and economic management. The law also upheld this position. Property
rights could have been imagined differently, as the right not to be excluded from
something that was held in common or as the limitation of excessive wealth, but
this would have deviated from the principles of capitalism to safeguard property as
a right that would enable surpluses of capital and indeed the inequality of possession in society.[36] One simple conclusion that can be drawn from this analysis is
that the "human nature" that Smith and other early liberal political economists
imagined to be manifested in the market system was historical. Marx made this
argument forcefully in his critique of what he took to be the ahistoricism of Smith's
political economy and its tendency to take the capitalist economy as an enactment
of the laws of nature, when in fact they were a product and manifestation of the
actual emergence of the social relations of capitalist production. I take the broader
conclusion to be that an emergent and then dominant liberal political economy
was shaped by, indeed built from, capitalist market logics and related conceptions
of the possessive, self-interested, and accumulative subject.

I shall leave this sketch of liberal philosophy there, and return to substantiate it
further in chapter 3, because I want to quickly outline the broad historical parameters and consequences of the liberal revolution across the long nineteenth century, which began with the publication of *The Wealth of Nations* and the US Declaration of Independence in 1776 and ended with WWI. I am doing so to clarify

both the *logics* of liberal political economy and the contingent *history* of its enactment, particularly its accommodation of liberal principles with the late nineteenth-century dawning of corporate and monopoly capitalism that is my principal focus. The scope of this is expansive, but it is integral to my argument that the
cinema and media I explore embodied and supplemented these logics and specific
historical practices. To give a simple example, beginning in the late eighteenth
century, a series of acts of enclosure in England terminated customary rights to
resources previously held in common, exemplifying how an emergent liberal, capitalist regime established legal protections for private property. Closing the commons required state-sponsored violence to transform a property regime to models
of capitalist production for exchange while destroying nonmarket forms of social
order.[37] The Radio Act of 1927 can usefully be understood as part of a direct line
extending from the principles of enclosing property that could be held in common—in radio's case, bandwidth and frequency—and its conversion into property
for purposes of economic exchange.[38] Radio as commercial mass media was born
liberal, and then became a component of a media system designed to sustain liberal political economy and foster the generation of capital. The logics of these acts
of enclosure were similar, even if the precise historical enactment of them differed
in significant ways. Because it has seemed to me imperative to pay attention to
both dimensions, I shuttle back and forth—in structure and argument—between
the broad dynamics of the processes I am exploring and the more specific and
contingent enactment of them across the precise period that is my principal focus.

The transformation of land *into* property and the destruction of nonmarket
forms of social order were exported across the expansive British Empire during
the nineteenth century in particular. It was a process driven by the twin imperatives of the expansionist logics of capitalism and corresponding liberal conception
of the role of the state in that expansion. Britain innovated a global, liberal free
trade regime in the early nineteenth century that framed informal economic control—in Latin America and parts of the Middle East—as well as direct territorial
control elsewhere, including Southeast Asia and Africa. Empire supported the
needs of industrial capitalism to gather in raw materials, through cheap or
slave labor, and to enable the global circulation of industrial goods that would for
a time dominate other economies. Liberalism and imperialism were, that is, constitutively enmeshed because both were shaped by the logics of capital and its
expansion across the world system.[39] Economic expansion has driven the destructive practices of empire, and this has been historically tied to racial logics that
structure an unequal and profoundly exploitative global division of labor. Quite
clearly the logics and practices of liberal imperialism continue in the expansion of
forms of what David Harvey, among others, has called "economic imperialism"
across the twentieth century.[40] (It was the dawning of this new form of economic
imperialism that caused such a kerfuffle among the British political and economic

elite as they panicked about the circulation of US corporate media as a Trojan horse for the coming American century and corresponding shift in the world system.) The brutal consequences of this "new imperialism" continue, of course, to be widely visible. I am exploring a part of this history of liberal capitalist imperialism and its enmeshing with/as media, but as I said at the outset, it is imperative to see that history in a broader framework across both time and space.

The global circulation of capital and material required a financial architecture and a communicative and transport infrastructure. Gold mined principally from peripheral colonized states loomed large with respect to the former and indeed would ultimately help establish the latter. (Copper dug up largely in central Africa would help the creation of the new communicative lines of telegraphs and telephones.) The gold standard established fixed exchange rates of currencies, tying the host society's monetary and banking system into an international system from the 1860s—with the expansion in particular of European trade—and becoming a global system enabling the unprecedented worldwide circulation of capital in the years 1880–1914.[41] Karl Polanyi has shown how the gold standard was integral to the liberal creation of a supposedly "self-regulating" market: "The expansion of the market system in the nineteenth century," he writes, "was synonymous with the simultaneous spreading of international free trade, competitive labor market, and gold standard; they belong together."[42] London's financial markets were central to the expansion of the capitalist market system, and the country exported capital to enable other countries to buy the machinery, equipment, and ships from the industries of the north, and Scotland in particular.[43]

Parts of this expanded imperial capital were invested in the United States in the 1860s, specifically to fund the building of transcontinental rail lines—capital becomes infrastructure—that necessitated the transformation of land into property and that was driven by the related interests of industrialists, financiers, and governmental elites. I will stick with the example of the railroads in the United States, because that will allow me quickly to sketch out the developments in governmental and corporate organization that frame the more precise history of how media facilitated parts of this corporate liberalism in the interwar years. The Railroad Acts of 1864–68 committed the US state to subsidizing the construction of transcontinental trunk lines, in particular to enable a national market.[44] Land confiscated or bought cheaply from indigenous peoples was turned over to private enterprises and formed the basis in particular of east-west rail lines—built principally by Chinese and Mexican migrant laborers—in another example both of how liberal states create property from land to generate economic "development" and of the centrality of infrastructure to liberal capitalist states.[45] Railroad transportation connected isolated local and regional markets to form a national network of economic exchange. Communication lines, starting first with the telegraph but expanding in the latter nineteenth century to the telephone, dovetailed with this process.

Capital from British markets helped establish rail networks, and by the 1890s most of the country's railway mileage was concentrated in six huge systems, four of which were controlled by the transnational banking House of Morgan and two by Kuhn, Loeb, the same investment bank that helped Paramount become the first corporate media entity in 1919.[46] James Livingston has suggested that the selling of government securities to finance train lines ultimately "made modern investment banking—and the post [Civil] war linkage between it and large industrial enterprise—both possible and necessary."[47] Bankers successfully pressured the United States into joining the gold standard in the mid-1870s. Railroads certainly established the framework for the large-scale corporate enterprises that emerged throughout the manufacturing sector later in the century. The business historian Alfred Chandler has shown how railroads were the first business to confront technical problems that were sufficiently complex to force them to articulate a managerial hierarchy, new organizational and communication systems, and new financing and accounting techniques that served as models for other large businesses.[48] Railroads also directly fostered the growth of large-scale iron, steel, and industrial machinery industries in the final third of the century. The dispersed economic ownership and managerial systems innovated for railroads marked a shift away from the forms of property typical of the small-scale proprietary capitalist economy before the Civil War toward a form of corporate capitalism. The transportation and communication revolutions in the nineteenth century enabled large, geographically (indeed globally) dispersed corporations to emerge in the latter parts of the nineteenth century.[49]

Political and legal conceptions of the corporation transformed under this pressure. Railroads were first built under the traditional Anglo-American common law of corporations that held a corporate charter was a grant from the government, a public creation for a public service that remained under the regulatory power of the state.[50] Legal decisions, including an important 1886 Supreme Court case regarding railroads, began to transform this conception of the public nature of the corporation and forced a newer definition of it as a "natural" or "real" entity with the legal status of a person within the meaning of the Fifth and recently enacted Fourteenth amendments of the US Constitution.[51] Corporations were essentially granted rights similar to those that were integral to liberal discourse and practice regarding individuals. The court elaborated also a more expansive definition of what property should be granted legal protection.[52] From once being a quasi-public entity, the corporation by the end of the century had been redefined in law as a form of private property, which was accorded the constitutional protections afforded individuals and property. Concurrent with these changes in legal conceptions, federal law regulating the market increasingly superseded state law and installed a legal framework at the federal level to support the emergence and spread of corporations.[53] Policy formation and legal frameworks thus tended to legitimize and recognize new conceptions of the form and role of the corporation, positioning it within the established framework of liberalism and defining it as analogous to the profit-seeking accumulative subject. Broadly speaking this development marked the adaptation of liberalism and the corporate form, and principles of this corporate liberalism would be central to the policy objectives of prominent political leaders. Ultimately, a new interventionist role for the government was shaped in ways that sought specifically to preserve private initiative and private-property ownership. The framing of this *corporate liberalism* would be a central task of the media texts and institutions I examine, and indeed of the broader corporate media culture that emerged in the early years of the twentieth century.

Let me take stock here: I have begun to explicate the *logics* of liberal political economy, and its contingent *historical* enactment across time and across the globe, because these logics and histories shaped practices of pedagogic and commercial media and a media system established to facilitate and supplement globalizing liberal political economy. I propose that we see this media as a significant component of the expansion of liberal logics, both domestically and across the world system. I endeavor here to explicate this history as one that encompasses the momentous shift in the world system that saw the decline of the British Empire and the rise of the United States to a position of global hegemony. The examples given already of how the British state used didactic film and media to transact a liberal, imperial political economy and the US government facilitated the global movement of pedagogic and commercial film indicate the directions of this argument.

But it is now time to quickly sketch out the more precise detail of what follows as a map also of how to use and read this book. I begin in the opening chapter, "The Panama Caper," with some concrete details on the elite use of cinema that emerged in 1913, just before World War I, and the exhibition of these at the Panama-Pacific International Exposition in 1915 celebrating the completion of the Panama Canal, which significantly reshaped global trade flows by connecting the Atlantic and Pacific oceans. I begin with the US Department of Agriculture, one of the first governmental film units in the world, as well as with the Ford Motor Company and a trade and lobbying group called the Bureau of Commercial Economics. Each of these groups began using cinema before World War, I thus marking the union of a specific form of liberal capitalism and the visual mass media that would thereafter be its cultural correlate. Pedagogic films celebrating new forms of economic productivity were widely exhibited at the exposition commemorating the completion of material infrastructure that would transform the global movement of materials and capital and position the United States as central to the capitalist world system.

These details help anchor the broader discussion that follows in "Empire of Liberty," which substantiates some of the arguments and history I have sketched thus far about the historical formation and transformation of liberal political economy. I conclude this expansive conceptual and historical discussion with further examples from the early political and corporate use of film on the eve of a war made particularly brutal by some of the same technologies that coalesced as media. Henceforth the book proceeds in largely chronological fashion, though with some back and forth within the chapters. Chapter 4, "Liberty Bonds," examines the propaganda institutions created in Britain and the United States during World War I, focusing on the Committee of Public Information in the United States, which used cinema, among other things, to foster the capital in terms of state debt necessary for fighting war. (The titular liberty bonds.) This chapter also explores the postwar counteroffensive against worker militancy, which had grown in the face of the transformation of labor practices required for new mass production processes. The concerted state and corporate counteroffensive used media in various ways to reestablish the precepts of a corporate liberalism. I believe this was an expansive project, beginning in significant ways here during World War but becoming important to the future shaping of a political economy attuned to the needs of elites, rather than of mass populations. One quick example can illustrate this. During the war, new "exceptional" state practices like the Espionage and Sedition acts in the United States (1917–18) radically limited the principles of "free speech" and expanded the police powers of the government to enable what started to be called "security." More recently, the US government convicted and imprisoned Chelsea Manning and has charged Edward Snowden for violating the Espionage Act, when they revealed information about the global spread of the "War on Terror" and the remarkably expansive government-sponsored surveillance of citizen speech and communication, in the name of security, made possible in the digital age. I make this simple observation here to note that the historical use of media and enactment of legislation that polices media began precisely to facilitate and supplement forms of governmental and corporate authority that continued thereafter.

In 1919, too, the US state began to create a pedagogical distribution network to circulate the films it had begun making to teach people how to be productive and loyal citizens. I explore these texts, institutions, and networks in chapter 5, "The State of Extension," arguing that this grew into a systematic project to create new figural resources as models for appropriate and productive conduct for working-class and migrant audiences, as well as the material networks for the circulation of these films as extensions of government. One simple example: the US Bureau of Mines began to make films in collaboration with large mining and oil corporations, exploring new industrial practices and the benign actions of corporations, and the bureau circulated these films through its twenty-three distribution centers "free of rental charges," to be "enthusiastically praised and regularly shown by technical societies and schools, commercial, industrial, educational, social and religious organizations."[54] The films circulated through an expansive "Visual Instruction" network established in the postwar years, making use in particular of educational institutions like land grant universities that functioned as an early liberal media network. Close ties between state and corporation were fostered to create peda-gogical films useful for the expansion of (in this example) extractive mining and the transformation of mineral and energy resources into property. Effectively this meant that the bureau was participating in the production and distribution of cor-porate propaganda, a fact that further illustrates the close ties among state, industry, and capital that were central to the emergence of a corporate liberal economy.

I pursue additional uses of media to foster new productive forms of interest to state and corporate elites in chapters 6 and 7, which explore (among other things) the use of film to help elaborate new road networks. *The Road to Happiness* (1924), for example, was a film made from collaboration between the Bureau of Public Roads in the Department of the Interior and the Ford Motor Company about the necessity of developing new farm-to-market roads. State investment in infrastruc-ture dovetailed—in classic liberal fashion—with corporate interest in fostering road networks to expand the consumption of automobiles. I begin examining this process in "The Work of Film in the Age of Fordist Mechanization," and I pursue the state's efforts to establish road networks further in "The Pan-American Road to Happiness and Friendship." The latter chapter explores the production and circu-lation of film to help create a Pan-American road network in the mid-1920s, which was carried out in collaboration between the US state and major industrial corpo-rations and banking interests, with some involvement from officials from Latin America. Road networks were significant material manifestations of the expan-sion of the economy integral to corporate and banking interests and the remit of the liberal state. Media was mobilized to supplement the creation of the infrastruc-ture key to the globalization of capital.

Ford also used films as part of its radical transformation of production and labor practices. The company began a film unit in the same year—1913—it established the practices of mass assembly, which transformed the speed of production to extract greater surplus value from laboring bodies while simultaneously de-skilling work-ers and enabling the mass production of a product—the automobile—that exempli-fied the time-space compression of advanced capitalism and transformed the built environment of modernity. For a time, film was integrated directly with the time-motion study integral to the development of the accelerated temporalities of production in mass assembly, because it enabled the close observation of bodily movement. Quickly thereafter the company began to use film as a communicative, rhetorical, and pedagogic medium that would articulate new positions about indus-try, work, and citizenship for audiences inside and outside factories. Writing in the early 1930s, Antonio Gramsci called these combined general practices "Fordist," the classic example of the production of hegemony and organization of consent in the service of a new industrial-productive historical bloc.[55] The company spent considerable sums on cinema, distributing these films at the outset free of charge and then cheaply through new pedagogic networks, making it likely these films were among the most widely seen in the 1920s. Little is known about these films or networks. But—to reiterate—close examination of media produced and circulated by one of the most significant corporations in the early twentieth century is important for understanding both the corporate reconstruction of the economy and the use made of media to facilitate that consequential development.

I shift focus from the United States to imperial Britain in chapter 8, "Highways of Empire," though analyzing how media was used to establish new pathways of circulation and economy remains a core concern. The British state initiated the use of film as mass media to buttress imperial economy quite late, but it developed the productive and regulatory strategies that I have sketched above beginning in the early 1920s. I survey the establishment of a film unit by the dominant Conservative Party in the early 1920s, the creation of the Empire Marketing Board film unit in the midst of broader shifts in global politics and economy, and the 1927 regulation of the movement of US films. Chapter 9, "League of Corporations," pursues some related issues, beginning with the expansive efforts of the League of Nations to facilitate the circulation of pedagogic cinema to help sustain a new liberal world order after the global and imperialist conflict of 1914–18. League officials, cooperating in the first global intergovernmental organization of the twentieth century, sought to develop a pedagogic cinema that would circulate outside commercial circuits and bypass the protectionist tariff systems of states, thus enabling "the mutual understanding of peoples."[56] Efforts toward these ends from 1926 to 1934 in particular motivated the establishment of numerous committees, international conferences, and memorandums, as well as scholarship, policy, and the creation of institutions to foster the usefulness of public and governmental cinema to sustain a liberal internationalism that would balance, if ultimately unevenly, welfare, collective security, and the mechanics of global trade. I take it that overall the league and its cultural, cinematic armaments were consistent with one of the fundamental dynamics of liberalism— the establishment of "security" to create the possibility for "freedom" which was, at the league and more broadly, ultimately winnowed down to a focus on "free trade."

The second part of chapter 9 explores the history of radio in the United States, showing it was initially a product of state-corporate interaction and geopolitical positioning but ultimately became a medium that brought consumers as audiences together with the products of a new corporate and consumer economy. The key period was from 1925 to 1934. This section is something of a pivot, because from that point on I begin to focus more on the corporate and commercial media system and its integration with new economic practices. Chapter 10, "The Silver Chains of Mimesis," explores ideas about the mimetic malleability of people that form the basis for many of the pedagogic and commercial uses of persuasive media. These ideas grew in the late nineteenth century, but they became more prominent after World War I as a result of the establishment of propaganda institutions and subsequently expanded in the 1920s into new practices of "public relations" and advertising which sought to use media to directly shape perception and influence conduct. Partly this registered a shift away from liberal conceptions of individual autonomy to new ideas and practices about the elite management of media as a way of "manufacturing" or "engineering consent."[57]

I analyze the corporate reconstruction of media in chapter 11, "The Golden Harvest of the Silver Screen," which explores bank investment in Hollywood and the syncing together of corporate and financial interests, most notably in the mid-1920s, when the syncing of sound and image became prevalent. I will be curious as to how the form of media produced by these corporate entities was shaped by the logics that produced and animated them. I argue that together these practices in relation to radio and cinema produced a mass media system that was closely tied to the generation of profit and consumption and was, and is, inadequate to the imagination of humane alternatives to the liberal orchestration of political economy.

Bank investment in Hollywood and corporate media expansion took place on the eve of the biggest economic depression (so far) of the modern age. It began in 1929 in the United States, largely because of an overheated stock market—in other words, because of the growing divisions between use and exchange value—and expanded thereafter across the globe. This was one indication of how central the United States had become to the global capitalist system by this point. The crisis was potentially system endangering, and in chapter 12, "Welfare Media," I explore the efforts to use film and media in the midst of this political and economic turmoil to buttress established forms of liberal political economy. In this chapter, I return my focus to how the US state and corporations, as well as corporate lobbying groups, used media to reestablish a corporate liberalism threatened by the inevitable periodic crisis of capital. In the midst of the Depression, significant elites began to argue for a more "militant" liberalism, which would mutate in the postwar years into what often now gets called neoliberalism. The history of that process is partly told in my final chapter, "The World of Tomorrow—Today!," which first examines the use of media in the important World's Fair of 1939–40 to articulate new positions on economic development, which were more broadly established in the postwar years. I sketch out some of the developments that took place thereafter, including the use (and regulation) of media during the Cold War, the integration of film and other media with efforts to rebuild capitalist economies, the Federal Bureau of Investigation's militant policing of progressive workers in media industries, and the Central Intelligence Agency's efforts to integrate the theme of "freedom" into the movies Hollywood made as part of the Cold War efforts to expand "security." I also briefly explore some of the significant media developments that expanded in the postwar years, including television, made global in the 1960s through satellite technology, and the subsequent emergence of "digital" technologies, which began in some of the same labs that developed corporate media (and weaponry). The *inter-net* (literally "inter-network," a product of the US Department of Defense) and *social* media that stemmed from the digital revolution construct people as data useful principally to corporate and political elites. Media, again, facilitates the expansion of consumption and the accelerated assaults of militant liberalism.

I cursorily examine the history of the corporate and state use of media after my principal period, roughly from the 1915 Panama-Pacific International Exposition to the 1939 World's Fair, because this book is a genealogy intended to explicate the forces that brought media and liberal capitalism/imperialism together and that shaped the use of media and framing of a media system beneficial to elite interests. I examine these histories not as abstract and academic exercises, but because they show the patterns and procedures established over time that positioned media as a supplement to political and economic practices that have been, and continue to be, profoundly damaging to people around the world and to the habitats we all share. What follows is a history, but it is a polemical one. I shall make no apologies for that, but I shall note that my focus is throughout on elite actors and their interests and goals. I spend little time on the resistance to those forces here, but all I have written was made possible only because of the praxis of the myriad people across time and the globe who have been and are committed to challenging and transforming exploitative political and economic practices. I have sought to explicate the broad arc of a history that encompasses liberalism and its mutations into corporate liberalism and neoliberalism, and of media's role in supplementing and facilitating exploitative political and economic practices. The situation on the ground, as it were, was and is no doubt often more messy, and contingent, but I believe focusing on the contingent at the expense of understanding the principal dynamics of these processes is a significant intellectual and political mistake. Probably it is clear that I have less faith that today's "convergent culture" fosters the kinds of agency others see in it. I propose, rather, to trace the emergence of an exploitative political economy and the use of media to supplement that system.

I see this investigation as a component of a properly radical media study that focuses (in part) on the use of media to supplement power as a contribution to the urgent necessity to foster resistance and bring about a more humane world where inequality is not so brutally present to so many people. I avoid the balkanization of media into separate subfields—hence I discuss both cinema and radio—and also take a necessarily multidisciplinary approach to fundamental questions about power and its consequences. (I focus principally on cinema because I am, for better and for worse, mostly a historian of that particular thing of darkness.) The study of media is a necessary component of that broader project. Relegating its study to the margins of the academy has been, and is, a mistake—albeit one consistent with how education has also been shaped to further economic and social reproduction, a subject of some interest to me in the following pages. I raise these issues here, and return to them at the end of this book, not to be prescriptive but rather—I hope—to be persuasive that the study of media should be integral to our efforts to understand the history and present reality of the political and economic forces that structure our profoundly unequal world.

One final word here on the title to this chapter. In 1927, the investment bank Halsey, Stuart & Co. wrote a report on investment opportunities in corporate Hollywood, which noted in passing that films use more silver than the US mint.[58] Presumably dug up from the imperial periphery, this silver went into the halogen silver salts that coated celluloid to register the (then) indexical images of moving picture cameras. Cinema, like other media, was (and is) integrated with extractive and exploitative practices, its materiality formed from the imperialism for which it was pushed into service. The reality of that only expands. Nowadays the digital imaging devices so central to a digital media system are built from minerals mostly dug up from African soils, often in exploitative conditions. The silver screen, I argue, supplemented a globalizing, liberal political economy that was for a time embodied in the gold standard. The media and media system that emerge most clearly in the interwar years were, indeed are, fundamentally liberal: dedicated to expanding the liberal logic of the market and, frequently, to the task of educating subjects in the new realities of liberal, corporate, and latterly neoliberal capitalism.

The Panama Caper

On the eve of World War I, a number of significant institutions began experiment-ing with film. In 1913, the US Congress made available funds for the exhibition at the Panama-Pacific International Exposition for "such articles and materials as illustrate the function and administrative faculty of the Government of the United States tending to demonstrate the nature and growth of our institutions, their adaption to the wants of the people, and the progress of the Nation in the arts of peace and war."[1] Moving pictures were a prominent aspect of government display at the exposition in 1915. In 1913, soon after the release of funds, the US Depart-ment of Agriculture (USDA) began "experiments to determine the feasibility of taking motion pictures and the educational and promotion value of these motion pictures," which led to the purchase and construction of the materials necessary for film production.[2] From this emerged what was probably the first governmental film unit.[3] In its first full year of operation, 1914, the unit produced a total of twenty-seven films, some of them for other government departments for display at the exposition; its budget in 1917 was ten thousand dollars, and in 1923 was thir-teen thousand dollars; by 1934, the unit had made approximately five hundred films.[4] Most of them promoted various aspects of state agricultural policy, for example, how to dip cattle to avoid ticks, while some included more general advice on how to live productively (how to mend clothes, set tables correctly, introduce labor-saving devices into the home, and so on).

The thrust of these state policies was to facilitate agricultural productivity and its integration with an industrial market economy. It worked principally through the application of new scientific knowledge to crop management and animal husbandry, alongside promotion of the mechanization of farm work. Economic modernization of farming was achieved through detailed reporting on markets and facilitation of bank loans for the maintenance and expansion of large farms and development of agribusiness.[5] The USDA was established by the US government during the Civil War, the same time the land grant universities and agricultural colleges were created, as the federal state expanded its role to invest in administration and education to facilitate economic productivity and the circulation of what the congressional decree called "useful information."[6] This is one example of how modern liberal states invested in pedagogic practices and institutions to facilitate economic productivity. Rationalizing rural practices in this way was also a common goal of modern states, as they converted land, which had often been occupied formerly by migratory people, into property, frequently relying on the legitimacy of science and technology.[7] The political scientist Daniel Carpenter has argued that the USDA was the foremost example of the establishment of stable and powerful administrative units as core elements of the modern bureaucratic and administrative state regime that emerged in the latter part of the nineteenth century.[8]

What came in the early years of the twentieth century to be called "agricultural extension" used this network of land grant state universities and agricultural colleges, alongside a system of model farms and mobile instruction, to disseminate knowledge about farming and economic management.[9] Governmental practices facilitated new forms of knowledge to enable a growth in food production to sustain the population, which is a crucial foundational task of states;[10] to establish a stable rural economy and simultaneously counter the agrarian "populist" insurgency of the turn-of-the-century period by integrating rural workers into a new national economy;[11] to buttress the urban and industrial expansion of the second-stage industrial revolution and sustain an industrial economy on a continental scale;[12] and to enable and sustain a mass economy of abundance that could, among other things, de-radicalize working-class opposition.[13] Legislation in 1914 created a federal extension service to further these goals, extending the reach of government into peripheral regions.[14]

The place accorded film in this expansive and extended economic, political, and pedagogic project was considerable. Making new productive practices visible, film was a form of communication that could be persuasive, pedagogical, and mobile. It could circulate through the agrarian and extraction-based peripheries of the South and the interior, bringing federal government advice to rural populations in a way characteristic of the liberal state's imperative both to facilitate economic productivity and to govern at a distance. Indeed, this is one of the ways liberal polities began to use technology to materialize forms of indirect rule.[15] USDA films circulated initially through the creation of a network of "extension departments," mostly at land grant institutions, which purchased films from Washington and disseminated them through their local communities. Later, the department's Bureau of Animal Industry innovated the use of a mobile cinema van that could carry films and a new

FIGURE 1. Cover, *Use of Motion Pictures in Agricultural Extension Work* (USDA miscellaneous circular, no. 78, November 1926).

mobile film projector to ever-more remote peripheral regions, and make use of electricity generated from its engine to project these films of government practice to isolated rural populations under the guidance of "extension" workers.[16] The state began to systematically make use of the supposed affective and pedagogic power of film, its mobility, its status as an emblem of a machine-made economic modernity, and its figural articulation of government to position movie watching as a technique of governmental management.

On the cover of the USDA's 1926 publication *Use of Motion Pictures In Agricultural Extension Work,* for example, the department's idealized image of an extension screening shows the USDA's car connected to a brick-built building by an extension cord, which is powering a light and a film projector that shows a film beginning with the USDA logo (fig. 1). The car's headlamps and the cone of light provided by the portable film projector outshine the dim moon, as government technology brings literal light to the pre-electrified countryside, metaphorically enlightening its population about productive ways to produce and live. Indeed, the lines of connection sketched in the drawing, which extend governmental oversight to auto-mobility, to electrical generation, and to portable film projection, mark an important nexus, a set of overlapping agendas and material forms. These positioned film and its ancillary technologies to supplement in important ways the work of the government to mold the conduct of (in this case, rural) workers to enhance particular economic and political agendas.

Various other bureaus and departments of the US government were similarly mandated and moved to make films exemplifying aspects of governmental policy from 1913 onward. Extractive economies were addressed in films made by the US Bureau of Mines within the Department of the Interior, including a series of films about safety-facilitating productivity, films about transport networks, and films made in cooperation with major oil companies.[17] The Department of Labor and Commerce made and used films directed at immigrant working-class audiences for the purposes of "Americanization."[18] The Bureau of Indian Affairs within the Department of the Interior made films recording Native American traditions and declarations of allegiance to the US flag, as well as films by religious groups that were used for "training for citizenship in Government Indian Schools."[19] The Department of Justice collaborated with Hollywood studios in the production of the fictional *G-Men* (Warner Brothers, 1935) and the nonfictional *You Can't Get Away with It* (Universal/Department of Justice, 1936). Public Health Service and Children's Bureau films instructed audiences in matters of social hygiene and public and individual health.[20] Road construction and maintenance, and the central importance of new roads to economic productivity, were addressed in films made by the Office (later Bureau) of Public Roads in the Department of Agriculture, sometimes in cooperation with major automobile companies. Indeed, the celebration of newly created transportation networks was a central trope in government filmmaking, including in a series of films about the Panama Canal and the related expansion of economic and infrastructural connections with Latin America.[21]

Developing alongside governmental film production were new ideas and practices about the pedagogic utility of cinema. The Department of the Interior's Bureau of Education began to explore the ways film could be integrated into the curriculums of various educational levels—both at schools and for adults—and facilitated the emergence of a "visual instruction" movement in the late teens.[22] "Visualization" was theorized as a new, powerful, pedagogical practice capable of productively shaping subjects.[23] The Bureau of Education collaborated with state universities, particularly those land grant institutions that were integral to the development of agricultural extension. Media networks were elaborated in this way as a collaborative effort between state departments and public educational institutions, one part of the broader "institutional matrix" that developed in the 1910s and 1920s among state, educational, and business organizations, to facilitate new economic and political realities.[24]

I mentioned in the previous chapter that the Departments of Commerce and State also began in the mid-1920s to provide global trade information to commercial film producers. In doing so, they worked under the explicitly articulated assumption— "trade follows the film"— that Hollywood would expand the interest in American goods and materials across the globe and thus supplement the broader, related goals of US businesses and the state to accumulate capital and influence. Commerce secretary, and later president, Herbert Hoover claimed that the global success of American film bore "very materially on the expansion of the sale of other goods throughout Europe and other countries."[25] The British colonial state, with help from manufacturing organizations, did its best to counter this. In all these examples, film as pedagogic text, as space-enabling governmental intervention, and as part of a newly elaborated media infrastructure extending the reach of government was utilized to establish and sustain biopolitical projects intended to shape the conduct of populations and further the economic objectives of the advanced, liberal, capitalist state.

· · ·

Various other institutions similarly began to conceive of film as a useful resource and form for expansive economic and political agendas. Also in 1913, the Ford Motor Company began a film production program. Ford was one of the most innovative manufacturing organizations in the world in the early part of the twentieth century. The company elaborated a mass assembly and mechanized industrial process from 1913 on, which radically transformed labor practices and deskilled workers by rendering them interchangeable cogs in a newly mechanized process;[26] compressed the temporality of production to extract greater surplus value from laboring bodies;[27] enabled the mass construction of a product, the automobile, that itself exemplified the space-time compression of advanced capitalism and transformed the built environment of modernity (and, incidentally, required the petrol developed initially by J. D. Rockefeller's Standard Oil, the sourcing of which would go on to dominate geopolitics thereafter);[28] and enabled this product to be produced cheaply to help facilitate the emergence of a mass consumer economy serviced by corporate and monopoly capitalism.[29] Ford also pioneered new forms of industrial "welfare" to defuse public criticism and to propose market solutions to the conditions of labor that would bypass state regulation.[30] It elaborated expansive programs of paternalistic worker education that strove to shape workers' lives outside factories.[31] The company sought in these ways to create a capitalist civics among working-class immigrant populations that would override the traditions of community and mutuality that characterized the unions banned by the company, replacing them with models of individualized consumption.

But it is now virtually forgotten that Ford was also a significant innovator in the production of "educational" moving pictures in the 1910s and early 1920s. The company became briefly one of the largest (and best capitalized) film production units in the world, making films that were among the most widely distributed and seen in the silent era.[32] In "taking these steps" in developing educational films, the in-house *Ford News* observed, "The Ford film department believes that the long-neglected and dormant educational value of the motion pictures . . . will be taken advantage of to carry out its fundamental purpose of true usefulness."[33] The parameters of this usefulness were broad. Ford's films frequently celebrated mass production processes, as well as its program of worker "education" and welfare.[34] The films taught workers how to function in the new configuration of mass assembly and how to consume in ways consistent with an emergent, mass consumer economy. Many of them focused on the emerging infrastructural networks of rural roads and highways, and as I noted above some of these were made in collaboration with the US government. Ford's factories screened its films to its captive audience of assembly-line workers.[35] The company also innovated distribution networks that circulated the films free of charge, initially to film theaters and nontheatrical exhibition spaces, such as schools and factories in the United States and as far afield as the important market of Latin America.[36] Together, the establishment of film production and new distribution networks and exhibition contexts marks a concerted effort, by one of the most significant industrial corporations of the era, to bend emergent mass media to expansive Fordist goals and transform workers, production practices, consumption, infrastructures, and (therefore) economic forms.

Ford's goals in these respects can be glimpsed in the accompanying image (fig. 2). It is an advertisement for the *Ford Educational Weekly*, a film series produced beginning in 1916 that was widely distributed to movie theaters and schools and other educational forums like the company's internal training schools.[37] In the image, a female teacher projects Ford films showing what I take to be the presentation of the Declaration of Independence—it seems to be modeled on John Trumbull's 1817 painting of the presentation that is displayed in the US Capitol rotunda—alongside a domestic scene where the father appears to read to his wife and child. The drawing proposes a connection between the patriarchal management of the nation and the home, relayed by a feminized but mechanized pedagogy. The founding fathers had received renewed attention in the war and postwar years, in a way consistent with a broader nationalization of public culture, carried through sundry Americanization projects fostered by the state and by corporate organizations to stimulate citizen loyalty and "educate" immigrant children and laborers in new kinds of capitalist production practices.[38] The latter imperative was essential to a company like Ford, which drew its workforce mostly from the migrant populations that moved to the urban industrial zones of the United States in great waves from the 1890s to the 1920s.[39] Worker turnover at Ford, after the innovation of mass assembly, was extraordinarily high.[40] Ford's sketch imagines an expanded pedagogical cinema that could train workers in the new productive practices of mass assembly and the obligations and responsibilities of liberal capitalist citizen-

Ford Educational Weekly

"Americanization"
—the Teacher's New Task

The hope of America lies in the prompt Americanization of the youth of the land. Can it be done—with the children of foreign-born parents running into the millions? Yes—*It can, and it must!*

FIGURE 2. Advertisement for *Ford Educational Weekly* (*Moving Picture Age*, January 1920).

ship. Broadly speaking, Fordist film was consistent with the imperative to reconcile the liberalism of the founding fathers—with its idealization (though certainly not enactment) of autonomy and individual rights—with the new realities of the corporation and its connection to emergent practices of *mass* assembly, production, and consumption. Movies helped make liberalism corporate.

. . .

In that same year, 1913, a small, somewhat shadowy organization called the Bureau of Commercial Economics was established in Philadelphia. It can stand as my final example, for now, of how institutions began to use cinema to shape the conduct of particular populations, be they the rural workers targeted by some government filmmaking or the working-class migrant populations that were frequently the focus of Fordist films. Little is known today about the bureau. The scattered materials I have come across in archives in Washington, New York, and Geneva confirm it was set up in 1913 as an "altruistic association" utilizing "the facilities and instrumentalities of governments, manufacturers, and educational institutions" to "advocate, stimulate, and encourage the making of motion pictures for free public instruction, to improve industrial relations, public health, sanitation, and to dispel ignorance."[41] Its charter from mid-1914 stated that the "Bureau is an association of the leading institutions, manufacturers, producers and transportation lines of America, to engage in disseminating geographical, commercial, industrial and vocational information by the graphic method of motography."[42] Moving pictures were purchased from industrial and corporate organizations, and from the government, and exhibited free of charge. Like the US government, the bureau developed the use of mobile exhibition vans and portable projection to circulate these films outside of cinemas and other nontheatrical spaces.[43] Extant photographs show the bureau's van projecting moving images on the steps of the New York Public Library, city squares, the campus of elite private universities like Yale, and the steps of the US Treasury building. This is one example of the way corporate images and messages began to penetrate the ostensible public sphere. The bureau was mysteriously well capitalized in this expensive endeavor, on which the historical record is silent, but its publicity listed connections with major extractive, transport, electrical, chemical, and banking organizations, and it seems reasonable to assume that it was at least partly funded by these organizations.[44] I take it then that the bureau was an early example of a corporate lobbying group using emergent visual mass media to proselytize for particular economic agendas. Later, the more established National Association of Manufacturers in the United States and the Federation of British Industries in the United Kingdom similarly integrated film with commercial imperatives to establish favorable policy decisions and "public relations" for large-scale industrial and corporate organizations. Together, these powerful organizations positioned movie watching as a significant supplement to the expansive project to establish new economic practices and forestall resistance from workers and unions.

Publicity materials from the bureau proposed that watching movies could "improve industrial relations," not only by helping workers and audiences understand new productive practices and the imperatives of capital, but also by showing films of "socialized" economies such as Soviet Russia "with the idea of instilling in the mind of the man in the United States by comparison with these conditions, the realization of how much better off the mass of humanity is here than anywhere else in the world."[45] Capitalism could be supplemented and sustained by movies extolling its values in contradistinction to those of socialized political economies. The "individual who sees" its motion pictures, the bureau's publicity materials claimed, "is not merely a more intelligent individual for so doing, he is a more valuable national asset."[46] Much of this was consistent with the industrial imperatives to Americanize immigrant workers glimpsed in the Ford advertisement. "The Bureau of Commercial Economics," its director Francis Holley said in an address to the Pan American Scientific Congress in Washington in 1916, will greet [immigrant workers] at the threshold and lead them to homes of opportunity showing them in motion pictures, films of the great American industries and the care and welfare work so manifestly apparent in so many of our workshops . . . showing what it means to be a citizen of this grand Republic, what responsibility is imposed upon the citizen, and what obligations he has assumed in coming to the new home of his adoption . . . [to] guard and ever protect his line of vision in correct and wholesome thought and action.[47]

Holley's rhetoric proposed that motion pictures could develop an industrial civics to underpin a particular form of industrial and corporate capitalism and forestall resistance to it.

Equally important to its guidance of populations at home, the Bureau of Commercial Economics began also to imagine that the films it gathered together could export "American ideals and ideas throughout the world" and so facilitate "world markets" and trade.[48] Its activities in this respect paralleled those developed by the US Departments of Commerce and State in the mid-1920s, which were endorsed by corporate Hollywood and its public relations agency. The bureau sought to innovate a global distribution network to show its films. "From Cape Town to Tokio [*sic*]— from Java to Lahore," claimed one of the bureau's publicity documents, "the world is eagerly awaiting the time when it can buy American goods."[49] Visual representations of those goods were regarded as integral to the efforts of US manufacturers and corporations to expand their reach across the globe. One of the significant functions of visual mass industrial media as a global form was the circulation of images of objects and lifestyles from core areas in the capitalist world system to peripheral regions. Electrical mass media, beginning with film, helped dematerialize use-value and produce it as spectacle to be looked at, as a silvery glimmer of lights, color, objects and impossible wealth. It may well be that this harnessing of the scopic to consumerism and economic globalization was, and is, one of the most significant functions of cinema and other mass media produced from within core economies.

Working on the widely articulated assumption that trade followed film, commercial and state organizations facilitated the global circulation of film. The bureau corresponded with the League of Nations to this end, explaining its investment in "the dissemination of useful information by the graphic method of motion pictures" to an organization that itself had begun to develop the use of film in the early 1920s, to help reestablish the geopolitical arrangements that enabled global patterns of trade but had been disrupted by the First World War.[50] I describe the league's use of cinema in the postwar years further in chapter 9, "League of Corporations." It is enough here to observe and emphasize that moving pictures came to be important to industrial organizations, lobbying groups, states, and interstate organizations that were in pursuit of related goals to facilitate the global movement of materials and capital.

A better sense of the bureau's use of cinema can be glimpsed from the accompanying images taken from the publicity materials it sent to the League of Nations.

FIGURE 3. Free public screening (*The Story of the Bureau of Commercial Economics* [Washington, DC: Bureau of Commercial Economics, 1920]).

Figure 3 shows one of the bureau's free public screenings, in a square in New York City, where a mobile projector and screen showed industrial films assembled by the bureau. Visible on the portable screen is the bureau's logo, a drawing of an eye, with the iris doubling as the globe, on which is drawn a map of North and Latin America that is partly surrounded by the words "The Eye Beholds" (fig. 3). While the audience watches the educational screen, its gaze is turned away from a different "globe," the name of a vaudeville theater, which can be glimpsed in the margins of the image. The framing suggests that a pedagogic cinema provides productive engagement with the actual world and, in "guarding" the vision and so shaping the actions of workers, is a useful alternative to lower-brow entertainment. The visual emphasis on North and Latin America in the bureau's logo was not accidental. Growing economic and infrastructural connections with Central America and South America, as significant sources for raw materials—notably rubber and oil— and as markets, were integral to the globalizing practices of the US state, industries, and banks.[51] Recall that it was at a Pan-American scientific congress that the director of the bureau outlined his view of the civic potential of film to socialize workers in the responsibilities and obligations of liberal capitalism.

Turn the pages of the same publicity pamphlet, and the accompanying image arrests attention. It shows an enormous film screen surrounded by a wreath placed at the foot of the Washington Monument in Washington, DC (fig. 4). On Memo-

WASHINGTON MONUMENT
The laurel wreath around the screen is thirty feet in diameter.

FIGURE 4. Washington Monument (*The Story of the Bureau of Commercial Economics* [Washington DC: The Bureau of Commercial Economics, 1920]).

rial Day, 1916, the bureau screened the films it had purchased from the US government and industrial organizations in front of an audience estimated to be over
three thousand.[52] The Washington Monument was the perfect backdrop for the
bureau's conception of the political and economic utility of cinema. Its location in
the US capital at the intersection of the axes of the White House and Capitol building, and thus of the executive and legislative branches of government, framed it as
a richly symbolic monument to liberal governance.[53] The film screen was thus
positioned by the bureau as an adjunct to the social and political functions per-
formed by public monuments (and celebrated national holidays), such as supporting the goals of social and national unity, patriotism, the continuity of existing
traditions, the shaping of memory in the public sphere, and the fashioning of loyalty to the economic and political status quo. Cinema, as the play of light and
shadow, merged with the built environment of government, literalizing the
bureau's conflation of eye, screen, and world and its conception of cinema as a buttress to economic and political forms. Projecting moving pictures, mostly celebrating industry and new economic practices, on this nationally significant monument acutely marked first, the convergence of economic and state interests that
exemplified an emergent corporate liberal political economy, and second, the
import attached to the visual—to public spectacle, symbolic power—in elaborating and sustaining that formation. The political has also always been semiotic. In
the period under scrutiny an emergent mechanical mass media began to take on
the role of visualizing power.

. . .

Further evidence of the power accorded visual display in the conflation of economic
and state interests can be seen clearly in the Panama-Pacific International Exposition
that began in early 1915. I noted above that the US government began its scattered
efforts to develop film production with a view to displaying them at this exposition,
clearly marking the completion of the Panama Canal as a significant indicator of the
burgeoning economic and geopolitical primacy of the United States.[54] Many of the
first films produced by the US government were exhibited at the exposition, some
for the first time. The USDA showed its own films, for example, as well as those it
produced specifically for the exposition for the Treasury, the Bureau of Education in
the Department of the Interior, and the Department of Commerce.[55] Quite a few of
them showed the building of the canal itself. Ford also occupied a significant place
in the exposition. The company built a working moving assembly line to demonstrate the recent radical advances in mechanized mass production that had dramatically cut the time and labor hours required to construct automobiles. Crowds
watched a Model T being constructed and driven off the assembly line, in a living
demonstration of a narrative of industrial process that was awarded prizes as one of
the most important exhibits at the exposition.[56] One could feasibly make the claim

that this exposition did for automobile technology what the 1893 Columbian Exposition in Chicago did for electricity. The public unveiling of Fordist practices of mass assembly and efficiency was accompanied by the exhibition of the first films produced by the Motion Picture Department of the company. *How Henry Ford Makes 1000 Cars a Day* (Ford, c. 1914), seemingly the first film produced by the department, showed how the mass assembly process at Ford's Highland Park factory increased production speed.[57] Its exhibition alongside the facsimile of the assembly line emphasized the new iterative and compressed practices of mass production, making this innovation visible and mobile through the technology of machine-made vision and mass reproduction. Gregory Waller has shown that many other industrial organizations and governmental institutions showed films at the exposition.[58] It marked a critical moment and space in the growing sense in rhetoric and practice that moving pictures could be useful in demonstrating the efficacy of liberal government and the "advances" of the Industrial Age.

The context for this proposed projection of industrial and state power was certainly an important one. Expositions from the mid-nineteenth century onward were generally sites for the display and diffusion of new forms of industrial and technological power, alongside an interconnected spectacle of white supremacy. The Panama-Pacific International Exposition was particularly significant because it celebrated the completion of a canal that connected the Atlantic and Pacific Oceans, which enabled the more rapid circulation of raw materials from Latin America to the United States and, in turn, the distribution of US-manufactured goods to new world markets.[59] Promotional posters illustrating the fair's defining theme, "The Land Divided—The World United," emphasized the canal's connection of oceans, and this was repeated throughout the exposition in sculptures and displays "tell[ing] the story of the unification of the East and the West through the construction of the Panama Canal."[60] (Fig. 5.)

Work on the canal was made possible by an aggressive and imperialist US foreign policy that had earlier intervened in Colombia. In the process, this created the nation of Panama, specifically to enable the construction of travel infrastructures that would support strategic and military agendas and facilitate economic growth and influence.[61] Large industrial and finance capital participated in the construction of the canal. Banker and controller of US Steel, J. P. Morgan, helped the government finance the construction and became, as a result, the chief fiscal agent on Wall Street for the new nation of Panama.[62] Workers digging the canal, who were divided into "silver" and "gold" payrolls, fared less well. The silver West Indian migrant laborers in particular died in great numbers.[63] The canal was a significant example of what sociologist Michael Mann calls "the infrastructural power" of states, as well as of the time-space compression that, David Harvey tells us, has remorselessly driven the "evolution of the geographical landscape of capitalist activity."[64] The infrastructural and coercive power that made the canal and extrac-

FIGURE 5. Panama Pacific Exposition poster, 1915.

tive imperialism possible was turned into symbolic power at the exposition. Completed in 1914, as Europe was convulsed in conflict, the canal marked acutely the moment when US investment and commerce, and the country's sphere of influence and geopolitical significance, extended outward, initially to Latin America—superseding British influence in the region—and afterward globally.[65] Scholars have claimed that the "Panama Canal elevated U.S. power in the western hemisphere for the entire century."[66] It was particularly useful as a conduit for the oil, rubber, and minerals from Latin America that would be crucial to US industrial and economic interests and to the expansion of trade in the Pacific.[67] In short, the Panama Canal helped enable US hemispheric dominance and control over the global flow of goods.

One of those goods was film. Hollywood became a fully global business from this point onward:[68] expanding first into Latin American markets, before its seductive corporate fictions were helped along their way across the globe by the US State Department and Department of Commerce. Globalizing capital, exemplified here by corporate media, required these new transport and infrastructural developments. Even further, that media was made possible only because of the hybridization enacted by global capitalism and the exploitation and transportation of particular mineral resources—for example, the silver needed for the photosensitive halogen silver salts that were essential to photographic film, the cotton essential to cellulose film stock, and the oil in acetate.

But I shall leave aside for now questions regarding the colonial materiality of film technology itself and the ties between film production and finance capital, noting simply that the emergence of a concerted effort to use cinema by states, corporations, and corporate lobbying groups began in the early 1910s *before* World War I and the establishment of state propaganda institutions. It marked the union of a specific form of liberal capitalism—shaped at this precise moment by corporations, nascent consumerism, and globalizing agendas—and the visual mass media that would thereafter be its cultural correlate. I believe it was no coincidence that this conjuncture was made particularly visible and concrete at the 1915 Panama-Pacific International Exposition celebrating the completion of material infrastructure, which transformed the global movement of materials and capital and positioned the United States as central to the capitalist world system. It is a fundamental tenet of my argument that the work proposed or imagined for government and industrial and corporate filmmaking sustained a particular form of liberal political economy and capitalist world system, which was predicated on circulation, display, and the compression of space and time and which was made material in the form of the Panama Canal and mobile in the circulation of film. The prominent display of state-made films celebrating the construction of the canal at the exposition stands as a useful example of this process: state-produced images of the technology and infrastructure made in collaboration by state and financial elites to facilitate the circulation of material, capital, and geopolitical power.

One final remark before I pursue the logics and histories that led to these developments in 1913–15. I spoke in the previous chapter of the imperative to explore genealogical connections with the present. Here is an opportunity. In April 2016, the release of a large cache of financial records labeled "The Panama Papers" revealed the offshore tax havens utilized by the wealthy elite and corporations to avoid paying taxes, which contribute to the public good and alleviate the murderous poverty that blights so many lives.[69] Why were the papers so called? Because the records came from a Panamanian law firm established to make use of the *liberal* regulations regarding tax and economy, which were largely set in place when the United States created the nation of Panama for the purposes of constructing the canal built in partnership with finance capital. "JP Morgan," writes journalist Ed Vulliamy, "led the American banks in gradually turning Panama into a financial centre—and a haven for tax evasion and money laundering—as well as a passage for shipping, with which these practices were at first entwined when Panama began to register foreign ships to carry fuel for the Standard Oil company in order for the corporation to avoid US tax liabilities."[70] Oxfam released a report in the midst of these revelations that estimated US corporations like GE and Apple have, collectively, hidden $1.4 trillion in offshore tax havens.[71] (Many other havens are located in British overseas territories like the Cayman Islands, which are now integral to the operation of finance capital in the City of London.) The invention of Panama and the building of the canal were significant to the orchestration of new trade flows and new patterns of liberal, economic imperialism, shared out by the state and financial and corporate entities. Capital courses through Panama still, as does a significant part of global trade. Media and the built space of expositions celebrated this at the dawning of a new era of economic imperialism that intensified thereafter. The political economy of liberalism, in its corporate, globalizing, phase, was scratched into the fabric of media like the images etched onto the photosensitive minerals and chemistry of celluloid.

Empire of Liberty

The parameters of what I have been calling liberal political economy, biopolitics, and the capitalist world system need clarification. Broadly speaking my interest is in the liberal configuration of economy and liberal practices of regulating and managing populations. I take it that there are core *principles* of liberal political economy and governmental rationality, but these were enacted across a particular and contingent *history* that spread and varied across the world. The broad parameters of that history—the *longue durée*—encompass the formation of a transnational economic system of empire, of what has been called British liberal free trade imperialism, and its supersession by the rise of the United States to a position of global economic and political hegemony.[1] The interwar years were crucial years for this shift in the world system, after the collapse of the Pax Britannica and its hundred years of (mostly) peace and before the rise of the American Century.[2]

The American state supported the globalizing agendas of the large and increasingly transnational corporations that emerged in the latter years of the nineteenth century, and developed an economic imperialism that was mostly divorced from the territorial. Many of those corporations built on the technologies of the second-stage industrial revolution and were driven by developments in electricity and chemistry.[3] The United States in particular innovated a new system of mass production, mass distribution, and mass media. Indeed, the support of the US Departments of Commerce and State for corporate Hollywood is a particularly visible example of the state support for transnational corporations and for the global mass distribution of an important (culture) industry.

Because of my interest in explicating principles and histories, this chapter begins by sketching out the logics of liberal political economy and governmental practices, before exploring the history of its formation and transformation across a period that saw radical changes in economic forms and organization and in what I have been calling the world system.[4] It does so because these principles and this history framed and shaped the state and corporate use of cinema to facilitate key aspects of economic practices and corresponding liberal management of populations. The account developed here of the principles, policies, and history of liberal political economy will necessarily diverge from film, in terms both of disciplinary focus and historical reach. I focus here in particular on what has been called the long nineteenth century, from the twin developments of the US Declaration of Independence and the publication of Adam Smith's *The Wealth of Nations* in 1776 to the beginning of World War I, and on the inter-relation of political, economic, technological and cultural formations and histories. It is important to explore this expansive context to discern the ways film was integrated with long-standing economic and governing practices of the liberal British and US states and was variously used to facilitate the specific configuration of late liberal imperialism and corporate capitalism that emerged in the turn-of-the-century period. I then return to the detailed and specific history of the ways film was put to work by powerful institutions to "manufacture consent" to forms of liberal capitalist order, which I began in the previous chapter.[5]

"LED BY AN INVISIBLE HAND"

The liberal conceptions and practices of political and economic organization and governance that emerged principally across the course of the eighteenth century privileged the limitation of state intervention into the economy and society on the assumption that this would enable forms of market and individual "freedom." The theoretical and practical elaboration of liberalism as limited government marked a break with absolutist forms of monarchical power and with the economic system of mercantilism that militarily exploited resources and markets—including colonial ones—principally to buttress royal dominance. Britain's industrial revolution from the mid-eighteenth century on created economic interests among manufacturers, who saw mercantilism as harmful, and led to significant pressure to develop forms of liberal free trade. Emergent conceptions of liberal freedoms in commerce, religion, and speech simultaneously broke the link between the maximum of regulation and the optimum form of government. Adam Smith argued in *The Wealth of Nations* that attempts by states to intervene in the operation of industry or the circulation of capital tended to retard the generation of wealth and the public good. The "mean and malignant expedients of the mercantile system" must be superseded, Smith argued, for the best mode of political and economic organization emerged when "systems either of preference or restraint" were removed to enable "the obvious and simple system of natural liberty [to] establish itself of its own accord."[6] By scaling the state back, Smith argued, the market economy would flourish, and this would produce general social advantages and "enrich both the people and the sovereign."[7]

What enabled this accord? Smith's answer was the principle of enlightened self-interest. The individual who seeks "his own advantage . . . and not that of society," Smith suggested, discovers that "the study of his own advantage naturally, or rather necessarily, leads him to prefer employment which is most advantageous to society." Indeed, Smith continued, in a now oft-quoted passage, the individual "is in this, as in many other cases, led by an invisible hand to promote an end which was no part of his intention. Nor is it always the worse for the society that it was not part of it. By pursuing his own interest he frequently promotes that of the society more effectually than when he really intends to promote it."[8] I take this to be a core definition of the principles of liberal political economy and its goals, as Smith framed and defined them, "first, to provide a plentiful revenue or subsistence for the people, or more properly to enable them to provide such a revenue or subsistence for themselves; and secondly, to supply the state or commonwealth with a revenue sufficient for the public services."[9]

Liberal theory and practice thus proposed that the maximization of private profit was a crucial function of government policy; the market mechanism functioned as a self-regulating system in which power ostensibly emanated from the mutual relations among constituent parts, rather than from a supervening authority; the market generated broad social advantages as well as individual and state wealth; and the mercantilist ideal of economic self-sufficiency was mistaken because greater divisions of labor and specialization made societies wealthier.[10] Together this all meant that states should accordingly restrain from arbitrary and "excessive" interference, particularly in the operations of the market. Laissez-faire in this sense was both a limitation of the exercise of political sovereignty and a positive justification of "market freedom"—and the market's rather miraculous ability to be self-regulating—on the grounds that the state would become richer and more powerful and stable by governing less. The classic "night watchman" liberal state limits the forms and domains of government action to create the minimal facilitative conditions for the global market and the simultaneous, intertwined, wealth of individuals and nations.[11]

It did not always work that way, for various complex reasons that are probably best regarded as both structural and historical. I am chiefly interested first, in the way liberal political economy was shaped by particular ideas about the motivation of individuals and the protection of property, which were derived from the operations of the capitalist market economy then operative in the Britain in which Smith and many other early liberal philosophers lived. Beyond that I am concerned with the complex balancing of state and economy that took place across a contingent and varied history, from the innovation of free trade liberalism in Britain in the early nineteenth century to a related (but mostly more protectionist) American variant in the latter part of the century, which became a global system by the mid-twentieth century.

A quick clarification: the liberal commitment to a scaled-back state was driven by concerns about the political consequences of being dependent on the state or repressed by it. It did not necessarily follow that the state should entirely avoid social provision, and liberal political economy was combined in Smith and other early liberal philosophers, such as John Locke, with older traditions of civic virtue and engagement in the common good and with newer conceptions of individual rights. A similar mix of liberal and republican traditions is visible in the US constitution, even if it is often argued that republicanism was superseded and liberalism ultimately prioritized in the US system.[12] The liberal position tended toward laissez faire, but residual conceptions of the common good that were mixed with emergent conceptions of individual rights sometimes mitigated the harsh edges of its economic logic and conception of the self-interested subject. Smith himself wrote about the bonds of "sympathy" that join people together.[13] The so-called new liberalism of the latter parts of the nineteenth century, from John Stuart Mill onward, transmuted into the "progressive" liberalism of the early twentieth century.[14] Democracy and liberalism also became aligned across the course of the nineteenth century, even if they were only reconciled when it was clear that democracy would not destroy the existing system of property and market competition.[15] In the 1930s and 1940s, progressive liberalism in turn informed the creation of liberal welfare states, which sought to complexly balance the principles of minimal intervention to facilitate the market with humane, or at least ameliorative, treatment for the less fortunate, even if ultimately this was only to enable the continuation of a particular industrial and economic system.[16] Beginning in the postwar years, and accelerating from the 1970s onward, the neoliberal project has eradicated, where possible, this humanism and state regulation to foster global free trade.[17] Central to this has been the diminution, destruction, and privatization of the liberal welfare systems erected in the first half of the twentieth century.[18] But that is a story for the conclusion of this book, not the beginning.

The liberal political economy articulated by Smith and subsequent practitioners of liberalism prioritized the individual, mostly unfettered by state regulation. Quite simply, individualism is "the metaphysical and ontological core of liberalism."[19] By this logic, the liberal revolution broke with dominant traditions in Western thought that viewed people as fundamentally social beings, defining *man* as an autonomous being, human because of "his" ownership of his own person and his own capacities—conceived of as "property"—and free in his lack of dependence on the will of others.[20] What political scientist C. B. Macpherson has called "possessive individualism" was at the core of liberalism and was formed from capitalist conceptions of property as private and exclusive, so that ownership was effectively imagined as constitutive of individuality.[21] Locke used property as a metaphor for all rights, and, as Anthony Arblaster observes, "It says much about liberalism that the philosopher who is often said to be its 'founder' should have placed property, even as a metaphor, at the heart of his philosophy of government and human rights."[22] Even further, early liberal philosophers imagined property rights as the prerogative to *exclude* others and as allowing unlimited appropriation—clearly registering the formative impact of capitalist logics on liberal conceptions and practices of government and economic management.[23]

Law upheld this position. *Commentaries on the Laws of England*, first published in the late eighteenth century and influential on the legal regime in the United States, stated simply that "So great moreover is the regard of the law for private property, that it will not authorize the least violation of it; no, not even for the common good of the whole community."[24] Property rights could have been imagined as the right not to be excluded from something held in common, or as the limitation of excessive wealth. But this would have deviated from the principles of capitalism to safeguard property as a right that would enable surpluses of capital and indeed the inequality of possession in society. Quite clearly, the liberal position assumed a "human nature" that was in fact a product and manifestation of the actual emergence of the social relations of capitalist production. Hence liberal political economy was shaped by, indeed built from, capitalist market logics and related conceptions of the possessive, self-interested, and accumulative subject.

"THE ROAD TO THE FREE MARKET"

The *history* of the enactment of some key liberal policies can help clarify this *argument* about the function of liberal political economy. I am mindful here of the need to historicize, to move away from a priori assumptions about the principles of capitalism and its political corollary, liberalism, to examine the particular and contingent ways in which a political and economic hegemony was constructed and, necessarily, reconstructed.[25] But I am also aware of the necessity to understand states and markets, politics and economics, as inextricably intertwined. Even property rights, the quintessential foundational category of capitalism, are conventions formed by rules that are often articulated by the law, and thus the state. Once again, my account strays some distance from the historical moment of cinema, but it offers a way of understanding both the expansive and the specific or conjunctural political and economic contexts that underpin and shape the ways states and corporations began to use media to facilitate key aspects of the advanced liberal capitalism of the turn-of-the-century period.

Enclosure acts in England across 1760–1830 exemplify how an emergent liberal capitalist regime of legal protections for private property terminated customary rights to resources previously held "in common."[26] Violence enabled "accumulation by dispossession."[27] The process simultaneously produced a displaced working-class wage labor force and a disciplinary system shaped by the imperative to regulate mobility and protect private property.[28] Destruction of traditional social relations in this way was integral to the effort to establish a "free" market in labor as one part of the broader liberal efforts to establish a self-regulating economy controlled by markets. "To separate labor from other activities of life and to subject it to the laws of the market," Karl Polanyi writes, "was to annihilate all organic forms of existence and to replace them by a different type of organization, an atomistic and individualistic one."[29] Displaced working-class populations rioted in protest at the enormous and terrible suffering created by the construction of a "free market," but they were savagely suppressed. Vicious new laws—most notably the New Poor Law of 1834—enacted the principles of a ruthless economic liberalism by giving laborers minimal poor relief in workhouses to ensure "security," while maintaining the liberal position that poverty was a consequence of individual failings, rather than structural economic causes.[30] The invention of new categories of personhood and indigence, such as the delinquent, the drunkard, or the criminal classes, became critical to liberal governing practices, motivating the creation of new agencies and institutions to expertly manage these dangerously "illiberal" individuals and groups.[31] It was in these ways (among others) that the "road to the free market was opened and kept open by an enormous increase in continuous, centrally organized and controlled interventionism."[32] By this logic the social order was reimagined as an adjunct to the market.[33]

The closure of commons, the simultaneous transformation of land into property, and the destruction of nonmarket forms of social order were exported across the British Empire in the early parts of the nineteenth century. The process was driven by the twin imperatives of the expansionist logics of capitalism and the corresponding liberal conception of the role of the state in facilitating that expansion. Empire supported the needs of industrial capitalism to gather in the raw materials, through cheap or slave labor, and to enable the global circulation of industrial goods that would for a time dominate other economies. English schoolchildren of my generation know well that the crucial piece of legislation here was the 1846 Corn Laws, which were driven by the interests of manufacturers and bankers to reduce protectionist tariffs in Britain as a strategy to fashion a global liberal free trade economy with Britain as its central fulcrum.[34] The example of Indian cloth is often taken as the archetype of some aspects of this liberal free trade imperialism and its simultaneous deindustrialization or underdevelopment or straightforward feudalization of colonial economies. In 1815, the value of Indian cotton goods exported from the country was £1.3 million, but this fell to less than £100,000 in 1832, while the import of British goods from the factories of the north, like those in Manchester in particular, increased sixteen times over.[35] Raw cotton produced cheaply with slave labor on Southern plantations in the United States was shipped through Liverpool to the factories of Manchester, and turned through industrial technology and exploited labor into cheap manufactured objects that were transported round the world. (The system broke down somewhat during the American Civil War [1861–65], and the British state and industrialists subsequently rushed to increase the planting of raw cotton in India to serve the interests of the British economy while further destroying the collective nature of Indian villages, instituting new regimes of "property rights," and replacing food crops in a strategy that led directly to devastating famine.)[36] Liberal "free" trade imperialism like this depended on a large naval and military force and on the technologies of the first stage of the industrial revolution, including automatic guns, ships, and the railways built to facilitate the movement of materials to market and these new transnational commodity chains. Much of this military force was constructed from Indian manpower, funded by the Indian taxpayer, and used throughout the nineteenth century in the long series of wars through which Britain "opened up" Asia and Africa to Western trade and investment.[37]

A few simple and relatively straightforward observations can be derived from this history lesson. The development of new transport and communication technologies greatly facilitated global expansion. Technology, globalization, and imperialism were inextricably intertwined. The development of new infrastructural technologies and connections, alongside the long economic downturn of 1873–96, motivated a new round of colonial conquest, in particular in Africa, the Middle East, and Asia in the late nineteenth century. The more intensive partitioning of the world into core and peripheral economies and the fusion of capitalist and territorialist logics of power served both industrial and finance capital. Both Marxist and anticolonial scholarship has clearly illustrated how the peripheral and semiperipheral regions of the world economy were exploited for cheap labor and mined for the energy and mineral resources needed to sustain industrial capitalism.[38] Frequently this imperialism "modernized" the host government's fiscal, budgetary, and taxation systems; laws of property and contract, along with their judicial administration; and class structures, through the commoditization of land and the creation of a wage-earning working class.

Vast wealth was generated through the global, colonial expansion of industrial capitalism. This led to a stage of finance capital, in which an expanded "mass of money capital . . . set[s] itself free from its commodity form, and accumulation proceeds through financial deals."[39] London became the "switchboard for the world's international business transactions" in the course of the nineteenth century.[40] Central to this was a gold standard that fixed value and currency rates to a gold parity, thus enabling global transactions and facilitating the kind of transnational commodity chains visible in, say, cotton in the nineteenth century or in the rubber gathered in Malaya in the early twentieth that was destined for the tires of new automobiles. By the latter part of the nineteenth century, the gold standard had enabled a global system of material and capital circulation that grew enormously in 1880–1914.[41] London's financial markets were central to this growth, and the control of "the international monetary network" was, Polanyi argues, one of the "instruments which made the voice of the City of London heard in many smaller countries which had adopted these standards of adherence to the new international order."[42] Britain's global hegemony was thus enabled by a combination of material and technological strength, command of the seaways and information networks, wealth, and control of the flow of international monetary transactions.

The accumulation of wealth through the industrial revolution and imperial expansion led directly to the investment of "surplus" capital in the "development" of the colonies in ways that straightforwardly benefited the British economy and state.[43] Most significant were the infrastructural developments of ports, communication lines, railways, and roads, which facilitated circulation of materials and people. Capital developed infrastructure to produce capital. Nowadays we can see many of these developments in the films the British state and large industrial firms made about the empire in the early years of the twentieth century. British colonial films were busy with roads and railways being built, with the large machines needed to facilitate extractive empire, and with the British-owned ships used to transport materials, goods, and colonial officers around the globe.

Still visible on screens, through the expensive technologies of the second-stage industrial revolution, is the world of "liberal" empire, etched onto and archived in the photosensitive halogen silver salts that were themselves likely mined from colonial territories. The Conservative Party built a mobile cinema van to exhibit its films outside theaters to the working-class populations of Britain. Visual record of the splendor of empire served to integrate the working classes into the modern capitalist market. Media and technology were made mobile to explain the circulation of imperial economics. I discuss these films and the institutions formed to make and distribute them in more detail in chapter 8, "Highways of Empire," because they are an extremely significant example of the way cinema was used by a liberal imperial and hegemonic state to distantly govern (and surveil) a diverse imperium, to spread instrumental modes of consciousness, and to facilitate the global economic project of capitalist imperialism. Winning hearts and minds to the project of liberal capitalism, after all, *demands* media—at least, a controlled and pliant media as the carrier of a particular model of economy and "development."

Likely it goes without saying, but as Michel Foucault used to remark, it goes even better with saying that much of this imperial expansion was justified—on the one hand, by a hateful "racial science" that imagined racial difference for imperial purposes and on the other by "liberal" homilies about "civilization" and "improvement" and "development."[44] One sees and hears this latter rhetoric repeatedly in the films of liberal empire. The dictates of liberal free trade over-rode such empty rhetoric when necessary, as the example of the famines in India suggested. Elsewhere and at other times sheer bloody racial murder and recourse to emergency and "exceptional" laws served the needs of economy and governance. It is sometimes imagined, Colin MacCabe reminds us, "that all this is one accident after another, the result of a temporary excess here, a misguided policy there, an unfortunate sequence of events in yet another place."[45] Or that it was "paradoxical" that a liberal regime ostensibly predicated on "freedom" and individual rights subjugated subaltern populations. Or that a liberal constitutional state like the United States prioritized individual rights while supporting a system of slave labor. But it was not paradoxical at all, because liberal political economy and violent imperial exploitation are inextricably, constitutively, enmeshed. It is imperative, rather, that we clearly see how the dictates of capitalist global expansion, marshaled by states working with industrial and financial organizations on the liberal assumption that the generation of individual and industrial wealth will lead to state wealth, motivated the systematic exploitation of large parts and many peoples of the world. Quite simply, the expansive process of accumulation by dispossession was central to imperialist practices, and indeed to the generation of wealth, like the closing of the commons. The political economy of empire was liberal, brutal, and at times genocidal, and it was facilitated by a concerted media strategy justifying the "benefits" of the "thriving trade" of imperialism to populations and audiences both in Britain and across its empire.

"THE CORPORATE RECONSTRUCTION OF AMERICAN CAPITALISM"

The closure of the commons and the simultaneous transformation of land into property took a slightly different but clearly related form in the United States. Westward expansion in the nineteenth century transformed the land formerly occupied by heterogeneous groups of often migratory people—Native Americans—into property, in "a preliminary capture of land that allowed the state to supervise and support continental occupation and sedentary settlement by its own subjects."[46] In the 1830s, American officials were willing to countenance permanent Native American territory in the West, but this was revised in the 1850s when Congress sought a route for a transcontinental railroad that would knit the East Coast to the Pacific and facilitate new trade networks.[47] Relations with indigenous populations turned on enforced transfers to Western reservations and their management through the Bureau of Indian Affairs.[48] Reservations functioned as places where Native Americans would be "de-tribalized" and individualized, thus adopting a liberal capitalist model distinct from traditional communal relations that some regarded as akin to socialism. Westward expansion and the institution of new property laws accelerated after the discovery of significant mineral resources in the West in the 1880s.[49] By and large this process, allied here with the genocide of indigenous populations, can be regarded as analogous to the contemporaneous practices of European imperialism.[50] Beginning mostly in the 1910s, popular fiction and the film genre of the "Western" repetitively celebrated this process.

Large tracts of this land/property were subsequently used by the liberal federal government to fashion a series of consequential and intertwined policies around agriculture, infrastructure, education, and the economy, which transformed the diffuse predominantly agrarian market economy of the antebellum period into an integrated urban industrial order characterized by a new "agro-industrial complex."[51] The state's activities in this respect were consistent with the political forces that contributed to the Civil War, which among other things marked a concerted shift away from an Atlantic economy predicated on the export of agricultural raw materials (and the import mainly from Britain of manufactured goods) toward "a political economy of continental industrialization" and a corresponding spread of capitalist social relations across the nation.[52] The overthrow of slavery and the destruction of the political power of slaveholders sped the economic development of the North and increased the political power of Northern industrialists and bankers over the federal government.[53] (The South would remain a largely underdeveloped region, an "internal analogue," historian Alan Dawley remarks, "of Latin America, producing raw materials and profits for absentee owners.")[54]

During and after the Civil War, the federal state created new administrative bureaucracies;[55] marshaled new "liberal" police powers;[56] established the framework for educating populations; and fashioned new travel infrastructures that marked one visible example of the alliance between Northern industry, finance capital, and the state.[57] Taken together, the related developments in administration, finance, education and research, and infrastructure marked a significant articulation and enactment of the principles of a liberal political economy that *bind* the goals and actions of the state with that of those of industrial and financial capitalists. The well-known "porosity" of the American political system to private economic interest and influence has deep roots.[58] Crucial alliances forged between state and capital, exemplified in these intertwined developments, had doleful consequences for the world more generally. The divergence from the Atlantic economy triggered Britain's more substantive exploitation of empire, India in particular; marked the moment when the United States moved from the semiperiphery to core region of the global capitalist economy; and established the terms for the state's support of transnational business organizations, from the late-nineteenth century onwards, which has shaped the economic imperialism and interconnected militant foreign policy of the United States thereafter.[59]

The liberal policy actions helped form a political economy ultimately dominated by large transnational corporations—with ties between industrial and financial capital—and by new practices of consumption. In 1862, the U S Department of Agriculture was formed to develop new knowledge about agricultural practices that would increase food productivity and profitability, including new chemical practices and efforts to adapt the natural world to machine processing.[60] Creating a layer of administrative bureaucracy within government is one way liberal states separate administration from politics and establish deep sediments of continuity underneath political change, thus insulating them from the reach of democracy. In that same year, 1862, President Abraham Lincoln bypassed Southern opposition to sign the Morrill Act.[61] Lincoln's largesse mandated the donation of public land "owned" by the federal government to the individual states, which could be sold as property for settlement. Receipts were to be used to endow, support, and maintain colleges of "agriculture and the mechanic arts" to "promote the liberal and practical education of the industrial classes."[62] Land-grant universities were founded in several states, while others used their land grants to support agricultural education at already established state universities. Both public and private higher-education institutions developed new knowledge about agriculture, industry, and economics that was crucial to the expansion of an agro-industrial complex and second-stage industrial revolution. Public school systems too became increasingly prevalent across the nation, innovating new practices of "factory-like" education to train workers in the skills and obedience needed for a new industrial economy.[63] Government at the federal and local levels started to fashion an educational system that provided the intellectual and disciplinary framework for the further expansion of a particular form of agrarian and, increasingly, industrial capitalism.[64] By doing so, the state fostered knowledge to enhance production processes, helping establish the rise of large-scale, science-based agriculture and industry to control competition, expand markets, protect and exploit inventions, and provide profits to Wall Street financiers and investors.[65]

In the following two years, 1863 and 1864, two banking acts established a uniform currency and a new stratum of bankers having vested interests in transportation and manufacturing in particular. James Livingston argues these acts created "banking techniques and institutions that could effectively underwrite large-scale enterprise in transportation and manufacturing."[66] Railroad acts across 1864–68 in turn committed the US government to subsidizing the construction of transcontinental trunk lines to facilitate a national market.[67] Land confiscated or bought cheaply from indigenous people was turned over to private enterprises and formed the basis of east-west rail lines in another clear illustration both of the practices of accumulation by dispossession and of the centrality of infrastructure to liberal capitalist states. Karl Marx, a contemporary observer, remarked that the transformation of industry and agriculture revolutionized "the means of communication and transport," enabling "the annihilation of space through time" that made the railroad so central to the transformation of isolated local and regional markets.[68] Railroad transportation connected these previously isolated markets into a national network of economic exchange and promoted the emergence of a national market structure.

But equally significant were the new forms of telecommunication technologies, beginning with the telegraph in the 1830s, that divorced physical from symbolic communication, further enabling the decoupling of spatiality and temporality, which would be important for the global expansion of the capitalist system.[69] Postal and electrical communication systems connected populations, enabling new conceptions of interconnectedness and national community. Indeed, developments like the transatlantic cable system—first laid by the British in 1858 but not fully workable until 1866—confirmed the importance of the Atlantic economy and a global network.[70] Transportation and information networks in particular allowed predictable and calculable circulation of materials and capital. The state's efforts to bind the Pacific states in particular to the East, to strengthen national bonds and facilitate a national industrial economy, were carried out in partnership with railways and, later, telecommunications corporations and with the banking sector, which helped finance these transport and communicative infrastructures. Bankers in turn successfully pressured the United States to join the gold standard after the Civil War. They were rewarded in the mid-1870s, when President Ulysses Grant prevailed on a weak Congress to adopt the standard. I will return to these transnational capital networks in the next chapter.

Big technologically advanced industrial firms frequently need considerable capital, necessitating connections with banks and other forms of venture capital to enable expansive investment. The ties between industrial and finance capital deepened in ways that tended to lead toward monopoly or oligopoly organization. By the 1890s, most of the country's railway mileage was concentrated in six huge systems, four of which were controlled by the investment bank House of Morgan— which had close ties to British capital markets—and two by the investment bank Kuhn, Loeb.[71] In short, then, the policies of the US state effectively catalyzed with emergent economic tendencies to consolidate connections between the state, large industry, and an increasingly global finance capital, which would be significant for the subsequent development of what economic historian Martin Sklar has called "the corporate reconstruction of American capitalism."[72]

Railroads certainly established the framework for the large-scale, corporate enterprises that emerged throughout the manufacturing sector later in the century. The business historian Alfred Chandler Jr. has shown the railroads were the first businesses to confront technical problems that were sufficiently complex so as to force them to articulate a managerial hierarchy, new organizational and communication systems, and new financing and accounting techniques that would serve as models for other large businesses.[73] Dispersed economic ownership and managerial systems innovated for the railroads marked a shift from the forms of property typical of the small-scale proprietary capitalist economy before the Civil War toward a form of managerial or corporate capitalism. The political and legal conception of the corporation transformed under this pressure. Legal decisions, including an important one involving rail companies that reached the Supreme Court in 1886, began to transform the public conception of the corporation and forced a newer definition of the corporation as a "natural" or "real" entity possessing the legal status of a person.[74] From once having been a quasi-public entity, the corporation had by the end of the century been redefined in law as a particular form of private property, which was accorded the constitutional protections afforded individuals and property. Concurrent with these changes in legal conceptions, the federal law regulating the market increasingly superseded state law and installed a legal framework at the federal level to support the emergence and spread of corporations.[75] Policy formations and legal frameworks first established for the railroads increasingly tended to legitimize new conceptions of the form and role of the corporation, positioning it within the established framework of liberalism and defining it as analogous to the profit-seeking accumulative subject. What Martin Sklar has influentially called a "corporate liberalism" emerged, becoming a prevalent ideology articulated by government, judiciary, and industrial and financial organizations "to transact . . . the mutual adaptation of corporate capitalism and the American liberal tradition."[76] It became central to the policy objectives of prominent political leaders, ultimately shaping a new interventionist role for the state in ways that sought specifically to preserve private initiative and private-property ownership.

By the 1880s, the corporate form had spread rapidly in the United States. (The situation in Britain was somewhat different because proprietary ownership continued for a longer time, the legal and policy framework tended to mandate looser organizational forms of cartelized self-regulation, and capital was frequently invested in the empire.)[77] "Almost non-existent at the end of the 1870s," Chandler writes, "these integrated enterprises came to dominate many of the [US's] most vital industries within less than three decades."[78] The number of corporate consolidations in industry began to increase noticeably during the late 1880s, culminating in a "merger movement" between 1898 and 1904 that effectively marked the fully entrenched corporate reconstruction of the nation's political economy and fixed ever-closer ties between industrial and financial capital.[79] Boards of large industrial organizations began to include representatives from banks, and investment bankers like J. P. Morgan commenced using capital to take over and merge companies, as he had when he created the first billion-dollar corporation, US Steel, in 1901.[80] (By that point Morgan was said to be sitting on the board of forty-eight corporations.)[81] The subsequent concentration and rationalization of entire industries under the direction of finance capitalists significantly increased the trend toward monopolization of manufacturing, mining, and transportation.[82] Big, horizontally and vertically integrated enterprises internalized transactions previously carried out by separate business units, enabling these integrated multiunit enterprises to reduce, and make more calculable, operational costs. Firms integrated backward toward the supply of raw materials and forward toward consumers.

Research and development laboratories were established at many of the new, large electrical and chemical firms, employing the scientists and engineers trained at the recently created state universities and at polytechnic institutions like the Massachusetts Institute of Technology. By the latter years of the 1890s, the legal protections for patents and intellectual property were extended from individuals to corporations, the latter of which used patents to monopolize crucial elements of technology or to suppress innovations.[83] The convergent visual and sonic media that became sound cinema in new corporate forms in the 1920s was a direct result of these histories.

Efficiency and technology allowed the exploitation of new economies of scale, and those economies in turn enabled the development and exploitation of new forms of technology and mechanization. The emergence of the corporation coincided with the mechanization of the labor process and the eclipse of skilled workers' control of machine production. Ford's innovation of the moving assembly line to rapidly construct the technologically complex automobile is an example of this. Mass production processes dissociated the labor process from the knowledge of workers, stripping them of craft skills and autonomous control, and consequently increased the authority of management over production and an alienated labor force.[84] Machines in this sense came to "embody" craft knowledge. Unions, particularly militant craft unions, were targeted, destroyed, and banned, a process I explore further in the following chapter.

"DOLLAR DIPLOMACY"

I will say more about the broad and specific goals of corporations and their deployment of media throughout this book. I turn now to explicating the ties between these organizations and the new forms of economic globalization and imperialism that were central to the history of the twentieth century. Because these ties between a liberal political economy, the growth of the corporation, and "globalization" are central to the history I tell of the liberal use of media, it behooves me to be as precise as possible here. Bear with me.

By the early 1890s, after a long economic downturn starting in the 1870s, many people in the United States began to argue that new practices of mechanization, efficiency, and concentration had resulted in the growth of productive capacity beyond effective demand. One prominent response to the so-called crisis of over-production was an argument for global expansion, and for the pursuit of new world markets to sustain the newfound productive capacity of the corporation and the mass assembly process.[85] Lobbying groups and trade associations like the influential National Association of Manufacturers emerged to pressure the government to improve transportation facilities—including the building of an isthmian canal that became the Panama Canal—support intellectual property rights, and reform the consular service to improve overseas reporting on markets.[86] "Between the late 1890s and 1913," historian Richard Hume Werking writes, "government officials overhauled and expanded the federal trade promotion apparatus."[87] Cabinet offices responsible for foreign trade and investment—Commerce, Treasury, and State—all expanded in the early years of the twentieth century.[88]

The imperatives of capital expansion directly powered imperial endeavors in the years spanning 1893–1904. During that period, the United States sent naval ships to Cuba, to protect US economic interests, particularly in sugar. The "mysterious" sinking of one of these ships triggered conflict with the fading Spanish Empire. But the conflict also mutated and stretched to battles with the Filipino resistance in the Philippines (up until 1902), and the annexation of Puerto Rico, the islands of Guam and Hawaii, and parts of Cuba.[89] (Guantanamo Bay, incidentally, was "leased" from Cuba in 1903, after the Platt Amendment of 1901 effectively enshrined US dominance over a nominally independent Cuba, a fact that can usefully alert us to the long arc of US militarized imperialism.) "Territorial expansion," said an official in the US State Department in 1900, "is but the by-product of the expansion of commerce."[90] Principally the separate conflicts were fought to foster trade routes and establish a global infrastructure of naval bases, treaty ports, shipping lanes, and coaling stations, which enabled the United States to achieve a territorial foothold and access to commodities, markets, and labor in Latin America and Asia, in particular through control of seaways in the Caribbean and Pacific.[91]

Cinema was quickly made useful for this fusion of economic, state, and geopolitical logics powering the intensification of capitalist imperialism. Edison Manufacturing Company (one of the pioneers of the second-stage industrial revolution) issued a special war catalogue of films showing troops leaving for Florida, and traveling from Florida to Cuba and the Philippines, and reenactments of key battles, including slow pans across the expanse of the new naval battleships that had been built in the early 1890s as the US military was "professionalized" to facilitate geopolitical security and protect the global spread of US capital.[92] The films *document* the birth of the modern US military as one part of the imperative to *display* state power, which has been integral to imperialism. Indeed, the films stand now as remarkable historical documents of a conflict between historical and emergent imperial powers and the birth of the US imperialism that radically transformed the global system thereafter. Charles Musser has shown how the films were frequently connected together in exhibition programs to narrate the story of the conflict from troop movement to battle to return home. Beginning, middle, and end—*a creative treatment of actuality*—enmeshing narrative form and imperial conflict together.[93] Even further, the films were wildly popular with audiences for the new phenomena of technologically advanced media that was cinema, so much so that Musser suggests that films of the conflicts played a significant role in entrenching the popularity of cinema itself in the United States. *Documenting* imperial expansion and the mobilization of nativist sentiment were important to the birth of cinema as a mass medium. The cultural work of cinema and other mass media was quickly assimilated into the sustenance of imperializing capital.[94]

Direct US territorial imperialism lessened after 1904, for various pragmatic and political reasons, not least because of the complexity of a postcolonial republic governing imperial subjects. But the pressing imperative to expand global trade only increased. Economic imperialism became the more significant strategy from this point onward. "Dollar diplomacy" opened up new markets and investment opportunities, particularly in Latin America, and began to supersede British informal imperial dominance of the region.[95] Loans from private US banks were used as "chosen instruments" of US state power to leverage the acceptance of financial advisors by foreign governments that US officials and investors considered unstable.[96] Bank loans established an imperial politics of debt. Broadly speaking, these efforts sought to use loans as entry points to establish regulatory and economic controls; create predictable global financial markets; assist the nations' expanding exportation of goods and investment capital; and create a gold-backed, dollar bloc, centered in New York, that could counter the financial and geopolitical primacy of London.[97] Hence when US business interests were threatened, in, for example, Nicaragua in 1912, Mexico in 1917, or Colombia in 1924, the US government flexed its growing military might in a way that made clear economic and state interests converged.[98]

New administrative bureaucracies emerged within the federal state to facilitate global trade. The Department of Labor and Commerce was established in 1903, and a Bureau of Foreign and Domestic Commerce was created within it that provided trade information to American businesses. (It was this bureau that helped corporate Hollywood studios distribute their films across the world in the 1920s, after Herbert Hoover became the secretary of commerce in 1921 and presided over a massive expansion of the bureau.)[99] In 1913, the creation of the Federal Reserve banking system brought federal elites and government officials together to exercise "expert" and ostensibly nonpolitical controls over the money supply and credit availability, "to answer the need for a banking and monetary system that could contribute to the stabilization of capital markets . . . [and] that could thereby facilitate corporate organization of enterprise."[100] These developments were key components of what historian Ellis Hawley has called "an associational state," predicated on the establishment of a cooperative system of self-regulating business associations and an expanded state bureaucracy in order to foster modern industrial and commercial practices and thus (it was hoped) to reconcile the emergent corporate form with the traditions of nonstatist liberal government.[101] Bureaucracy worked to reduce the structural contradiction between capitalism and democracy. It was predicated on the liberal capitalist assumption, or theory, that the expansion of private wealth was beneficial to national interests, and the state's goals should be aligned with the generation of wealth.

Even though these assumptions were widely shared by industrial and financial capitalists, and powerful state officials, the corporate reconstruction of liberalism and capitalism was not uncontested. Sklar, for example, makes clear that the adaptation of corporate capitalism and the liberal tradition was a complex and fluctuant process.[102] The replacement of the "invisible hand of the market" by the "visible hand of management" challenged long-standing liberal ideals of a self-regulating market system, as well as republican ones about the concentration of power.[103] The Sherman Anti-Trust Act of 1890 sought to deny companies colluding in loose horizontal combinations, charging that such trusts unfairly controlled markets. But the act had contradictory effects, because the groups of companies denied the opportunity to collude in horizontal combinations instead merged into tight, horizontally and frequently vertically integrated giant corporations.[104] In 1895, the Supreme Court also ruled that a monopoly on sugar refining was a monopoly in manufacturing and not commerce, and so could not be regulated through the Sherman Act. But the act could be used against interstate strikes, because they were "restraints of trade," and it duly was invoked in the railway strike of 1894.[105] Equally significant to the entrenchment of corporate power was the "rule of reason" doctrine articulated by the Supreme Court in 1911, which granted legitimacy to the form of the vertically integrated corporation.[106] Law effectively sanctioned and legitimized the corporate administration of the market.[107]

"YOU SHALL NOT CRUCIFY MANKIND
UPON A CROSS OF GOLD"

But worker resistance to this reorganization and the corresponding new practices of industrial efficiency were less conflicted. The battle to contest the corporation as it emerged in the 1890s was carried out both in the agrarian periphery and urban north. I take these to be significant struggles over the organization of political economy, and I briefly examine here the role played by media in helping establish the cultural conditions for the establishment and expansion of corporate liberalism.

The Populist movement, principally in farming areas in the United States in the late 1880s and 1890s, spawned farmer's organizations that challenged the ascendancy of a new industrial economy, and its ethic of unlimited acquisitiveness, and articulated the varied concerns of rural populations. Among those were struggles against rail carriers, banks, other big business, and tariff policies that protected manufacturing but compelled farmers to sell their crops on what purported to be the open market.[108] The gold standard also loomed large in the Populist critique of liberal political economy. In the mid-1870s, the Rothschild's banking dynasty in particular had pushed the United States to join the gold standard.[109] But when prices began to fall steeply in the early 1890s, at the end of a long period of economic depression, farmers and miners in particular believed that going off gold would push the prices of their goods higher. The gold standard became a symbol of the Pax Brittanica, of a global economic conspiracy led by Britain and bankers that enforced what we might now call "austerity" on working populations. Faced with destitution, farmers organized into a mass movement of protest and demanded that the United States leave the gold standard. The Populist movement elected state legislators and national senators and congresspersons all over the country's southern and western agricultural regions. After 1893, as the antigold movement swept the country, foreign investors started selling off dollars to guard against the threat of devaluation. The US government began to run out of gold and turned once more to Nathan Rothschild, who authorized his representative August Belmont Jr. to ally with American financier J. P. Morgan Sr. to form a syndicate to provide the Treasury with all the gold it needed up until the looming presidential election.[110] Plus, to make out like, well, bankers by turning a quick six or seven million dollars in profits.[111]

But at the Democratic National Convention in 1896, antigold activists succeeded in nominating a senator from Nebraska to rival Republican William McKinley in the presidential election of that year. William Jennings Bryan challenged gold backers at home and abroad and championed free coinage of silver against supporters of the gold standard, arguing that only eastern moneyed interests benefited from the standard and its framing of global trade. "You shall not press down upon the brow of labor this crown of thorns," he famously said, "you shall not crucify mankind upon a cross of gold."[112] Northeastern businesses and banks contributed fortunes to McKinley's campaign, making this the most expensive presidential election until the 1920s. Campaign contributions were thought to be instrumental in persuading McKinley to champion the gold standard.[113] Bryan's defeat in the election was accompanied by so-called sound money propaganda in the form mainly of pamphlets and cartoons that were widely circulated at the time, and this marks one example of an emergent corporate propaganda that sought to facilitate the modern corporate-industrial investment system.[114]

Quick thinking by Republican political strategists integrated the new technological marvel of film into the election campaign. The American Mutoscope and Biograph Company filmed McKinley on the front porch of his home in Canton, OH. It was the first time moving images of a presidential candidate had been used as part of an election campaign.[115] The film was one of the central attractions of the first showing of Biograph films in New York City, just one month after Edison's vitascope had been unveiled as one of the new technological marvels of the age. McKinley is seen opening a telegram, meant to represent the moment he received the Republican nomination, though it was filmed after the fact and taken by contemporary reviewers to be news of the progress of the election. *McKinley at Home— Canton—O* (Biograph, 1896) associated the presidential nominee with modern technology and enabled the circulation of his image through emergent mass media.

It was part of an election strategy, developed by the chair of the Republican National Committee Mark Hanna, to use the media of newspapers and film to disseminate carefully controlled media events to shape electorate/audience perception of the candidate. "Hanna's strategy," Jonathan Auerbach writes, "thus paved the way for a new style of modern presidential campaigning that more and more has depended on the power of abstracted images produced by 'pseudo-events.'"[116] Indeed, the initial film of McKinley and its exhibition played knowingly with the seeming paradox that enabled the candidate to be at home in Ohio while on a screen in New York City, presaging the way the visual mass media would transform contemporary conceptions of the private and public sphere. The process would ultimately create a new culture of spectacle and pseudoevents that would damage any robust sense of a public sphere as a critical space of discussion and debate.

The silver screen helped sustain the gold standard. McKinley narrowly won the election, buttressed by the enormous sums of money "donated" by corporations and banks to protect their interests, particularly adherence to the gold standard. Bryan's loss is now often read by historians as a crucial moment in the defeat of the Populist insurgency. Even further, it was ultimately the "elimination of populism," Norman Pollock writes, that marked "the historical condition that made possible modern corporate liberalism."[117] Quite simply, the destruction of worker radicalism around the turn-of-the-century period was a crucial foundational moment in the establishment of a corporate-driven political economy. I shall argue in the following chapter that the films the USDA made from 1913 onward were also a part of that expansive strategy.

In late 1901, McKinley gave a speech at the Pan-American Exposition held in Buffalo, where he had talked of the growing economic connections between North and South America and of the "genius of the inventor and the courage of the investor" in hastening global communications and trade. "The World's products are exchanged as never before," McKinley said, "and with increasing transportation facilities come increasing knowledge and larger trade."[118] But the very next day, he was assassinated by Leon Czolgosz, a former steel worker from Detroit, who had been made unemployed after his company was "downsized" following the Morgan-financed creation of US Steel. Czolgosz seemingly saw his act as one of protest at McKinley's economic policies, and he quickly became a symbol of "the dangerous mobility and degeneration ascribed to the unskilled labor increasingly displaced and disposed by manufacturing technologies."[119] The specific context for this was significant. The 1901 exposition was held to celebrate the ascendancy of the United States to a position of global power, which followed directly from the spurt of territorial imperialism I mentioned earlier. (The exposition featured reenactments of the genocide of Native Americans, and it was briefly mooted that the recently captured Filipino resistance leader Emilio Aguinaldo be put on display at the fair.)[120] It marked the efforts of the US state to facilitate closer economic ties across the

American continent, and in this respect it prefaced and paved the way for the Pan-ama-Pacific International Exposition in 1915. Like that event, the exposition cele-brated technology, principally the electricity that lit up the night sky, which was provided by Edison after he had been financed by J. P. Morgan to develop the tech-nology. Electricity enabled the dissociation of light from time, a further subordina-tion of nature to the power of industry and those courageous investors that McKinley talked about. Electricity in turn enabled the development of a whole host of linked phenomena, which harnessed the power of electricity and integrated numerous technologies of communication and transportation into new networks of circulation. Edison's film company shot scenes of the exposition at night to advertise electricity, turning investment and technology into aesthetics at a moment when Edison was aggressively pursuing patent litigation against other film compa-nies to profit from intellectual property rights.[121]

Czolgosz circulated no more, though, because of electricity: quickly convicted, he was sentenced to death by electric chair. Edison had cannily sought to position Westinghouse's alternating current system as dangerous and had lobbied for elec-tric chairs to use that system as clear evidence of this.[122] Czolgosz's death at the hands of the state was reenacted by Edison in the film *The Execution of Czolgosz with Panorama of Auburn Prison* (Edison, 1901). The linked technologies of the electric chair and cinema financed by courageous investors killed, and visualized the death of, this seeming radical in an expanded mobile public display of techno-logical power and discipline.

Two examples can quickly illustrate how the government further supported corporate property rights. The first is the Homestead Massacre: Pinkerton detec-tives were hired by the Carnegie Steel Company to break a strike by workers at a factory in Homestead, PA, in 1892.[123] The battles resulted in a number of casualties. Eventually the Pennsylvania militia took over the plant and helped Carnegie bring in nonunion workers, effectively destroying the union and keeping unionization out of the Carnegie plants until well into the twentieth century. The second is the Ludlow Massacre: miners and their families in Colorado protested against the work conditions imposed by absentee owners, and this grew in intensity in the winter of 1913–14. One particularly bitter strike erupted at the Colorado Fuel and Iron Company, a Rockefeller subsidiary, when the company refused to deal with the United Mine Workers Union. The governor of the state supported the com-pany by sending in the militia, which was gradually taken over by company guards and used as a strikebreaking force. In April 1914, the militia attacked a tent colony of miners' families, who had been evicted from company housing, killing sixty-six people. The president of the United States was compelled to act. Wilson withdrew federal troops from Mexico, where they were busy protecting Standard Oil interests, and sent them to Colorado, where they restored order on terms that permitted the mines to reopen on a nonunion basis.[124] What connected these examples, and many others, was the alliance of large industrial organizations and the state and the use of violence to destroy union resistance—to prioritize property rights over worker rights—and establish the conditions for corporate liberalism. The state made its most formidable resource—the coercive powers of its armed forces—available for the protection of corporate property. The destruction of effective resistance to capitalist hegemony, in particular with the defeat of broad-based industrial unions like the Knights of Labor and the Industrial Workers of the World, was of epochal significance.[125]

PUBLIC RELATIONS

The interests and agendas of corporations were from this point onward increasingly framed by "public relations" experts and departments. The history is very precise on this shift and merits recounting. Public outrage about the Ludlow Massacre led to the formation of a US Commission on Industrial Relations. Evidence began to emerge that suggested the Rockefeller family was complicit in the decision to deploy the militia, and in response they hired a man called Ivy Lee to deflect attention and change the news agenda. Lee was one of the first influential practitioners of corporate public relations.[126] He set to work producing a series of circulars blaming the atrocity on the actions of strikers and the union, effectively initiating some of the strategies that subsequent corporate and state public relations drones have used to shape the news to benefit their clients and interests. Public relations and corporate propaganda emerged to support the destruction of the collective power of unions, to further the protection of corporate property and the enormous profits generated from the exploitation of workers. It was part of the battle to establish the principles and operations of corporate capitalism at the crucial and fateful moment of its inception. Nowadays "public relations" is an integral part of the work of most multinational corporations. Indeed, there is plenty of evidence to suggest that states also make use of public relations "experts" to frame news agendas.[127]

Cinema was quickly used as part of the public relations agendas of corporations and to help establish and visualize the corporate reconstruction of liberalism and capitalism. Ford's initiation of its film production program in 1913 should be read in this light, as should the actions of the Bureau of Commercial Economics. But other examples abound. Take the 1913 film *An American in the Making*, produced by the United States Steel Corporation, which was part of the J. P. Morgan financial group established after Morgan combined Carnegie Steel with other significant steel producers, to establish the world's first corporation with capital of over one billion dollars. The company approached the Thanhouser Company to make a film extolling the virtues of the steel industry that would respond to criticism in the press and to labor disputes at the company, which was fiercely antiunion.[128] The resulting film told the story of a peasant immigrant leaving his parent's rural shack in, it seems, Hungary, to work in the steel industry in Gary, IN. Upon arrival at the steel factory, he is schooled in the various safety features of the plant. Later, he romances his English teacher and, in a conclusion evidently set a few years later, settles down to dinner with his wife and child in a spacious house.

An American in the Making mixes fiction and actuality in a way quite characteristic of nontheatrical films seeking to tie the emotional registers of fiction together with didactic rhetoric. The middle part of the film presents an extended "actuality" showing the various safety procedures of the factory that allegedly keeps workers healthy, industrial property safe, and productivity high. This is inserted into a narrative that sees the migrant swap a humble rural shack for a bigger, modern home in the company-built town named after attorney Elbert H. Gary, who cofounded US Steel with Morgan. Indeed, the film's narrative of romance and the sanctity of property was quite consistent with narrative fiction films of the period. The film presents the corporation as a form that enables the global migrant to marry and become a property owner with a stake in the capitalist and American future, which supersedes the European peasant past. What "makes" this migrant worker "American" and what stops him from following the example of the Colorado miners? The answer appears to be, principally, owning property, or rather the debt that comes from "owning" property.

The film's message about pastoral corporate oversight precluding the need for unions was helped along its way by the US Bureau of Mines, who distributed the film through its own institutional networks. The bureau was established within the Department of the Interior just three years earlier, in 1910, to oversee the extractive industries central to the second-stage industrial revolution and to conduct scientific research and disseminate information on the extraction, processing, use, and conservation of mineral resources.[129] In 1913, at the same time that the USDA began film production, the Bureau of Mines started sponsoring a series of films about the petroleum, steel, mineral, rubber, and automotive industries, which explored the remit of these new industrial processes and repeatedly emphasized the benign actions of corporations and their role in producing American citizens. Most of these films were financed by major corporations but were disseminated from the Bureau of Mines through its twenty-three distributing centers "free of rental charges" to be "enthusiastically praised and regularly shown by technical societies and schools, commercial, industrial, educational, social and religious organizations."[130] The production, circulation, and exhibition of *An American in the Making* exemplified the alliance between the state and corporate capital—a visual machine of sorts, circulating through a pedagogical network to help *make* the conditions necessary for the primacy and longevity of belief in the corporate model of political economy.

Lobbying groups like the powerful National Association of Manufacturers (NAM) also played a role in that process, and it is no surprise that they likewise distributed *An American in the Making* through their networks. NAM was one of the most important of the new business associations that had mushroomed in the turn-of-the-century period to help establish the machinery that would enable business cooperation.[131] When shown under the auspices of the bureau or the National Association of Manufacturers, the film became a part of an emergent pastoral network shared out between corporations (US Steel), the state (Bureau of Mines), and nonstate lobbying groups (NAM). They suggested that a watchful, caring, industry and government ensured the safety of workers and citizens and that this underscored economic advancement imagined as the ownership of property. The film and its distribution network mark a particularly canny example of the broader corporate reconstruction of the political-economic order, placing property at the center of the adaptation of liberalism to corporate capitalism.

Such a process of adaptation was predicated on the destruction of workers' rights, be those rural or industrial workers, and a corresponding reorganization of labor practices. This process of adaptation was smoothed over by various forms and uses of a mass media that was—is—frequently the site and space where the contradictory imperatives of liberalism, democracy, and corporate capitalism are played out and imaginatively resolved. The films, institutions, and networks I examine were part of the process of adapting liberalism to corporate capitalism. It is in this context too that the esteemed professions of "public relations" and also that of advertising begin. This was a precise historical process that was started most clearly in the latter years of the nineteenth century in the context of the broader transaction of liberalism and corporate capitalism and of the formation of a mode of power for which the distinction between state and market was steadily eroded. These developments and these uses of media played important roles in the establishment and entrenchment of particular long-term political, economic, and media structures whose continuation extends beyond the focus of this book.

LIBERAL GOVERNMENTAL RATIONALITY

I have so far examined the principles of the liberal configuration of political and economic order and the (truncated and contingent) history of the enactment of those principles across the long nineteenth century. I have begun to suggest cinema, as a form of persuasive mass media, was integrated with the particular formation of corporate liberalism that began to dominate the capitalist world system from the late nineteenth century on. Further, I maintain there is indeed a shadow history of cinema, which does not find its place in textbooks about cinema history and in the narratives of the great movements of national cinema and art practices usually contained therein. It did, however, *participate* in the processes and history—in the elaboration of a form of economic and political power—that formatively shaped the modern world.

I now slightly shift the terms of this emphasis, though, to focus briefly on the governing rationality of liberal regimes and, ultimately, on the place of cinema and other media therein. Liberalism produced a new ethos and practice of government that marked a distinct shift from regimes dominated by structures of sovereignty, and was characterized by a "frugality" that sought consistently to minimize government to enable forms of "freedom."[132] I have argued that the birth of political economy—exemplified by Smith's *The Wealth of Nations*—can be read as a crucial dividing line in this reformation of principles of governance and the idealization of a free and self-regulating market economy. Distinctive governing rationales emerged with new conceptions of political economy.[133] Henceforth, liberal governance "places at the centre of its concerns the notion of population and the mechanisms capable of ensuring its regulation."[134] Various epistemological and institutional practices focused on the management of bodies and populations emerged so as to shape, guide, correct, and modify the ways individuals and groups conduct themselves. It is one of my central arguments that film and media became an important component of these practices.

Foucault and subsequent scholars of liberal governmental rationality discern a slippery dynamic between the liberal injunction to govern through freedom—with the self-regulating free market as the archetype of this—and the innovation of new ways of knowing, classifying, examining, policing, and shaping individuals and populations. Political economy was born in this context and was accompanied by a spectacular growth in new ways or technologies of statistically mapping populations;[135] in new kinds of knowledge needed to understand the psychology of individuals and the sociology of crowds (e.g., the social sciences, in particular psychology, sociology, social psychology, psychoanalysis);[136] in the production of new forms of "expertise" to administer diverse aspects of conduct (e.g., social workers, juvenile court officers);[137] in the creation of public education systems (from schools to universities, including the land-grant universities in the United States);[138] and in the myriad interventions into the "welfare" of populations that stretched from poor laws in England in the early nineteenth century, through "Victorian" philanthropy, the "progressive" undertakings at the turn of the century, and the innovation of state welfare liberalism in the 1930s and 1940s.[139]

The various components of these interventions can be called "bio-political," in that they sought to bring "life and its mechanisms into the realm of explicit calculation" in order to "control and modify them" in ways consistent with the dictates of the liberal configuration of political and economic order.[140] One simple example is consistent with the history I have recounted thus far: in 1915, the Ford Motor Company established a "sociological department" to investigate workers' eligibility for a new higher wage and their embodiment of "good" citizenship. Workers were visited in their homes by "investigators," who interviewed family members to ensure they conformed to the standards established by the sociological department.[141] They were not supposed to drink alcohol and were encouraged to maintain a clean "well conducted home" (without boarders or extended family), to regularly deposit money in a savings account, and to have a "good moral character."[142] It was believed these characteristics would increase efficiency and create "the proper kind of citizen."[143] The management of "Human Resources" beginning here extended control beyond the factory gates.[144] It was in this context that the head of the sociological department told the National Education Association, "As we adapt the machinery in the shop to turning out the kind of automobile we have in mind, so we have constructed our educational system with a view to producing the human product in mind."[145] By these methods, the company fostered a bio-political intervention aimed at reshaping subjectivity and increasing the usefulness of bodies in accordance with the goals of Fordist mass production. It was an important context for the company's production of films and thus its use of culture as a form of liberal bio-politics.

Work on the political rationality of liberalism frequently suggests that it was constituted in what Patrick Joyce has termed an "agonism" of freedom—that is, the invitation to freedom (of markets, of civil society, of the press, of rights, and so on) alongside the anxiety that such freedom would overwhelm governmental order.[146] Hobbes, for example, examined carefully what the frightening consequences of freedom as the "warre of every one against every one" could be.[147] Two principal dynamics amid the liberal innovation of governing practices are often identified. The first centered on the production of subjects capable of the *self-regulation* necessary to function productively, to effect "by their own means or with the help of others a certain number of operations on their own bodies and souls, thoughts, conduct, and way of being."[148] While the second focused on the innovation of "mechanisms of security" or on "the establishment of limitations, controls, forms of coercion, and obligations" to fashion stability and order.[149] Foucault's well-known and oft-used example of the "Panopticon" prison devised by liberal philosopher Jeremy Bentham illustrates both dynamics. Bentham's plan was innovative for its attempt to orchestrate space and visibility to generate the reformation, or self-regulation, of the prisoner. The recalcitrant, illiberal, prisoner was accordingly placed in a cell that circled a central watchtower. Guards could look into the prison cell but could not themselves be seen by the prisoner—who would then, Bentham proposed, have to assume they were being watched, and who would accordingly regulate and monitor their own behavior in ways that conformed to the (imagined) interests of the guards.[150] "Hence the major effect of the Panopticon: to induce in the inmate a state of conscious and permanent visibility that assures the automatic functioning of power."[151] Foucault saw in this "analytical arrangement of space" a sort of diagram of the logics of liberalism and its doubled imperative to produce self-regulation as a form of "freedom" alongside a correlative investment in institutions and practices of discipline and security that simultaneously individualizes and makes visible.[152] By these techniques, liberal governance enables "governing at a distance," which tends to eschew the impositional logic of previous regimes, of rule d'état, and aims instead to induct individuals into programs of self-management through which specific governmental objectives will be realized by the "voluntary" activities of individuals, who are thus conscripted as agents for the exercise of power on and through themselves. The human, or social, sciences play a central role in this, as we shall see. But when this fails, a host of more directly disciplinary mechanisms ensures security. It bears emphasizing that many of those practices of discipline and security were innovated first in colonial territories and were buttressed by the bio-political logics of racism, which animated eugenics in Britain and the United States and in turn the atrocities of fascism, in Germany in particular.[153]

I argue that film as the first visual mass media played specific roles in the elaboration of liberal governmental rationality and, indeed, that mass media and culture became significant spaces through which government as the shaping of the conduct of self and other operated.[154] We can discern two principal dynamics in the liberal management of media. The first is the censorship and regulation of media. I have elsewhere argued that censorship is one example of how governments interact with media in order to regulate populations.[155] Censorship is in part a bio-political practice, and the broader regulation of media—in particular through the creation of policy—is integral to the establishment of particular configurations of political economy. The second is the growing use of mass media—its governmental deployment—to convey information and shape the ways subjects and citizens think and behave. The examples examined here are more clearly related to this second dynamic, which is more central to this book than is the further substantial exploration of the liberal regulation of media. But the two dynamics are interrelated, indeed intertwined, and must be read together as aspects of the dialectic of liberal governmental rationality in the management of media as a crucial component of the governance of populations.

Liberal philosophers certainly pondered the consequences of a mass media—exemplified initially by the press—on newly literate laboring populations. John Stuart Mill, for example, in his *Principles of Political Economy* published in that auspicious year of 1848, wrote,

> Of the working men, at least in the more advanced countries of Europe, it may be pronounced certain, that the patriarchal or paternal system of government is one to which they will not again be subject. That question was decided, when they were taught to read, and allowed access to newspapers and political tracts . . . The working classes have taken their interests into their own hands, and are perpetually showing that they think the interests of their employers not identical with their own, but opposite to them.[156]

Even more threatening to liberal order would be a media form that did not rely on literacy and that appealed to young, working-class, and migrant populations: the cinema. In the United States, this produced a series of governmental responses that empowered police and government officials to regulate cinema in ways that certainly pushed at the borders of the liberal principles of freedom and frugal government. When film industry entrepreneurs challenged this "illiberal" regulation, ultimately by arguing that film could be seen as analogous to the press, the justices of the Supreme Court flatly denied their claim. Justice Joseph McKenna issued a significant unanimous decision that classified cinema as distinct from the press and thus in a realm outside that protected by the liberal guarantees of free speech enshrined in the First Amendment of the Constitution. The state's "police powers" were thus appropriate for the expanded regulation of media as a cipher for the regulation of particular populations. No doubt the decision was legally flawed, as historians and legal scholars have observed, but no matter: the overriding imperative was to regulate cinema because of concerns about what McKenna called its "capacity for evil," meaning its appeal to a mass heterogeneous and impressionable public.[157] Moving pictures became the first and only form of communication subject to legal prior restraint in the United States. Regulating a mass and commercial media in a liberal state in the midst of the fundamental transformations mandated by the establishment and expansion of a new industrial economy necessitated the suspension of the liberal ideal—and of the fiction—of minimal intervention.

By doing so, this "exceptional" regulation delimited the possible social and political function of mainstream cinema, thus mandating its marginalization from the public sphere of "metatopical" common debate.[158] The regulation of cinema depoliticized a popular media form that threatened to disaggregate and demoralize particular populations in ways that were imagined to be disabling to an unstable political and economic order. Censorship and regulation of cinema should be seen as part of a broader strategy to manage, shape, and use media to establish and sustain economic and (bio-)political objectives.

Hollywood studios mostly enthusiastically adopted the logic of this regulatory regime as they entered a corporate phase in the late 1910s, which prioritized profits and the circulation of their films across the nation and the world. In the early 1920s, the studios established a self-regulatory public relations and lobbying body, led by a prominent elite politician (former postmaster general and Republican Party chair Will Hays), which busied itself with ensuring the studios avoided controversial or political subjects to evade further regulatory intervention. It also lobbied the state to provide trade information that would help circulate studio films around the globe. Corporate collusion kept political material from most cinema screens. Threats of antitrust action kept the studios in line. The commercial form of a cinema produced by corporations telling particular kinds of "harmless" stories, and helped along its way by the state, did not happen "naturally" but was a consequence of a series of contingent regulatory decisions and accommodations between commerce and the state. The configuration established for moving pictures influenced future state media policy. I will examine later how this framed the state's orchestration of radio in the 1920s and its production of a media form financed and shaped by corporate capital. The media ultimately produced was (and is) indeed *liberal*—but not in the sense that the Conservative Party in Britain or Fox News in the United States understands that term.

I now come more directly to the ways in which cinema was used by elite organizations to sustain social, political, and economic order. Various arguments were made from the nickelodeon era onward (1907–) in the United States, and to some extent in the United Kingdom, about the ways in which moving pictures might help fashion "productive" subjects and "good" citizens from among its audiences. It was widely argued that cinema could function as a "counterattraction" to other more dangerous forms of working-class and immigrant leisure activity—the saloon was often singled out—and so could become a useful and "healthy" moral force.[159] Even more widespread were conceptions of the possible educational role of cinema. Entrepreneurs (e.g., Thomas Edison, George Kleine) and religious and "progressive" social reform organizations (e.g., the Young Man's Christian Association [YMCA], the People's Institute) began to establish institutions and networks to mold a pedagogic cinema.[160] YMCAs showed industrial films to immigrant audiences and distributed them widely within their network;[161] the self-regulatory and "progressive" National Board of Censorship (established initially by the People's Institute) circulated lists of films that would work well in schools and libraries; settlement houses in the United States began to program films as part of their remit to integrate migrant populations into the social order;[162] and so on. What emerged was a series of discourses and practices—albeit fragmentary ones—that proposed cinema could be a productive tool to shape the working-class, migrant, and young populations, who were drawn to its attractions. It was in this context that states, corporations, and corporate lobbying groups also began to use moving pictures as part of their remit to shape the way people thought and behaved.

There are two main tributaries to these conceptions of the usefulness of media— the sense that it might be operationalized as a technology of governance—that began in the years immediately before World War I. The first is consistent with the nineteenth-century liberal argument that culture could combat civil disorder and establish shared common values and cultural cohesion. The former school inspector Matthew Arnold's 1869 book *Culture and Anarchy* is often taken as the emblematic example of this argument. Written in the context of political turmoil in England, which had resulted from demands for working-class suffrage, Arnold's book argued that culture—defined as "the best which has been thought and said in the world"—

could encourage "reasonable" and prudential conduct and ultimately "do away with classes."[163] Arnold's influential argument proposed that culture could become a pedagogic exercise for the self, to establish a shared set of national values that would counteract the dangerous threat of collective action. Literature was frequently imagined as a form that could help cultivate these practices of self-reflection and self-regulation, arguably because the form of the novel itself was intertwined with the historical shift away from lineage and inheritance to self-development, in the context of capitalist production and private property, and thus with the establishment of the liberal conception of the individual subject.[164] Ian Hunter has shown how this conception of literature as a "technology of the self" was central to the establishment and expansion of a new discipline—English—that could help form the practices of ethical self-management imperative to liberal governance.[165]

Variants on this conception of the utility of culture for liberal governance informed the establishment in the nineteenth-century of institutions of cultural reproduction like the school, university, museum, and library.[166] The example of the philanthropy of Andrew Carnegie is instructive. In the wake of the aforementioned Homestead Massacre of impoverished striking workers at his factory near Pittsburgh, Carnegie began using his vast wealth to endow public libraries, an early example of corporate public relations that was predicated on the assumption that libraries were "instruments for the elevation of the masses of the people."[167] Carnegie understood implicitly what Antonio Gramsci would later theorize as hegemony, and he gambled forty-one million dollars on the idea that cultural hegemony and symbolic culture were probably ultimately more productive than beating and killing workers. Something like this specific logic—whereby capital becomes cultural capital to sustain the hegemony of capital—and the more general conception of the governmental utility of culture were at work in many of the examples of film production that I have given thus far. Ford's film production, for example, began at exactly the moment the assembly line was created.

Carnegie's philanthropy, like Arnold's concept of "culture," worked mostly with a liberal idea of the rational, self-interested, and autarchic subject. Educated readers used culture to fashion prudential conduct. Worryingly, though, this notion of the rational liberal subject came under intense scrutiny in the latter years of the nineteenth century, when it began to seem that the subject was not rational and straightforwardly self-interested, as Smith had surmised, but was in fact "suggestible" and easily influenced to "imitate" the ideas and actions of others. This raises the second principal tributary to the idea that film could help fashion the conduct of conduct. The social sciences, formed as part of the expansive rationality of liberalism, began to examine how people were formed, how and why they behaved in certain ways, how they functioned in groups, and how social order was constituted. The disciplines of crowd psychology, sociology, psychology, and social psychology all emerged in this context and became entrenched in "useful" universities. Psychoanalysis and the Freudian conception of the unconscious was a related phenomenon. What developed was a growing consensus that the subject was not simply autarchic—the bounded and rational subject of Cartesian and classical liberal logic—but instead was divided, was essentially social, and thus was derived from relationships with others.

Questions of mimesis accordingly became central to the explosion of work in the social and human sciences from the 1880s onward.[168] It was widely argued that the individual developed a self through mimetic contact with others and thus was what psychologist James Mark Baldwin called "a veritable copying machine."[169] "The self," Baldwin wrote, "is realized in taking copies from the world."[170] Even further, mimeticism was at the base of social order, crowd and social psychologists argued, because society itself was but "a group of beings who are apt to imitate one another."[171] What this work suggested was that mimetic relations with others constituted both the individual and the social order. The logical consequence of this was academic and, more broadly, social and political engagement with the question of subject and social formation and particularly with what came widely to be called "social control."[172] We can see this as part of the broader response to the transformations of industrial modernity and economy that gathered pace, notably from the 1880s, when crowd psychology began in France and mutated into sociology and social psychology, in particular in the United States.[173]

This intellectual and political context framed the doubled liberal response to cinema as both a regulatory problem and a potentially persuasive tool of governance. Indeed, the regulatory debates about cinema as what one prominent reformed called a "mimic stage" were a—if not *the*—principal public forum for these debates about subject and social formation.[174] I examine this intellectual history further in chapter 10, because it is a crucial context for the articulation of influential ideas and practices about the danger *and* usefulness of media for managing mass populations.

The idea that cinema might be operationalized as a technology of governance for the self and other—which began around 1907 in ad hoc fashion after the expansion of cinema,— was expanded and made more substantive when the liberal and partly democratic states of Britain and the United States entered World War I in 1914 and 1917, respectively. Both states quickly innovated new "propaganda" practices and institutions to persuade populations at home and abroad about the causes of the conflict. War gave new, urgent, currency to the ideas about the suggestibility and irrationality of people and crowds. Liberal ideals about the rational and self-interested subject and social order, and about the hierarchy of Western modernity, took quite a beating in the brutal industrialized killing of roughly twenty million people, in a conflict that was largely caused and made global because of rivalry between European imperial systems (particularly over the resources of Africa). War exemplified also the fusion of politics and economics in the age of empire.[175] I next examine this hinge point of the long nineteenth and twentieth centuries, and the pivot from British to American global hegemony. The ideas and practices developed during the war had a clear, direct influence on the further development of practices of "propaganda" and their mutation into other state and corporate media institutions and practices that set out to teach people how to live and consume.

4

Liberty Bonds

I return now to a more precise exploration of the state use and management of mass media and communication that grew rapidly after the scattered developments of 1913 in the context of World War I. I focus in particular on new practices of media production and control, which were innovated during the crisis of wartime but which expanded in the process to become integral to the *security* of state and capital. My earlier example about the innovation of new police powers in the United States to target dissident and mostly socialist opposition to the conflict, inscribed in the 1917 Espionage Act and 1918 Sedition Act, illustrates the dynamics of this process. New, "exceptional" practices of media control were invented to support wartime exigencies but exceeded them in the effort to secure the prevailing political and economic order.[1] I maintain that the creation of new state institutions and practices to control, produce, and distribute media—what came to be called "propaganda"—was integral to the intensification of exceptional state practices to regulate populations to secure the continuity of the liberal state. The management of media came increasingly to seem integral and fundamental to the management of populations.

To explore this expansive praxis of production and regulation, I begin with Britain in 1914 and then explore further the developments in the United States in 1917–18. Cinema in commercial and nontheatrical iterations will come in and out of focus in this exploration, but ultimately I am interested in the broader framing of a media system to be useful to state and capital interests. Regulation and production crossed modes and mechanisms of expression, and other media technologies and forms—notably radio—were designed to be useful in this conjuncture. The state use and regulation of media to foster its security that was gathering pace in the 1910s did not recognize the borders later set around the study of separate components of that media system. Because this process was driven by the expanding, exceptional logics of state and economic power, it continued beyond wartime, becoming part of a host of new practices to deploy media on behalf of the intertwined interests of the state and large economic actors. Consequently, I take up subsequent state developments in the United States in the following chapter, and I consider the use of media to support corporate interests, and in particular the counteroffensive against new ideas and practices of democracy and worker's rights in the "Red Scare" of 1919, in chapter 6. In chapter 9, I pick up on the history of the state and corporate development and use of radio beginning during wartime, and in chapter 10 I look at the innovation of new practices of "public relations" that also grew directly from state propaganda initiatives during the war and expanded in the 1920s alongside radio and the new corporate media entities that were Hollywood studios. *Exceptional* practices to utilize and regulate media put in place under the cover of wartime became ever less exceptional thereafter.

"THE FLAG FOLLOWED THE DOLLAR"

War began in Europe with the control of communication infrastructure. The British ultimatum to Berlin expired on August 14, 1914, and a British General Post Office ship was immediately dispatched to cut Germany's five Atlantic submarine telegraph cables, which linked the country to the United States and the world.[2] Britain's carefully planned destruction of the cables debilitated Germany's diplomatic and commercial relations and enabled the British state to mostly shape the news agenda in the United States. Cutting the telegraphic cables marked concretely the import attached to the control of communication and media. Britain had dominated the construction and deployment of submarine cables partly because the materials needed for them were sourced principally from its colonial "property."[3] Ownership and control of a global communicative infrastructure from the latter half of the nineteenth century—the first successful transatlantic cable was laid in 1866, the continuous line to India in 1870—had been central to the country's administration of its far-flung empire and its position as global hub of free trade. It enabled Britain to monitor messages and control information and thus hold the relational power to enforce decisions and the structural power to set diplomatic and media agendas.[4] Global trade relied on a communicative infrastructure dominated by Britain.

Even so, the cutting of the cables that connected the world's two fastest-growing economies—Germany and the United States—marked clearly the growing realization in Britain that the United States had become increasingly crucial to the balance of power. Clear evidence of the rising geopolitical, commercial, and infrastructural power of the United States came the very day after the cutting of the cables, August 15, 1914, when the first ship sailed through the just-completed Panama Canal. One could feasibly make a case for this being the precise moment when the balance of power between Britain and the United States shifted. US government planners had developed the canal to establish new infrastructural and economic connections with Latin America and the Asian Pacific in particular, and this was supplemented with the construction of telegraphic cables that linked the imperial possessions in the Pacific that had been gained during the complex conflict of 1898–1901.[5] Elite politicians in the United States had begun to see the British control of the submarine cables that connected the global economy as materially significant to the economic and political power of Britain. By this logic, the canal and the Pacific telegraph were part of the effort to forge new transport and information infrastructures.

During the war, it had become clear that the British were monitoring the information that passed through the cables that connected the United States to Europe. New infrastructure and communication technologies were developed to bypass this control and to expand US-dominated communication networks. Radio became significant here. US naval officials had become interested in the potential of radio technology around the turn of the century to better facilitate point-to-point communication, which bypassed the British-controlled underwater cable networks.[6] Working closely with the corporations busy buying up the patents associated with radio technology—in particular GE, Westinghouse, AT&T, and United Fruit—the navy constructed a high-powered radio chain in 1915, with stations adjacent to the Panama Canal and in Pearl Harbor, Puerto Rico, the Philippines, and Guam.[7] Communicative networks closely mirrored the quest to achieve a territorial foothold and access to commodities, markets, and labor, in particular in China and Latin America. (It was, incidentally, a similar situation with regard to new telephonic networks, and the US Navy collaborated in particular with AT&T in its aforementioned experiments to develop cross continental and transatlantic communications in time for the celebration of technology and circulation integral to the Panama-Pacific International Exposition of 1915.)[8] Cooperation between the military and new corporate entities turned into partnerships when America entered the war. The government instituted a freeze on the amateur radio broadcasting that had emerged in scattered fashion in the early years of the twentieth century and a moratorium on patent infringements that enabled GE, Westinghouse, and AT&T in particular to advance technological developments free from litigation and with financial support from the military.[9] Civilian-military cooperation produced technology capable of distant point-to-point communication, which was initially prioritized, but was also capable of "broadcasting" messages to diverse audiences. GE was prompted by the military to establish the Radio Corporation of America (RCA) to maintain US control of radio technology after the war and thus counter Britain's control of cable networks. Capital from banker J. P. Morgan was used to enable GE to buy out British interests in American Marconi, and this formed the core of RCA.[10] The history is a textbook example of corporate liberalism in action.

I will return to the history of radio when I explore how it was framed as a media form directly linked to the fostering of consumption and how related forms of sonic technology, controlled by large technology corporations, were synchronized with moving images to create sound cinema in the later 1920s. For now, it is enough to note that battles over communication infrastructure were intertwined with geo-political positioning and the control of the circulatory networks central to glo-balizing capital.

Britain's cutting of submarine cable networks to control the circulation of infor-mation and media was supplemented with the passage of the expansive Defense of the Realm Act immediately upon declaration of War. The act was designed princi-pally "to prevent persons communicating with the enemy or obtaining informa-tion for that purpose . . . to prevent the spread of false reports or reports likely to cause disaffection to His Majesty's forces . . . or to prejudice His Majesty's relations with foreign powers."[11] It was consistent with the emergence of new state security practices in the prewar period, which had increasingly focused on the mainte-nance of public order and targeted working-class and socialist opposition to new industrial practices and to the war. New "secret state" practices began in the early twentieth century, including for example the creation of the special branch of the metropolitan police in London and the security agencies that came to be called MI5 and MI6.[12] The war ensured these agencies were strengthened and expanded, buttressed by the Defense of the Realm Act, and this was sustained in the interwar years, when the state continued to monitor civilian unrest.

Exceptional state regulation during the war was supplemented with media pro-duction when a War Propaganda Bureau was established in the Foreign Office in September 1914.[13] The bureau began to issue pamphlets, pictures and cartoons, books, and films that proposed Germany was responsible for the conflict, the war was a fight to protect democracy and liberty, and the German army was responsi-ble for grotesque atrocities such as the killing of babies. Propaganda established principles that continue to be used, including the framing of war as protective of democracy and the demonization of opponents as inhuman. By and large it had two overarching imperatives: to convince British and colonial subjects to sacrifice for the war effort (a necessity in the age of total war and [partial] democracy); and to shape opinion in the United States with the goal of drawing the country into the conflict on the side of Britain.[14] Later in the war the state's propaganda efforts were collated into two new institutions, the Ministry of Information and the Depart-ment of Enemy Propaganda.[15] German and American politicians would subse-quently claim this British propaganda had drawn the United States into the war and played a decisive role in the conflict.[16]

I doubt we can parse the effects of propaganda quite so clearly and directly. By the time the United States did enter the war, in April 1917, the motivation was more directly connected to the question of global trade and finance. German war planners had gambled in January 1917 on a strategy of unrestricted submarine warfare to destroy the supply chain to Britain and by targeting ships in this way threatened America's trade links with Britain.[17] The related so-called Zimmerman telegram also played a role in drawing the United States into the conflict. Zimmerman was a German diplomat, who sent a telegram in early 1917 as part of this renewed military strategy inviting Mexico to join Germany's side of the war in exchange for the restoration of Mexican territory lost to the United States in 1848.[18] Germany thus contravened the Monroe Doctrine, opposing European colonialism in the Americas, and compounded this by also encouraging insurrection in Cuba, Haiti, and Santo Domingo. But Britain intercepted the telegram, making good use of its control of global communication infrastructures, and carefully leaked it to the Associated Press in the United States, where it generated newspaper and public outrage and further prepared the ground for US intervention.[19]

By 1917, the ground had already been prepared pretty thoroughly. Bank loans taken out by the British state in the United States to buy, among other things, the munitions being produced on the mass assembly lines of US factories were directly threatened if Germany prevailed. J. P. Morgan, whose financial house was the chief conduit for the money from the United States to Britain—that averaged about a billion dollars a year during the war—and other financiers pressured the government to intervene.[20] "The flag," Horace Cornelius Petersen later drily remarked, "followed the dollar."[21] Simply put, the needs of finance capitalists helped shape foreign policy, making it extremely difficult for the United States and its financial houses to remain outside the conflict. By the end of the war, Britain had become a debtor to the United States for the first time, marking a momentous shift in the center of the global capitalist system.[22]

"THE WAR IS ESTABLISHING THE SCREEN FIRMLY AS A PART OF GOVERNMENT WORK"

President Woodrow Wilson established the Committee on Public Information (CPI) immediately after the United States entered the ongoing conflict between the European states, in April 1917, to shape public opinion about the far-flung conflict and to communicate strategic state goals.[23] The new institution was created by executive order, on the basis of the expansion of powers delegated to the president during wartime, and was established without congressional approval. Wilson had previously corresponded with influential journalist and political commentator Walter Lippmann on the subject of mobilizing public opinion.[24] Lippmann had proposed a clearinghouse for information on government activities, the monitoring of the foreign press, and the need to rally a wide range of communications specialists, including people working in the motion picture industry.[25] George Creel was appointed to head the CPI, and he quickly created divisions relating to film, news, and "pictorial publicity." Creel argued at the outset that the CPI should principally avoid censorial actions and instead work to disseminate publicity and media, not least because censorship would inflame the troublesome socialist critique of the war that argued it was driven by the needs of business and banks.[26] "Better to have the desired compulsions proceed from within than apply them from without," Creel wrote, in a pithy summary of the logics of what Foucault would later call liberal governmentality.[27] Wilson, Lippmann, and Creel thus innovated a new governmental media agency as a concrete ideological state apparatus, which worked to shape perception and allegiance in accord with state policy and to protect the forms of exchange and circulation integral to the liberal capitalist world system.

Cinema became increasingly central to this "new public relations state" endeavor.[28] Creel orchestrated an extensive architecture of information, publicity, and persuasive argument that was directed particularly at the migrant working-class audiences, who were drawn to the cheap mass visual media that was cinema and had complex allegiances to Europe or its empires. Vast numbers of public speakers drawn from "bankers, professional or business men" were organized to facilitate this work and sent to cinemas to speak on topics relating to the war.[29] The four-minute men, as they were called, got their name both from the minutemen militia of the Revolutionary War, who had reputedly stood ready to fight at a moment's notice, *and* from the amount of time it typically took for movie theatres to change reels.[30] Creel's naming of them connected ideas about national birth, anti-colonial struggle, and the defense of nation (propelled, ironically, by a conflict caused in large part by European colonial expansion and interstate rivalry), with the space and time accorded their sustenance by the relatively new space of cinema.

Brief gaps between filmic entertainment were filled by legions of four-minute men delivering short talks on topics such as the reasons the United States entered the war, the draft, the necessity of buying Liberty bonds to finance the war, rationing food to support the war, "the meaning of America," and so on.[31] The state's agenda was sutured into cinema. Speakers worked from scripts and guides circulated by the CPI, many of which were written by advertising executives and carefully supplemented publicity and information with emotional rhetoric that drew sharp distinctions between the political and moral positions of the combatants. Wilson and Creel's army of citizen business speakers connected the seat of federal governance in Washington to peripheral regions through the space of cinemas. Occasionally the speeches addressed the perception that the war was "a capitalist's war," an argument that was, it was claimed, "constantly whispered by German sympathizers."[32] Creel also encouraged the creation of a special propaganda arm within the Department of Labor, which flooded factories with posters and speakers designed to defuse the radical charge that the conflict was fueled by the demands of industrialists and finance capitalists.[33] Democratic questions about the economic motivations for war were repositioned as undemocratic, disloyal, and dangerous to the state in a rhetorical move that later administrations and other regimes would learn well from.[34]

Quickly thereafter, the CPI began to produce and distribute film material at no charge. Beginning in September 1917, it launched what media historian Stuart Ewen has described as "an unprecedented effort to deploy movies as implements of war."[35] The CPI's Division of Films had an educational department that initially distributed films made by the US Army Signal Corps, circulating this military film material through movie theaters and nontheatrical networks made up of patriotic organizations, educational institutions, chambers of commerce, political and social clubs, training camps, and hospitals.[36] Various films produced by industrial corporations were also utilized and widely disseminated by the CPI, including in particular those made by Ford and (the Morgan-dominated) International Harvester and US Steel.[37] The "screen carried the story of America," Creel wrote, "flashing the power of our army and navy, showing our natural resources, our industrial processes, our war spirit, our national life."[38] Crucial alliances between state and significant economic institutions were fostered to advertise the technological strength of the state, and this is a concrete example both of the forces that brought state and large industry together and the nascent formation of what would later be called (by a five-star general and president of the United States) "the military-industrial complex."[39]

By the summer of 1918, the CPI had created a scenario department that worked closely with commercial film producers, working on the "theory," as Creel framed it, that "propaganda pictures had never been properly made, and that if skill and care were employed in the preparation of the scenarios the resultant pictures could secure a place in regular motion-picture programs."[40] CPI officials sought in this way to draw on the expertise of Hollywood, blending the nonfictional and didactic with the emotional and immersive registers of commercial film. By *learning* from Hollywood to supplement its own persuasive powers, the state became increasingly filmlike.

Domestically the CPI's films reached many of the nation's theatrical film screens, and the committee also disseminated film material principally from the Signal Corps to major newsreels.[41] CPI films made in collaboration with commercial film producers tended to focus on fictions of national inclusion. *The American Indian Gets into the War Game,* made with Universal, and *Our Colored Fighters,* made with producer C. L. Chester, showed the activities of native and black Americans in support of the war effort.[42] *Labor's Part in Democracy's War* and *Woman's Part in War* had similar objectives. Collaborations with the Food Administration and the US Public Health Service sought also to use cinema directly to sustain bio-political objectives. Herbert Hoover, the director of the Food Administration, sought to "make motion pictures a valuable adjunct to our campaign of education throughout the country."[43] The latter collaboration produced films about sexually transmitted diseases widely shown to soldiers in training camps to bolster the military efficiency of the population.[44]

Creel began also to elaborate what he called a "world machinery" to enable "the story of America" to circulate across the globe.[45] Essential to this was the control of export licenses, through the War Trade Office, such that Creel was able to ensure that every shipment of commercial film included 20% "educational matter" and that foreign exhibitors would not be able to show US film without also showing the films produced and/or circulated by the CPI.[46] The films created and approved by the CPI thus circulated internationally because of the state's control of export licenses during wartime. Because "exhibitors simply had to have our comedies and dramas," Creel later wrote, "we soon had sole possession of the field. Much as they may have disliked our propaganda features, Douglas Fairbanks, Mary Pickford, and the Keystone Cops were a necessity."[47] Creel was innovating here a practice that shortly thereafter came to be called "block booking": the use of popular, usually star-led, films to dominate distribution networks and exhibition spaces that effectively marginalized the exhibition of other films. But note that Creel is orchestrating this as a political and ideological project just before it became standard commercial practice in the film industry, in 1919. From that year on, the film company that came to be called Paramount used the capital from newly expanded securities markets to fully control production, distribution, and exhibition networks in one corporate form. Creel's practices innovated a controlled global system of circulation and exhibition that used the popularity of industrialized commercial cinema to further merge the emotionally persuasive registers of fiction cinema with the "pedagogical" material produced by the state (and its industrial collaborators) to explicate policy and (in Creel's words) "advertise America." The CPI thus played a significant role in helping establish the subsequent dominance of American film in the global marketplace. Creel's book about the CPI includes remarkable material on its efforts to circulate films in a crumbling tsarist Russia and in Latin America, where American mining companies also used CPI films:[48] cinema, again, as the avant-garde of expansionist economic policies and geopolitical agendas.

Executives in Hollywood grasped the opportunity to ally with the federal government as a concrete way of ensuring business during wartime and to uplift the cultural status of the hitherto rather beleaguered industry. Creel had cannily sweetened the pill of the control of export licenses with a promise "to expedite film shipments," making sure there was space on boats for commercial film.[49] Protecting the material infrastructure of circulation was crucial during wartime. (It was, after all, largely the reason the United States entered the conflict.) Creel's innovation was simultaneously beneficial to the commercial interests of the film industry and the ideological interests of the state. From this point the global center for film distribution shifted from London to New York, and Hollywood became the world's dominant film industry.[50] Following in the wake of the ties established between state and film industry, in the summer of 1917, the mainstream film industry's trade organization, the National Association of Moving Picture Industries, was elected to membership in the US Chamber of Commerce, a key sign of stability and recognition within the wider business and financial community. By the winter of 1917, the film industry was granted the status of "essential industry" from the War Industries Board, despite the fact that the nitric acid in celluloid was a crucial component of high explosives.[51] The ties forged between the state and media industry were thus directly beneficial to that industry in two concrete ways: by bringing it into the orbit of the established industries in the Chamber of Commerce, a factor that would be useful to the industry shortly thereafter when it was sourcing pools of capital to become fully corporate; and by enabling the industry to stay open during wartime, when other businesses were forced to close to conserve resources.

Close ties between the government and cinema industry were forged around the Liberty bond campaigns that began in 1917 and had the immediate goal to generate debt securities to help finance the conflict. Treasury secretary William Gibbs McAdoo wrote to the president of the National Association of Moving Picture Industries in mid-1917 to enlist the film industry's support in the first campaign.[52] Responding to the Treasury's request, the film industry produced slides and short films about the campaign and distributed them widely. Wilson's speech about the importance of "Liberty loans," for example, was filmed, and eight thousand copies appeared repeatedly in cinemas and other nontheatrical spaces.[53] Creel's army of four-minute men was equipped with speeches about the importance of the bonds. The National Association of Moving Picture Industries organized to attach Liberty loan trailers to the start of film programs.[54] Private organizations sponsored open-air showings of films to support Liberty bond drives, and some of the films produced through the cooperation between state and film industry were screened in the rotunda of the Capitol building: a fitting image of the enmeshing of media and state.[55]

Movie stars were also enlisted to give speeches and then appear in short films that urged people to buy bonds. Mary Pickford toured widely, attended rallies for Liberty loans, and met with wealthy investors, lending her persona as "America's sweetheart" and celebrity to the goals of the state. Pickford and Charlie Chaplin made short comic films to support the bond drives. *100% American* showed Pickford learning to eschew consumer pleasures for the greater need to buy bonds. Chaplin's *The Bond, A Liberty Loan Appeal* dramatized the ways bonds functioned (see fig. 6). Chaplin stands between figures representing Uncle Sam and Industry,

FIGURE 6. Still from *The Bond, a Liberty Loan Appeal,* directed by Charlie Chaplin (Liberty Loan Committee, 1917).

and when he buys a bond from Uncle Sam, Industry sets to work to provide military materials to soldiers. At the close of the film, Chaplin hits the Kaiser over the head with a large mallet bearing the words "Liberty bonds." It is a film that comically sketched out the economic model of government debt that supported US military intervention. The media celebrity was put to work to sustain the warfare state and to exemplify the kind of liberty that was coming to be best exemplified by debt.

The Liberty bond campaigns were partly driven by the necessity to innovate new governmental financial practices to sustain the military. Sixty percent of the cost of the conflict was raised in this way, about $21.5 billion, through purchases by about one third of the population.[56] But the loan drives also put into practice new ideas about securities ownership, which surfaced first around the turn of the century to foster new forms of "investor democracy," designed to bind citizen to state and to expand and "deepen" the capital necessary to the growth of corporate and financial capital.[57] Bond campaigns during wartime followed these political and economic logics, and they were a part of the larger dynamic in which the state worked to expand securities ownership and innovate a new investor-centered theory of political economy as one way of updating older notions of proprietary democracy to bind the heterogeneous population to the state through the matrix of the market. Policy makers, historian Julia Ott writes, argued that "Universal ownership of federal securities would stabilize society by forestalling radicalism and curbing inflation. . . . By extending the opportunity to acquire property in a new form, the wartime state aimed to nudge those prone to radicalism into a classic liberal social contract, in which individuals submitted to the rule of law in order to preserve their property."[58] Bonds bound together state interests to finance the military and warfare and, therefore, foster its own security, as well as that of the economic institutions like investment banks, which relied on that expansion of securities. By the 1920s, after the success of the wartime bond drives, an expanded securities market buttressed by new cognate ideas about investor democracy was firmly established. Over the decade, and thereafter, these ideals and practices formed the "basic economic precepts of modern conservatism," principally that laissez faire financial markets best allocate capital and risk and that the maximization of shareholder value is the proper goal of state and corporate policy.[59] Capital in the form here principally of bonds (but mutating also into new forms of equity financing in terms of stocks) expanded through the process established by the state in compact with financial elites and innovated initially to finance military expansion and warfare.

I contend here that this extremely significant transformation of political economy was created by the state during the exceptional crisis of wartime to foster expansive political and economic ends. This process used media as space and form, and included the new phenomenon of persuasive celebrity, which was enmeshed with the growth of corporate media. It is a central tenet of my argument that the state utilized media during the exigencies of wartime to establish forms of governmental rationality that exceeded the immediate requirements of combat and expanded thereafter. The process further established significant ties between political and financial elites, including for the first time those who controlled the new media that was cinema. For those media entrepreneurs, the expansion of finance capital in the wake of these developments during the war enabled them to attract the pools of capital necessary to create new national networks of distribution and exhibition and connect these together with production in one corporate entity. Corporate cinema and other media settled thereafter into an oligopolistic market, which marginalized alternative forms of media culture and thus radically limited the public sphere.

Wilson declared himself very satisfied with the results, and with the contribution of cinema to the bond campaigns and war effort. In a letter sent in the summer of 1918 to the head of the film industry's central trade body, he echoed Hoover's conception of cinema as a "valuable adjunct" to the work of government by writing,

It is my mind not only to bring the motion picture into fullest and most effective contact with the nation's needs, but to give some measure of official recognition to an increasingly important factor in the development of our national life. The film has come to rank as a very high medium for the dissemination of public intelligence and since it speaks a universal language it lends itself importantly to the presentation of America's plans and purposes.[60]

Wilson's letter indicates the importance attached to cinema as a form of mass media at the highest level of state. The president's conception of cinema as a form of communication that crossed linguistic barriers made cinema especially important for the project both to shape the attitudes and conduct of the diverse population's drawn to the United States from the late nineteenth century on *and* to facilitate the globalizing agendas of the state and the large corporations that had flourished since the turn of the century. In the wake of this, in the 1920s, offices in the Department's of State and Commerce worked to aid the global circulation of corporate Hollywood as one strand of the new forms of economic imperialism led by the United States, which repositioned it as the world's exceptional state thereafter. Quite clearly the use and deployment of media were integral to expansive political and economic objectives in a process that began most concretely during wartime but then expanded.

"SUCH A NATURE AS TO CREATE A CLEAR AND PRESENT DANGER"

The production of propaganda to facilitate military and state goals was twinned with the significant expansion of state censorship and political policing most clearly in the years 1917–19. New policies and practices were innovated and sustained by the judiciary in significant and far-reaching decisions on free speech. Like the activities mapped above, the establishment of new exceptional practices to police political and economic opposition began under the cover of wartime and expanded in the immediate aftermath, becoming central to the agenda of the federal police force in the Red Scare of 1919–20. Union members and socialists received the most scrutiny in a process that radically limited dissident speech to further cement the primacy of liberal capitalism. The innovation of a militantly liberal praxis, including broadly the framing of a media system, was a crucial, *formative,* episode in the entrenchment of state power and corporate, liberal political economy.

Wilson's administration passed the Espionage Act in June 1917, which made it a crime to convey information or false statements that could interfere with military operations or promote the success of enemies. Particularly significant to the act was the outlawing of speech—broadly conceived—that could "willfully cause or attempt to cause insubordination, disloyalty, mutiny, or refusal of duty in the military or naval forces of the United States, or shall willfully obstruct the recruiting or enlistment service of the United States."[61] The clause specifically targeted socialist and pacifist opposition to the war, members of which had argued that the conflict was a consequence of the globalizing expansion of capital and had at times urged men to resist the draft. Eugene Debs, the leader of the Socialist Party, which had polled around 1 million votes in the election of 1912, gave an antiwar speech in Ohio in 1918, which noted (among other things) that the "ruling class" has "always taught and trained you to believe it to be your patriotic duty to go to war and have yourselves slaughtered at their command."[62] Debs began his speech with the prescient observation "that it is extremely dangerous to exercise the constitutional right of free speech in a country fighting to make democracy safe in the world." But truth and irony did not keep him out of prison. By the next day, the speech had been scrutinized, first by the US attorney in Cleveland and then by the attorney general. Debs was arrested, indicted, and ultimately imprisoned with a 10-year sentence under the terms of the Espionage Act.[63]

Expanded restrictions on speech and media to protect state and economic interests and to sustain military action were elaborated thereafter, most notably in a revision to the Espionage Act commonly known as the Sedition Act. Passed in May 1918, this revision prohibited "any disloyal, scurrilous, or abusive language about the form of government of the United States, or the Constitution of the United States, or the military and naval forces of the United States."[64] By this expanded definition, *sedition* included criticism of the liberal capitalist state *and* its military, positioning the two as essentially intertwined. Particularly significant were clauses regulating speech about economic practices. Banned speech included that which manifested "intent to obstruct the sale by the United States of bonds or other securities of the United States or the making of loans by or to the United States," or that advocated "any curtailment of production in this country of any thing or things, product or products, necessary or essential to the prosecution of the war."[65] Questioning the economic motivation for war, the expansion of the securities markets to finance warfare, and the nascent form of the military-industrial complex was outlawed. But the act did more than enable the ex post facto regulation of speech, in that it gave the postmaster general enlarged powers to police the circulation of materials "in violation of any of the provisions of this Act" through the mail system.[66] By this clause the act specifically targeted the circulation of ideas, information, and media through the federal government's control of mail networks and interstate commerce.

Both acts were specifically used to target socialist opposition to the war as one part of the broader imperative to entrench the corporate reconstruction of American capitalism. By September 1917, the Espionage Act was invoked by the Department of Justice to raid the offices of the Industrial Workers of the World union around the country, arresting 166 union officials and simultaneously destroying printing presses and private correspondence.[67] Postmaster General Albert Burleson used the sedition revision to quickly ban socialist publications from the mails, including the journals *American Socialist* and *The Masses,* as well as *Solidarity,* the publication of the International Workers of the World.[68] Regulation to sustain the militarized state was simultaneously targeted at the socialist and unionist challenges to liberal political economy. Over nineteen hundred prosecutions were carried out under the terms of the Espionage and Sedition Acts during the short time the country participated in the war.[69] Debs was but one high-profile example of this extraordinary policing of peaceful dissidence. The radical economist Scott Nearing was also indicted for scholarship that explored the connections among capitalism, imperialism, and war that I too have been exploring, using some of his scholarship in the process.[70] By early 1918, the mass targeting of International Workers of the World members led to a series of political trials, which handed out heavy sentences of as much as ten years imprisonment for circulating material that was often simply pacifist and antiwar.[71] Simultaneously the director of a film about the Revolutionary War of 1776 was jailed in 1918 under the terms of the Espionage Act, because the film showed scenes of British brutality and so, it was claimed, undermined support for the alliance with the imperial British state.[72]

Quite clearly the state's intensified and exceptional surveillance targeted speech, broadly conceived to include print publications and film, that questioned the motivations for war, or otherwise undermined support for it. Speech challenging the ascendancy of the forms of corporate liberalism that led to what Nearing labeled "dollar imperialism," and that underpinned the militant and militarized foreign policy of the United States beginning in the latter years of the nineteenth century, was particularly targeted. It marked what must be understood as a deformation of the principles of liberal democracy to foster free speech as a necessary and crucial component of any conception of liberty. By radically limiting the possibility of speech that challenged the primacy of the prevailing political and economic order, and its militarized sustenance, the legislation and its policing were consistent with the broader winnowing down of the progressive components of liberalism by the logics of capitalism and its mutation into the "national security liberalism" established in incipient form here and more fully and expansively in the aftermath of World War II.[73]

Debs and other convicted socialists challenged the legality and constitutionality of the state's extraordinary policing of speech. But when the cases reached the Supreme Court in early 1919, they were dismissed in rulings that upheld the constitutionality of the Espionage and Sedition Acts and delegated authority to the government and the courts to police speech that could present "a clear and present danger" to the "nation" during wartime.[74] New practices of policing, internment, denaturalization, and deportation were simultaneously initiated that specifically targeted migrant workers and those suspected of harboring socialist tendencies.[75]

In 1919, Attorney General A. Mitchell Palmer created a new division of the Bureau of Investigation specifically to target suspected radical groups. Palmer organized a series of raids on meetings held by the Union of Russian Workers, which were timed to coincide with the second anniversary of the Bolshevik regime in Russia. In January 1920, Palmer's Department of Justice collaborated with local police forces to round up members of the Communist Party.[76] The bureau became a political police force that targeted radicalism of various types. Chaplin, for example, was investigated by the bureau in the early 1920s, after his progressive political views became apparent: quite a comedown from his role as heroic exemplar of state debt in 1917–18.[77]

Policing media dovetailed again with its deployment. Right at the beginning of 1919, in the immediate aftermath of the war, Wilson authorized the creation of a "visual instruction" section of the Bureau of Education to be a "clearinghouse," through which films produced by the government during the war would be widely circulated so they could have what one bureaucrat called "greater usefulness."[78] Following this the secretary of the interior asked the secretary of war for cooperation in passing the films produced for the war effort over to the Bureau of Education, from where these films would be distributed to schools and colleges to foster "Americanization."[79] Over one million feet of film were salvaged from the military and CPI and circulated through these emergent nontheatrical networks, created by the government in partnership with educational institutions in particular.[80] Simultaneously motion picture exhibition equipment used abroad by the government during the war was also dispersed at cheap prices to a wider nontheatrical network after the end of the conflict.[81] Both the propaganda films produced by the CPI and the material means for their projection were thus put into circulation as concrete—material—examples, both of the extension of the state of exception in the interwar years and of the twinned dynamic of media production and regulation that I have been exploring thus far. I turn now to examining the expanded deployment of cinema by the US state, principally in the interwar years.

5

The State of Extension

Protest at exploitative labor practices and the pressures and brutality of total war simmered during the conflict of 1914–18 but exploded in its immediate aftermath. In January 1919, for example, 35,000 textile workers in New York went on strike; in February there was a general strike of 60,000 union personnel in Seattle; in the autumn, a steel strike drew together 376,000 workers.[1] Police, and rail, transport, dock, and coal workers struck in Britain between 1918 and 1921, culminating in a general strike in 1926.[2] By that point, the enormous expense of war, alongside the continued repayments to American financiers and the death and injury to over 3,000,000 people, had left the British economy in tatters. (New policies of "imperial preference," alongside new cultural practices like documentary filmmaking, emerged in this context, a subject I explore further in chapter 8.) In the United States, an economic depression in 1920–21, caused in part by the reduction of agricultural exports to Europe and the partial breakdown of the prewar, liberal free trade system, triggered economic deprivation and worker protest in the rural periphery in particular.[3] Labor, socialist, and communist parties gained support and became—in Britain, at least—a viable electoral alternative to conservative and liberal parties.[4] (Labor formed a minority government in Britain for the first time in 1924, helped by the expansion of the democratic franchise under the pressure of war in 1918.)[5] Overseas the Soviet experiment with collective ownership of the means of production visibly challenged the primacy of private property in liberal capitalism. In March 1919, the Third International, a worldwide body of Communists from forty-one nations, met in Moscow and proclaimed worldwide proletarian revolution as its goal, threatening nation-based political order and global trade.

Responses by political and economic elites in both Britain and the United States were expansive. The experiments in exceptional "illiberal" state practices innovated during wartime were extended. Britain's Emergency Powers Act of 1920 continued the exceptional police power of the state, granted by the 1914 Defense of the Realm Act, by enabling the government to declare a state of emergency for one month and to make any regulation necessary to secure "essential services."[6] (Emergency powers were quickly invoked to deal with the coal strike of 1921.) New powers for the political oversight of the police were granted in the Police Act of 1919, which also barred police from belonging to a trade union or striking.[7]

In that same year, 1919, the Red Scare in the United States produced a brutal clampdown on workers and unions, which continued the quashing of dissent encoded in the Espionage and Sedition Acts and extended it to include new policing institutions and practices of internment, denaturalization, and deportation. Migrant workers in particular were targeted. In late 1917, an Immigration act specifically excluded migrants suspected of membership in revolutionary organizations, as well as those who had advocated socialist or revolutionary sentiments after being granted entry.[8] In October 1918, the Alien Anarchist Act further asserted federal authority to deport any alien or recently naturalized citizen who believed in the overthrow of the government, even if that person had never actually acted on that belief.[9] In 1919, Attorney General A. Mitchell Palmer created a new division of the Bureau of Investigation, specifically to target suspected radical groups, as I noted at the end of the previous chapter. (J. Edgar Hoover, long-standing head of the subsequent Federal Bureau of Investigation, played a central role in this division, which also assumed responsibility for enforcing that other product of racial nationalism known as Prohibition.)[10] Quasi-governmental "loyalty" and "security" organizations likewise proliferated during the war and postwar period amid widespread anxieties about the divided loyalties of "hyphenated" immigrant groups.[11]

By the end of the war, the project to "Americanize" the economically displaced populations, who had been drawn to the United States as the central pole of attraction in the world system, had become a crucial task carried out by federal and state governments, civic groups, and corporations, often acting in concert. The "pressing need"—as the Ford advertisement for its films from 1919 framed it—to Americanize foreign workers led to a host of educational programs and endeavors. Workers at Ford, overwhelmingly drawn from migrant populations, were taught by the company how to maintain a clean "well conducted home," in ways that sought specifically to reorient immigrant traditions of extended families and communities, just as the fictional Hungarian migrant in the US Steel film *An American in the Making,* discussed in chapter 3, learned how to love his English teacher and property.[12] Violence, deportation and a restrictive racial nationalism as a form of racialized social control clearly dovetailed with this expansive pedagogic project in a further illustration of the dialectic of liberal governmentality in the service of maintaining a particular political and economic system. The dovetailed joints were sometimes visible. Upton Sinclair, for example, called the beating by state police of mourners at a funeral of two immigrant anarchists, who had been executed by the state in 1927, "the process known as 'Americanization.'"[13]

In the years from 1917 to the mid-1920s, then, state and corporate forces, frequently in collaboration with each other, mounted a counteroffensive against worker militancy and the expansion of democracy. I will first concentrate on the situation in the United States, and the actions of federal bureaucracies, before returning in the next chapter to the corporate counteroffensive against union activism—known as "the American plan"—and turning in chapter 8 to the response in the mid-1920s of the British state to domestic and subaltern dissent and to the growing economic and geopolitical primacy of the United States. The elaboration of pedagogic and policing institutions and practices in the United States in the postwar period marked the second stage of the corporate reconstruction of liberal capitalism, after its inception in the 1890s. Evidently the parameters of this encompassed both the bio-political and the economic, with the two modalities of governance dovetailing in—for example—the project to Americanize migrant populations. The *pressing need* for "reliable" citizens and workers in the integrated global system of liberal capitalism became a disciplinary and pedagogic project.

Visual mass media was consistently used in this counteroffensive. Movies were widely deployed in particular because of their popularity with working-class and migrant audiences. Numerous branches of the US government began to elaborate new production facilities and establish new distribution and exhibition networks that made considerable use of state educational institutions like land-grant universities. "Visual instruction" networks emerged, amid much rhetoric about the pedagogic value and impact of the "universal language"—as Wilson had framed it—of visual materials on particular populations. The movies these administrative bureaus produced were often undertaken in partnership with corporate organizations, especially those in extractive and industrial economies. Indeed, these collaborations themselves stand now as visible evidence of the close ties between state and corporate organizations, as they set about teaching people how to work, live, and consume. The movies the state produced sought to be directly instructional, but increasingly they also visualized the structures of *allegiance* to the nation and its political and economic institutions and practices. The state's use of media grew into a systematic project to create both the new figural resources needed to model appropriate and productive conduct for working-class and migrant audiences, as well as the material networks to circulate these films as the extension of the work of government.

War intensified this process, but it did not produce it. I started this history with a series of examples from 1913 that showed how various institutions had begun to use film to achieve particular but broadly related pedagogic goals. The significant precedent for the development of government filmmaking as part of an "extension" network to educate populations in productive ways to work and live was carried out by the US Department of Agriculture (USDA). I explore here further the beginnings and operations of the agricultural extension system and the role that film played in instructing rural workers in new productive and frequently mechanized practices. Visual instruction emerged as a broader movement out of the extension network elaborated initially by the USDA and thereafter also by the Division of Educational Extension in the Department of the Interior's Bureau of Education. Educational "extension" built also on the emergence of extension departments at universities, in particular land-grant ones, which sought to bring the academy into closer relationship with populations outside its walls in order to make education more directly "useful."[14] Extension became in this way a broader pedagogical project across various departments of the state, as well as of educational institutions, to enable government to intervene in the conduct of populations. Visual materials, including film, became important to this project, particularly in the years from 1919 on, when the Visual Instruction Section of the Bureau of Education was established. It was proposed that the bureau was the appropriate central organizing body for the elaboration of an extension and visual instruction network at this moment, because it was, its own reports suggested, "that branch of Government most intimately connected with the making of good and patriotic citizens" and in particular "for transforming our foreign-born residents into 'loyal, literate, and efficient citizens.'"[15] It was also the case that the Bureau of Education had close ties with corporate philanthropic educational organizations, like the aforementioned Rockefeller-financed General Education Board and the Carnegie Trust, and played a significant role in establishing what Clyde Barrow calls "the corporate ideal" of the university during the war and interwar years.[16] Extension merged with this ideal in making knowledge practicable and useful.

The postwar establishment of this extended visual instruction circuit radiating from Washington and implemented by universities took place in the midst of the Red Scare and the reestablishment of corporate liberalism. It marked a shift toward integrating film and its perceived pedagogic power with the expansive state and corporate efforts to educate and interpellate *urban* working-class populations— particularly economically displaced ones—in the responsibilities of liberal, capitalist, American citizenship. By doing so, it supplemented the agricultural extension network. Related rhetoric about the pedagogical efficacy of movies, which developed within these networks, built on the new theories about the malleability of subjectivity that were emerging in the human sciences, as well as from the purported success of propaganda during the war, and merged with the wider discussions about the place of media in pedagogy and in "manufacturing consent" in newly expanded liberal democracies that proliferated in the 1920s. I look at this specific history of visual instruction and educational extension later in this chapter as a crucial part of my broader examination of the way film and other media were used to help establish a particular modality of political and economic power.

"SPECIAL PROPAGANDA"

Chapter 3 discussed the formation of the USDA in 1862 as part of the federal state's investment in administration and education to facilitate economic productivity. Land "granted" by the federal government in the Morrill Act in the same year was used by individual states to endow and support agricultural colleges and universities. The USDA began with a largely practical agenda in gathering and disseminating knowledge about seeds, animals, and agricultural machinery to farmers, but this agenda began to shift in the late nineteenth century toward the development of applied and pure scientific research and a more activist intervention into agricultural practices and market planning, which established the department as "the principal scientific agency of American government."[17] Federal funds from the 1887 Hatch Act created further agricultural "experiment stations," which provided research information to universities and farmers.[18] The USDA created the Association of American Agricultural Colleges and Experiment Stations in 1888 to coordinate research between itself, the colleges, and the experimental stations.[19]

Plant breeding was innovated to adapt the natural world to machine processing, to facilitate the mechanization of farming.[20] In the early twentieth century, USDA scientists were assembled into a host of bureau that propelled research into entomology, soils, plants, animals, and, slightly later, patterns of rural life, markets, and agricultural economics.[21] It was a significant component of the creation of the associative state in the United States, whereby "ordering systems" were created "while sustaining self-government, private decision-making, and a limited formal state apparatus."[22] The scientific innovations of the USDA marked the convergence of pure and applied scientific knowledge to expand governmental oversight and facilitate economic productivity and the welfare of populations. Knowledge created circulated among government agencies, research and teaching institutions, the research and development arms of chemical and industrial manufacturers, and farmers.

The efficacy of the USDA was tested when a boll weevil infestation destroyed large swathes of the southern cotton crop beginning in 1892. Cotton had long been critical to the southern economy and indeed to the liberal world system. The boll weevil ruined parts of the cotton crop in 1892 and began spreading at the culmination of a long period of economic downturn, which stretched from 1876 to 1893, and at the height of the populist insurgency. "We know of no single subject," the journal *Science* wrote, "that contains more of importance to the entire country's economic interests than the devising of methods to arrest and, if possible, eradicate this scourge."[23] It was from this problem that the USDA established an extension system to rapidly circulate information to farmers. Government officials in the Bureaus of Plant Industry and Entomology established experimental demonstration farms to test methods of weevil control.[24] In 1902, the project to counteract the damaging effects of the weevil was assigned to Seaman A. Knapp, who devised a system whereby farmers followed exactly his advice in cultivating parts of their land, and any losses incurred were made good on by a fund supported by the USDA and local businesses.[25] Knapp proposed ways both to reduce the weevil damage, principally by developing new seeds and early harvesting, and to improve southern agriculture, generally through crop diversification and rotation and new cultivation techniques. Local farmers were invited to observe the methods and copy them. Extension and its pedagogical methodology were predicated in this way on the valorization of direct experience and of practices of imitation. Knapp's system enlarged the power of the USDA and facilitated the further elaboration of modern scientific farming practices in the South.[26]

In 1904, Congress agreed to allocate $250,000 to combat the weevil, and the USDA expanded its extension work, employing twenty-four new demonstration agents and creating more than seven thousand demonstration farms.[27] In 1906, the government's money was supplemented by large grants from the General Education Board (GEB), a philanthropic group that had over $50 million in funding from oil baron John D. Rockefeller Jr.[28] Altogether the GEB contribution to southern extension work totaled almost $1 million over a nine-year period.[29] Rockefeller's philanthropic investment was designed to facilitate the economic productivity of the South.[30] GEB money also helped support new programs for the systematic education of farm youth as one aspect of the extension project. "Children's clubs" encouraged boys to study "agricultural science," while girls were taught "domestic science," the latter of which dovetailed with the emergence of "home economics." Also pioneered by the USDA, home economics taught women new practices of efficiency and rationality that mirrored those being developed in agriculture and in the Fordist practices of industry.[31]

In 1914, Congress institutionalized and nationalized the USDA's southern extension system. The Smith-Lever Agricultural Extension Work Act in that year inaugurated a large-scale system of practical education for farmers, conducted by the USDA "in cooperation" with the land-grant colleges.[32] Large numbers of these colleges already had extension departments—there were forty-three by 1912—and this legislation positioned these departments as central to the "nexus of institutions" that developed to manage and expand the agricultural economy in the early twentieth century.[33] It was these extension departments at universities that would become important to the general distribution of nontheatrical films in the later teens and 1920s. In 1916, the government's educational programs were further extended, when the Smith-Hughes Act created a new and unprecedented federal role in promoting agricultural, industrial, and home economics education at the high-school level.[34] Extension work carried out through the institutional nexus of the USDA and the land-grant colleges, and supplemented by money from industrial philanthropy, marked an extremely significant pedagogical intervention into the conduct of workers and the organization of the rural economy.

The political and economic logics subtending this investment in agriculture, science, and education can usefully be quickly recalled. Governmental practices took cognizance of the fact that food was of paramount importance to populations, and so its availability and cost were a critical index of the legitimacy of political regimes. The imperative to balance cheap and plentiful food production through advances in science and technology and distribution networks to facilitate population (and urban and industrial) growth, and yet maintain profitability for farmers, was a central task of macro economic policy.[35] It was essential to keeping urban wages low, to keeping exports competitive, and, more broadly, to sustaining the political economy of abundance that was becoming central to the emerging urban consumer economy. Simply put, the scientific development of agriculture became an important source of primary accumulation for advanced industrial capitalism.[36] Governmental interventions into the agricultural economy from the 1890s in particular sought also to negate the "extreme demands" of farmers and populists into what political scientist Elizabeth Sanders calls "the moderate, discretion-laden programs of an expanding bureaucratic state."[37] Destroying populism was critical to the establishment of corporate liberalism. Rockefeller's GEB was unsurprisingly also wedded to this project. Populists protested at the increasing cost of machines, chemicals, and transport, the combined effects of which were driving many farmers to become tenants or sharecroppers or to work in industrial factories and which lead to the concentration of farmlands in the hands of rich landowners.[38]

The policies of the state with regard to land, property rights, and new chemical and mechanical practices led to the growth of what came to be called "agribusiness."[39] New, large chemical and biotechnology corporations began to form and became increasingly influential, often working in concert with the USDA. (Monsanto, for example, was created in 1901 and is now a multinational chemical and biotechnology corporation heavily invested in pesticides and new genetically modified seed technologies, some of which were developed in collaboration with the USDA.) The growth of agribusiness was also predicated on the casualization of labor and the creation of a migratory agricultural proletariat, which in the large farm states of California and Texas was made up principally of Filipinos and Mexicans.[40] Corporate-style agricultural businesses proliferated in the 1910s and 1920s, after the effective destruction of the Populist Movement. In 1923 the USDA established a Bureau of Agricultural Economics to further the economic modernization of farming through detailed reporting on markets and the facilitation of the use of bank loans to enable farm expansion and the purchase of expensive seed and mechanical technology.[41]

The state innovated the use of film to further these expansive political and economic goals. It began to do so in late 1913, when a Temporary Motion Picture Committee was established to consider "the development of moving pictures dealing with agricultural subjects and the method of agricultural education" and "to report plans whereby the use of motion pictures in agricultural education could be placed on a stable basis as a Departmental project."[42] It met just five times, after which members "asked to be discharged and recommended that a permanent committee be appointed, and the Department at once install, in the Division of Publications as a feature of the Section of Illustrations, a complete laboratory for the taking, developing and printing of its own films."[43] The secretary of state for agriculture approved these recommendations in December 1913, and the permanent Committee on Motion Picture Activities met for the first time in January 1914.[44] Quickly thereafter the committee set about establishing a film laboratory and testing and purchasing the materials necessary for government filmmaking. Memorandums document the details of tests on arc lights, cameras, and portable projectors, as well as the costs of their purchase.[45] In its first few months of existence, up until November 1914, the film unit produced twenty-seven films, ranging from those for the Bureau of Animal Industry (e.g., *Cooperative Cow Testing in Vermont*), Bureau of Plant Industry (e.g., *Congressional Seed Distribution*), Bureau of Chemistry (e.g., *Destruction of Condemned Goods*), Forest Service (e.g., *The National Forests*), and the Office of Public Roads (e.g., *Road Building and Testing Scenes*).[46] It is likely that these films were the first produced by an established filmmaking unit in the cabinet offices of a liberal democratic state.

The speed of the decision to establish motion picture production within the department, and the film unit's alacrity in equipping a laboratory and making films, was a consequence of three related developments. First, the Panama Exposition Board prompted various departments to make films for the 1915 Panama-Pacific International Exposition, as visible evidence of the modernity and efficacy of the American state. The board asked the USDA, as the most advanced of the state's administrative units, to produce films for other government departments, including the Treasury, Bureau of Education, Department of Commerce, and Post Office.[47] Indeed, the purchase of a second motion picture camera by the USDA in May 1914 was made in order to "enable the Department to cooperate more effectively with the Panama Exposition Board"—that is, to use film to visualize the display and reach of government work so central to the exposition.[48]

Second, the USDA was clearly given this responsibility because it had already experimented with the use of film and its integration with its extension work. The department had begun to collaborate with commercial filmmakers and had used films as "adjuncts to the work of their speakers at conventions or in connection with special propaganda carried on by the field force."[49] Toward the end of 1913, just before the establishment of the Temporary Committee, the Bureau of Animal

Industry showed widely a film called *The Life of the Cattle Fever Tick and the Method of Dipping Cattle* (1913). Also produced were films by the Office of Public Roads, which were shown, the department noted, "at gatherings of highway commissions and other road building conferences" and were intended "to interest the public in road improvement."[50] I will come back to some of these road films in the following two chapters because they were significant examples of the way film was put to work to help transform infrastructure. Evidently the USDA's extension project to educate populations in the rural periphery prompted the early adoption of film as a medium of persuasive communication.

Third, the department's investment in film was also driven by the simple fact that films were popular with rural audiences, some members of whom were illiterate, and thus were a useful mechanism for conveying government information in its extension network. The report on the first showing of *The Life of the Cattle Fever Tick and the Method of Dipping Cattle,* for example, observed that it was so popular it was shown three times.[51] The imperative to enumerate and document that characterizes administrative governance is visible in scattered letters and memorandum. "Motion picture exhibit[s]," a 1914 report on the workings of the film unit observed, "brought out 75 to 100 people, where stereopticon talks attracted only 10 to 20."[52] It is clear that the drawing power and popularity of motion pictures were crucial advantages to their "extended" dissemination, for they functioned in this way as a means to bring government and particular populations—here, rural workers—together: a literal and figurative site of government work.

Evidence suggests that the rapid development of filmmaking from the beginning of 1914 was substantially funded from money allocated to the USDA by Congress through the Smith-Lever Act, to develop and expand the extension program.[53] Money disbursed through the Smith-Lever Act was also invoked by the USDA as a way for university extension departments to buy its films, as well as other government films, to set up film libraries to further establish and develop moving pictures as part of the extension work of government departments and educational institutions.[54] In 1922 the utility of film for extension work was further recognized when the filmmaking unit was relocated from the Division of Publications to the relatively newly created Office of Cooperative Extension Work.[55] In 1924 a separate building housing a studio, a processing laboratory, vaults, cutting space, projection theater, and offices was built.[56] It seems that the film activities of the USDA were driven and supported principally by the department's extension work to facilitate particular kinds of welfare and productivity and that this encompassed several related developments: Extension work informed the department's film production, in terms both of the content and form of the films it made; created a network of film distribution, making use in particular of the extension departments of state universities; and motivated the creation of new technologies like mobile projection equipment and electric generators to facilitate the movement of these films along an extension network that radiated outward from Washington to agricultural communities.

"THE FILMS ARE OF GREAT SERVICE . . . TO THE EYE-MINDED"

In 1913, right at the start of the process that led to the establishment of the Temporary Motion Picture Committee later that year, the USDA began showing *The Life of the Cattle Fever Tick and the Method of Dipping Cattle.* Its goal was to explain to farmers the cause and treatment of so-called Texas Fever, a disease that affected cattle in the South because of particular climactic factors.[57] Texas was particularly hard hit because of the number of large cattle ranges in the state. In 1889, USDA scientists in the Bureau of Animal Industry had discovered that the disease was caused by cattle ticks, and they subsequently innovated treatment that entailed dipping cattle in particular chemicals. It was a significant scientific advance, clear evidence of the value of government-led and financed scientific investigation for agricultural productivity. It was imperative that the information be communicated widely because the cattle tick had disastrous consequences not only for cattle-rearing in the South but also, and even more importantly, because the southern cattle—which had developed limited forms of immunity—infected and killed northern cattle when driven to markets in the North.[58] The Bureau of Animal Industry accordingly began tracking the movement of southern cattle and the federal government delineated a quarantine line following the known northern border of permanent cattle infestation.[59] It was developed specifically to sustain a cash economy in cattle-rearing, in ways that directly supported the capital-intensive commercial farming of large corporate-style ranches.[60] Smaller-scale farmers, particularly the tenant and sharecropping farmers, who in the South were frequently African-American, raised cattle mostly not as a cash crop but for purposes of subsistence. Many of these farmers complained bitterly about the considerable expense of dipping cattle. Violent refusal was not uncommon. The rather prosaic cattle tick film was produced and shown in the context of the federal government's support for capital-intensive commercial farming—to the exclusion of other farming practices—and the sustenance of the interconnected national market. It directly intervened in an ongoing and complex negotiation between farmers and government, albeit one that was clearly heavily weighted toward the authority and power of government. Right at the start of its experiment with film production, the USDA began to put film to work to bolster its support of particular agricultural and fiscal practices and economies of scale.

Bureaucratic reports and memorandums from this point discuss the nature and utility of cinema for the department's work. It can be seen as a form of film theory, albeit one that unusually carried some real-world consequences. In a letter in

March 1914, for example, the assistant secretary of state for agriculture, B. T. Galloway wrote, "We have yet to decide, however, whether films can be developed to a point where they will *actually teach* agricultural processes."[61] Galloway's words implied a distinction between pedagogy and the representation of processes. But his initial uncertainty gave way to a growing consensus in the department that film had concrete effects, and thus could be considered directly pedagogical. In the 1914 annual report on the activities of the new film unit, the committee claimed, "Pictures enabled those who saw them to visualize into concrete action the otherwise abstract points of the propaganda."[62] In the 1915 report, it was similarly proposed that "Film . . . does give an excellent idea of the plan to be followed, puts the spectators in a more receptive frame of mind, breaks ground for the demonstrator and his practice work, and stimulates intelligent reading of bulletins."[63] Visualization leads away from abstraction, these reflections suggested, and directly to concrete action. In the same report the department stated, "The films are of great service to those who are not fond of reading and to the eye-minded who do not readily digest a lecture. They are especially useful in planting ideas in the minds of young people."[64] Evidently the department's bureaucrats saw in the "concrete" visualization of film—what later theorists would call its indexicality—a useful pedagogic tool that enabled its audience to move beyond the visual toward direct action. Indeed, the state's theorizing proposed that the "eye minded"—meaning the largely illiterate poor migrant and black farmer audience—were more easily reached and influenced by moving pictures, as indeed were the young, whose minds were particularly ripe for the "planting" and cultivation of ideas and practices of government. "Visual Instruction," predicated both on ideas about the impact of film and about the plasticity of subjectivity, emerged in this precise context as a pedagogical idea that sought to use visual forms to reach marginal populations in order to socialize them in various productive and civic practices.

What these bureaucratic reflections on the ontology and form of film "revealed" was its unique suitability for extension work and so for the expansion of government pedagogy and oversight to ever-more remote regions. Knapp's demonstration farm system worked under the straightforward assumption that farmers would observe new practices and then imitate them, and that this would in turn generate new productive practices. In its annual report in 1915 the Motion Picture Committee directly stated that "Films explain the methods to be taught, in a concrete form, and bring to the people of one neighborhood direct evidence of the measures in successful practice in other localities."[65] The indexical concreteness of film could carry its demonstrations to widely dispersed farmers, so overcoming the resistance or difficulty that they had in traveling themselves to demonstration farms.[66] Examples of this type of USDA film were produced right at the beginning of the work of the department. These included, for example, *Silo Construction, Poison Effects on Sheep, Commercial Canning of Corn, Spraying and Pruning of*

Trees (all 1914), as well as the later, more elaborate films, such as the four-reel *The Government Poultry Farm* (c. 1917) from the Bureau of Animal Industry, which showed how poultry was raised on a government farm as an example of best practice. Various other films extended this logic from farming practice to the economic exploitation of products, most notably those from the Office of Markets, including the long, multireel film *Cotton* (c. 1917),which encompassed cultivation, ginning, marketing, and manufacturing uses of this crucial cash crop.

Movies made extension possible through a mechanic indexical reproducibility that could circulate in ways land could not. To be effective in this way, though, moving pictures had to become fully mobile. In the early discussions within the USDA about the utility of film, bureaucrats began to ponder the vexed question of how film could be used by its demonstration agents in remote areas. The problems were considerable. Not only was this before the establishment of extensive road networks, but it was also before the widespread dissemination of electricity, as well as the standardization of currents and the development of reliable portable projection equipment. In late 1914, therefore, the committee announced "some method of projecting which does not call for electric current from public-service mains must be devised."[67] Government employees investigated portable projection units and had manufacturers come to demonstrate them in the department's offices. Likewise, the Motion Picture Committee investigated "the possibility of equipping an ordinary automobile with an electric generator which will supply the small amperage needed" for portable projectors.[68] Various machines were examined, including demonstrations by companies in 1917 of portable electricity-generating machines.[69] In the same year, the Motion Picture Committee committed to buying a number of portable projectors and recommended that "experimental work" be carried out by the Office of Public Roads and Rural Engineering, "to equip automobiles cheaply and effectively to generate electric current for projectors and thus to make it possible to give satisfactory motion-picture exhibitions out of doors and in rural schools, churches and halls where no commercial current is present."[70] In a memorandum of 1921, the chief of the Photographic Division of the USDA stated that "Types of apparatus which use current generated by automobile engines [were] now being perfected."[71] The department also innovated the use of portable screens.[72] In order to establish the efficacy of these technologies, the department issued a questionnaire in January 1922.[73] The results showed that 332 extension agents out of 982 were using motion pictures in their extension work.[74]

These developments constituted a significant effort to combine figural and material/machinic resources to establish new communication channels to influence the conduct of—here—rural populations. The department's conception of movie watching as a form of modern pedagogy is well illustrated on the cover of the 1926 publication *Use of Motion Pictures in Agricultural Extension Work* (see fig. 1, chapter 2.) In the picture, movies and ancillary technologies come to *embody* a machine-made modernity. Electrical, modern technology transforms traditional rural practices and makes them modern in ways similar in some respects to the way Fordism transformed industrial practices. Indeed, we can glimpse something of the effects of these government-sponsored electrical technologies on remote rural populations in a remarkable account of film extension work by Fred Pickering, who had become special assistant to the secretary in charge of the Motion Picture Department in 1919. In a 1921 letter, Pickering wrote of what it was like to enter a remote town with the department's mobile film truck: "The children . . . when they see the Government truck go by with a lot of strange equipment in it, they look upon it very much as they would a truck loaded with toys on Christmas Eve, and they regard those in charge as a kind of sublimated Santa Claus."[75] Wary initially of government workers, the men in such locations, Pickering writes, become "very much interested in the cable which carries the current to the picture machine" whilst "the bright eyes of the children, and the tired eyes of the women . . . are made to sparkle by their first sight of an electric light."[76] The state's film project exemplified a technological modernity characterized by electricity, mechanization, mobility, and a government-directed vision that supplemented the particular policies of the bureau with regard to the modernization of agriculture, as well as to the broader governmental efforts to direct the conduct of workers to establish and entrench new productive practices.

In the early days of its experiments with moving pictures, the USDA also began circulating its films "through lending, renting or selling films to private agencies, such as schools, churches, farmers' and other organizations, county fairs, conventions, etc.," so that its films could be "shown at country schoolhouses and churches, as well as in towns and villages, over a wide area in the South and in the Northwest," as well as at state and county fairs.[77] By around 1918, this effort shifted toward the more substantive use of extension departments at the state universities and agricultural colleges, which were central to the institutional nexus established for shaping research and policy. Extension departments of particular universities became distribution centers for the department's films and for a burgeoning nontheatrical film sector. In 1918, the University of Wisconsin at Madison, for example, had a Department of Visual Instruction that collaborated with its Extension Division to circulate "educational motion pictures" free of charge "to public schools and qualified civic organizations."[78] Universities, particularly midwestern land-grant institutions, quickly followed suit, and by 1920, the extension departments at Indiana, Kansas, North Dakota, Missouri, Arkansas, and others as far afield as California, Florida, and Massachusetts purchased and circulated films from the USDA, other government departments, and other nontheatrical film producers. This process was facilitated also by the Division of Educational Extension office, set up within the Department of the Interior, the aims of which were "to establish a national system whereby pictures, both of an educational and industrial character, produced not by Government departments only, but by any other available agency, may be distributed throughout the schools, colleges, universities, and other educational institutions of the country."[79] In a 1921 USDA memorandum, the department also proposed that land-grant universities use Smith-Lever money to become distributing centers.[80] Extension departments at universities supplemented the mobility of the extension agent. Machines and networks joined the federal state to specific regions to shape the conduct of populations and "modernize" economies.

Indeed, the developing connections with extension departments marked also an effort to circulate film more broadly, extending outward from rural workers and specific government projects to communicate ideas about general government practice. This marked an important expansion of how government film functioned. It now included films that publicized the work of government and circulated among broader publics. In a 1917 report on extending its film program in order to better facilitate the goal to "supply films to outside agencies," the department outlined two broad classifications of films.[81] The first group was defined as those films "designed primarily for use in direct agricultural education."[82] But the second category was broadened out to encompass "films designed to make clear certain functions of government, to convey information as to public resources and facilities, to promote the protection of public property, and to develop an intelligent and constructive citizenship."[83] Visible here was an emerging conception of government film as a publicity medium conveying broad ideas about government practice and appropriate citizen conduct.

It seems that this more expansive conception of the pedagogical work of film also led the department to seek to increase the distribution of its films by developing ties with commercial film distributors. In March 1917, a subcommittee was formed to "survey the commercial motion picture field" and report on how the department could effectively partner with a film company to distribute its films in the wider commercial networks that had been established by 1917.[84] Universal was chosen. The company began to distribute some of the USDA films to commercial cinemas, and in early 1918 it began to "abridge" some of this "material" and circulate it in its widely seen *Screen Magazine* newsreel.[85] The USDA's shift toward a broader conception of the publicity work of film coincided with the presidential establishment of the Committee on Public Information and the closer ties between Hollywood and the state.

THE OLD AND THE NEW

Various USDA films exemplified this publicity logic in advertising the work of the government in nascent form from the outset, and this became more widespread after 1917. *Government Meat Inspection* (Bureau of Animal Industry, c. 1914), for example, shows the ways in which healthy and diseased meat was inspected and what happened when disease was discovered. "Under Uncle Sam's Eye," a title exclaims, "From Hoof to Meat Ready for the Table." *Destruction of Condemned Goods* (Bureau of Chemistry, c. 1915) advertises the government's protective powers. *Clean Herds and Hearts* (Bureau of Animal Industries, c. 1924) tells a story about how the children of a county persuaded their parents to submit their cattle for tuberculosis testing. Uncle Sam regulated commercial practices, these films suggest, for the purposes of welfare. (Despite the reality that these regulations were established in partnership with major American meatpackers in order to protect exports).[86] Publicity segued into advertising for both specific products and for the work of government in protecting and developing farming. *Dates—America's New Fruit Crop* (Bureau of Plant Industry, c. 1922) shows the "establishment of a new industry through Government effort."[87] *Uncle Sam, World Champion Farmer* (Bureau of Plant Industry, c. 1922), for example, demonstrates "how the United States leads the world in food production."[88]

Government media extolled the varied benefits of the productive oversight and economic development fostered by the state. *Tree Planting in the National Forests* (Forest Service, c. 1917), *The Work of a Forest Ranger* (Forest Service, c. 1917), and *Winged Guardians of the Forest* (Forest Service, c. 1922) all show aspects of the workings of the Forest Service. Numerous films, including films on mountains and a series on national forests in Colorado, New Hampshire, New Mexico, and Oregon (e.g., *Trails that Lure* (Forest Service, c. 1919), *Outdoor Life in the Rockies— National Forests of Colorado* (Forest Service, c. 1919), *The Santa Fe National Forest* (Forest Service, n.d.)), reveal the splendor of national lands and scenery. Quite a number of films display the benefits of the extension system itself and thus the efficacy of governmental networks to revitalize and sustain agricultural life. Kids benefit from extension work in *Boy's Pig Club Work* and *The 4-H Camp for Boys and Girls* (States Relations Service, c. 1922), which shows "work and play at one of the camps where club boys and girls learn better farming and home work, and the meaning of 4-H—Head, Heart, Hand, and Health Development."[89] *Helping Negroes to Become Better Farmers and Homemakers* (States Relations Service, c. 1921) demonstrates how USDA extension agents helped African American farmers. Women likewise benefit in the three-reel *The Home Demonstration Agent*, which shows the agent's work with women and girls and in *The Happier Way*, which introduces labor-saving devices for the home (both States Relations Services, c. 1926). Finally, the whole community benefits from extension work in *The Farm Bureau Comes to Pleasant View* (States Relations Service, c. 1926).

Let me take one example in detail: *Helping Negroes to Become Better Farmers and Homemakers* tells of the benefits the extension system brought to black tenant farmers in eastern Alabama. It was made with some form of cooperation with the Alabama Polytechnic Institute and the Tuskegee Institute. At the outset we are introduced to "Rube Collins, typical of many Negro tenant farmers in the South" and his family, including his youngest daughter, who is introduced simply with an intertitle reading "Etc" while eating a large watermelon.[90] Typicality and the generic example of the "etc" function to generalize the narrative and the moral of the story. Collins is a character but is one broadly drawn to exemplify a particular position—the initially poor black tenant farmer—and the film is split between the poles of individualized narrative and generality and iteration that are characteristic of many nontheatrical educational films in the period. Collins is clearly poor, as indicated by the sparseness of his family's shack. After his introduction, and a scene of his family working in the field and subsequently relaxing, a neighbor appears and tells Collins that he has found a pest in his cotton crop. Collins and his colleague travel to tell their white landlord, who immediately summons the white extension agent, who tells them they have boll weevils. A microscopic close-up shows the weevil, as the film inserts informational detail into its story. The agent explains to the two farmers the way to control the boll weevil pest, following the methods of early cultivation and crop diversification established by Seaman Knapp at his demonstration farm.

Three instructional vignettes show the black farmers following these instructions and, "with their landlord's approval," beginning to "diversify their farming and to grow food and feed crops." All of this leads directly to economic betterment. "Two years later," an intertitle tells us, "better farming has given the Collins family a better home, and a local Negro agent to assist the White agent has become necessary." Collins and his family now live in a larger farmhouse, containing several rooms. The contrast is made explicit in a brief sequence that starts with the intertitle "The Old," followed by a shot of the family's previous shack, and then proceeds to "The New," which features a slow pan of their more prosperous home: the old ways are superseded by the new, made possible by government intervention. This film, with its shift from the old to the new, has quite a different valence than, say, Sergei Eisenstein's contemporaneous film *The Old and the New* (1929) about the collectivization of agricultural practices. In the USDA film, the slow pan of Collin's new and large house uses camera movement to carefully and slowly present the material benefits brought about by government extension. It is not particularly surprising that such benefits are measured in terms of property, just as they were in US Steel's *An American in the Making*.

The dictates of liberal political economy shaped film form. The temporality of *Helping Negroes to Become Better Farmers and Homemakers*, the articulation of time passing, marks the presence of a narrative form that meshed with the governmental purpose to show the economic benefits of state-led farming practices. Government and narrative intertwined, exemplified by the temporality of the before-and-after structure. The film shows the progress of Rube Collins and his family, who learn to make baskets and set a table and benefit from flypaper, fireless cookers, and a new poultry house. Collins brings a gramophone home at the very end of the film, a symbol of the mechanized modernity and new consumer power that government and business imagined for peripheral economies. But the song he plays, "Suwannee River," was a staple of blackface minstrel shows and tells of a roaming black slave who misses his happy life working on the plantation. The old remains, necessarily, a part of the new.

Collins is made modern, and becomes a prosperous homeowner, because of the intervention of white extension agents. J. Emmett Winn has astutely shown how this film ignores a longer history of black-led extension and community work to locate governmental agency in white authorities and institutions.[91] The representational excess of stereotypes, such as the young black children eating watermelons seen at various points in the film, positions black subjects and workers as particularly in need of governmental intervention. Typicality in this way connects also to racist logic, particularly baldly present in the "Etc" intertitle. Winn suggests the film was more widely shown among white audiences.[92] It may in this way have sought to be equally educational for white landlords, for the film publicizes the power of government to transform not only the economic conditions of black tenant farmers but also the economic potential of the white-owned land.

The growing realization that film could supplement the work of government, particularly through widely distributed fiction and narrative, prompted the department to once again revise its conception and practice of filmmaking. In a 1923 policy document, the categories of the department's films were broadened to better reflect this effort to communicate widely among diverse publics. As before, films were categorized as "didactic or teaching films" and "publicity films," but now two categories were added: "propaganda films," in "which the aim was to arouse public sentiment to a beneficial end," and "semi-entertainment films . . . which have a definite entertainment value when they are shown in company with the heavier and less popular films."[93] Once again the goal was clearly connected to the imperative to distribute the films ever-more widely, so as to expand the usefulness of the department's films. Further to this, the department also wrote to the Motion Picture Theater Owners of America in early 1923, in advance of their annual meeting, to sound out possibilities to show their films in commercial theatres.[94] Evidently the department continued to expand the distribution and exhibition networks its films moved through and carried on innovating new forms and practices to shift beyond teaching particular practices and publicizing the work of the state to include the imperative to "arouse" audiences to follow particular practices and ideals in a form that would frequently balance nonfictional didacticism with narrative and fiction. Later this hybrid form was frequently called "documentary." It is enough here to note that this form was innovated by the state to establish the ways film could pedagogically shape the conduct of audiences and populations.

Updated tick-eradication films and a series of films about extension work blended the department's four categories in somewhat characteristic ways. In 1919 the department commissioned an outside studio, Bray Studios, to make a cartoon about tick eradication. *The Charge of the Tick Brigade* (1919) was written by Max Fleischer and tells the humorous story of a cow couple pursued by ticks.[95] Toward the end of the film, a mother tick shows a short film-within-the-film about her prolific reproductive ability. Cartoons by this point already connote humor and a playful inversion of the real world; here its entertaining playfulness is connected to the ongoing problem of ticks destroying the economic value of cattle. The same story is rendered melodramatic in *Mollie of Pine Grove Vat* (1923), in which the eponymous heroine eventually foils the bad Ledbetter gang, who had selfishly destroyed the cattle-dipping vat because it was angry at the cost of cattle dipping. The quarantine is lifted after the vat is rebuilt, and the final shots show healthy cows and Mollie's farm transformed because livestock now supplement its farming income. Cows have become a cash crop. The final shots of a more prosperous-looking farm directly mirror the opening shots of Mollie's then rundown farm, where she had discussed with her husband their economic problems. It is a familiar narrative form, not only following the before-and-after structure of the didactic text but also the narrative dynamics of fiction texts, which frequently conclude by returning to a state that approximately replicates the beginning of the story. Indeed, as Jennifer Zwarich has observed, the film "mirrors the style and narrative arc of popular prewar heroine serials."[96] *Mollie of Pine Grove Vat* ties narrative order together with economic wellbeing, all made possible by the agency of Mollie supplementing that of the state and its particular policies around cattle, which here results in wealth and expanded property.

Various films told stories about the benefits of extension work, in particular to women and to the revitalization of community life. Many of these were produced in the context of the agricultural depression of the early 1920s. *The Farm Bureau Comes to Pleasant View* begins with a shot of a disused community hall, showing, the title observes, "a lack of social life" in the town. The film shifts attention to Grandpa Little, who enthusiastically goes to meet with extension agents and is told "his State Agricultural College and U.S. Department of Agriculture are cooperating with the county in the employment of extension agents to help farming people." Walking home, Grandpa stops outside the boarded-up and dilapidated community hall and begins to play a fiddle. "Old times," the intertitle exclaims, and we see momentarily Grandpa's memories of a community dance at the hall. Grandpa's enthusiasm for extension work persuades others to attend a meeting with the agents, who suggest solutions for the community's problems in dialogue with the members of the community. "Grandpa's vision realized," a title reads at the end of the film, as the community mingles and dances at the now revamped community hall. The rundown community, an oblique reference to agricultural depression, is revitalized by government intervention.

The Farm Bureau Comes to Pleasant View inaugurated a series of films on the same community, through which Grandpa weaves in and out. *A Matter of Form*, for example, shows the home demonstration agent helping women in the community make clothes. *Layers and Liars* shows "good poultry practices." *Food for Reflection* shows how home demonstration agents advise women about nutrition and help them organize to raise money to install machinery in the school to give the children hot school lunches. The young children of the community begin to grow and put on weight, becoming, the catalogue observes, "the best crop the farm produces."[97] Government intervention here is directly bio-political. *The Happier Way* focuses on women. Women "fall short of real enjoyment in country living," the film asserts at the outset, because they lack the "labor saving machinery" that is increasingly commonplace on the farm. The home demonstration agent organizes a questionnaire on labor-saving devices on the farm—shown in close up, as again extratextual detail becomes enfolded in the story—and Grandpa Little begins what is described as "a scientific study" of the water supply to their house in consultation with the extension agent. Grandpa's plans to modernize, and to some extent Taylorize the house (the language of "scientific study" seems to deliberately reference Taylor's *The Principles of Scientific Management*) is made more urgent when Louisa Little collapses carrying water into the house from an outside well.[98] Louisa is visited by the doctor, and told she must rest. Grandpa and his son, Louisa's husband, are comically inept at carrying out the household tasks, but with the help of the extension agent they do succeed in constructing a water system that effectively modernizes the house. Louisa returns from her enforced rest to marvel at this, and the film ends with her on a rocking chair on the porch: "a better housekeeper than ever," the final title reads, she now "found opportunity and leisure to enjoy country life." *The Happier Way* is found through the modernization of domestic life and the government-led expansion of "prosperity" and revitalization of community. The later USDA film *Poor Mrs. Jones* (1925) underscores this objective by telling a story of a woman who grows tired of life on the farm and demands to move to the city. But after taking a vacation in the city, staying with her sister, "she gets a sample of life in a crowded city flat, learns of the taste of food not fresh from the farm, the hazards to children, of the traffic." She is, the USDA's press release for the film notes, "happy to commit her 'vacation' short and return home— convinced that her lot is not so bad as it had seemed."[99] Louisa and Mrs. Jones discover that life on the farm can be made modern and compares favorably with crowded cities, as the films tell stories that clearly seek to counteract the movement of populations from farms to cities to underscore economic, regional, and national stability.

Mobile movies supplement state policy. The USDA's films teach specific farming practices, publicize the work of the department and state, and proselytize for the importance of extension work for improving "prosperity" and happiness. The delineation of empathetic characters and a narrative structure strongly driven by a before and after logic, which positions government as the motor of narrative and general progress, works to begin to bend film form to the task of "arousing" public sentiment in favor of the extension of government intervention. Collins, Mollie, and Louisa all find new enjoyment and prosperity through the intervention of government, and all happily end up with larger or much-improved houses. Property underscores stability. The enhanced enjoyment enabled by government is enfolded into the film's "semi-entertainment" form, the curiously hybrid structure that is characteristic of the nontheatrical film and that balances narrative and singularity (and comic hokiness) with detail, typicality, and the didactic or propagandistic. Experiments in form mirrored those in the construction of material networks for the circulation of these films, under the pressure also of the economic depression in agricultural regions in the early 1920s. In these ways the department's films became more mobile and visible just as their usefulness was expanded from the teaching of particular practices, such as dipping cattle, to a broader bio-political and economic intervention into the lives and practices of rural populations.

"TO ALLAY THE SPIRIT OF UNREST WHICH SEEMED SO PREVALENT"

Visual instruction and extension networks expanded in the immediate aftermath of the war. I noted at the end of the previous chapter that Woodrow Wilson authorized the creation of a Visual Instruction Section in the Bureau of Education at the beginning of 1919 to be a "clearing house," through which films produced by the government during the war would be widely circulated to generate "greater usefulness."[100] In early 1919, the secretary of the interior asked the secretary of war for cooperation in passing the films produced for the war effort over to the Bureau of Education, from where these films would be distributed to schools and colleges.[101] Over one million feet of film were salvaged and circulated, along with projection equipment.[102] By doing so the state sought to use the media produced during the exceptional crisis of wartime to help (re)establish liberal political and economic order in the midst of ongoing rural and urban crises and in the shadow of the Soviet revolution. Media became a regularized part of the armory of the "disciplinary state."[103] What follows traces the dialectic of media pedagogy and state discipline in the highly charged years of the so-called Red Scare, 1919–20, and the consequences of this through to the mid-1920s

In the early months of 1919, the newly formed Visual Instruction Section of the Bureau of Education began to quickly gather information about "the channels of distribution available" for film and other visual materials and to survey "universities, colleges, schools, clubs, community centers, industrial plants, stores and other organizations and institutions," so as "to locate projection machines in use for educational purposes."[104] Working speedily under the pressure of the postwar crisis, the bureau produced a series of reports and bulletins about "the visual method in group teaching and promotion," the "motion picture activities of the Departments of the government and allied organizations," and the "associations and industrial and commercial companies having motion pictures in their possession with lists of these motion pictures and explanations as to how they might be obtained for use."[105] In turn the bureau established connections with state universities, in particular with the extension departments that had begun to form in the 1890s and had expanded thereafter with federal funding in 1914 and 1916. Visual instruction departments had begun to form at some of these universities, sometimes affiliated with extension departments, particularly in the postwar period, and there emerged a network of participating institutions that acted as state distribution centers for the circulation of "educational" films produced by the government *and* related industrial and civic organizations.[106] In its annual report in 1920, just one year after its establishment, the bureau stated,

> The Visual Instruction service of the Bureau of Education, Department of Interior, received 2,160,000 feet of film during the fiscal year ending June 30, 1920, and deposited 982,000 feet with its State distributing centers . . . The film material was received through the very courteous cooperation of the departments of the government, of allied organizations and industrial companies.[107]

Bureaucrats in the Visual Instruction Section sourced films produced by the government, industrial companies, and "allied organizations" and circulated these through a newly created network of educational institutions, from where the films could be used by other related institutions like schools or YMCAs. The result was the creation of a media infrastructure that stretched from federal to local governments, and from industry and related civil organizations, and made use in particular of educational institutions. Movies were circulated through this network and were regarded by many as a powerful new pedagogic form, particularly after the perceived success of propaganda during the war.

Visual instruction proliferated as a loosely configured movement from this point, 1919, onward.[108] In that year alone, two organizational bodies were established—the Society for Visual Education and the National Academy of Visual Instruction—and *Educational Film Magazine* and *Moving Picture Age* was created.[109] In 1920, the Society for Visual Education began publishing the journal *Visual Education*, and *Moving Picture Age* began to assemble its important annual guide to nontheatrical films—*1001 Films*—, with the subtitle *Suggestions for the Compilation of Film Programs for Americanization, Boy Scouts, Churches, Clubs.*

At its inaugural meeting in July 1920, held at the University of Wisconsin, the National Academy of Visual Instruction included papers on the "Visual Instruction Service Available from the United States Government," the "Work of the Y.M.C.A. in Visual Education," "Visual Instruction in Agricultural Education," and "What the University Extension Divisions of the Country Are Doing to Supply Schools and Welfare Agencies with Visual Instruction Materials." On the agenda also was a symposium on the "Ideals and Purposes of the National Academy of Visual Instruction" and, indicating the level of government support for this, an address by Philander P. Claxton, the US commissioner of education.[110] Quickly thereafter, other related organizational bodies began operation: the Visual Instruction Association of America in 1922 and the Department of Visual Instruction within the National Education Association in 1923. (The three national visual instruction organizations merged in 1932.)[111] The Educational Screen began publication in 1922. The four nontheatrical journals begun in the years between 1919 and 1922 played an important role in relaying information about the production, distribution, and exhibition of films for pedagogic and "civic" purposes. In 1924 the Bureau of Education published a guide to visual instruction departments in universities and school systems as a further step in the orchestration of a visual pedagogic network.[112]

Why this sudden expansion? Partly these developments drew directly on the experience of the state in its "exceptional" experiment with the Committee on Public Information and expansive policing of speech and dissidence. But they responded also to the specific conjuncture of the postwar years. Eugene Debs, recall, was imprisoned in 1919 under the terms of the Sedition Act. The movement of the migrant populations, who were drawn to the United States as the main pole of attraction for the labor, entrepreneurial, and capital resources of the world economy, was increasingly regulated and policed. The restrictive immigration acts of 1917 and 1918 were supplemented in the wake of the Red Scare of 1919–20 with the passage of the Emergency Quota Act in 1921 and the Immigration Act of 1924, which radically reduced the movement of particular immigrant groups to the United States and in doing so effectively halted the great wave of migrant movement to the country that had begun in the 1880s.[113] Legislation founded on pernicious racial logic borrowed from the pseudoscience of eugenics merged with the imperative to produce "loyalty" to the reigning political and economic institutions of the nation.

In 1919 a special unit to police radicals was formed within the Bureau of Investigation, and this innovated new practices of denaturalization and deportation. New state police forces were implemented in several states.[114] In 1919 also the Senate introduced an Americanization bill calling for federal support for English-language instruction, education in principles of government and citizenship, and instruction "in such other work . . . for successful living and intelligent American citizenship."[115] In that same year, a Joint Legislative Committee to Investigate

Seditious Activities in New York State, known as the Lusk Committee, devoted half of its four-volume—one-million word—report, *Revolutionary Radicalism,* to Americanization, drawing special attention to the failure of the public schools to instill loyalty and calling for teacher training in Americanism, immigration control, and public education.[116] Americanization laws designed to inculcate allegiance to the nation's political institutions and to the prevailing economic order had been passed in more than thirty states by 1921.[117] Quasi-governmental and "loyalty" organizations were formed. In 1919, for example, the veteran's organization the American Legion was established, with a constitution pledging "to foster and perpetuate a one hundred-percent Americanism"; it quickly established a National Americanism Committee.[118]

But Americanization was also enthusiastically endorsed and practiced by corporate industrial organizations seeking to reorient the labor and consumption practices of their largely migrant workforces. Chambers of commerce and the powerful lobbying group the National Association of Manufacturers commended Americanization to their members and marshaled a corporate counteroffensive against union action, which came to be called the "American plan," in a way that made clear the manner in which nationalism was being used to sustain particular economic practices.[119] Americanization campaigns sought to dissolve immigrant and working-class traditions of mutuality to establish new patterns of individual consumerism and acceptance of the principles of liberal, capitalist political economy. In all these examples, and more, exceptional state, corporate, and civic practices were implemented to destroy growing opposition to the reigning political and economic order. Opposition was coded as un-American.

Visual instruction, the creation of new networks to circulate pedagogic culture, and the rapid expansion of a nontheatrical film culture responded directly to these contexts. In December 1919, the secretary of the interior, Franklin Lane, called a meeting of film producers and "laid before them a project to employ motion pictures in the promotion of a true spirit of Americanism among the people, and by this means to allay the spirit of unrest which seemed so prevalent."[120] New forms of visual pedagogy, new production units, new distribution networks and exhibition contexts—all were developed, in part, at least, as components of the ongoing and conjunctural counteroffensive against opposition to reigning political and economic norms. Media and the institutional networks that framed and circulated it was put to work to sustain the particular configuration of corporate liberalism that emerged in the 1890s and was re-established—in the face of considerable opposition—in the postwar years in particular.

Visual instruction emerged as a loosely configured movement shared out between federal and state governments, educational institutions, corporations, and related civic organizations in the precise context of the postwar crisis. But different lines of genealogical descent can also be observed. The proponents of visual instruction drew on a loosely configured mixture of pedagogical and psychological theories to argue that visual material and concrete imagery were closer to experience than the more abstract and traditional verbalism that dominated teaching. The prospectus of the National Visual Education Association, for example, proposed that moving pictures "make a deeper *dent* or more lasting impression on the memory than any other method."[121] Visualization provided richer and more useful pedagogical experiences for students, many argued, and this perspective informed the integration of museum materials, still images, and moving pictures into the classroom.[122] Visual instruction in this way merged with the "Progressive" shift in educational philosophies in the turn-of-the-century period, which increasingly valorized experience in education and deemphasized book and rote learning.[123] Motion pictures were prized in particular for their ability to re-present movement, mimicking phenomenological experience in a way that was distinct from still images and objects. Visual materials, and moving images in particular, "spoke" to those populations of immigrants whose English-language skills were unformed, the very groups that were frequently singled out as most in need of education as socialization in the ways of America. "Pedagogical cinematography" could transform curricula, experiences, and institutions, thus underpinning a newly efficient and productive educational system.[124] This was, indeed, a partly mechanized pedagogy, as suggested in the 1919 Ford advertisement for its films, in a way that became a significant visual trope from this moment: a classroom of pupils looking toward the screen, rapt with attention, focused on the mechanized pedagogy of the new school.

Liberal political philosophy had long declared the importance of education in developing the cognitive and moral qualities seen as necessary for citizenship in a liberal and democratic polity. Locke, for example, had talked of education imprinting upon the "wax" of the child, and similar conceptions of the necessity of "civic" education framed Jacques Rousseau's reflections on the place of pedagogy in shaping subjective and social order.[125] Liberal ideals of self-government and individualism dovetailed with the developing economic principles of laissez faire capitalism. Education in these values became increasingly important in the context of the radical changes of industrialization and the corresponding political threat of an expanding working class in the course of the nineteenth century.[126] Public education systems were innovated and established in the United States in the mid-nineteenth century, and universities were developed in collaborations between federal and state governments in the latter half of the nineteenth century.[127] "Extension" would be a significant component of the imperative to make education "useful."

Partly this marked a mutation from the ideal of "philosophic education" to "civic education." William Galston has argued that liberal states increasingly valorized civic education as "the formation of individuals who can effectively conduct their lives within, and support, the political community" over the more abstract philosophical education as "the pursuit and acquisition of truth."[128] In 1906 the United States Bureau of Naturalization was created precisely to promote civic education to Americanize migrants and simultaneously supervise the citizenship process. Early experiments focused on language as imperative for naturalization, and simultaneously "civics" classes became increasingly important at both public schools and in the flourishing adult education system.[129] The Bureau of Naturalization played a coordinating role in prodding local school authorities to provide classes to educate foreigners. It produced a widely used "citizenship" textbook, offering guidance on ways of living—including sections on home economics and hygiene—and discussions of the duties of citizenship.[130] The privately funded Division of Immigrant Education was set up within the Bureau of Education in the Department of the Interior, providing yet further evidence of the close links between corporate organizations and the federal government.[131] It worked to promote educational extension work and adult education in particular. During the war, a National Historical Service Board established by the Carnegie Institute was put to work by the Committee on Public Information and the Bureau of Education to transform history teaching and the social science curriculum to establish new forms of patriotism.[132] Philander P. Claxton stated clearly that the "success or failure of the Nation may turn very largely on the proportion of its citizens in whom the essential historic conception of their membership in a continuing community, is more important than their own individual fortunes."[133] Visual Instruction and History would be pressed into service for these civic purposes.

The final related intellectual context for the shifting conception of pedagogy in the period was the fore-mentioned revolution in conceptions of subjectivity that transformed the human sciences in the latter years of the nineteenth century. In the linked fields of psychology, sociology, social psychology and educational research the individual was increasingly imagined as a malleable "copying machine."[134] Visual instruction proponents argued that visual materials were particularly powerful in their imprint on the "plastic" minds of children and related other groups, like the allegedly racially inferior immigrants drawn to the United States. Tests seeking to prove this were carried out in the 1920s, and numerous groups—including Hollywood's public relations arm—argued that film was a particularly useful technology for imprinting the values of what was repetitively called "good citizenship." I will come back to those developments in chapter 10.

Visual instruction emerged, then, when there was a confluence of several complex developments that valorized civic and experiential education and that reached a kind of tipping point in the immediate postwar years. The screen was widely used, as Arthur Edwin Krows framed it, as "an effective conveyor of information" that would be integrated with the interpellation of migrant—and—working-class populations to the liberal political and economic norms of the nation.[135]

Lest this sound unnecessarily abstract, consider these simple examples. In 1917 the National Americanization Committee produced a film called *The Immigrant in America,* which presented "in sequence the forces which influence the Americanization of the immigrant" and which was "exhibited by Young Men's Christian Associations, Chambers of Commerce, at conventions and in outlying mining districts."[136] The Bureau of Naturalization in the Department of Labor began a Motion Picture Section in 1918 and "selected and edited" a set of "educational motion picture films" to "visualize the activities of the Federal government ... as an aid to the public school teacher in the preparation of candidates for the responsibilities of citizenship."[137] By the end of 1919, Secretary of the Interior Lane was encouraging film producers to assist the government in using film "to carry on a nationwide campaign to combat Bolshevism and radicalism," in stories that would "have an intense human interest in addition to a visualization of the principles and theories underlying the representative republication form of government."[138] Lane's National Americanism Committee had a logo with a film reel wrapped around the Statue of Liberty (see fig. 7). *World Aflame* (1919), one of a number of antiradical films produced in the wake of the government's efforts, was shown at the Department of the Interior.[139] The film dramatized the smashing of the Seattle general strike in that year: a film made in collaboration between the government and the film industry, glorifying the destruction of worker and union resistance, was projected in government offices. Once again media helped legitimate the state.

Early bulletins from the extension departments at universities included lists and programs for Americanization and civics classes. To take but one example, the Department of Visual Instruction within the University of California Extension Division's 1922 catalogue had a section on "civics" that was organized into seven film "lessons" tracing the migration of a family from a farm in Western Europe to the United States. Each step of their journey to a new life in the United States is accompanied by an elementary civics lesson extolling appropriate economic and civic conduct. Lesson 1 is a "direct comparison of economic conditions" for farmers in Europe and America "showing the advantages of Americanization."[140] When they arrive in the United States, the father of the family purchases a farm and builds it up, forming as he does so a "Good Roads Club" to better facilitate economic movement. The "civic content" of this lesson, as the catalogue frames it, centers on "the civic and economic betterment due to owning your own home." The necessity of property was of course a wider lesson in liberal political economy. Later lessons demonstrate how "service" is "the keynote to good citizenship," and offer exemplary brief lessons in liberal philosophy. Lesson 4, for example, was on "Obedience": "We cannot always do as we please because little would be accomplished; the stronger would get all ... In every group some one must be in authority; in the home, father and mother; in the city, the police-

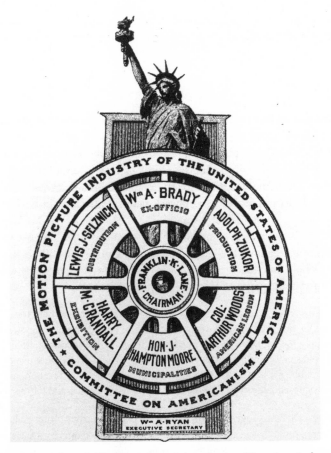

FIGURE 7. Logo for the Committee on Americanism (Department of
the Interior, in collaboration with the Motion Picture Industry, 1919).

man; in industrial life, the foreman; no one is above authority. Freedom does not
mean to do as one pleases. It ceases when in so doing it interferes with the rights
of others."[141]

The logic suggesting that obedience to the authority of the foreman will produce freedom is nicely illustrative of the ways in which liberalism was attached to
industrial capitalism. Lessons in "Thrift," "Physical and Mental Fitness," and "The
Beautiful School" follow, all showing how the children of the family are instructed
in better and more productive forms of conduct. Kids stand, usefully, metonymically for those populations needing visual civic education to become efficient and
loyal subjects. The push to integrate moving images into school and adult education
marked a significant moment, then, in the effort to orchestrate the use of modern

media for the purposes of socialization in particular attitudes and conducts relating principally to political and economic forms and institutions.

"THE GREAT TASK OF PROTECTING LIVES AND PROPERTY"

I will now focus on four types of films produced for the purpose of civic education: 1) films produced about the workings of government in North America; 2) films about safety, oversight, and material progress that were collaborations between the government and major corporations; 3) films on the history of the United States; and 4) films about the geography of the country. Broadly speaking, these film cycles and practices were used as a bulwark against radicalism and to further facilitate and sustain corporate liberalism.

In the first category were a number of films that provided exemplary lessons in liberal governance, and in the kinds of freedoms and responsibilities expected for and from American citizens. *Government* (Society for Visual Education, c. 1922) was described in the pages of *Moving Picture Age* like this:

> American workingman demonstrates to newly arrived immigrants the different functions of our republican government, such as, police protection; street light, water supply, foodstuffs inspected, freedom of religion, free education, traffic regulation, free hospitals, fire protection, no child labor, safety devices and insurance for workers, public parks and playgrounds . . . paper currency, low taxation, independent ownership, equality, republic is of the people, by the people, and for the people.[142]

The brief description suggests a story designed specifically to interpellate migrant workers into a democratic and liberal order, narrated it seems by a satisfied American worker. *Romance of a Republic* similarly offered "insights into the various departments of the government" over ten reels, while *A Citizen and His Government* (Society for Visual Education, c. 1922) "visualizes the many services our government performs" to offer a "lesson in Americanism."[143] *Growth of Cities and Their Problems* (Society for Visual Education, c. 1922) similarly demonstrated government oversight of roads, bridges, street cleaning, traffic rules, water systems, and "well equipped schools [to] make better citizens."[144] In these civic lessons the benign liberal state regulates in order to produce freedom and prosperity.

In the second category was a series of films about the benevolent oversight of industrial organizations that were made or distributed in partnership with the government. The connections are particularly visible in a series of films made in collaboration between the Bureau of Mines and related industrial organizations. The bureau was established in 1910 within the Department of the Interior to conduct scientific research and disseminate information on the extraction, processing, use, and conservation of the mineral and energy resources central to industrial

capitalism.[145] By providing new scientific information, the bureau helped transform natural materials into property. In 1913, at about the same time that the USDA
began film production, the Bureau of Mines sponsored a series of films about the
petroleum, steel, mineral, rubber, and automotive industries, which explored the
remit of these new industrial processes and repeatedly emphasized the benign
actions of corporations and their role in producing American citizens. I used earlier the example of the US Steel film *An American in the Making*, which was produced in collaboration with the Bureau of Mines to promote this idea. In other
films produced and distributed by the Bureau of Mines from the midteens onward,
the emphasis on the safety procedures of industrial organizations was more clearly
directed at the recalcitrant and dissolute worker who endangers the health of
workers, property, and productivity. In these films, the narrative transformation
that shows workers learning how to be safer is heavily overdetermined, for this
marks their socialization into the American economy and construction as efficient
cogs in a complex industrial system. *The Miners Lesson,* for example, was made by
the Bureau of Mines in collaboration with Anthracite Coal Operators in 1914 and
showed, the extant synopsis observes, "The safety practices observed in coal
mines, with emphasis on the danger from gas, and shows the penalties incurred
[by individual miners] when regulations are disregarded."[146] Government regulates, corporations happily concur, but workers at times dangerously fail to adhere.
In *Safety Lessons in Metal Mining,* produced in 1914 in collaboration with the New
Jersey Zinc Company, the extensive safety procedures of the zinc mine are com-
promised by what the synopsis describes as "careless, selfish and drunken
women."[147] Mining companies work together with the government to heroically
minimize the dangers of mining and counteract the actions of dissolute workers.
Evidently there were a lot of lazy and drunken workers, as a report on the Commission on Industrial Relations in 1914 stated that thirty-five thousand workers
were killed in industrial accidents and seven hundred thousand were injured
annually.[148] But happily for the caring mining and industrial firms, workers' com-
pensation had been declared unconstitutional by the Supreme Court in 1910,
because it deprived corporations of "property" without due process of law.[149] The
bureau distributed the films through its twenty-three distribution centers "free of
rental charges" to be "enthusiastically praised and regularly shown by technical
societies and schools, commercial, industrial, educational, social and religious
organizations."[150] Effectively this meant that the Bureau of Mines was distributing
corporate propaganda, further illustrating the close ties between government,
industry, and capital that were central to the emergence of a corporate liberal
economy.

Bureau collaborations with industry began in 1913, but they accelerated in the
postwar years, in the context of the broader corporate "American plan" to counteract worker radicalism and enforce discipline and productivity. *Live and Let Live: A*

Story of Safety in the Oil Fields, produced in 1924 in collaboration with the Humble Oil and Refining Company, the Gulf Production Company, and Magnolia Petroleum, showed a "careless smoker" dropping a match and causing a dangerous fire.[151] *When Wages Stop, or, Safety First in the Petroleum Industry* was produced in 1925 by a number of California oil companies, including the Rockefeller-owned Standard Oil. It tells the story of a careless worker learning the error of his ways after a minor accident and is described in an intertitle as "the simple, homely story of the great task of protecting lives *and* property."[152] Various other films produced collaboratively, and distributed by the bureau, emphasized progress and positioned industry as the central motor of a productive American modernity. *The Story of Transportation* was produced in 1922 "through the cooperation of the Westinghouse Electric and Manufacturing Company." It recounted the *longue durée* of transportation, from walking to sleds pulled by dogs to railways powered by the electricity supplied by Westinghouse. "Modern industrial efficiency" necessitated greater capacity and speed, and Westinghouse's innovations supplied this.[153] Likewise, *The Story of the Gasoline Motor,* made with the cooperation of the Continental Motors Corporation, told what an early intertitle described as "A story of progress—a romance of achievement." Numerous other "story of" films were produced, including *The Story of Steel,* again with US Steel; *The Story of Petroleum,* with the Sinclair Consolidated Oil Corporation; *The Story of a Motor Truck,* with General Motors; and so on—all encompass historical accounts of mostly extractive and transportation industries to emphasize the progress brought to the country by large industrial organizations.[154] Quite clearly these and other similar films are visible evidence of the ways in which the state and large corporations worked to socialize migrant and working-class populations in the system of wage labor and property rights central to liberal political economy.

"TO MAKE BETTER CITIZENS"

I will shift now to the role played in this process by educational organizations, for the threads that tie government, economy, and pedagogy together have been central to the history recounted here. Visual instruction, and extension departments, flourished as we have seen in land-grant institutions such as those in Indiana, Iowa, Minnesota, and Wisconsin. But the example I use is from Yale, an elite private institution buoyed by money from major industrial philanthropists invested in the business of social reproduction. In 1923, Yale University Press began to produce a series of films collectively called the Yale Chronicles of America Photoplays. The press produced fifteen four-reel films over the next two years that narrated significant incidents from the history of the United States, beginning with Columbus and ending with the Civil War. The films encompass settlement, the American Revolution, "the struggle for supremacy along the frontier" in the face of "Indian depredations," and Alexander Hamilton's successes as the first secretary of the Treasury in "stabilizing the currency of the new government and formulating its financial system."[155] The films were promoted vigorously to schools and were frequently central to rhetoric about the efficacy of visual instruction and the *pressing need* for the Americanization of migrant populations. In a pamphlet produced to advertise the films, the connections between history and the formation of a liberal civility among diverse populations were made clear. Viewed together, the press asserted, the films constituted a "powerful instrument for the stimulation of patriotism and good citizenship among native Americans and foreign born citizens alike" that would enable "millions of new citizens" to gain "a true understanding and a real appreciation of American institutions and ideals, and of the sacrifices made so that these might endure."[156] Publicity positioned the series of films as "a way to make better citizens."[157]

Yale's considerable investment in the representation of history was consistent with the imperative shared out by state, industrial, and educational institutions to fabricate the "fictive ethnicity" of the nation state which began most substantively in the context of the waves of migrant movement needed to sustain advanced industrial capitalism, starting in the late nineteenth century and becoming particularly urgent during the war and the immediate postwar years.[158] "Pastness is," Immanuel Wallerstein usefully reminds us, "a central element in the socialization of individuals, in the maintenance of group solidarity, in the establishment of or challenge to social legitimation."[159] Various other organizations produced history films also and particularly during the postwar years. The Society for Visual Education, for example, produced a series of films entitled Foundation and Settlement of the United States, which included *English Settlements in North America, War of the American Revolution, Settling the Ohio Valley, The Louisiana Purchase and the Lewis and Clark Expedition,* as well as a subseries on the Economic History of the United States that included *Canals in United States History, Railroads in United States History, Immigration to the United States,* and *The Panama Canal and Its Historical Significance* (all Society for Visual Education, c. 1922). Ford too produced a series of films about the nation's past, particularly from 1919, some of which I will talk about in the following chapter. Civic organizations like the American Legion and the Ku Klux Klan also used film extensively to establish restrictive forms of national identity.[160] In short, the flurry of historical representations in movies created by government, industrial, civic, and educational institutions in the 1910s and thereafter marked a moment when mass media was bent to the task of promoting allegiance to a state and its political and economic practices and institutions.

Visual displays of the past were central to the Americanization project. In the catalogues and reviews in the nontheatrical trade press, one also comes across repeated examples of films about the geography of the United States, which suggest that the representation of the space of the nation also played a role in the efforts to construct a fictitious national identity. "The nationalization of nature," historian Ian Tyrell tells us, began most clearly with the creation of national parks in the 1890s as "part of the quest to sharpen American identity."[161] This nationalization of the spaces of nature accelerated with the creation of the US Forest Service in 1905, the 1906 National Monuments legislation, and the creation of a unified National Parks Service in 1916, all of which strengthened the "nationalistic aspects of the federal state."[162] These efforts led to the creation of what historian Bruce Shulman has called "a resource management state" with expanded federal power.[163] It was in this context that the Forest Service and the National Park Service of the Department of the Interior became significant film production units.[164] *The Story of Our National Parks,* for example, was produced in 1925 by the National Park Service in collaboration with the White Motor Company, continuing the trend of government-industry collaboration (and cannily tying together the display of national space with its appreciation from the window of an expensive automobile). Regular showing of these films in schools and in other nontheatrical exhibition spaces provided further evidence of the ways in which the pedagogical media produced in collaborations between the state and large industry was utilized to help socialize particular populations in the fictions of national identity.

Representational practices and mass media played a role in the socialization of populations into liberal capitalism. Also important was the guided encounter of audiences with film material that positioned the watching of movies as a pedagogical exercise. Visual instruction rhetoric and practice frequently imagined the film experience as a way to guide particular populations in understanding new productive and civic practices. I will take an example from the work of the YMCA, a civic organization that can be seen as part of the broader liberal network of pastoral and welfare institutions that flourished in the turn-of-the-century period. In an early issue of the nontheatrical journal *Moving Picture Age,* there is this description of the "Americanization" work of the Y:

> Forty per cent of the programs being provided by our service are being used in Americanization work ... An interesting way in which films are being used was noted at one Sunday meeting, where 250 non-English-speaking men, representing nine nationalities, were witnessing a melodrama. It was a story of a moonshiner in the Tennessee mountains. For one hour the secretary talked with the picture, reading the titles in very simple English, composing short sentences from the picture action, such as, 'The door opens,' 'the man comes out,' 'he looks around,' 'he hears a noise,' 'he grabs the gun,' 'he shoots the men,' 'he is a bad man,' 'he breaks the law,' 'he is not a good citizen,' 'a good citizen will not break the law,' etc. Those men went home with higher ideals of citizenship that afternoon.[165]

In this way the Y official supplemented the political logic of the film, thus transforming movie watching, as Ronald Walter Greene has insightfully framed it, "into a domain and technique of social management."[166] The YMCA incorporated a sig-

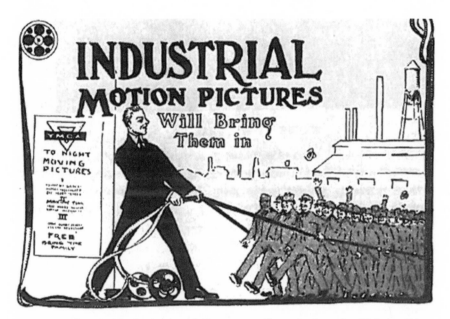

FIGURE 8. Advertisement for the YMCA's film program ("Use of Industrial and Educational Motion Pictures in the Y.M.C.A. Practical Program" [New York: YMCA, 1919], 3).

nificant film component into its undertakings, working in tandem with government and in particular with industrial organizations to fashion a film service that helped supplement new practices of mass production and the political economy of advanced capitalism. Look at figure 8 for example, which is a picture from publicity for the YMCA's film program. Workers are "reeled in"—captured even—by a smartly dressed man with a film reel.[167]

Various significant industrial corporations began film production in the early years of the twentieth century with similar interpellative imperatives. Westinghouse, US Steel, International Harvester, and General Electric, for example, all dabbled in film production, beginning around 1904.[168] Vast quantities of films exploring new industrial processes, and corresponding transformations in labor practices, were produced and circulated through the networks established by the state in collaboration with educational institutions and related industrial and civic organizations like the YMCA, the National Association of Manufacturers, and the US Chamber of Commerce. Moving pictures were produced and circulated by corporations and related organizations as part of the shared imperative to visualize new productive practices and construct new ideals and enactments of subjectivity and allegiance to support emergent economic and political realities. These practices began after the emergence of the corporation of the second-stage industrial revolution, but they became more pressing in the postwar years in the context of the reestablishment of corporate liberalism in the "American plan" and the related construction of practices and fictions of national identity.

I have in this chapter concentrated principally on the state orchestration of economy, pedagogy, and the policing of political and economic opponents of liberal capitalism. In the next chapter I will consider further the industrial and corporate use of film. Frequently this was undertaken in collaboration with state departments, as we have seen, in a clear indication of the close ties between state and corporate goals in the political economy of corporate liberalism. What follows examines both the specificity of industrial-corporate filmmaking and its points of connection with the broader political and economic orchestration of infrastructure and worker-citizen conduct in particular.

6

The Work of Film in the Age of
Fordist Mechanization

One of the most significant and remarkable experiments in the systematic production of industrial and "educational" moving pictures was undertaken by the Ford
Motor Company. I have already observed that the company began using the serialized indexical photography of moving pictures in early 1913, as part of the "time-
motion" studies that minutely documented worker movement, and what the in-
house newspaper *Ford Times* called the "problem of 'waste motion,'" to propose
practical methods for the most efficient movement and use of laboring bodies.[1]
Evidence suggests that the Time-Motion Study Department at the company continued to use moving pictures to monitor productivity, as indeed did other time-
motion experts, who helped rationalize production and labor practices at other
corporations.[2] Time-motion study, Fordism, serialized photography, and film
emerged in a particular conjuncture of capital and shared significant objectives in
the segmentation and compression of space and time.

Ford's use of time-motion study was combined with the innovation of machine
tools, which enabled the standardization of mechanical tasks to establish an
assembly line, beginning in 1913, that enabled the speeded-up production of the
company's Model T. Labor hours to produce a Model T decreased from 400 in 1910
to 130 in 1916, while production went up from 21,000 to 585,000 cars in the same
period.[3] Ford's momentous innovations enabled the direct and mechanized control of the movement and pace of workers, and so dramatically increased productivity and the extraction of surplus value from laboring bodies.[4] Labor practices
were transformed as workers were de-skilled and increasingly rendered interchangeable cogs working on isolated parts of the production process. Workers
were forced to become more machine-like as "living labor" was transposed into

the activity of the machine.[5] Ford's innovative, coercive architecture of mass production thus enabled cars to be produced "like the successive negatives on a motion picture film."[6] We can turn that contemporary observation around. The successive frames of motion pictures participated in the process by which the outputs of the laboring body could be maximized to produce quickly the identical Model Ts, which rolled off the assembly lines as perhaps the most emblematic image of the age of mechanical production. Ford's use of motion pictures as a form of surveillance of laboring bodies dovetailed with the imperative to increase production pace and reduce costs, which underpinned the emergence of a new mass economy of consumer abundance thereafter.

But Ford's use of motion pictures quickly shifted. The creation of a Motion Picture Department in late 1913 marked a switch in the principal use of moving pictures at the company, away from their integration into time-motion studies and production practices toward a communicative, rhetorical, and pedagogic form that would articulate new positions about industry, work, and citizenship for audiences inside and outside factories. Ford's films rhetorically supplemented Fordism. The films produced from early 1914 were initially grouped into a newsreel-like series entitled The Ford Animated Weekly, which was innovatively distributed free of charge by Ford dealers to movie theaters and nontheatrical exhibition spaces in local communities.[7] In 1916 a new series was produced called The Ford Educational Weekly, which from 1918 was widely distributed at low cost to cinemas by a commercial distribution company.[8] Ford's films were throughout a "loss-leading" proposition that exemplified a different commercial logic of exploitation than the commercial film industry in a way that was a testament to the translation of surplus value into rhetoric and the conception of the importance of this for Fordist practices of hegemony. Indeed, some accounts suggest the company spent as much as six hundred thousand dollars annually on film production, at a time when the average budget for commercial features was probably around fifty thousand dollars.[9] The final Ford series, The Ford Educational Library, began in 1921, and the company claimed that the "films will be made to correlate with the textbook."[10] Many of these films were aimed specifically at the burgeoning nontheatrical sector. University extension departments in particular were encouraged to purchase The Ford Educational Library cheaply, and to distribute the films widely within their region to schools and other nontheatrical exhibition spaces like factories, churches, YMCAs, chambers of commerce, agricultural colleges, community halls, prisons, and so on. Ford's films were significant to the visual instruction networks that emerged most substantively in the postwar years.[11]

What scattered evidence exists suggests the Ford films were very widely seen. Ford Times, for example, claimed that the films were by 1917 being shown in three thousand theaters a week to between four and five million people;[12] the trade journal Reel and Slide wrote in 1918 of the innovative system of film distribution through Ford dealers, claiming the films reached six thousand exhibitors a week and thus an audience of between five and six million;[13] in 1920, the company was claiming a minimum of four thousand theaters and a coverage of one-seventh of the weekly motion picture audience in the United States;[14] and by 1924, *Ford News* asserted that the films had been seen by sixty million people worldwide.[15] The low cost of the films meant they were especially attractive to part-time exhibitors, and nontheatrical groups, and the films were widely seen in small towns and rural areas.[16] Ford distributed the films outside the United States also, and there is some evidence to suggest they were widely distributed in the important market of Latin America.[17] The films were seen in many different spaces, circulating well beyond movie theaters to other public or civil spaces as one concrete realization of the expanded role for cinema in civic life widely discussed at this time. Indeed, Ford showed its films in its own factories. The company's Highland Park Factory, where mass assembly was established, included a screening space, and a cinema was also built in the famous sprawling River Rouge complex, which replaced Highland Park beginning in 1917 and became one of the most visible symbols of the new age of mass industrial production.[18]

Ford's figures for the dissemination of their films cannot be simply verified and were clearly part of public relations rhetoric. Even so, the Ford films were referenced regularly in the emergent nontheatrical trade press, from around 1918, and frequently singled out as evidence of a newly productive and useful cinema. The Ford Company was also one of the most widely discussed in the period. Henry Ford was perhaps the most visible exemplar of the new industrial age, a public figure and, in the words of his most recent biographer, "the prototype of the mass culture celebrity," who was also widely quoted on aspects of industrial and governmental order at a time of tumultuous change in early twentieth-century America.[19] In his 1922 autobiography, *My Life and Work,* for example, Ford extolled the values of thrift, hard work, the land, and industrial production unfettered by government involvement, and the book became an international bestseller that was translated into twelve languages.[20] (Ford's brand of industrial rationality was particularly attractive to fascism, and it is said that Adolph Hitler kept a picture of Henry Ford by his desk.)[21] In the late 1920s, intellectuals like Walter Lippmann and Herbert Croly took the company as a model of efficient government, presaging the now common liberal argument that markets and managerial and economic "expertise" can transform government and public services.[22] One of the most significant corporations of the age, that is, began producing films that were among —if not simply—the most widely seen in the silent era and were complexly connected to the radical transformations of industrial, labor, and consumer practices that ushered in the modern world. It behooves us to think about these developments carefully.

Ford "spoke," then, through moving images. What did this corporation say? I discern two broad trends in the integration of film into the Fordist project. Many of the films produced within the Ford Animated Weekly and Ford Educational Weekly series documented and celebrated new industrial practices and the infrastructures of advanced capitalism. Central here were a number of films about communicative and transport infrastructures. Emerging in the postwar period, though, was a second strategy that formed the Ford Educational Library of films and mapped out new practices of worker and citizen conduct that were connected to the Fordist imperative to transform industrial and labor practices and the broader trends of Americanization and the related reestablishment of corporate liberalism after the war—part of my subject in the previous chapter. The company began to pioneer new forms of industrial "welfare" and corporate liberalism to compensate for the newly restrictive and repetitive work practices in the age of mass assembly, as well as to defuse public criticism and effective government regulation. Worker education programs strove to shape workers' lives outside factories and create a capitalist civics among working-class immigrant populations, which would override the traditions of community and mutuality that characterized the unions banned by the company.[23] Broadly speaking, this was an attempt to obviate class-based political action and create what Michael Buroway has called an "industrial citizenship," which constituted workers as individuals with specific rights and obligations and displaced a generalized and unionized battle over capitalist relations to limited skirmishes over individual rights.[24] Watching movies was imagined as one component of this critical transformation of labor practices and political action, which was capable of shaping new modalities of "useful" consciousness and conduct for the working-class and immigrant groups that would form populations fitted to the new era of mass production. The production, dissemination, and exhibition of movies dovetailed with the biopolitical management of workers in the service of the construction of a new industrial and consumer economy.

"DISCIPLINE, ORDER AND SYSTEM PREVAIL EVERYWHERE"

In 1913, after a moving-picture company had visited Ford's newsworthy factory and after encouragement from Henry Ford's former employer and friend Thomas Edison, the Ford Company established a Motion Picture Department.[25] *How Henry Ford Makes 1000 Cars a Day*, seemingly the department's first film, was produced and exhibited in early 1914. It showed the new practices of mass assembly begun at Ford's Highland Park factory in 1913, which had radically speeded up production and transformed labor practices. Ford films thereafter disseminated the new ideals and practices of what came to be called Fordism, teaching, in the words of Henry Ford himself, "the lessons of modern efficient" work practices that would change the way many audience members worked and lived.[26] The novel circuits of distribution quickly established by the company through its extensive network of dealers carried the films' lessons about new industrial and labor practices across the country, through rural areas and small towns, often in the very Model Ts that could be seen being built on cinema and makeshift cinema screens. Early Ford films such as *How Henry Ford Makes 1000 Cars a Day* functioned as very visible illustrations and harbingers of what one of the Ford films modestly called "the Ford age." Movies announced the age of mass assembly.

One of the most visible sites for this display of modern industrial practices was the Panama-Pacific International Exposition in early 1915. Ford built a replica of the recently innovated assembly line at the exposition and simultaneously showed some of its first films, including *How Henry Ford Makes 1000 Cars a Day*. Movie exhibition alongside the facsimile of the assembly line emphasized the new iterative and compressed practices of mass production, making those practices visible and mobile in particular through the technology of machine-made vision and mass reproduction. It is worth recalling that it did this in the context of the expansive celebration of new capital-intensive technology and new transport infrastructures that transformed the movement of materials and capital and helped position the United States at the center of the global economy. Fordism was celebrated as a particularly American contribution to the new age. Exposition goers traced out a dizzying relay between the demonstration of mass-assembly processes, of affordable automobility, of mass reproduction through moving images, and of the newly enabled and rapid circulation of goods and capital. Together this marked a significant articulation of the varied compression of spatiality and temporality integral to advanced capitalism.

Movies exemplified the compression embodied in mass-assembly practices. Early rhetoric from Ford positioned its film production as consistent with the new practices of mass assembly, and thus in some respects as a Fordist cultural form. In an early account of the functioning of the new department published in the in-house *Ford Times,* for example, emphasis was placed on the "high degree of manufacturing efficiency" needed in the "production of moving pictures."[27] "Discipline, order and system prevail everywhere," the paper asserted, and "as far as possible nothing is left to chance and the human element is eliminated in the making of Ford moving pictures."[28] Ford's idealization of the rationalization of production, and the replacement of human labor with machinery, was made particularly visible in the publication of a number of images of the machinery used by the company in motion picture production. Photographs of the machines that perforate raw film, print positive film, develop negatives, and dry the film reels work to illustrate a production process from raw film to finished motion picture that emphasized the salience of the machines and their potential to reproduce negatives, like Model Ts rolling off the assembly line (see fig. 9).[29]

Look, for example, at the most intriguing of these images of the company's film production processes in the *Ford Times* (see fig. 10). Entitled "Assembling the film,"

Where the motion picture film is developed

The drying reels carry 1600 feet of film each. Connecting with each reel is the forced draft
from the humidifier apparatus which aids in drying the film

FIGURE 9. Machinery used in motion picture production (*Ford Times* [July 1916]).

Assembling the film

539

FIGURE 10. Assembly line film editors at a Ford factory (*Ford Times* [July 1916]).

the picture shows film "assemblers" working together in a line—a literal illustration of a mass-assembly-line for film, of the work of cultural production in the age of mechanical reproduction. Economic and cultural logics intertwine in the picture. The assembling of film from disparate images to create a coherent whole resembles the practices established for the mass assembly of the automobile. Even further, assembling and editing film compresses and reorders space and time in ways that were analogous to the logics and practices of mass assembly, and even automobility itself. Fordist films like, for example, *How Henry Ford Makes 1000 Cars a Day* compressed even the quickened pace of mass assembly, transforming the lived time and space of the assembly line through shot duration and the dissection and reassembling that is film editing into what we might in this context call the Fordism of filmic time and space.

Ford's films from a cinematic shop floor rolled off the motion picture assembly line after the company's twinned public unveiling of new practices of mass production and reproduction. Many of these worked to visualize and explain the advances in capital-intensive mining, manufacturing, and construction processes in ways that frequently focused upon the speeded up circulation of materials and production practices. *How Henry Ford Makes 1000 Cars a Day* was followed by a number of films that showed aspects of automobile construction, including A *Visit to the Ford Motor Company* (c. 1917), *Ford Plant, Tractors, and Workers* (c. 1917), *Where and How Fords Are Made* (c. 1919), *Industrial Working Conditions* (c. 1921), and *Making Rubber Tires* (c. 1922). Numerous other films showed aspects of the mining of materials for industrial production, including *Coal Mining* (c. 1916), *Iron and Steel* (c. 1920), *Ford Way of Coal Mining* (c. 1923), *The Ford Age* (c. 1923, a summary of Ford's mining, lumbering, and manufacturing), and *Modern Oil Refining* (c. 1925). The industrialization of farm work is visible in, for example, *The Story of a Grain of Wheat* (c. 1917), *Electricity for the Modern Farm* (c. 1919), *Food for Thought* (c. 1921, on how milk is manufactured), and *Farm Progress* (c. 1924). New systems of communication and the production of mass media are visualized in (for example) *Telephone and Telegraph Communication* (c. 1917), *Benjamin Franklin and Modern Communication Systems* (c. 1918), and *The Romance of Making a Modern Magazine* (c. 1926). Construction projects or feats of technological engineering are demonstrated in (for example) *Water Power* (c. 1916), *Ship Construction* (c. 1919), *Tokyo, Japan: Transportation Methods* (c. 1920), *A Century of Progress* (c. 1921, including sequences about the construction of a dam and the use of water power), *Panama and the Panama Canal* (c. 1922, including maps of the trade routes facilitated by the canal), *Cities: New York City* (c. 1922, including a lengthy sequences on bridges), and *Sanitation and Health* (c. 1924, on the building of sewage systems). Technology was central to these films. Workers appear in them only as cogs in an expansive mechanical system. Together, these typical Ford films participated both in an "operational aesthetic" that sought to make visible the new advances of technology and in the broader technological utopianism celebrated at the 1915 Expositions and more widely in the period.[30] The idealization of circulation, and the facilitation of various forms of traffic, was a common trope in the films. Sequences on the movement of materials through factories, by means of roads, bridges, canals, sewage systems, and the circulation of information abound.

Benjamin Franklin and Modern Communication Systems, for example, presented an object lesson in the way new communication systems enable the speeded up transmission of information. Franklin is schooled in how telegraphs, telephones, and radios work, and there is a reenactment of Franklin's famous electricity experiment, with rudimentary special effects to re-create lightning. Franklin reappears in a later film, *The Romance of Making a Modern Magazine,* observing the techniques of newspaper production (in the offices of Ford's own paper, the *Dearborn Independent,* a canny synergistic connection between media elements of the company). The opening title connects Franklin's pioneering *Gazette* to contemporary newspapers, emphasizing the shift in technology away from "hard presses and wood type" to wax molds, electric type, and modern printing presses. "Modern magazines," a title observes, "are produced with amazing speed to handle tremendous circulations."

Ford's savvy "casting" of Franklin as observer to how communication systems facilitate faster and wider circulation of information enables audiences to see both the scope of contemporary developments in the Ford Age and the processes by which disembodied and instantaneous communication works.

Indeed, Ford's Franklin films supplemented the operational aesthetic frequently central to industrial film with the "character" of Franklin, as exemplary early capitalist inventor, who interacts with modern technology in his eighteenth-century costume and is clearly incredulous at the wonders of modern industry he witnesses. Franklin stands in this way as an avatar for an audience being schooled in modern mass communications, and he is also an element, or figure, who unifies disparate forms and processes and so shapes them into a form of narrative.[31] *Benjamin Franklin and Modern Communication Systems* and *The Romance of Making a Modern Magazine* both shift then from the representation of industrial actuality onto the terrain of narrative and what we might call, in that well-known and almost contemporaneous phrase, "the creative treatment of actuality."[32] One of the things that narrative does in this context is individualize technological transformations and work practices in a way consistent with Ford's broader efforts to construct an industrial citizenship opposed to the collectivity of union organization. In these examples it is clear also that actuality and narrative were bent toward idealizing communication's transcendence of space and time in ways consistent with the industrial practices and economic logics of Fordism.

Ford's early films did frequently overlay narrative form on industrial and economic processes, so that the films developed partly fictional scenarios in which technology and new infrastructure overcome problematic traditions to enable happy endings that combine individual and familial fulfillment and profitability. Two examples of the way the Ford films travel into fictional terrain to develop a narrative machinery merit particular attention here. *Farm Progress* contrasts two ways of tending farms. "Brown's way is hard work," the initial title observes, before we see a farmer manually cutting down corn. Providing a contrasting view, the film shifts attention to Brown's neighbor Anderson who uses a Fordson tractor on his farm, both to plow the field and husk the corn. "The Fordson cuts down the working days," a title observes, "thereby allowing time for recreation and self-improvement," exemplified by Anderson sitting and reading the *Dearborn Independent*. Anderson also plays baseball with one of his sons. "Remove the drudgery by using Fordsons and your sons stay at home," the film observes, positioning Fordist technology as a way to "self-improvement" and familial unity. Ford's films participated in this way in the broader economic and political imperative to mechanize farm work, which was particularly visible, as we have seen, in the actions of the USDA and in the state's use of film to enable new "productive" practices. Ford's imperative to mechanize and modernize farming was consistent with state objectives in a further illustration of the hybridity of corporate liberalism.

In the extant script for *Farm Progress* in the Benson Ford Research Center, there are specific directions for casting that show a shrewd sense of the physicality of actors in delineating the distinctions between the old and the new, which were not unlike the contemporary Soviet experimentation with "typology."[33] The guidelines suggest that Brown should be "rather thin, showing lines in face . . . old wrinkled clothes, showing lots of wear," and his wife should be an actress "whose face is careworn from worry and hard work." By contrast, Anderson should be a "typical well-to-do rural type," with a wife who is a "healthy, intelligent, matronly type of woman" and sons who are "healthy country types . . . Intelligent, snappy and ambitious." The lack of Ford technology has deleterious effects on the body. Visible here is clear thought in the production process about the supplementary effects of characterization and the creative treatment of actuality for the pedagogical and persuasive effects of the film in winning audiences to the side of the technologically savvy Anderson.

Farm Progress could end, as contemporary fiction films surely would, with the happy family Anderson, but the Fordist emphasis here necessitates a shift away to other conceptions of value and utility. Titles directly state the different amount of time it would take to plow thirty acres of corn with a tractor (eleven days) or with two or three horses like Brown does (thirty days). Variants of mass-production processes are transferred to the farm through technology consistent with the Ford Company's rhetoric about the advantages mechanization could bring to farm work. Anderson consequently can enjoy the kind of leisure time that was increasingly available to industrial workers after the initiation of the eight-hour workday. The conclusion sees Anderson visiting his bank, and in the final image, and the only extreme close-up in the film, we see his account book showing a healthy profit—a literal *money shot*, using the technological capabilities of cinema to make visible the economic benefits of Fordist technology and practices.

Other Ford films focus on the accelerated circulation of goods, rather than on accelerated production. In *The Road to Happiness* (c. 1924), for example, a young farmer is instructed by his bad-tempered father to deliver eggs to market, but he misses the connecting train because the roads are so bad, and his eggs are destroyed along the way. The father blames the boy for being lazy and dismisses his argument for the need for better roads. Later, at school, the boy is invited to enter a competition to write an essay about his local community, and he writes about the need for good roads to enable the easy transportation of rural goods. The sequence in the rural school emphasizes the importance of education (a recurring theme in the Ford films) and implicitly draws connections between the school and the function of the Ford film as a pedagogic form. The lesson learned by the young farmer, and hopefully by the film audience for whom he serves as an exemplar, was about the commercial necessity of improving roads to enable the smoother flow of commerce and the integration of rural spaces with the national market. The young farmer's essay is the winning entry in the competition, and he accepts his award from President Calvin Coolidge on the lawn of the White House.

Coolidge's appearance was possible because *The Road to Happiness* was produced with the cooperation of the Bureau of Public Roads, a division of the Department of Agriculture.[34] The film's arguments about the necessity for a new material infrastructure for the transport of commerce dovetailed with emergent governmental practices to better facilitate a national and global market. In 1916 a Federal Aid Road Act supplied federal money to states building new roads, administered by the newly created Bureau of Public Roads; and this policy was continued and extended with the 1921 Federal Aid Highway Act.[35] The governments at the state and federal levels were fully committed to organizing technology and infrastructure—creating over four hundred thousand miles of highways in the 1920s, the "golden age" of highway construction—to enable the more efficient flow of commerce and the emergence of a national market.[36] Commercial automobile manufacturers such as Ford were invested in the project to establish "better roads" to facilitate the sale of automobiles to new markets. (Indeed, some of those same corporations were simultaneously engaged in projects to destroy public mass transit systems, with far-reaching consequences for the transportation structure of the country and global ecology.)[37] What was at stake here was the innovation of a new technological space, a networked infrastructure shared out between corporate and governmental forces that would enable market expansion and the incorporation of rural America into an emergent consumer economy. Ford's happiness is akin to the states. The road to happiness is born from the union of the political and economic forces that prioritized the mobility of goods and capital. Here media was put to work to help facilitate the travel infrastructures and modes that subsequently have proven to be integral to the escalating threat of climate change. Key decisions in modern history were formulated and visualized.

The road that led to the happiness of efficient distribution and profitability also led away from the troubling figure of the authoritarian, backward-looking, overbearing father. Fordist film again trips over into fictional scenarios, combining here the delineation of particular ideals of governmental intervention for the smooth functioning of the economy with a partially formed fictional scenario shot through with an Oedipal and narrative dynamic. Overcoming the traditional ways of the father was necessary to unblock the traffic of commerce and capital and to innovate better models for the economic future of Fordism. Quite clearly, the articulation of character and narrative in Fordist films delineated technological futures and related character types, which dovetailed in specific ways with the expansive goals of Fordism to reshape production efficiency, political economy, infrastructure, and subjectivity and citizenship.

"THE PROPER KIND OF CITIZEN"

Ford's mass-production processes came at the cost of a radical dissociation of the labor process from the knowledge of workers, stripping them of craft skills and autonomous control and consequently increasing the authority of management over both production processes and an increasingly alienated labor force. Workers resisted this in various ways, most simply by leaving the company in massive numbers but also by absenteeism, by strikes, and later by efforts to unionize and challenge the open-shop policies of the company.[38] Corporate managers at Ford regarded worker turnover, resistance, and organization as critical problems, as did their contemporaries at other corporations. Executives began to develop policies to counteract the instability of production and to make the largely immigrant workforce more acquiescent, efficient, and productive. The solutions the company devised involved innovations in wage structures and a host of welfare and "educational" initiatives to "Americanize" immigrant workers, to "repersonalize" aspects of the workplace, and more generally to shape worker attitudes and conduct with respect to the new Fordist logics of production and consumption. Together, the company's efforts to establish forms of worker welfare and to educate its workforce sought to increase worker productivity, to forestall union and government involvement in labor practices and welfare programs, and to foster a consumerist ethos to support mass production. "The business of benevolence," as historian Andrea Tone has called it, supported the corporate reconstruction of political economy that prioritized the authority of corporations over workers.[39]

In January 1914, shortly after the initiation of mass-assembly processes and the investment in motion picture technology, the Ford Company dramatically announced it would increase worker wages to five dollars a day and reduce the working day to 8 hours. Its policy increased the wages of its workforce, roughly doubling existing paychecks, and generated a storm of publicity that also drew vast crowds of hopeful employees to its factories. "The Ford Five Dollar Day," labor historian Stephen Meyer claims, "is the most famous labor-management reform in the annals of American business."[40] Ford's goals in increasing wages were varied. Executives hoped it would increase worker loyalty to the company and offset the damaging turnover of the workforce attendant upon Ford's new industrial practices. It would also hopefully dissipate worker radicalism. James Couzens, an influential business manager at Ford and architect of the five-dollar-a-day wage, asserted that with the wage rise "the follies of socialism and the terrors of anarchy will fade away."[41] What would replace these follies? In a word: *consumerism*. Ford's managers hoped the new wage would enable workers to participate in the emergent consumer economy, and this would obviate or overcome worker radicalism. Ford's central product, the Model T, would ultimately be produced at a cost within reach of the company's workforce. Indeed, the automobile would come to exemplify and make material the new conception of self-realization through consumption. Ford's Model T was a complex sign in this respect, produced through the elision of individuality in mass-production processes but sold in part on the basis of the "freedom" it seemingly, though chimerically, enabled. Cars embodied, we might say, the muted "freedoms" of liberalism and consumerism.[42] In any case, what is clearly evident is that the initiation of consumerism functioned quite precisely as a panacea for the de-skilling of a workforce and the circumscription of worker agency in the new Fordist production practices. Gramsci, to reiterate, called these programs of high wages and consumption, and the effort to establish a "consensual" capitalism, "Fordism."[43]

Worker's needed to demonstrate their fitness in "coming up to certain standards of cleanliness and citizenship" to be eligible for this new wage.[44] The company established a Sociological Department to investigate workers' eligibility and "good" citizenship. Workers were visited in their homes by "investigators," who interviewed family members to ensure they conformed to the standards established by the Sociological Department.[45] Employees were not supposed to drink alcohol and were encouraged to maintain a clean "well conducted home" (without boarders or extended family), to regularly deposit money in a savings account, and to have a "good moral character."[46] It was believed these characteristics would increase efficiency. In a 1916 account of its "sociological" and "educational" work, for example, the company remarked that it had "discovered that home conditions, domestic relations, and neighborhood environment, in case they were not right, had a great tendency to lessen a man's efficiency in the factory and to make him an unreliable factor in the organization."[47] To create what the department described as "the proper kind of citizen" necessitated a policing of conduct and internalization of discipline that extended the Fordist goals of utility and efficiency beyond the factory walls.[48] "We want to make men in this factory as well as automobiles," Henry Ford was quoted as saying.[49] Or, in the words of Samuel Marquis, the head of the Sociological Department, "As we adapt the machinery in the shop to turning out the kind of automobile we have in mind, so we have constructed our educational system with a view to producing the human product in mind."[50] Marquis's words make clear how "sociology" segued into an expansive conception of "education," as a reshaping of "productive" subjects, and this was made further evident when the Sociological Department changed its name to the Educational Department in 1915. Elsewhere in this period, these functions were beginning to be carried out by "industrial psychologists," who advised companies on how to make their personnel more "efficient" in ways that paralleled Fordist practices. (One of the better known of these, a professor of experimental psychology at Harvard, was also in his spare time a film theorist.)[51]

"Americanization" was a key facet of the Ford Company's social and educational work. Workers at the company were primarily foreign-born laborers and internal migrants. In 1914, for example, 71 percent of the workforce at Ford's main auto-assembly factory was foreign-born (of these 53 percent came from Russia, Romania, Italy, and Austria-Hungary).[52] Ford's educational program sought to educate these migrant workers in American industrial practices; standards of consumerism; and ideals of morality, civility, and citizenship. It was in this way that the Sociological Department intervened in dictating living arrangements for workers, reorientating immigrant traditions of extended families and communities by valorizing specific and historically middle-class domestic structures as markers of civility. In 1914 the company established an English school that connected language learning with the expansive goals of Americanization. Table etiquette, how government works in the United States, and ideals of citizenship were common classroom topics.[53] Marquis stated that the curriculum overall sought to "make the men more efficient in our work in the shop, but also to prepare them for better citizenship. The first thing we teach them to say is, 'I am a good American,' and then we try to get them to live up to the statement."[54] Likewise, a series of classes on "Pay Day," "Going to the Bank," and "Buying a Lot" taught "the foreigner . . . the meaning of the phrase 'American standard of living'" and thus how to consume "productively."[55] Living up to the difficult task of being a good American meant buying things. When classes on language and the ideals of liberal capitalist citizenship concluded, a graduation ceremony was constructed that had workers arriving on stage in national costume, passing through a melting pot and emerging, changed, as Americans, singing "The Star Spangled Banner." Land of the free, home of the Model T.

Ford's Motion Picture Department started producing films at the same time that the five-dollar-a-day wage was established, the Sociological Department was set up and the Ford English School began to teach immigrant workers how to be good Americans. The department's films were frequently connected to the broader pedagogic goals of the company to reshape worker subjectivity and to interpellate working-class and immigrant populations into a liberal capitalist civility. Ford's use of moving pictures as part of its expansive pedagogical aims was intensified when the company began producing the Ford Educational Weekly series in 1916, explicitly connecting its film production to its educational department and goals. Numerous films produced for the series told stories specifically intended to school young and immigrant audiences in aspects of American history, ideals, monuments, and geography that were widely regarded in this period as subjects of critical importance for the pedagogic project of "Americanizing" diverse populations. *The Story of Old Glory* (c. 1916), for example, documented the history of the American flag, *Where the Spirit that Won was Born* (c. 1918) showed the historic sights of Philadelphia, and *Landmarks of the American Revolution* (c. 1920) was a series that showed the historic sites associated with the revolutionary war. *Presidents of the United States* (c. 1917) briefly recounted the purported major issues facing each president since Madison, particularly those connected to aspects of economic history and to the articulation of a corporate conception of political economy. The entry for John Quincy Adams (president from 1825 to 1829), for example, observed, "Tariff and the means of communication were the great questions of the day. Protection of America's 'infant industries' was secured through the tax on certain imports and the Erie Canal opened up the Northwest Territory to more rapid development." Ford's position was consistent with other northern industrial corporations in calling for tariff barriers to protect American industry.

Various other Ford films showed the grandeur and impressive modernity of American cities. *Pittsburgh, Pennsylvania* (c. 1917), for example, presented grand public institutions such as the Carnegie Library and Institute, museums, and the university; *Washington, D.C.* (c. 1918) likewise pictured Washington, showing in particular a number of imposing government buildings (the Departments of State, Army, Navy, and Treasury; the Patent Office; and the White House); and *New York City* (c. 1919) showed images of the skyline and Statue of Liberty. *Detroit, Michigan* (c. 1921) was made in the context of the economic recession of 1920–21 to specifically encourage consumption. The film celebrates the dynamism of the city, showing the impressive railway station, monumental civic buildings, schools, and various banks, alongside churches and playgrounds and parks. "The downtown pulsates with business activity," a title observes. "Unbelievable tales of coming months of idleness and other propaganda are being swallowed up, and the strings on the money wallet have tightened. Business depends on our buying and spending reasonably to avoid boomeranging another depression on ourselves." Fordist film directly encouraged consumption to sustain economic expansion. Together the historical films and the Fordist symphonies of the city spun a narrative about political and material modernity that extended the coverage of industrial progress to the terrain of the historical and contemporary nation.

The most intriguing of the films delineating a political history and positioning it in a complex internal narrative was produced initially in 1919 and repackaged as a volume of the Civics and Citizenship series of the Ford Educational Library series in 1922.[56] *Democracy in Education* (c. 1919) begins with the revolutionary establishment of a liberal republic, made up of a "sturdy race of resourceful, independent, clear-thinking men, who rebelled at tyranny" and signed the Declaration of Independence. This history of freedom, liberty, and self-determination is rapidly brought up to date by reference to the travails of World War I and images of soldiers marching and fighting. "In 1916," a title observes, "many felt city life had destroyed ideals. Liberty took up arms, making the world safe for democracy." *Democracy in Education*'s abbreviated political history connects the autonomous, independent liberal self that was enshrined in the Declaration and Constitution to political independence, to global assertion, and to a liberty or democracy imagined principally as security. Education is positioned as central to this form of democracy. "America must be prepared," a title tells us, and "her public schools must make Democracy safe for the world." Wilson's rhetoric upon the declaration of war is repeated twice. Between shots of classrooms, the film tells us that "school training must result in the development of those qualities which are essential both to the happiness of the individual and to the strength and vitality of the nation." Ford's arguments about civic education, democracy, and security were clarified in a guide to the film included in a 1926 book on visual instruction. The "exercise of the fundamentals of democracy in the schools," the guide asserted, "lays the foundation for a free and independent nation."[57] *Ford News* similarly observed that the "importance of school training to the individual's happiness and success and to the nation is shown."[58] The concluding sequence shows the US Capitol building as evidence of the "the genius of government" and so underscores the connections that the film proposes must run between the shaping of independent selfhood, nation, and political order.

What to make of the political philosophy of this brief, episodic, and enigmatic film? Broadly it exemplifies the larger goals of corporations in seeking, as historian Martin Sklar frames it, to "transact the corporate reconstruction of the political-economic order on the basis of the mutual adaptation of corporate capitalism and the American liberal tradition."[59] The films' portrayals of a history of freedom and self-determination work to propose that the subjectivity exemplified by revolutionary subjects can survive the transition to corporate capitalism. It is education that must facilitate this shift between historical forms of subjectivities. To do this, schools, and also implicitly cinema as a form of mobile school, must teach "methods which will result in SELF DIRECTION . . . SELF APPRAISAL . . . [and] SELF CONTROL." Fordist "methods" produce a selfhood understood as self-possession and self-discipline. Education sustains a political and economic technology of individualization. But the transition is complex, for Fordist rhetoric and culture must also necessarily revise the liberal idealization of autonomy for the new machine or mass-assembly age. Education, in the Ford films and in the company, functions as the pivot between liberal ideals of self-determination and the necessity of "self-control" to produce social, economic, and political order. The balance tips in favor of a muted version of classical liberal conceptions of self-determination befitting the truncated form of autonomy integral to mass-assembly industrial practices.

Ford's rather complex argument about democracy, liberalism, and education draws explicitly on what seems at first glance a rather unlikely source—the liberal educational philosophy of John Dewey. Dewey's 1916 book *Democracy and Education: An Introduction to the Philosophy of Education* appears to be the source of the film's title, a connection suggested also in the short document the company produced to accompany the film, when it was reissued as part of the Ford Educational Library.[60] Dewey argued for the import of education in the "enlisting of the person's own participating disposition in getting the result desired, and thereby of developing within him an intrinsic and persisting direction in the right way."[61]

Liberal educational philosophy had long declared the importance of education in developing the cognitive and moral qualities seen as necessary for citizenship in a democratic polity and had pondered the complexity of combining self-determination with the social contract. Dewey's work in this period updated this dialectic with reference to the new social, economic, and political conditions of the early twentieth century. "When the school introduces and trains each child of society," Dewey wrote in 1915, "saturating him with the spirit of service, and providing him with the instruments of effective self-direction, we shall have the deepest and best guarantee of a larger society which is worthy, lovely, and harmonious."[62] Ford simplified Dewey's complex pondering of the mix of self-direction and self-control in liberal education. The Ford films use aspects of liberal pedagogy but frame that, or cathect that tradition, to the needs of mass-assembly practices and corporate capitalism. Movies and media helped visualize and transact that critical connection and transformation.

Workers challenged this association. Many of them saw Fordism as a destructive transformation of preexisting work practices and a radical reduction in the promises of liberalism. In the war period, criticism intensified amid a widespread sense that industrial cooperation and the fight for what *Democracy in Education* called "liberty" and "democracy" would result in a fairer future. Workers called for an "industrial democracy" that they defined as "trade union power, even workers' control, at both the point of production and the nexus of ownership."[63] Unionism increased considerably during the conflict. But in the immediate postwar period, corporations invested very different meanings in the phrase "industrial democracy," reusing it as part of a counteroffensive that came to be called the "American Plan" and that attempted not only to "roll back trade unionism" but also "to reconstruct their legitimacy by incorporating the rallying cry of the wartime union upsurge into their managerial lexicon."[64] Widespread use of espionage within its own factories, coupled with strike breaking, countered efforts at Ford to unionize and battle for better working conditions.[65] Workers responded with a series of strikes in 1919, which took place at automobile part shops and factories and, more widely, which registered laborers' investment in reorientating capitalist and Fordist practices.[66]

Clearly it was in this precise context of a battle over the definition of "industrial democracy" that the company first produced *Democracy in Education*, which was part of a shift toward the "American Plan" at the company, which marked its intensification of antiunion practices. The connection of this to the organization's broader goals of Americanization was clear in the film's history and civics lesson. It was also apparent in the short document the company produced to guide educators in how to exhibit and describe the film when it was reissued in 1922, in the shadow of the economic recession of 1920–21. Where the film's titles had observed that in 1916 "many felt city life had destroyed ideals," the teacher's guide clarified how those ideals had been challenged: "The city congestion has been complicated by large immigrations from Europe, which have planted foreign customs and languages in large areas of some cities."[67] The deprivation of life in industrialized urban cities, and the "congestion" that troubled the circulation of materials and people, was clearly the fault of migrant workers and their foreign customs. Ford's broader goal here was to align worker unrest with attitudes and conduct that could be thought of as "un-American." The company banned union membership and clamped down violently on attempts to unionize its workforce.[68] By doing so it was consistent with the governmental interventions that produced, for example, the Palmer raids in 1919. Together these practices marked a critical moment in the discursive construction of "America" as embodying particular political and economic logics and institutions and in portraying beliefs contrary to those as "un-American." It would not be the last time these arguments were made.

Ford simultaneously made overtly anti-Soviet and antiunion propaganda, using film to educate the public about the "evils" of Communist economic and political systems. The tissue of connections running from immigration to unionism to socialism that underlay the managerial counteroffensive against worker radicalism was made particularly apparent in another 1919 Ford film, *Uncle Sam and the Bolsheviki* (c.1919). In this short animated film, an American farmer stands behind grain bags, with the words "American Institutions" written on them, and beats a rat bearing on its back the words "Bolsheviki (IWW)" (see fig. 11). Uncle Sam's defense of American institutions necessitates the defeat of the unions, here the Industrial Workers of the World, who had attempted to unionize at Ford as early in 1913.[69] Ford's rhetoric connected them to Soviet radicalism. The IWW rat—complete with eugenic overtones—is a carrier of the Communist ideology posing radical challenges to the political economy of liberal capitalism.

Ford began at this point advertising its films as adjuncts to the "pressing need" to Americanize migrant populations (see fig. 2 in chapter 2). Its endeavors dovetailed with the state's efforts, which began in 1919, to use film to support "Americanization," a further illustration of the shared goals of governmental and corporate institutions. Earlier, I talked briefly about this particular advertisement and its canny articulation and condensation of ideals of civility and political belonging relayed through a newly corporate and mechanized form of pedagogy. Ford began a concerted effort to disseminate its films to schools. The company's final series of films, the Ford Educational Library, emerged in 1921 in the midst of economic depression and heightened antiunionism. Ford Educational Library films were directed specifically at the young audiences seen in the Educational Weekly advertisement, those who would, the *Ford News* observed, "tomorrow . . . be citizens."[70] Ford Educational Library films were distributed especially to schools by universities at a time when extension departments at state schools in particular were purchasing and distributing increasing numbers of nontheatrical films. Ford's own newspaper, the *Dearborn Independent,* likewise ran a promotion that promised

FIGURE 11. Still from *Uncle Sam and the Bolsheviki* (Ford Motion Picture
Laboratories, 1919).

free projectors to schools based on subscriptions to the newspaper.[71] Henry Ford,
as quoted in the nontheatrical trade publication *Moving Picture Age,* claimed that
the objective of this new series was to "establish the foundation for a reference
library of motion pictures to be used by schools."[72] Ford sought in these ways to
transform education through the form of mechanized culture to better serve
industrial and corporate goals.

Ford Educational Library films were even described as "organized visual
instruction."[73] In a catalogue produced to advertise the films, the company talked
of a tradition of "visualization in education" begun by John Amos Comenius—
"the father of visual instruction"—in his 1657 book *The World of Sensible Things
Pictured.* In a drawing on the cover of its catalogue, a film reel is shown wrapped
around Comenius's book, illustrating the purported potential of moving pictures
to supplement the book as a central element of the school system (see fig. 12).
Ford's rhetoric about the place of vision in pedagogy dovetailed with the emergent
visual instruction movement, and the films the company produced were important to the functioning of that network. Various Ford films, including *Democracy
in Education,* were shown at the National Education Association meeting in 1922.[74]
The films' accounts of the importance of education for the shaping of selfhood
and democratic order, and their embodiment of the ideal that education could be

FIGURE 12. Cover from Ford Educational Library catalog (Ford Educational Library, 1922).

supplemented with a newly mechanized rationality, seemingly found a receptive audience. In the immediate aftermath of the meeting, the National Education Association formed a committee to survey the field and in 1923 established a Department of Visual Instruction.[75] Visual instruction promised to revitalize education for the Ford Age. Ford's filmic contributions sought specifically to educate workers and their children in the realities of mass production and its transformation of work practices, as well as to participate in the broader reconciliation of liberalism with corporate capitalism.

"TRUE USEFULNESS"

But the Fordist dream of a productive pedagogical cinema began to recede in the late 1920s and early 1930s. The company stopped adding films to the Ford Educational Library series in 1925 and abandoned its Motion Picture Laboratory in 1932.[76] Technology played a role in this, for there were practical problems in using films in educational institutions before 16mm had become a major factor (beginning in 1923), and the emergence of sound cinema in 1927 increased the costs associated with filmmaking. The corporate power of Hollywood, modeled in part on Fordist mass-assembly practices, marginalized alternative formations of cinema, most clearly by controlling distribution and exhibition and by the actions of its own industrial relations committee, the Motion Pictures Producers and Distributors of America. Ford's investment in nontheatrical cinema had sought to counter the dominance of Hollywood. Workers and young people voted with their feet, though, filling their leisure time with the more enjoyable and seductive articulation of liberal capitalism and the pleasures of consumption found in mainstream American cinema of the 1920s.

Ford's cultural attitudes engendered other problems as well. Henry Ford purchased the newspaper the *Dearborn Independent* in 1919 and began a vitriolic anti-Semitic campaign that dovetailed with the increasingly restrictive definitions of citizenship visible in Ford's Americanization programs in the postwar period. Across a two-year period starting in May 1920, the paper published a series of "exposés" about Jewish influence in American life, notably in respect to purported Jewish control of financial markets and unions.[77] Henry Ford buttressed this by purchasing and publishing the fraudulent *Protocols of the Learned Elders of Zion*.[78] Hollywood was also targeted by the *Dearborn Independent* as part of its exposé of Jewish influence. The "financing of motion pictures from the production angle has been almost entirely in the hands of Jews," the paper claimed, leading to the production of "reels . . . reeking with filth . . . slimy with sex plays."[79] Ford's paper reported approvingly on conservative moral reformers battling with Hollywood.[80] In the wake of these arguments, the company's educational films were repositioned as responses to the degraded products of Hollywood. *Ford News* thus suggested in 1922 that, in developing educational films, "the Ford film department believes that the long-neglected and dormant educational value of the motion pictures sacrificed in the desire for money grabbing, will be taken advantage of to carry out its fundamental purpose of true usefulness."[81] Ford's considerable economic and symbolic investment in producing and distributing "useful" films in the postwar period thus sought in part to challenge the values enshrined in the "useless" commercial cinema controlled by purportedly "money grabbing" Jewish entrepreneurs.

But the controversies that ensued over the vicious anti-Semitism of the *Dearborn Independent* damaged the reputation of Ford and of the company in the early 1920s. The controversy was publicly revisited when Henry Ford was sued for libel in 1927, and in that same year he closed down the *Dearborn Independent*.[82] Ford's controversial and unpopular anti-Semitism was certainly damaging to company film practices. The socially conscious and progressive groups interested in cinema's potential to be useful for the shaping of "good citizenship" began to distance themselves from Ford. Cinema exhibitors who had shown Ford films, many of them Jewish, also began to refuse to show the films. Hollywood retaliated too. Upton Sinclair wrote a book about Ford, supported by the United Auto Workers Union, where he alleged that Ford stopped the *Dearborn Independent* articles after the Jewish film entrepreneur William Fox threatened to release newsreels of Ford cars in serious accidents.[83] Charlie Chaplin lampooned the dehumanizing effects of the Fordist assembly line in his 1936 film *Modern Times*.

Ford faced even graver business problems in the late 1920s. General Motors had maneuvered into a position of industry dominance by changing the car designs each year and developing different cars for different population segments.[84] GM's business model better resonated with the new consumer culture and its ethos of self-realization through consumption. I shall come back to this, and to GM, in chapter 13, but here it is worth noting that Ford was more innovative in mass-assembly practices than they were in actually developing new strategies of mass consumption that segmented populations according to particular products and product lines. Partly this was connected to the different corporate forms of Ford and GM. Ford functioned as a sort of hybrid corporation. It was connected to familial ownership and capital, and it had begun to develop the bureaucratic form of the corporation. Before Henry Ford's death in 1947, however, it did not achieve the separation of ownership and management that characterized new corporate forms. GM and its long-serving president Alfred P. Sloan Jr. innovated a modern bureaucratic form, including the development of research laboratories and innovations in marketing that encompassed the annual model change and such things as installment credit.[85] Companies like GM also began to develop new personnel departments and company unions to acknowledge but forestall worker discontent.[86] GM, in short, overtook Ford in the new consumer economy that had been partly initiated by Ford's innovation of mass assembly. Ford began to respond. It stopped production of the Model T in 1927 and halted production for six months to retool the River Rouge factory to produce the Model A.[87] The (partly) post-Fordist practices of GM, predicated on a "flexible specialization" to enable constant innovation, spread across the automobile sector and to other industries.[88] Ford was no longer the industry leader.

Ford's economic problems only got worse. The Depression of 1929 challenged the idea of consumption as self-realization and the Fordist idealization of industrial as opposed to governmental welfare and management of the economy. Henry Ford refused to cooperate with the New Deal and continued to valorize the formation of laissez faire liberalism, which was being tested and partly revised by the Depression.[89] Economic depression led also to more organized efforts to unionize auto workers. Opposing these efforts was the Ford "Service Department," established to carry out industrial espionage and described by the *New York Times* as "the largest private quasi-military organization in existence."[90] In March 1932, a march of auto workers sponsored by the small Auto Workers' Union and the Detroit Unemployed Council was brutally suppressed by the Service Department, which was responsible for the deaths of four marchers and the serious wounding of twenty-eight others. Dearborn's police force was seemingly complicit. Carl Raushenbush, of the League for Industrial Democracy, claimed that Ford controlled the police and the whole government of Dearborn.[91] The leftist filmmakers of the Detroit and New York Workers Film and Photo League captured the events on film in *Detroit Workers News Special 1932: The Ford Massacre*, offering a rare filmic glimpse of the underbelly of the Fordist dreams of industrial and worker efficiency that appeared in the company's films. Later, the Service Department disrupted a union-led film screening at Ford of a prolabor film called *Millions Like Us* in Dallas. Union members who attended the screening were savagely beaten.[92]

Violence marked the nadir of the Fordist engagement with cinema, as brute force temporarily replaced the potential for cinema as a consciousness industry to establish hegemony. The company stopped regularly producing films. Various other forms of media stepped into the breach. Ford sponsored, for example, Charles Sheeler's photographs of the River Rouge factory in 1927, images that reinforced the ideal of rationality that subtended the organization of space in the factory.[93] The pictures make clear the connections between modernism and Fordism, a connection that was perhaps most visible in modernist architecture.[94] Charles Sheeler's images of the modern factory contained few workers, supporting, if only ambiguously, the idealization of mechanization so central to Fordism. Later the company began a radio show, inaugurated at the Century of Progress Fair in Chicago in the summer of 1934. The *Ford Sunday Evening Hour* continued until 1942 as a weekly show on CBS that included music and comment on public affairs.[95] The Ford Foundation began in 1936, one of a number of liberal foundations that worked to manage liberal capitalism and ensure its continuity.[96] The foundation later sponsored a television program, *Omnibus* (1952–59), that offered liberal arts instruction for viewer improvement.[97] Ford began with film, that is, but moved to other media to supplement its economic goals. The shift from film to radio and eventually to television was a significant one, as the corporation utilized the successive formations of popular mass media to further its interests.

Ford also started another media project in 1927, the same year that the company stopped production of the Model T, Henry Ford stood trial for libel, the *Dearborn Independent* closed, and Sheeler took photographs of the Rouge—a museum village to be called Greenfield Village. The museum was completed in 1929, on the eve of the economic depression that would threaten the model of Fordist mass production. Ford's museum village celebrated traditional industry, farming, and crafts, displaying a series of outmoded mechanical devices and buildings, ranging from a traditional village church and schoolhouse to the courthouse where Abraham Lincoln argued law, the bicycle shop of the Wright brothers, and Thomas Edison's Menlo Park laboratory. The bucolically named village, described in a guidebook as "Henry Ford's fantastic time machine," marked Henry Ford's own gathering sense of personal nostalgia, a growing retreat from the travails besetting Fordist mass production amid the sense that it had come at the cost of great damage to traditional ways of life.[98] The efforts to connect rural and modern traditions were apparent also in Henry Ford's establishment of a series of small factories in rural communities encircling Detroit and in the Muscle Shoals project on the Tennessee River to utilize water-power for electricity.[99]

Greenfield Village as built environment and material (and acquired) history embodied a mediation between, and stabilization of, the relationships between "tradition"—loosely, a nineteenth-century small town, untouched by the forces of industrial modernity or worker solidarity and oppositional movements—and the transformation of that space and social order by modern innovations like electricity, mechanics, the airplane, and the automobile. In its ethos of the preservation of indexical traces of the past, the village museum sought to immobilize historical temporality and yet simultaneously exhibit forms that spoke to the transformations wrought by an ascendant advanced capitalism and its modern technologies. Philip Rosen's insightful reading of the village proposes that it functioned as a fetish, as acknowledgment and disavowal of difference and of "corrosive temporality."[100] Indeed, one of the exhibits at the village marks this dynamic of nostalgia and fetishism particularly acutely. Ford's own childhood home was reassembled there because it would otherwise have been destroyed by a highway construction project necessitated by the growing use of the automobile.[101] Automobile manufacture in this respect exemplified the ruthless destruction of the old endemic to capitalism—severing people from one another across time and space—and the village and historical projects of Ford emerged as reflexive desires to reestablish links to a past occluded by the onrushing present.[102]

Fordist film might perhaps be read a little differently in this context. The films themselves functioned in some respects as a time machine enabling the restitching together of both past and present—most notably perhaps in the Franklin films—as well as the work tasks separated out by the process of mass assembly. The company's films of industrial processes and mass assembly reconnected the fragmented parts of those processes, thus making visible the connection of part to whole that had necessarily been rent asunder by the mass-assembly line. Ford's anonymous "assemblers," working in a line to thread together the films made by the company, were able to restitch together the work practices of Fordism. Workers could then see the entirety of their work practices, as film reflexively resisted the economic imperatives of mass assembly—even if only to re-present a fiction of coherent time and space, tied together by Fordist editors on an assembly line.

One film project carried out by Henry Ford himself at this point had particular resonance in relation to this reflexive turn to a past occluded by Fordism and by the automobile's destruction of traditional patterns of sociality and its fueling of individualism and consumerism (not even to mention oil-related military expansion). Henry Ford had apparently become increasingly convinced of the idea of reincarnation, and he came, it seems, to believe that his niece was the reincarnation of his mother. He made a film starring his niece celebrating his mother's life.[103] I suppose we might see it as a companion piece of sorts to the curiously Oedipal narrative submerged in *The Road to Happiness*. Cinema functioned, for Henry Ford, finally, as a literal "mummification of change" in the face of the rapid and violent transformation of the world in which the automobile and the Ford Company—and indeed cinema—would play such a central role.[104]

The Pan-American Road to Happiness and Friendship

Ford's 1924 film *The Road to Happiness* was made in collaboration with the Bureau of Public Roads. The film's production history and form embodied the points of connection between state and corporate efforts to facilitate new transport infrastructures and the mobility of materials. It was made in the wake of the 1921 Federal Aid Highway Act when the "extended" state disbursed considerable funds to construct a network of roads that would enable the incorporation of rural markets into a new national market.[1] Road networks facilitated the emergence of an industrial and consumer economy predicated on the rapid transit of produce, raw materials, and manufactured goods. The creation of what historian Jo Guldi has recently called an "infrastructure state" became more pressing because of the depression of 1920–21 that hit rural areas particularly hard and because of the emergence and development of automotive technology.[2] Ford and other automotive corporations lobbied for the extension of road networks. The Fordist compression of spatiality and temporality and the creation of infrastructural networks was crucial also for all those myriad businesses that required mobility to extract materials, some to manufacture objects, and all to distribute materials or objects or information both nationally and increasingly internationally. Road networks began to supplement rail networks in this respect (and in fact began to overtake them in terms of amount of material and people transported toward the ends of the 1920s) and dovetailed with other expanded transportation networks that included subway and mass transit systems.[3] Material networks of infrastructure dovetailed with the more immaterial networks of communication such as the long-distance telephonic communication that enabled coast-to-coast calls first publicly demonstrated at the 1915 Panama-Pacific International Exposition (and transatlantic calls from 1926) as well as the expansion of radio in the 1920s.[4] In short, a complex interconnected system of material and more immaterial wired and wireless infrastructures emerged to facilitate the relatively rapid circulation of people, goods, and information that was essential to the particular form of advanced industrial, consumer, and global capitalism that emerged in the latter parts of the nineteenth century and that began to spread and intensify in the interwar years.

What follows examines the ways film was used by the US government to facilitate the material networks of transport that supported economic expansion domestically *and* globally. I explore both the ways that film as an informational form was used to help construct stable all-weather roads capable of carrying heavy automobiles and how film as a rhetorical form was used to persuade various domestic and international populations of the necessity of expanded road networks. I begin with the domestic situation by looking at the Office of Public Roads' use of film to disseminate information on road-building practices and, after its transformation into the Bureau of Public Roads in 1918, the films it made in collaboration with major automobile manufacturers that focused on the varied benefits road-building would bring to people and communities. But thereafter I explore the role the Bureau played in the attempted creation of a Pan-American road network in the mid-1920s, carried out with the collaboration of major industrial corporations and banking interests alongside Central and South American governments. Numerous films were made by the Bureau of Public Roads both for the Pan-American Highway conferences that began in 1924 and for "distribution . . . in the countries of South, Central, and North America" to be used "in educating the people to the value of better highways."[5] Communicative and infrastructural forms intertwined in pursuit of expansive political and economic goals.

Efforts to use film as an informational and rhetorical form in these ways were significant because they played a role in the orchestration of networks of circulation that went hand-in-hand with new economic practices both domestically and globally. In the U.S. there was considerable attention paid to problems of distribution, leading to an inaugural National Distribution Conference organized by Secretary of Commerce Herbert Hoover in 1925 and a Census on Distribution orchestrated by the federal government from 1928.[6] Trucks and roads were political technologies, enabling expanded consumer networks, and radical transformations in built space. In the 1930s both would come to be used by agribusiness instead of unionized railroads "to craft 'free market' solutions" to the distribution of "the products of factory farms and food processors to the new supermarkets of booming suburbia."[7]

Remember that the markets and materials of Latin America came to be ever more important to the United States in the context of its rapid industrialization in the latter parts of the nineteenth century. The completion of the Panama Canal in 1914 enabled expanded and accelerated movement of raw materials and manufactured goods. In 1915 an important Pan-American economic conference discussed economic ties, and thereafter a series of Pan-American conferences in the 1920s focused on travel infrastructures.[8] The central objective of the US state in developing economic ties with Latin America was in opening access to raw materials as well as new markets and investment opportunities. Raw materials associated with automobility were particularly prized, notably including oil in Colombia, Venezuela, Peru, Mexico and rubber in Brazil. The US government countered local efforts to nationalize mineral resources by organizing private loans from banks. The historians Scott Nearing and Joseph Freeman called this "dollar diplomacy" (before, that is, Nearing was jailed for his views under the terms of the Espionage Act).[9]

Two examples can quickly illustrate this. In 1917 the Mexican government asserted sovereignty over mineral rights but the United States government forced the country to grant legal guarantees of American property by organizing a banking consortium that promised much needed loans in return for such safeguards.[10] (The House of Morgan was central to this, and in return the US government recognized the Mexican government and supplied it with arms.)[11] Colombia reformed its subsoil laws in 1919. The US government collaborating with Gulf Oil's attorney (and future director of the CIA) Allen Dulles worked to safeguard US investment. The Department of Commerce cautioned American investors about loaning to Colombia until their government agreed to safeguard Gulf's properties—at which point they received a loan from National City Bank.[12] The state, large extractive corporations and finance capital colluded to safeguard the plundering of the material resources needed for economic expansion.

Global expansion also in terms of markets was mandated by the contemporary idea that high levels of production needed new global outlets—the previously discussed so-called overproduction thesis—and this shaped the practices of large corporations and trade associations like the United States Chamber of Commerce and the American Manufacturers' Export Association (established, respectively, in 1912 and 1913). The federal government supported this agenda by acting as what economic historian Emily Rosenberg calls a "promotional state."[13] Cartels engaged in foreign business were accordingly exempted from US antitrust law in the Webb-Pomerene Act of 1918, and this was a crucial motor for global expansion and the vertical integration of large US corporations (including the mainstream film industry).[14] Certainly, there was a history of US global economic expansion that predated the 1910s and 1920s, visible in the previously discussed imperial agendas that sustained the so-called Spanish-American War of 1898 and the beginnings of the Panama Canal from 1904. But the developments in the 1920s in particular marked a (partial) shift away from a European style colonialism and its territorial logics of power towards the economic and capitalist imperialism and what Rosenberg calls the "liberal developmental paradigm" that sustained the United States' rise to global hegemon in the interwar years.[15] It is a central tenet of my argument that media played varied roles in that complex and globally significant process, and I now add further detail to this by focusing closely on the mid-1920s and the precise connections between the material and semiotic networks that underscored the United States' centrality to an ever expanding market driven modernity.

ROAD BUILDING AND TESTING SCENES

In early 1914 the Office of Public Roads (OPR), located within the Department of Agriculture, produced a number of films that documented the testing and building of durable road surfaces. Among the films produced, at the very beginning of the USDA's experiment with filmmaking, were *Road Building and Testing Scenes, Macadam Road Construction, Gravel Road Construction,* and *Road Conditions and Maintenance* (all OPR/USDA, c. 1914).[16] Together these were designated "films designed for popular agricultural education," defined in internal USDA documents as those "designed (1) to illustrate progressive agricultural methods, (2) to arouse general interest and lead to community adoption of these methods, (3) to 'break ground' for the work of the personal demonstrator or county agent, and (4) to familiarize people with activities of the Department which directly touch their daily business."[17] Also available were three "professional films" entitled *Testing Rock to Determine Its Value for Road Building, Rock Tests with Traction Dynamometer,* and *Cement and Concrete Tests* (all OPR/USDA, c. 1914). "These films," the department's annual report stated, "are designed to show specialists the exact technical methods employed by the Department or to give those interested in an industry an accurate idea of the best practice of their field."[18] Film was integrated in this way directly into the scientific-testing procedures of the Office of Public Roads. "Educational" and technical "professional" road films from the OPR sought in this way to shape new road-building practices by specialists and to educate rural populations in the methods for constructing and maintaining farm-to-market roads.

Experimentation with surfaces and materials had been central to the scientific agenda of the OPR since its creation in 1905, and this necessitated closer ties with the USDA's Bureau of Chemistry.[19] Government experts examined different materials, from asphalt to concrete to gravel to macadam, and different construction processes.[20] Expanding after 1905, partly to accommodate the arrival of the automobile, the OPR constructed a new laboratory to test materials and began to disseminate information about standards.[21] Its goals were consistent with those of the USDA more broadly, that is, to orchestrate scientific knowledge in a robust bureaucratic form to foster a market economy in agriculture—here, specifically to enable the speedy distribution to urban areas of crops that could sustain both farm production and the rapidly expanding urban society.

To accomplish these goals, the Office of Public Roads constructed a number of roads as what they called "object lessons."[22] Like Seaman Knapp's extension farms, these were constructed for local rural communities, which were encouraged to visit them to observe construction and maintenance practices and thus to move forward in constructing local roads themselves with assistance from the OPR. Celluloid's storage capacity, and indexicality, again made film a useful supplement to the state use of extension models to facilitate new productive practices. *Concrete Road Construction*, for example, was described in a later USDA catalogue like this: "*Illustrates* the essential requirements in the design of concrete pavements to provide the necessary stability to resist the destructive action caused by the volume, weight, and speed of modern motor traffic. Shows the principal operations in the most advanced methods of concrete-pavement construction."[23] Likewise similar films, such as *Hot-Mixed Bituminous Pavements, Penetration Bituminous Macadam, Low-Cost Road Surfaces—First Stage*, and its no doubt eagerly awaited sequel *Low-Cost Road Surfaces—Second Stage*, all "illustrated" methods of road construction advocated by the OPR to local communities and states.[24] Film was in this way a useful informational medium, capable of concretely illustrating the materials and methods needed for the construction of a new transportation infrastructure. Valued for its indexicality, its ontological ties to objects, and its mobility, film was put to work to help facilitate the new farm-to-market road construction that would connect rural and urban markets and so grease the wheels for the expansion of markets.

Later films made by the OPR, mostly after it became the Bureau of Public Roads in 1918, supplemented this agenda by extolling the virtues and benefits of road construction to rural communities and, in the 1920s, urban workers. They did so in lockstep with the federal policies that began to establish new road networks, beginning with the 1916 Federal Aid Road Act, which supplied up to seventy-five million dollars in federal monies to states to build new roads. The act proposed a model of federal-state collaboration, whereby the federal government carried out fundamental research, and provided matching funds, and newly formed state highway departments carried out the road construction.[25] Roads were mostly constructed at this point in order to enable farmers to move produce to markets, increasingly to urban ones.

Rapid rises in individual car ownership, from 78,000 in 1905 to 3.3 million in 1916 and 8.1 million in 1920, also pushed federal and state governments to devote resources to road building. Car corporations and trade groups, like the American Automobile Association, lobbied for road construction, including new intercity roads. Firestone, an important early innovator in rubber tires with close connections to Ford, organized a transcontinental publicity tour in the summer of 1920, which included films, speakers, and a handbook about the necessity of road construction.[26] After these developments, the 1921 Federal Aid Highway Act "fulfilled some of the objectives of the automobile industry" in supporting limited interstate road building, as well as supplementing the extant focus on farm-to-market roads.[27] After passage of the act, a series of state conferences with the Bureau of Public Roads and American Association of State Highway Officials created new maps of how the road network interconnected, effectively creating a national road infrastructure.[28] State highway budgets increased from $430 million in 1921 to $1.3 billion in 1930.[29] New roads were to be monitored by the Bureau of Public Roads, which had been granted bureau status in the USDA in 1918, in recognition of the growing importance of road networks for economic expansion. Federal monies, state bonds, and gasoline taxes supported the emergence of a vast automotive infrastructure thereafter, with deleterious consequences for the environment and global ecology but profitable results for automobile manufacturers and related industries like steel, iron, rubber, and oil. Gasoline taxes, beginning in 1919, were earmarked specifically for new road construction in a "self-replicating system," which was, Christopher Wells has argued, "designed explicitly to stimulate near-constant growth in American demand for gasoline."[30] US foreign policy and military expansion in the twentieth century would be intimately tied to securing this crucial resource.

But for now let us stick with a few of the films the bureau produced in the wake of the 1916 and 1921 federal legislation, beginning with *The Road to Happiness*, which I will now explore from the perspective of the state that collaborated with Ford in its production. In the state's archives there is a memorandum from the director of the USDA's Extension Work, C. W. Warburton, in which he recounts how the Bureau of Public Roads helped "in the location of suitable scenes for picturization and in the loaning of one or two members of the staff of that Bureau to act in the picture." Warburton revealed that the "Motion Picture Laboratory" of the USDA "was also used by the photographers of the Ford Motor Company in developing the film." Ford's resources mingled together with the state's to tell a story that carefully orchestrated allegiance to the cause for road building embodied in the young farmer. Policy was encoded in character and became narrative. Warburton concluded that the "film itself is entirely commendable and it is quite in keeping with those produced by the Department. As a matter of fact the Department might have produced the film in exactly its present form."[31] His remark in this respect makes clear that the film perfectly illustrated the mutuality of interests between state and corporation.

Warburton's memorandum even revealed that bureau officials acted in the film, in front of Ford's cameras, before the celluloid was developed with the help of USDA chemicals. *The Road to Happiness* embodied the goals of what Rosenberg calls "the cooperative state" that promoted industry and trade in the liberal belief in the mutuality of public and private interests.[32] Ford and the bureau distributed the film through their own networks of distribution. The bureau circulated the film in particular through the Highway Education Board, which had been set up

FIGURE 13. Title card from *The Road to Happiness* (Ford Educational Library, 1924).

by the chief of the bureau in 1923 to disseminate information about road building, chiefly to schools. The Highway Education Board is listed on the title card of the extant copy of the film, alongside the National Automobile Chamber of Commerce, which functioned principally as a lobbying group for the automotive industry and had close ties to government (see fig. 13).[33]

In a press release to accompany the film on its way through these networks, the bureau even imagined a future for the character of the young farmer. Escaping the grumpy backward-looking father, anointed by the president as the good father of the nation, he "becomes a highway engineer," as the bureau's PR had it, and "is privileged to bring about such changes in the condition of the roads of his community that even the most skeptical opponents of road improvement are brought to a realization of the truth of the maxim which forms the moral of the picture that 'we pay for improved roads whether we have them or not, and we pay less if we have them than if we have not.'"[34] In the context of the Highway Education Board's work with schools, the young farmer becomes an exemplar of the technocratic management of an emerging networked society.

Various other films produced by the Bureau of Public Roads narrate a story of progress and happiness that culminates with the car and the paved road. *Highways of Service* (Bureau of Public Roads, c. 1927), for example, tells the history of transport from pioneer days to modern roads and in doing so connects road building to national progress and the kind of frontier mobility widely celebrated as constituent of the American national experience. In one sequence, a car struggles to traverse a mud road, before the next shot shows the same car smoothly motoring down a newly built road, a before-and-after editing pattern that was a common trope in nontheatrical films emphasizing the transformative power of government. Many films celebrated the technological achievements that enabled government engineers to build roads in treacherous conditions. *A Road Out of Rock* (Bureau of Public Roads, n.d.), for example, shows "how engineers and road builders overcome huge obstacles to construct a modern highway through Glacier National Park"; *Building Forest Roads* (Bureau of Public Roads, n.d.) shows "men and machinery at work in the national forests, pushing good highways through the great mountains and woodlands"; and *Highways and Skyroads* (Bureau of Public Roads, n.d.) is described in a USDA catalogue like this: "Building Government roads through the national forests; obstacles overcome and scenic beauties reached."[35] Government and advanced construction technology intertwine, these films suggest, the one strengthening the other, establishing the networks that facilitate commercial and personal movement across the nation. "Education" through mobile media sought to facilitate the kinds of mobility and circulation integral to this particular formation of liberal capitalism.

ROADS FOR ALL AMERICA

In these representations of technological advancement, as well as in their circulation, the state advertised and emphasized its power and modernity. This became particularly important with respect to the US government's efforts to establish a Pan-American road network that would enable the hemispheric circulation of raw materials and manufactured objects. In 1919 a Pan-American commercial conference presented the need to disseminate information among Latin Americans about the "superiority" of US road-building methods as a prelude to exporting those methods, along with the machines that made roads and drove across them. Participants were told also of the effectiveness of "publicity films" to present US firms and products more effectively to Latin American markets.[36] In 1923 the efforts to foster road construction in South and Central America, and to connect roads across the continent, were addressed at a conference of American states in Santiago, Chile. Delegates passed a resolution calling for a Pan-American Highway Commission that would observe the US highway system and US means of financing, administering, constructing, and controlling modern highways and work to establish similar road networks.[37] Quickly thereafter the National Automobile Chamber of Commerce in Washington began arranging funding after the

Bureau of Public Roads and the recently formed Department of Commerce endorsed the notion. It received funding from the bureau's Highway Education Board and pledges of a thousand dollars or more "from prominent bankers and leading automotive and road machinery manufacturers of the United States."[38]

Indeed, members of the Pan-American Highway Commission's executive committee had strong ties to US automotive and banking interests. Roy D. Chaplin, chairman of the board of Hudson Motor Car Company, chaired the committee, which included Fred I. Kent, vice-president of Banker's Trust of New York, and W. T. Beaty, president of the Austin Manufacturing Company in Chicago, which made road maintenance equipment. Among those on the advisory committee were representatives from the American Manufacturers Export Association, Atlas Portland Cement Company, Barber Asphalt Company, First National Bank of Boston, General Motors, Mack Trucks, Inc., Standard Oil, and B. F. Goodrich Rubber Company: all large corporations with clear economic interests in the expansion of road networks.[39] US government–sanctioned encouragement of investment in transportation infrastructures filled the coffers of the companies that made the machines and materials for road building, automobiles, and the banks that invested in these construction projects. US support for Pan-American road networks also supplanted previous British investment in expensive rail networks in Central and South America. The emergence of cheaper road-building projects, supported by the US government and US corporations, is a concrete example of the way US economic imperialism supplanted the extant economic exploitation orchestrated mostly by the British. I talk further about that in the following chapter.

Businessmen and engineers from Latin American countries were invited by the commission to consult with the Bureau of Public Roads and to travel on an expenses-paid excursion through the United States, focusing on highway construction and automobile manufacture. Coolidge gave an address of welcome to the delegates when they arrived in June 1924: "We see today, more clearly than ever before, that the improved means of communication is not only one of the great forces making for cultural and economic advance, but it is also one of the basic factors in the development of Pan-American unity."[40] Likewise, Secretary of State Charles Evans Hughes told the delegates, "Highway construction enlarges the market for your products which in turn stimulates production and leads to general economic advance."[41] Liberal developmentalism was supplemented by a political argument that road systems—operating as what Coolidge described as communication networks—were "closely related" to what Hughes called "democratic development." The secretary of state accordingly proposed that "Improved communication means the elimination of sectionalism and contributes in no small degree to the formation and construction of an intelligent and controlling public opinion."[42] Economic arguments dovetailed with political ones in a way that presented road networks as the magical solution that both kick-started economic development and stabilized political regimes—and no doubt ideally precluded the socialist reorganization of property rights that caused the US government and US corporations such problems in, for example, Mexico and Colombia.

Visits were arranged for the delegates to tour automobile manufacturers in Detroit, including meetings with General Motors and with Henry Ford himself "for the serious study of the manufacture of the automotive vehicle designed to run over the highways they had seen in course of construction and maintenance."[43] Also included in the itinerary were visits to the rubber-manufacturing companies located principally in Cleveland and Akron, OH. US automotive and rubber corporations had begin to invest in Latin America, notably in Brazil, where Ford established an assembly plant in 1919 (and a disastrous rubber-processing plant in 1928) and where the Goodyear Tire and Rubber Company, United States Rubber Company, and General Tire and Rubber Company all opened businesses in the 1920s.[44] The agents for US firms associated with road building began to crisscross Brazil and other oil- and rubber-rich states in particular, offering their wares, often with a letter of introduction from the US ambassador.[45] Corporations were helped by the "cooperative" US government to source the materials necessary for car and road construction from the mineral and plant resources of Latin America and then to sell the technologies of cars and roads back to the countries from whence much of the material came. It was in this way a textbook example of an economic imperialism that relied on the cheap extraction of primary materials and their transformation into expensive technologies to be exported from the metropole to the periphery, using the very road networks created from (and for) the endeavor.

Toward the end of the tour by Latin American engineers and businessmen, the USDA organized a film screening. Among the films screened in the summer of 1924, to persuade these men to establish a network of roads connecting their countries to the United States with US materials and machines purchased to accomplish that, was a film of the tour itself. It was carefully planned. Fred Perkins of the USDA Motion Picture Laboratory was appointed a member of the Pan-American Highway Commission and accompanied the delegates on their tour to film it. The resulting film was no doubt partly a diplomatically flattering use of government film technology, but it functioned also as a way of circulating the agenda of the commission across the hemisphere. "The motion picture record of the trip and a handbook on the underlying reasons for highway development," the official account of the tour observed, "are two outgrowths of the tour now in preparation, which will unquestionably find a wide circulation here as well as abroad."[46] It functioned, then, as both a reminder of the "highways of friendship" built by the money invested by the US government and its industrial and financial collaborators and a mobile and visible way of circulating knowledge about the tour and the effort to orchestrate new road networks.

Also screened for the delegates was the Ford-financed *The Road to Happiness*, for which the titles were specially translated into Spanish. The film was to be "sent to their countries for use in educating the people to the value of better highways," a central part of the broader imperative to "arouse public interest" and provide "education in the effects of highway development" in Latin America.[47] It is not clear if the film was produced with this purpose in mind, though it is possible given that the Highway Education Board began planning for the tour in late 1923, the film was made in March 1924, and the tour began in June 1924. The films' narrative of economic advancement to rural and peripheral areas, and of the progress and modernity brought by road networks, could well have been seen by those delegates in allegorical and hemispheric terms. *The Road to Happiness* clearly connected to the goals of the tour to convince the Latin American delegates of the advantages to be gained from building roads and using automobiles. The film's composite production, whereby it was financed from the money accruing from new mass assembly practices and was made with equipment and personnel from the US government, makes abundantly clear the close ties between government and industry in orchestrating new transnational markets. Here, remarkably, was film as a "cooperative" endeavor between state and business operating as bridge-head to foreign economic policy and being integrated directly with the economic imperialism that was repositioning the United States as global hegemon. In this context, indeed, the movement of young, progressive farmers from the sphere of their old-fashioned, bad fathers toward that of the enlightened president of the United States was invested with geopolitical resonance. Oedipal narrative was replayed as geopolitics and economic imperialism.

In the wake of the decisions made at the 1923 Conference of American States, and after the 1924 commission, a Pan-American Congress of Highways was organized in October 1925 in Buenos Aires. US interests dominated the congress. The Highway Education Board, which as we have seen was an "associationalist" organization made up of members drawn from government, industry, and finance capital, formed the executive committee of the confederation and shaped the agenda. Accordingly, the central goal of the congress was to establish "a network of connecting highways for the American hemisphere," and its "primary purpose" was defined as "the dissemination of the fundamental principles of highway construction, finance, administration, and maintenance, and the advancement of the social and economic uses of the highway and the automotive vehicle."[48] Keeping with the film and extension practices of the Bureau of Public Roads, and those of the Highway Education Board, Congress proposed that these principles could be disseminated through "the distribution of a series of new films in the countries of South, Central, and North America."[49] Among these were Perkins's film of the 1924 tour, a film called *Wheels of Progress,* and a film called *Building Roads in North America,* which appears to have been one of the Bureau of Public Roads' "popular agricultural education" films demonstrating "progressive" methods of road construction "to arouse general interest and lead to community adoption of these methods."[50]

Also taken to the conference was a film entitled *Roads for All America,* which was subsequently used, the director of the United States Bureau of Foreign and Domestic Commerce observed, "to inform American firms of road conditions in Latin-America."[51]

Wheels of Progress was more expansive in its arguments. It surveyed the long chain of transportation that stretched from horse-drawn carriages to bicycles and from bicycles to cars and buses. Workers benefited the most from this progress, the film argues, for better roads, cars, and buses enabled them to relocate from the crowded tenements clustered around factories to new suburban developments. In a brief sequence toward the middle of the film, a worker leaves his detached house and walks to his car, before driving to work: property and the automobile mesh as the embodiment of modern progress. Motors, "good roads," and "personal transportation" enable "fresh air and attractive surroundings for the workers" in new factories built out of town. Workers mill about these factories, in a shot framed with leaves on branches blowing in the foreground in an image that replicated some of Ford's efforts in the 1920s to imagine and reconnect industry and the natural environment. By this logic cars and road networks enabled new forms of individual *freedom* for the workers, who labored on the mass assembly lines first innovated for those same cars and then expanded to be integral to new forms of corporate and consumer capital.

Directly following on from the nameless worker who leaves his house to drive to work, another sequence connects cars and property but now shifts to the symbol of national domesticity, the White House, where Coolidge and his wife get into an open-top car and drive away. Coolidge was becoming quite the educational film star. The logic of the film connects in these ways with Secretary of State Hughes's welcome to the 1924 Congress, in which he proposed that cars and roads not only lead "to general economic advance" but also eliminate "sectionalism" and stimulate "democratic development." Viewers are told that worker disaffection and calls for a socialist rearticulation of political economy, say, are offset by the progress and happiness provided by cars, roads, and property—good "neighborly" advice that, from a US government working in conjunction with industry and finance capital to export "progress." The film ends with a curiously modernist, low-angle shot of car wheels running across paved roads, a now disembodied space showing only the abstract movement of machines. Its image of the wheels of progress powered by state, capital, and industry makes the film an example of a government-mandated modernism—literally in the service of the construction of the material means to compress space and time to enable the expansion of markets.

Numerous films produced by the Bureau of Public Roads, and interested corporations like Ford, were thus put into circulation principally by the US state, starting in the early 1920s, to help expand material networks of circulation across the continent. Here was cinema being used to elaborate infrastructural pathways of circulation for American capital and machines. Was it successful? The question is not easy to answer. The success of the road-building efforts was only ever partial, hampered always by the parlous economic situation in many states in Latin America and by imperatives for those states to build domestic roads.[52] Roads would be overtaken in the later 1920s by the emergence of air networks and the creation of the airline—with support from the US Air Force and capital from J. P. Morgan— that would come to be called, fittingly, Pan American Airlines.[53] But it is quite clear, as economic historians emphasize, that US economic hegemony over Latin America increased during the 1920s, and this supplanted British interests.[54] Road networks replaced British-financed and built rail networks. Even further, this economic imperialism, formed through a complex "cooperative" effort among state, corporations, finance capital, and associated lobbying groups, was a crucial precondition for US global economic hegemony and a liberalized world order from circa midcentury onward. The films and institutions I have explored thus far were made to facilitate US economic expansion.

"TRADE FOLLOWS THE MOTION PICTURES"

By the early 1920s, then, senior government officials quite clearly began to consider film as an important supplement to US economic advancement and to act on those beliefs. Hollywood in particular came to be seen by some influential state officials as a useful adjunct to US economic interests. Creel's experiments at the Committee on Public Information helped with this, and together with the destruction in other countries that had been wrought by imperial war they had positioned Hollywood as a globally powerful cultural industry.

The US state began thereafter to innovate practices and institutions of cultural imperialism. These endeavors can be linked also to the broader governmental efforts of the US state to control communication and transportation infrastructures, including, as we have seen, the development and spread of radio, beginning during World War I, and such things as the establishment of hemispheric and transpacific cable networks.[55] Coolidge's conception of the importance of "improved means of communication" for "cultural and economic advance" was suitably capacious.[56] The movement of immaterial images of abundance, of what the Ford Educational Department would call "the American standard of living," was joined to the control of the material means of transport and communication to help establish American global economic hegemony.[57]

In 1922, the Department of Commerce began to suggest that "trade follows the motion pictures," and its spokesmen thereafter frequently repeated the claim that for every foot of film exported, a dollar was earned for the United States in sales of other goods.[58] (The same department also played a crucial role in the formation of the Pan-American Highway Commission.) After this, the Department of

Commerce began reporting on conditions affecting movies abroad in its *Daily Consular and Trade Reports*. It is worth underscoring that both the State and Commerce departments conceived of the film industry in broad terms, not simply as film production but also in terms of the material means of production and exhibition that were dominated by US businesses. Kodak, for example, manufactured 75 percent of the film in the world; RCA and Western Electric later monopolized the production of sound equipment for film production and exhibition; and US studios, backed by US finance capital, owned many of the most profitable cinemas in the world, which were outfitted with US equipment.[59]

In the 1920s the Department of Commerce emerged as the central conduit through which the US state promoted global trade. Herbert Hoover, then head of the department, established a Bureau of Foreign and Domestic Commerce within the department to supervise overseas trade promotion in particular. The bureau expanded dramatically during Hoover's tenure by boosting the number of foreign offices from twenty-three in 1921 to fifty-eight in 1927 and quintupling the staff of the bureau.[60] (Thus was born the "commercial attaché.") Testifying before a US Senate committee on appropriations in 1925, Hoover claimed that the global success of the American film industry bore "very materially on the expansion of the sale of other goods throughout Europe and other countries."[61] In the aftermath of Hoover's enthusiastic liberal championing of global trade promotion, the head of the mainstream film industry's public relations arm, the politically well-connected Will Hays, began pressing the Department of Commerce to establish a special Motion Picture Section within the Bureau of Foreign and Domestic Commerce. Hays imagined this would function as an information service, helping counter adverse censorship and tariff legislation and smoothing the movement of American films across the globe. In 1926, Congress responded to Hays's request, appropriating twenty-six thousand dollars for the purpose of creating a Motion Picture Section within the Bureau of Foreign and Domestic Commerce.[62] In 1929, the section was "made a division in its own right," Ulf Jonas Bjork has observed, "Placing films on the same level as major export commodities such as machinery, minerals, automobiles, textiles, chemicals, and electrical products."[63] State and film industry officials worked collaboratively to maintain "free" and "open" markets, a further concrete example of the way the associational state worked to promote global trade.

"The American Motion Picture Industry stood on a mountaintop," Hays wrote in his memoirs, "from which the beacon of its silver screen was sending rays of light and color and joy into every corner of the earth."[64] Commerce more than joy motivated the US state to begin supporting the commercial film industry, on the assumption that the visual representation of goods and consumer durables would support American business by stimulating interest in their products. Hollywood's silver screen became a global advertisement for the American standard of living. The

Motion Picture Section of the Bureau of Foreign and Domestic Commerce supplied information about foreign censorship regulations, tariffs, and duties, as well as trademark, copyright, and taxation—the matters of international political economy and the economic substrate of global commerce. It also published lists of producers, distributors, and exhibitors in foreign markets and kept track of theater capacity and construction.[65] In a letter to the National Board of Review in New York, the chief of the Motion Picture Section explained that the bureau produced pamphlets to help different parts of the film industry, including, for example, the "Market for Industrial and Educational Motion Pictures Abroad," and the "Chinese market for motion pictures."[66] (This was probably not the last time the Chinese market was considered by what is now called the United States Commercial Service.)

Hollywood was the chief beneficiary of these developments, but industrial and educational films were also included in the bureau's remit, as North made clear in his letter. Director of the bureau, Julius Klein, suggested that US industrial films helped spread the news of American industrial advancement across the world. *The Story of Steel*, for example, produced by the Morgan-financed US Steel and distributed widely by the Bureau of Mines, was one of the industrial films singled out for praise. Klein reported that the film was "effectively distributed throughout the world, so much so that a certain brand of pipe has become almost a by-word in Japan."[67] In a 1923 editorial in the bureau's official publication, *Commerce Reports*, Klein also imagined an American film being shown in Argentina, in which the husband admired the clothes worn by the male stars while his fictional wife was "in rapt contemplation of the leading woman's gowns." Klein concluded, cheerfully, "Two prosperous residents of Buenos Aires now purchase their clothes in New York rather than Paris."[68] In this way industrial and commercial film became a global shop window for the innovations of US technology and the products of US consumer industries.

Latin America was again imagined as an important market for those industries. But the Hollywood film studios' displays of gowns and goods fared less well in those markets, it seems. The director of the Moving Picture Section of the Bureau ruefully observed that as a "result of low purchasing power" the "rentals in Latin-America are considerably lower than in many parts of Europe." China too, he remarked, might become a "much larger motion picture market if the scale of living of its tremendous population were higher, if transportation conditions were better, and if political conditions were more stable."[69] Curses that the iniquities of global capitalism and the hegemony of US economic interests meant that foreigners were not able to pay as much to watch films celebrating American consumerism.

In the memorandums, internal reports, diplomatic correspondence, and scattered public statements of government officials, we can discern the articulation of a theory of cinema as a critical infrastructural mechanism enabling the expansion of industrial commodity culture. The US state began to develop theories *and* practices that proposed that film elicited desire, seduced affect, and dematerialized the commodity form. The state had infrastructural power to act on its theories to create institutions, using and retooling extant diplomatic and commercial ones to facilitate the movement of industrial films advertising American modernity, the machines and materials for making and projecting films, and commercial fiction films in order to support industrial exports, the growing film industry, and, at its broadest, the global hegemony of American consumerism. Film as a dematerialized, easily transportable commodity worked as what the chief of the Bureau of Foreign and Domestic Commerce called a "silent salesman," and it was accordingly supported by a state "extending" its reach across the globe in the 1920s.[70]

But these practices would not go unchallenged. The British state still had pretensions to be a globally dominant power, even if after the war some of the realities of that had begun to fade. The British government began to propose regulations to halt the movement of US films across its sprawling empire and to produce films that would, it was hoped, help establish an imperial economy walled off from the influence of emerging US economic dominance. It is to that part of the story of cinema's place in the global political economy in the interwar years that I now turn.

8

Highways of Empire

In the mid-1920s, the British state and political elite began to make use of film to support a political economy increasingly predicated on colonial territory, imperial trade, and the utility of a newly configured Commonwealth bloc of predominantly white settler Dominions. It did so in part in collaboration with British industry and finance capital and with the goal of sustaining an economic and geopolitical primacy that had began to fade in the early years of the twentieth century in the face of the emerging industrial, economic, and—therefore—political power of the United States in particular. New institutions of film production housed within political parties and state offices created a series of films visualizing the import of empire trade, and in the process innovated the film form and practice that came later to be called "documentary." While doing so, the state worked to establish new global networks of distribution; novel practices of exhibition in various nontheatrical spaces like mobile cinema vans, schools, and factories; and legislation to regulate the transnational movement and purported effects of non-"empire" films—principally Hollywood—on metropolitan and colonial subjects and on economic and political order. Britain's state-directed formation of cinema sought to make visible and material a political economy of early twentieth-century imperialism that was driven by what David Harvey has described as a "dialectical relation between territorial and capitalist logics of power."[1] Cinema was utilized, that is, to respond to and reorientate economic and political problems in the metropolitan center and, incipiently, the so-called colonial periphery; to support the expansionary global goals of large industry and finance capital and, relatedly, the infrastructures of circulation central to capitalist modernity; and to build and strengthen ties, in particular among the Commonwealth bloc, in order to respond to global shifts in trade and power and to shore up a hegemony rendered increasingly shaky by the transformations of the second-stage industrial revolution, global conflict, and the growing economic and political strength of the white settler colony of the United States. New forms of state-directed, nontheatrical cinema, alongside new practices of cultural policy and regulation, emerged, then, within the wider logics of capital accumulation, which subtended the liberal political economy of capitalist imperialism in the interwar period in particular.

The broad outline of that political economy is this: the British state's response to the growing economic power of other industrialized nations, to the cost of war, and to the devastating economic depressions that opened and closed the 1920s was to develop a partial shift away from the classical free trade liberalism, which had been the guiding principle of economic strategies since the mid-nineteenth century, toward a policy of protectionism and "imperial preference." In this new economic configuration, tariffs were placed on goods imported from outside the territories of the empire, and new institutions were formed to market empire produce in Britain to reduce a reliance on foreign imports, as well as to stimulate colonial economies and enable them to purchase British-manufactured goods. In the 1920s the British government also constructed new economic and political structures for the elaboration of a Commonwealth bloc. The political and capitalist logics underlying this radical shift in macroeconomic policy, away from classical liberalism toward a more protectionist variant, were varied. It was hoped that these strategies would support a faltering British industry, which was slow to innovate in the technologies of the second-stage industrial revolution—notably in relation to electrical, chemical, and mass-assembly industries—by delineating a protected empire market for the exchange of raw materials and manufactured goods, while simultaneously reinforcing the underdevelopment of peripheral economies. The resulting stronger exports would thus ideally lower the levels of unemployment in the metropole and counteract the political radicalism that accompanied worker disaffection with new Fordist manufacturing practices and resulted in proposals for socialist alternatives to a liberal, capitalist political economy. Likewise, the state's strategies would help protect the finance capital that had been central to Britain's geopolitical primacy, which had long been dependent upon the empire. Finally, the economic and political ties with the industrializing settler Dominions—the Commonwealth—would ideally fence off an economic bloc that was imagined as a way of sustaining British geopolitical hegemony in the face of the broader transformations in the world system that were mandated by the second-stage industrial revolution and the rise to prominence of the United States in particular.

The emergence of film production, distribution, and exhibition within the confines of, first, the dominant Conservative Party and, second, the machinery of state was a consequence of these precise economic and (geo)political contexts. Indeed, the investment in culture and development of cultural policy are two aspects of the new interventionist liberal state in the interwar period, marking the ways in which culture and, in particular, its mass variant were reconfigured as aspects of governance. The broad contours of this film history can be quickly delineated to guide our exploration: the Conservative Party established a film unit in 1925 to exhibit and produce films extolling principally its policies of protectionism to working-class British audiences; the Conservative government established a film unit within the newly created Empire Marketing Board (EMB) in 1926 to support the board's wider goal of establishing networks of economic ties within the imperial and Commonwealth bloc; and, after lobbying in particular from the Federation of British Industries, the Conservative government enacted a form of tariff legislation for the film industry in 1927, which sought to counteract the perceived economic and political effects of the global movement and success of Hollywood. In the midst of these developments, a series of films visualizing economic relations, and the global flow of raw materials and manufactured goods, were produced and widely circulated through networks of global distribution. "Documentary" cinema emerged and was established in the space shared by state and corporate entities.

I explore here, then, the history of the complex enmeshing of cinema and liberal political rationality and liberal imperial economics in the interwar years within the context of the British state's efforts to sustain an imperial economy and to use this to contest the growing economic and political power of the United States. It is a history that remains largely unwritten, one that has been reduced in the extant literature mainly to accounts of the formation of documentary cinema in the confines of the Empire Marketing Board and even then largely without substantive engagement with the centrality of the economics of imperialism.[2] It is a central tenet of this book that we urgently need to rethink the history of the state use of cinema as mass media in this period in the context of the broader political and economic goals of crucial state and economic actors. Part of this requires situating documentary cinema within the sponsored and nontheatrical cinematic culture that flourished in the 1910s and 1920s as one component of the wider governmental use of media for the purposes of shaping the attitudes and conduct of populations and facilitating new economic practices—in this case, new imperial economic practices. Such an examination will not only deepen our knowledge of cinema and media history but also our understanding of the enmeshing of political, economic, and cultural apparatuses of hegemony and—specifically—the way cinema as a form of mass media was utilized by state and economic elites to articulate perspectives that supported imperialist or "globalizing" practices.

"IMPERIALISM OF FREE TRADE"

In early 1920s Britain, after the destruction of war, the dominant Conservative Party began to propose a newly interventionist protectionist regime of tariffs on imported materials, alongside a system of "imperial preference" that would lower or withdraw those protectionist measures for countries within the empire.[3] Its policies marked a shift from what has been called the "imperialism of free trade,"— which had from the mid-nineteenth century positioned Britain at the hub of global circuits of commercial and financial capital, as the first large transnational economy of the industrial age—toward a revised political economy that would necessitate Britain's partial withdrawal from the global economy and the establishment of an imperial economic bloc, with Britain at its political and financial center.[4] Conservative policy was designed specifically to support finance capital and large-scale industry, as they both had become increasingly dependent upon the empire, starting in the latter parts of the nineteenth century, when other countries, in particular Germany and the United States, began to rapidly industrialize. The policies were electorally unpopular, largely because of their potential impact on the price of everyday goods; the fading Liberal Party and the emergent Labour Party both opposed the policies.[5] In the absence of a clear mandate, the Conservative government used a series of imperial economic conferences throughout the 1920s to foster intraimperial economic connections (where film was a hotly debated topic); set in process the formal establishment of a Commonwealth bloc; and supported the creation of a number of other policy and cultural initiatives, to foster the establishment of this newly configured emphasis on global political economy. Later, in the aftermath of the cataclysmic global collapse of 1929, the Conservative-dominated national government withdrew Britain from the gold standard, the very symbol of liberal internationalism; formalized the statutory identity of the Commonwealth in 1931; passed the Import Duties Act of 1932, which introduced a general tariff of 10 percent; and, also in 1932, introduced a system of imperial preference that supported quotas and other bilateral arrangements at an important imperial economic conference held in Ottawa in the strategically significant nation of Canada.[6] Elsewhere the developments of the early 1930s prompted innovations in governmental welfare to ameliorate the worst excesses of economic collapse, which in other countries proved to be a fertile breeding ground for the atrocities of fascism.[7]

The governmental logics underlying this critical shift of emphasis in economic policy and in the elaboration of an imperial political economy were varied and expansive. It was closely aligned with the support of finance capital, a crucial part of the Conservative Party's support base in London and the southeast of England.[8] Tariffs were designed to protect an ailing British industrial sector from the growing strength of other industrialized nations, particularly with respect to the chemical and electrical products generated from the second stage of the period of capitalist industrialization.[9] It would consequently foster the growth of large-scale and export-dependent monopoly capitalism.[10] The support of a faltering economy, and correlative formation of the conditions subtending corporate capitalism, was critical to the governing agenda of the Conservative Party, which was to advance propertied interests.[11] It would also, it was hoped, go some way toward resolving the vexatious and seemingly related problems of unemployment and working-class radicalism, put firmly on the political agenda because the Representation of the People Act of 1918 had extended the franchise to most working-class adult males.[12] The signs of that radicalism were increasingly visible in the interwar years, in the shadow of the Russian Revolution: trade union membership increased in the early 1920s,[13] the Labour Party became a viable political alternative, and the militancy of workers produced a series of industrial disputes (including most notably a general strike in 1926 that threatened to disrupt the infrastructure upon which the country depended).[14] By introducing tariffs, the government hoped to tackle unemployment and thus, in the words of one of the policies' chief architects, Secretary of State for the Colonies Leopold Amery, detach "the working people in this country from the anti-imperialist leaders of Socialism."[15] Tariff reform (and, later, empire settlement) sought to renovate both British global primacy and the liberal capitalism that had been profoundly damaged by the war and related shifts in the world system.[16]

The correlative system of imperial preferences buttressed the metropolitan economy by sustaining the lucrative flow of raw materials for industry and energy from the "periphery" and their transformation into the more expensive manufactured goods created, sold, and exported from the "core." Quite clearly, the "development of underdevelopment" of colonial economies, and their construction as "complementary" to that of the advanced industrial core, was central to imperial political economy.[17] Its principles guided the creation of the system of "development" economics, and imperial preferences, along with the resulting imperial- and Commonwealth economic and political bloc. The former, as evidenced for example in the 1929 Colonial Development Act, helped finance economic and physical infrastructures in colonial spaces that specifically facilitated the expansion and circulation of British products and finance capital.[18] (Many film cameras turned their machinic gaze on these developments, as a way of offering visual evidence of the modernity produced by British imperialism.) The latter strategy subtended the "Balfour Declaration," which was issued after the 1926 Imperial Conference and which declared Dominions "autonomous communities," and the Statute of Westminster, which legally enshrined this conception of the Commonwealth in 1931.[19]

Economic ties, developed with, in particular, the semi-industrialized and predominantly white settler Dominions of the Commonwealth across the 1920s and at the Ottawa conference, were regarded as central to the establishment of an imperial economic and territorial bloc.[20] It was thought these ties would straightforwardly bring benefits to the core economy; would help cathect the new working-class electorate to the Conservative Party and a newly emergent consumer economy; would conciliate the rising nationalist and anti-imperialist sentiments in colonized countries;[21] and would simultaneously help resist the growing economic and political dominance of the dollar and the United States, particularly as large amounts of private bank loans were being directed by the US State Department to help rebuild Germany and Europe.[22] Canada would become particularly important for Britain's attempted containment of the world's next great hegemon (and was consequently included in the imperial preference system, despite opting out of the sterling area).[23] In short, the British state, frequently with the prompting of large industry and finance capital, innovated political, economic, and cultural responses to the transformations in the capitalist world system that was positioning the United States as the world's dominant economic and political power. What follows traces the imprint of these agendas—of liberal, imperial political economy—on celluloid and cinematic and media institutions and policy.

"THE CINEMATOGRAPH IN EDUCATION"

Economic crisis, and military conflict and colonialism more broadly, mark limit points of liberalism as theory and practice, generating new agendas of intervention that also penetrate the cultural sphere. (The Committee on Public Information is one example of that process.) Efforts to manage opinion became integral to the newly interventionist practices of the liberal state around the turn of the century. The work of communication and culture assumed new priorities for political parties, the state, and corporate organizations interested in sustaining a liberal imperial economic order.

In the immediate postwar moment in Britain, a number of cultural forms and institutions were innovated to utilize media to sustain state policy and in particular to foster intraimperial connections. The Foreign Office, for example, took over some aspects of the supervision of publicity and propaganda in 1918 from what was called the Ministry of Information during the war.[24] Foreign Office officials began to closely monitor nationalist and radical movements in the empire. In 1924 the government met half the costs of a large imperial exhibition held in London that was designed "to foster inter-imperial trade and open fresh world markets for Dominion and home products."[25] The British Broadcasting Company began broadcasting in 1922, including, significantly, King George V's opening address at the imperial exhibition of 1924; was constituted as a public utility in 1927 (when it became the British Broadcasting Corporation, or the BBC); and began an "Empire Service" in 1932, to broadcast through the empire and so cultivate ideas of "imagined" imperial unity.[26] Note again how liberal polities began to use technology to materialize forms of indirect rule, here, specifically, to foster a media connectivity that paralleled an economic one. In 1930, the British Empire Games began, not coincidentally in Canada, generating and promoting a Commonwealth union then in the process of formation. And the British Council, an international cultural relations organization, was established in 1934 as the institutional embodiment of what Nicholas Pronay has called the "cultural propaganda approach."[27] Together, the efforts to foster new cultural forms and build new media systems sought to generate an economic and political unity, all the while sustaining an imperial order and forestalling subaltern resistance.

Cinema became particularly important to the political economy of inter-war capitalist imperialism, largely because it was widely seen as the most popular and powerful form of mass media—a specifically visual media—that reached the newly politically important working-class audience in Britain. The idea that film was a pedagogic form that could be utilized for the broader governmental project of fostering and stabilizing imperial economic and political union gathered pace in the early 1920s. In 1923, at an Imperial Education Conference in London, for example, a day was devoted to discussing "The Cinematograph in Education," accompanied by a screening of appropriate films and an exhibition of projectors suitable for educational uses.[28] The conference set up a committee to study the question of the pedagogical value of film further and published the *Report on the Use and Value of the Cinematograph in Education,* which argued for the integration of film into school education.[29] Later in 1923, another imperial conference focusing on the development of empire trade discussed the "utilization of the cinematograph films as an instrument for disseminating knowledge both here and overseas," and also as a supplement to aid British emigration to "new lands."[30] The conference issued a report that generated interest in the press and suggested that film was uniquely positioned to show "the benefit of educating the young and of strengthening the ties of sentiment, which mainly rest upon our knowledge of each other."[31]

In early 1924, the Treasury appointed a "cinematograph advisor" whose "duty it is to assist Government Departments generally in questions relating to cinematography and to supervise the preservation and use of films in the possession of the government."[32] In that same year, a report initiated by the Board of Education asserted that film was a powerful form for shaping the attitudes of its audiences and concluded that the "the time has fully come when the British and Dominion Governments should combine to produce a library of Imperial films to circulate around the Empire."[33] In the 1924–25 Imperial Exhibition in London some of these ideas about the usefulness of film in educating audiences about the empire, and fostering intraimperial unity, were put into play. *Highways of Empire* and *Resources of Empire,* for example, both produced by the Department of Overseas Trade and both examining the infrastructure and resources of the empire, were shown at His Majesty's Government Pavilion. By the end of the exposition, a touring program of films produced through collaboration among the British Colonial office, colonial governments, and corporate sponsors was released theatrically. *Tin Mining in Nigeria* (1925), *Zanzibar and the Clove Industry* (1925), *Black Cotton* (1927), *Oil Palm of Nigeria* (1928), *Gold Mining in the Gold Coast* (1928), and others principally "defined the colonies by products and industries," Tom Rice has argued, "emphasising a post-war imperial identity centred around trade and economics."[34]

But it was the powerful Conservative Party itself that at this point pursued most fully this conception of the economic and political usefulness of film, wrapping it together specifically with the party's efforts to communicate with the new, nearly mass electorate and to establish a revised imperial political economy. The party established a film department within its central office in 1925, the first political party in Britain to do so. It stands as an important, if largely unknown, moment in the political use of film and media.[35] The department initially distributed and showed films in Britain that were "mainly pictures of British industries and of the Empire," likely including a number of those sponsored and produced for the Imperial Exhibition by the Colonial Office, Dominion governments, and business organizations like the important Federation of British Industries.[36] The filmed "views of Britain's imperial glory" were shown in mobile cinema vans, at political meetings, and in schools.[37] In 1926 the party started producing its own films. In 1930 its Department of Film was replaced by the ostensibly independent, but party-financed, Conservative and Unionist Film Association (CFA). These films were made also with advice and help from the film producers Alexander Korda and Michael Balcon, whose own series of films on the adventures of empire in the 1930s, which included *Sanders of the River* (Korda, 1935), *Rhodes of Africa* (Balcon, 1936), *King Solomon's Mines* (Balcon, 1937) and *The Four Feathers* (Korda, 1939), was a significant articulation of the logics of colonial rule.[38]

The party's establishment of a film unit was driven by the belief that film had been useful to the British war effort, and thus also supported what the *Times* called films "utility for political work" with respect to the new working-class electorate.[39] J. C. C. Davidson, party chairman, said in 1926, "The first job on which I set my mind was to apply the lessons of the Great War to the organization of political warfare."[40] Many associated with the film unit had indeed worked on war propaganda.[41] In turn, the party's chief publicity officer, Joseph Ball, later noted that the "enormous increase in the popularity of cinemas particularly among the working classes, pointed the way . . . to the cinema film as a method of placing our propaganda before the electorate."[42] It was the pressing need to address the new working-class electorate, and to articulate in particular the political economy of imperialism as distinct from that of socialism, that pushed the party to its considerable material and ideological investment in cinema. Consequently, the films made by the party frequently offered images and accounts of the productivity of capital investment and selective state interventions, showing in particular how this facilitated the development of colonial economies for the advantage of the British worker and economy.

West Africa Calling, for example, was made in 1927 by the Conservative Party in Britain to show how "workers at home benefit by the policy of developing the

Empire."[43] The economic development led by Britain, the film proposes, made West Africa productive in various ways, and this in turn generated economic benefits in Britain. "Years ago," the opening intertitles claim, "West Africa was a country of forest . . . swamps . . . and desert," where "national conditions made communications almost impossible." The introduction of "British enterprise has changed all this," creating a "thriving trade" that both improves conditions for the "native population"—the film shows schools and hospitals—and generates employment for British workers and profit for British industry and capital. Lumber is "turned to account with the help of British machinery," and huge mechanical diggers aid the "British engineers . . . developing the tin mines." The shift from unproductive natural spaces (forest, swamp, desert) to exemplary spaces of liberal civility (hospital, school) is facilitated by capital, engineering, machinery, and state intervention.

West Africa Calling's account of this imperial political economy came thereafter to focus on the creation of new infrastructures that facilitated mobility and the circulation of goods and capital. It is in these images, and in the connections made between them through editing, that the film effected a visual corollary to liberal imperial political economy. Cameras wielded on behalf of the ruling British political elite traversed the new harbor at Takoradi in Ghana, as boats moved past the huge cranes that load them with raw materials bound for England. Railroads were built, using "British steel sleepers and lines . . . and rolling stock." It is "British cement," the film asserts, that is used in bridge building, and the newly constructed "roads create a demand for British motor cars to run along them." One brief scene shows British cars moving across the frame, with the margins at the front and the side of the frame occupied by an African woman carrying a basket on her head and by a slow moving cart. The familiar dichotomy between technological modernity and tradition, so central to imperial rhetoric and iconography, is meshed here with an emphasis on the way the British state, finance capital, and technology transform the space of West Africa to facilitate the circulation of, as the film puts it, "food stuffs and raw materials" to Britain and "increased employment in British workshops" to sustain imperial development. The sequence that comes after the one of cars traveling across African roads shows cars being constructed in British factories, by workers using modern technology (and the use of materials produced in colonial spaces, like the Malayan rubber central to tire production). Earlier the sequence showing African workers laying railway sleepers switches to three shots of those sleepers being produced in a British factory. Here the emphasis on the infrastructure of roads, bridges, and waterways as the material form that allows exchange over space is carried through and emphasized toward the end of the film in the editing of shots that switch between colonial spaces and the factories that the film proposes are mutually constituted and sustained. It is in these ways that the images of material connections, emphasized through the connective tissues of editing, are central to the visualization of a political economy that positioned empire development and markets as integral to the sustenance of the wealth of the nation.

The fascinated gaze of the camera machine at the various industrial machines that litter the film offer exemplary instances of what Brian Larkin has called "the colonial sublime," which he defines as the "effort to use technology as part of political rule."[44] *West Africa Calling* lingers over machines in motion. The film makes a distinction, though, between the way workers interact with machines. In the sequences in colonial Africa, the machines—like cranes—dwarf workers, who are always supervised in their relatively menial work of fetching and carrying by British officials, whereas in the short sequences in British factories the workers are unsupervised and demonstrate a mastery of complex technology. The gulf of technological superiority legitimizes colonial rule; racialized labor supports the British working class. If this representation straightforwardly belies the history of how new technologies of mass production and Fordist work practices deskilled working-class populations, it does so in the goal of a political logic that seeks to cathect the working class to technological modernity and simultaneously to associate the power of machinery with that of capital and state. *West Africa Calling,* like the liberal political economy of the Conservative Party, imagines that the machinery of state powers industrial machinery—witnessed and facilitated here by the actual and figurative machinery of film.

West Africa Calling's narrative of progress and modernity stretching from swamps to railways was an early example of a set of films, financed and produced mostly by the Conservative Party, that presented lessons in political economy and idealized the creation of infrastructures for the mobility of capital and goods. Many of these were produced in the early 1930s, in the context of the global economic depression and as an explanation for the shifting contours of economic policy, which saw the introduction of tariffs and imperial preference by the Conservative-dominated National Government in 1931. In the animated *The Right Spirit* (1931), for example, John Bull's damaged car can only be fixed at Conservative leader Stanley Baldwin's "Prosperity Garage," when it is filled from pumps labeled "Safeguarding" (a term for the introduction of protectionist tariffs), "Empire Unity," and "Reduced Taxes" (fig. 14). The facilitation of the movement of the car by the Conservative garage is metonymic for the regeneration of the mobility central to economic well being. *The Price of Free Trade* (1932) shows the advantages of the British production, rather than importation, of steel. When steel is imported, there is a line drawn simply between port and factory, yet when it is produced at home, we see a multiplying series of lines drawn that connect quarries, mines, steel works, and factories. The emerging web of lines portrays the connections between productive sites and spaces, of the circulation of materials that facilitates employment and profit. *Two Lancashire Cotton Workers Discuss Safeguarding* (1935) is a short, scripted conversation between an older and younger

FIGURE 14. Still from *The Right Spirit* (Conservative and Unionist Central Office, 1931).

worker taking their lunch break. "We shall have to look more to the empire," the older worker tells the younger one, "and them more to us." The tutelary role of the experienced worker explaining the complexities to the younger one, standing in for those newly admitted to the electorate, was a common characteristic of Conservative propaganda and stood here as metonymic for the role of Conservative film more generally.[45]

Empire Trade (1934) focused specifically on the Dominions (as well as India), which had gathered in Ottawa, at a time when those (semi-)industrialized economies were particularly important to the proposed creation of an autarchic imperial bloc. Voiceover commentary explains how colonies or Dominions purchase manufactured goods from Britain and thus maintain employment in Britain. "By purchasing our goods," the Malay states "create regular employment in this country"; Australia keeps "77,000 British workers regularly employed through buying British goods," and Canada "gives employment to 67,000 Britons."[46] *Empire Trade*'s remarkable opening cuts from the launch of a ship to several shots of a fast-moving train—recalling the opening of the modernist *Berlin—Symphony of a Great City* (1927)—that stand as visual markers for the speed of the circulation of goods and capital. After this, the film's account of the economic interconnection between the core and periphery is supplemented by a message about the territorial import of the empire. Britain's naval base in Singapore, we are told, "keeps watch over the Malay states," while Aden (in present-day, war-ravaged Yemen) is "guarding the Suez canal, our trade route to the East." Naval bases were integral to British efforts to rule seaway traffic and the Suez Canal was an indispensable infrastructure for the movement of materials (and particularly oil) between Europe and Eastern Asia.

Conservative Party elites began then to use film as part of their remit to communicate with a new nearly mass electorate and to draw working-class populations in particular into an idea of imperial unity and utility. Cinema operated for a time as part of a wider networked infrastructure, which worked to facilitate the movement of the materials and goods that traveled along the same pathways. Connections can be drawn here to the related use of media by the US Department of Agriculture and the Ford Motor Company. Little surprise, then, that the Conservative Party innovated a "special machinery" of distribution and exhibition to show its films—a fleet of mobile cinema vans that toured Britain (fig. 15).[47] Bypassing extant cinemas, the party invested in the design and construction of a number of mobile cinema vans, which had projectors that back-projected film onto a hooded screen at the back of the van, thus enabling daylight projection. The elaboration of new machinery to foster the actual mobility of the virtual mobility of film was testament to the party's investment in the import of film as critical to its elaboration of economic policies in the interregnum before the establishment of those policies as legislation. And this was emphasized when the party fitted the cinema vans in 1927 with an early and expensive sound system, just at the time the well-capitalized Hollywood studios were also investing in sound technology.[48] That it was able to invest considerably in the capital-intensive business of film production and exhibition was a consequence of the party's financial backing by the city and big business. In other words, the capital visible on screen, in the filmed accounts of the import of capitalist and imperialist economy, circulated through expensive machines of distribution and exhibition made possible by the support of capital and industry similarly invested in the imperial economy.

Vans were first used in August 1925, and were thereafter sent out in particular to rural areas and through small towns that had limited access to the cinema. Other vans carried film projection equipment that could be set up in villages and town halls and other public spaces. The films were most frequently shown before a political meeting, which would expound on the themes of the films.[49] At times, the vans also carried with them "a number of showcases containing samples of Empire products in order that Empire food demonstrations may be combined with the film programme."[50] Vans functioned in this way as mobile display and exhibition spaces, combining visual and material culture to encourage intraimperial trade. And they did so as mobile spaces that extended the reach of government, making

FIGURE 15. Conservative Party mobile cinema van, 1927 (Courtesy Modern Records Centre, University of Warwick, UK).

government mobile and capable of circulating among the new electorate. The conception of film as a way to enlarge the public sphere was elaborated in part in recognition of the way cinema had been constructed as an apolitical space of entertainment.[51] Later, the use of mobile cinemas was imported to the empire, with the intention frequently of using film to "educate" colonial populations, to create modern colonial subjects, and to bind populations into an imperial collectivity.[52]

But the Conservative Party and the British state came to the realization that movies helped mobilize capital rather late in the day, and it turned out that audiences curiously seemed to prefer elaborate and expensive fictions of abundance more than they did accounts of imperial economic conferences. The corporate managers at Hollywood studios knew this, and so did their expensive public relations and political lobbying organization (the "Hays Office") and the state officials in the Department of Commerce. The Department of Commerce had begun to suggest that "trade follows films" as early as 1922, and as we have seen its chief Hoover had begun to make similar arguments from 1925 and had responded to the lobbying efforts of the politically well-connected Hays by establishing a special

Motion Picture Service within the Bureau of Foreign and Domestic Commerce in 1926 to assist the global circulation of images of America and its goods. Indeed, the European representative of the mainstream US film industry's trade association observed, when surveying the concerns in Britain and Europe about American media, that motion pictures "are demonstrably the greatest single factor in the Americanization of the world and . . . fairly may be called the most important and significant of America's exported products."[53] The endeavors of state officials and political and trade lobbyists to globalize cinema helped make the century American—or, at least, that's what prominent British elites and politicians began to think. The perceived economic and ideological dangers US films posed to the model of British liberal imperialism pushed the British state into action. New structures of film policy and regulation were established to protect the imperial economy, mirroring the broader protectionist logic that began to become state policy in the 1920s, as Britain withdrew from the precepts of classical liberalism to try to ward off the visible transformations in the capitalist world system. It is toward an account of this regulation and censorship as a practice of political economy and imperial governance that I now turn.

"THE AMERICANIZATION OF OUR EMPIRE"

The facilitation *and* regulation of the movement of film, as a form of both material and cultural capital, became an issue for government debate and legislation starting in 1925, the same year the Conservative Party began its own film unit and in the midst also of the ongoing debates about protectionism that followed the party's election victory in 1924. Calls to regulate the movement of American films into Britain and across its empire were twinned with efforts to foster a better capitalized British film industry and the movement of those films across the commonwealth and empire, principally as markers for and generators of the intraimperial movement of capital and manufactured goods. In a series of debates and policy decisions on cinema and its mobility in the mid-1920s, the British state thus tried to innovate a political space to foster the economic usefulness of cinema. The formulation of film policy became one aspect of the broader struggle to foster the British model of territorial imperialism in the face of the rise of the deterritorialized American variant of economic imperialism.

Not all of this was state led. It was an influential business organization, the Federation of British Industries (FBI) that did most to initiate the debate and to push for state legislation. In a memo written in 1925 to Philip Cunfliffe-Lister, president of the Board of Trade in the Conservative government, the organization called for protection for the British film industry and the increase of capital for British film production through the creation of a new British film studio and a finance company, or a "Film Bank."[54] Films produced by what the memorandum proposed to call the "Imperial Cinematograph Corporation Ltd." would "use to the full the marvelous and varied resources of the Empire [and] could include subjects relating to British history and industry."[55] The FBI's engagement with cinema extended beyond the goal to protect the British film industry for its own sake and was driven also by the conception of the importance of film as a form of advertisement and propaganda, which had gathered pace in the postwar period. It was this logic that prompted the organization to sponsor a number of short films in 1924, some of which were shown at the British Empire Exhibition in London. Cinema had a wider economic significance, the FBI began to propose, and the growing global dominance of American films thus threatened to damage British commercial interests at home and in the empire markets that were so important to a British industry facing intense competition from other industrialized nations.

FBI members set up a series of meetings in 1925, to discuss the problems facing the British film industry and the impact of this on industry more broadly. "The influence of American fashions," the organization noted in its first meeting, "was beginning to affect the markets for goods even in this country and in the Dominions the tendency was even stronger than here."[56] In a later letter to the *Times*, the president of the FBI, Max Muspratt, offered a sharp economic analysis of some of the factors that supported the global circulation of American films and its "stranglehold over the film business throughout the Empire."[57] If Britain were "to stand up against the ever-growing flow of foreign rubbish and to check the gradual Americanization of our Empire," it would need to draw on the resources of the state to establish a protectionist tariff and to facilitate a heavily capitalized industry like the one that had developed in the early 1920s in the United States, when Eastern finance capital supported the establishment of an oligopolistic studio system.[58] Muspratt called for the kind of state intervention in the economy that industrialists often demand when the "free" market does not work out the way they want it to.

Cunliffe-Lister responded to the FBI's analysis of the economic force of cinema by calling meetings with representatives of the production, distribution, and exhibition sectors of the film industry and with the FBI to formulate a policy to counteract the dominance of American film and its impact on business and empire markets. In a memorandum to the cabinet in early 1926—about the same time Hays was lobbying the Department of Commerce in the United States—he mapped out the problem film posed to economic order and the reasons underpinning American economic dominance. "In Great Britain and throughout the Empire," he wrote, "nearly every film shown represents American ideas, set out in an American atmosphere . . . The accessories are American houses, American motor cars, American manufactures and so forth."[59] Later, he astutely described film as "the greatest advertising power in the world."[60] Moreover, the widely shared assumption that audiences for moving pictures were "composed largely" of what Cunliffe-Lister called—in eugenic tinged language—"young and 'low-brow' people" intensified these concerns, for it was those audiences and populations at home and across the empire that popular and academic thought imagined to be particularly malleable, even as they also needed to be cathected to British imperialism for the political and economic system of liberal imperialism to work.[61] Both regulation and production, note, pivoted on the economic and biopolitical management of populations. No doubt action needed to be taken, but Cunliffe-Lister was distracted by the General Strike of those pesky lowbrow workers and was still beholden to the lingering dictates of laissez-faire liberalism, which continued to have some hold over prominent members of his party.[62] In accordance with that logic, he proposed initially that the film industry should itself take action to bolster its efficacy in advertising empire produce and British goods.

Economic impact and political allegiance were frequently balanced in these debates about the function and impact of cinema. Widespread anxieties about the effects of film on lowbrow, working-class and colonial populations—who were often implicitly connected—centered on their proposed capacity to displace British national culture, to foment political resistance, and so to potentially disaggregate populations. In a meeting held by the FBI to consider the problem of film, Professor A. P. Newton of the Royal Colonial Institute bemoaned how American films that circulated widely in the Dominions "hold everything British up to ridicule" because this had "a very bad influence on the comparatively plastic minds of the young."[63] Newspapers picked up on these debates and circulated them widely in the public sphere. In an editorial in early 1927, for example, the *Times* asserted that it was a "public danger" that the "false values of film" promoted the importance of "wealth, luxury and notoriety" to audiences made up of "the many newly enfranchised [with] slightly educated minds."[64] In March 1927, the film columnist G. A. Atkinson for the *Daily Express,* in a now oft-quoted statement, wrote, "The plain truth about the British film situation is that the bulk of our picturegoers are Americanized . . . They talk America, think America, and dream America. We have several million people, mostly women, who, to all intent and purpose, are temporary American citizens."[65] Atkinson's choice of the word *citizen* was surely not coincidental, for the promise of liberal citizenship held out by American films could be seductive and disruptive for those varied populations in Britain and its empire that were not citizens but *subjects.* In a pithy and perceptive observation on this problematic, the London *Morning Post* observed, "Film is to America what the flag once was to Britain."[66] Or in other words, the global circulation of the filmic representation of American "modes of life" and "standards of living" symbolized, and participated in, the transition from a British imperialism formed on the basis of territorial power and the flag to the coming American-dominated world of economic and political power that was (partly) dislocated from geographical possession and rerouted through media.

Widespread concerns about the political and economic effects of cinema on populations at home and abroad led to the issue being put on the agenda of the

Imperial Economic Conference held in London in late 1926. The conference principally addressed economic issues, and it was the site where the preliminary organization of a Commonwealth economic union was elaborated. Here was film being debated at the high table of imperial economic organization. FBI members had continued to lobby Cunliffe-Lister, and he agreed to add film to the conference agenda in a further recognition of the economic and political importance of mass media. "The Committee view with great alarm," the FBI wrote, "the practical monopoly which has been obtained by foreign film production concerns of the kinema programmes of the British Empire. They consider this must have a most detrimental effect on British prestige and must be seriously prejudicial to the best interests of the Empire, especially in those parts of the overseas Dominions which contain large coloured populations."[67] To counteract these detrimental effects, the FBI submitted a memorandum to the conference recommending an immediate quota for the exhibition of 12.5 percent of British films in the British market.[68]

When the conference convened, a subcommittee was established to investigate film and its place within the empire. "It is a matter of the most serious concern," the committee reported, "that the films shown in the various parts of the Empire should be to such an overwhelming extent the product of foreign countries . . . powerfully advertise (the more effectively because indirectly) foreign countries and their products." The report concluded by calling for "suitable Government action" to encourage "private enterprise in its efforts to place the Empire film industry on a sound footing."[69] It was no surprise that the tenor of the report closely followed the logic of the FBI and Cunliffe-Lister's efforts to establish state aid to the British film industry, in a way that was consistent both with the broader logics of liberal governmental investment in cultural forms to generate economic and social and political stability and with the specific efforts to establish a Commonwealth market to counter American dominance. The FBI accordingly issued a manifesto on how to market films in the crucial markets of the Dominions, proposing the formation of a central distribution company to facilitate the movement of British and Commonwealth films, and an empire-wide quota scheme to regulate the movement of American films.[70] Lobbying groups, trade associations, and the state combined to fashion film production and policy to establish and support an imperial political economy.

The tipping point for state intervention had been reached. Cunliffe-Lister responded to the conference report, and to the failure of the film industry to voluntarily reduce American film imports, by introducing a bill into parliament in March 1927 that would compel renters to acquire, and exhibitors to show, a prescribed number of "British" films.[71] It defined a British film, significantly, in terms principally of employment: the "film must have been made by a British subject or a British-controlled company; the studio scenes must be photographed in a studio in the British Empire; the author of the scenario or of the original work must be a

British subject; and not less than 75 percent of the salaries, wages and payments for labour and services."[72] At the same time, the bill sought to address the question of block- and blind-booking, those trade practices established by dominant American studios to force exhibitors to book a raft of films at the same time, frequently sight unseen, in order to establish a trade monopoly. British government officials hoped that the respective governments of the Dominions would establish reciprocal agreements, thus supporting a film economy along the lines of the mooted imperial preference system. In this way the bill closely followed the position staked out by the FBI, showing not only the close relation between the organization and the Conservative Party but more broadly the import accorded to economic expansion by the liberal and imperial state.

Quota legislation did effectively support the production section of the film industry over that of distribution and exhibition, in a way analogous to how tariff legislation worked more generally in supporting large export industry. It was partly for this reason that the Labour Party refused to support the bill, and that some commented that it was driven entirely by the demands of the FBI and by the interests of business and finance capital.[73] Philip Snowden, former Labour chancellor, accused Cunliffe-Lister of "being simply a tool in the hands of the Federation of British Industries."[74] Certainly the act was successful in, as the *Times* predicted, attracting "new capital . . . to the British industry."[75] The vertically integrated film companies Gaumont-British and British International Pictures were established in 1927, with a capital investment predicated on the stable markets created for British films by the quota legislation.[76] Quota legislation helped foster the capital investment in the film industry, which had been a core concern throughout the process.

Economic ties and common markets were complexly enmeshed with the imperative also to forge political and affective "bonds." After reading the already-cited resolution of the imperial conference into the record of the debate in Parliament, Cunliffe-Lister asserted,

> Everybody will admit that the strongest bonds of Empire—outside, of course, the strongest of all, the Crown—are just those, intangible bonds— a common outlook, the same ideas, and the same ideals which we all share and which are expressed in a common language and a common literature. Should we be content for a moment if we depended, upon foreign literature or upon a foreign Press in this country? From the trade point of view, the influence of the cinema is no less important. It is the greatest advertising power in the world. Just let the House imagine the effect upon trade of millions of people in every country, day after day, seeing the fashions, the styles, and the products of a particular country. It inevitably influences them in their trade purchases.[77]

Cunliffe-Lister referred also to the dominance of American films and its effects on trade with Latin America, pointing out that the economic influence of the United States in the region was superseding that previously enjoyed by the British. In his remarks he showed how closely elite British politicians had been watching the development of the US state in elaborating the machinery to help films circulate the globe:

> I wonder if hon. Members have seen the evidence which was given by the Department of Commerce of the United States before a Committee of the Congress, I think, in January, 1926. The Department was justifying to the Committee an appropriation for the cinema section, and Dr. Julius Klein, in charge of the Department, said this: I do not think it is any exaggeration to say that the motion picture is perhaps the most potent single contributor to a better understanding of the United States in Latin America . . . It is invaluable in all markets where there is a high percentage of illiteracy among the people, for from the pictures they see they get their impressions of how we live, the clothes' we wear, and so forth. In fact, there has been a complete change in the demand for commodities in dozens of countries . . . That is completely borne out by our own representatives in these countries.[78]

Cunliffe-Lister referenced here specifically the moment when the Department of Commerce established a Motion Picture Section after lobbying from Hays. Movies were seemingly tipping the global economic balance in favor of the United States. Cunliffe-Lister, the president of the Board of Trade for an imperial superpower, was effectively theorizing cinema as a sort of gateway drug leading to American capitalism—a definition shared by his peers in the United States, including Klein at the Department of Commerce and the political lobbyist Hays. Early significant theorists of cinema as an ideological object were the state and quasi-state officials working to establish or contest its efficacy.

Economic "influence" was therefore yet again supplemented in these debates by concern about ideological influence, by the potential power of film to destroy the hierarchies of difference and the bonds of deference essential to colonial governance. "I do not suppose that there is anything which has done so much harm to the prestige and position of Western people and the white race," said the Conservative former president of the Board of Trade and Chancellor Sir Robert Horne, "as the exhibition of films which have tended to degrade us in the eyes of peoples who have been accustomed to look upon us with admiration and respect."[79] What was implicit in these concerns about misrepresentation was the idea that there was a form of representation that would best sustain Britain's "prestige" and the right to govern. "The success of our government of subject races depends almost entirely on the degree of respect which we can inspire," a report attached to a Colonial Films Committee established by the government in 1929 stated. "Incalculable is the damage that has already been done to the prestige of Europeans in India and the Far East through the widespread exhibition of ultra-sensational and disreputable pictures."[80]

Debates in the offices of trade and lobbying associations, in the offices of state, and in parliament and associated committees, began to produce a conception of film as a commodity and as a symbolic and ideological object. The latter concerns about representation and ideology were particularly pressing for an imperial state that necessarily relied on spectacle and deference to maintain the apparatus of colonial governmentality. (Early British films had played a role in this in circulating spectacles of imperial splendor that were frequently connected to royalty.)[81] Political and economic elites argued that mimetic responses to films were more evident in subaltern populations, be those of the lowbrow domestic working classes or what a government-sponsored report in 1933 described as the "backward races within the Empire" who "can gain and suffer more from the film than the sophisticated European, because to them the power of the visual medium is intensified."[82] Visible also in the margins of these debates were nascent concerns not only about the representation of misbehaving white characters but also about the structures of empathy that were so central to the textual economies of American fiction film and that enabled positions of alignment and allegiance between populations, which undercut the premises of colonial logic and practices. The problem of film was, in Babli Sinha's suggestive phrasing, its "threatening deterritorializing potential" and its capacity to mix spaces and populations, to undercut boundaries, and to foster utopian possibilities that ran counter to economic and political structures of imperial hegemony.[83]

Elite politicians innovated film regulation in this period in a way that made manifest the close ties between ideas about film as a form of cultural imperialism, evident in debates about quota legislation, and the establishment and sustenance of institutions to curtail the visibility and mobility of forms that were potentially threatening to economic order and governance. The self-regulatory British Board of Film Censors quickly agreed with the need to regulate film images to sustain the spectacle of British probity and authority. In 1923 the board banned any films showing British officials in "equivocal situations" involving colonial women, and a new series of injunctions was elaborated in 1926–30 that banned "the showing of white men in a state of degradation amidst Eastern or Native surroundings," "liaisons between coloured men and white women," and "equivocal situations between white men and coloured people."[84] The Colonial Office wrote to all colonies and protectorates asking them to outline the censorship measures in place,[85] noting that colonial governments needed to begin to provide films as counterattractions: "It is, I am afraid, clear that private enterprise does not provide Colonial Dependencies with the best class of film, and consequently it may become necessary for Colonial Governments themselves to provide films."[86] Government intervention was needed to supplement the free market. The Colonial Office recommended the use of mobile cinema projection like that pioneered by the Conservative Party.[87] (Later, the Colonial Films Committee worked to set up a machinery of distribution within the colonies, with the help of the FBI.)[88] In 1929, the British Board of Film Censors turned to the politically well-connected Edward Shortt to become its second president. Shortt had previously been home secretary tasked with dealing with industrial unrest in the immediate postwar years and the threat of a General Strike. He was notable, Nicholas Pronay observes, for his mastery of "internal security, counter-subversion and counter-insurgency."[89] Censoring cinema was tied to these governmental aims. Regulating Soviet film and its articulation of a radically different political economy also became important in this context.[90]

Censorship became significant to the imperial state, then, and tied together with the broader problematic of regulating the global flow of media culture as one aspect—albeit a particularly visible one—of the global economy. Elite state officials and industrialists and lobbyists in Britain began to piece together a conception of cinema as a particularly important symbolic and ideological commodity, responding as they did so to the practical enactment of those ideas by US state officials and industrial lobbyists. The affective power of film, and the malleability of subaltern audiences and populations, made film policy a component of imperial governmentality. Censorship practices intersected with those that underpinned film production by the Conservative Party, linked by the imperatives to facilitate capital flow, protect industry, and govern working-class and colonial populations, and thus to sustain liberal and colonial governmentality.

"THE ART OF NATIONAL PROJECTION"

Conceptions of the economic and political import of film emerging in the 1920s in the context of the economic and political logics of imperialism led also to the establishment of a state-run film unit in early 1927, while the debates about the economic and ideological effects of film rumbled on in Parliament. The film unit was housed within the Empire Marketing Board (EMB), a department established by the Conservative Party—with support from the Board of Trade and Cunliffe-Lister—to promote interimperial trade in lieu of the formal establishment of a protectionist economy that would be postponed until the onset of the Depression. Film production was to be directly tied to the sustenance of an imperial political economy, to the visual illustration and elaboration of imperial economic relations. The establishment of the EMB film unit was consistent with the Conservative Party's own use of film, and with the widespread belief in the economic and political usefulness of cinema for the maintenance of liberal economic and political order. Its subsequent history is relatively well known, for the film unit is often seen as the starting point for the history of British documentary cinema. But here I am arguing that the formation of the aesthetics and institutions of documentary must be seen as one strand in the broader history I have been exploring of the forces that brought cinema and the political economy of liberalism—and here specifically late liberal imperialism—into close association.

The history of the EMB was itself tied up with the Conservative Party's strategy to elaborate a new imperial economy in the interwar period. When it returned to power in late 1924, on the back of a renunciation of the direct imposition of tariffs, the party sought other ways to encourage a protectionist economy and closer economic ties within the empire. One of these was the establishment of an Imperial Economic Committee, which had a budget of one million pounds per annum to be spent on finding "entirely new and untried ways of developing trade with the Empire, trade which will bring in Empire stuff in lieu of foreign stuff." The committee recommended in 1925 that the money be spent by an "executive commission" to produce "continuous publicity on a national scale with a view to spreading and fostering [the idea] that Empire purchasing creates an increased demand for the manufactured products of the United Kingdom and therefore stimulates employment at home."[91] Cunliffe-Lister at the Board of Trade supported this version of what has been called "non-tariff preference," arguing that the improved marketing of empire foodstuffs in Britain would reduce a reliance on nonempire imports—and thus the dollar gap with the United States—as well as stimulate colonial economies to enable them to purchase British manufactured goods.[92] The board, the Imperial Economic Committee recommended, "should be charged with the duty of conducting the movement for trade in Empire produce."[93] Leopold Amery at the Colonial Office supported this also, and the executive commission to carry out this economic task was established as the EMB in May 1926, with Amery as its first chairman.[94]

Gathering together for their first meeting in June 1926, the members of the EMB observed that they would be implementing a new government policy of publicity that was unprecedented in peacetime.[95] In this respect, the EMB marked a significant moment in the connection of state economic goals with cultural work that was clearly informed by the new ideas about government, "public relations," and the sustenance of liberal democracies, which had proliferated in particular in the immediate postwar period. The membership of the board reflected this too, a number of whom were drawn from the BBC—the institutional embodiment of ideas about culture as public utility—and from the advertising profession, the other crucial industry that mushroomed in the 1920s and was predicated on ideas about the effects of media and its economic usefulness.[96] The publicity goals of the board were managed by its secretary, Stephen Tallents, who had played a significant role in the management of the General Strike in 1926, as secretary to the cabinet committee that dealt with the strike, which had supported in particular government use of the BBC radio network to elaborate its response and its political critique of union action.[97]

Tallents elaborated on the logic that animated his and the EMB's sense of the governmental import of culture in a pamphlet entitled *The Projection of England*, published in 1932. "When England by her sea power won her place in the sun,"

Tallents wrote, "her shadow was the longest of them all. To-day that morning of the world is past . . . The shadows of the peoples are more equal and the long shadows have grown less."[98] England needed to elaborate "the art of national projection" to "create a belief in her ability to serve the world under the new order as she has served it under the old."[99] New practices of national projection—of propaganda— were necessary to maintain "supremacy" in the revised geopolitical configuration marked by transformations in imperial rule and by the emergence of a "new order" dominated by the United States and to some extent Soviet Russia.[100] Tallents bemoaned how American dominance had "turned every cinema in the world into the equivalent of an American consulate."[101] The projection of geopolitical suprem- acy needed to be supplemented by the communication of economic "qualities" and primacy. "If we are to win their custom, we must first win their minds," Tallents wrote. "And to win their minds we must set ourselves to project by all means of modern international communication a picture of England's industrial qualities."[102]

Visual culture was important to the EMB, and its goal of "winning" minds, as Tallents's use of "projection" suggested. The board commissioned modernist art- ists to produce posters, which were displayed widely and which made beautiful aesthetic images out of imperial economics.[103] It quickly discussed the possibility of using film to support establishing a system of non-tariff preference and to "sell the idea of Empire." Tallents had discussed this with the famous author Rudyard Kipling in August 1926, immediately after the formation of the EMB and shortly after the end of the General Strike, which was also around the time the Conserva- tive Party was beginning its own film program.[104] Kipling suggested that the EMB should undertake the production of a major feature film "in which intrinsic enter- tainment value would be paramount, and which would be suitable for distribution on its merits in the ordinary commercial way to the trade."[105] Kipling also pro- posed the board hire Walter Creighton to carry this out. Creighton had produced the Wembley Tattoo at the 1924 Imperial Exhibition, with help from Kipling, and was thus well versed in the production of imperial spectacle. After a film commit- tee was established at the EMB in February 1927, Creighton was appointed in March, with the support of Colonial Secretary Amery. Creighton had no actual knowledge of film production and was employed because of his connection with Kipling, whose fame and association with imperial storytelling would, it was thought, help guarantee the film's success.[106] This was elite nepotism in action. Kipling was also very closely associated with the Conservative Party, which was led by his cousin Stanley Baldwin. The board proposed that Creighton travel to Canada and the United States to gain knowledge of film production, from both commercial studios and from the Canadian Motion Picture Bureau, and to scout locations for the imperial epic he and Kipling imagined.

While Creighton was away, John Grierson was employed by Tallents to develop the EMB's film activities, initially on an ad hoc basis but his participation grew so that he became the dominant figure in the operations of the EMB.[107] Grierson's intellectual history is now relatively well known, at least in the discipline of film studies: a Glasgow philosophy graduate, he had recently returned from the United States, where he had been a Rockefeller-funded scholar based initially at the famed sociology department at the University of Chicago.[108] Grierson had become interested in the social psychology of popular media, like others within the social sciences at Chicago, and during his time in the US he also met with Walter Lippmann, whose work on public opinion and democracy was widely influential. Tallents commissioned him initially to write a report for the EMB on "popular appeal in cinema" and its potential use by the government. The lengthy "Notes for English Producers," written between February and April 1927, was influenced by the social science work Grierson had studied in the United States. It would be an influential document for the establishment of a theory and practice of what later came to be called documentary cinema.

"Cinema is recognised," Grierson began, "as having a peculiar influence on the ideological centres to which advertisement endeavours to make its appeal . . . because it is an ideal medium for all manner of suggestion."[109] Grierson's conception of "suggestion" here came directly from work in sociology, psychology, and the emergent discipline of social psychology, which argued that individuals and social groups were "suggestible" and so were formed through mimetic contact with others. Theories of suggestibility, sympathy, and mimesis were directed at that central liberal problematic—the question of how individuals were bound into social order—in the context in particular of the migratory movement and the establishment of urban democracies characteristic of the early twentieth century. I shall talk more about this in chapter 10. Here it is enough to note that Grierson and Tallents wrapped their immediate aim in assessing how film could foster imperial economic cooperation in the broader question of how the suggestive and ideological power of cinema could be cathected to liberal governmental rationality.

Grierson dismissed the usefulness of the preexisting models of film form exemplified by commercial American cinema, state-financed Soviet cinema, and to a lesser extent actuality cinema. "American producers," Grierson wrote, "are so bound up with what they call 'human interest,' and so insensitive to the dramatic importance of scene and setting, that they invariably allow the more private preoccupations of their characters to destroy the sweep of events."[110] But he continued, the "Russians, to take 'Potemkin' as a guide, have gone to the other extreme. Communist interests have made them somewhat blind to personal themes," and this finds its "cinematic expression in an emphasis on crowds, ships, streets and factories, to the almost complete exclusion of individual life."[111] Grierson's political theory of film sought to articulate a space for state-sponsored British cinema and for its enactment of the liberal problematic to form the interdependence of individual and social formation. The appropriate register for this was a realism that meshed "scene and setting," and "the sweep of events," with a proper focus on aspects of individual life. Grierson's argument, in this government-sponsored memorandum, for the establishment of a practice of cinema that was positioned between the poles of economic individualism and collectivism, was clearly driven by the same logics that shaped the British state's efforts in the interwar period to establish a political role for the country, in what Tallents had described as "the new order" dominated by the coming hegemons, the United States and Soviet Russia. Grierson's efforts to clear the theoretical grounds for a specifically British film form that would embody and manifest something like classical British liberalism was a subset of the economic and geopolitical problems facing the imperial British state.

No surprises then that the examples of this new state-mandated political formation of cinema, which emerged from Grierson's paper and indeed later became practice, were closely tied to the imperative to elaborate a new imperial political economy. It was that task that was central to the Conservative Party and government and to the institution that Grierson worked for to further those aims. EMB films could thus create "original scenarios round the adventures of the great explorers, around the different phases of Colonial life, and round the great commercial and industrial enterprises of the time."[112] Exciting "true" stories of conquest and exploitation were awaiting the film cameras. Likewise, the intertwined stories of "discovery and colonisation" and the establishment of infrastructures should, Grierson asserted, be central to the films the Board produced. Its films could thus utilize "the visually dramatic material in which the Empire is so rich" to show and develop accounts of "the sweep of commerce . . . the ships, the docks, the factories, the furnaces, the streets, the canals, the plans, the plantations, the caravans, the parades, the dams, the bridges, all over the earth ball that carry the flag of English energy."[113] Cinema and infrastructural movement were again aligned in the service of the imperial movement of materials, people, and goods.

Grierson's paper on the proposed usefulness of cinema was circulated widely, at the same time the debates on the economic and political effects of cinema were taking place in Parliament and in the pages of the press. Cunliffe-Lister praised the report as he worked on framing the quota legislation that was predicated on similar ideas about the suggestive power of cinema.[114] Grierson was subsequently employed by Tallents to help establish the EMB's use of cinema, a job that entailed both a theoretical and practical elaboration of the effective use of cinema by the state to further its economic and political goals. Quickly setting to work, he had by late 1927 arranged a series of screenings at the Imperial Institute, inviting members of the government to attend and to participate in a discussion about the films and "the various possibilities of the film in educational, scientific, marketing and propagandist work."[115] In October 1927, Grierson organized a screening of films on a train carrying members of the Imperial Agricultural Committee from Edinburgh to London. Among the films was one "showing the saving of labour and greater efficiency which comes with the electrification of the land."[116] Watching the pictures of the USDA-like modernization of farming on a speeding train was uniquely appropriate for the government and the EMB's goals to establish infrastructural networks to facilitate imperial economies and to rationalize imperial production. The close ties between cinema and the railway, often commented upon by contemporary and subsequent observers, were forged here on the rails of imperial economics and the sustenance of the imperial, "complementary" economy by which colonial economies were tied to agriculture and raw materials.

The innovation of new nontheatrical exhibition spaces, like the Imperial Institute and the train, was quickly established as a critical task for the EMB's elaboration of the filmic corollary to the projected imperial economy. Grierson wrote another position paper, "Further Notes on Cinema Production," to assess the situation. "All those interests which do not (and cannot) find their ends satisfied by the commercial industry," he wrote, "are beginning to look elsewhere; and this they must do."[117] He commented approvingly on the FBI's efforts to utilize cinema by drawing "up a list of films for the encouragement of private and institutional exhibitions."[118] The crossover between the goals of the FBI and the EMB to foster imperial trade was considerable.

In mid-1928, the EMB innovated the use of "automatic projectors" in public spaces to show short "poster" films, which advertised some element of imperial produce like South African fruit or Canadian apples. The first of these was positioned in Victoria train station in London, an appropriate space of transit. "The model" of the poster film, Grierson wrote, "is the American 'trailer,'—the short film advertisement which heralds the 'coming soon' of another Hollywood masterpiece."[119] Hollywood's advertisement for itself was a successful model to be copied for the advertisement of imperial goods. In 1928 too the EMB sponsored a mobile cinema van in Leicestershire—once again linking cinema with mobility in ways that refracted the idealization of economic mobility visible in the films of imperial produce it was showing.[120] Grierson referenced the Conservative Party's successful pioneering use of mobile cinema vans.[121] The elaboration of mobile cinema networks, and nontheatrical exhibition spaces, was a formative moment in the establishment of a media infrastructure to facilitate the flow of goods and thus an imperial economic bloc. The long-term goals of the EMB in respect to nontheatrical distribution and exhibition centered on the use of its films by teachers, either the practice of bringing schoolchildren to the cinema established by the EMB at the Imperial Institute or of circulating films to schools, which would use them in classes on geography, economics, and the empire.[122] This was analogous to the more decentered visual instruction movement in the United States. The integration of film, pedagogy, and imperial economics was pursued consistently in the early 1930s by the EMB, operating on the assumption that film was most appealing to children—who were, it was argued, particularly suggestive subjects—and that it could thus be utilized as a pedagogical technology. Its ideas and assumptions in this respect supported the British government's later development of film production for colonial populations, which were similarly regarded as particularly susceptible to the suggestive and persuasive powers of cinema.

"A DRAG ON THE FISCAL HEALTH OF THE EMPIRE"

I have thus far examined the production, dissemination, and regulation of film to supplement and transform imperial economic relations. Most of these film texts were directed at working-class audiences in Britain and were designed to interpellate them into a newly configured imperial economic bloc, even if many of them were also exhibited across the empire principally to facilitate intraimperial trade. But there were also scattered efforts to utilize film initially as part of the spectacle of colonial rule marked by a technological disparity exemplified by cinema but underscored by armaments, and subsequently as part of attempts to "educate" the "backward races" in the new realities in (mostly) modern medical, labor, and state practices.[123] Broadly speaking this was consistent with the integration of film and other media with liberal governmentality traced out in this book, inflected here in particular by the biopolitical, economic, and communicative practices and exigencies of the colonial state.

I will concentrate on one influential example, mostly located in East Africa in the mid-1930s, with the development of what came to be called the Bantu Educational Kinema Experiment (BEKE). The history and logic of this experimental use of cinema to educate Africans can be briefly recounted and woven into the fabric of the institutional history articulated thus far. In the wake of the passage of the British Cinematograph Films Act, the Colonial Office convened a film conference in late 1927, at which a colonial films committee was formed to discuss the circulation of British films in the empire, the control of films already circulating, and the production of educational cinema for the "benefit" of the colonized. The Federation of British Industries played a considerable role in the 1927 conference, where they affirmed the importance of cinema for trade and education and advocated the compilation of a catalogue of educational films already in existence.[124] In the wake of the conference, the Colonial Advisory Committee on Native Education sent the noted biologist Julian Huxley to Uganda, Kenya, Tanganyika, and Zanzibar to "advise upon certain aspects of native education."[125] Huxley took with him a projector and a selection of films supplied by the EMB to various educational institutions. Cinema's usefulness for colonial pedagogy was further buttressed by the Colonial Office's support for a plan from missionary John Merle Davis to show and produce films for the regions around and including the copper belt mines in what was then Northern Rhodesia.[126] Davis allied with Major Leslie Alan Notcutt, a sisal plantation owner in East Africa, who himself had previously "thought that an estate cinema might be an effective method to help maintain a contented labor force."[127] Davis secured funding from the Carnegie Institute, as well as other mining operations in the region, and began an experiment to produce and exhibit "cultural, recreation and educational films for the Bantu" people.[128] He was supported by a somewhat cash-strapped Colonial Office in London, which was grateful for American corporate philanthropic money.

What brought the missionary, plantation owner, corporate American philanthropy, and the Colonial Office together? If that sounds like the setup for a joke, the short answer is a little more prosaic—the management of African mobility and labor in the midst of the massive social transformations wrought by large-scale mineral extraction to serve transnational capital. Davis's proposed project was motivated by an interest in the social impact on local villages of mass labor migration to Northern Rhodesia's Copperbelt, which was the subject of his influential 1932 report *Modern Industry and the African*. In this sense he was part of the wider shift in the interwar years toward new conceptions of colonial "development," albeit one predicated in this case on finding ways to educate Africans in their "natural" roles as agriculturalists and to disrupt the drift of African farmers and laborers from land reserves to employment in mines and other jobs in cities, or at least to minimize the deleterious consequences of this for migrant laborers, colonial rule, and the imperial system.[129] Rural development in this way sought to align African production to the global market and simultaneously minimize the emergence of forms of political nationalism, contestation over land rights, and an incipient Pan-Africanist movement among the migrant laborers. Carnegie and the British colonial state found common ground in these objectives, and the connections among missionary, state, and American corporate philanthropic capital are one example of an expansive associationalist or development apparatus intended to manage the "modernization" of African populations and economies and facilitate their integration into a transnational liberal economy. Violent police reprisals against the 1935 strike of workers in the Copperbelt were the flipside to this project of pedagogical hegemony.

The thirty-five films made by BEKE in 1935–37 included several on agricultural matters, including films about crop rotation, seed selection, soil erosion, and cooperative marketing. Other films advertised the colonial government's departments and services. In the very first film of the experiment, *Post Office Savings Bank* (1935), two African men working on a plantation handle the salaries they are given differently. One buries his money in the floor of his hut, and later has it stolen, but the other agricultural worker takes his straight to the colonial post office bank. The structure of wise and foolish choices, usually embodied in character positions, was a very common one in colonial pedagogy produced by state and quasi-state institutions. In this example it works to support a colonial banking system and so, therefore, the extraction of further profit from colonized labor.[130]

Likewise, the third BEKE film, *Tax* (1935), contrasted the precolonial and colonial methods of taxation. The first system is one of tributes paid to a tribal chief, while under colonial rule taxes are shown being used to provide services, such as medical attention and education, and to finance the infrastructure that develops agricultural economies. (Never mind, as Aboubakar Sanogo remarks, that colonial taxes essentially paid for the cost of colonization and subsequent administration.)[131] Various other BEKE films focused on hygiene and disease preventions. *Tropical Hookworm* (1936) showed the step-by-step process of constructing a pit latrine to avoid the hookworm infection that proliferated in rural areas in sub-Saharan Africa, rendered sufferers exhausted, and so constituted "a drag on the fiscal health of the empire."[132] In these direct ways, film was integrated with the biopolitical project to manage colonized populations and in particular to ensure laborers were productive.

Quasi-state officials, missionaries, anthropologists, and philanthropists all worked from similar assumptions that there was a unique "African mind" and that education should take these race-based proclivities into consideration. William Sellers, a medical officer with the Nigerian government, had first begun to articulate this biopolitical conception of "the African" in his experiments with film as pedagogy in the mid-1920s, and it became axiomatic in these colonial circles that educational films should take these proclivities into consideration (and so, for example, should be minimally edited, should unfold at a slower pace, should remove extraneous material from the frame, and so on).[133] Indeed, one aspect of the BEKE project was to study how African audiences responded to films in order to understand how to make them more pedagogically effective. Watching Africans watch movies became an ideologically charged anthropological and state intervention—an early reception studies project, though one that was, unusually, somewhat interesting and consequential. Everyone already knew, of course, that the racially inferior Africans were more prone to mimetic responses to cinema, and the BEKE project was "partly designed," Glenn Reynolds has argued, "to 'capture' African viewers and correct the 'falsehoods' perpetuated by the Hollywood dream machine."[134] James Burns suggests that the BEKE sought to produce enough films to completely restrict the exhibition of commercial productions, and the project "was not merely an attempt to teach through films, but was also a form of proactive censorship."[135] Certainly the films were widely disseminated in East and Central Africa, traveling through Kenya, the mining towns of the Copperbelt in Northern Rhodesia, Tanganyika, Nysaland, and Uganda in following the same migratory patterns exploited by global capital and on the back of—what else?—"a two-ton Ford lorry, with the cinema unit engine mounted on a trailer bounding behind."[136] (See fig. 16.) Vans like this enabled the government to take its message to areas often beyond government supervision, thus both extending the visibility of government and expanding the ability of the state to see. The report written on the

FIGURE 16. Mobile cinema van (L. A. Notcutt and G. C. Latham, *The African and the Cinema: An Account of the Bantu Educational Kinema Experiment during the Period March 1935 to May 1937* (London: Edinburgh House Press, 1937).

project suggested that the mobile cinema van traveled "9000 miles by road in addition to short trips by rail and lake," giving ninety-five performances to approximately eighty-thousand Africans, thirteen hundred Europeans and a "large number of Indians."[137] Exhibitions frequently used a sound-on-disc system and often ended with a short film of London, a picture of the king, and the national anthem.[138] Many of these audiences had never seen moving pictures before, and it seems likely that the films came themselves in some ways to stand metonymically as representative of the technological power of the colonial state—a form of technological shock and awe in the service of the biopolitical and economic management of empire.

The experiment mirrored in some ways that enacted by the USDA in relation to the agricultural periphery of the United States. Using cinema to educate rural populations in productive agricultural practices, and related ways of living, took some similar forms and prompted related developments in mobile cinema technology and exhibition. US corporations, and their related foundations, were becoming increasingly invested in the resources located within the British Empire in the interwar years.[139] Concrete connections existed between some of these projects to use media to foster the biopolitical and economic usefulness of populations. The Rockefeller-financed International Health Board, for example, made a film in 1920 called *Unhooking the Hookworm,* meant principally for distribution in the American South to counter the deleterious effects of the hookworm on rural workers. International Health Board officials subsequently worked with the British Colonial Office to distribute the film across its empire.[140] Rockefeller's investment should be read as one of the ways that corporate philanthropy supported projects that increased the productivity of rural workers. The investments of Rockefeller and Carnegie, with a compliant Colonial Office, tell us something also about the shifting configuration of power way from the state—and the colonial state—and toward new corporate wealth in the period. But also something of the deeper structural continuities between these projects, for the interventions of Rockefeller and the USDA were frequently designed to manage the descendants of African populations forcibly removed from their homelands to serve transnational capital just as the British colonial efforts sought to manage displaced African populations.

Indeed, the site of these experiments in pedagogy and governance was extremely significant. The discovery of rich copper deposits in Northern Rhodesia, on the border with the Belgian Congo, in the early 1920s, was a crucial economic and political boon to the British, because copper was crucial to the wired communicative networks that themselves were central to imperial governance and economic globalization. Local "instability" demanded state action. Telecommunications, "capitalism's essential lubricant," required the resources dug up from African soil by an occupying power.[141] (Nowadays the neighboring Democratic Republic of Congo is one of the central resources for the coltan that is integral to mobile and smartphones, and the legacies of imperialism have resulted in atrocious mining conditions and ongoing brutal and devastating armed conflict.) The innovation of a pedagogical film project for African audiences in the crucial region of the Copperbelt is another example of the ways in which film as mass, mobile, media was integrated with the efforts to sustain governance and facilitate the global flow of information and materials.

"COMMON ALLEGIANCE"

EMB films did something similar for the global movement of materials and capital. The EMB has a rather typically British ring to it, almost as if the word "marketing" were shyly hiding its actual purpose—the *advertisement,* as Americans would rightly call it, of imperial produce to foster the unequal circulation of raw materials and manufactured objects and capital that sustained imperial power. Documentary cinema was born as advertisement for empire. The strategy initially innovated by Grierson and Tallents was to use preexisting film, principally from the Dominions, that showed examples of agricultural produce or raw materials. The poster films *Canadian Apples, Lumber,* and *South African Fruit,* for example, functioned as short advertisements for these products, in line with the EMB's rhetoric on the importance of buying empire goods to better sustain the British and imperial economy. *Conquest* (1929) was a more expansive project, a compilation film on "the pioneering development" of Canada that reused scenes from Hollywood westerns and from footage shot by the Motion Picture Bureau in Canada to tell a story about the settlement and "conquest" of Canada.[142] The film drew, if probably unwittingly, links between the western genre and the "drama" of "discovery and colonization" that Grierson had written about in government memorandums on the economic and political use of cinema.

Grierson and the young filmmakers he employed produced a number of compilation films in the early months of the EMB's film production, reusing existing footage drawn mainly from the Commonwealth and innovating new practices of editing that were partly influenced by Soviet cinema. The compilation film pioneered by the EMB marked in its very form the imperative to elaborate the imperial political economy, which the board sought to visualize and foster, for in the mingling of footage from across the nascent Commonwealth the films made concrete the idealization of the circulation of goods and capital at the base of the efforts to create the British-led imperial economic bloc. Grierson discovered, in his theory and practice, that montage could be divorced from its radical function in Soviet film, where at base it articulated the Marxist dialectic, and repositioned in the service of the closely linked imperatives of the consumer and imperial economy. Advertising executives would learn well from this innovation.

Visualizing the "complementary" imperial economy, and its usefulness for Britain, was established as a central goal of the EMB's film production right from the outset. The first film the board commissioned was the one imagined by Kipling, Creighton, and Tallents, though it was not finally completed and released until 1930. *One Family*, as the film came to be called, presents an elaborate fantasy of Commonwealth economic integration.[143] It tells the story of a young boy who imagines visiting various Commonwealth countries to collect the ingredients that go to make up the king's Christmas pudding. The film begins with the boy getting ready to go to school, as his mother chivvies him along and his father reads the newspaper. On the way to school, he sees a shop window advertising the empire produce that goes into making a Christmas pudding, directly connecting the film to a broader EMB campaign about the pudding, which took it as a concrete symbol of the way empire goods could be used to produce an object that marked in its nature the comingling of produce central to the nascent Commonwealth-bloc imagination and yet was also specific to British traditions. The latter was further marked by the fact that the pudding was being made for the head of the Commonwealth, the king. In his classroom, the boy asks about the empire but is bored by the teachers dull recounting of territories and falls asleep. The film sets out to teach a better, more engaging, lesson about empire, enacting the pedagogical value of film proposed by government supporters of the use of cinema and its integration with schools. The boy dreams of entering the grand space of Buckingham Palace to meet the king (who remains unseen) and sets off on an adventure to gather the products that make up the Christmas pudding, guided by a set of women dressed in robes, who symbolize different commonwealth spaces. Typically the boy looks outward from the palace to magically gaze upon a colonized state, before entering the frame to be shown and told about some aspect of the farming and harvesting of foods. Other sequences show the produce being transported to England: a small cask of brandy is lowered from a huge steamer ship, docked in England; ships dock at large grain factories in Canada to gather flour for the pudding, before setting off for England, where the products are fed into huge machines that produce the pudding.

This industrial process narrative is enfolded within a domestic narrative, for the film begins with the young boy getting ready for school with his mother and father and ends with his realization that the Dominions are "a family too." The domestic narrative so central to narrative fiction is translated to a geopolitical narrative of proposed Commonwealth unity, imagining a family of nations gathered together under the benevolent patriarch of the king and Britain. If its principal goal was to advertise the importance of imperial produce and economy, the film also worked to visualize and produce the "common allegiance" within the Commonwealth bloc that the 1926 Balfour Declaration on the formal establishment of Commonwealth ties had affirmed as critical, as indeed had those who sought to elaborate the quota and regulatory framework for Commonwealth films. In this way the film visualizes the ties that were being delineated at the state level, and its shifting between fantasy and reality is eloquent testimony in itself to the way that the film was positioned and imagined as a text and form that could translate fantasy—or political will—into the real world.

Central to many of the EMB films were images showing the harvesting of products in colonial spaces and their transport and arrival in the metropole. This is a dominant trope across the board's work, indeed across the colonial archive in the interwar period more generally, for it offers the clearest visual record or account of the efforts to establish the so-called complementary imperial economy. *One Family* is consistent with many other EMB films in this respect. *Cargo from Jamaica* (1933), for example, directed by Basil Wright, shows the harvesting of bananas and their transport, on the heads of colonial subjects, to be manually loaded onto a large ship (fig. 17). Arriving in London, the cargo is transported efficiently by conveyor belts from the ships to warehouses (fig. 18). The contrast between the use of bodies and technology—not only the conveyor belt but also the ships, which were undoubtedly built, owned, and insured by Britain—marks acutely the standard contrast between an advanced technological modernity and its double, the "primitive" economy of colonized labor and agricultural produce. The ubiquity of large transport ships in EMB films and a great number of British colonial films is in this way instructive, for they mark not only the idealization of technology and trans-

FIGURE 17 *(top)*. Still from *Cargo from Jamaica* (Empire Marketing Board Film Unit, 1933).

FIGURE 18 *(bottom)*. Still from *Cargo from Jamaica* (Empire Marketing Board Film Unit, 1933).

port but stand also as concrete symbols of the literal mobility of the British finance capitalism that sustained the shipping industry and thus British economic control of the global circulation of materials and goods in the nineteenth and early twentieth centuries.

The elaboration and sustenance of the economic and political ties of the Commonwealth, played out on the film screen, were enabled also by networks of exchange in film institutions established in particular between Canada and Britain. Canada's position was uniquely significant to the establishment of a Commonwealth bloc, for it offered a bulwark against the expansionist United States. The director of the Canadian Government Cinema Bureau, Captain Frank Badgely, had visited the EMB in May 1928. Badgely shared with Tallents, Grierson, and others on the film committee the experience the unit he led had gained in elaborating a state-financed film production unit and distribution and exhibition network that sought to use film to, in part, articulate a national perspective countering the economic and media dominance of the United States.[144] Creighton had visited Canada immediately upon his appointment by the EMB. Grierson likewise visited Canada, and the USA, in 1931, approvingly surveying film production methods in the Canadian unit.[145] The EMB unit authorized him to purchase "film material suitable for the Board's purposes."[146]

In 1932 Grierson and the EMB set about organizing a film screening at the crucial imperial economic conference in Ottawa, in discussion also with the Federation of British Industries and the Canadian Government Motion Picture Bureau.[147] A "further plan was to supplement" these screenings with "shows throughout Canada from the rear of Canadian Pacific Railway trains."[148] In many ways these plans marked the culmination of the EMB's efforts as regards cinema, for they connected film directly to the political project of establishing an imperial economic bloc, which was itself concluded at this conference when the "imperial preference" system was established. Watching films of economic projection, of the circulation of goods, and of the creation of an imperial political economy, projected in the conference halls and from the back of a train traveling across the economically and politically crucial space of Canada marks a significant moment in the conception and practice of the economic and geopolitical use of British colonial cinema.

"STRENGTHENING THE LINK BETWEEN BRITAIN AND THE DOMINIONS"

But the EMB's finest hour was one of its last. It was disbanded shortly after the establishment of an imperial preference economic system, because its function to establish nontariff forms of preference was thus rendered redundant.[149] Key personnel—Tallents and Grierson—moved to the auspices of the post office, setting up the general post office film unit that would itself make the idealization of forms of circulation a central task. Various other documentary and marketing film units were established from the ashes of the EMB, and many of these worked in conjunction with corporate sponsors. For example, Strand Films, led by Paul Rotha, was commissioned by Imperial Airways in 1936 to produce a cycle of documentary films about air travel and its imperial networks. The airways cycle included *Air Outpost* (1937), *The Future's in the Air* (1937), and *African Skyways* (1940).[150] The company also produced a film for Anglo-Iranian Oil called *Dawn Over Iran* (1938). One dominant trope, as Martin Stollery has observed, was the picturing of air planes flying over pyramids, in part to recognize the centrality of Egypt to imperial networks of transport but also clearly to play with the contrast between the past and modern technology that underlay colonial rhetoric and practice.[151]

The imperial dream of the economic and geopolitical utility of cinema lived on. In 1938 Grierson was commissioned by the Imperial Relations Trust to travel to Canada, New Zealand, and Australia to survey the possibilities of setting up a film center in each of these countries with a view in particular of "strengthening the link between Britain and the Dominions if war came."[152] The Imperial Relations Trust was administered by Tallents and was seemingly connected to Britain's secret service as part of the propaganda efforts to establish Commonwealth and colonial unity for the war hovering on the horizon. Grierson's assignment was, Gary Evans has shown, specifically "to set up a Northern American propaganda base to urge Canada and (more important) the United States into an active partnership with Britain at war, if war should come."[153] Grierson was commissioned also by the Canadian government, and the report he wrote for them about film in mid-1938 was enthusiastically received. He returned in late 1938 to draft the legislative bill that created a National Film Board, and a year later he was invited by the Canadian government to take up the position as first director of the board.[154] Grierson's further elaboration of documentary cinema, supported by state authority, was connected directly to the geopolitical goals that had partly subtended the establishment of the Commonwealth.

But the economic and political realities of this dream of "commonwealth" unity and British primacy floundered amidst growing resistance to colonial oppression and also because the United States directly countered the British economic project. Hollywood films offered seductive visions of liberal capitalism somewhat at odds with its colonial formations. Colonial and Dominion states began to resist Britain's entreaties to forge imperial connections to counteract American and Hollywood dominance.[155] Later, the United States made the dissolution of the system of imperial preferences, and the opening up of the British Empire to US economic capital and trade, a condition of its economic support to Britain in the post–Second World War settlement. By doing so, the United States created a new liberal economic world order, with the United States at its center.[156]

If film seemed to offer, for a time, a way of sustaining British economic and geopolitical primacy, it could not resist the sweeping changes that altered the economic and political landscape in the interwar years. The films of the 1920s and early 1930s analyzed here came to look ever-more fictional, divorced as they were from the realities of Britain's economic and geopolitical position. "Documentary" cinema indeed tries to "mummify" change.[157] The complex indexicality of the cinematic image, and of documentary, came to be ever-more bent toward the fantastical maintenance of a dying dream of economic and geopolitical dominance. Archives institutionalized this position on cinema's potential to mummify change. The maintenance of empire in fact underlay the creation of what came to be called the British Film Institute. The sequence of events that led to its creation, which have already been mostly outlined, looked like this: the 1927 Colonial Office conference on film in the empire led to the formation in 1929 of a Colonial Films Committee, which sponsored the 1932 report *The Film in National Life,* which called for the formation of a national film archive and institute. The British Film Institute was established in 1933 and became, first, a space for the promotion of the pedagogic potential of cinema and, second, a repository for the "national" moving images that helped form the imagined community of nation.[158] The archive, which was formed in part to help halt the forces that repositioned Britain's hegemony, now houses the films that register those same forces, even if this is frequently only through their purposeful absence. In the now decaying film cans of the archive and in the currently pristine digitized "copies" of some of this material we can still witness what territorial imperial power *looked like*—albeit power that mostly tried to hide its purposes and operations across the period of the "slow, fractious, blood-soaked decomposition of the British empire" and its replacement by an alternative but still bloody configuration of economic imperialism.[159]

9

League of Corporations

I will now sketch out the history of two further developments in the late 1920s that took place about the same time as the British state innovated the use of film to support liberal imperialism. Both are significant to a fuller understanding of how media was used to supplement liberal governance and a particular form of corporate and consumer capitalism. The first is the efforts made by the League of Nations to integrate film in various ways into its expansive agendas to establish a new liberal, and peaceful, world system after the global and imperialist conflict of 1914–18.[1] League officials, cooperating in the first global intergovernmental organization of the twentieth century, sought to develop a pedagogic cinema circulating outside commercial circuits, and bypassing the protectionist tariff systems of states, that would be capable of enabling "the mutual understanding of peoples."[2] Efforts bent toward these ends motivated numerous committees, international conferences, memorandums, scholarship, policy, and the creation of institutions to foster the public and governmental utility of cinema to help sustain a liberal internationalism to balance, if ultimately unevenly, welfare, collective security, and the mechanics of global trade. Cinema was integrated with geo- and biopolitical and economic agendas that transcended the nation-state to try to help establish a new, global, liberal capitalist world order. Humanitarian endeavors and successes coexisted, complexly, with biopolitical and economic agendas. Overall the league and its cultural, cinematic, armaments were consistent with one of the fundamental dynamics of liberalism—the establishment of "security" to create the possibility for liberalism's central tenet of "freedom." But this dynamic produced ever-increasing demands for "security," visible clearly in the "state of exception" emerging in the World War I years and intensifying thereafter, and this "freedom" was increasingly imagined in terms of the "free trade" that structurally benefited "advanced" industrial powers.

I am reluctant to give the end of this particular story away before we begin, but it is no great secret that these efforts to foster peace and provide global security did not turn out so well in the 1930s. The league, and its media culture, failed to sustain a liberal internationalism built shakily from old (mostly British and French) and new (American) imperial systems, in the context of the complex and partial transition from the world of formal empires to ostensibly sovereign states and national self-determination. Throughout the process, the league was hamstrung by the absence of the newly hegemonic United States from its official operations and challenged by the devastating economic crisis of the early 1930s and the (related) rise of fascism.[3] Even despite this failure, though, the league's extensive engagement with cinema across the tumultuous years of the 1920s and 1930s certainly marked a significant effort to use mass media to supplement a capacious liberalism. In the margins of these complex and sometimes contradictory efforts were new ideas about culture as a "public utility" that were distinct from the mostly already-established conceptions and practices of mass media as a commercial form, even if—as with the aforementioned example of the British Broadcasting Corporation—these practices were at times coarticulated with imperialist and economic agendas to "modernize" particular populations. Moreover, despite the fact the league ceased to be an effective force for global security in the mid-1930s, some of these conceptions of a cultural system complementing an interconnected capitalist world system were revived in the post–World War II settlement. The creation of the United Nations and its cultural arm UNESCO grew directly from the league, with significant transfer of personnel.[4] Recent scholarship on the league has examined it as part of a complex shift from formal empire to new patterns of economic imperialism.[5] In the aftermath of the league, its economic functions were hived off to other ostensibly international organizations—now though controlled largely by the United States—like the International Monetary Fund and the World Bank.[6] In this revised configuration of the liberal world system, with the United States now firmly central, the utopian—if always also flawed—inter-war dreams of cosmopolitan internationalism and of alternative media networks and structures of regulation were mostly cast aside to support the circulation of commercial American mass media that was integral to economic globalization and the spread of US "soft power" through the world system.

The second development, beginning in the late 1920s, examined here is the establishment of a policy for radio in the United States. I explore the debates about the financing and functioning of radio, which ranged from positions that regarded the medium as a public utility to those emanating from recently established telecommunications corporations, which proposed that radio be controlled by them and financed by corporate sponsorship and advertising. The Radio Act of 1927 and the Communications Act of 1934 in the United States enshrined this latter perspective into law. Radio and subsequent mass media—for example, television—emerged from this context as commercial forms tied into new forms of consumer capitalism, in contradistinction to the ideal of culture as a form of public utility embodied in the aforementioned example of the British Broadcasting Corporation and in some of the activities of the League of Nations.[7] The consequences of these debates about the function of media, solidifying into policy, were extremely significant. What started in the 1920s to be called "mass media" was increasingly aligned with the generation of capital and was tied into a globalizing system of corporate and consumer capitalism. It is axiomatic that advertiser-sponsored media designed to bring consumers together with corporate sponsors tends to be affirmative and rarely, if ever, challenges the configuration of the economic system it is tied to.

I make no pretense that these two examples from the same years of the late 1920s are directly connected. Even further than that, from some angles these two examples can be seen as diametrically opposed: one was the continuation of a dream of pedagogical culture that could be socially and economically useful for a global liberal order, while the other was the obsolescence of that conception of media as a public utility and the establishment of a form of commercial, privately owned media culture that mostly cast aside ideals of pedagogy to establish a model of corporate-financed media, which became increasingly dominant in liberal capitalist states thereafter. In some ways this can be seen as a story of failure and "success," in which the idea that media might be integrated into practices of pedagogy that were *somewhat* utopian and ethical were ultimately overridden by the use of mass media to supplement and straightforwardly expand corporate and consumer capitalism. (The detail of the history of the league in particular is more complicated than that suggests, since it was established as a component of a liberal, capitalist world system and, as I shall show shortly, became increasingly focused on reestablishing the mechanics of global trade.) Certainly, the parameters of these debates about media and culture, solidifying into policy, institutions, and established practices, marked crucial moments in residual and emergent and increasingly dominant conceptions of the function of culture and media for liberalism and a globalizing liberal capitalism.

"VISUAL ESPERANTO"

Cinema was quickly identified by the league's founders as a cultural form that had significant impact on the world system. This position was formed from the growing realization in the interwar period—after successful experiments with wartime propaganda—that cinema and mass media were crucial to the management and shaping of the attitudes and conduct of populations. British politicians and industrialists, for example, bemoaned this state of affairs in the 1920s while simultaneously working to establish new practices of regulation and cultural production. League officials similarly set to work to integrate "culture," and particularly cinema as a visual and ostensibly "universal" language, with the efforts to secure a new, liberal world order.

The participants in the first meeting of the league in 1919 discussed a proposal to establish a technical committee for culture alongside those for economic and social affairs, effectively proposing that the circulation of culture would function as a form of liberal security. In September 1921, the French representative Lèon Bourgeois, the first president of the league council, submitted a report on intellectual organization "urging improved and fuller exchange of documents in all branches of knowledge and calling upon the League to fortify its ideals through the intellectual life uniting the nations and favor educational enterprises and research study as important influences on opinion among peoples."[8] Bourgeois concern for the shaping of opinion was consistent with the widespread reflection on propaganda and what Walter Lippmann began calling "public opinion" in the aftermath of war.[9] League officials thus began from the recently established position that propaganda influenced public opinion, to propose the establishment of a forum for propaganda for peace and global security. Later, in 1924, the French government offered to permanently house an institute to foster "intercultural" interaction in Paris, and by 1926 the International Institute of Intellectual Cooperation had begun operations.

Right at the outset, the director of the institute, Julien Luchaire, submitted a report titled *Relations of the Cinematograph to Intellectual Life,* which acknowledged cinema as "a powerful medium for the diffusion of moral, social and even political ideas or modes of thought" and proposed that it might function as a form of visible liberal internationalism.[10] "This new and extraordinarily efficient instrument of intellectual action is intrinsically international," Luchaire wrote. "The mere possibility that the cinema might become a great new universal art should be the attention of all who have the intellectual future of humanity at heart."[11] Luchaire's conception of (then still silent) cinema as a form of universal language was consistent with earlier discussions of cinema as a form of what was sometimes called "visual Esperanto" but was now connected directly to a project of liberal internationalism. Luchaire proposed that the Committee for Intellectual Cooperation prepare the grounds for "a permanent international organization . . . to study all questions of interest in connection with the cinematograph industry," by holding an international congress.[12] It convened in Paris in 1926.

Luchaire and others hoped the congress would provide a forum to establish the efficacy of cinema for furthering the goals of the league. Many of the attendees similarly proposed that a new educational cinema could help international understanding and indeed that cinema might be reimagined as a public utility that would supplement forms of liberal welfare and internationalism. William Marston Seabury, whose 1926 book *The Public and the Motion Picture Industry* was widely distributed at the congress, put forward the most prominent argument for that perspective. Seabury, who had previously been a lawyer for the mainstream US film industry's first two trade associations, had participated in the founding of the Motion Picture Producers and Distributors of America (MPPDA), but he had grown disillusioned with the industry's economic structures of oligopoly and vertical integration and had turned himself into a prominent critic of the industry.[13] The motion picture had attained an "immense and virtually unchecked, uncontrolled and unregulated" power to "influence the masses of the world for good or evil," Seabury wrote, but the existing industrial and commercial regime militated against the appropriate use of this power.[14] What was needed, Seabury asserted, was an international movement to establish the legal status of the motion picture as "a new public utility" that could compel the industry "to consecrate its service to the cultivation and preservation of the world's peace and the moral, intellectual and cultural development of all people."[15] Seabury argued that cinema could be established as a public utility that could "uplift" populations in a way that was clearly consistent with "progressive" ideals and was connected to the broader investigation of the consequences of the newly emergent corporate economy, which flourished in the early years of the twentieth century, in the United States in particular. In making this argument, he took aim at the central economic structures of the mainstream American film industry, proposing that European states erect laws to disable vertical integration, the ownership of cinemas by foreign nationals, blind- and block-booking, and taxation on gross rentals.[16]

Seabury's argument, at its most radical, proposed a fundamental reorganization of the capitalist basis of media production. It was supplemented at the 1926 congress by more familiar calls for a moral regulation of cinema as a component of liberal biopolitical security. The primary contributor to that position came from the League's Child Welfare Committee, which had commenced investigating the effects of cinema on the "mental and moral well-being of children" in 1925, drawn up a list of global censorship statutes in advance of the congress in 1926, and produced further critical reports in 1928 and 1932.[17]

Both positions—on economic and moral/biopolitical regulation—spelled trouble for the mainstream film industry, and it is no surprise that the MPPDA in particular lobbied to dilute the resolutions of the congress and to sideline in particular Seabury's conception of cinema as a public utility. In his 1929 book *Motion Picture Problems* Seabury talked of the "secret trade diplomacy" of the MPPDA, which influenced the congress to propose that any concrete league body on cinema should centrally address "protecting in general the interests of the cinema industry."[18] Corporate power works to further its own interests. More recently cinema historian Andrew Higson has similarly discerned "a clear tension between the official League of Nations discourse of the conference and the discourse of business which came to dominate much of the proceedings," which confirms parts of

Seabury's account.[19] The possibility of a Pan-European trade agreement that would limit the incursion of US cinema was raised repeatedly in the 1920s, but it was never realized, a reflection Higson suggests of the lobbying power of the politically well-connected MPPDA, the economic interests of factions of the European film industry, and the general inefficiency of the bureaucratic league.

Equally important was the fact that Seabury and the Child Welfare Committee's call for regulation and protectionism ran directly counter to the aims and policies of the league as a whole to oppose national economic protectionism and foster a newly reconfigured liberal world system. The history of the establishment of the league and of its economic operations is key here. Woodrow Wilson mapped out the terms of a postwar settlement to the US Congress in early 1918 in his famous Fourteen Points address, which included the principle of maintaining open seaways to facilitate global trade; the "removal, so far as possible, of all economic barriers and the establishment of an equality of trade conditions;" and the founding of a "general association of nations" to establish new patterns of diplomacy, to further national self-determination, and to provide a forum for collective security.[20] Wilson's agenda helped frame the Paris peace talks in 1919 and the establishment thereafter of the League of Nations.[21] The overriding objective of the US position was the reestablishment of a liberal capitalist world system that had been substantially damaged by the war and challenged directly by the Soviet revolution.[22] (Wilson's Fourteen Points declaration was in this respect a clear response to Lenin's call for the rise of a global proletariat—all the while many Western powers were supporting both counterrevolutionary forces in Russia and newly created states in Eastern Europe as bulwarks against communism.)[23] Liberal internationalism was predicated on the establishment of an "open door" economic policy that envisaged a world of free trade, with economic progress emerging from equal competition in world markets.[24] In this way the liberal agenda of minimal government intervention cooperating with private industrial and capital interests to facilitate economic expansion was transferred from the domestic sphere to the international arena. Wilson's delegation to Paris accordingly included "such internationalist representatives of Wall Street as Morgan's Thomas Lamont," who was charged with reestablishing a system "similar to the classically liberal British" world order, albeit one with the United States now established at the commanding heights of the world economy.[25]

Wilson's Fourteen Points declaration had been produced by a cadre of advisors working in a secret group, called "the Inquiry," which had been set up by Wilson and his chief advisor "Colonel" Edward House.[26] (Walter Lippmann, incidentally, was recruited to a central role within this group, and I shall return to Lippmann's related influential thinking about the postwar transformations of democracy and the necessity of establishing an administrative technocratic elite using media to govern mass populations in the following chapter.)[27] Wilson and House's Inquiry proposed the partial expansion of the ideal of "freedom" and "rights" intrinsic to liberalism to a global stage—for example, new conceptions of national self-determination, albeit in practice principally only for white populations—and fused this with the classically liberal emphasis on the "free" movement of materials and capital across the globe.[28] Liberal internationalism sought thereafter to "balance" ethical principles in foreign policy with the imperatives to protect and foster trade and capital flows.[29] But this was, and has subsequently been, an uneven balancing act, heavily weighted toward the latter imperatives, even if the league's liberal internationalism did produce progressive transformations of international law; of the management of displaced people; and of humanitarian developments, in particular in terms of social, labor, and health problems.[30]

In any case, in order to forestall a longer discussion, let me simply state that I am positioning the league as a component of a "liberal internationalism" that framed the capitalist world system in both its territorial (and British) and economic (and American) imperialist formations and generated new apparatuses of "security" principally (though not solely) to uphold open markets.

Recent research on the league has indeed emphasized the increasing centrality of economic analysis and policy to its central operations and even "self identity."[31] The Economic and Financial Section (EFO) of the league had been set up in 1920 to help prepare an International Financial Conference, to be held in Geneva to reestablish global trade. In 1923 the EFO worked together with the Bank of England, and the House of Morgan, to devise a multilateral program of private and intergovernmental financial support to bail out the struggling postwar economy of Austria.[32] Unsurprisingly, the country was required to establish a central bank and return to the gold standard. Very similar conditions were imposed on Hungary and Greece in 1923.[33] (Morgan also helped finance the US Dawes plan in 1924, which committed two hundred million dollars to help stabilize the German mark and regularized reparations payments).[34] League officials cooperated also with significant banks and multinational corporations to reestablish the mechanics of the gold standard, beginning most substantively in 1924 (and so preceding the short-lived British return to the standard in 1925).[35] Bureaucrats within the league worked also to try to reduce the economic protectionism that increased in the postwar moment and threatened the global movement of materials and capital. In 1927 the league convened the World Economic Conference with experts in social science, finance, industry, and agriculture advocating for the reestablishment of a liberal world system. The director of the Federation of British Industries, for example, spoke at the conference in support of free trade—albeit at about the same time the federation was lobbying the British government to curtail the movement of American films.[36] Following on from this, in London in 1933, the league called for the abolition of tariffs and quota legislation.[37] The MPPDA specifically cited this position when it opposed the efforts of the British and French to limit the circulation of the products of its corporate sponsors.[38]

In short, the league took on central roles in reestablishing a liberal internationalism predicated principally on trade and monetary policy. Economic questions were fundamental to the design of the organization and became increasingly central to its functioning, particularly in light of the economic depressions of the early and late 1920s. In this respect the broader goals of the league to establish the terms of a peaceful global system were framed increasingly by the imperatives of maintaining and extending the circulation central to economic globalization.

Quite clearly, then, the failure of the 1926 Paris congress to enact protectionist legislation, and to further Seabury's radical conceptions of cinema as a form of public utility, was of a piece with this increasing focus on engineering economic globalization. Cinema was ultimately more "productive" as a component of that process, as the State and Commerce Departments of the United States had began to realize beginning in the mid-1920s, closely followed by worried British imperial administrators. When the inconclusive 1926 congress ended with a resolution to hold another conference about cinema the following year, then, the lobbying power of the MPPDA in particular helped force a delay.[39] In response to this commercial intervention into the workings of the league, the representatives of the International Institute for Intellectual Cooperation resigned en masse. By the time the conference took place, in Berlin in 1928 it was, as Higson remarks, "entirely a trade organised event."[40] League officials thereafter mostly avoided engagement with the economics of the mainstream US film industry. Cultural protectionism, as a component of the response to economic globalization, remained outside the jurisdiction of a league increasingly invested in fostering "free" trade.

In the midst of these delays and struggles, the league instead took up an offer by Benito Mussolini and the Italian state to establish a permanent home for consideration of the global pedagogic use of cinema, to be called the International Educational Cinematographic Institute (L'Instituo Internazionale di Cinema Educativo, or L'IICE). Mussolini gave a speech at the opening of L'IICE in 1928;[41] and was apparently a regular attendee of the film screenings it put on in a newly established film theater in the grand Villa Torlonia in Rome, which Mussolini gifted to the institute.[42] What did the fascist dictator see in liberal, educational, cinema? Quite a number of things, it seems. Mussolini's establishment of the Rome Institute was part of a strategy to insert Italy into the heart of Europe, in particular here through contesting French and German dominance of European film production.[43] Likewise, the institute advanced the efforts of the fascist state to establish film as part of its media agenda. In this respect, L'IICE carried on from "L' Unione Cinematografica Educativa" (LUCE), the Italian state film agency set up in 1924, which began producing and distributing newsreels and documentaries from 1927.[44] L'IICE, for example, had its director, Luciana de Feo, drawn directly from LUCE.[45] Both institutions were clearly part of the Italian fascist state's recognition of the necessity to produce and manage mass media. Indeed, given that LUCE was partly inspired by the Soviet experiments to use cinema as an ideological weapon (as to some extent was the British innovation of documentary), we can discern a rather dizzying mix of state systems—communist, fascist, liberal, liberal imperialist—investing in cinema as mass media as a component of governance in the 1920s.[46]

What did the institute do? Various things designed to foster cinema's utility for "education" broadly conceived. It established committees to examine the use of film in the fields of health and hygiene; it promoted the modernization of agricultural practices (with echoes of the earlier agendas of the USDA and its media strategies); it drew up lists of educational film groups; and it fostered the study of the effects of cinema (sending out two hundred thousand questionnaires to children) and of global censorship statutes.[47] Along the way it established a monthly multilingual cinema studies journal, which included varied investigations of the utility and sometimes the danger of cinema that stands now as a fascinating glimpse into a moment of global media analysis long since fragmented and dissipated.[48] Readable still, albeit in now mostly dusty and unused volumes, are accounts of censorship in Lithuania, military instruction by means of film, labor contracts in the German film industry, hygiene films in Latin America, religious cinematography in India, the contribution of cinema to public health in rural districts, authors' rights in Iraq, and so on, mostly in a sustained effort to figure out how cinema could be regulated and made useful for various projects of governance.

L'IICE's rhetoric around regulation in particular was more voluble than its actions, in part because the MPPDA "had taken early action to defuse the Institute's dangerous potential and attach de Feo to its own public relations campaign."[49] When de Feo visited the United States in the winter of 1928–29, he was given "every aid and help" by the MPPDA's staff, who took him also to Washington where "a number of days were spent . . . going through different government departments interested in motion pictures."[50] The connection between a corporate lobbying organization and government departments is but another example of the corporate-state nexus in action. And also, incidentally, of how widely influential the model of pedagogic filmmaking established by the US state was. After this visit, Carl Milliken, the MPPDA's secretary, was appointed to the institute's governing body, and George Canty, the Department of Commerce's trade commissioner for Motion Pictures in Europe, became a member of L'IICE's executive committee.[51] In this way the MPPDA and its allies in the US state effectively obtained considerable influence over the workings of L'IICE. Richard Maltby has suggested this influence was used to defuse growing criticism of the morality and effects of Hollywood film and the trade policies of US studios. One example of this, he proposes, is the scant attention paid to a major multivolume critical study on the effects of cinema on children that was sponsored by the philanthropic Payne Fund in the late 1920s and early 1930s in the pages of the *International Review of Educational Cinematography*.[52] (I discuss those investigations in the following chapter, as well as the

MPPDA's efforts to discredit them.) With Milliken and Canty's input, de Feo steered L'IICE away from activities that affected the economic objectives of corporate media.

Even further, some of the league and L'IICE's work in relation to film straightforwardly buttressed the economic agendas of other corporate lobbying groups in ways that were consistent with the broader remit of the league to reestablish and stabilize a liberal capitalist world system. Quickly after its establishment, for example, L'IICE began examining how cinema could be integrated with new practices of scientific management to rationalize work practices and make them more "efficient." We can see this as consistent with some of the Fordist practices examined earlier in this book. The second session of the governing body of L'IICE in October 1929 noted that the institute had "entered into relations" with "the Scientific Management Institute," and this was further buttressed with a report in the *International Review of Educational Cinematography*.[53] "The cinematographic projections used for educational purposes are a means of propaganda," said the journal, "they improve the methods of production, discern childish tendencies, spread the knowledge of machineries with their various systems and the means by which labour accidents are prevented, becoming thereby a real benefit to modern society."[54] Likewise the journal published an article entitled "The Film in the Service of Scientific Management" in January 1930 that referenced Henry Ford's "masterly description of the advantages of scientific management" and explained how films were made of "employees engaged on their particular jobs" which were "later shown in slow motion to the individuals concerned, who were thus able to study their own actions while at work, to observe defects, and correct wasteful or unnecessary movements."[55] The technology of film was harnessed to the extraction of surplus value from laboring bodies, and the "benefits" of this were circulated through the auspices of the League of Nations. A special issue of the journal was devoted to "The Cinema and Scientific Management."[56]

Our old friends the Federation of British Industries was involved with this endeavor to make cinema useful for new industrial practices.[57] Titles for the films listed as useful in the pages of the *International Review of Educational Cinematography* were drawn principally from those produced or distributed by the federation evangelizing for new industrial practices, including *The Magic of Nitrate of Soda, Reinforced Concrete, Modern Lighting,* and *The Romance of Oil* (which I strongly suspect was not quite as "romantic" and, shall we say, interesting as it sounds).[58] In short, a powerful industrial lobbying group, which had the clout to influence public policy in Britain, proposed that the league be a useful space to disseminate films that could make workers more efficient and that could work as propaganda for a procorporate worldview. The league supported this endeavor, for it was fundamental to its remit to restart a liberal capitalist world system.

The "educational" goals of the league carried through cinema were in this way straightforwardly utilitarian and developmental. Similar imperatives were at play in the league's orchestration of both the study of the effects of cinema on "backward races" and the circulation of films to those populations as part of the imperative to "modernize" them enough to participate in the operations of global capitalism. These efforts were carried out in cooperation with the imperial British state, which were similarly invested in this period in examining how films were received by subaltern African populations in particular, in order to better use the technology of cinema to further practices of imperial extraction and exploitation. Accordingly the British League of Nations wrote to the League's Committee on Intellectual Cooperation in April 1932, drawing attention to the ongoing British investigation of the effects of cinema on African audiences, including in subsequent correspondence material from the Colonial Office and the aforementioned Commission on Educational and Cultural Films.[59] Responding to this, the governing body of L'IICE included the issue in its agenda for its annual meeting in 1932, wherein it resolved that "the adjustment of cinematographic production to the needs and mentalities of different peoples is a question deserving of the attention of all official administration or specialised associations which are anxious to prevent the cinematograph having a pernicious influence, whereas a judicious utilisation might, on the contrary, have beneficial effects in developing the native culture of different peoples."[60] L'IICE liaised with the Mandates Commission about this question of the biopolitical regulation and use of cinema—the same commission, that is, that enabled the continuation of European colonial practices under the guise of benevolent guidance while marking the gradual shift toward new models of economic imperialism run by ostensibly neutral international institutions.[61]

Following on from this, L'IICE circulated questionnaires in 1933 to its corresponding members about the effects of cinema on "peoples whose civilization and mentality differ from those of the western world." Over fifteen hundred replies were received, giving "serious food for thought," the chairman of the Institute wrote, "as to the disastrous effects which the cinema has had on a number of countries and even throughout whole continents as regards the manner in which our western civilization is conceived of and judged by peoples who may have identified it with the more or less immoral, doubtful and amoral vision which the screen conjures up for them."[62] The British Bantu Educational Kinema Experiments to work out the ways cinema might be utilized to further the productivity and docility of workers in the East African Copperbelt were shared with the league.[63] In short, a league ostensibly marking the end of the organizing principles of imperialism helped the circulation of studies about the regulation and production of cinema and other media to foster the utility of colonized populations.

Circulation of pedagogic filmic material of various kinds was central to the league's long-running efforts to enable "educational" films to escape the tariffs associated with protectionist state policies. Finally signed in 1933, by representatives from the governments of twenty-three states, after four years of debate, the Convention for Facilitating the International Circulation of Films of an Educational Character exempted from customs duties films intended for use in education and research.[64] Its preamble stated that the league was "convinced that it is highly desirable to facilitate the international circulation of educational films of every kind, which contribute towards the mutual understanding of peoples, in conformity with the aims of the League of Nations and consequently encourage moral disarmament or which constitute especially effective means of ensuring physical, intellectual and moral progress."[65] Cinematic liberal internationalism was enabled, appropriately enough, by a free trade agreement fostered by a league increasingly focused in the early 1930s on economic matters.[66] Even here, the high point of a cultural liberal internationalism, the language of "progress" betrayed the imperialist and "modernizing" logic at work and the fundamental sense that Western culture equaled universal culture.[67]

L'IICE's shepherding of the convention through a long process of negotiation was celebrated at the International Congress on Education by the Cinematograph held under the auspices of L'IICE in Rome in April 1934.[68] Educational cinema helping various populations "develop" now circulated free of the economic protectionism that, as we have seen, rose dramatically in the wake of the catastrophic depression that began in the United States in 1929 and spread across the world in the 1930s. But the institute's finest hour was one of its last. The dream of a liberal internationalism reborn from the ashes of World War I began to fade with the rise of fascism, partly from the embers of the demands of liberal states and their bankers for excessive reparations and the repayment of war debts. Hitler acceded to power in 1933. Italy invaded Ethiopia in 1935, in pursuit of empire, using chemical warfare and killing perhaps hundreds of thousands of Ethiopians.[69] (News footage of Italian journalists shamefully barracking Ethiopian emperor Haile Sellassie while he was condemning the brutal Italian invasion before the League of Nations in 1936 still exists on YouTube.) But league inaction, aside from a few modest sanctions, compounded their inability to respond to the earlier Japanese invasion of Manchuria and effectively marked the end of its functioning as a forum for global security.[70] Germany, Italy, Japan, and even Soviet Russia for a time, fostered an alliance that challenged the hegemony of liberal capitalism, amid growing signs in the 1930s that such a system was foundering. L'IICE closed its doors in 1937, when Italy withdrew from a league now described by Mussolini as a "tottering temple," as the end of this experiment with a cultural liberal internationalism was transformed into autarchic fascist cinema and media systems that seemed to be terrifyingly powerful in their abilities to persuade mass populations of the virtues of violent, barbaric, racially defined nationalism.[71] I return to some aspects of, and reflections on, that history in the next chapter.

"GOVERNMENT SANCTIONED MONOPOLY"

Before that, though, I want to examine another forum for debates and decisions about mass media as either a form of public utility, as pedagogy, or as a commercial form fully synced together with the rise of a new form of consumer economy. The example is now radio, another media form dependent on the technological developments of the second industrial revolution, and the policy decisions made specifically in the United States in the aftermath of World War I and in the 1920s and early 1930s. I explore how radio developed ultimately as a communicative form controlled by corporations in terms of ownership—by significant institutions like General Electric (GE) backed with money from finance capital—as well as in terms of the financing system for radio supported by advertising that was solidified in policy decisions between 1927 and 1934, despite considerable opposition from various people and institutions arguing that radio should be constituted as a public utility. Elsewhere, in Britain and other parts of Europe, in Canada, and in the Soviet Union, for example, radio was established along "public service" lines. Lobbyists for technology and emergent technology and media corporations in the United States, however, wielded considerable power in enacting the privatization of the electromagnetic commons and framing a system that maximized the role of the market in defining the function of radio. In doing so they were supported by government officials like Herbert Hoover at the Department of Commerce, who constructed a liberal "associative state" characterized by close ties between (supposedly) self-regulating corporate and financial institutions and the state.[72] The "American system" of broadcasting, as it came to be known, became widely influential over the course of the twentieth century, tied together with corporate-led and state-supported practices of economic globalization.

What follows examines the development and use of radio technology as a crucial part of the history of corporate and state cooperation in elaborating new communicative and media systems that were functional for liberal political economy. I stray some distance from cinema, again, and while this is consistent with my interest in film as a component of mass media and in the corporate and state uses of media, it is worth noting at the outset three points of direct connection between radio and cinema in the 1920s and 1930s. Hollywood stars were frequently central to the new advertising practices of radio in the 1930s (as they had been to the state practices to sell war debt in 1917–18). Stars became exemplars of a new consumer economy and one of the primary spaces for that enactment was a radio system financed through advertising. Likewise, genres established in film were often transported to radio, creating new intermedial forms.[73] Finally, the corporations developing radio played significant roles in establishing the sonic technology that was welded to the visual technology of moving pictures to create a "synergistic" sound cinema in the late 1920s. Consequential ties were established here between finance capital, large technology companies, and media corporations. I explore that history further in chapter 11.

How the chaotic development of radio technology around the turn of the century, often driven by independent inventors, was transformed into corporate property is certainly a useful lesson in how state and corporate objectives combined to retool media to make it useful for particular geopolitical and economic goals. US naval officials became interested in radio technology around the turn of the century, to better facilitate point-to-point communication that bypassed the British controlled underwater cable networks.[74] The navy fostered the development of radio technology, then, as part of a broader geopolitical strategy to challenge the British control of the communicative networks important to state communication, "national security," and the circulation central to new patterns of global capitalism. Working closely with the corporations busy buying up the patents associated with radio technology—in particular GE, Westinghouse, American Telephone and Telegraph (AT&T), and United Fruit—the navy constructed a high-powered radio chain in 1915, with stations adjacent to the Panama Canal and in Pearl Harbor, Puerto Rico, the Philippines, and Guam.[75] Communicative networks closely mirrored the quest to achieve a territorial foothold and access to commodities, markets, and labor, in particular in China and Latin America.

Cooperation between the military and new corporate entities turned into partnership when America entered the war. The government instituted a freeze on the amateur radio broadcasting that had emerged in scattered fashion in the early years of the twentieth century, another example of the state control of communication and media as an aspect of "national security," which developed in the war years. Wartime exigencies led the state to bypass European companies, notably the powerful British Marconi and German Telefunken, and to a moratorium on patent infringements that enabled GE, Westinghouse, and AT&T in particular to advance technological developments free from litigation and with financial support from the military.[76] Civilian-military cooperation produced technology capable of distant point-to-point communication, which was initially prioritized, but also capable of "broadcasting" messages to diverse audiences. Woodrow Wilson's aforementioned Fourteen Points address extolling the virtues of a liberal system of global free trade was thus broadcast widely, including to Germany, and the navy reported that it was "cooperating with the State Department and the Committee on Public Information in the broadcasting of information of advantage to the United States in all parts of the world by high-power radio."[77] Radio broadcasting emerged rather as an afterthought to point-to-point, "narrowcasting," communication, but it quickly became apparent that control over communication and media was integral to various military and state objectives.

Wilson had reportedly been greatly impressed with the reach of the broadcast of his Fourteen Points address, and while he was in Paris in 1919 negotiating the Versailles Treaty, he cabled back urging GE not to sell its technology to the American subsidiary of the British Marconi Company.[78] GE's corporate officers were encouraged instead to establish a new American-controlled company, with significant support from the military and the state. In October 1919, the Radio Corporation of America (RCA) was established, with GE owning 25 percent of the shares, with Westinghouse owning 20 percent, with AT&T owning 4 percent, and with the rest held by individuals and smaller companies.[79] (GE, Westinghouse, and AT&T, you will recall, all received significant backing from the House of Morgan, and bankers from Morgan played significant roles on the board of RCA.)[80] The state effectively backed US corporations, and finance capital, in the creation of a hugely significant communications and media organization—what Susan Douglas has called a "government sanctioned monopoly"—as part of its geopolitical objectives.[81] Corporations cooperated with the military and the state to further their economic interests. Media was made corporate, and American, in ways that illustrate again the import of the control of media to states; the emergence and intensification of military-industry cooperation; and, relatedly, the developing corporate/state nexus and oligopolistic corporate practices of the interwar period.

Cross-licensing agreements to share patent technology and maintain oligopolistic control were worked out in the immediate postwar period, initially between RCA and GE, then between GE and AT&T, and finally with the addition of Westinghouse and United Fruit, which also owned significant patents, to form what was called the Radio Group in 1921. Radio technology was now embedded in interlocking corporate grids, making RCA "a civilian version of the military monopoly that had controlled radio during the war."[82] GE, Westinghouse, and AT&T began to set up initial broadcasting stations amid uncertainty about how the patents agreements extended to broadcasting and about the nature of that broadcasting. WEAF, established by AT&T in New York City in 1922, was among the most significant, because it sold airtime to companies wishing to promote products—so-called toll broadcasting—that provided a model for later developments. In January 1923, AT&T linked WEAF first with its Boston station, then with its station in Chicago, and by 1924 it had an experimental coast-to-coast operation consisting of twenty-three stations, inaugurated with a speech by President Calvin Coolidge.[83] GE and Westinghouse established broadcast stations but struggled to create as effective a network because AT&T controlled the long-distance telephone wires connecting cities.

Various other broadcast stations emerged, run by amateurs and other institutions, including universities and labor, civic, and religious groups. Universities used radio technology as part of their extension remit, as they had done with moving pictures.[84] Likewise, the USDA, such a significant early innovator of pedagogic moving pictures, used radio to broadcast weather and market prices to farmers in rural America, as well as instructional "messages about how farm families should behave."[85] Much of this repeated the efforts to utilize cinematic technology to educate particular populations. Indeed, some reformers saw in radio the perfect mechanism to "uplift" the cultural tastes of the masses, as they had with "educational" and nontheatrical cinema.[86]

The chaotic cacophony of the electromagnetic commons emerging after the war, divided broadly speaking between commercial and nonprofit imperatives, required government regulation to ensure broadcast clarity. Hoover's Department of Commerce initially allocated to amateur broadcasters the less powerful shortwave spectrums and to corporate stations the more powerful media-wave spectrums, and then established a series of annual radio conferences, which ran from 1922 to 1925, to further clarify how the electromagnetic spectrum would be used and to enable the commercial broadcasters to establish a system of self-regulation.[87] Hoover relied on the technical expertise supplied by the research departments of RCA, AT&T, GE, and Westinghouse. In 1923 the conference divided radio stations into three classes—high, medium, and low power—assigning the most-preferred and least-congested wavelengths to the stations owned by AT&T, GE, and Westinghouse and the lower-power stations to universities, churches, and labor unions. These station were also required to time-share, and many were allowed to broadcast only during the day. In this way the "state remained an important ally of corporate interests, legitimating their often preemptive claims to the spectrum, and constraining the transmitting activities of those with less power and money," in the process straightforwardly marginalizing diversity in the public sphere.[88] The third conference in 1924 focused on the establishment of radio networks, which effectively supported the model of broadcasting being developed by AT&T, not to mention their monopolistic control of wired networks.[89] Local specificity would be overridden in the creation of national networks controlled by corporations.

Beginning in the late 1920s, and more substantially through the 1930s, these networks were used to promote newly national brands and thus played a crucial role in the dissemination of the ideals of a consumer culture. The network system dovetailed with other aspects of state policy—from the creation of railroads to road networks—creating interconnected material and symbolic networks that facilitated the circulation of people, goods, messages, and capital. Applying a metaphor making some of these connections apparent, in the aftermath of the 1921 Federal-Aid Highway Act, the celebrated president of RCA, David Sarnoff, talked at the 1924 conference of the development of "national highways of the air."[90] (It seems to be from about 1929 on that these highway networks were synergistically connected—when the first car radios were installed.)[91]

Hoover and Sarnoff's shared dream of national network broadcasting came closer to realization in the aftermath of the final radio conference in 1925, when further intracorporate patent agreements ironed out ongoing disputes between AT&T and RCA, GE, and Westinghouse. AT&T sold WEAF to RCA and agreed to stay out of the ownership and operation of broadcast stations in return for RCA's pledge to keep out of wire transmission. In exchange for guaranteed access to lines, RCA agreed to pay AT&T a minimum annual fee of $1 million for ten years—quite a significant sum, indeed, for a media form whose profit-making potential was still somewhat uncertain.[92] RCA clearly operated on the assumption that a networked system, whereby programs were relayed from station to station, could make an advertising-supported model of broadcasting sustainable and profitable, because it offered advertisers access to a national public.

In 1926, after signing the agreements with AT&T, RCA created the National Broadcasting Company (NBC), relaying programs mostly produced in New York City across its developing network. Sarnoff envisaged NBC supporting mostly institutional advertising through program sponsorship.[93] The following year a second national network was created, Columbia Phonograph Broadcasting System (CBS).[94] CBS was run by cigar magnate William Paley. In early 1929, Paley convinced Adolph Zukor, head of Paramount, the largest studio chain in Hollywood, and owner of the largest chain of movie theatres in the world, to invest $3.8 million for a 50 percent ownership stake. Zukor imagined the network could help advertise Paramount stars and films. In the early 1930s, suffering losses in the depression, Paramount went bankrupt and Paley collaborated with Wall Street banking firm Brown Bros. to buy back its shares. (The banker's representative on the Columbia board was Prescott S. Bush, father of President George H. W. Bush and grandfather of President George W. Bush, an interesting conjuncture of finance capital, media networks, and political power.)[95] CBS included institutional advertising, like the aforementioned "Ford Sunday Evening Hour," which ran from 1934 to 1942, but also pioneered direct advertising that offered advertisers sixty-second ads unrelated to the program.[96] Hollywood stars were regularly used to advertise a wide range of products.[97] Particularly significant were products, such as new beauty products, directed at women, part of the effort to incorporate women into an expanding consumer culture—predicated frequently on display—that made use of radio technology to penetrate the domestic sphere. Radios themselves were frequently advertised as a form of domesticated, feminine technology.

In 1926 the *U.S. v. Zenith Radio Corporation* case, disputing the organization of frequency assignments, effectively disbanded previous legislation over radio and so speeded the passage through Congress of the bills resulting from the fourth radio conference, helped along its way by the powerful commercial industry's lobbying arm the National Association of Broadcasters (NAB).[98] The 1927 Radio Act established the Federal Radio Commission (FRC) to provide regulation of broadcasting. With barely any congressional or public oversight, the procommercial broadcasting FRC instituted a general reallocation in 1928, which assigned all stations to new frequency assignments. CBS and NBC were the clear victors in the reallocation and assignment of property rights in the electromagnetic commons.[99] Indeed, the FRC opposed some noncommercial broadcasters, like the nonprofit "Voice of Labor" WCFL station in Chicago, which had its power allowance and broadcast hours limited by the FRC, by defining them as "propaganda" stations because they articulated particular viewpoints.[100] Education was redefined as propaganda, and the FRC worked from the liberal capitalist assumption that the market was best equipped to allocate interests and resources. CBS and NBC, financed by corporations and fully synced up with corporate America, had little interest in broadcasting the voices of labor, though they were happy to broadcast profitable corporate propaganda like the "Ford Sunday Evening Hour."

In the wake of this, a sophisticated media critique and broadcast reform emerged, arguing—like Seabury had with moving pictures—for the idea of culture as a form of public utility. Robert McChesney outlines the compelling arguments, made by individuals and institutions about the dangers of a corporate-controlled media system, that he believes have continuing validity today in the face of the ongoing urgent need to transform corporate media to enable democracy to be established and to flourish.[101] The commercial broadcasters, and their well-connected and funded lobby group NAB, thwarted these efforts, supported by powerful members of Congress and indeed by Presidents Hoover and then Roosevelt. (CBS, incidentally, hired the pioneer of public relations Edward Bernays as part of this campaign. I examine the work of Bernays and the emergence of public relations as a way of using media for probusiness goals in the following chapter.)[102] In 1934 the Communications Act was passed, which restated the radio charter of the Radio Act of 1927 and created a permanent Federal Communications Commission that functioned as an industry-controlled, self-regulatory body and effectively removed fundamental broadcasting issues from congressional consideration thereafter. "The political battle for the control of U.S. broadcasting, including television as well as radio," McChesney explains, "was now concluded. The various elements of the broadcast reform movement unraveled and disappeared in short order."[103] Corporate interests, with close ties to the political system, now controlled a crucial forum for the shaping and control of public opinion. Broadcasting policy embodied the corporate, liberal ideal of a benign cooperation between a supposedly self-regulating corporate sector networked with the state.[104]

The decisions about radio and mass media made and enacted in this period were probably the most consequential of the modern age: they enabled corporations to gain control over a newly emergent mass media and so, simply, extended corporate influence and power; they defined the principle role of media as bringing audiences as consumers together with corporate capital, in the process producing persuasive forms beamed into homes to incite the desire to consume that is fundamental to the expansionary nature of corporate-consumer capital; they ensured that mass media—owned and financed by corporations—would principally support the goals of corporations, in the process also increasing corporate influence over the political process; and they removed debate about the private control of media and communication from that "democratic" political process. Finally and simply, the decisions made about radio in this period shaped the subsequent decisions made about television, the most significant form of mass media in the second half of the twentieth century, which joined the technologies and practices of cinema and radio together. Ownership and "sponsorship," or advertising, shape media, as Noam Chomsky and Edward Herman, among others, have made evident in compelling, empirical detail, and constrain the possibility of democracy.[105] Civic, labor, religious, and reform groups all fought to oppose corporate domination of the mass media, particularly after the 1927 Radio Act, believing—correctly—that independent media is crucial to the enactment and practice of democracy. Corporate power, supported by the policies of the liberal associative state, won out, and the results were a radical diminution of the prospects for establishing and sustaining democracy. The arguments of the broadcast reformers of the 1920s and 1930s, that corporate media radically limits the public sphere, remain as true today as they were then. Democratic governance, the rule of the many as opposed to the few, requires the transformation of this media system and the fostering of alternative, noncommercial, media.

The corporations and policy makers invested in controlling media, like the businesses that were spending millions by the late 1920s on advertising, worked on the assumption that media shapes the attitudes and conduct of people. Beginning in the 1920s, corporate philanthropies began to investigate those assumptions. The next chapter examines the ideas that informed these conceptions of the power of media and the malleability of people, as well as the ways they were developed into new persuasive strategies and systems to try to "engineer consent" to the new corporate and consumer order of things.

The Silver Chains of Mimesis

I return here to the history of the ideas that people are suggestible and imitative and to the related practices of mass persuasion carried through media that grew from those ideas. Earlier I suggested that emergent ideas in what came to be called crowd psychology, sociology, psychology, and psychoanalysis in the late nineteenth century began to challenge and transform preexisting liberal and Cartesian conceptions of a bounded rational subject—including the Smithian self-interested individual—and instead began to suggest that the subject was divided, irrational, and essentially social and was thus derived from relationships with others. Questions of mimesis became central to the liberal human and social sciences as they expanded in universities in the latter years of the nineteenth century. New ideas about suggestibility and imitation functioned as something like a pivot, or hinge point, for the liberal management of media, for on the one hand they underpinned regulatory concerns about the mimetic mass audience, while on the other they suggested that media might be used as part of the management of populations. Ideas about the malleability of people and the mimetic power of media were put into play in early propaganda organizations like the vast exercise of mass persuasion that was quickly pioneered as the Committee on Public Information (CPI). These ideas were further reflected on and refined in the post–World War I years, in particular with respect to "propaganda" and the practices of public relations (PR) and advertising.

What emerged were new ideas about, and strategies of, governance that used symbolic communication and mass media to try to shape what started to be called "public opinion." "Propaganda is a concession to the wilfulness [*sic*] of the age," Harold Lasswell concluded in his 1927 book *Propaganda Technique in the World War.* "The bonds of personal loyalty and affection which bound a man to his chief have long since dissolved. Monarchy and class privilege have gone the way of all flesh . . . If the mass will be free of chains of iron, it must accept its chains of silver."[1] The rise of "mass society" and the slow spread of forms of democracy called for new practices of state control and use of media that encompassed censorship, policy, and production. Lasswell's influential reflections on the necessity of propaganda rhymed with broader revisions of the tenets of classical liberalism emerging in the turn-of-the-century period, which began to shift away from the rather abstract conceptions of "freedom" toward the proposition that "social control" and the (silver-tinged) "manufacture of consent" were necessary to the security of an already-existing political and economic order.[2] Broadly speaking, this marked a shift within and mutation of liberalism toward the security-based problems of protecting US society from ostensibly antidemocratic or otherwise threatening forces that emerged in the "Progressive Era." The shift was particularly visible during the war, during the Red Scare of its aftermath, and arguably thereafter in US political liberalism, particularly from the Cold War through the War on Terror.[3] In such "exceptional times," the state takes on greater responsibility for controlling, monitoring, and producing media.

Simultaneously the new PR professionals and the growing advertising industry began to use the insights from the psychological and social sciences, together with media, to accustom people to the new order of corporate capitalism and to try to persuade them to cast away ideals of thrift and self-sufficiency, which were ill suited to an age of mass production, and instead to want consumer objects they did not necessarily need and frequently could not afford. Wartime propaganda was copied and retooled for business. "The World War," Edward Bernays wrote, "left business astounded at what the technique of propaganda had accomplished in the conflict."[4] Visual, "persuasive," mass media, exemplified initially by cinema but fundamentally transmedial, was frequently central to this process. Cinema and the stars of the silver screen were deployed by Wilson and Creel during World War I and were subsequently used to visualize, embody, and "engineer consent" to the transformation of democracy into consumerism and the related replacement of citizen with consumer, which took place most clearly in the 1920s.[5] (At this point the divisions between wealthy and poor became the most extreme in the twentieth century; they have, though, recently been surpassed.)[6] Lines of connection can be drawn quite precisely from new ideas about malleable and irrational people and crowds, to new disciplinary configurations in the university, propaganda, new state practices, PR, and new strategies of advertising—including political advertising—as well as to the policies that shaped popular media as a form that was financed by corporate capital to turn audiences into consumers.

One simple and small example of a part of that PR process in action can be useful for orientation here before the more complex and wide-ranging discussion to follow. In 1924 CPI alumnus and "counsel on public Relations" Edward Bernays was engaged to help presidential candidate Calvin Coolidge with his reelection campaign.[7] Bernays later told the story, in his memoirs and in interviews, of how he set to work to persuade a host of stage and screen stars to visit Coolidge for breakfast at the White House and then to have the news and photographs of this "pseudoevent"—to borrow Walter Lippmann's term—distributed widely to media outlets.[8] Coolidge was serenaded on the White House lawn by Al Jolson, soon to be star of convergent sound cinema. Bernays reflected that this "spectacular publicity"—meaning, publicity through spectacle—"jutted out of the routine of circumstances and *made* news."[9] Writing about this event a few years later, in an article baldly titled "Putting Politics on the Market," Bernays suggested that associating Coolidge with stars appealed to the populations that liked "amusements."[10] Coolidge was "humanized"—one of the common goals of political and corporate PR—and lightly dusted with the glamour of stardom for the mass audience for "amusements." Bernays benefited because he cannily represented some of the stars. Coolidge was reelected to his second term and famously declared shortly thereafter that "The business of America is business." In 1929 this was followed by another Republican administration, headed by the former commerce secretary Herbert Hoover, toward the end of the first period of the ascendancy of a new kind of managerial liberalism, which took the corporation as a model for the state.[11] New persuasive practices of PR and advertising became central to the political process thereafter, which increasingly became a species of market-based entertainment. Democracy withered behind the silver screen.

What follows starts earlier than that, though, as part of a genealogy of the fateful intertwining of the human and social sciences (particularly the "psy-sciences") with politics (and new governing practices), media, and consumer capitalism, which transformed political and economic strategies and realities thereafter. I begin again with the latter years of the nineteenth century, when a new form of corporate capitalism began to surface on the eve of the birth of cinema. Below I examine the emergence of new ideas about people, sociality, and crowds, which shaped the human and social sciences and in turn affected the liberal practices of governance, which that had assumed a stable, mostly rational, self-seeking individual. The stability, rationality, even individuality of that liberal subject were buffeted by work on hypnosis, "suggestion," the mind of the crowd, and the unconscious, all of which began to imply that the subject was divided, frequently irrational, driven by primal instincts, and malleable. Contingent historical events played a role also. The barbarous tragedies and shocks and traumas of World War I, together with the apparent success of propaganda during the conflict, had seemingly proven the validity of some of those ideas about the primal, irrational, and malleable nature of people. Sigmund Freud, for example, returned to thinking about group psychology in the early 1920s, dolefully concluding that the human is a primal and largely irrational animal capable of great violence and destruction.[12]

In the midst of this, "progressive" ideas about mass education—which helped form some of the film institutions and texts I have been examining—began to mutate into new conceptions of an atavistic mass that needed to be controlled by a cadre of experts.[13] Freud's reflections grew gloomier still when the rise of fascism in the 1930s provided further evidence of the seemingly latent irrational violence of the mass.[14] Joseph Goebbels, the head of the Nazi propaganda machine, read the two books Bernays published in the 1920s and used Bernays's insights into the practices of mass persuasion to develop the "spectacular publicity" that contributed to Hitler's rise to, and consolidation of, power.[15]

One of the early *public* forums for these debates about the mimetic and dangerous masses was the contestation over cinema. Early reports on the new technology of cinema in the 1890s frequently remarked on its startling mixing of the illusory and the real, recurrently telling stories of audiences apparently confused by the technology into believing the illusion was real. Reform and regulatory reports from the period, beginning around 1907, after the emergence of cinema as a separate space and entertainment form, commonly also reported that cinema was a peculiarly mimetic form—a "mimic stage"—that appeared to be capable of shaping the attitudes and conducts of its audiences.[16] Some of this rhetoric was associated with conservative and religious disapproval of modern mass media, its audiences, and societal change. But academic human and social scientists began also to empirically investigate the mimetic power of movies, and mass media, beginning most substantively after the war and the state experiments with mass propaganda and persuasion and in the context of a broader disciplinary shift away from religious authority and moral philosophy toward empiricism.[17] The nascent study of film and communication was framed, initially, by work in the human and social sciences on the nature of human beings and social groups. Knowing what people thought and how they acted, their "attitudes" and conduct, became increasingly important to political and economic elites. The social sciences, particularly the psy-sciences, were allied with new governing rationales. Corporate-financed philanthropic foundations and new disciplinary configurations in the university played important roles here.

Even as mimetic media influenced populations, and seemingly rendered liberal order fragile, then, they also presented new possibilities for the "education" and political and economic management of mass populations. Creel's use of cinema and the seemingly magnetic power of film stars during the war was an important precedent for this position, and this contributed to new ideas about, and practices of, "visual instruction" in the interwar years. Grierson's late 1920s experiments in film form to "market" colonial produce were also significant. Both were examples of how liberal states began to use movies as mass media and persuasion. In the aftermath of war, the success of state propaganda institutions also generated novel theories and practices of consumer persuasion driven by new PR and advertising professionals.

Bernays and other influence professionals used cinema and its "charismatic" and "influential" stars in particular to sell all sorts of consumer objects, including those, like make-up and fashion associated with self-presentation but extending even to presidential candidates. "Celebrity culture," functioning frequently as the articulation of new models of selfhood and display in an emergent society of the spectacle, began here. The stars of the silver screen frequently became transmedial, crossing from the screen to the ether of radio and the pages of magazines and newspapers in "commercial tie-ins" that positioned them as significant nodes in networks of capital mobility. Bernays would also pioneer what came to be called "product placement" in movies, thereby turning the expensive corporate spectacle of moving pictures over to the advertisement of the new objects of mass production. Doing so literalized the conception of the function of the movies held by State and Commerce Department officials and petulant British politicians. "Culture," in its mass variant in particular, was harnessed to persuasion and capital generation.

I chart that rather complex intellectual, political, economic, media, and disciplinary history below. It is a story that underpins much of what I have said thus far, because the efforts to use cinema and shape media policy emerged from an amalgam of ideas about pedagogy, malleable people, and persuasive media in the context of transformations in practices of liberal governance and economy. It comes at this point in my historical account because I will ultimately be most interested in the post–World War I reflections on media and propaganda, their practical use by new persuasion professionals in the 1920s and their sedimentation into new disciplinary configurations thereafter. It will take us a little while to get there, though.

"INTERPSYCHICAL PHOTOGRAPHY"

Work on the mimetic basis of subjectivity became widely influential in what became the human and social sciences in the latter years of the nineteenth century, becoming a key structuring principle for the explosion of theories of subjectivity and social order in the disciplines and practices of psychology, sociology, and psychoanalysis.[18] Early work on the phenomenon of hypnosis was critical to the initiation of this new discursive formation.[19] It is "suggestion that rules hypnotism," said Hippolyte Bernheim, defining "suggestion" as "the production of a dynamic change in the nervous system of a person . . . by another person by means of the calling forth of *representations* or ideas."[20] Representations thus "created" in the minds of people are "like a living memory, which governs them to such an extent as to appear an incontestable reality."[21] Everyone is open to this power of suggestion, Bernheim proposed, for at base the subject is a highly plastic, receptive material, bearing the imprint of the other as suggestion. Or put another way, as (Bernays's uncle) Sigmund Freud observed in the preface to his translation of Bernheim into German: suggestion forms the subject.[22] Bernheim's argument was influential across the human and social sciences and had profound implications for the liberal conception of the autarchic and rational individual. If suggestion were central to the formation and functioning of the subject, as Bernheim surmised, then that subject would be penetrated by the discourse of the other and hence not fully conscious to him- or herself.

Early work on suggestion, hypnosis, and the mimetic relation to others effectively offered a model of the mind as doubled or fragmented, leading to a reconceptualization of mental topography (most notably in the "discovery" of the unconscious), to a revaluation of the sovereignty of the Cartesian and liberal subject, and thus to a conception of a lability central to identity. The power of suggestion and of the related phenomenon "imitation" came to be widely regarded as the basis of subjectivity, suggesting that the subject was socially formed, assuming a broad definition of "the social" as the effect of others. The mimetic paradigm was integral to the development of the human and social sciences thereafter. Indeed, similar ideas about the suggestibility of people migrated across media and became widely visible in news reports of "hypnotic" crimes and in novels and film.[23]

One immediate consequence of the new ideas about suggestibility and mimesis was the development of theories of collective psychology in the 1890s. Collectively, the work of scholars such as Scipio Sighele in Italy, Gabriel Tarde and Gustave Le Bon in France, and Robert Park and Boris Sidis in the United States used ideas about suggestion and imitation to argue that groups of various kinds were drawn together by the power of suggestion and could consequently act impetuously, as if in fact hypnotized.[24] Even further, this work began to propose that society itself was predicated on mimetic connections. The criminologist Gabriel Tarde, in his influential 1890 book, translated into English as *The Laws of Imitation* in 1903, used ideas of hypnotic relations to develop an account of the interdependency of sociality and mimesis. Tarde wrote, "Society may . . . be defined as a group of beings who are apt to imitate one another," and thus imitation was "the elementary social phenomenon," the "fundamental social fact."[25] Tarde's account of the import of mimesis to collectivities and to sociality thus effectively extended Bernheim's account of the centrality of mimesis to subjectivity, to propose that it stood at the center of subject *and* social formation.

Crowd psychologists viewed with considerable alarm the suggestible and irrational nature of collectivities.[26] Crowds were, it was argued, easily influenced by powerful leaders and by images and spectacles. Gustave Le Bon's popular 1895 book *La Psychologie des Foules,* translated into English in 1896 as *The Crowd* and quickly appearing in other languages, suggested that the individual in the crowd behaved like "the hypnotized subject," undertaking the "accomplishment of certain acts with irresistible impetuosity."[27] Crowds of working-class populations, emboldened by the expansion of rights and extension of suffrage, hovered "on the borderland of unconsciousness, readily yielding to all suggestions," and so were prone to irrational, dangerous, and impetuous *antisocial* acts.[28] Writing on the eve of the mass distribution of images that seemed to move (though they were in fact only a *suggestive* collection of still images), Le Bon proposed that "whoever can supply" the crowd "with illusions is easily their master," and thus that "to know the art of impressing the imagination of crowds is to know at the same time the art of governing them."[29]

Crowd psychology was clearly constituted out of anxiety about new mass groupings of people and the spread of democracy from elites downward. Work emanating from Britain began to articulate similar conceptions of the "herd instinct," particularly after the violence of the Boer War in 1899–1902, when the British innovated new practices of confining enemy populations into "concentration camps" as part of the desperate attempt to maintain imperial rule.[30] The emergent human and social sciences were allied to the efforts to establish new liberal governing rationales in the age of mass democracy and media, which threatened traditional rule. Le Bon cautioned that a "knowledge of the psychology of crowds is today the last resource of the statesman who wishes not to govern them—*that is becoming a very difficult matter*—but at any rate not to be too much governed by them."[31] Le Bon's book, part fearful jeremiad and part how-to manual, was very widely read: Benito Mussolini, Hitler, and Theodore Roosevelt were all said to have read the book.

Processes of suggestion and imitation were repeatedly connected, in work on hypnosis, psychology, and crowd psychology, to images and spectacles. Gabriel Tarde defined imitation as "the action at a distance of one mind upon another," or "the quasi-*photographic* reproduction of a cerebral image upon the sensitive plate of another brain," and so as an "impression of inter-psychical photography, so to speak, willed or not willed, passive or active."[32] The social psychologist George Elliott Howard described processes of suggestibility as like "a motion picture stamped on the film of associative memory."[33] Bernheim's account of suggestion, Le Bon's of the mass mind, and Tarde's of imitation all suggested that "representations" and images were crucial to the processes of mimesis that formed the subject and the social bond.

Work on mimesis from Europe, particularly from Le Bon and Tarde, transformed American social thought from the late nineteenth century, informing the establishment of the human and social sciences as university disciplines.[34] Psychologist James Mark Baldwin utilized Tarde's work on mimesis to develop an account of mental development in children. Mark Baldwin argued that imitation and "ideo-motor responses" were critical for the development of selfhood in a process that passes through the "projective stage," where the child receives impressions "of a model as a *photographic plate* receives an image," to the "subjective stage" where the child assumes the movements and attitudes of the model and becomes what Baldwin termed a "veritable copying machine."[35] "The self," Baldwin wrote, "is realized in taking copies from the world."[36] Once again mimesis was positioned as central to subject formation in a process akin to the projection and reception of images. Language used by scholars posited a connection between the subject and the photographic medium, as if the subject were molded like the photosensitive silver salts that produced images.

The mimetic paradigm, and its influence over both crowd and individual psychology, informed also the establishment of sociology in the United States and the emergence of the discipline of social psychology, both of which gained presence in academia, as universities modernized, expanded, and reorganized disciplinary divisions in the 1880s and 1890s and as new professional organizations were created.[37] Work in sociology developed in the late nineteenth century as one way of understanding the formation of social groups and social order and disorder, in the face of anxieties about the breakdown of primary groups and local communities and in the context of the emergence of an increasingly industrialized and urbanized culture.[38] Edward Ross's work, bearing a direct relation to Tarde's, is critical here.[39] Beginning in 1896, Ross published a series of influential articles in the recently formed *American Journal of Sociology* on the subject of "social control," and the articles were collected together as the book *Social Control: A Survey of the Foundations of Order* in 1901.[40] Ross's work was premised on the idea that there is a fundamental conflict between individual and social interests and that in order to maintain itself society has to modify individual feelings, ideas, and behaviors By arguing thus, Ross effectively reversed the valences of nineteenth-century philosophical liberalism, for it was now social control that was sought, and individual autonomy became a subsidiary theme. The pressing question of "social control," of how society modifies individual desires to conform to sociality, defined early twentieth-century American sociology and the quest to, as philosopher John Dewey framed it, "gain control of the forces forming society."[41] By 1921, in the very widely used and influential textbook *Introduction to the Science of Sociology,* Robert Park and Ernest Burgess of the University of Chicago could simply state that "all social problems turn out to be problems of social control" and thus that the issue of social control should be "the central fact and problem of sociology."[42]

Ross, Park, Burgess, and many others, regarded the question of how to bind liberal individuals into a harmonious society as preeminently a psychological one.[43] Questions of suggestibility and imitation were critical to this binding process, seen by Ross as central mechanisms by which individuals shaped their conduct in accord with the desires and expectations of others and society but, potentially, also as problematic stumbling blocks for the foundation of social order.[44] Controlling those processes to effectively govern individuals and mass groups was a critical task, Ross argued, calling for the establishment of what he described as an "ethical elite" and the development of "the state in its administrative side."[45] Work in the human and social sciences thus connected subject formation to social order, in the process inaugurating the discipline that came to be called social psychology.

The connection between sociology and psychology, through conceptions of mimesis, was guided by practical concerns in governing individuals and masses, and it formed one significant part of the invention of the new epistemological and institutional practices to govern individuals and populations that flourished in turn-of-the-century modernity. By this process, liberalism was updated and revitalized by new knowledges about people and social groupings in the human and social sciences: knowledge and its sedimentation into institutions like universities helped form the new art of liberal bio-power.

Early accounts of the technological and later institutional phenomenon of cinema frequently drew on this expansive discursive context. The cinema came to be an example, a diagram even, of suggestion in action.[46] Language about suggestion anticipated cinema, as the mass production of spectacle; the language used to describe cinema borrowed from the terrain of the human and social sciences: cinema came to be seen by many as a mimetic machine. Certainly much of this was constituted negatively, as concern about its impact on displaced laboring populations. But it came also increasingly to be configured—during wartime and thereafter—as a component of new strategies of governance and of consumer persuasion. Both these strategies were part of the effort to make cinema functional for liberal governmental rationality and political economy.

"THE ENLISTING OF INTEREST"

Various kinds of reports about the phenomenon of "nickelodeons"—cheap moving picture shows—flourished in the United States from late 1906 on. Early studies of this new phenomenon frequently posited the direct impact of moving pictures on the behavior of audiences and thus on what social reformer Jane Addams called their "working moral codes."[47] By doing so, they drew on the currency of popularized ideas of hypnotic suggestion to propose—at their most extreme—that cinema itself was a form of hypnosis. I have explored some of this work elsewhere.[48] Here a few examples will suffice to explicate the joins between ideas about the malleability of people and the danger and utility of media.

"Modern thought has been keenly aware," social reformer John Collier remarked in an address given about cinema to an audience at a child welfare conference, "that all influences which reach the child, make more than a transitory impression . . . We are reminded that the child is *imitative,* that he is *suggestible.*"[49] Professor of philosophy William A. McKeever articulated similar anxieties in *Good Housekeeping* in 1910, contending that cinema had deleterious effects on "plastic youth."[50] In a lecture in 1911 to the People's Institute, a progressive reform organization involved in the regulation of cinema, Reverend H. A. Jump asserted that movies operated through "psychologic suggestion."[51] George Elliott Howard's 1912 article "Social Psychology of the Spectator" argued that sometimes "under the spell" of the motion picture "the 'gash' in consciousness is so deep, the 'mental disaggregation' so complete, the entire obsession of the mind by the momentary suggestion so profound, that the spectator is hypnotized."[52] William Healy, director of the Psychopathic Institute in Chicago's famed Juvenile Court, included in his 1915 book *The Individual Delinquent* several case studies concerning the "peculiar plasticity" of children allegedly influenced by "pictorial suggestions" to commit criminal acts.[53] Wary of the "motor consequences of imagery," Healy wrote, "The strength of the powers of visualization is to be deeply reckoned with when considering the springs of criminality . . . It is the mental representation of some sort of *pictures* of himself or others in the criminal act that leads the delinquent onward in his path."[54] Watching criminal acts leads to imitative acts; visualization is a critical component of mimesis, a literal "inter-psychical photography" triggering imitative acts and, crucially, conditions of personhood. The first significant "theorist" of cinema in English was a trained hypnotist and industrial psychologist interested in how film rendered spectators "spellbound."[55] Time and time again, ideas about "impressionability," "plasticity," "suggestion," and "hypnosis" informed the study and conception of cinema and its psychic and social effects. Quite clearly, the governmental context for the emergence of the human sciences as practical epistemology in managing mass publics also shaped the establishment of studies of cinema and its purported mimetic effects. Cinema became a site around which these new arguments about mimetic individuals and the fragility of social order were transferred from the rarefied atmosphere of the academy and played out in the public sphere.

The logic ran two ways. One direction led toward intensified regulation, culminating in the Supreme Court decision of 1915 that denied film the liberal constitutional guarantees of "free" speech because of its potential to influence audiences.[56] Commercial cinema was pushed outside the public sphere and rendered as a depoliticized space of entertainment. (This preceded, and helped to frame, the shaping of radio as a commercial and corporate medium in the 1920s.) But the other consequence of the argument that cinema was a particularly powerful mimetic form was the growing integration of cinema with various forms of pedagogy, made clearly visible in the establishment of the Committee on Public Information in 1917 and its use of media to shape perception and conduct. Recall that Lippmann, a public intellectual well versed in debates in the human and social sciences, advised Wilson on the setting up of the committee. Quickly thereafter human and social scientists, as well as people drawn from the advertising profession, were recruited to work in the CPI, which became for a time an experiment in applied human and social science. Media was central to this. Lippmann's plan spoke of the need to rally a wide range of communication specialists and included people working in the "motion picture industry."[57] The growing consensus that people were mimetic, and shaped and influenced particularly by representations, was put into practice: movies and media were pressed into political and economic service to become a part of new governing practices in the age of mass democracy. Creel effectively put symbols and "suggestion" to work to sustain state interests (indeed to support also the financial interests of the banks protecting loans to Britain in particular). And it seemed to work.

Certainly according to Creel, who made much of his contribution to the war effort as befits good PR practice. In his book about his time at the CPI, eloquently titled *How We Advertised America,* he described his job as "a plain publicity prop-osition, a vast enterprise in salesmanship, the world's greatest adventure in adver-tising," and proclaimed that propaganda worked very effectively.[58] But many oth-ers agreed that mass-mediated propaganda was a newly powerful force in modern society. "Never before in history," wrote Charles and Mary Beard, "had such a cam-paign of education been organized; never before had American citizens realized how thoroughly, how irresistibly a modern government could impose its ideas upon the whole nation."[59] Yale psychologist Raymond Dodge observed, in an arti-cle in 1920 entitled "The Psychology of Propaganda," that "It has been discovered by individuals, by associations, and by governments that a certain kind of advertis-ing can be used to mold public opinion and democratic majorities."[60] Propaganda began to appear to many as a way of regimenting the mimetic mass mind. Graham Wallas, in his influential 1920 book *Human Nature in Politics,* stated simply, "The empirical art of politics consists largely in the creation of opinion by the deliberate exploitation of subconscious non-rational inference."[61] Lasswell similarly defined propaganda as "the management of opinions and attitudes by the direct manipula-tion of social suggestion." He argued that the attempt to control opinion through the manipulation of "significant symbols or . . . by stories, rumors, reports, pic-tures and other forms of social communication" had become routine and thus propaganda was "one of the most powerful instrumentalities in the modern world."[62] Numerous other works on the suggestibility of the crowd, with titles like *The Psychology of Persuasion, Our Unconscious Mind and How to Use It,* and *Man the Puppet: The Art of Controlling Minds,* emerged in the 1920s.[63]

Wallas in particular had influenced Lippmann, and it was Lippmann's trilogy of books on media, public opinion, and democracy, in particular the 1922 *Public Opinion,* that framed the terms of much of this debate in the United States in the 1920s.[64] (James Carey, for example, has called *Public Opinion* "the founding book in American media studies.")[65] After advising Wilson on the establishment of the CPI, Lippmann worked during the war to produce and disseminate propaganda in Europe with the Military Branch of the War Department. He thereafter became convinced, his biographer observes, that "public opinion could be molded."[66]

Lippmann articulated a position that has subsequently been called "liberal real-ist," standing as a significant revision of liberalism that took new conceptions of the irrational subject and mass as a basis to argue for new forms of elite manage-ment of democracy. In making this argument, Lippmann suggested that people understand the world according to the "pictures inside" their "heads," which are largely made up of stereotypes and beliefs rooted in myths, dreams, and traditions.[67] The gulf between these "pictures" and reality had widened significantly in the complex modern world. Lippmann argued that mass-mediated "pictures" constitute a credible but often fallacious "pseudo-environment" that inform ordinary thought and behavior.[68] "For the most part we do not first see, and then define, we define first and then see," Lippmann wrote. "In the great blooming, buzzing confusion of the outer world we pick out what our culture has already defined for us, and we tend to perceive that which we have picked out in the form stereotyped by our culture."[69] What this meant was that public opinion is malleable, and the mass "might be placed at the disposal of those who stood for workable law as against brute assertion" if carefully managed and orchestrated.[70] "What is propaganda," he asked, "if not the effort to alter the picture to which men respond, to substitute one social pattern for another?"[71]

What was needed to counter the confused and dangerous suggestible "irrational" mass, who saw the world not as it was but through the "habits of [their] eyes," was a technocratic elite to assess and interpret the potentially dangerous public opinion objectively and to work through organizations of independent experts to make "the unseen facts intelligible to those who have to make decisions."[72] Public opinions "must be organized *for the press* if they are to be sound, not *by the press* as is the case today."[73] Lippmann drew on the work on the suggestible and irrational nature of the subject and the mass to propose that the modern mass media system be carefully regulated and used to "manufacture consent" to liberal order. Once again, this pivoted on the idea that media needed to be censored *and* shaped as propaganda. "Without some form of censorship," Lippmann wrote, "propaganda in the strict sense of the word is impossible. In order to conduct a propaganda there must be some barrier between the public and the event. Access to the real environment must be limited, before anyone can create a pseudo-environment that he thinks is wise or desirable."[74] Likewise, "He who captures the symbols by which public feeling is for the moment contained," he proposed, "control by that much the approaches of public policy . . . A leader or an interest that can make itself master of current symbols is the master of the current situation."[75] Lippmann here effectively observed how the state had functioned during wartime, with both the regulation of speech (in the Espionage and Sedition Acts) and media and symbolic production (in the form of the CPI) and proposed this as a working model for how elites should control media thereafter.

Lippmann's thinking about propaganda, media, and democracy positioned cinema as an important new form in modern mass society, positing it as a model for how mediated democracy could work. In the midst of an influential and significant revision of the tenets of classical liberalism, that is, the cinema was invoked as an important component of the transformations of the modern world that both necessitated rethinking the framework of liberal democracy and presented itself as a model for understanding how symbolic communication could shape perception and opinion. In a chapter entitled "The Enlisting of Interest," Lippmann took the fictional film of classical Hollywood, of the recently formed "studio system," as a way of understanding how "identification" is orchestrated. "Pictures have always been the surest way of conveying an idea . . . But the idea conveyed is not fully our own until we have identified ourselves with some aspect of the picture . . . the handles for identification are almost always marked. You know who the hero is at once."[76] Politics needed to become more cinematic in marshalling patterns of identification. To illustrate his remarks on moving pictures Lippmann quoted Frances Taylor Patterson's early screenplay writing guide, *Cinema Craftsmanship*, going so far as to propose that the suspenseful narrative form of cinema is a good model for framing politics for mass audiences. In a footnote he quotes Patterson advising screenplay writers that if "the plot lacks suspense: 1. Add an antagonist, 2. Add an obstacle, 3. Add a problem, 4. Emphasize one of the questions in the minds of the spectator," and remarks in the main text that "in order to make politics popular, issues have to be found, even when in truth and justice, there are none."[77] Lippmann's analysis here of how Hollywood films functioned, in particular as "handles for identification" that shape the perspective of audiences, effectively began to see the narrative form of this mass-produced spectacle as integral to new practices of persuasion and to the modeling of appropriate conduct. The particular mode of popular narrative fiction cinema, its invitation to identify or ally, became a model for imagining the identification with political leaders and the state. Liberalism became cinematic.

Lippmann's articulation of a form of liberal "realism," better called democratic elitism, supposed that the masses were not really capable of judging the newfound complexities of the world and so should be guided by others. The control of symbols, of spectacle, was integral to the control of populations. Hence the most effective politicians are "'cinematographic'" in their ability to "visualize for us."[78] Lippmann's arguments, from his 1914 book *Drift and Mastery* through his trilogy of books on media and democracy in the 1920s, were widely discussed, and influential, and his close ties to policy-forming elites helped shape the way the CPI functioned in 1917, as well as Wilson's famous Fourteen Points address calling for a new liberal world order in 1919 (and the related 1921 formation of the still influential Council on Foreign Relations).[79] Broadly speaking this position held that the radical potential of mass democracy must be made safe for an elite society and its existing political and economic organization. By this logic liberalism overrode the idealization of participatory democracy.[80] Lippmann's argument, or insight, that democracy in mass society is only possible if decisions are made by the few, with merely superficial mass participation, preceded also C. B. Macpherson's powerful critique of the deterioration of liberalism and democracy under capitalist auspices.[81]

Lippmann's careful thinking about how pseudoenvironments control access to the real, and how identification can be marshaled, took cinema as a model and metaphor for the transformation of democracy into technocratic management. It was consistent with the reframing of liberal democracy as "social control," as articulated particularly bluntly and vividly in Ross's influential work in sociology and social psychology. Lippmann shifted, if somewhat anxiously, away from the concern about the manipulated public, which underlay crowd psychology and early accounts of the phenomenon of cinema, toward an acceptance of the malleability of the individual and mass and examination of how the public could be influenced and managed. Subsequent scholarship on the perils and possibilities of the "chains of silver" of mass persuasion drew on this framework. Lasswell's influential work on propaganda in the later 1920s and thereafter, for example, took this position on the modern political necessity to shape perception and opinion as a starting point and further explored how propaganda could effectively manage mass populations.[82]

What emerged from this intellectual and always simultaneously political context was a clear consensus among significant intellectual and political elites that mass media needed to be shaped and used to manage perception and frame the political sphere. It was in this context, for example, that the Conservative Party in Britain began to produce films and distribute them through new nontheatrical networks, while simultaneously innovating new regulatory frameworks to curtail the mobility of commercial American films. Corporations too increasingly began producing PR films and sponsoring other media to articulate the corporate point of view. New ideas and practices of a form of mediated and attenuated "liberal democracy" had a significant impact on the subsequent shaping, and narrowing, of media, as well as on the political and public sphere in liberal states thereafter.[83]

"ENGINEERING CONSENT"

Lippmann's anxiety about the potential for mass media to disaggregate political order unless it was carefully orchestrated was palpable, tinged, as Mark Crispin Miller frames it, "with the melancholy of a disillusioned socialist."[84] Even more anxious was Lippmann's chief interlocutor, John Dewey, who described *Public Opinion* as "perhaps the most effective indictment of democracy as currently conceived ever penned" and who worried that mass society would lead to a decline in participatory democracy.[85] European variants on that position, emerging in the later 1920s and early 1930s, began to see forms of mass media as key components of a new regimentation of political order that led directly to fascism.[86] But, as I have suggested, many embraced the possibilities of mass persuasion through media. Chief among those were the new persuasion professionals and "symbol specialists," who grew rapidly in numbers in the immediate aftermath of the war. Propaganda techniques successfully innovated by the US and, to some extent, the British states mutated directly into "public relations" and new practices of advertising.

Edward Bernays was one of the most visible practitioner's of the new art of state and corporate mass persuasion. Bernays learned directly from his time at the CPI and put his ideas into practice in postwar PR work for significant corporations such as General Electric, American Tobacco, General Motors, United Fruit Company, and others. In period commentary (not least his own), and in subsequent scholarship, Bernays was singled out as probably the most visible and influential practitioner of the new profession of PR counselor, and some of his schemes to shape perception and manage opinions have gone down as classics in PR textbooks and the playbook of subsequent PR workers.[87] The new methods of PR that Bernays pioneered were not based on a mechanistic reaction of stimulus-reply—on straightforward media effects—but on a more complex procedure that worked by suggestion to "create the circumstances that will make emotional desires merge with appeals to buy" or to support particular political and economic positions.[88] By this logic the PR practitioner sold soap, for example, not as something that got you clean but more likely as something that gave you sex appeal. I want now to substantiate those ideas and practices in a little more depth, as they developed from the intellectual contexts sketched in thus far—from Le Bon, to Freud, to Lippmann—to make increasing use of spectacle and the "subconscious" manipulation of media and symbols to "engineer consent" to a corporate dominated political economy. I shall pay particular attention to the place cinema occupied in that process, but it is worth reiterating that PR is fundamentally transmedial: cinema was frequently invoked as exemplifying the new society of the spectacle, and its stars in particular were used to model new identities and products, but they did so frequently in newspapers, in new image-dominated magazines, and on radio.

In his memoirs, Bernays tells his life story in a way that reads something like a fable for the age and indeed this book: after dull years spent as an undergraduate at the school of agriculture at Cornell, he escaped to New York City and fell into the profession of press agent for theatrical stars. This led him circuitously to volunteer to work in the Committee in Public Information, from where he was sent to the Paris Peace Conference in 1919. From there he returned to set himself up as a "counsel on public relations" and worked with various corporations and, from time-to-time, with particular agencies of the state up to the years of the Cold War. In the year he worked with the CPI, he "planned and carried out a campaign directed at Latin American businessmen" that both countered German propaganda and clearly connected to the goals of the US state and corporations to establish economic hegemony in the region by superseding the British in particular.[89] No surprise, then, that the "American Manufacturers Export Association willingly co-operated" with his state-sponsored campaign, as did corporations like Ford and International Harvester, in a way that Bernays took as illustrative of a significant principle—that "political propaganda and commercial advancement can go hand in hand."[90] Writing shortly after his campaign, Bernays reflected on this happy confluence of state and economic objectives: "We sold them [Latin American populations] American war aims, and concomitantly they learned to be enthusiastic about American manufacturers and were won over to a desire to deal further with American business men."[91] These principles connected state and corporate interests, imagining them as essentially isomorphic. Military conflict was directly utilized to expand commercial spheres of influence. Collaborations between Hollywood and the CPI worked on a similar logic, as did the efforts of the State and Commerce Departments to help facilitate the global circulation of the products of corporate Hollywood as a sort of mobile window space for America and its commercial objects and objectives.

What Bernays described as the "astounding success of propaganda" during the war "opened the eyes of the intelligent few in all departments of life to the possibilities of regimenting the public mind."[92] Reflecting on this, Bernays made use of his familial connection with Freud, whose work he helped popularize in the United States, as well as some of the work described and analyzed thus far in this chapter. "Walter Lippmann's book *Public Opinion,* was published in 1922 and made a great impression on me," he wrote. "So had William Trotter's *Instincts of the Herd* ... and Le Bon's book *The Crowd.*"[93] Well versed in the expansive mimetic paradigm—such even that his repeated imagery of "impressions" being made mimics its logic— Bernays himself published two books in the 1920s and wrote countless articles that drew on these ideas about malleable people, and the power of propaganda "to mold the minds of the masses," and proposed some practical applications.[94] *Crystallizing Public Opinion* in 1923 and *Propaganda* in 1928 were both part theoretical reflection, part PR for his own practices, and part how-to manual for shaping opinion in ways consistent with the goals of political and economic elites. *Crystallizing Public Opinion* was written in the context of the widespread debate about Lippmann's book— Bernays cannily used the title to jump on that particular bandwagon—and agreed with its central contention that "the conscious and intelligent manipulation of the organized habits and opinions of the masses" had become an indispensable feature of "democratic society."[95] *Propaganda* likewise baldly took this position as its starting point: "The conscious and intelligent manipulation of the organized habits and opinions of the masses is an important element in democratic society. Those who manipulate this unseen mechanism of society constitute an invisible government which is the true ruling power of our country."[96]

But theoretical reflection on this state of affairs went only so far, Bernays argued, and "discussions of public opinion" that emerged from Lippmann and subsequent commentators "referred little to the application of their findings to everyday use."[97] PR was not to be simply academic: it was a radical hybrid of scholarship and "activism," of a sort, that excavated the mimetic paradigm for its practical use in using media to shape the attitudes and conduct of people in ways that conformed to those desired by political and economic elites. The practices of the CPI were in this way disseminated to become standard corporate practices. Bernheim, Le Bon, Freud, and Lippmann were made practical in "taking the risk out of democracy" for liberal political economy.

A few examples show what this looked like in practice. In late 1917, the film producer William Fox approached Bernays after learning of his successful work as a theatrical press agent to employ him to promote the film *Cleopatra* (Fox, 1917), starring Theda Bara, who had made quite a splash as a "vamp" in her 1915 film *A Fool There Was* (Fox, 1915). Bernays set to work to design a publicity campaign that made use of both sex and education to sell the film. In doing so, he clearly followed some of the principles he had established at the beginning of his career when dealing with the controversial play *Damaged Goods* in 1913, which he had promoted by emphasizing its value in addressing the "social problem" of venereal disease and by inviting along respectable members of the medical profession and society to lend their support to the play.[98] Cannily mixing sex with a serious agenda, or with pedagogy, became a standard practice quickly thereafter in both Hollywood and the margins of exploitation cinema, including directly a cycle of "white slave" films from 1913 onward, which straightforwardly mimicked this approach.[99] Bernays's strategy had another angle to it, though, for he designed his publicity for *Damaged Goods* and *Cleopatra* with the guidance of the discoveries of crowd psychology. It "is one of the most firmly established principles of mass psychology," he remarked when recalling the example of *Damaged Goods* in his 1928 book *Propaganda*, that in "making up its mind" the "first impulse" of the crowd "is usually to follow the example of a trusted leader."[100] It was this logic that motivated, for example, his invitation to medical and society elites for *Damaged Goods*, to high-school principals for *Cleopatra*, and to doctors for a PR campaign for bacon that claimed it to be particularly nutritious.[101] In his memorandum mapping out his strategy to Fox, recalled in his memoirs, he advised him to reach out to high school principals and scholars of Egyptian and Roman history while also not neglecting the mass audience looking for "easy stimulation of the senses and the imagination."[102] Not a bad strategy for an industry predicated on that stimulation but navigating the complex cultural terrain of early twentieth-century America. Will Hays, the politically well-connected master of public relations for the corporate film industry from the 1920s through the 1940s, adopted many similar strategies in allying Hollywood with religious, civil, and educational authorities in order, principally, to draw the state's attention away from the industry's economic practices. The circumvention of state regulation is frequently central to the practices of public relations. PR as the alchemical transformation of private interest and profit into ostensible public good through the orchestration of media spectacle is in this respect fundamentally liberal.

Elsewhere in his memoirs, Bernays recalled observing "how people feel towards movie stars"—"identifying" with "focused . . . attention"—and recounted scattered examples of using stars in particular publicity campaigns.[103] Working for a textile and fashion company, for example, he offered "stars free dresses" and had them model them and developed a stage revue featuring the dresses that played as "adjunct to movie" bills in the significant Paramount, Loew, and Stanley exhibition chains. Likewise for fashion items for men he "supplied radio stations and motion-picture newsreels with features"—creating "newsworthy events" was one of the central definitions of PR for Bernays—and for another company he provided fashionable luggage to be used by stars on screen. Working to promote a book about love he got "America's reigning movie queens" Mary Pickford and Lillian Gish to write about "their definition of love."[104] Will Rogers was hired as "master of ceremonies" alongside a host of Hollywood stars—including Harold Lloyd, Clara Bow, Greta Garbo, and Tom Mix—for an elaborate radio show on the recently completed National Broadcasting Corporation network that was designed to, "in the words of Walter Lippmann . . . 'jut out of the routine of circumstances'" and create a "favorable climate of opinion" for a new Dodge car. Charlie Chaplin recorded a radio ad for the car.[105] In all these examples, public relations used the visibility of movie stars and the identification of mass audiences with them in synergistic tie-ins with the corporate studios beginning around about the same time these studios were themselves discovering the economic utility of stars for the film industry. What emerged was the incorporation of cinema and its stars—functioning as something like the "leader" or as the object of libidinal identification in theories of crowd psychology—into an emergent culture of consumption ever-more predicated on display and spectacle. Cinema was central to the emergence of that culture, even as it crossed media forms—radio was also important to this as some of the examples above suggest—becoming increasingly powerful later with the emergence of the "cinematic" domestic form of television and ever more so through the more pervasive spectacles of public and mobile screens in the digital era.

Indeed, in a brief passage in his memoirs, Bernays recalled advising the head of the Columbia Broadcasting System, William Paley, in the complex negotiations that made radio a commercial form financed by corporate capital. In advance of Paley appearing before a congressional committee in 1930, Bernays—as he tells the story—sent him a statement that defined "radio broadcasting [as] a private business, based on coincidence of the public and private interest."[106] The statement is a characteristic one in his memoirs, and speaks to the centrality of the standard Smithian liberal position that private interests effectively served the public interest to the conception and practices of PR.[107] PR in this lofty conception helps self interest become public interest, in the process becoming crucial to the liberal order of things and the alchemy that supposedly makes selfishness and greed good. PR helped radio in the United States became a commercial form fully networked into the new consumer economy, which urged people to buy things. PR and media facilitated the beginnings of the damaging and unsustainable economic system of consumerism.

One other quite well-known final example from Bernays' practice can help illustrate how PR used persuasive practices to expand consumption. In 1929 Bernays was asked to help overcome the cultural taboo on women smoking in public to enable American Tobacco Company to increase its sales of cigarettes to women. Bernays paid to consult with the psychoanalyst A. A. Brill, who had been the first translator of Freud into English, and who (rather predictably) advised him that cigarettes could symbolize the missing penis that Freudian psychoanalysis makes so much of and thus that "Cigarettes, which are equated with men, become torches of freedom."[108] Combining many of the techniques he had been innovating since the war, Bernays staged a "pseudoevent" on Easter Sunday in New York City with a group of debutantes, who were coached in lighting up cigarettes all at the same time as they left church and strolled down Fifth Avenue. Newspapers were primed for the event.[109] Cigarettes became symbolic "torches of freedom" in a way that brilliantly connected the consumption of cigarettes with a broader feminist movement—indeed even with the ideal of liberty monumentalized in the nearby Statute of Liberty—and that thus mingled the hidden private interests of large tobacco companies to enlarge profits with the public interests of women to establish new forms of subjectivity and independence. Quite clearly feminism was repurposed to serve the interests of profit-seeking corporations.

I shall leave Bernays for now, though he shall reappear in the conclusion to this book advising General Motors on their PR films as part of a corporate fight back against some aspects of the New Deal, in the latter 1930s, and thereafter helping US corporations and the state frame the massive PR exercise that was the Cold War. Keep that dial locked on *Cinema and the Wealth of Nations* for more on corporate PR, after a considerable break for other messages about the philanthropically financed human and social science investigations of the mimetic movies, and later radio, in the latter years of the 1920s. These stand as significant articulations of ideas about media influence and of the practical demonstration of the mimetic paradigm. Both sets of investigation also shaped new disciplinary frameworks for the study of film and communication, though as we shall see somewhat differently when under the particular pressure of corporate PR and the financial interests of corporate funding institutions.

"DO MOTION PICTURES DIRECTLY OR INDIRECTLY AFFECT THE CONDUCT OF CHILDREN?"

Numerous efforts to empirically document the mimetic power of the movies, as part of "influence" broadly conceived, flourished in the aftermath of the war. They did so in the context of the widespread discussions about propaganda and the new practices of public relations as well as of the broader disciplinary shift toward empiricism taking place in the human and social sciences. The upsurge of work on media and mimesis in this period should also be situated in the context of the state and corporate crackdown on labor activism that, for example, produced the Palmer Raids by the FBI in 1919 to break up radical groups and that mutated into cultural form in, for example, Fordist film from 1919. Empirical verification of the impact and influence of media was significant to interested political and economic elites and this—plus the materiality of this interest in the form of funding— solidified into the emergence of new disciplinary frameworks for the study of film and communication.

Verification of the impact and influence of film grew from ongoing and intensi- fied concerns about the governmental management of diverse populations in urban modernity, which had motivated much of the initial work on crowds and social control, and found institutional manifestation in the creation of propaganda bodies and censorship boards. But it began also to merge with the new empirical orientation of the human and social sciences in the university. Evidence, rather than simple assertion, became the order of the day, even if that evidence was pro- duced entirely from within the mimetic paradigm. Likewise the practices of new social and psy-sciences began to be used more substantively as part of the impera- tive to know people in particular as consumers. Communication studies emerged in these contexts, in the United States at least, and was formed into a discipline with the help of corporate philanthropic money, which focused in particular on the study of persuasive media.[110] Cinema was a part of that discipline, but for vari- ous reasons the study of film was ultimately repositioned as part of the humanities that deemphasized the study of its influence on people.

In late 1918, immediately after the end of the war, a Motion Picture Commission was convened in Chicago to consider the regulation of moving pictures in the city. Testimony at the hearings, running every Friday until May 1919, was given from exhibitors, producers, social reformers, and social scientists about the effects of moving pictures on audiences. Much of this repeated long-standing assertions about the deleterious effects of the movies. George Kleine, for example, quoted the industrial psychologist and film theorist Hugo Münsterberg on the possible hyp- notic effects of commercial movies.[111]

But beyond these familiar assertions of influence and mimesis, the commission sought empirical verification of the effects of moving pictures in a way illustrative of the broader shift from "philosophic" concerns about crowds and mass publics toward the more precise measurement of "effects." Ernest W. Burgess, University of Chicago sociology professor and coeditor of the influential textbook *Introduction to Sociology*, was commissioned to quantify the effects of motion pictures on school children. Questionnaires were produced by Burgess, asking kids and teachers about the attendance of the young at moving picture shows and the effects of this on schoolwork, home life, and morality more broadly. Teachers in particular complained in familiar ways that moving pictures induced in young girls the "vampire attitude," taught young boys "bandit games," and stopped children from becoming "good citizens."[112] Burgess tabulated these responses; authority was reconstructed as knowledge in new forms of disciplinary power. What emerged was a meshing of long-standing ideas about mimesis, subjectivity, and social order and the newer imperative to empirically measure audiences and the effects of media. It was no coincidence that this and other investigations focused on the situation in Chicago, as that city became a hub for the national and global movement of materials—in particular farm produce—and consequently one of the central poles of attraction in the migratory movement of people across the capitalist world system.

Various studies emerged in the 1920s that drew on the concepts and research protocols of the human and social sciences and began to retool the mimetic paradigm with forms of empirical verification. In 1920 the prominent behavioral psychologists John B. Watson and Karl S. Lashley undertook an investigation of the effects of films used during the war in campaigns against venereal diseases. Watson and Lashley showed the film *Fit to Win* (1919), about the perils of venereal disease and one example of bio-political uses of cinema during wartime, to "many groups of individuals of various economic, social, and educational status" and posed four central questions for their study:

1. What amount and kind of information can the film give and how accurate is it?
2. What emotions do the films arouse?
3. What transitory and permanent effects do the films produce in the behavior of those who see them?
4. What are the probable social effects of any such permanent modifications in behavior that may be made?[113]

Watson and Lashley proposed to answer those questions by conducting a "thorough analysis" of the film itself and pursuing audience research through the observation of audience response, personal interviews, questionnaires, and "inquiries as to results in communities after a lapse of some months."[114] It was an early "reception studies" project combined with some longer-term attitudinal study predicated, in this example, on discerning the impact of the film—first on soldiers and second on other audiences, the latter when the film was briefly released more widely after the war.

Watson and Lashley's research was financed and carried out under the aegis of the United States Interdepartmental Social Hygiene Board, a governmental organization that sought to investigate and ameliorate the problem of venereal disease. Quite clearly this investigation of the emotional and social effects of film emerged from the governmental imperative to produce *and* regulate cinema in accordance with bio-political objectives. Indeed, their conclusion was that cinema should not engage with the problems of venereal diseases in "dramatic form" because of problematic "emotional reactions" with "erethitic effect."[115] In this way the argument buttressed the broader redefinition of cinema's place in the public sphere, which took place after the war and the evident success of propaganda and which returned commercial mainstream cinema to its function as "entertainment." as opposed to as an overtly pedagogical and political form.[116]

Cinema became an object of analysis for scholars within the human and social sciences. In a 1923 article, for example, social scientist Joseph Roy Gieger adopted the concepts of imitation and suggestion to argue that moving pictures lead the "individual to experience the emotional states and instinctive behavior" of those "other individuals who come under his observation," and this results in the implantation of "false standards of value" and, most worryingly, "the ways and means of accomplishing antisocial ends."[117] Chicago sociologist Frederick Thrasher's ethnographic account of gang culture in the city observed that "many of the exploits of the gang undoubtedly involve imitating the movies," before quoting criminologists and newspapers that asserted direct links between movies and crimes of murder, blackmail, and burglary and concluding that movies induce "imitative conduct."[118]

But the amalgam of governmental anxieties about cinema with the nascent scholarly study of cinema from within the human and social sciences was visible most clearly in the so-called Payne Fund Studies, which were initiated in 1927 and resulted in the publication of a series of books on the question of cinema's impact on young people in the early 1930s.[119] The studies emerged from the work of the National Committee for the Study of Juvenile Reading to develop a program of reading materials promoting citizenship. This committee was funded by philanthropist Frances Payne Bingham Bolton, who used her financial fortune from steel, oil, and tobacco production to fund social science research concerned with discerning the workings of society.[120] Reverend William H. Short, who had worked briefly with the Study of Juvenile Reading, proposed establishing a Motion Picture Research Council with funding from the Payne Study and Experiment Fund (as the original committee was renamed in 1927). The council conducted a nationwide study to determine the degree of influence and the effect of films upon children and adolescents and ultimately to lobby for more stringent forms of legalized social control over the film industry.[121] Short published *A Generation of Motion Pictures: A Review of Social Values in Recreational Films* in 1927, as part of this project to lobby for the regulation of cinema, bringing together existing work from sermons, articles and books on the negative role and impact of films.[122] Yet, conscious of the paradigm shift in the social sciences towards empiricism, Short became increasingly convinced that more precise and empirical work was necessary to generate further measures of social control.

Casting about for empirical verification (of what he already "knew"), Short met with social scientists in Chicago in the summer of 1928, including Jane Addams (a formative influence on the policy activism of social scientists at the university) and faculty at the University of Chicago.[123] Werrett Wallace Charters, professor in the School of Education; attitude psychologist Louis Leon Thurstone; and Robert Ezra Park in the School of Sociology were particularly helpful.[124] With their guidance, to pursue a precise study of the effects of moving pictures, Short proceeded to enlist the expertise of a number of social scientists, several of whom were associated with the social sciences at Chicago—widely regarded as the most important social science program—and others who were at major public and private research institutions.[125] Cutting-edge research protocols and technologies in the human and social sciences were trained directly at discerning the influence of the movies.

When the group of scholars gathered together for the project from the disciplines of sociology, psychology, social psychology, and education met for the first time, Short presented a document entitled "What We Need to Know as a Basis for a National Policy in Motion Pictures," which listed six categories of research:

1. The number of children reached by the movies
2. Their influence, using a quantitative measure
3. The positive, negative, or neutral qualities of their influence
4. Differentiations of their influence ascribed to gender, age, intelligence, level, and temperament
5. The influence of cinema on children's information processing, attitudes, emotions, conduct, and aesthetic and moral standards
6. The influence of cinema on "such important matters" as respect for authority, marriage, forms of crime, hero worship and international understanding.[126]

The document formed the basis for the subsequent studies, translated into a series of questions articulated by Charters in his preface to the published volumes:

> What sorts of scenes do the children of America see when they attend the theaters? How do the mores depicted in these scenes compare with those of the community? How often do children attend? How much of what they see do they remember? What effect does what they witness have upon their ideals and attitudes? Upon their sleep and health? Upon their emotions? Do motion pictures directly or indirectly affect the conduct of children? Are they related to delinquency and crime, and, finally, how can we teach children to discriminate between movies that are artistically and morally good and bad?[127]

Collectively, Short and Charters contended, the studies would "provide a composite answer to the central question of the nature and extent of [the] influences" of moving pictures.[128]

Quite clearly the studies were formed out of the intellectual, disciplinary, and political context discussed thus far, and they were principally designed—at least at inception—to empirically verify the already "evident" deleterious effects of moving pictures on vulnerable and simultaneously dangerous audiences. (Even a scholar in the humanities can recognize the flaws in that methodology.) The Payne Fund Studies were in this respect one concrete example of the ways in which the human and social sciences were deployed to produce knowledge about the psychology and sociology of individuals and groups in their relationship with media, so as to better manage problematic conducts. Cash from corporate capital was turned into "knowledge" positioned at the interface of morality, governance, and the academy. It is certainly not without its ironies that studies funded in part from money made from tobacco concluded that movies were a harmful narcotic.

The psychological studies suggested this most clearly. Psychologists at the University of Iowa wired children up to a machine called a "psychogalvonometer," which measured the changing galvanic resistance in their skin as they were shown exciting and somewhat risqué fiction films from Hollywood (see fig. 19). Movies, they concluded, "are a powerful stimulus, especially at certain ages and notably at the pre-adult ages, to conduct and behavior."[129] Wiring up children to machines was intended to translate the hidden emotional and psychological responses to movies into legible and actionable data. Elsewhere in the studies, the prominent attitude psychologist L. L. Thurstone, and his graduate student Ruth Petersen developed scales for measuring the influence of motion pictures on young viewers' attitudes about racial prejudice.[130] The attempts to render through machines and gradated attitude scales what was seemingly invisible—the engagement of individuals with cinema, the hidden processes of media influence—into a form that could be recorded and classified made clear the way knowledge about cinema was being inserted into circuits of knowledge and power about particular populations. In this way, as Mark Lynn Anderson has astutely noted, the studies contributed to "the development of modern methods of social control" that have required ever-greater collection of "data" about the interiority and conduct of people for the purposes of "social administration."[131]

Work on delinquency and behavior once again exemplifies the connections between these studies and long-standing ideas of mimesis and the problem of liberal governance in the age of mass society. Robert Ezra Park initiated this work. After graduating from the University of Michigan, and working briefly as a journalist, Park conducted graduate work in Germany, finishing a thesis entitled *Masse und Publikum* in 1904 (translated as *The Crowd and the Public* in 1972), which surveyed the work on crowd psychology and mimetic effects, including that of Tarde, Le Bon, and Sidis.[132] Later, this perspective on collective behavior informed the *Introduction to the Science of Sociology*, which included work by Le Bon and extensively surveyed work on collective behavior as a critical component of

FIGURE 19. Psychogalvonometer (Wendell S. Dysinger and Christian A. Ruckmick, *The Emotional Response of Children to the Motion Picture Situation* [New York: Macmillan, 1933], 17).

understanding the problematic of social control, defined as the central task of sociology.[133] Park's enthusiasm for the Payne Fund project was important to Short at its inception, and he himself intended to conduct work on cinema as a component of collective behavior and its impact on the creation of delinquency. In early correspondence about the project, for example, he wondered whether the University of Chicago students Leopold and Loeb, infamous for the shocking murder of a young boy, had been influenced by the movies.[134]

Granted a fellowship in China, Park reluctantly withdrew from the project, passing the study of cinema and delinquency over to his colleague Herbert Blumer, then a young social psychologist at Chicago (and later well known for his work developing "symbolic interactionism," the sociological paradigm examining how individuals and groups interact).[135] *Movies, Delinquency, and Crime,* co-authored with Chicago graduate student Philip Hauser, pursued a more qualitative and ethnographic approach to research by including questionnaires and interviews with male and female prisoners, former criminals on parole, children who frequently truanted from school, and children who resided in areas designated as high-rate delinquency areas.[136] The authors drew precisely on models of suggestibility and imitation, showing, using the accounts of their subjects, the "imitation of criminal techniques" that followed from watching movies, how moving pictures "furthered and fortified the development of criminal conduct," by presenting "disciplinary problems" and functioning as a "sexual excitant" producing "sexual delinquency."[137] Movies, they concluded, have both readily observable effects in producing and contributing to delinquency and "unconscious" effects, disposing or leading "individuals to various forms of misconduct"; they are "problems of social control."[138]

Movies and Conduct, Blumer's second study for the Payne Fund project, pursued this argument about the direct and expansive influence of movies on conduct. Blumer inquired "into intimate experience" by conducting interviews with undergraduate, college, junior college, and high school students, as well as with young office and factory workers about their cinema-going. Blumer's account of what he called "emotional possession," where the "individual" spectator (particularly the adolescent) "loses self-control" directly mimicked accounts of suggestibility and imitation, perhaps most notably Le Bon's ideas about "emotional contagion" in crowds.[139] Movies induced, then,

> emotional agitation . . . while in this condition the observer becomes malleable to the touch of what is shown. Ordinary self-control is lost. Impulses and feelings are aroused, and the individual develops a readiness to certain forms of action which are foreign in some degree to his ordinary conduct. Precisely because the individual is in this crucible state what is shown to him may become the mold for a new organization of his conduct.[140]

Blumer feared this "new organization of . . . conduct" would transform traditional sexual morality in particular. The research "into intimate experience" and media use through confessional-like interviews marked the acute convergence of the histories of sexuality and cinema in the early twentieth-century, which formed one part of the broader liberal imperative to discern the truth of the subject in order ultimately to better manage conduct. Knowledge produced in the human and social sciences dovetailed with this objective.

Not all of the studies suggested such a direct media impact on conduct. Many of the scholars began to suggest that media was one influence, albeit a powerful one, among many. Garth Jowett, Ian Jarvie and Kathy Fuller's invaluable reevaluation of the studies shows in compelling detail the difficulties that some of the researchers had in squaring their research findings with the objective of Short in particular. In doing so they single out the unpublished study by Paul Cressey as exemplary of a more complex and nuanced approach to the question of media influence. Cressey's study was to be coauthored with Frederick Thrasher and was part of Thrasher's research project on the broader environment of boys and young men in a neighborhood of East Harlem in New York City. Cressey is praised for his attempt to study "the movies as one part of a total 'social situation' or 'configuration' in which they are experienced."[141] Jarvie suggests that this research "promised to be the most fruitful of all the studies, and . . . might have provided continuity with media research to come."[142] By situating influence in a broader context, Cressey's research rhymed with the dominant paradigm in communication studies as it grew in the latter 1930s and 1940s into a discipline predicated on "selective influence theories."[143] But from a different vantage point, one that is more focused on the way disciplinary knowledge and the expansion of "expertise" connected to liberal governmental rationalities, Cressey's broadening of the object of study represented (in Anderson's words) "not so much a reversal of the bureaucratic impetus of the original studies as an elaboration on and extension of the sites of observation and of social control."[144]

Blumer's perspective on the relatively direct impact of media on conduct rhymed most precisely with Short's, who commended his work wholeheartedly as revelatory of the profound and dangerous effects of cinema on young people. It was this sense of the mimetic and deleterious effects of cinema that was most widely publicized from the Payne Fund Studies, notably through the publication of a popular summary commissioned by Short and written by journalist Henry Forman.[145] *Our Movie Made Children,* as the book was called, simplified the complexity of some of the studies, though it was entirely consistent with the preexisting accounts of mimesis and the movies that informed many of the studies and were most clearly apparent in the work on delinquency. Forman asserted that the studies provided evidence for "the influence of motion pictures and their impersonations upon the character, conduct and behavior of vast numbers of our nation and especially upon the more malleable and younger people."[146] So much so, in fact, that the "conclusion appears inescapable," Forman wrote, "that to show certain types of pictures—so numerous in the current output—in what are known as high-rate delinquency areas, in cities, is in some measure like selling whiskey to the Indians, against which there are quite justly severe laws and sharp penalties."[147] Whiskey, in this turn of phrase, is equivalent to the narcotic effects of movies, rendering kids as undisciplined – and uncivilized – as "Indians." Quite clearly the innovation of new knowledge about cinema was rooted in the same soil as that of regulatory practices for the maintenance of social control in a liberal polity among undisciplined, potentially dangerous subjects.

"ARE WE MOVIE MADE?"

Short had hoped to use the studies to kickstart a regulatory clampdown, and he mounted a PR offensive that sought to disseminate the findings through the mass media of the press in particular. Countless articles suggested the studies showed the movies had deleterious effects on young people. "Overexcitement is seen," the *New York Times* exclaimed.[148] But overall the studies had little direct impact on the regulation of cinema and, in the main, did not initiate the sustained examination of cinema from within the disciplinary boundaries of the human and social sciences. The majority of the scholars involved did not continue with the study of film—some of them were disaffected with the popularization of the studies in Forman's book and with the uneasy mix of research and policy activism that constituted the project overall.[149] When the study of film developed further, it did so in the humanities.

One can speculate on the reasons for this limited impact. Certainly the Production Code established by the mainstream film industry's trade organization the Motion Picture Producers and Distributors of America (MPPDA) in 1930 had already incorporated some of the logic underpinning the studies. The code's preamble acknowledged the great "emotional appeal" of moving pictures, their "affect [on] moral standards," and (in a nice though unacknowledged nod to Adam Smith) the process of "sympathy" generated for its characters or stars.[150] In this way the political goals of the studies were already partly realized, or at least deflected, in the code. Which is another way of saying that theories about cinema—beginning almost with the birth of cinema itself but continually rolling and gathering disciplinary moss—had considerable impact on US commercial film. The code formalized and advertised the industry's investment in the policing of the social and political function of mainstream cinema, making sure in particular that cinema avoided any overt controversial political engagement, to smooth its passage across the world and avoid drawing unnecessary state attention to the industry. Media worked better as a commercial entity when it was apolitical.

The Payne Fund had hoped to avoid antagonizing the mainstream film industry's powerful lobbying and trade organization, the MPPDA.[151] But it failed. Will Hays began to orchestrate a direct attack on the studies and the ideas about the mimetic movies that they continued and deepened. University of Chicago philosopher Mortimer Adler published a book in 1937 called *Art and Prudence*, likely with encouragement from the MPPDA, wherein he argued that the Payne Fund Studies were methodologically flawed (which they were); that they had discovered little or no harmful effects (arguable); and that, in any case, no value conclusions could be drawn from empirical research and thus social science was poorly equipped to make moral and political judgments.[152] (The argument here was part of a broader disciplinary skirmish between philosophy and the human and social sciences.) Adler's argument was useful indeed for the mainstream film industry as it battled ongoing regulatory interventions, particularly those about ownership and oligopoly, which eventually resulted in the initiation of antitrust proceedings against the studios in 1938. Censorship skirmishes were, as Richard Maltby in particular has emphasized, often a smokescreen for the industry's investment in deflecting state intervention away from its core economic practices.[153] Industrial self-censorship was in this respect frequently straightforwardly PR.

Even so, a dense philosophical critique of the reasoning protocols of the human and social sciences was unlikely to shape public opinion. Hays took a leaf out of

Short's book to overcome this and commissioned a popular summary of Adler's arguments, written by Raymond Moley, a former member of the Roosevelt administration and professor of public law at Columbia. In a Bernays-like reference to Forman's title, Moley called his book *Are We Movie Made?* and put Adler's argument in a more accessible form. The question posed by the title was emphatically answered in the negative.[154] Corporate Hollywood thus sponsored philosophy, and what nowadays gets called "research impact," to argue that movies do not have direct and deleterious effects. The argument here had a direct economic determinant.

Going even further than this, the MPPDA sponsored forms of film study that countered the mimetic logic, which had been central to regulatory and scholarly accounts of cinema up to this point. In 1934, after the publication of the studies and the same year as a PR revision of the Production Code, the organization sponsored the educational psychologist Mark May to develop a program of film education in concert with Yale University.[155] May had been one of the Payne Fund Studies scholars, and his volume *The Social Conduct and Attitude of Movies Fans* was one of the studies that deemphasized mimetic effects. Later May, in his role as director of the Institute of Human Relations at Yale, developed a series of short films drawn from Hollywood called *Secrets of Success,* which used extracts from Hollywood films to tell moral stories about how to behave appropriately and achieve personal and public success. The *Secrets of Success* series was a significant example of the way Hollywood sought to present itself as a form of character education and to intervene in the corporate management of "human relations."

Likewise, educationist Edgar Dale, whose (best-selling) volume for the Payne Fund Studies was called *How to Appreciate Motion Pictures,* developed a program of film education in concert with the National Council of Teachers of English and Ohio State University. On the one hand, these two programs promoted a sense of film as art and discussion subject, with Dale, for example, commending a canon of approved films, such as the adaptations of *A Tale of Two Cities, Great Expectations, A Midsummer Nights Dream,* and *Anne of Green Gables.* The educational programs were also conceived of as a way of destroying the mimetic effects of cinema, thereby enabling adolescents to control their response to cinema and to not fall foul of what Blumer had termed "emotional possession." Lea Jacobs thus rightly observes that the programs Dale and May devised follow directly from the model of spectatorship advanced by the Payne Fund Studies as a whole.[156] Cinema study in this sense became an "appreciation" of movies as art and pedagogic administration of psychological and aesthetic disciplines for forming sensibility and managing the self and problematic conducts. Given this, it made perfect sense that Dale's program of "appreciation" was developed with the National Council of Teachers of English, for English had itself become a discipline centered on the formation of the practices of ethical self-formation imperative to liberal governance.[157] Later experiments with establishing film studies frequently connected to disciplinary organizations in English studies; and this tended to produce the idea that film studies was best allied to the humanities and to practices of close textual reading and "appreciation."[158]

Clearly the corporate film industry's trade organization saw in this alliance with the humanities a way of further solidifying their argument—made for political and economic purposes—that film was essentially nonpurposeful, and apolitical, being at its worst simply harmless entertainment but at its best a form of art. Elsewhere, other developments like, for example, the creation of the Film Study Division at the Museum of Modern Art furthered this growing conception that film might be a form of art and thus would be best "appreciated" as part of the humanities.[159] The movies achieved the dream of some of those early migrant entrepreneurs, and of the film industry that developed—a form of cultural capital that ultimately helped marginalize the long-standing concerns about mimesis and the cinema as a troublesome agent of socialization and propaganda.

But those concerns about mimetic media did not disappear but instead mutated into a discipline of communication studies, which began in scattered form in the 1930s as part of the social and human sciences and which ultimately embraced a model of selective and limited effects in its analysis, initially of radio and later television. (The Payne Fund itself shifted its attention away from cinema and toward the analysis of radio in the 1930s.)[160] Communication studies developed in particular with the help of the Rockefeller Foundation, one example of the growing significance of such foundations in the model of corporate liberalism established in this period. Recall that the Rockefeller Foundation supported the production of educational films such as *Unhooking the Hookworm*, which was discussed in chapter 8. In this spirit the Rockefeller Foundation officer John Marshall suggested that the foundation could play an innovative role in the development of radio and film in particular as tools for public education. "But," Brett Gary writes, "as their interest in the connections between media technologies and education expanded, so did awareness of the inadequacy of existing theoretical and empirical knowledge about mass communications."[161] In order to rectify this inadequacy, the foundation sponsored a variety of mass communications research projects, including significant ones on propaganda, public opinion, and effects studies. Using this largely empirical and behaviorist approach, the foundation innovated a series of questions—Who? Said what? To whom? With what effect?—and began to establish a model of limited media effects that mostly remains dominant in communication studies to this day.[162] Quite clearly the corporate interest in producing pedagogic texts to better "educate" mass audiences tripped over into the establishment of research protocols to understand media and its social and political roles.

"From its outset," Gary shows, "the Communication Seminar was decidedly interventionist and policy oriented" and "identified its agenda . . . with the state's agenda, in terms both of offensive and defensive propaganda intelligence work."[163]

Communication studies in this respect came to be seen as important to the national security state that had emerged in early forms during World War I and expanded in the late 1930s and thereafter during the Cold War. The Rockefeller funds supported work on propaganda and in the process established the American Film Center in 1938, which liaised with some of the institutions examined thus far—for example, the film division of the Department of Interior, the Division of Cultural Relations in the Department of State—to help produce and circulate media supporting state objectives. One example is the organization of an exchange of cultural and educational films between North and Latin America that was intertwined with broader economic and geopolitical imperatives and that again made clear the importance of media to those objectives. Grierson's documentary film units in England and Canada were models for the American Film Center, evidence of the transnational exchange of expertise in developing the utility of film for liberal objectives.[164] Marshall helped initiate the establishment of a film library at the (Rockefeller-funded) Museum of Modern Art as well, and as part of that the foundation financed Siegfried Kracauer's fellowship at MOMA, which began in 1941. During that time, he produced his now canonical analysis of German film, *From Caligari to Hitler*, as part of the agenda shared between corporate foundation and state to examine and utilize propaganda.[165] Kracauer's work on German film helped concretize the argument that totalitarian states—not liberal democratic ones—produce propaganda, and this position would be central to the propaganda the United States produced about the Cold War in particular. The Rockefeller Foundation also funded Paul Lazarsfeld's well-known radio research project and Hadley Cantril's public opinion research project, both at Princeton University and both of which were significant to the corporate and state elites' investment in discerning the nature of media influence on public opinion.[166]

Communication studies as it developed under the aegis of corporate and state sponsorship concentrated on the question of influence, ultimately concluding in large part that the media had limited but significant effects. Lazarsfeld discerned a varied communicative process that was filtered through familial and social groups and was not that dissimilar to the model Cressey had proposed in his study of boys and movies. Equally significant, this research tradition effectively supported what Lazarsfeld called "administrative" as opposed to "critical" research.[167] Lazarsfeld drew a distinction here between the developing empirical work in the United States and the traditions of progressive political analysis that were associated in particular with European émigrés to the United States. While some of those émigré scholars—like Kracauer—were used in this project, others were unable to translate a leftist critique of the dangerous power of mass media into administrative work on its muted effects. Theodor Adorno, for example, worked for a brief period of time on the Princeton Radio Project but left amid disagreements about methodologies and political purposes. Adorno and Horkheimer's subsequent scathing critique of the culture industries marks a very different conception of media and its ideological role than that advanced within mainstream communication studies.

The emergence of models of film and communication studies that de-emphasized ideological effects supported the maintenance of the corporate-controlled system of mass media. I follow in this James Carey, who has, for example, cogently argued that the shaping of communication studies as mostly a model of limited effects de-politicized the potentially radical Progressive critique of media and "legitimated a different form of research and a different role for social scientists in the apparatus of government and rule."[168] One concrete example here of this process can usefully loop back to the discussion in the previous chapter. In 1927, right at the outset of the Payne Fund Studies, William Short corresponded with William Seabury. This was at about the same time that Seabury was busy thinking about the place of film in the work of the League of Nations. Seabury argued that the Payne Fund Studies should include analysis of the ownership of the film industry. It "is more important to study the causes of existing conditions which involve the economic and commercial phases of the subject," Seabury wrote to Short, "than it is to examine further into the effects of motion pictures."[169] But Short marginalized Seabury, and this agenda completely dropped from the studies, likely it seems because of Short's and the Payne Fund's fears about the lobbying power of the film industry under Hays's leadership. The central question of the Payne Fund Studies became one of media influence and not the question of ownership and related questions about corporate- or public-financed media. Communication studies as it emerged in particular in the significant Rockefeller-financed communication seminar also deemphasized questions of ownership and instead focused on questions of limited effects and the utility of media in corporate and state communication. The study of film was increasingly hived off even from that paradigm and relocated—and "appreciated"—in the humanities.

Deemphasizing the question of influence and ownership in traditions of film and communication studies thereafter has been dangerously politically disabling, mistakenly ceding the ground of necessary debate about media power to the conservative (and frequently censorial) agenda, from where much of it originated in the first place. But it behooves those of us interested in the place of media in shoring up exploitative political and economic practices to take more seriously the ideas about the malleability of people and related practices of mass persuasion carried through media, which began to emerge in late nineteenth-century modernity. And to explicate the practices and history, whereby media was put to work to facilitate the governance of mass populations and the expansion of a corporate and consumer economy as precisely, empirically, as possible. Our children might not be movie made, or straightforwardly media made; "effects" are not direct or unmediated. But it would be naïve to think that the systematic and repetitive nature of a media system largely captured by corporate capital is adequate to meet the communicative needs of democracy and has little impact on socialization and attitudes. It has seemed to me (among others) that the now mostly conservative and fragmented discipline of film studies might *collectively* muster better responses to the political and economic uses of media and culture and the related ongoing devastating consequences of globalized capitalism on people and the world than it currently does. One consequence of my argument—that we need to collectively think more carefully about the ways in which film and other forms of mass media have been used to build and support a system that is profoundly destructive to individuals, social groups, populations, and even the planet we share—is the book you are now reading.

The Golden Harvest of the Silver Screen

In the same year—1927—that William Seabury unsuccessfully urged the Payne Fund to examine the existing ownership structures in Hollywood, and the Radio Act consolidated corporate ownership and control of radio, two investment banks issued prospectuses evaluating "motion picture securities," which effectively channeled significant amounts of finance capital toward established film studios.[1] Both bank reports recounted the history of moving pictures (with varying degrees of accuracy) that charted the rise and *stabilization*—a key term in both reports—of the industry, so that by 1926, a total of $1.5 billion was invested in the business of cinema.[2] Much of this was in property, particularly the theater chains that studios had been buying and constructing since the first influx of finance capital into the film industry, amid the rise of securities ownership in the immediate postwar period. In some of the theaters built with this money, other office and retail spaces were included. The history of cinema is rarely written as a history of property, but the fact that the ephemeral pleasures of the silver screen were anchored in the materiality of property—"real, unquestioned values"—was significant to finance capitalists.[3] In the accompanying image from the Californian investment bank Hunter, Dulin and Co's report *The Golden Harvest of the Silver Screen*, the rise in investments in property and "subsidiaries" just between 1924 and 1926 is rendered graphically (see fig. 20).[4] The subsidiaries included such things as finely calibrated distribution and logistics networks, relying on the material and communicative networks of railroads, roads, telegrams, and telephones, that marked the establishment of a national and global infrastructural system for the rapid circulation of film through a complex tiered system of exhibition. Bankers quickly realized that the establishment and control of distribution systems—what we might call

Showing increased investments in theatres and subsidiaries from 1924 to 1926 by Paramount, Loew's, Stanley, Orpheum, Fox and Universal. Buildings show combined investments in theatre properties— money bags, combined investments in subsidiaries. (Based on Wall Street Journal figures.)

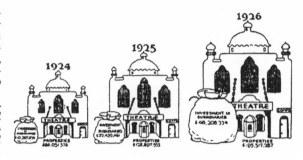

FIGURE 20. Graph showing rise in cinema theater investments, 1924–26 (Hunter, Dulin and Co., *The Golden Harvest of the Silver Screen* [California, 1927], 9).

infrastructural power—were integral to the profitability of film businesses. Quite possibly these "subsidiaries" also included the silver consumed in the manufacture of motion pictures, noted by investment bank Halsey, Stuart and Co to be greater than that used by the US mint in its production of the currency.[5] The suggestive connections among film, silver, and money in this bank report on investing in media can remind us again how cinema was enmeshed with wider practices of extractive imperialism, as well as the finance capital that frequently drove the spatial expansion of the capitalist world system. The golden *harvest* of the silver screen, indeed.

Both prospectuses told a story of massive growth, of (an almost Fordist) rationalization of work practices, and of the establishment of a "well organized and integrated" industry, accomplished in particular through the operations of the "very effective trade association" established in 1922.[6] Liberal "self-regulation" was then, as it is now, the preferred form for corporate and financial entities. The reports are clear sighted about the advantages brought to the industry by the Motion Picture Producers and Distributors of America (MPPDA), which were principally the stabilization of economic relations between its constituent parts, efficient "arbitration of disputes," and "improvement of *public relations.*"[7] Quite clearly the so-called Hays Office functioned chiefly as a forum to stabilize economic relations and to better enable oligopolistic control by major producers and distributors, consistent with the interests of finance capitalists in establishing stable and controlled markets. Praise was issued, for example, for the studio control of distribution and exhibition, so that out of "425 pictures . . . sent to this country . . . only six were successful in winning a showing in American theatres," while the "constant and mighty stream of wealth" that was the cinema industry in the United States was "further enriched by the pesos and lire and gulden and yen that steadily flow into it from all portions of the globe."[8] Will Hays's regularly issued refrain, "trade follows the film," was repeated in an observation likely of some interest to finance capitalists.[9] Indeed, the influx of finance capital in a second wave of investment, beginning in 1925 and exemplified by these prospectuses, clearly indicates the success of the studios and the MPPDA in establishing the kind of "stable" oligopolistically controlled market that investment bankers preferred for themselves, even while they simultaneously advocated for "free trade" for the global movements of capital.[10] The studio creation of the Academy of Motion Picture Arts and Sciences, also in 1927, principally to suppress unionization in the industry was also a part of that process.[11] Written two years before the Great Depression made clear the stark division between "real, unquestioned values" and what Marx called "fictitious capital," the prospectuses predicted "boundless" growth for the film industry in the future.[12] Graphs "confirmed" the remarkable investment opportunity that was corporate media, and the Halsey, Stuart report concluded with a useful summary of why motion picture bonds were a good investment (see fig. 21).[13]

What did bankers want with "Hollywood"? The answer is on one level excessively obvious. Finance capitalists generate money from money. Karl Marx's formula, tweaked and historicized by Giovanni Arrighi in his remarkable history of the cyclical rise of financialization, is operative here: M-C-M', in which money is transformed into commodity capital, which then generates supplementary money in an expanding dialectic of accumulation.[14] I outlined earlier in this book the significant roles played by investment banks as intermediaries between industry and capital in the rise of large corporations and of corporate mergers in the 1890s. Quite clearly the film industry began to seem like a productive site for investment, most notably after the war and the demonstration of the utility and influence of cinema in helping sell state debt. Bond issues in general increased dramatically after the success of the Liberty Bond campaigns.[15] In 1919, the significant and influential investment bank Kuhn, Loeb issued a bond prospectus for the film studio that came to be called Paramount, the capital from which was used by the firm's chief executive, Adolph Zukor, in the purchase and construction of cinemas to tie exhibition and distribution networks together with production in one corporate structure.[16] Zukor's goals here, to consolidate manufacturing, wholesaling (distribution), and retail (exhibition), were consistent with the imperatives of other capitalists in control of large industries that, beginning in the latter years of the nineteenth century, had produced the corporate-dominated economy. Likewise they connected with the aims of financiers to use capital to create large corporate entities that controlled markets, either singularly or in oligopolistic structures, like those seen initially in the first wave of corporate growth and corporate mergers in the 1890s (eg, the House of Morgan's roles in the creation of US Steel and GE). Kuhn, Loeb had played an important role in the consolidation of large railway networks, and now seemingly turned their attention to the circulation of signs and meanings, rather than of people and materials.[17] What began to emerge through

SUMMARIZING—

Why Well Chosen Bonds

in the

MOTION PICTURE INDUSTRY

Are Deserving of the Investor's Confidence

1. *A BASIC INDUSTRY*—the demand for entertainment and recreation is instinctive and universal.

2. *A PRODUCT WITHIN THE REACH OF THE MASSES*—The motion picture satisfies this universal demand for entertainment at prices within the reach of all.

3. *AN EXPANDING MARKET*—Improvements in both the production and exhibition phases of the industry have produced, and give promise of continuing to produce, substantial annual gains in theatre attendance.

4. *FIRMLY ENTRENCHED*—American films dominate the world markets, and are so entrenched as to be able to meet successfully all competition.

5. *WELL ORGANIZED AND INTEGRATED* — production, distribution, and exhibition are generally well coordinated.

6. *CAPABLY MANAGED*—concentration of control provides the usual advantages of large-scale production, one of the most important of which is sound, able management.

7. *CONSTANT EARNINGS*—demand in the exhibition field varies little in dull times; seasonal fluctuations are being steadily eliminated.

8. *A CASH BUSINESS*—in both the exhibition and production ends, the product is largely paid for as delivered.

9. *SUBSTANTIAL FIXED ASSETS*—largely in real estate; about five-sixths of the total investment of the industry is in theatre properties, mostly in important business centers where land values are well stabilized or increasing.

10. *ATTRACTIVE YIELDS*—being a new industry, yields are somewhat more attractive than in older and more conventional investment fields.

FIGURE 21. Halsey, Stuart Co. summary on motion picture bond investment (Halsey, Stuart Co., *The Motion Picture Industry as a Basis for Bond Financing* [1927], 28).

this alliance of studios, investment bankers, and the capital located principally in banks and large institutional investment structures was a corporate, vertically integrated studio system, which came to be parceled out in the 1920s among a small number of large combines with access to capital. The history of that process, and the consequences that followed this merging of media and capital, chiefly in the period from Kuhn, Loeb's 1919 report to Halsey, Stuart's 1927 prospectus, is my principal subject here. This history contributes to my broader goal of discerning how media was made useful and functional for forms of corporate and financial liberalism.

I mention the 1927 Radio Act here, then, not merely as contextual detail, and for at least two reasons. One, the control of large well-capitalized corporations over popular forms of mass media was a transmedial phenomenon in the 1920s. The developments with respect to both radio and cinema marked the colonization of media by corporate and financial entities and the concomitant marginalization of alternative conceptions of the possible functions of media. Given that, the trenchant critique of the consequences of that control by radio reformers, and by some scattered critics of the film industry like Seabury and others in the early 1930s, bears repeating, and even heeding: the corporate and capital control over media—its construction as a commodity form, synced to the varied generation of capital—marks a radical diminution of the possibilities of media, culture, and the public sphere, which is corrosive to the possibility of democracy. Cinema history has often been written as if the studios were the organizations that invented vertical integration, when this was actually consistent with a longer history of the corporate form and its ties to capital. Even worse, this phenomenon is described neutrally, without any explication of how this form (in this instantiation) radically limited the possible uses and functions of cinema and expanded the cultural power of capital.[18] The capital made material in ornate corporate "palaces" of consumption, made visible on screens through expensive machinery and the sumptuous shaping of electric light bent toward the spectacular fetishism of commodities (and people as commodities), was synced to the generation of further capital. (M-C(inema)-M'). In the process, the cultural was made economic, just as the economic was made cultural.[19]

Two, the second wave of investment in Hollywood, exemplified by the two prospectuses I began with here, took place on the eve of the consolidation of the convergent media technology of sound cinema. The large electrical, technology, and telecommunications corporations involved in the establishment, consolidation, and control of radio as a technological commodity synced to the consumer economy were similarly *invested* in the creation of sound cinema. I mapped out some of the histories of those corporations (and their close ties to US state agendas and finance capital) in chapter 9. GE and its partly owned subsidiary Radio Corporation of America (RCA) and American Telegraph and Telephone (AT&T) and its wholly owned subsidiary Western Electric played significant roles, both in developing the technologies that enabled the syncing of sound and image and in buying and controlling the patents ("intellectual *property*") that generated profits shared out between these corporations and the phalanx of investment and commercial banks with which they were allied. Cinema became a part of the corporate strategy to turn technology and its intellectual property into profit. The complex ties between film studios (media corporations), electrical/technology/telecommunications corporations, and investment and commercial banks bear exploring in the context of the interlinked rise of the corporation, mass media, consumer economy, and practices of financialization.

Consequential ties among capital, electrical and telecommunications corporations, and media were established here that significantly framed the operating assumptions about how media should function thereafter. One might think of this as something akin to a Big Bang for media. Cinema and radio began this process, becoming convergent—with the backing of finance capital—in the 1920s, but this expanded thereafter to include television, satellite-enabled communications and media, the Internet, the smartphone, and so on. The media produced from these interlocking relations among telecommunications, media corporations, and finance capital became convergent in the mid-1920s because of the related goals of the corporations and banks that established these relationships. Even further, the networks created by electrical and telecommunication corporations, intertwined with media and supported by finance capitalists from this precise point onward, were integral to the astonishing expansion of capitalism and new patterns of consumption across the world system in the twentieth and twenty-first centuries.

What follows tracks the lineaments of this Big Bang. In some senses the story I tell in this chapter is disarmingly simple, for banks, corporate studios, and technology and telecommunications corporations all had similar goals in the minimization of regulation and maximization of profit. This is corporate liberalism in action, with the replacement of market mechanisms to ensure corporate orchestration and control. But the interaction among these profit-seeking entities, across a particular history and within a particular regulatory regime, means that these goals were not always simply aligned, and struggles ensued among these institutions for control and larger shares of profits. In the early years of the Depression, for example, Fox Studios overextended and was taken over by bankers, while a new major studio, RKO, was formed by GE and RCA as a consequence of the complex battles for precedence in sound technology. The history of these imperatives and interactions is both structural and contingent.

One way to conceive the complex relations in the history I recount below is to separate out the imperatives of the constituent forces. What did film entrepreneurs and studios want? What did banks want? What did technology and telecommunication corporations want? How did these entities go about achieving their goals?

Where do these goals align, and where do they diverge? But we must also factor into this history the goals of the state and its regulation of the economy, exemplified by the initiation of antitrust proceedings against Paramount in 1921, after the first tranche of investment capital had enabled the studio to expand across all sectors of production, wholesaling, and retailing.[20] What regulatory policies affected the economic practices of studios, banks, and corporations? How did the corporate studios respond? Finally this specific history of media and capital must be linked back both to a broader history of the corporation and capital and to the specific rise in securities ownership, debt, and the consumer economy that emerged after the war only to be derailed (for a time) by the Great Depression of the 1930s.

The history that follows traces out the intricate connections that developed among corporations, media, and finance capital. What, though, resulted from these interactions? What were the consequences of the growing ties between banks and media, in the first instance, and then electrical and telecommunications corporations? I have begun to suggest some specific ones, like the creation of vertically integrated corporations and an oligopolistic market patrolled by a powerful trade organization, but I propose to probe further the ways the broad and specific practices of these new media corporations were influenced and shaped by the imperatives of finance capitalists, many of whom sat on the boards of studios representing substantial shareholdings.[21] I rely on period and subsequent accounts of the consequences of "financial control" of business practices, though much further research and reflection will be needed.[22] But answers to these fundamental questions about control and consequences will help us better discern the expansive ways in which media was made functional for the system of corporate liberalism and finance capital that was elaborated as the foundation of our contemporary modernity.

"NETWORK OF A THOUSAND THREADS"

In 1919, the investment bank Kuhn, Loeb commissioned a report on the corporation that came to be called Paramount.[23] The report was outlined in detail by Howard T. Lewis in his 1930 book *Cases on the Motion Picture Industry,* published while Lewis was a professor of marketing at the Business School at Harvard, and in the aftermath of a series of talks given by motion picture entrepreneurs at the university in 1927, which themselves marked a significant moment in the consolidation of the cultural and economic status of cinema. (These events, and Lewis's two useful books on the economics of the industry, were financially supported by Joseph P. Kennedy, then a banker and investor but better known now as the father of John F. Kennedy: finance capital, media, and politics have a long and complex history.)[24] Lewis tells us that Zukor approached the bankers because he needed financing to purchase and construct theaters in "key locations in order to protect the producing and distributing activities of the business."[25] Various banks turned Zukor down, until the venerable Kuhn, Loeb expressed interest. Zukor provided comprehensive financial statements, but the bank "desired to have more information on the industry as a whole," and so hired American International Corporation (AIC) to investigate Paramount and the industry with a view to determining whether it represented a sound business opportunity.[26] The choice of AIC was likely not coincidental. The company had formed in 1915 specifically to develop trade connections in foreign countries and promote the investment of American capital abroad.[27] Written by a vice president of the company named Harris H. D. Connick, who had (appropriately enough) previously been "director of works of the Panama-Pacific International Exposition," the report emphasized the possibilities for the global dominance of US media.[28] Kuhn, Loeb in turn had significant connections to German capital.[29]

Connick's report for the investment bank surveyed the growth of the industry using concrete, material indices (such as the amount of celluloid used, projection machines sold, and fan magazines consumed) and examined Paramount's distribution records and financial statements to trace the number of cinemas existing in the United States and the world.[30] Connick quickly established that control of distribution infrastructure and exhibition was integral to the realization of rental values. Numerous other financial reports on cinema in the period similarly identified distribution as key to profitability.[31] The large domestic market for moving pictures (15,000 cinemas in 1919) meant that those films could be sold relatively cheaply abroad, Connick observed, thus undercutting foreign competition and permanently establishing the precedence and profitability of US media.[32] (Connick's report revealed also that Paramount had bought a lot of Liberty Bonds and that it had created corporate subsidiaries in such a way as to avoid paying what he called "excessive taxes.")[33] The detailed survey of the growth of the industry; the profit potential; and the assets, liabilities, and strengths of Paramount convinced the investors and bankers that "the industry as a whole had reached a point in its development at which *stabilized* earnings were to be expected in the future," and thus that media was a sound investment.[34] Indeed, profits were so high, Connick wrote, that the industry "deserved to be taken in hand by business men of high standing and made respectable."[35] Kuhn, Loeb accordingly established a financial syndicate to float a ten million dollars preferred stock issue on the stock exchange in late 1919, and Paramount used the money to buy and construct cinemas.[36] By 1921 the company owned 303 theaters, ensuring first-run exhibition in most significant markets.[37] Capital enabled the company to vertically integrate, tying production, distribution, and exhibition together in one corporate form in ways that enabled the company to *capitalize* on previous success and develop new economies of scale that gave it first-mover advantage in the coming era of corporate media.

Connick's report praised the stability brought by vertical integration, and was one example of the way in which capital supported the establishment of large corporations with significant market dominance. It was in this respect consistent with the corporate and financial reconstruction of liberalism. The capital supplied principally by investment banks helped substitute "the visible hand of managerial direction" for "the invisible hand of market forces."[38] Movies became fully corporate at this precise moment. The report, written by a global financier for an investment bank (with significant ties to transnational capital), concluded by proposing that the board of directors of Paramount "should be reorganized and a different class of men should take the place on the board now occupied by the executives of the Corporation" and that a "finance committee" be established to help guide corporate policy.[39] Connick himself took the position of chairman, alongside "a representative from each of the security distributing firms in the syndicate, and the president of a commercial bank."[40] The *Wall Street Journal* named these members as F. G. Lee, president of the Irving National Bank, G. G. Dominick of investment bank Dominick and Dominick (later to lead a $50 million stock offering for General Motors), Maurice Wertheim of investment bank Hallgarten and Co., and Zukor himself.[41] Commercial and investment bankers, and global financiers, would sit around a table with media entrepreneurs, plotting strategy for control of the circulation of media as a profitable commodity through complex national and global networks.

Quite clearly Zukor had approached the bankers as part of an unfolding strategy to expand his business and also to respond to particular domestic and global issues in the film industry in early 1919, in the wake of the emergence of opposition to Paramount's control of distribution and the reopening of European production and markets.[42] Writing to existing stockholders in mid-1919, around the time of Kuhn, Loeb's investigation, Zukor proposed that "world conditions, as related to the motion picture industry, are ripe for legitimate and healthy extension which can best be provided for by the increase in capital."[43] His letter makes clear that global economic conditions at the end of the war were significant in attracting capital investment. Connick too agreed that the war had enabled the expansion of the film industry both domestically and globally: "The foreign producers practically stopped production during the war and it will take them several years to create organizations of stars, special writers and directors necessary for the work."[44] We can see this merging of corporate media and transnational capital as a significant effort to establish domestic and global control of this form of popular media at a moment of particular import in the transformation of the capitalist world system.

The strategies and developments that led Paramount to its position of primacy in the film industry by 1919, and to the doors of Kuhn, Loeb, are relatively well known and can be told quite quickly. But they butt also on to more expansive questions about film form and liberal and consumer culture that merit some attention.

In his talk before the professors and students of business at Harvard in 1927, Zukor recalled the success he had as an exhibitor with a three-reel film of the Passion Play made by the French company Pathé in 1907. "I stood at the door eager and anxious to hear the comments. People with tears in their eyes came over to me and said, 'What a beautiful thing this is.' I felt instinctively that this was the turning point, that my rent would be paid from now on."[45] Emboldened by the revenues realized through this commodification of religion, Zukor decided in 1911 to begin to "to take big plays and celebrities of the stage and put them on the screen."[46] *Queen Elizabeth,* starring the venerable stage actress Sarah Bernhardt, was the first of these films, and it was quickly followed by others that Zukor started exhibiting in large vaudeville and legitimate theaters.[47] He called the company Famous Players.

The developments brokered the transition from a film system formed on the basis of the rapid turnover of a program of several one-reel films (each lasting about 12 minutes) to the feature-length film as the central and concluding element of a film program.[48] Zukor told his privileged audience that he listened to the responses of audiences to these early feature films and became "sure then that *personalities* plus a good story were all that were needed in pictures."[49] Quickly thereafter he put this logic to work to develop "famous players" specifically for the cinema, beginning most significantly in 1914 with Mary Pickford. The Canadian-born actress had worked both on stage and previously for D. W. Griffith at Biograph, and so (in Zukor's words) "knew the camera."[50] Pickford's remarkable popularity with audiences led Zukor to offer her ever-more lucrative contracts, effectively marking the beginning of a star/celebrity system that became integral to commercial media.[51] The shift from legitimate theater (Bernhardt) to cinema (Pickford) was a significant one in the context of the mechanical reproduction of forms of theatrical entertainment—the reconstitution of live entertainment through the machinery and chemicals of the second-stage industrial revolution—alongside the concomitant commodification of "personality" and celebrity.

In that same year Zukor contracted with the distribution company Paramount Pictures to circulate the feature films his company was producing through the national network of film exchanges that constituted Paramount.[52] The aim was, in Zukor's quasi-Fordist parlance, "to completely *systematize* the distribution of feature films."[53] W. W. Hodkinson had started Paramount in 1914, merging eleven regional exchanges to create what the Federal Trade Commission later described as "unique facilities for nation-wide distribution."[54] Various other production companies contracted with Paramount at the same time to guarantee a steady supply of product to exhibitors—two films a week was the initial goal, booked in a large block—that would in turn help producers finance and advertise their pictures with advance rental money.[55] Paramount charged production companies a distribution fee of 35 percent of the gross to cover operating costs and profit. Cinemas were quickly graded, based on size, location, and condition, and labeled from first-run to fifth-run. The films distributed by Paramount circulated initially to first-run cinemas, usually in urban areas and located close to transport hubs, and thereafter through the tiered system of distribution that left "clearance" time between exhibition sites. Normally films would open at first-run houses in large cities, followed by second-run, third-run, and so on until they eventually reached the neighborhood theaters in small towns and rural areas.

In 1916 Zukor proposed that Paramount and its producers merge, but Hodkinson refused, believing instead that production, distribution, and exhibition should remain separate and that the film industry could not be converted to practices of mass production.[56] Zukor disagreed, and in turn engineered a hostile take-over of the distributor by secretly buying the company's stock, "with the intent," as the Federal Trade Commission later framed it, "of perpetuating and making more effective" the "conspiracy" to "create a combination in restraint of competition and trade" and "of creating a convenient, permanent, and efficient instrumentality for the maintenance and operation thereof."[57] Hodkinson was deposed in a "well-orchestrated putsch" at the company's annual meeting in July 1916.[58] Quickly thereafter Zukor merged with the Lasky Feature Play Company, forming Famous Players–Lasky, and began, from 1917, establishing economic relationships—mostly through stock ownership—with significant regional exhibition chains.[59] The control over distribution and stars enabled the company to dictate favorable terms to exhibitors, particularly through the practice of block-booking, whereby independent theaters were strongly encouraged to rent movies in blocks in order to obtain the particularly popular star-led vehicles. This enabled the producers to begin to guarantee exhibition for all studio product, regardless of quality.

"The production of films by the major companies is not really an end in itself," Mae Huetting observed in her pioneering study of the economics of the industry; rather, "It is an instrument directed toward the accomplishment of a larger end, i.e., domination of the theater market."[60] Lower-budget films made by the major studios and booked alongside higher-budget star vehicles allowed the studios to occupy exhibition time and so foreclose entry into the market by independent producers and distributors. Exhibitors either acquiesced to these practices, or they resisted, and the most significant iteration of the latter imperative was the formation of First National in 1917 by a group of disaffected exhibitors.[61] First National created a distribution network of its own through its chain of theaters and began to contract with film producers and significant stars to supply films to them. In 1918 the company poached Pickford from Paramount and Charlie Chaplin from Mutual.[62] What emerged was a loose form of vertical integration, tying exhibitors—who acted as distributors in their particular regions—to production subsidiaries.[63]

Zukor approached investment bankers, then, in this precise context, as part of an ongoing and intensified struggle to control distribution and access to exhibition.[64] From mid-1919 on, the Federal Trade Commission reported, Paramount "adopted a progressive and increasing policy of building, buying, owning or otherwise controlling theatres" for "the purpose of intimidating and coercing exhibitors to lease and exhibit films" produced and distributed by the corporation. Capital released by investment bankers funded the construction of new "picture palaces" located near good transport links, which made use also of the economies of scale outlined in Connick's report for Kuhn, Loeb.[65] These picture palaces are the ones now often celebrated in historical accounts of the so-called golden age of Hollywood. Many of them were the materialization of capital—made into property, shaped as a consumer utopia, and constructed as part of a bitter struggle for control over a media industry.[66] Zukor and Paramount later "induced" affiliates of First National to "enter employment under the control of Mr. Zukor," seemingly infiltrated the board of directors of the company, and effectively destroyed it in 1926 by taking over its significant Midwestern exhibition chain of Balaban and Katz.[67]

Two lessons from this compressed history of the enduring shape of Hollywood merit emphasis. The first, to reiterate, is simply that vertical integration significantly marginalized alternative formations and imaginations of cinema. Making media corporate in this way radically limited the public sphere. For example, the flourishing union and progressive filmmaking of the 1910s, surveyed by labor historian Steven Ross, found no place in the distribution and exhibition networks of a corporate industry.[68] The second follows: the realization that distribution was integral to profitability and control. Establishing a complex and indeed expensive system for the selling and movement of film across the nation (and the globe) was central to the industrial primacy of Paramount. Distribution remains central to the economics of the mainstream film industry.[69] Paramount innovated a *national* distribution system in the first instance. In doing so it replaced local and regional distribution in ways analogous to the growth of mass national marketing and distribution of brand name goods in this period.[70] Chain stores, emerging in the 1920s, relied on the economies of mass distribution, selling nationally advertised brands in a way that substituted the consumerist "parable of the Democracy of Goods" for republican expectations of "an equality of self-sufficiency, personal independence, and social interaction."[71] Indeed, Paramount utilized in particular national magazines in its advertising campaigns, the same magazines—like *The Saturday Evening Post*—that Richard Ohmann considers integral to the establishment of a national consumer culture.[72] Will Hays praised the consequences of this new national image market in his talk before the future business leaders of the world at Harvard: "Through motion pictures we are bettering living conditions everywhere, especially in the small towns. No longer does the girl in Sullivan, Indiana, guess what the styles are going to be in three months. She knows, because she sees them on the screen . . . There are no more out-of-date towns."[73] From the late 1920s and early 1930s, the networks of radio became increasingly significant. The *nation* was increasingly imagined there-

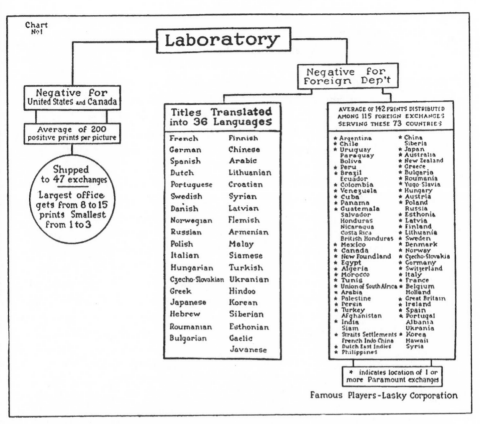

FIGURE 22. Global film distribution (Kent, "Distributing the Product," in Kennedy, *Story of the Films*, 211).

after as a collective through media and consumer goods. Global distribution began to expand that imagination further afield.

The distributional system elaborated by Paramount in the 1920s is mapped and explained in a talk by the company's "general manager," Sidney Kent, before the students and professors at Harvard in 1927. Two negative prints were received by the distribution arm, and from there about 200 positive prints were circulated to the 47 U.S. and Canadian exchanges controlled by the company and 142 prints circulated to the 115 foreign exchanges the company controlled.[74] The accompanying chart mapped out how the company distributed its film across the world (see fig. 22).[75] Films were screened initially in the central office—and an estimate of how much money the film would realize was made, using statistical information gathered over the years—and parceled out initially between the three large sales divisions. Exchange offices took orders, negotiated with exhibitors, and advertised pictures both to them and to audiences.[76]

The mechanics of the system required "the scientific system of supervision," an in-house 1919 publication on "the story" of the corporation stated, built through "a prodigious amount of labor possible only to a corporation directed by wise foresight and backed by ample resources."[77] (It revealed also that the distribution arm of the organization published a weekly "internal house organ" called *Pep*, "devoted to what its name implies—stimulating the exchange force.")[78] Corporate size and reach, and an almost panopticon-like surveillance system, was needed—the corporation said—to facilitate the complex "network of a thousand threads" that enabled the distribution of media through the carefully delineated networks of space and time integral to the economic practices of the studio.[79] Telephones, railroads, and Paramount-owned automobiles facilitated this ceaseless, rapid movement and the imposition of a kind of economic order on space. The position of the person in charge of all this, the corporation stated, "is analogous to that of vice-president in charge of traffic on a railroad."[80]

Perhaps, though, the most important figure in this system was the humble "shipping clerk," who acted speedily to ship the print out, get it back, pass it over for inspection, and then ship it out again through the descending zones of profitability. "Time is what we sell," Kent stated bluntly.[81] Rhetoric emphasized Fordist efficiency:

> Nothing is done by hand that machinery can do. Powerful tabulating machines, an improvement on similar apparatuses used in the US Census Bureau, tabulate data from the exchanges in a small fraction of the time needed to perform the same operations by hand. Book-keeping machines, adding and computing machines, addressographs, duplicating machines, interoffice phones, and kindred appliances are used wherever possible to save time, effort, money.[82]

The system of distribution was predicated on "novelty," the speeded up circulation of texts and objects that was becoming crucial to the consumer economy. The run zone "protection" accorded first-run theaters, predominantly owned by the major studios, enabled the extraction of further surplus value from film predicated on temporality that dovetailed with new national advertising campaigns.[83] In action here is the elaboration of a very complex *logistics* system, which functioned with the accelerated work processes of a Ford factory to extract profit quickly from a product that had a somewhat limited shelf life.[84] Value came here to reside in speed, and topicality: time becomes money, and so distribution becomes part of "production," a phenomenon significant to this particular formation of capitalism and intensifying with film.

The 115 exchanges Paramount operated across the world likely functioned in similar fashion. The US film industry became global, at least at the level of distribution, from this point onward (the changing geographies of production, in search of cheaper labor, mostly came later, though the shift to California in the first place was a part of that imperative). Global profits amounted to about 25 percent of overall profits, Kent observed, so the films Paramount produced should first satisfy the domestic market yet always be mindful that "the profit in these pictures is in that last 25%."[85] The history of "distribution" and "logistics" in this expanded sense, with its knock-on effects on the definition of value, is integral to the history of the expansion of capitalism. It is part of the story of the creation of national and global markets.

"BONDS OF SYMPATHY"

Why, though, were "stars" integral to the "value" of cinema? Cinema historians have taught us that the efforts to stabilize and expand film production in the period, stretching from approximately 1903 to 1909, produced a new formal system formed on the basis of linear temporality and the subordination of such things as editing, camerawork, and composition to the demands to tell a story.[86] The emergence of what Tom Gunning terms "the narrator system" around 1908–09 was enmeshed with the presentation of psychologically individuated and internally motivated characters, who drove narratives forward in the production of a causal chain of events. Writes Gunning, "The approach to characterization in the *narrator-system* asserts its hold on *story* through an expression of *psychology*, by which I mean the portrayal of interior states, such as memories or strong emotions, which are then seen as motivation for the action of characters."[87] The narrator system reveals the motivations and desires of characters and thus draws spectators into the unfolding action, intensifying the "bonds of sympathy"—to invoke Adam Smith—between characters, or actors, and audiences. Various other formal developments intensified the focus on individuated characters and actions. The shift toward closer views of actors, the careful use of electric lighting to position those actors as the center of attention, produced new forms of emotional engagement that spread from character to actor. With the advent of the feature film, from around the time of the formation of *Famous* Players (c. 1912), the formal orchestration of emotional engagement was expanded and intensified. Point of view constructions, eye-line matches, and shot-reverse-shot structures all helped guide audiences through films and position them—optically and emotionally—with the central character and star.[88] The intensity of the emotional bonds established between audiences and stars was visible in the fan magazines that began to emerge in this period, the precursors to the myriad magazines and websites that today peddle stories about the celebrities of an expanded electronic and digital media culture.[89]

Quite clearly, the formal orchestration of emotional engagement dovetailed with the strategies of entrepreneurs like Zukor to use stars to publicize films and attenuate risk. In this way the star became something like a trademark and a brand, conveying information quickly to consumers, or audiences, that generated demand in particular to see the stars at the more expensive and lucrative first-run theaters controlled by the larger studios. Publicity strategies in the 1920s in particular came to focus ever more on stars. What this also enabled was a more careful planning of costs and the form of market stabilization favored in particular by bankers. Indeed, the AIC report on Paramount for Kuhn, Loeb had a section on the huge salaries that stars soon commanded; introduced with a note of anxiety—the costs were enormous, as the example of Pickford showed—the report quickly identified the star system's usefulness to the studio in terms of visibility and "the drawing value to the box office of the *personality* of the stars," before concluding that it "is sound and will continue to be used by the most successful producers."[90] By 1927, in investment bank Halsey, Stuart's prospectus, the benefits brought to the industry by the star system were more clearly delineated: "In the 'star' your producer gets not only a 'production' value in the making of his picture, but a 'trade-mark' value, and an 'insurance' value, which are very real and very potent in guaranteeing the sale of this product to the cash customers at a profit."[91] How surprising that the bankers justified excessive salaries ... but clearly the import of various forms of *value* brought by the star to the economics of the industry was evident to both entrepreneurs and financiers.

Three principal axes of value can be discerned here. In the first instance, the star brought "spectacular publicity" to a film, to invoke one of Edward Bernays's definitions of PR, which generated attention in the crowded world of mass-mediated spectacle.[92] In turn, this enabled the forms of market control for producers and distributors embodied in the practices of block booking. Finally, the massive costs paid in establishing stars, on the publicity that centered on them and on their salaries, functioned as effective barriers to competitors. In the early 1920s, the studios extended these efforts by embarking on a global recruitment strategy that used expensive stars—in particular young European female stars—to help extend market control and the supremacy of US commercial media in viable global markets.[93] Global media stars were created through this process.[94]

Why, though, were audiences drawn to stars? What models do we have for understanding why film audiences came to be emotionally invested in actors and actresses whom they were likely never to meet? I suggest that we might productively think about these relations as examples of mimesis in action and therefore as practical demonstrations of the kinds of emotional engagement explored more abstractly in the social science investigations of cinema in this period, as examined in the previous chapter. Zukor et al. were practical, entrepreneurial, social scientists, who built on the mimetic and affective relations central to the particular narrative form established as dominant in the 1910s and embodied by the figure of the star. Bond campaigns during wartime had begun to use these bonds of sympathy in the service of state debt, and PR and advertising pursued this thereafter, using stars to sell the new products and brands of the consumer age and to personalize and embody corporations.[95] Government functionaries, executives in film studios, PR gurus, and advertisers all used the emotional engagement of audiences with stars, the *sympathy* accorded them, to sell things to audiences, who were also consumers. Connections between stars, created mostly for purposes of profit and control by film executives, and the emergent culture of consumerism are concrete examples of the convergence of spectacle, of cinema, and of a corporate-driven consumer economy. Yet again, it is important to remember the simple fact that mass media and consumerism were and are inextricably linked. The corporate film star advertising merchandise on radio networks designed to bring audiences together with those products and owned by some of the same banks and corporations that were invested in cinema, is one of the clearest examples of that process.

The star helped personalize and humanize corporations, be they cinematic ones like Paramount or other kinds (eg, say, GE's employment of Ronald Reagan in the 1950s).[96] In this regard the star was a form of PR in action, embodying an idea of corporate personhood that was legally established in the late nineteenth century as a crucial precondition of the emergence and expansion of the corporation and the consumer economy that form helped establish. What often gets called (if not always accurately) "classical" narrative, emerging in nascent form from around 1907, was formed from the articulation of individual psychology and agency. The star system dovetailed with that form. Put bluntly, this is a liberal form, repetitively telling stories about individual desire that is usually imagined as realizable by all, irrespective of the conditions of exploitation and exclusion experienced by many. It is not a neutral form but is rather one fully consistent with the liberal conception of the monadic, self-interested subject.

Paramount's successful 1927 film *It* can function as a very quick and well-known example. The film told the story of a young woman working at a large department store, who pursues a relationship with the owner of the store that has its ups and downs (the engaging narrative) but ends happily with them declaring their love for each other. (The film itself actually ends with the Paramount logo of a snow-capped mountain surrounded by stars, which functions both as a form of corporate branding and as protection of property rights.) Clara Bow starred in the film. Bow had been "discovered" in a fan magazine competition that suggested that stardom was realizable to all, just as the rise of the lowly shopgirl to a member of the property-owning class was possible if one possessed the "it" imagined in the film as the form of personal "magnetism" supposedly possessed by people like film stars. The stories told about stars like Bow by the large PR departments of studios in this period frequently showed them basking in a success imagined as both personal and material.[97] Corporate media peddles the affirmative culture of acquisitive and possessive liberal individualism integral to the corporate economy, formed into narrative and sundry myriad publicity texts affirming that fiction. Bow embodied the *personality* that was consistent with the shift toward a "culture of personality" and, in turn, with the broader conceptions of mimesis circulating in the period. The story came from one written by the popular writer Elinor Glynn, for the magazine *Cosmopolitan,* itself a significant player in the formation of a national consumer market. Both the magazine and Glynn are featured in the film as an example of the cross media tie up common in the era to garner visibility for commercial media and sundry related products. *Cosmopolitan,* the film, and cinema more broadly all linked "commodity-based happiness with the 'modern' sexuality of the American girl" and made this integral to a "newly integrative national consumer culture."[98]

Certainly, classical cinema requires a sleight of hand to prioritize the individual, more so than the novel, which was born from the liberal revolutions of individualism, because it was a form and object produced and mechanically reproduced by large corporations. The star sumptuously illuminated by the careful orchestration of electric light, singled out from the crowd, their unique "aura" proclaimed through the mechanized fiction of "exploitation," helped with that particular card trick. Cinema of the studio era marked the cultural correlate of the broader corporate reconstruction of liberalism. The star frequently *embodied* this. Even further, the "network of a thousand threads" elaborated by media corporations for the circulation of this culture across the globe, supported by the state and star in significant ways, worked to try to universalize this particular (and contingent) form of subject and economic entity.

I am going to quickly give two further examples from corporate film of the early studio era because they help me illustrate other aspects of the argument I am making about the form, content, and function of corporate media, and they loop back to the broad context of settler colonialism and the establishment of a national transport infrastructure explored earlier in this book. *The Iron Horse* (Fox, 1924) told the story of the construction of the transcontinental railroad in the 1860s, which characteristically merged the action story of the completion of the railroad with that of heterosexual romance. The film celebrated the creation of a nation through transport infrastructure, built despite the savage attacks of the indigenous populations, who mysteriously opposed the modernity exemplified by the railroad and the private appropriation of land. *The Covered Wagon* (1923), another Paramount film, similarly told a thrilling story of settler colonialism and the "civilization" of the West, becoming one of the most profitable films of the era. Both films mixed narrative drive with melodrama and spectacle, exemplifying the emergent fusion of "classicism" and melodrama, and both metareflectively allegorized the establishment of "order" from "chaos" as a story of nation-building and of the creation of a "stable" film industry with national reach.[99] Even further, both films, made by corporations with close ties to banks, told a story that was foundational for capital—that of the usurpation of common lands and its re-creation as private property in a process of (to borrow again Harvey's words) "accumulation by dispossession" that was accompanied by state violence in order to create "the system of private property rights that gives a legal basis for the operations of capital."[100] The western repetitively told parts of this story, powerfully revising historical truth—the destruction of indigenous populations and the transformation of common lands into property—into stories about the establishment of "civilization" and modernity threatened by savage others. (Quite a common story, that, in US fiction, and indeed current political rhetoric). Capital needs fictions to sustain it, and mass-distributed fictions need capital to triumph: the marriage of these interests, like those of the characters at the end of all three of the fiction films I have briefly explored, has been my subject thus far in this chapter.

Now let us take stock of the situation after Kuhn, Loeb underwrote the issuance of $10 million preferred stock for Paramount. In 1919, Paramount began to actively purchase and construct new first-run cinemas, usually near transport hubs, thereby knitting together its production system and distribution network with exhibition outlets. The company had gained control of over 300 theaters by mid-1921. Reports in the financial press of the time talk of its expansion into India and Canada and of new distribution offices in Japan, Australia, Mexico, Brazil, and so on.[101] The "mighty stream of wealth" that flowed rather resembled a scene toward the end of *The Covered Wagon,* when the hero finds a literal golden harvest, in the California gold rush, and gathers it up before heading off to rescue the wagon train and "win" the heart of the young female star.[102] Zukor used the profits accruing to the company in the 1920s to construct a new financial headquarters in Times Square, almost within touching distance of Wall Street, with a flagship theater illuminated by crystal chandeliers. Paramount created a vertically integrated cultural system that tied production, distribution, and exhibition together, and so enabled a form of control that marginalized competitors and alternatives to the corporate system of media.

Various other companies began to imitate this corporate and textual model. In 1921, for example, the banking firm Merrill-Lynch acquired the significant distribution firm Pathé Exchange.[103] Loews Incorporated combined Marcus Loews chain of theaters with the producer-distributor Metro in 1920, Goldwyn Pictures in 1924 (previously backed by Chase National Bank), and the Louis B. Mayer unit that same year to establish what came to be called MGM. (PR tagline: "more stars than there are in heaven.") Loews external financing was indicated by two of its board members, W. C. Durant, head of General Motors, and Harvey Gibson, president of Liberty National Bank.[104] Warner Brothers bought Greater Vitagraph (previously financed in part by American Tobacco, one of Bernays's clients) and parts of First National in the mid-1920s with backing from Goldman Sachs.[105] Finance capital enabled Warner Brother's to expand into synchronized sound technology from 1925 on, a subject I take up in the final section of this chapter. By around midpoint in the decade, then, the corporate and financial reconstruction of cinema appeared complete. Each of these emerging corporate entities controlled significant first-run theaters, often in particular regions, and rented films from each other to fill exhibition time in a form of oligopolistic collusion that further marginalized alternative formations of cinema and enabled the kind of stable market required by bankers for so-called capital deepening.

But problems emerged and deepened. In 1920, the former Paramount star Mary Pickford's divorce and quick remarriage created ripples of scandal, which expanded in late 1921, when current Paramount star Roscoe "Fatty" Arbuckle was accused of raping and murdering a young actress at a booze-filled party (this during Prohibition), and in early 1922, when Paramount director William Desmond Taylor was found murdered at his home under suspicious circumstances.[106] The mass commercial press spent quite some time speculating on these scandals and told stories of salacious carryings-on and in particular of debauched star behavior, which helped increase circulation figures. Even Zukor himself was not immune to scandal when it emerged that he had attended a party with young women who were apparently working as prostitutes.[107] In 1921 a censorship law was passed in the state of New York, and legislation pended in several other states, further threatening the profitability of an industry suffering also because of the recession of 1921–22.[108] Henry Ford's newspaper the *Dearborn Independent* began its vicious and anti-Semitic campaign against Hollywood. Cinema came for a time to be a central node around which the broader cultural shift away from local, rural, republican traditions toward a modernist, consumerist, liberal, and metropolitan culture was negotiated.

Even worse than all these scandals, for the corporate industry, was the decision by the Federal Trade Commission in August 1921 to undertake an investigation of the business practices of Paramount. The FTC charged the company with violating the terms of the Clayton Antitrust Act of 1914, which sought to closely regulate mergers, stock pooling, and other practices that restrained trade. The investigation marked a significant intervention into the business practices of a corporate media industry. What happened as a consequence follows next. In the form of the melodrama integral to the narrative formulae of corporate Hollywood, our plucky hero, Zukor, wishing to establish order in the industry and best his rivals is thwarted by star scandals, mostly through no fault of his own, and worse even!, by the pesky government seeking to regulate markets to ensure they are "fair" (boo, hiss), But, phew, he is rescued by a goofy looking, jug-eared religious Republican politician hired at great expense to ward off all this unnecessary meddling in private business and corporate property. Will Hays, for it is he of the ears and PR skills, was perfectly cast, even if he did not look like a leading man. Watch this thrilling drama of intrigue, sex, corruption, committee work, and lobbying to hijack the political process for the benefits of (media) corporations unfold.

"THE BEACON OF ITS SILVER SCREEN . . . SENDING . . . JOY INTO EVERY CORNER OF THE EARTH"

In late 1921, the chief executives of the major production and distribution companies wrote a letter inviting Will Hays to head up a new trade organization, which would come to be called the Motion Picture Producers and Distributors of America. The facsimile of the letter reproduced in a significant early history of the film industry reads, in part,

> In order to attain complete *accord* in our industry . . . it will be necessary to obtain the services of one who has already, by his outstanding achievements, won the confidence of the people of this country, and who, by his ability as an organizer and executive, has won the confidence, admiration, and respect of the people in the motion picture industry. We feel that our industry requires further careful *upbuilding* and a constructive policy of *progress*.[109]

In January 1922, Hays met with executives in New York and accepted the offer, along with the enormous salary attached to it.[110] (Later he would say he made up his mind to do the job after overhearing his son playing a game *mimicking* film stars William S. Hart and Douglas Fairbanks.)[111] The new trade association of the producers and distributors was to be located in New York City, the industry's financial and distribution center. It was "incorporated" in March 1922, with a board of directors including Hays, studio chiefs, and their lawyers and with the stated goal (as the *Wall Street Journal* reported it) "to foster common interests of those engaged in [the] motion picture industry."[112] Quite clearly some of those interests were more common and equal than others, and the efforts to establish "accord" to enable further "upbuilding" were driven by the demands of the large production-distribution combines.[113] Established right at the outset of the FTC investigation into Paramount, in the midst of the deepening relations between the industry and finance capital that enabled extensive theater building, the organization was chiefly concerned initially with "harmonizing the domestic business practices of distribution and managing the distributor-exhibitor interface" to "safeguard the political [and economic] interests of the emerging oligopoly."[114] Nowadays the "Hays Office," as it was sometimes called, tends to be known as the censorship body that elaborated the Production Code from 1930 on, which helped shape the form and content of Hollywood in its classic—which is to say, its corporate—phase. Censorship though was only ever a minor part of its work, a subset always of what Hays would consistently call (*pace* Bernays) *public relations,* and it was significant to the industry only for its impact on the widespread circulation of its products. One of the chief successes of that expensive PR work for the corporate industry, however, was to divert attention away from the economic base of its operations "to the ideological superstructure of movie content"—a PR move so persuasive most subsequent film historians have been happy to repeat it.[115]

Will Hays was a savvy choice to facilitate the varied goals of the corporate and oligopolistic industry on several counts. He had the look of someone, and the religious credentials as a Presbyterian elder, which (back then at least) suggested he probably would not be involved in a sex scandal. Before taking on his well-remunerated work for the film industry, he had, beginning in 1919, been the Republican National Party chairman and had played a central role in Warren Harding's successful presidential campaign of 1920. It was said, if mostly by Hays himself, that he originated the maxim "that what America needed was 'more business in government and less government in business,'" the standard refrain of first the Republican Party and thereafter of pretty much all parties in liberal democracies.[116] The affiliation with free trade and the largely laissez-faire Republican Party turned out to be useful to a corporate industry fighting federal regulation. In his memoirs, Hays portrayed these political campaigns largely as exercises in PR, and a compelling case could be made for this postwar election to be the first one thoroughly shaped by the dictates of the emerging "professions" of image management.[117] In the aftermath of the election, Hays was given the job of postmaster general, in charge of "the biggest distribution business in the world."[118] The corporate media industry predicated on the orchestration of distribution paid handsomely for the kinds of political connections *and* evidently successful PR *and* logistics skills Hays possessed—an early example of the "revolving door" between political and corporate elites that helps entrench policy decisions beneficial to capital. The MPPDA can be situated in the broader context of the corporate reconstruction of liberalism and the growing ties between business and the state, exemplified in the idea and practice of industrial self-regulation as obviating "unnecessary" state intervention into the economy.[119] The MPPDA was fundamentally a liberal entity, though its liberalism was the product of expensive political lobbying that would require extensive state-industry coordination to keep open the global channels of distribution for US corporate media.[120]

In the summer of 1922, shortly after beginning work, Hays organized a conference in New York with representatives from civic, fraternal, welfare, religious, and professional organizations, thereafter established as what he called a Committee on Public Relations. The goal was ostensibly to bring the public and the industry closer together, to *arbitrate* disputes, and to create a virtuous associational network that would defuse the gathering clouds of censorial rhetoric and action. Quite quickly the strategy proved successful for the industry in blocking the passage of several state censorship laws pending after the 1921 New York legisla-tion, a matter of considerable import to the corporate industry because local cen-sorship damaged the circulation of its products. Indeed, this aspect of censor-ship—as a block on distribution *movement*—was always the most significant to the organized film industry because it was fundamental to its economic model. What Hays did in this respect was straightforwardly PR, and it is worth pausing over the naming of this committee, as Hays drew on this new form of corporate image management, borrowing (or just stealing) the very term—PR –Bernays was trying to popularize and using similar strategies of "respectable" endorsement to facilitate the economic goals of his employers.[121] Later several subcommittees were created, including ones seeking to establish further the respectability and utility of cinema. These included the Committee on Pedagogic Pictures and the Committee on Historical and Patriotic Information, the latter of which cooperated with the elite group Daughters of the American Revolution to help produce the D. W. Griffith–directed *America*.[122] PR helped defuse censorial interventions that were ultimately problems of distribution and so-called free trade.

The consequence of the necessity of creating products that could avoid censo-rial intervention and the costly brake on circulation it entailed was a radical nar-rowing of the form and function of cinema—not so much in terms of this or that thing that could not be shown but more broadly in the framing and codification of the social function of mainstream cinema. Corporate media circulated best when it offended as few significant markets as possible, offering instead a harmless and culturally affirmative form of entertainment consistent with the liberal consensus of a corporate and consumer economy. In 1938, for example, the Institute for Prop-aganda Analysis highlighted some of the common value judgments of this consen-sus, including "the successful culmination of a romance will solve most of the dilemmas of the hero and heroine"; if you "catch the criminal you will solve the crime problem"; that "the good life is the acquisitive life, with its emphasis on luxury, fine homes and automobiles, evening dress, swank and suavity."[123] It is axi-omatic that corporate-sponsored and produced media tends to be affirmative and rarely if ever challenges the status quo. The majority of Hollywood films end hap-pily, for example. The framing of cinema as "merely" entertainment was integral to corporate goals to smooth the circulation of film to maximize audience reach. When that argument needed supplementing, as it occasionally did, the *value* of this kind of entertainment could be emphasized, as in the above examples about cinema and education. The MPPDA sponsored conferences, publications, com-mittees about the pedagogic potential of cinema, marking the corporate sponsor-ship of "educational cinema," when it served the broader PR goals of the industry but without contravening the fundamental designation of cinema as a space of harmless *entertainment*. Quite often this meant Hays had to walk a tightrope and suggest that Hollywood was not influential and was mere fluff and entertainment.

(It was in this context, for example, that the MPPDA sponsored research to "disprove" the Payne Fund Studies, as shown in the previous chapter). But now and again, it helped the interests of his corporate paymasters to suggest that Hollywood could be a useful pedagogic form for educating and uplifting the masses. Fortunately for Hays, it did (and does) not matter if PR is consistent or truthful.

But it is important to remember also that the Committee on Public Relations was only one of six committees established in the original bylaws of the MPPDA, codified in March 1923, even if it is now by far the best-known one. At the same time committees on banking and finance, membership, foreign relations, law, and title were also created.[124] In early 1923, Hays called a meeting of the financial and accounting offices of the member companies "for the purpose of giving detailed consideration to the attitude in general of banks towards the motion picture industry."[125] The Committee on Banking Procedures and Finance was subsequently formed, and meetings were held during which balance sheets of member companies were examined and samples were drafted, with definition of terminology suggested for use in accounting processes. Evidence uncovered by Janet Wasko suggests the committee cooperated with the Federal Reserve Bank of New York, the New York Clearing House, and public accountants and banks familiar with film financing.[126] In this way the committee fulfilled one of the central objectives of the formation of the MPPDA more broadly—the establishment of a "respectable" trade association to better facilitate relations with banks and enable the capital deepening that established control for the corporate industry. Indeed, in one of his early speeches after agreeing to head up the MPPDA, Hays traveled the short distance to the Bond Club of New York City—established in 1917 to "promote . . . dialogue among those engaged and interested in the distribution of investment products and services"—to tell the bankers and investors gathered there that "Unless people are properly entertained this country may go Red."[127] The conversations between industry executives and bankers, beginning in 1919, may indeed have contributed significantly to the very establishment of the MPPDA. In an article in the financial journal *Barron's* by banker John E. Barber in early 1922, for example, the industry is advised to form a "trade body" like that of the American Bankers Association or the National Association of Manufacturers to "end . . . factional strife . . . [and] obtain fair treatment for the industry in Congress and other legislative bodies."[128] Likewise, the first treasurer of the MPPDA, J. Horner Platten, made clear the utility of the organization for bankers in an article in the *Banker's Magazine* in late 1926: "The significance of this movement was clear to the banking interests of the country. Bankers had a responsible headquarters to go to for information on financing certain phases of the industrial operations."[129] And the bank prospectuses from 1927, with which I began this chapter, heap considerable praise on the MPPDA and the "improvement of public relations," "promotion of more friendly relations within the industry," and "improvements in business practices, such as standardized budgets, uniform cost accounting and the arbitration of disputes."[130]

The latter two of these points were extremely significant to the work of the MPPDA and its utility for the industry and its financiers, as it began its work after the initiation of the FTC investigation of the complaints made by exhibitors about the trade practices of Paramount. Richard Maltby has underscored the significance of the Uniform Exhibition Contract, quickly established by the MPPDA in 1923, soon after its formation. The contract "established consistent terms of trade and included a provision for the compulsory internal arbitration, at a local level, of contractual disputes," and so helped defuse some of the disagreements between distributors and exhibitors, albeit in ways that "operated overwhelmingly to the benefit of the major distributors who ran it."[131] Much praise was heaped on the use of arbitration, which was seen as evidence of the industry's adoption of modern business practices and as obviating the need for federal regulation. Like with the Committee on Public Relations, the corporate industry's trade association used liberal models of arbitration to defuse more stringent regulation and legal accountability. The Standard Exhibition Contract, as it was renamed in early 1926, further helped stabilize business practices in ways that both assisted in setting the framework for further capital investment and worked to undermine the FTC investigation into the business practices of corporate media. I will return to both these points presently.

The golden harvest possible from the silver screen was also enabled by facilitating the global circulation of US media, which was central to the purview of the Committee on Foreign Relations. Hays and the MPPDA turned their attention to this subject in 1924, after industry efforts to defeat state censorship, foster relations with banks, and establish mechanisms to help defuse the tensions in the relationship between vertically integrated corporations and smaller independent theaters and theater chains. European concerns about the impact of US commercial media on its populations (or imperial subjects) produced varying responses, beginning notably with a quota system in Germany before similar models in France and the United Kingdom threatened to curtail the global circulation of Hollywood. Hays and the MPPDA lobbied for state support, and a Motion Picture Division of the Bureau of Foreign and Domestic Commerce was established in March 1925.[132] In early 1926, Hays asked the State Department to file protests with countries passing legislation that harmed the commercial interests of the producers and distributors. The state helped with the collection of information and data of use to the industry and disbursed these to help facilitate the movement of US media. Diplomatic assistance was rendered too. The trade commissioner specializing in motion pictures for Hoover's Department of Commerce attended significant meetings in Europe, including those at the Imperial Conference in London in 1926 and in Geneva under the aegis of the League of Nations.[133] Hays too discussed trade policy with foreign state officials, for the significant markets of England in 1923 and

France in 1928 with support from the US ambassador.[134] The corporate industry's lobbying group, run by a well-connected member of the Republican Party, helped in orchestrating state support for squeezing the final 25 percent of profitability from the global circulation of its products. The "American Motion Picture Industry," Hays later wrote in characteristically religious-tinged language, "stood on a mountaintop from which the beacon of its silver screen was sending rays of light and colour and joy into every corner of the earth."[135]

Visible here is the formation of significant ties between a corporate industry (now backed by finance capital) and the state in globalizing its operations in ways beneficial to all parties. Even more expansively: the origins of a process of globalization facilitated by image capital and carried out by corporate and state officials working frequently in tandem. The American film industry used the infrastructural and intelligence-gathering power of the state to establish and entrench global dominance. But the other side of this equation also merits emphasis, as it syncs with the history of state-media relations I have been examining and the arguments I have been making in this book about how the US state sought to put film to work to facilitate particular economic and political objectives. The state had, in fact, been lobbying the film industry to offer its support for quite some time before the MPPDA turned its attention to the foreign distribution of its products. In late 1916, the State Department wrote to US consuls to provide information on the "market for American films," right at the moment that the US industry acceded to the commanding heights of mass media production. Recall also that Creel had cannily gathered support from the film industry in 1917 by promising space on ships for the distribution of their films. (Logistics was a military phenomenon before it was utilized by industry.)[136] The head of the Bureau of Foreign and Domestic Commerce, Julius Klein, wrote in 1921 to the executive secretary of the industry trade association that preceded the MPPDA, noting, "I may say that Mr. Hoover and I have discussed on several occasions the significance of motion picture exporting both as a straight commodity trade and as a powerful influence in behalf of American goods and habits of living."[137] Likewise, Klein wrote to Hays, again *before* the establishment of the Motion Picture Section, in 1923, "We have been giving considerable thought to this subject and our plans for the new fiscal year contemplate some special effort towards making the pictures even more effective on behalf of our trade in foreign countries."[138] Government officials, particularly from the State Department, negotiated with foreign counterparts to benefit the corporate industry.

Once the state began to take the promotion of foreign trade as integral to its remit, film and media became something of a special case because of its perceived centrality to the broader semiotic promotion of US-manufactured objects. These ideas and practices were consistent with the more profound transformation of the conception of the function of the state in the emerging era of corporate globalization. The idea that mass media was itself a significant commodity, as well as a display mechanism for other commodities—what Hays called "an animated catalogue"—was taken seriously enough to shape state policy.[139] Later, Hays would smugly describe the MPPDA as "almost an adjunct of our State Department"— corporate lobbyists and state officials working together, side-by-side, to facilitate the circulation of commodities that housed within them, like Russian dolls, other commodities and *habits of living*.[140]

But perhaps the true test of the utility of the MPPDA was in the services it could provide to help Paramount, and by extension the corporate industry, defeat the Federal Trade Commission investigation into its business practices. To reiterate, the FTC had the power to intervene in the distribution practices of the studios because it policed interstate commerce—a consequence of the federal-state division of powers in the US political system—and so could transform the way the industry operated. Or, more simply, the FTC had the power to halt the growth of a corporate oligopolistic industry and instead promote a more genuinely open market for film, which could perhaps have fostered alternatives to the corporate form of benign, banal, affirmative commercial entertainment that has mostly constituted the history of corporate Hollywood (give or take). In its brief, the FTC argued that the practice of block-booking effectively destroyed the open market for film and so competition. "In order to control a theatre," part of its main brief stated, "it is not necessary for a producer-distributor to own or lease the theatre because if all, or substantially all, of the exhibition time of the theatre is taken up in showing the product of one producer-distributor the theatre is ipso facto closed to all other producers."[141] In the other corner, chief counsel for the MPPDA, Charles Pettijohn, argued that the "abolition of these price-fixing provisions [ie, block-booking] would be an unwarrantable interference with private business."[142] What right, asked the corporate lawyer, does a state have in regulating business and "open" markets?

In the short term Pettijohn's arguments, supplemented by those made by Zukor's expensive lawyers, failed. The FTC decision rendered, finally, in 1927 was trenchant in its critique of the business practices of Paramount and the corporate industry. It is worth quoting at some length the first clauses of the decision. Paramount and its various subsidiaries

(a) Conspired to create a combination in restraint of competition and trade in the production of motion-picture films, and to create a monopoly therein and in pursuance of said conspiracy, which they consummated, and with the intent and effect of creating a combination of producers of feature pictures, to produce and lease full programs sufficient to use all of an exhibitor's available time, and thereby exclude such exhibitor from showing competitive films;

(1) Entered, through their respective corporations, and along with said third corporation, into an agreement with a concern engaged exclusively in distributing pictures for it its corporate distribution owners, under its well-known and established

trade-mark and with unique facilities for nation-wide distribution, giving said distributing concern the exclusive right to distribute all their films, each exhibitor to receive a full program of 104 pictures to be produced and furnished by them for such purpose; with the result that they thereby created in and for themselves a complete monopoly in the production and distribution of motion-picture films;

(2) Acquired 50 per cent of the stock of the aforesaid distributing concern, which had theretofore acquired control of its distributors;

(3) Incorporated a holding company . . . to acquire and hold the stock of their two companies, of said third corporation, and of a subsidiary created by it to produce feature pictures; with the intent of perpetuating and making more effective their aforesaid conspiracy, and of creating a convenient, permanent, and efficient instrumentality for the maintenance and operation thereof.[143]

Later in the text of the decision, the specific actions of Paramount from 1919, around the time it was seeking capital from Kuhn, Loeb, were condemned: "On July 22, 1919, the board of directors of Famous Players-Lasky Corporation . . . for the purpose of modifying, perpetuating and making more effective its said distribution policy . . . and for the purpose of intimidating and coercing exhibitors to lease and exhibit films produced and distributed by Famous Players-Lasky corporation, adopted a progressive and increasing policy of building, buying, owning or otherwise controlling theatres . . . It was the openly and publicly avowed purpose . . . to dominate the entire moving-picture industry."[144] The results of this forceful decision, by a significant federal commission, were the break-up of the corporate system of Hollywood, and the flourishing of a thoughtful, independent cinematic culture open to various perspectives on the nature of the good life and the correct and equitable political and economic forms of a just society . . . except neither, of course, happened. Why?

In furtherance of its decision, the FTC issued a "cease and desist" order to Paramount in July 1927, and when the company simply refused to comply, the FTC organized a trade practices conference in October of that same year.[145] The conference established a committee that drew up a new standard exhibition contract. In the midst of the complex negotiations about corporate trade practices, the MPPDA produced and tabled a document called "Don'ts and Be-Carefuls," a list of subjects frequently censored by local, state, and national censor boards and a direct precursor to the Production Code in 1930.[146] It did so in response to some of the exhibitor's arguments that block-booking forced them to book films inappropriate for their communities. But this was only ever a marginal part of the more substantive argument about monopolistic business practices. Yet again, censorship as corporate self-regulation was offered by the industry's PR and lobbying group as a way to escape economic regulation.

Even so, the FTC continued to press its cease and desist order. Paramount further denied the charges, and the FTC subsequently filed for judicial enforcement of its decision with the US Circuit Court of Appeals.[147] In early 1932, in the midst of a severe economic depression, the court denied the FTC and sided with Paramount.[148] Partly this was because significant competition to Paramount's dominance had emerged in the intervening years, notably with the transformations in the industry attendant upon the introduction of sound. It probably helped also to have some of the most expensive lawyers money could buy on its side—indeed, the same lawyers who were counsel for Kuhn, Loeb, suggesting that the bank assisted Paramount in its defense.[149] In a report made public in December 1932, the FTC announced it would make no further efforts to enforce its decision.[150] Paramount escaped. Corporate and oligopolistic practices of control continued.

Not all of this success for the corporate industry can be attributed to the MPPDA, or to Paramount's expensive phalanx of corporate lawyers. The powers of the FTC to regulate trade practices were significantly winnowed down in the 1920s, in the midst of the broader corporate reconstruction of liberalism. In 1925, a number of probusiness appointees of the Harding and then Coolidge administrations replaced the tenure of some of the progressive members of the FTC.[151] This was also the year, incidentally, that a second tranche of significant bank capital was disbursed through Hollywood, a subject I will address below. I have no evidence that the two events were connected, and perhaps they were not. But it is surprising that major investment banks were willing to underwrite significant capital expansions *while* the FTC investigation, with its power to radically transform Hollywood's business practices, was ongoing—unless those banks were not unduly worried about the result of the decision and its enforcement. In any case, the waning efficacy of the FTC in regulating large corporate business practices was one symptom of the broader dynamics of the growth of corporate power and the significant rearticulation of the role of the state in respect to this that gathered pace in the 1920s. The failure to take seriously the state regulation of media, as radio was establishing itself as a form to bring consumers together with corporate PR and advertising, set the terms for the expansion of corporate media thereafter. By the time the FTC decision was made, indeed, the separate elements of media and the corporations and banks that were significantly invested in them were converging, creating new configurations of visual and sonic media and new alliances across media, electrical, and telecommunications companies that now merit our attention.

"THE VOICE FROM THE SCREEN"

Late in December 1924, Harry Warner, president of Warner Bros. (then a small production company), met with Waddill Catchings, head of the investment division of Goldman Sachs. In the aftermath of the meeting, and the due diligence investigations by the bank, Goldman established firstly a revolving credit line for Warner's of three million-dollars and then raised four million dollars through a bond issue.[152] Capital swept through the industry in the same period, particularly from 1925 onward, marking the second wave of finance expansion and culminating in several new bond issues like those examined at the beginning of this chapter.[153] In 1925, for example, Fox Film floated six million dollars of new common stock and used the capital to purchase theaters and theater chains in California and elsewhere.[154] William Fox developed close relations with Halsey, Stuart, and the investment bank's prospectus of 1927 was issued principally on behalf of Fox. Bankers began to play significant roles in the boards of directors at film studios. Cinema was accordingly increasingly Fordized, a process carried out also with the help of the young graduates of business schools (eg, Harvard) who began in this period to work in the film industry. "Efficient" practices, making of culture an industrial product, helped pave the way for further capital investment, enabling the expansion into property and global distribution, as well as into new forms of technology and convergent media.

Warner Bros. thus used the money enabled by (the appropriately named) Goldman to open new distribution exchanges in the United States and across the world, joining these together with the international network of exchanges purchased in early 1925 from Vitagraph.[155] In this their model was similar to that of Paramount's, which is to say to that of other corporate entities seeking vertical integration to control and expand markets, reduce costs, and eliminate competitors. But some differences of strategy emerged, largely as a consequence of Warner's being a smaller and later entrant to an already-established market. Warner Bros. bought a Los Angeles radio station, an early example of transmedial interaction and ownership, which continued thereafter more widely when studios and exhibition entrepreneurs used radio to advertise film shows and to broadcast music and live performances from them.[156] Ownership of the station brought the Warner brothers into contact with Western Electric radio equipment and personnel. Early in 1925, the brothers attended a demonstration of Western Electric's newly established system for recording and reproducing sound motion pictures. The company devised a strategy to use this new technology to record musical and vaudeville acts that would lessen the costs of live entertainment in theaters—by mechanizing it—and provide added, unique, attractions to its output, so that it might compete with the still larger Paramount and Loews-MGM combines. By June 1925, an agreement was signed between Warner Bros. and Western Electric, mediated by the latter's agent, who marketed its new sonic technology to film companies. Warner's created a new subsidiary, Vitaphone, and in early 1926 signed a further agreement with Western Electric, which gave the former an exclusive license to use the technology and the latter an annual royalty fee and the profits accruing from the sale of new technological apparatuses to theaters. Western Electric insisted that it be given a permanent representative on Vitaphone's board of directors and that Goldman, Sachs guarantee the company's debts for a period of five years.

Vitaphone's August 1926 premiere began with a short filmed introduction by Will Hays. Keeping on-message, the first remarks Hays made epitomized the idea of a cinema self-reflexively talking about only itself, not the world outside of its screens: "my friends, no story of the screen is as dramatic as the story of the screen itself." Hays briefly outlined the "mighty growth" of this industry, now helped along its way by the scientists of Western Electric and Bell Labs, all while standing in front of the corporate trademark of Vitaphone, which embodied in its very name the convergence of cinema (vita, life, movement) with telecommunications (phone, from *phonos,* sound). Otto Kahn, of bankers Kuhn, Loeb, and Zukor were in the audience to hear this paean to corporate research and convergent media forms.[157] What would be its result? The spread of culture and "civilization," of course, most notably by bringing symphony orchestras to small towns as a "service" to society. Hays was a pretty savvy PR operative, and he cannily conjoined a religious sense of service to the technological sublime to facilitate the goals of telecoms and media corporations. Rhetoric about beneficent and necessary technology in particular had become increasingly significant to large media, telecoms, and electricity corporations after the emergence and spread of science- and technology-based corporations in the broader context of the second-stage industrial revolution. Corporate propaganda began then (and continues) to routinely present the technologies produced in their research laboratories as services for the social good.

Vitaphone's system grafted electrical sound technology together with cinema, syncing the phonograph with moving picture projection in a form of analogue convergence. What it enabled media corporations to do was cut down on the costs of live entertainment in cinemas, so reducing labor costs in a way that also straightforwardly standardized—and made national—a cinematic experience, which up to that point had retained some organic connections to locality (eg, in the musical and stage accompaniment to "silent" films). The introduction of sound further centralized media production. In this it demonstrated continuity with the earlier creation of national distribution networks controlled by large corporations and was consistent with the logic of the policy decisions around radio, which concentrated longwave frequency allocation among corporate stations with a national reach.

William Fox similarly invested capital in new convergent technologies. Fox had allied with the inventor Theodore Case from 1926, after Case had developed a way of encoding sound on celluloid, rather than by using the more unreliable syncing of moving pictures to the phonograph.[158] The Fox-Case Corporation also bought important sound-on-film patents—the so-called Tri-Ergon patents—developed by German scientists. Courtland Smith, the president of Fox newsreels, devised a strategy to create synchronized sound newsreels to differentiate its products from those of Warner's and the other film studios. Smith approached GE to work out the amplification problems of the system, but they opted against collaborating as they were developing their own sound-on-film system. Fox instead paid a licensing fee to Vitaphone, which at this point held exclusive licenses to all Western Electric patents. In April 1927, the Fox system was premiered, at its recently purchased first-run theater in New York, the Roxy. The first film showed West Point cadets marching with synchronized sound, no doubt an impressive demonstration of military force married with the technology that could trace significant parts of its genesis back to the military (through the development of radio in particular). One month after its premiere, the Fox Movietone newsreel presented pictures with sounds of Charles Lindbergh's historic solo flight across the Atlantic on the very same day that his plane took off.[159] Lindbergh's 1927 flight had "marked the apex of the adulation of the modern as embodied in innovative technologies that swept America in the decade after the war."[160] Once again, as was the case with the earlier example of the Panama-Pacific International Exposition, this presentation proposed a dizzying set of relays across new technology and transport; the compression of space and time; and the speeded up circulation of images, sounds, people, materials, and (consequently) capital.

The story, as told next in countless histories, tends to concentrate on the subsequent period of sound expansion in the film industry, from *The Jazz Singer* to the industry-wide adoption of the technology and the technological, formal, and market-based complexities that followed. I am more interested in the story of how far larger, and in many respects more powerful and significant, corporations and financial institutions invested in technology and new forms of telecommunications and media. It is not so much a story about how silent cinema became sound cinema but more a history of the convergence of capital, technology, and media forms. I have already argued that we can profitably think about radio and cinema together, shifting beyond a media-specific focus to examine the larger constellation of forces—both political and economic—that produced new technologies and framed the ways they would be used as profit-generating media. What emerged from these convergences were significant corporate and capital tie-ins that crossed various forms of visual and sonic culture, their material manifestations (such as loudspeakers, radio sets, projectors, phonographs), and the intellectual property rights and patents that produced surplus value from technology and culture. The *syncing* of sound and image was made possible by a complex set of developments that encompassed the emergence of technology-based industries; the close ties developed between these industries and finance capital; and the creation of technology-based communication networks, which came together in new media forms, of which cinema, sync-sound cinema, and radio were the earliest iterations. This history marks the precise moment when capital and the interests of large, well-capitalized corporations penetrated the cultural and media sphere and bent it extensively toward their own (mostly) related ends.

Indeed, this history necessarily takes us back over some of the ground examined already, notably radio and, a little more sketchily, telephony. Western Electric was a wholly owned subsidiary of AT&T, the enormous corporation that operated a virtual monopoly on telephonic communication in the United States during most of the twentieth century. How that came to be can only be sketched out here, though the story is an instructive one in terms of what it reveals about the connection of capital, technology, and communicative infrastructures, as well as the way these connections created new forms of media. In the aftermath of the invention of the telephone, attributed mostly to Alexander Graham Bell in the 1870s, a brief battle for primacy in its development was waged between the very large corporation Western Union and the "tech start-up" that was the Bell Telephone Company. Both developed technology and owned patents related to telephony. In 1878 the financier and "stock manipulator" Jay Gould sought to control Bell by buying stock, hoping to challenge the primacy of Western Union by making his telegraph company (American Union Telegraph) a combination telegraph and telephone corporation. Western Union directors decided that it best served their interests to strengthen the Bell Company in order to keep it out of Gould's hands, while simultaneously keeping Bell away from competing with its telegraphic business.[161] The directors accordingly sold the patent rights on the technology it had developed to Bell, for a fixed royalty, and agreed thereafter to keep out of the telephone business if Bell kept out of the telegraph business.[162]

To continue to grow, the Bell Company required a large injection of capital, beginning in the latter years of the nineteenth century.[163] In 1885 Bell established a subsidiary, which it called the American Telephone and Telegraph Company, incorporated under the laws of New York State to build, own, and operate the long-distance lines that became increasingly central to its control of the network. New York's laws "were much more permissive regarding capitalization," so when the corporation needed additional financing in 1899, the company's assets were transferred to AT&T and the former subsidiary took over as the parent company of the entire Bell system.[164] Put simply, the looser regulation of capitalization in New York better enabled the influx of capital needed to create a complex national network of communication. AT&T was thereafter increasingly allied with, and partly controlled by, financial interests, most notably by House of Morgan after the bank took a lead in a stock offering in 1902 (for $7.7 million) and again in 1906, when $100 million of convertible bonds were sold to finance expansion.[165] The financial "panic" of 1907 left Morgan in particular with a large amount of AT&T bonds, and he used this to leverage control of the corporation and install Theodore Vail as its president. Moreover, in 1910 Bell acquired a 30% share in Western Union, part of a drive by Morgan to consolidate telecommunications like the bank had with, for example, steel and electricity.[166] Vail established the centrality of long-distance telephone lines to the corporate strategy, not least because this enabled the company to dictate terms or deny access to local independent operators, who needed to connect to this network to enable their customers to communicate outside of their localities.[167]

The corporation was investigated as a trust in 1913, largely because of this aggressive policy with regard to independent operators. Vail responded by agreeing to sell its share of Western Union, to seek the agreement of federal regulators before buying more independent operations, and to allow other companies access to Bell's long-distance lines.[168] The antitrust suit was defeated (as it would be in regards to Paramount a little later), and AT&T was free to develop as a virtual monopoly in telecommunications in the United States. Perhaps having Morgan on the board and as the controlling interest in the corporation helped with this, in the same year the bank played a formative role in establishing the Federal Reserve Bank system in the U.S. What is clear is that a telecommunications network was created through the development of technology and control of patents, supported and shaped by finance capital, and framed into a corporation that had significant monopoly power.

Western Electric was purchased by Bell in 1882 and established as a wholly owned subsidiary to manufacture and install equipment. Beginning in 1912, the Western Electric Engineering Department, under the direction of Frank B. Jewett, began experiments with the amplification of sound technology that would support long-distance telephony, a crucial goal of the parent company. Indeed, the results of some of this research were demonstrated at the 1915 Panama-Pacific International Exposition, with the successful completion of a transcontinental telephone call, amidst the wider celebrations of the new transport infrastructure of the Panama Canal and the merging of technological, communicative, and material networks. Jewett's experiments were helped considerably by AT&T's 1913 purchase of the patent rights to a particular piece of technology, the audion tube, designed initially by Lee De Forest. The details of how the technology functioned do not need explication here. What does bear examination is the process by which large corporations began to buy the patent rights to various forms of technology from lone or poorly capitalized inventors in order to control technological transformation and to profit from ensuing royalties and subsequent developments. Patents functioned as a form of what Leonard Reich has called "corporate insurance," helping yield "important ammunition in wars for market control."[169]

Early in the twentieth century, then, large technology corporations like AT&T and GE began to construct well-capitalized in-house research laboratories to establish patent controls, hiring the graduates of science and engineering departments from universities like MIT and Chicago—Jewett had studied at both—to develop applied forms of scientific knowledge. AT&T accordingly expanded its investment in research from 1909, and Bell Labs was established as a separate division in 1925.[170] Engineers and scientists working in these corporate research laboratories were encouraged to develop technology and patents germane to the central business strategy—in this case, telephony—but also, in what the executive in charge of Bell's sound motion picture activities described as the "'no mans land'" between engineering fields, "to maintain such strong engineering, patent, and commercial situation in connection with these competitive activities as to always have something to trade against the accomplishments of other parties."[171] Patent rights were used to develop and commodify technology and as bargaining chips in the battle to control how technology would be operationalized and turned into capital. Recall the previous example from the history of radio: for the deals eventually signed between—chiefly—GE and AT&T to cross license each others patents separated out their interests, so that AT&T agreed to eschew owning radio stations if GE similarly kept away from the wired transmission of sound. Patents and selective cross-licensing agreements thus came increasingly to favor large, science-based, well-capitalized corporations, which used their positions to try and dominate the ways technology was deployed and used. Furthermore, "the agreements through which the efforts of individual companies were coordinated in the interest of all" helped insulate these companies "from national and international competition in particular fields" and also circumvent antitrust laws.[172] At the same time, the development of corporate propaganda frequently emphasized the socially beneficial nature of corporate research and technology. Will Hays did something similar for the major studios, keeping one eye warily on the implementation of antitrust regulation.

But it is worth recalling that the state also played a role in the development of technology and in the framing of policy decisions that helped large corporations profit from scientific and technological innovations. Radio is again a useful example here, for as we have seen, the state played a significant role in marshaling technological development and creating research partnerships that helped facilitate its development. Certainly the role of the state intensified in wartime, as it directed companies like AT&T and GE to research such things as searchlights and radar detection. But it developed before that, in the significant state funding given to research at universities and in the development of infrastructural systems like railroads and roads, which were so integral to the demands of liberal capitalist states. The expansion of proprietary rights to technological and cultural forms similarly expanded in the early twentieth century.[173] One of the results of the shared corporate, banking, and state *investment* in technology was the creation of monopolistic and oligopolistic markets dominated by large, well-capitalized corporations.

But back to the history at hand: to test the apparatus for amplifying telephonic sound, Jewett proposed to develop new methods for recording sound and simultaneously began testing sound on phonographic discs and on celluloid. The research was somewhat delayed by the war, when Western Electric was asked by the state to develop airplane and submarine detection systems, but it resumed in the postwar period.[174] Jewett's experiments led quickly to the development of the loudspeaker and public address system, used successfully at the 1920 Republican national convention—when Hays was still the party chairman—and at Harding's inaugural address in early 1921. Late in 1921, AT&T added this amplification system to its long-distance telephone lines. By doing so it was able to broadcast a speech given by Harding to audiences in New York and San Francisco, demonstrating the viability of long-distance transmission and presentation of electronically augmented sound. The corporations developing these sonic technologies made them available to politicians, a savvy merging of corporate and political interests to the mutual benefit of both (what liberals call "enlightened self-interest"). When sound synced with film became a possibility, some of the very first examples were of politicians, including Calvin Coolidge speaking in 1924, at about the same time that Bernays was organizing a pseudoevent for him on the White House lawn, which featured Al Jolson on the eve of his becoming a star of Vitaphone shorts and hugely lucrative Warner Bros. features.

Our history necessarily dovetails here again with the history of radio. The rudiments can be quickly recalled: the state's interest in creating a communicative system beyond the control of the British, in particular, led to support for the corporate development and control of patents and technology. Cross-licensing agreements between, mostly, electrical and telecommunications companies paved the way for accelerated development, and these separate investments were eventually orchestrated in accordance with the specific interests of those corporations. The example above, of GE and AT&T agreeing not to compete with each other's core business strategies, illustrates how this process worked. GE created RCA and NBC, and its national system of broadcasting—superseding local alternatives— was facilitated by use of the wired networks controlled by AT&T. The various possibilities enabled by the creation of radio technology were gradually winnowed down, so that by 1927 the state's policy directives in the form of the Radio Act supported the strategies of its corporate partners. Communication became media and media became integral to a consumer and corporate economy, operating first on a national scale, before spreading (its joy) across the globe.

Western Electric, and its corporate parent AT&T, began exploring other commercial uses of its newly developed sound technology. GE did too. Western Electric pursued the merging of sound and vision through the initially more reliable sound-on-disc system, which worked by electronically synchronizing the phonograph and the projector. It produced a corporate PR film, *Hawthorne*, that showed its own factory in a self-reflexive celebration of corporate efficiency and technology. *Hawthorne* was similar to those Ford-produced films that celebrated the beginnings of mass assembly. Quickly thereafter AT&T made another film to help market its technology. *The Voice From the Screen* begins, as most films do, with the identification and assertion of property rights of its corporate owners: "The Vitaphone Corporation presents . . . *The Voice from the Screen*, by Edward B. Craft, Executive Vice President Bell Telephone Laboratories Inc." Craft starts with a lecture describing sound cinema as a "new application of the telephonic principles," marking the central objective of the film to assert the primacy of AT&T and its research laboratories in developing synchronous sound films. It is an example of film being used by a corporation to frame its proprietary control. Craft's lecture traverses varied developments identified by AT&T as integral to sound cinema, and thus to its control of the technology, beginning with the amplification processes that enabled public address systems to function and then moving to electrical recording and finally to electrical sound reproduction.

Craft then moves to a Vitaphone-equipped studio and talks the audience through the simultaneous photographic and sonic recording of action—in this case, a song sung by the male vocal duo Witt and Berg—which is staged in cross section to demonstrate, as Steve Wurtzler insightfully observes, "the *simultaneous* recording of sound and image and thereby to distinguish the Vitaphone from several earlier sound film processes that relied upon post-synchronous strategies of recording."[175] Later the singers are shown to us in closer frontal view, an example of the short, filmed music and vaudeville acts that were integral to the commercial strategies of Vitaphone in reducing the costs of live performance, which were henceforth rendered mechanical and reproducible. Craft talks loftily at the end of the film of the wondrous advances that technology brings to the world—repeating the ones often used for cinema in the first place, the ability to record and preserve events—and praises the inventive corporate scientists who have made all of this possible. But perhaps the real interest in the film lies in the remarkably prescient set of relations and ideals it maps. *Voice* sells technology, as well as the image of an advanced and benign corporation, but syncs this also with music and thus with the phonograph corporations that Western Electric had secured licensing agreements with, as well as with the sale of sheet music.[176] I have proposed the metaphor of *syncing* here, extending from the successful syncing of sound and image to the synergies created between technological and "cultural" corporations to expand technology (as material culture) and the more immaterial but still profitable forms of media and culture.[177]

Paramount was approached to partner with Western Electric, but, mindful in particular of the history of failures in successfully syncing sound and image, Zukor declined, leading the telephone company to the smaller Warner Bros. studio. The situation within AT&T changed in 1926, notably with the appointment of a new director of Western Electric called John Otterson. Otterson formed a new subsidiary, Electric Research Products Incorporated (ERPI), and pressured Warner's to renegotiate its exclusive agreement because he believed it threatened to slow down development and prevent AT&T from establishing a monopoly on the technology.[178] Warner's countered, and with the help of its bankers at Goldman Sachs sought to maintain its position of primacy in the diffusion of sound technology. But the asymmetrical power relations between a relatively small film studio and investment bank and an extraordinarily powerful technology corporation backed by Morgan and other significant banks could lead to only one outcome. Warner's agreed to a new contract as a nonexclusive licensee, pocketing a little over $1 million for doing so, not an insignificant sum for the film studio but rather a drop in the ocean for AT&T, which had assets in 1925 totaling $2.9 billion.[179] ERPI, its parent Western Electric, and its parent AT&T used their combined size and power to pressure a much smaller media corporation into accepting its terms.

But all was not plain sailing for ERPI and AT&T thereafter. GE had also begun to develop a sync-sound system, similarly buying up patents along the way and developing research laboratories to capitalize on scientific and technological developments.[180] These developments were interconnected with those concerning radio during World War I and with the subsidiaries of GE in the form of RCA and later NBC. Cooperation between these very large electrical and telecommunications networks extended only so far, though, and both GE and AT&T competed directly with each other to innovate and expand the syncing of sound and image to capitalize on their patents and technologies. Otterson had sought to tie up licensing agreements with Paramount and Loews/MGM, but these two studios refused to sign—mindful in particular of the high royalty rates demanded by AT&T—and instead used the fact that GE had a competing system to propose and enforce a year-long moratorium (beginning February 1927) for the decision on which system to use. The studios created a committee that explored all options and narrowed the decision down to GE and AT&T; after a to-and-fro struggle between the two technology corporations, AT&T was eventually chosen, mostly it seems because it had the technological capacity, through Western Electric, to produce the amount of equipment needed and to quickly wire the theaters owned by the studios.[181]

GE responded by quickly forming a major vertically integrated studio of its own, RKO, born from RCA's purchase of stock in the production company FBO, which was largely controlled by Joseph Kennedy. Kennedy had cannily connected FBO first to the Keith-Albee vaudeville chain in early 1928 and then to the Orpheum vaudeville circuit, thus establishing R(adio) K(eith) O(rpheum) as a vertically integrated studio to use GE's technology. Various forms of media, past and present, converged here, particularly radio, vaudeville, and film. Banking interests were integral to the studio, and various bankers sat on its board—one example of how the new requirements for capital in sync-sound cinema intensified banker participation and control in media corporations.[182] Kennedy later sold up, exiting a rich man, and RCA and GE competed thereafter with AT&T to wire theaters for sound cinema. GE and AT&T controlled electrical and telecommunications networks and now also had significant tie ins with various film studios, making money from the material and immaterial culture of technology (and the patents filed on them) and media. Cinema in its classic and convergent form was synced to far larger technology and capital networks. The voice from the screen spoke the language of corporate and financial wealth.

Douglas Gomery concludes his meticulous history of the emergence of sound cinema by suggesting that Paramount and Loews in particular had expertly played GE and AT&T off against each other, remaining "in the driver's seat" in marshaling "orderly technological change."[183] Clever, rational, sensible film entrepreneurs carried the day. But the story is murkier and less clear-cut than that. Certainly, the development of mechanized sonic culture enabled these large media corporations to reduce labor costs and create further barriers to entry for competitors, ones so high that many independent producers and exhibitors were squeezed out of the business. The "introduction of sound" was in this respect a crucial step in the consolidation of both the large corporations that produced, distributed, and exhibited film and the banks that supplied capital for them to do so. Zukor used some of this capital to purchase, in 1929, a half interest in the Columbia Broadcasting System (CBS), evidently mindful of the cross promotional and convergent possibilities of a larger media corporation such as that established as RKO.[184] The further consolidation of studio control, and in turn an oligopolistic market, also enabled studios to resist the process of unionization. Workers in the studio system were pushed toward the company union, the Academy of Motion Picture Arts and Sciences, but actively discouraged from joining more effective and militant unions. Entrenched corporate and oligopolistic control helped the studios discipline and control workers.

But for all these "benefits," film studios were now synced together with far larger telecommunications and electricity corporations. Capital flowed to the latter through licensing agreements with film studios, through the material production of technology, and film became enmeshed with broader networks of technology and capital that were not controlled by film corporations. Even further, the large pools of capital needed to convert to sound—across production and exhibition—tied the film studios to banks and rendered them vulnerable to fluctuations in the stock and bond markets. When the stock market crashed in 1929, the studios were threatened with catastrophe, leading even the mighty Paramount to declare bankruptcy in 1933. The taxicab and rental car tycoon John Daniel Hertz was persuaded to chair the finance committee of Paramount. Hertz sold the CBS stock back to CBS and installed a "board of directors consisting of bankers, lawyers, realtors—in general, Wall Street types, most of whom knew nothing about movies but enough about business to turn Paramount-Publix around."[185] Otterson of AT&T assumed the presidency. Fox was taken over by the banks and ERPI (under the direction of Otterson), in part to control the Tri-Ergon patents that were useful for the consolidation of AT&T's control of sound technology. Fox's own account of this, as told to Upton Sinclair, presents a murky tale of bank and AT&T malfeasance as they sought to increase control and profitability.[186]

Control of media corporations, once they were synced to finance capital, became a matter for financial speculation. What happened to the film studios in the Depression was one example of what happens frequently to individuals and companies reliant on bank mortgages and the stock and bond markets in periods of financial downturn, when banks reclaim property and materiality. If the film studios won, as Gomery wants to insist, it was a pyrrhic victory, bringing them into ever-closer collaboration with large technology corporations and the banks, which now exercised significant control over both technology and media companies. I contend that the convergence of capital and technology in the second-stage industrial revolution, along with the consolidation of corporate capitalism, produced a convergent set of relations between technology, telecommunications, and media corporations and banks. Within this configuration, media came to play specific roles in the generation of profits for bankers, corporate executives, and holders of capital. It was one part of an emergent complex network that would become further entrenched in particular with the establishment of television, then computer and digital technologies. The marriage of media and technology corporations, officiated by the banks, brought enormous "benefits" in the form of expensive technology and telecommunication contracts. Who reading this does not have some of this technology, of screens synced with sound, and contracts with telecommunication corporations? The backstory of those forms properly begins with the history of capital and technology that shaped radio and sync-sound cinema in the early years of the twentieth century.

In the chapter that follows, I take up some aspects of the subsequent history of these convergences in the 1930s. I shall explore also the state response to economic depression and the consolidation of the state's use of media to shape its populations and maintain stability. The fictitious value of capital, its formation in part as fiction, butted up against reality, as it cyclically does: the varied consequences of this exceptional economic crisis, for the film industry, and also for the ways in which media was used to stabilize a damaged liberal system, is the subject of the next and final substantive chapter of this book.

Welfare Media

Late in 1929, the public relations (PR) campaign for General Electric's "celebration" of the fifty-year anniversary of Edison's "invention" of the electric light bulb reached its conclusion with the "Light's Golden Jubilee" event at Henry Ford's Greenfield Village. Edward Bernays had orchestrated events for GE throughout the year, including the production of a commemorative stamp and the saturation of news media with stories of Edison's inventive genius as one aspect of the broader PR goal to humanize and individuate the corporate form. Quite a familiar cast of characters watched on in October 1929 as Edison repeated his famous experiment, in his old laboratory that Ford had removed from New Jersey and rebuilt as part of his obsessive monument to technology and the past.[1] In still-extant newsreel footage, shot by the moving picture companies invited specifically by Bernays, it is possible to make out Edison as he is feted by the great and the good, including titans of industry, finance, and state such as Ford, John D. Rockefeller Jr, J. P. Morgan Jr., and Thomas Lamont (partner in the House of Morgan, the bank central to the initial creation of GE, which still maintained significant financial control), Gerald Swope and Owen Young (president of GE and chairman of RCA), treasury secretary Andrew Mellon, and President Herbert Hoover.[2] Bernays cannily also arranged for Albert Einstein to call from Germany to congratulate Edison, merging theoretical and applied conceptions of the movement of light and compression of space and time that was relayed through the transoceanic cables controlled by AT&T.[3] Parts of the proceedings were also broadcast over the GE-controlled NBC radio network, itself reliant on the corporate agreements between GE and AT&T that had parceled out radio and telephonic communication and established the grounds for the syncing of media and telecommunication networks. Electrical, telecommunications, and media networks converged. Or, put another way, inter-locking corporate agreements, underwritten by a state supporting the so-called natural monopolies of electricity, radio, and telecommunications, enabled the private control of power and communicative networks.

Owen Young's and Hoover's speeches were the two included in the radio broad-cast, exemplifying the fusion of corporate and state interest that underlay corporate liberalism, all the while carried on the networks established through that asso-ciation.[4] Hoover praised Edison's role as innovator of industrial research, like that subsequently carried out by GE in the corporate labs that had, for example, "built the worlds largest electrical installation" at the Panama Canal, had innovated radio technology, and had just a few years earlier successfully synced sound and vision on strips of celluloid.[5] The audience listening at home had been instructed to turn off their electric lights, and then to turn them on again at the precise moment in the broadcast when Edison reenacted his famous experiment. Homes moved, lit-erally, from darkness to light, premodern to modern, led by Edison as personifica-tion of corporate power, *binding* the nation together through the matrix of priva-tized electrical, media, and communicative forms.

General Electric's PR campaign for electric lighting was consistent with the broader campaign of the electrical industry's trade association, the National Elec-tric Light Association, which had worked assiduously in the largest PR campaign of the decade to argue for private ownership of electrical networks.[6] (The association's campaign made some use of film, too, but was fundamentally multimedial.)[7] "Light's Golden Jubilee" came after congressional investigations of the electrical industry and its PR campaigns, in 1925 and 1928. The campaign was part of a corpo-rate counteroffensive against state oversight, which clearly enlisted significant state support in the form of the immensely rich treasury secretary (and former banker) Mellon, who had in 1923 massively reduced higher-end tax levels (on the theory, central to modern conservatism, that wealth would "trickle down"), and the presi-dent, who in his previous role as commerce secretary had supported corporate con-trol of radio.[8] GE's arguments were consistent with those made by AT&T when it successfully defended its control of long-distance telecommunication lines.[9] The company developed sophisticated "institutional advertising" in the 1920s that focused on glorifying electricity in general and making a virtue of the size of the corporation.[10] Quite clearly the multimedia spectacle orchestrated by Bernays was consistent with the imperative to forestall state regulation, or ownership, of electri-cal networks and the strategy of individuating the company and associating it with the general advantages of light/enlightenment it brought to people and the nation. PR accomplished, again, the alchemical transformation of private interest and profit into ostensible public good through the orchestration of media spectacle.

Equally significant to GE was the expansion of electrical networks that pro-duced profits both in terms of electricity *and* the machines—such as radios—that plugged into those networks and revolutionized domestic life in the 1920s, by which point around 70 percent of homes in mostly urban areas were electrified.[11] The head of GE's lighting division had described electric lighting as "the entering wedge" for other electrical technologies in the home.[12] By the 1920s, GE had shifted its attention from the creation of turbines and power stations to the profits to be realized through the innovation of domestic electrical technologies.[13] Perhaps the most significant of those were radio and then later television, which also enabled the continuous link between corporation and home. This fulfilled Edison's initial dream for what cinema would be around the time he sketched out the legal caveats, in the late nineteenth century, that his company would use as the basis for its enforcement of patent rights in the early years of the twentieth century.[14] Electrical, telecommunications, and media networks connected the home to the outside, relaying corporate messages to the private sphere, which were mediated by the corporations controlling those networks.

But . . . the timing for Bernays's magic trick of dazzling electric light and personification of corporate culture was not propitious. "Light's Golden Jubilee" took place on October 21, and on the 29th, the stock market began to crash, signaling the severest economic depression (so far) of the last two centuries. (Lamont had written to President Hoover on the 19th, assuring him that the present financial system was sound. He perhaps even repeated this in person on the 21st. Oops. But as more recent history rather suggests, investment bankers might not be the best judges of the systemic failures of financial capitalism.)[15] The preceding years of the decade had witnessed a massive rise in stock ownership, particularly of new technology companies like GE (and subsidiaries like RCA), AT&T (and Western Electric), International Harvester, and indeed film studios. It was what we might now call a tech bubble. Electricity had also massively increased the productivity of manufacturing and the amount of goods produced by industry. The astonishing rise in productivity levels at Ford's iconic River Rouge factory, for example, were facilitated by the use of flexible electrical motive power.[16] New forms of credit, and installment credit, enabled people to purchase the latest objects of technological capitalism, notably the automobile, and fueled also a real estate boom, beginning in Florida, which was enabled in part by the expansion of car ownership and road networks, and then moving to the commercial property markets of the Northeast and North Central regions.[17] (Part of that boom was in new cinema theaters and related office blocks, including the Paramount building in Times Square, and other iconic buildings like the Chrysler Building, begun in 1928 as a concrete symbol of the new forms of capital and technology transforming the economy.) But much of this was a speculative bubble bearing little relation to the more prosaic and concrete realities of use and value. Credit could only absorb parts of the surplus produced by monopoly capital and its newly created productive practices.[18] The stock market crash wiped fictional figures off balance sheets, bankrupting countless individuals, companies, and banks– starting with the small-scale investors, often drawn into the market through their Liberty Bond purchases back in 1917—and this spread first to the real estate markets and then widely from there across the economy, nation, and globe.[19]

Writes Eric Hobsbawm, "Banks, already hurt by the speculative real-estate boom which . . . had reached its peak some years before the Big Crash, loaded with bad debts, refused new housing loans or to refinance existing ones. This did not stop them failing by the thousands, while (in 1933) nearly half of all US home mortgages were in default and a thousand properties a day were being foreclosed. Automobile purchasers alone owed $1,400 million out of a total personal indebtedness of $6,500 million in short-and medium-term loans."[20] Vast numbers of people became homeless, as the banks liquidated their loans and took hold instead of the materiality of property. (It happened to film studios too, including to the mighty Paramount, which declared bankruptcy in 1933, principally because it had borrowed heavily to purchase theaters, as well as to Fox, after the company overextended itself and was taken over by the banks and AT&T. In 1934, RKO also went bankrupt.) Estimates put unemployment in 1933 at nearly 12 million people, as much as a quarter of the entire workforce.[21] Ford, for example, had employed 128,000 workers in Spring 1928, but that number was down to 37,000 by August 1931.[22] Workers in the urban North experienced an average wage cut of 40 percent between 1929 and 1933. Farm prices tumbled catastrophically too, hitting sharecroppers and tenant farmers hardest and leaving countless families homeless and destitute. In some states one-quarter to one-third of all farms were foreclosed between 1928 and 1934.[23] Farm income dropped from $11 billion in 1929 to $5 billion in 1932.[24] The country's overall gross national product—the market value of all products and services—fell precipitously from $104 billion in 1929 to $56 billion in 1932. Quite simply, the financial system of lightly regulated liberal capitalism in the era of the intertwined growth of corporate and financial capital, reached what seemed to many to be a breaking point. The intricate global system of capitalism began to collapse too, as countries around the globe experienced economic crises—these hit those countries reliant on the production of raw materials hardest—and withdrew from the gold standard into forms of economic autarky and nationalism.[25] Britain, recall, decoupled sterling from gold in 1931 and fashioned new forms of "imperial preference."[26]

The prevailing economic orthodoxy at the start of the crisis—a fusion of classical and associational liberalism—suggested it would correct itself. Mellon (in)famously advised Hoover, "Liquidate labor, liquidate stocks, liquidate the farmers, liquidate real estate . . . purge the rottenness out of the system."[27] Workers and the disenfranchised were more proactive in their response, where possible. In 1932, for example, as many as twenty thousand war veterans who held government bonus certificates due years in the future descended upon Washington to demand that Congress pay the money immediately. (Hoover ordered the army to evict them, a task carried out with ruthless efficiency by General Douglas MacArthur, with assistance from future president General Dwight Eisenhower.)[28] Vast numbers went on strike, across different industries, so that by 1934 1.5 million workers were striking for more humane conditions.[29] The strikes spread also to the new mass production industries—notably automobile and rubber—where unions had largely been banned. Violent responses by police, state militia, and the National Guard were not uncommon. Protest in the agricultural periphery in particular was widespread. When patrician Franklin Delano Roosevelt (FDR) came to office in early 1933, he identified the threat of "an agrarian revolution" as imminent.[30] Radical revisions to liberal political economy were widely mooted. "Probably for the first, and so far the only, time in the history of capitalism," Hobsbawm suggests, "its fluctuations seemed to be genuinely system-endangering."[31] FDR wrote in his own journal of the possibility of a "violent and disorderly overthrow of the whole capitalist structures."[32] Outside the United States the specters of communism and fascism spread in part as responses to the apparent breakdown of liberal capitalism.[33]

Roosevelt's so-called New Deal eventually prevented such a breakdown in the United States, albeit ultimately only after the war of 1939–45 kickstarted a new round of industrial, technology, and finance capital expansion.[34] The results of a flurry of social democratic reforms in the 1930s undoubtedly improved the lives of many working populations and marked a significant restructuring of the remit of the liberal state. The 1935 Social Security and National Labor Relations Act, for example, established forms of social welfare and new rights for labor organization that were innovative and significant.[35] Quite clearly a regulated and more humane capitalism is better than a less humane capitalism. But equally clearly the broad thrust of governmental response worked principally to safeguard the functioning of the corporate- and finance capital–dominated liberal political economy rather than to revise its essential predicates. Contemporary commentators like, for example, banker and film financier Joseph Kennedy recognized this.[36] "Exceptional" state practices, including those that led to a proliferation of state media texts and institutions, were designed principally to safeguard a political and economic system, rather than to revise any of its structural logics and operations.[37] The goals were to foster social *security* not social *equality*.[38] Executives from GE and the Chamber of Commerce, for example, helped design the National Industrial Recovery Act, which "effectively legalized cartels in American industry," while significant trade associations—like that established by the mainstream film industry—wrote the codes governing their industries in ways that favored large corporate industry and circumvented antitrust regulation.[39] Even further, the Roosevelt administration turned, beginning around 1935 (and the election in 1936), in what is often called the second New Deal, toward alliances with new capital-intensive industries—like the electrical and telecommunications industries—and associated investment and internationally orientated commercial banks. From this point onward, as Thomas Ferguson has influentially argued, a new configuration of free trade "multinational liberalism" and globalism developed in the United States, cut to the interests of globalizing economic entities.[40] This coalition became an "organizing principle in American politics" thereafter.[41]

What follows explores the ways media was deployed to help respond to this political and economic crisis and to begin to visualize the future of a new, neoliberal capitalism. In the first part of this chapter, I examine the uses made of film and other media by state agencies to try to shape the attitudes and conduct of vulnerable and "dangerous" populations in order to shore up a liberal political economy. Here again I am interested in state-produced "pedagogical" film and media, and I discern two broad logics: media was utilized as part of biopolitical measures of *security* that cross over from *social* security to the continuation and extension of the surveillance and policing of populations that had begun most significantly in the post–World War I years; and it was used as a symbolic, informational, and rhetorical form to help reinvigorate the moribund economy, in particular by facilitating new infrastructural projects such as expanded road, air, and electrical networks, which were increasingly regarded as essential to the circulatory logics of capital. The form that came to be called "documentary" begins in the United States in these contexts, which are not dissimilar in some respects to its origins in Britain, as that country sought to innovate new forms of persuasive media and symbolic culture to sustain liberal (and imperial) political economy.

The latter parts of this chapter begin to examine the corporate counter-offensive against labor radicalism and state regulation that too began from around 1935 and that produced film and media that began to articulate the principles of a "new" liberalism, which became the foundation of modern conservatism. This "neo"-liberalism, or conservatism, championed the cutting back of state regulation and the radical expansion of free trade and the market across the globe. It began to be most clearly articulated in the midst of the economic crisis, notably in significant campaigns by the influential trade organization the National Association of Manufactures (NAM), but it stretched also to events like the 1939 World's Fair in New York, where an array of corporate spectacles and experiences were on view, presenting a glittering and technologically mediated "world of tomorrow." The arguments gathered pace in the postwar period, after the second global conflict of the twentieth century ended the Depression and in the process taught (or reminded) state managers of the lesson that war is good for high-tech industries and financiers and thus "the economy." New institutions, such as the World Bank, were created at the war's end, which were designed to shape and govern a new capitalist world system. Economists began to argue that unfettered markets equal freedom.[42] One of the most influential architects of this neoliberal position, Milton Friedman, later argued that the Depression was caused ultimately by mismanaged state and central-banking policies and was not a consequence of the inherent instability of finance capital.[43] Quite clearly the precepts of these lessons in free trade and war-making were repeated across the long Cold War, reaching fuller expression in the 1970s and thereafter with the fusion of neoliberalism, neoconservatism, and endless war, which has grown and expanded further from 2001. The "neo" in this configuration of liberalism fought back against state (social) welfare and regulation of "free" market forces, sometimes presenting itself (albeit falsely) as a return to the "classical" liberalism of Adam Smith.[44] (I emphasize social because the massive rise in military spending during the Cold War and War on Terror periods has functioned as a form of state welfare for arms and technology corporations, carried out alongside the kinds of state aid and trade support that have historically also helped the globalizing ambitions of US corporate media.)[45] I shall have more to say about that neoliberal configuration, and the role of media in articulating and supplementing it, in the next and final chapter of this book. Before that I will first sketch out the state and corporate responses to economic depression, out of which new and "exceptional" media texts, institutions, and policies emerged.

"CREATING MONOPOLY SUSTAINED BY GOVERNMENT"

The largely laissez-faire initial response to the economic crisis from the Hoover administration, clearly articulated by Mellon's call for the "liquidation" of "rottenness" in the system, crumbled in the face of systemic economic collapse. Guided by the principles of an associational liberalism, which fostered a compact between state and large industry, Hoover reacted slowly to the novel scale of the crisis and was soundly defeated in the election of 1932. Roosevelt, when taking office in early 1933, fashioned a now rather fabled series of state responses to the crisis to forestall further economic and political breakdown. In his first one hundred days in office, his administration passed emergency relief bills for the unemployed; the Agricultural Adjustment Act, which restricted farm production by paying farmers subsidies; the US Banking Act, which separated commercial and investment banks (better known more recently, after its neoliberal dissolution, as the Glass-Steagall Act);[46] the Securities Act, which reformed the New York Stock Exchange; and the National Industrial Recovery Act (NRA), which offered limited legality to unions and simultaneously legalized cartels in American industry.[47] The Roosevelt administration's responses were varied, indeed somewhat haphazard, but the broad thrust of them built initially on the array of "extended" administrative capacities, policy tools, sources of expertise, and patterns of state-interest group "associationalist" relations, which dominated public policy during and after World War I.[48]

Wilson's War Industries Board (WIB) was, for example, a significant precedent for the early New Deal's management of the economy. The WIB had accelerated war production in 1917 by effectively suspending antitrust laws and allowing large firms to dominate their industries.[49] FDR's NRA was partly modeled on this.[50] The NRA was also partly developed out of a plan formulated initially by Gerald Swope, the same chief executive of GE who had traveled to watch Edison reenact his experiment with electric light on the eve of the stock market crash.[51] It was led by General Hugh Johnson, who had served with the WIB during World War I, and who followed the WIB precedent of recruiting officials from business and delegating enforcement of government regulation of industrial practice to code authorities dominated by representatives selected by trade associations or other major interests within each industry.[52] In this it was consistent also with Hoover's longstanding support for trade associations, which had further entrenched corporate and oligopolistic power in the 1920s, during his tenure at both the Department of Commerce and the White House.[53] Quite simply, then, the NRA sought to respond to the economic crisis by further orchestrating associational and oligopolistic practices and, in turn, delegating "state authority to business."[54] Typically the code authorities to which code enforcement was delegated replicated the existing distribution of power among firms within each sector.

Indeed, the NRA code for the mainstream film industry can serve as a useful guide to this process in action, clarifying also how the corporate film industry's lobbying and PR group sought to influence state policy to sustain monopoly practices. The former Republican Party chairman Will Hays had been hired at great expense for just such purposes. I described earlier how Paramount had successfully bypassed antitrust regulation in 1932, when the Federal Trade Commission decision against the company was declared null and void, in part because of the economic depression. Emboldened by this, the Motion Picture Producers and Distributors of America (MPPDA) presented a code plan in the summer of 1933 that sustained the interests and practices of the vertically integrated studios that the MPPDA represented and that would also suspend any further antitrust actions.[55] It was opposed by independent exhibitors in particular, who called again for the end of practices such as block- and blind-booking. Hugh Johnson appointed Solomon Rosenblatt, a New York lawyer, to draw up a code, and Rosenblatt called public hearings in September of that year, before sanctioning a code that effectively supported the oligopolistic practices of the corporate industry. Adolph Zukor himself wrote an article in the 1934 edition of the *Film Daily Yearbook* entitled simply "Faith in the NRA," and the implementation of the code warded off any further state regulation of the business practices of the major studios during the Depression.[56] (It also outlawed most of the rebate schemes introduced by independent exhibitors to drum up business, including such things as lotteries and prize giveaways.)[57] Early in 1934, an independent National Recovery Review Board, led by the famous lawyer Clarence Darrow, issued a report that concluded the codes it had considered provided "an opportunity for the more powerful and more profitable interests to seize control of an industry or to augment and extend control already obtained."[58] Darrow condemned the NRA for "creating monopoly sustained by government," and identified the film industry code as one of the most oppressive.[59] But the Darrow report was ignored by the Roosevelt administration because its principal objective was sustaining the power of trade associations and monopoly capital, which was consistent with the precepts of corporate liberalism as elaborated principally across the 1920s.

Rural regulation had similar in-built flaws and biases. The Agricultural Adjustment Act aimed to raise prices by taking land out of production and providing subsidies to make up for lost income.[60] But this New Deal legislation ignored the three million agricultural wage earners, a large portion of whom were poor black tenant farmers, and funneled subsidies through the larger landowners. The act's benefits consequently gave large agribusiness capital to mechanize, further displacing labor and reinforcing class domination within agriculture.[61] Landmark social welfare legislation in the New Deal also reflected the interests of large manufacturers and employers. The Social Security Act of 1935 provided a complicated federal-state provision of unemployment insurance and federal old-age insurance known as social security. Provision was sketchy, though, and Social Security excluded all agricultural and domestic workers—that is, most African-Americans and women—and payments did not begin until 1940.[62] Let me reiterate that this does not mean that these measures were devoid of humanitarian intent or did not also materially and significantly benefit many workers. But they were shaped also by political expediency (eg, agricultural workers were excluded to appease Southern Democrats) and by the interests of large industries anxious for the federal state to take over this welfare role.[63] And they were framed also through extant ideological norms, which, for example, presumed that married women were dependents of their husbands and excluded large groups of the lowest-paid women workers, including the three million domestic servants, from protection.[64] The developments marked a mutation within liberalism toward what historian Alan Brinkley calls a rights-based liberalism that "left little room for the broad efforts to reshape the capitalist economy that concerned previous generations of reformers."[65] Indeed, it has been argued that "the 'welfare state' was expressly designed by its chief architects to encourage and stimulate mass consumption," thus taking the recently established consumer economy as a given and building from that policy levers that would encourage consumer spending.[66] Broadly speaking, then, the New Deal innovated forms of regulation that sought to balance competing interests without either infringing on the "rights" of the wealthy or fundamentally reorientating the political and economic system in order to buttress the "security" of liberal capitalism.

The massive investment in infrastructural projects in the New Deal to regenerate the circulation essential to advanced capitalism further illustrates this logic. In

1933, the Public Works Administration received an initial appropriation of $3.3 billion, a figure over 165 percent of the federal government's revenues for that year.[67] The well-known Tennessee Valley Authority emerged from this development, becoming a government-owned corporation that provided flood control, electrical generation, and economic development in the distressed Tennessee Valley region. Partly these developments were symbolic, functioning as visible examples of the power of government to reshape the built environment.[68] Media would be important to that too. In 1935 the Works Progress Administration received an initial appropriation of $4.88 billion and used the money to employ workforces to build light construction projects, including 480 airports, 78,000 bridges, and nearly 40,000 public buildings.[69] Vast new road networks were also built, as FDR presided over a period of massive public spending on infrastructural projects that sought to stimulate employment and the circulation of people, goods, capital, and electricity integral to advanced capitalism. Substantial governmental spending on infrastructure sought also "to create long-term markets . . . in undeveloped regions," marking further and materially enacting the spatial expansion of the logics of the market.[70]

By the end of the 1930s, these measures to foster "security" and infrastructure produced a new historical compact, or bloc, between the state and capital-intensive industries and (parts of) finance capital. To cut a longer story short, it is also clear that the war and the massive increases in military and "defense" spending finally ended the Depression, after the severe "recession" of 1937–38, and would remain central to the subsequent growth of the US economy in the postwar years. The establishment from the war years on of what President Dwight D. Eisenhower later called the "military-industrial complex" traded on ideas of "security," which intensified in the New Deal but were expanded globally in the 1940s, notably because of the National Security Act of 1947 and the establishment of institutions like the National Security Council and the Central Intelligence Agency.[71] Cold War "development" carried these imperatives forward as the US state exported the lessons learnt from the New Deal investment in infrastructure to expand its remit and its global reach (particularly in southeast Asia) and to further the circulation of investment, materials, and capital.[72] It was accompanied by another "Red Scare," like the one after World War I, which was in part directed toward purging Hollywood of leftist influence and which later prompted the CIA to form a program called "Militant Liberty" to try to insert the theme of "freedom" into movies.[73] I shall talk a little more about that history in the chapter that follows.

"A SPECTACLE OF MOBILITY"

Various forms of media and symbolic culture were deployed as technologies of governance in the New Deal era. Photography, cinema, radio, sculpture and other forms of public art, and the built environment were all operationalized to help secure the welfare and allegiance of populations and the future of liberal capitalism. The New Deal state also built on the management and use of media that had been innovated by political parties and state managers in earlier years, and which has been my subject here and there in the preceding pages: for example, the Republican Party's canny use of film in the 1896 election; the creation of the Committee on Public Information (CPI) in 1917; Bernays's use of film and stage stars to "humanize" Coolidge in 1924; and the UK Conservative Party's creation of a film production unit in 1925 and the Empire Marketing Board in 1926. Quite clearly, the New Deal state managers learned specifically from Wilson's experiment with the CPI, a development consistent with the way Wilson-era policies and practices were retooled in FDR's first administration in particular. Equally clearly this deployment of media developed also from the mutation of the CPI into the broader practice and culture of PR in the interwar years. The Democratic Party had itself established a publicity bureau in 1928 and presided over the significant expansion of press offices within government agencies in the 1930s.[74] FDR became the first president to employ a press secretary.[75] Radio was widely used by the administration, connecting the White House directly to houses across the nation through the recently synced together telecommunication lines and media networks.[76] Government departments produced films to "educate" citizens about the crisis and the state response, some of which were circulated through the pedagogical networks— schools and extension services— established earlier, and some of which were circulated using the distribution networks of corporate studios.

Roosevelt's use of the media was certainly *exceptional* and in many ways unprecedented. FDR's first-ever presidential press secretary, Stephen T. Early, coordinated Roosevelt's relations with the media, alongside the president's personal secretary, the former journalist and CPI alumni Marvin McIntyre.[77] The attention paid to the management of media exposure and imagery was testament to the growing recognition of the necessity of framing and managing the news cycle in the new era of modern media systems. Lippmann's lessons were learned well. Both Early and McIntyre had worked with newsreel companies in Hollywood—Early even with Paramount—and thus expertise imported from the film industry was positioned right at the center of the administration's management of PR.[78] FDR's press managers worked to shape positive coverage, across the press, radio, and newsreels and policed visual imagery in particular to ensure that the extent of Roosevelt's disability caused by polio was largely shielded from the public. In 1936, Roosevelt fell on his way to the podium at the Democratic National Convention, but none of the journalists took pictures, despite many of them being in a position to do so.[79] Cameras turned away from the president's disabled body to foster instead an image of a dynamic and vigorous leader, standing—almost invariably literally, as his wheelchair was practically never pictured—as metonymic for the hoped-for healthy body politic. Ewen, with characteristic insight, calls this a "spectacle of mobility";[80] this works as a pretty good description for much of the New Deal state-produced films, too.

Radio also became a significant part of the new PR state. The extent of FDR's use of the relatively recently established radio networks has been seen by communication studies scholars and others as a significant moment in the political use of nascent media technology.[81] The president practiced an informal, friendly delivery, in speeches that had been polished by the playwright Robert Sherwood, using the medium to connect the White House directly with the houses of citizens and to reassure the populace that governmental action would restore economic and social order.[82] Various government departments also produced radio shows, most notably the Office of Education within the Department of the Interior. Soon after taking office, FDR gave a radio talk on the banking crisis that is now commonly regarded as a significant moment in forestalling further bank closures.[83] Banks were sustained, that is, by the president's using media networks that government had helped to establish, in partnership with large technology corporations, which were themselves closely allied with significant investment and commercial banks. Quite a dizzying set of connections. The mobile, wireless, "extended" media networks created through complex partnerships among the state, tech corporations, and finance capital were pressed into service to maintain the liberal capitalist political economy from which they emerged. Media provided security and helped foster the "confidence" integral to the complex system of fictions that is "the market."

Visual symbols of the state's power, of modernity, and of governmental efficiency and utility were particularly significant to the New Deal state's PR in keeping with the broader emergence of the new forms of a "spectacular" culture of consumption, exemplified by cinema and the new illustrated magazines, such as *Life,* which became such an important part of media culture in the 1930s. The investment in sculpture, painting (including murals), built space, and photography has been relatively well addressed by photographic and art historians.[84] The destruction of rural economies and the terrible impact of this on people caught up in this crisis were pictured in now-famous photographic work sponsored by the state. Photographs like the well-known "Migrant Mother," by Dorothy Lange, accord a remarkable dignity to their subjects. The photographic record of the devastation caused by catastrophic environmental degradation and economic collapse was part of a socially progressive humanitarian project of realism and empathetic engagement. For the state that sponsored them, they were also designed to help secure the population's allegiance to the state in its efforts to secure social and political and economic order.[85]

Less is known about the extent of the New Deal state's investment in the mobile and purportedly powerful form of visual display that is film. Certainly, we know a great deal about a couple of documentary films produced under the aegis of the state—*The Plow That Broke the Plains,* and *The River*—and about Hollywood's allegorical representation of, for example, chorus girls and gangsters. But we know almost nothing about the more mundane use of film to *sustain* the New Deal order. It is this use of film to publicize the work of the state, enlist support for its policies, and visualize new practices of exceptional governance that I shall examine in the rest of this section.

Your Job Insurance, Social Security Benefits, Social Security for the People, Old Age and Family Security, and *Federal Old-Age Insurance* (all produced by the Social Security Board in 1935–39) seek to explain the practicalities of claiming the new (if restricted) Social Security benefits elaborated by the state to protect some vulnerable populations and the state itself from radical agitation. Voiceover directs attention in all the films, guiding the viewer through texts that seek to be directly pedagogical in explaining significant shifts in the liberal state's relationship with its populace mandated by welfare legislation. The sound of the state shapes a narrative form that is straightforwardly didactic. Both *Social Security Benefits* and *Social Security for the People,* for example, correlate images and voiceover to carefully map out the procedure for applying for a Social Security card, explaining what documents are needed, who is eligible, how the forms look, and how they should be filled out. Welfare recipients are only lightly individualized—"let's call him Joe," the voiceover in *Federal Old-Age Insurance* jokingly observes—for they function not as characters per se but as representations of particular positions of citizenship (unemployed, retired, widow, etc). The administrative function guides a narrative form that has little use for individualized "characters" in order to better cathect citizen audiences to the machinery of the state.

Part of the imperative was simply to explain policy and to use film to instruct the population, but the films also segue into generating support for the actions of the state and contain fascinating glimpses into the way the New Deal state imagined itself and its biopolitical objectives. Much is made in this way of filing processes and the literal machinery of the biopolitical state. "Joe's" form in *Federal Old-Age Insurance,* for example, is filled out, and then converted into a punch card that can be read by filing machines, photographed by cameras, and put on microfiche. Machines do much of the processing in this advanced technological state. One of the women workers (it is an almost entirely feminized workforce in all the Social Security films) holds the original form next to the microfiche of the form, demonstrating the administrative efficiency of the government in rendering the statistical matter of life into ever-more precise and processable forms. Each of the films shows the forms entering vast filing cabinets, part of what the voiceover for *Old Age and Family Security* calls the "biggest bookkeeping job in the entire world." The Social Security cycle frequently lingers over filing processes and cabinets, illustrative of the way the "high modernist state," in James Scott's formulation, processes information and catalogues and stores "legible people."[86] Visible across the cycle is the state's careful attention to its populace, which makes use of high-tech machinery combined with a care personified as feminized—even partly maternal—to present the state as benign, caring, rational, and modern. Quite clearly film was utilized as part of the state's exceptional expansion of new forms of state and social security. It was in this respect a form of welfare and biopolitical media.

The state's modernity and "infrastructural power" were also emphasized in films of its public works developments. *Uncle Sam the Greatest Builder* (1937), for example, surveys irrigation projects and dams, including the recently completed Boulder Dam, labeled the "Eighth Wonder of the World" and a "lasting *symbol* of the power and might" of the nation [my emphasis]. The Tennessee Valley Authority development was pictured again and again in newsreels commissioned by Washington.[87] Dams feature in the public works films as often as filing cabinets do in the Social Security films. It has been argued indeed that the dam "became the central emblem of the New Deal," as the "concrete and steel realization" of the "New Deal's successful regulation of liberal capitalism."[88]

Take the ending of the canonical *The River* (1938) from this perspective. The film was financed by the Farm Security Administration, which sought to rehabilitate rural areas damaged by flood, the dust bowl, and the economy. The film is read and remembered mostly for its account of ecological destruction, and its poetic images and voiceover foregrounding the cost of farming practices that destroyed topsoil and contributed to devastating flooding. The film begins, though, with sequences celebrating the historical circulation of materials, a sort of hymn to the mobility that underpinned the industrial revolution. Cotton is shown being shipped along rivers and overseas, to mills and factories in the north of England (the steam from the ships visually rhymes with the images of clouds, suggesting a connection between the natural and the industrial); iron and coal to the steel mills in Pittsburgh; lumber along flumes and rivers. Certainly the costs of this movement and of destructive farming practices are severe. Floods destroy communities and agricultural land is rendered barren. But the final third of the film suggests that modern construction can restore natural balance and successful commerce. It is this ending that is often seen by subsequent scholars of documentary as somewhat at odds with the rest of the film, tagged on, it is suggested, to keep the sponsors happy.[89] It is not that. Rather, this final sequence is integral to the formal and ideological organization of the film. The sequence emphasizes the scale and historic import of the building of the Tennessee Valley Authority, of its series of dams shown from aerial perspective—no doubt at considerable cost—to emphasize their enormity, and of the vast cranes and drills that enable them. Dams protect farmland from flooding and also provide hydroelectric power to modernize rural spaces and economies. In the final sequence we see water bursting forth from the dams, a series of electric pylons carrying electricity across the land (a modern corollary to the circulation that begins the film), and a final image of water burst-

ing out again from one of the Tennessee Valley Authority dams: a close relationship of the money shot of pornography, aptly named, for here the final orgasmic
images emphasize the generative power of government to transform environment
and economy.

The narrative form of *The River* thus makes greater sense, and is more coherent,
in what is a pretty classic three-act structure than subsequent accounts allow, for it
starts with the excitement of industrial revolution and material circulation and
traverses the problems of ecological disaster before presenting the resolution of
state action.[90] Government is narrative resolution; narrative resolution is only possible because of government. If the film is a documentary, as opposed to "nontheatrical," as many curiously want to insist,[91] it is so because it orchestrates very carefully a narrative form to support state action and because it uses the poetry of the
voiceover and other forms of expensive aesthetic embellishment—a carefully constructed score, a visual aesthetic alive to the poetry of imagery that was only possible with a very high shooting ratio—to effectively sugarcoat the governmental
message about state power and its transformation of land and construction of
power networks. Expensive aesthetic documentary is better PR, as subsequent
scholarly commentary confirms.

Work Pays America is a rather more prosaic account of the myriad activities of
the Works Progress Administration, the largest agency of the New Deal state,
which employed workers on public works projects. It too is a celebration of infrastructure. It begins, rather curiously, with a biopolitical image: a map of the United
States that becomes a frame around actual workers, seemingly emphasizing that
the people literally embody the land and nation in a way quite consistent with New
Deal rhetoric (and, indeed, that of other states undergoing economic crisis, perhaps most notably that of the fascist state in Germany). What follows is a tour of
the Works Progress Administration's investment in roads, sewage systems, reser-
voirs, and airports, as well as its support for buildings like community stadiums
and for cultural practices like theater and public art. The emphasis is on mobility,
on infrastructural networks, a focus on "getting the nation moving," for it is of
course circulation that is fundamental to the operations of advanced capitalism.
The road construction shown is principally that of farm-to-market roads, continuing the pre-Depression emphasis on integrating a rural-urban market, though
there is a short sequence about roads being built to carry motorists to vacation
spots, which has a different conception of land and its utility as spectacle. Airports
appear as the technological future. The construction of new airports in Newark,
Philadelphia, and Cleveland connects the industrial heartland with the accelerated
mobility of air transport. Together, networks and associated buildings emphasize
circulation and the infrastructural power of the state. Moreover, they do so in a
form that carries the images of the buildings and networks beyond that imaginable
for the material structures themselves: mostly immaterial, mobile (through

already-established networks of distribution), film became a form of what one commentator at the time called an "architecture of public relations."⁹²

Perhaps the clearest articulation of the governmental imperative to foster new advanced infrastructural networks came in *The Power and the Land* and its picturing of the process of rural electrification, which effectively connected the agricultural periphery to a newly emerging national network.⁹³ The film was made by the radical filmmaker Joris Ivens, and it is clear sighted about the myriad benefits electricity brought to rural populations. One of those is the spread of radio itself, while another is the refrigeration that enabled farmers to produce and sell more milk before it turned sour. Electricity in this example resembles the good roads in the Ford film *The Road To Happiness,* which allowed the young farmer to transport eggs more efficiently. Corporate and state rhetorics of "development" intertwine. The before and after narrative—from sour to fresh milk—appears again as a common form in the liberal and governmental use of film and other media, extolling a liberal developmental paradigm, which structured earlier state-produced films like those of the USDA, as well as those constructed by the British state to facilitate global imperialism. The extant digital copy of the film has an opening that maps the subsequent progress of the electrification project across the agricultural regions of the nation. Lines of connection proliferate, made possible by the material infrastructure of the electricity pylons we see erected in the film.

The starkest delineation of the circulation essential to the economic system is visible in the Works Progress Administration film *Hands* (1934). Each shot is simply of a hand holding and passing on coins and bills to other hands. The film celebrates the mobility of the dematerialized and symbolic object of money. *Hands* is a further example, then, of a governmental modernism directed at fostering, and lubricating, the circulation of capital fundamental to the "stability" of the system.

One final example from the New Deal–produced media combines several of the tropes seen thus far, such as the maps and filing cabinets from the infrastructure and Social Security films, which aligned with new conceptions of the state's role in protecting property and maintaining economic security. *You Can't Get Away with It* (1936) was produced through collaboration between the Department of Justice and Universal, with the agreement specifically of the attorney general of the United States, Homer S. Cummings, and the active cooperation of the director of the Federal Bureau of Investigation (FBI), J. Edgar Hoover. The film presents the image of a hyperefficient surveillance agency that makes use of myriad modern technologies to bring criminals to justice, in particular notorious gangsters like John Dillinger, "Baby Face" Nelson, and Ma Barker. In one sequence toward the beginning of the film, Hoover stands in front of a large map on a wall, which shows the locations of federal agents and FBI offices, and dictates to a (male) secretary orders for the deployment of the agents. The FBI's reach is *national.* Its "scientific crime detection" is also seemingly infallible: a long sequence thereafter shows the way the agency gathers fingerprints and how those are stored in a large room, with long rows of filing cabinets housing the biopolitical data of parts of the population. Machines of enhanced vision, microscopes, help identify fingerprints and evidence like dust and blood. Even more effectively, a machine is able to sort through the fingerprint archive to find matches from crime scenes and so provide what a contemporary account of the film called "infallible means of identification."[94] Radio too helps the government agents communicate with each other across the nation. The technologically advanced state agency uses machines and data to police the interstate and mobile crime, which was fundamental to the remit of the FBI as a national policing agency. Hoover's *CSI*-like FBI protects the movement of interstate commerce. *You Can't Get Away with It,* indeed.

You Can't Get Away with It can be situated both within a longer history of the FBI and the more immediate context of a 1934 crime bill, which responded in particular to a spate of bank robberies and kidnapping crimes in the early years of the Depression, especially in parts of the rural periphery.[95] The FBI had specifically worked to police radicalism in the post–World War I Red Scare, resulting in the deportation of a number of members of the Union of Russian Workers. J. Edgar Hoover played a central role in that process, and this effectively marked the beginning of the overt anti-Soviet logics that would be central to the Cold War and to various other operations of the FBI. The FBI functioned thereafter as a state surveillance and policing agency, which frequently targeted radical opposition in the form of individuals and groups—from Chaplin to the Black Panthers and beyond—using methods that have recently involved the radical expansion of Internet surveillance carried out in the name of security. *You Can't Get Away with It* was media produced by the state to sustain a policing and surveillance organization that covertly targeted radical opponents of the existing political and economic system. The expansion of the FBI, and the right of agents to carry firearms mandated by the 1934 legislation, was part of the *exceptional* state practices that accompanied economic crisis. Quite clearly the film also directly sought to strengthen the protection of property and the policing of crimes against capital in the early years of the Depression.

The imperative to produce media extolling the authority of state policing was happily taken over by the corporate media system thereafter. Indeed the FBI's film was even preceded by a 1935 Warner Bros. film called *G-Men* (1935), made in close collaboration with the FBI. The film stars James Cagney, well known for his role as a gangster in *Public Enemy* (Warner Bros., 1931), but now playing a lawyer from the wrong side of the tracks. He becomes a crack FBI agent and destroys a criminal network, just in time to rescue the sister of his boss at the agency, who is also his love interest. *G-Men* played a useful role for the corporate industry's trade and lobbying agency, the MPDDA, because it advertised the industry's compliance with the regulation of stories about gangsters and criminality, which had brought welcome profits in the early years of the Depression but unwanted attention to the political and economic role of mass media.[96] *G-Men* replayed the story of the gangster—urban, ethnic, disaffected—as that of the "government man" heroically upholding the sanctity of property. It was produced by a studio with close ties to banks and technology corporations and with the encouragement of a lobbying and trade organization that continually sought to advertise Hollywood's compliance with moral, political, and economic norms. The FBI and the MPPDA found considerable common ground here.

The New Deal state, then, increased media and film production to communicate its objectives to its population. Broadly, these were directed at supplementing the security of the extant political and economic system by shaping new biopolitical norms and extolling the virtues of new infrastructural developments, which extended as far as the policing of criminality. New media production from agencies like the WPA supplemented extant production from administrative authorities like the USDA and the Department of the Interior. Collaboration with corporate media facilitated the production of films like *G-Men* and *You Can't Get Away with It,* as well as, briefly, the distribution of a state-produced film like *The River,* which was circulated through Paramount networks. The success of these developments, and particularly the theatrical and PR triumph of *The River,* prompted the Roosevelt administration to create in 1938 a centralized film unit, which would gather together the filmmaking activities scattered across the administrative functions of government. The United States Film Service (USFS), as it was called, can stand, albeit only momentarily, as the end point of the experiments with state-produced film and media that began in 1913.

Lorentz, the director of *The River,* headed up this unit. In its day-to-day operation, the USFS's relationship to other government bureaus and departments was primarily curatorial and advisory.[97] It distributed the popular *The Plow That Broke the Plains* and *The River* and acted as a clearinghouse for the distribution of other government-made films to schools, community organizations, business and professional organizations, labor groups and farmer cooperatives, and other civic institutions. The USFS was also responsible for the design and publication of study guides and other materials to accompany film screenings, thus turning screenings into pedagogical events. It was tasked also with developing a Latin American "Good Neighbor" film program, which was consistent with the earlier efforts to use film to secure economic relations with Latin America and with the Roosevelt administration's foreign policy focus on securing close relations with the countries of Latin America.

Roosevelt located the USFS within the Office of Education, and it was allied also with the National Emergency Council. In his instructions to the head of the latter body, Roosevelt asserted these goals for the utility of film:

> It has been found advantageous for these agencies to produce motion pictures, sometimes with sound accompaniment, illustrating the physical and human problems

confronting the country and the methods adopted by the Government for their solution. Such pictures serve a double purpose. For the people as a whole they make understandable the basic causes of present conditions. For the government employees in the relief and work relief programs, there is provided, not only the invaluable aid that results from this understanding by the general public, but the clarification of the purposes of the relief statutes which they are engaged in administering.[98]

For the president, then, film was useful both as an outward-facing form, providing information to the public about government "solutions," as well as a sort of internal communicative system that explained state objectives to its workers. Together this dual focus as articulated by the head of state positioned cinema and other media as integral to the state's management of the national emergency.

But Roosevelt's optimism about the possibility and utility of the centralized USFS was short lived. The USFS produced Lorentz's next film, *The Fight for Life* (1940), which was about maternity care, for the US Public Health Service, as well as Ivens's *The Power and the Land* and Robert Flaherty's *The Land* (1941). But by the time the latter was nearing completion, Congress had decided that government film production was unconstitutional. In the debates in the now Republican-dominated House (after elections in 1940), opponents raised a series of objections, arguing that the government was using funds set aside for the administration of relief programs for "propaganda" and that this usurped the authority for education explicitly given in the Constitution to the states.[99] For the opponents of the New Deal, and of the government's use of new mediums of symbolic communication, the films of the USFS in particular transformed the informational work of publicity into *propaganda,* which sought to shape public opinion and was thus inconsistent with the principles of liberal and democratic governance.

Lorentz's USFS was disbanded. Corporate Hollywood, incidentally, rejoiced, for it regarded government filmmaking as unfair commercial competition, and in any case its studio heads, as well as Will Hays, had opposed some aspects of the New Deal, particularly the right for workers to unionize.[100] Executives in Hollywood had even banded together to finance a number of fake newsreel films depicting California's borders being flooded by incoming migrants, who were escaping drought and poverty in the East and Midwest, in order to besmirch progressive Upton Sinclair's efforts to become governor of California.[101] Corporate-produced fake newsreels—fiction masquerading as fact, "fake news" –mixed with a flourishing procorporate media culture, which gathered pace in the second half of the 1930s to extol the virtues of free trade and the utility of corporate business in revitalizing the economy. Powerful lobbying and trade promotion groups like NAM played expansive roles in fostering the production and circulation of media, outlining the centrality of business and commerce to what the NAM campaign called "the American way." I turn now to a brief examination of some aspects of this media history in the latter years of the 1930s, when a narrative began to be articulated that was counter to that of the broadly associational liberalism of the New Deal and when the proposal began to be made that business alone was the most effective solution to economic crisis and to the fostering of economic security. Such ideas gathered pace in the late 1930s and became increasingly central to the articulation of new forms of "militant liberalism" calling for the "freeing" of global commerce from the restraints of regulation, which gained prominence during the rest of the American Century.

"PROGRESS ON PARADE"

The corporate pushback against state regulation of the economy began in the depths of the Depression and expanded in the latter years of the 1930s. Broadly speaking these arguments proposed that business was best equipped to reestablish domestic economic security and "free enterprise" was thus a foundational cornerstone for "freedom" itself. Various forms of media and corporate display and mediated experience were pressed into service to facilitate this. New film technology, in the shape particularly of the 8mm gauge established in 1932 and the first cheap 16mm sound projector from 1933, began to be widely used, and this was circulated through some of the nontheatrical circuits used to establish a form of conservative media network, which I examined earlier in this book.[102] Film, in various forms, and radio dovetailed in significant ways here. I focus first on the campaign of the NAM because it was a significant cross corporate lobbying and trade association, the operations of which have been examined here and there in the preceding pages. But I also take up some of the other dynamics of these forms of militant liberalism in the 1930s, exploring briefly other campaigns and the efforts expended to circulate these films among various publics. I pursue the subsequent history of these efforts, in the late 1930s and beyond, in the following chapter.

NAM and "cinema" both began in 1895, in the midst of the rise of the corporation, and the former became a visible and influential procorporate lobbying group thereafter. The organization "was influential in establishing public relations as a permanent fixture in the American corporation and trade association."[103] In the face of the crisis of the Depression and the New Deal, the association reorganized, when a small group of executives from some of America's largest corporations took control, with the goal to "build a powerful, militant voice for American industry, one which would advocate specifically on behalf of open shop ideology and against the New Deal more generally."[104] In some ways this resembled "the American plan" elaborated in the aftermath of WWI. "Business" operated collectively as a *political* unit."[105] In 1934, NAM also participated in the founding of the Liberty League, another conservative lobbying group that campaigned in particular against New Deal labor legislation. The Liberty League was financed from the wealth amassed by the Du Pont family's investments in chemicals, explosives, and automobiles.[106] It sponsored radio shows beginning in 1934, making use in particular of time given freely "with the compliments of the radio companies."[107] NAM too began to use radio. *The American Family Robinson,* which began airing in late 1934, was a weekly radio program sponsored by NAM. Carried by radio stations owned by NBC and CBS, it functioned as a kind of soap opera teaching economic lessons favorable to business.[108] Various other corporations similarly began to sponsor radio shows in this period, part of a broad-based conservative movement to use mass media to sustain economic conditions favorable to large business. Ford, recall, began a radio show on the CBS network, which also began in late 1934, in the midst of its battle to oppose unionization. GM, Chase National Bank, DuPont, Texaco, and Firestone all underwrote radio programs in this period too.[109] The DuPont show, *Cavalcade of America,* beginning in 1935, concluded each episode with the slogan, "Better Things for Better Living with Chemistry."[110] Corporate-owned media in the form of radio articulated positions favorable to the economic interests of corporations.

The NAM campaign was multimedial. Indeed it took its inspiration from the CPI apparatus created during World War I. Local leaders were recruited to head up other committees on public information and were encouraged to speak in various public forums—again including movie theaters—and to disseminate NAM materials, in schools and public libraries in particular.[111] The organization produced pamphlets articulating its position on free enterprise and freedom, which made clear its central argument that the two were inextricably enmeshed. Destroy the basis for free enterprise, this logic ran, and freedom itself evaporates. *What is Your American System All About,* a 1936 NAM pamphlet, thus contrasted "two kinds of government," the American system, in which "the citizen is supreme and the government obeys his will" and alternative forms, in which "the state is supreme and controls the citizen."[112] The logic of this critical argument—contrasting freedom for the individual with unfreedom managed by the state—was made apparent in a 1937 internal planning memo, which outlined organizational goals to establish "the inter-relation and inseparability of free enterprise and democracy" to prove that "free enterprise is as much an indivisible part of democracy and the source of as many blessings and benefits as are our other freedoms of speech, press, and religion."[113] Positions similar to these were circulated to five thousand newspapers across the country by NAM.[114] Elsewhere, very visible public billboard campaigns used PR and advertising techniques to invade public space and populate it with procorporate business messages. The campaign received a combined $3,250,000 in free print, radio, and billboard advertising from corporations that supported its aims.[115] The thematic slogan "What's Good for Industry Is Good for You," chosen by a PR advisory board at NAM, was a pithy summary of the logic of the campaign, which was headed up by a senior executive from GM.

Film was significant to these campaigns, but in partnership with other media, and not always *film* in the way we typically use that term. New forms of "talking-slide film" were established, for example, which functioned like a moving-slide machine but with synchronized sound. These "hybrid media machines," as Haidee Wasson calls them, were widely used by businesses to sell products, as well as the "business idea" more broadly, and also to communicate with internal workforces.[116] Ford, for example, had sixty-five hundred dealers equipped with sound-slide-film projectors, through which they could show old and new films.[117] NAM made a series of talking-slide films in 1936. *Flood Tide*, for example, "warns against rising costs of government," while *American Standards of Living* "forcibly portrays what the American working man enjoys as the fruit of his labor under the American system."[118] This is a "film" history that so far remains mostly unwritten.

The procorporate and probusiness agenda extolling ideas about freedom, democracy, and the individual was marshaled in response to the economic crisis and to the limited forms of social democracy established during the New Deal. Business leaders used film, as well as radio and other forms of media, and worked to circulate media as broadly as possible to articulate ideas about what I shall call simply "militant liberalism." With film this involved using the networks that were partly established in the 1920s, particularly by the state, in combination with educational institutions and with other significant players like the YMCA. For example, the United States Bureau of Mines circulated films through its networks as long as those films were not direct advertisements for particular services.[119] For NAM and its members, this worked well because the battle at this point was to articulate the probusiness position more expansively. It was a broader ideological battlefield, and many of the films produced by business and NAM were more PR for the forms of militant liberalism emerging as modern conservatism than they were adverts for particular products. Hence many of the NAM films were distributed through the networks established by the government, a further illustration of the close ties between state and business at this point. Even further, NAM was able to distribute its films directly to the extension departments of universities and to the broader "visual instruction" network, as well as through the auspices of the YMCA. These networks were significant because they were trusted and used by educational and civic groups when they sought to use films with their particular publics. It was in this way, for example, that corporate PR films made by organizations like GM, Westinghouse, DuPont, Ford, and so on were widely shown in schools and at educational and civic forums.[120] To cut a longer story short, probusiness organizations used the combined nontheatrical networks that began to be established, mostly in the 1920s, as a conservative media network. The intention was to influence opinion and conduct in the battle over ideas about the proper role of business and government, which was waged particularly bitterly during the Depression.

GM is a useful quick example of this process, not least because the company was closely connected to the Du Pont family—and so to the Liberty League and NAM—and because it played an innovative role more generally in the generation of procorporate media in the midst of the depression.[121] In 1935, the president of GM, Alfred Sloan, told the NAM convention they were facing a battle to protect the "very foundation of the American system," defined as "private enterprise," from the encroachment of "political management."[122] The following year the company began a multimedia PR campaign with a traveling exhibit called "Parade of Progress," which included a film called *Previews of Science* that "offered an inspirational narrative of America's future."[123] *Progress* was enabled by corporate innovation and technology, the campaign argued, in rhetoric very similar to that of the media produced by other corporations such as Ford, GE, AT&T, and Westinghouse. The modern "scientific" and "progressive" technologies of radio and film in particular were pressed into service to articulate and embody this position. GM sponsored a number of corporate propaganda films, beginning notably around 1936, in the midst of strikes called by the United Auto Workers for the right to organize and negotiate with management. Once again, as with Ford, this marked the use of expensive forms of mass media to articulate procorporate positions in the public sphere in the midst of ongoing bitter labor disputes.

Quite clearly there were close ties between GM and NAM, and between the various corporations that sought PR advantages using institutions like NAM to engage in the same kind of collective organizing these same entities were busy trying to deny their workers.[124] It was a united (in the main) corporate front to help structure and shape the public sphere. There is a further twist to this that merits brief explication. *Progress on Parade,* a GM film made as part of its "Parade of Progress" jamboree, was produced by a company called Audio. This company made a number of significant corporate PR films in the 1930s for organizations such as Westinghouse (*The New Frontiers*), DuPont (*The Wonderful World of Chemistry*), and Ford (*Symphony in F,* discussed further in the next chapter). What was Audio? It turns out the company was owned by ERPI, a subsidiary of Western Electric, which was itself a subsidiary of AT&T.[125] Audio had a licensing agreement with "Modern Talking Picture Service," through which their films were widely distributed using nontheatrical networks. In short, ERPI, Western Electric, and AT&T profited further from the technological developments of cinema and sound in the production of corporate PR, which began to function as a united front of the large technology and chemical corporations. These corporations had became ever-more central to the economy in the early twentieth century, that had become more closely allied with corporate media in the form of radio and sync sound cinema, and indeed with the Roosevelt administration from the mid-1930s onward. The films embody, then, the complex ties between significant large corporations, in the midst of efforts to articulate and spread the forms of militant

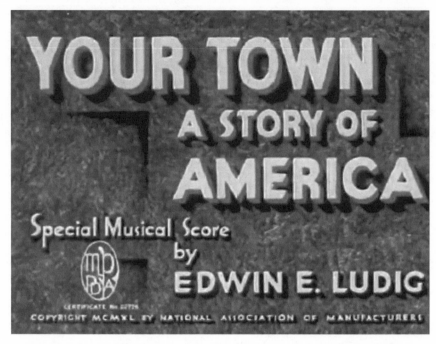

FIGURE 23. Title card from *Your Town* (Audio Productions/National Association of Manufacturers, 1940).

liberalism—often through governmental networks—that would ultimately become the dominant political and economic form in the latter parts of the twentieth century.

I discussed the GM films earlier, and I will return to them briefly in the following chapter.[126] I will conclude this brief outline of the gathering forces of conservative PR and militant liberalism carried through mass media with a closer look at an example in the form of the NAM-sponsored and Audio-made 1940 film *Your Town* (see fig. 23). Right at the outset, the film has a series of dissolves, from the flag, to the statue of liberty, to the Capitol building, and finally to the local town hall, which function as a form of political editing articulating in its very form the idea of interconnection that is so central to the liberal logic the film espouses. *Liberty*, the film argues, is indivisible from free trade. But the smooth transition at the outset from flag, ideals of liberty, and national and local government is disrupted when the story itself begins. A teenage boy is brought home in a police car by a kindly police officer, who explains to the boy's grandfather that the boy had gotten caught up in a protest at the local factory. Jerry, the boy, talks enthusiastically to his grandfather about the protest, but he is cut short, and the grandfather takes him on a walk through the town to explain to him the significant role the factory has played in the historical growth and present wealth of the town. The dissolve gives way here to a long tracking shot to better illustrate the grounded connections between people and businesses in the town.

Grandfather NAM explains how the town grew because the factory was located there, by the foresight of its individual owner and the people who helped him finance it, and how the wages and wealth generated from the factory circulate through the town. The film here purposively links industry to an individual, a maneuver that is consistent with the argument made about the corporation as an entity in the early twentieth century and that is significant thereafter to its legal definition, including that which granted it the same rights to "free speech" as the individual. Local businesses emerge to serve the growing population, the grandfather explains, as the two of them walk through the town. Professionals like doctors and lawyers populate the town because of the factory. Indeed, the hospital where Jerry was born and the school where he was educated were established only because of the factory. Even the newspaper can exist only because of the advertising in it, which can be traced back to the factory and the businesses that started to serve the workers of the factory. The film makes here a compelling argument for the way capital generates capital to establish community, which is also fostered through advertising-dependent media and is extolled here through corporate- and trade association–financed visual media. The tracking shot is the formal corollary of the argument about economic circulation. "Everybody's welfare" is linked to the factory and the capital it generates, grandfather says, in words that were surely very carefully chosen. *Welfare* is properly sustained by industry, not the state.

Wise old grandfather NAM's persuasive rhetoric convinces Jerry, who relinquishes his childish attachment to radical rhetoric. The ending carefully traces the reverse of the opening in a formal conclusion that would not be out of place in a film produced by the well-capitalized corporate media entities that were film studios. Now the image dissolves from the town, to the Capitol building, to the statute of liberty, to the flag, returning to the opening of the film and the idealized image of the connections between town, nation, government, and economy that was briefly disrupted by Jerry's selfish radicalism. Quite clearly, the dissolve functions again as the visual articulation and embodiment of the idea that democracy, liberty, and capitalism are inextricably enmeshed. NAM worked hard to circulate this film and the others it financed in schools and other educational forums to get that idea in front of as many people as possible.[127]

I turn now to some related aspects of the corporate use of media and the elaboration of forms of militant liberalism and globalism in the years both immediately preceding and following World War II. The history will be necessarily sketchy and more suggestive than fully substantiated. But it is integral to my argument that media has been utilized and shaped in various ways to facilitate and sustain a globalizing capital that has been profoundly destructive to the peoples and habitats of the world. This history began with the emergence and shaping of new forms of mass visual media in particular and expanded thereafter through other media systems, encompassing radio, television, and the various convergences of the digital.

NAM, incidentally, has continued to play some role in the subsequent expansion of neoliberal logics and practices. The organization now lobbies and campaigns to limit environmental protections, for example, which damage the profits of its corporate paymasters.[128] In one case NAM lobbied against legislation that would compel companies to declare if conflict minerals are used in their technologies. The minerals from the Democratic Republic of Congo, for example, are frequently integral to the proliferating digital media and screen technologies that are now central to the current stage of capital. Why would NAM oppose legislation that sought to compel companies to use reputable and humane supply chains? Because such legislation violates the "free speech" guaranteed to corporations as part of their legal definition as individuals.[129] For corporations such as AT&T, Loews, GE, and the Edison Electric Institute, all of which continue to contribute funds to NAM, this is money well spent.

Plus ça change . . .

The World of Tomorrow—Today!

In the midst of the explosion of corporate propaganda and PR in the mid-1930s, a group of businessmen in New York came up with the idea of a technology fair to bring business to the city and to contribute to ending the depression. The New York World's Fair opened for two seasons in 1939 and 1940, projecting an image of a new world of technology guided by benign corporations. Indeed, the theme of the fair, "The World of Tomorrow," had been carefully chosen to position technology—and the corporations that designed and produced it—as a solution to the Depression more powerful than New Deal state intervention (see fig. 24). Edward Bernays and other PR professionals played a central role in this.[1] The director of PR for the fair described it as "the greatest single public relations program in industrial history," and he encouraged corporate exhibitors to use the fair as a space to battle the influence of "New Deal propaganda."[2] Vast corporate displays told stories about the ways new forms of technology would improve lives and create a new utopian world. The spectacles and spaces that housed them were designed not so much to sell particular products "than to synthesize the technological, electrical and geometrical sublimes into one form that modeled the future."[3] Together the corporate displays bypassed the social realism of the New Deal for a "colorful corporate Oz," staging a symbolic reconciliation of the egalitarian dreams articulated in the midst of depression and the shiny new world offered by large tech firms staking a claim on the frontier of the future.[4]

"Cinema," radio, television, and related forms of mediated and material immersive experience were integral to this. The demonstration of television, triggering the sale of television sets, marked a significant moment in the early history of the medium.[5] Portable screen technology was widely integrated with the imperative to

FIGURE 24. Poster, New York World's Fair, 1939.

display, sell, make visible, and invoke desire that was fundamental to the expanded model of consumption elaborated across the fair as the solution to the Depression.[6] Media technologies embodied and articulated the techno-fantasies and newly intensified practices of consumption that became integral to the coming American century.

General Motors (GM), to pursue the example begun in the previous chapter, sponsored a very popular exhibit mapping out an imaginary future of friction-free road circulation. Parts of the exhibit were designed by celebrated "industrial designer" Norman Bel Geddes, and it took spectators on a moving journey that merged immersive and "filmic" entertainment together to extol a vision of the future characterized principally by ease of movement.[7] Bel Geddes later stated that a "national motorway system will maintain the flow of goods to the consumer without interruption."[8] Visitors entered the "Futurama" through a lobby featuring a huge map that started out showing the highway system in 1939 and then switched to reveal first, the projected traffic congestion by 1960 and second, the proposed solution in the form of a new network of superhighways. From that point on, audiences were ushered into chairs on a moving conveyor—each of them with "individual, synchronized sound equipment"—that moved them around an enormous and detailed model of the city of the future.[9] Expansive seven-lane freeways solved the problem of congestion and impeded circulation. The imaginary model city was a form of immersive, hybrid, sonic spectacle, celebrating the "freedom of movement" that the accompanying soundtrack described as essential to "progress." GM, DuPont, Liberty League, NAM, all of them interconnected, supported this idealization of friction-free movement and the necessity, as GM chairman Alfred Sloan described it in a pithy summary of militant liberalism, to "destroy the economic barriers that now prevent the essential expansion of enterprise . . . and that repress the spirit of individual initiative."[10]

The corporation produced a film called *To New Horizons* as a touring and mobile version of their future fantasy. It begins with a brief account of the accelerated progress of the second-stage industrial revolution, which celebrated various forms of technologies—gramophone, telephone, hydroelectric power—before shifting to explore GM's Futurama exhibit. Color photography erupts at this point as a visible marker of technological progress. The film explores the model's freeways and the rotary systems that allow cars to join these roads without slowing down. Outside the model, the camera is, for much of the film, fixed to the front of a (presumably) GM car, a return of sorts to the "phantom ride" cycle so popular at the outset of cinema itself as a material enactment of its status as *moving* pictures. But here the camera movement embodies the circulation and interconnection that GM proposed as the motor of what the accompanying PR–written script called "new horizons of better living."[11] Perhaps the images seen from the front of a GM car moving sinuously through real and imaginary space come the closest to picturing what the circulation Marx described as fundamental to capital *looks* like. Certainly they mark a further embodiment of the intertwined material and symbolic media infrastructure that has frequently been my subject in the preceding pages. The pedagogical corporate and state media examined in this book regularly focused on forms of infrastructure—canals, roads, railways, electrical networks, and so on. Media itself became a part of the circulatory networks integral to this particular form of capital, visible, for example, in the complex distribution networks established by corporate studios and in the interlocking agreements between telecommunications and media corporations integral to radio. Both pedagogical and commercial corporate media were key to the establishment and supplementation of a global, liberal political economy reliant on the orchestration of circulation, which encompassed material and capital and was also predicated on the innovation of new forms of consumer desire.

But let me emphasize again that this was not simply and solely a representational exercise. GM's vision of a new freeway system crossed over from science fiction to fact in the postwar years of interstate road construction, notably after passage of the Interstate Highway Act of 1956, just as Ford's imagination of farm-to-market roads dovetailed with policy in the 1920s. Bel Geddes had made this integral to his initial pitch to GM, proposing that a model of a "scientific" motorway system would demonstrate the need for its construction.[12] Right at the end of the exhibit, the audience was swung round from the model to a full-sized, real-life replica of the intersection they had just been looking at in the model. Brought *into* the spectacle, audiences left the fictional space for a "real" one mirroring the transformations proposed by the corporation as essential to the new horizons of better living. These were to be realized by the expansion of car ownership, creation of freeway systems and the corresponding destruction of public transport networks, and establishment of an oil-dependent economy. Cars, those made by GM in particular, had been integral to the establishment of a new consumer system—a model for individual preference, rather than the one-size-fits-all Model T—and car ownership was crucial to the expansion of twentieth-century industrial capitalism, in general, and to capitalism's postwar boom in particular.[13]

GM's exhibit was supplemented by Ford's, which included an elevated road system on the top of its pavilion called "The Road of Tomorrow," which enabled "driving with as little interference from traffic."[14] (See fig. 25.) Inside the building a theater showed Ford films, including *Symphony in F,* which was produced specifically for the fair to demonstrate "the Ford cycle of production" and the ever-widening circle of employment and wealth it supposedly generated. Right at the outset, the film announces its interest in the transformation of raw materials into industrial product: "From the earth come the materials to be transformed for human service by Ford men, management, and machines." After this, paper accounts that show how much Ford uses of each material—for example, 2,350,000 tons of coal were needed to produce one million cars—become animated, marching in precise military formation. Then we switch first, to animated models of workers across the globe gathering the materials that become Ford cars and second, to real scenes of materials arriving at the factory, and workers using machinery to transform it. The film offers a remarkable glimpse into the extraction and global supply chain elaborated to produce cheap cars. (Nowadays the celebration of the exploitation of cheap overseas labor regimes is generally kept offscreen, usually with the help of PR professionals.) The end of the film shows a car being magically built by itself, without workers, similar to that of the popular Chrysler/GM

FIGURE 25. *Ford Exposition Booklet,* New York World's Fair, 1939.

3-D stop motion film at the fair, which also used filmic technology to picture the corporate dream of an invisible, compliant, nonunionized workforce.[15]

Westinghouse also produced a color film called *The Middleton Family at the World's Fair* specifically for the exposition. It showed a Midwestern family visiting the Westinghouse pavilion and marveling at how electricity was powering new consumer technologies like dishwashers and television. Expensive new color technology exemplified in its materiality the technological sublime articulated at the fair. Central to the exhibit and the film was an exposition of how electricity enabled the "transformation of life." The family visits the celebrated competition orchestrated by Westinghouse between a woman washing dishes by hand (Mrs. Drudge) and a dishwasher (Mrs. Modern). Once again, as it was in USDA films like *The Happier Way,* technology enables people—and here, once more, specifically women—to become *modern.* But not too modishly modern. The daughter attends the fair with her current boyfriend, a radical abstract artist who describes the Westinghouse building as a "temple of capitalism." But he is discredited and replaced in the film by a young Westinghouse engineer, who talks about how the corporation's technology has created jobs and protected workers. The shift from radicalism to enlightened corporate management resembles that seen in *Your Town.* Babs, the daughter, finally ditches the churlish radical and chooses the engineer. The two of them get together at the conclusion, appropriately enough during the dazzling Westinghouse electric light show. Electric light, corporations, the formation of the couple = cinema . . . Radical abstract art cannot compete with the hybrid spectacle of corporate PR as entertainment; consumer technology and acquisitive individualism obviate the need for anything as old-fashioned as class solidarity.

Numerous other iterations of the argument that technology benignly serves people by ushering them into a new world of plenitude and pleasure were articulated at the Fair. GE's exhibit featured a model "electric home" stuffed with new domestic electrical technologies that clearly connected to the focused and general efforts to reestablish and expand consumption as the solution to the depression.[16] RCA, closely tied to GE, displayed television at the fair, framing it as an extension of radio—adding "sight to sound," as the president of the company said—and as "an art which shines like a torch in a troubled world."[17] The company began selling television sets the day after the fair opened.[18] (But when the United States entered World War II in 1941, the manufacturing of radio and television was officially banned as the industrial capacity was needed for arms manufacture:[19] a precise example of the close ties between military, industrial, and media companies.) Visitors to the AT&T pavilion could make free long-distance calls, with the destination lit up on a huge map for the crowds to see.[20] Quickly thereafter the company produced the remarkable film *Long Distance* (1941), celebrating the role the corporation played in establishing long-distance telecommunications that enable people to connect—through the friendly women operators—and facilitate business, security (telecommunications enabled interstate policing), and ultimately the nation itself. *Long Distance* extols the centrality of the corporation to the nation, showing they are essentially isomorphic. *Your Town* becomes your nation.

But outside the specific imperatives to sell the expensive technology of the second-stage industrial revolution, the broader themes of "Building the World of Tomorrow" were perhaps most brilliantly realized in the fair's central buildings, the now iconic "Trylon" and "Perisphere." The circular Perisphere housed a diorama called "Democracity," which displayed the future through an immersive experience that projected enormous images using purpose-built powerful projectors and lenses on the walls of the building as fairgoers walked among them. The connections, extolled in the very name of the exhibit, between electricity, the cities that were now served by the new road systems imagined by GM and Ford, and the political order positioned the corporation as integral to the liberty supposedly encoded in the nation's "democratic" political system. Expanded "cinema" as immersive experience and "science" fiction sought to remake the political system more responsive to the economic goals of corporations. Connections between the economic system and democratic order were stressed as part of the broader corporate campaign, which intensified during the Depression, to propose the two were inextricably enmeshed. That fiction was (and is) integral to pedagogic and commercial corporate media. Democracity can join the list of examples in this book that chart how the *spectacle* of democracy came ever-more frequently to stand in for any substantive form of democratic decision making.

Part of all this expensive effort to imagine and define the shape of the world of tomorrow was quite clearly a battle to take charge of that definition and assert the centrality of business and the corporation to the future. But some of this vision required restorative historical work too. For this the corporate studio system's PR, lobbying, and trade organization the Motion Pictures Producers and Distributors of America (MPPDA) marshaled the production of a collective film by the studios specifically for the fair called *Land of Liberty*. The film was a fictional essay film of sorts that collated scenes of US history from 112 different studio-produced fiction films in 1915–37, with some newsreel and stock footage, into a narrative about the progressive unfolding of "liberty" in the United States as the unique motor of the country's "story." The emphasis on liberty dovetailed with the broader strains of corporate PR in the period, which argued for the inextricable enmeshing of *freedom* and *free* trade. *Land*'s earliest newsreel footage appropriately enough was from the construction of the Panama Canal—the material realization of the militantly liberal foreign policy central to the establishment of new US-centered global circulatory networks. The final part of the film, which was simultaneously PR for corporate media and for the nation itself, argued for the national, political, and economic utility of media. Radio "made the world one neighborhood," the film proclaimed, while the motion picture, "the mirror of the world," had produced visions of distant and heroic pasts that worked to engender collective sensations of belonging.[21] *Land of Liberty* was exhibited in the film theater established within the federal building at the fair, making apparent the close ties between corporate media and the state.[22] It mingled with the kinds of state-produced media that began in 1913 and proliferated across the interwar years. When the fair was over, the MPPDA worked to circulate the film through schools by means of an affiliate it had established, with the help of Rockefeller monies, to disseminate corporate media through schools to shape "character education."[23] *Land* came to be useful, then, for the MPPDA's specific efforts to position cinema as a force for social good to obviate the need for state regulation and for the broader efforts to use media to shape a pedagogy fit for the interests of political and economic elites which were examined in the previous pages.

Land's reference to the Panama Canal can usefully remind us of the myriad connections between the 1915 Panama-Pacific International exposition, which celebrated new forms of industry and communicative and transport infrastructure, and the 1939 fair, which displayed the fusion of technology and infrastructure built into various forms of symbolic space and culture. Both events stand as dense sites for the articulation and enactment of new practices of circulation, underscoring the expansions of capital powered by corporations and banks and mandating forms of territorial and economic imperialism. But differences emerge too. The 1915 exposition spent more time on examining processes, like the mass assembly of the Ford Model T, while the 1939 fair tended to picture technology as a form of modern magic.[24] The differences register the impact of a shift from the celebration of new mass production processes to the knock-on imperative to expand consumption. By the 1939 fair, it was also apparent that screens and media culture were becoming more integral to the expansions of capital. Mobile projectors and screens proliferated at the fair, and indeed thereafter, marking the expansion of a screen-based culture that began to insinuate screens into all sorts of public and private spaces. Television played a significant role here, following the policy frameworks established for radio to become a form financed principally through corporate advertising and sponsorship.

Broadly speaking, to reiterate, media came to play central roles in the sustenance of a consumer culture that was integral to a particular phase of liberal capitalism. That phase was driven by the rise of the corporation, tied together with finance capital, that mandated intensified forms of economic imperialism (what latterly gets called globalization), new processes of mass production, distribution, and consumption. Up to this point I have focused principally on the period bookmarked by the 1915 exposition and the 1939 fair. But I have imagined this task as a genealogical one to explore (at its broadest) the place of media in the orchestration of a liberal political economy that has been, and continues to be, profoundly damaging to peoples and habitats across the world. I shall conclude, then, with a brief and partisan sketch of some of the continuities in the post–Second World War period and of the enmeshing of media and global, liberal (and latterly neoliberal) political economy, as the United States assumed the role of global hegemon and established institutions and policy frameworks to bring about a new global liberal order.

"MILITANT LIBERTY"

Expensive forms of technology did in fact help usher in the end of the Depression, but this initially owed less to the consumer technologies displayed at the fair and more to the military technologies produced by some of the same corporations—GE, Westinghouse, DuPont—that were consumed by allied and thereafter US military forces. FDR's late New Deal alliance with capital-intensive tech firms paid off. GNP doubled in 1938–45.[25] The establishment of what president Dwight Eisenhower later famously called the "military-industrial complex" gathered pace from this moment onward.[26] It did not originate there, and there is a long history of the enmeshing of military and media technologies in the second-stage industrial revolution that encompasses such things as lights, explosives, and lenses and that straightforwardly gave birth to radio. But it expanded. Vast sums of money were spent in the United States on arming the largest and most costly military ever assembled. The tech industry grew exponentially, becoming ever-more significant during the symbolic war that was the Cold War. Computing and an early version of the Internet were developed, some of it in the same Bell Labs that had developed the visual and sonic technologies that coalesced as sound cinema, radio, and television.[27] The industrialization of warfare turned it into a powerful engine of technological innovation. New regimes of accumulation were thereafter closely tied to warfare.[28] Weapons of mass destruction, and new imaging and sonic systems, were developed hand in hand, both helping to resolve the crisis of capital that was the Depression and both integral to the future of technology, endless war, and expanded media.

If the World's Fair was the benign, shiny, version of this new technologically mediated world, it found its darker twin in the display of high-tech force that effectively ended the war, when the United States—with the consent of the British—dropped nuclear bombs on Japan, killing over 129,000 civilians. This was largely a symbolic act to both *represent* the state's power and minimize Soviet influence in the postwar Pacific.[29] War, state terror, and murder as semiotic act.

But just as the military-industrial-tech complex geared up in the 1940s—accompanied by another round of propaganda institutions established in liberal-imperialist, fascist, and communist states alike—so too did the powers of liberal states to police media and communications. Warfare produces the conditions for *exceptional* state power, a process that began in the post–World War I years and has expanded exponentially thereafter, in particular as a result of the post–9/11 intensification of the security state. Connections can be drawn precisely here from World War I to World War II. The Red Scare of 1919 triggered a militant response from the Federal Bureau of Investigation (FBI), which orchestrated a campaign to target union and progressive activists. In the 1930s, in the midst of the Depression, the FBI collaborated with filmmakers, including those from Hollywood, to glorify the efficacy of national policing (see chapters 4 and 12). But on the eve of the US entrance into World War II, in 1942, the FBI began an intense surveillance of Hollywood because it had become convinced that leftist and communist supporters were using film to influence audiences.[30] The bureau wrote reports about the industry and specific films. FBI agents became film scholars. (Not very good ones, mind, for they, like many film studies scholars still do, remained wedded to a banal representational analysis, which paid very little attention to the political economy of the industry: it was, for example, absurd to imagine that a corporate industry synced together with finance capital would become a radical one.) The efforts mutated into the well-known House Un-American Activities Committee (HUAC) investigations of the film industry, which began in 1947 and culminated in ten writers and filmmakers being imprisoned for refusing to answer questions about their political beliefs or to name others who were active in the progressive cultural front of the 1930s.[31] Once again it is worth simply observing that powerful institutions both *produce* and *regulate* media in pursuit of broader objectives.

The FBI and HUAC investigations of cinema must be understood in the context of a longer history, some of it visible in these pages: a militant national policing organization that targeted radicalism as part of a state project to support the continued functioning of liberal capitalism. (White rule, too, as the FBI had historically targeted black radicalism, from Jack Johnson in the 1910s to the Black Panthers in the 1970s and beyond.)[32] Obviously there is a direct line of continuity here from the Americanization campaigns in the 1910s, which became tied to the militant policing of immigrant radicalism, in particular in the aftermath of World War I. The argument that the nation was embodied principally in its political-economic organization was also consistent with the corporate counteroffensive in the mid-1930s, as seen in the NAM campaign and in a movie like *Your Town* or AT&T's 1941 *Long Distance*. Believing that other forms of political and economic organization were possible rendered a person *un-American*. Quite clearly the FBI-HUAC nexus was an effort to police the public sphere and to continue the militantly liberal counteroffensive against progressive forces, which began in the turn-of-the-century period when the FBI was created and intensified in cyclical spurts after World War I, the Depression, War World II, and beyond.

The corporate studio system happily acquiesced in this remarkable extension of police power to shape media culture in accord with a particular theory and practice of political and economic organization. Jon Lewis has brilliantly outlined how the corporate industry and its trade and lobbying organization, renamed in 1946 as the Motion Picture Association of America, opportunistically used the HUAC investigations to discipline its unionized workforces.[33] Parts of this policing of radicalism also registered a pervasive anti-Semitism, Lewis explains, and the process helped consolidate the power of the corporate management of the studios. The blacklist enabled management to discipline and police its workforce, which was particularly necessary given the significant transformations Hollywood was undergoing. During this period, suburbanization and the spread of television began to affect box office, and this was also on the eve of the eventual 1948 antitrust regulation of the studio's monopolistic practices. Will Hays resigned in 1945 and was replaced by Eric Johnston, a man with similarly impeccable political and economic credentials to help "grease the wheels and smooth the road" for the industry, using *Variety*'s suitably automotive and infrastructural language.[34] Johnston had been president of the powerful US Chamber of Commerce four times, had worked in the FDR administration (eg, as chairman of the US Commission on Inter-American Development), and had close ties to the State Department.[35] In his first year in office he established the Motion Picture Export Association to help orchestrate global film distribution and merged this with the federal government's overseas branch of the Office of War Information, exemplifying further the close ties between corporate Hollywood and the state.[36] The studio's corporate lobbying institution now negotiated directly with foreign governments, with the support of the State and Commerce Departments. Johnston quickly came to support an industry blacklist of film workers tainted by association with views about political and economic organization that differed from the state's. Even further, he specifically counseled studios to avoid making any films, like some of the social realist films that had emerged in the 1930s, that could be regarded as "political" or somewhat critical of the state.[37] The FBI and congressional campaigns helped further the imperative to produce an apolitical media system that would not challenge the prevailing political and economic orthodoxy.

The Cold War that began in the latter parts of the 1940s intensified these imperatives and produced new policies and state agencies. Broadly speaking *security* became a keyword, and focus, across a range of policies and practices stretching over the Cold War of the second half of the twentieth century, which justified in particular a militant *containment* of socialism and communism. In early 1947, as President Harry Truman articulated that imperative in the Truman Doctrine, the National Security Act created the Defense Department, the Joint Chiefs of Staff, the National Security Council (NSC), and the Central Intelligence Agency (CIA). "Around this institutional complex," Perry Anderson remarks, "developed the permanent ideology of national security presiding over the American empire to this day."[38] The CIA became the avant garde of this global militant liberalism, complementing the FBI and its focus on domestic security. For large parts of the latter half of the twentieth century, the CIA was busy fomenting coups around the world to better secure the goals of security, of "freedom," and of the globalization of capital.[39]

Examples from, say, Iran, Indonesia, Chile, Venezuela, Afghanistan, and so on are myriad, but for my purposes the somewhat lesser-known case of Guatemala in 1954 is more immediately germane. That country was in many respects a classic example of the underdevelopment of the imperial periphery of the United States, operating largely as a primary producing nation dominated by capital, in particular from the large US corporation United Fruit, which bought up the country's productive land at cheap prices and controlled shares in its railroad, electric utility, and telegraph industries. (This is where the phrase "banana republic" originates, before it was stripped of its history as a descriptor of economic imperialism and mutated into the name of a clothing chain.) United Fruit had owned significant radio patents and was a part of the radio group established by the US state to pool patents and develop the technology in 1921. The corporation had such patents because of its need to coordinate communication among its imperial "properties": communication and imperialism were intertwined. In the 1930s, Guatemala's ruthless dictator Jorge Ubico allied with the company, for their mutual benefit, with the support of the US Embassy.[40] But after the 1944 revolution, a new president, Jacobo Arbenz Guzman, began, in 1950, to implement some modest land reforms, which would have nationalized some of United Fruit's "properties." The company vigorously opposed this.

Bernays reappears here. He was hired by United Fruit and began a savvy campaign that proposed the regime was essentially communist.[41] It was not, but

Bernays succeeded in branding those who opposed United Fruit's liberal conception of land as property and investment as communist. To cut a longer story short,[42] in 1954 the CIA proposed to President Eisenhower that they depose President Arbenz, and the agency orchestrated a coup, installing a new regime that "rescinded the nationalization, liberalized conditions for foreign investment, curtailed democracy, and severely repressed its opponents."[43] The idea that land might be socially useful and not simply property needed to be resisted with military force.[44] The example could be joined by others—for example, Iran in the same year, in pursuit of oil—and together they can be instructive in various ways: they illustrate how PR functioned to support corporate property rights; how the expropriation of global resources was essential to corporate wealth; how the United States' new global security agency directly supported the goals of corporations; and, more broadly, how the ties between corporate and state objectives and elites furthered the orchestration of a new global liberal order in the early stages of the Cold War. PR as the management of perception and media was central to the conflicts between economic systems over the latter half of the twentieth century.

Guatemala was but one part of the broader reorganization of the liberal capitalist world system that accompanied the end of war and the final ascent of the United States to the commanding heights of the global economy. CIA agents stepped in when that process threatened to break down, but its smooth operations were encoded in policy and institutions that sought to ensure the stability and expansion of the liberal capitalist system. I shall not explore those in any substantive detail here. But a cursory survey would include the Bretton Woods institutions established at the war's end, notably the International Monetary Fund and the International Bank for Reconstruction and Development (better known today as the World Bank), which sought in broad terms to reestablish global capital flows, now routed through the United States, to secure the stable market conditions important to banks and corporations and to ensure capitalist states had funds to draw upon when they had balance of payment deficits.[45] Together with the establishment of the United Nations in San Francisco in 1945, these institutions replaced the failed League of Nations, and were designed to provide "security" to the global system. The UN Educational, Scientific, and Cultural Organization enshrined the liberal "free flow" principle that the league attempted to enact, enabling transnational media firms in particular to operate globally with minimal governmental intervention.[46] Efforts to "secure" the global capitalist system were supplemented in 1947 by the Marshall Plan, according to which the United States disbursed monies through Europe and parts of Asia to rebuild capitalist economies in contradistinction to communist ones and as essential trading partners to the economically dominant United States.[47] The monies came with strings attached, principally the lowering of protectionist measures in other economies and the purchase of US-made goods. Also in 1947, twenty-three Western countries signed the General

Agreement on Tariffs and Trade (GATT) to reduce trade barriers and thus foster trade "liberalization."[48] Two years later, the North Atlantic Treaty Organization was created as a US-led military bloc to accompany its sphere of economic influence.[49] In that same year, 1949, President Truman unveiled a plan to industrialize the economies of the "Third World," as a means of opening up opportunities for US capital.[50] Britain played some role in the design and functioning of the new postwar economic institutions, but it was a subordinate one. By 1944, at Bretton Woods, the United Kingdom was obliged to abandon its imperial preference system, elaborated in the early 1930s with media integral to its orchestration, because it impeded the circulation of capital.[51]

The imperatives of *security* and what nowadays gets called *globalization* were intertwined, then, in the establishment of a new geopolitical and economic hegemony. Media and culture played varied roles in that process, encompassing the circulation of information that segued into propaganda, or PR; into public opinion "management"; and into what started to be called "psychological warfare." The Marshall Plan to rebuild capitalist economies, for example, was accompanied by films explaining the advantages brought to all through free trade. *World without Fear* (1951), to take one example, proposed that the eradication of economic borders would enable trade that would produce peace. Marshall Plan films were widely disseminated in Europe and in parts of Asia as visible and material supports for the dissemination of capital itself. Radio—including Radio Free Europe, begun in 1949, and Radio Liberty, which starting in 1951 was directed toward the Soviets—was also used for this purpose.

Elsewhere film was used more expansively to rebuild the shattered states of Germany and Japan. "U.S. authorities shipped close to two hundred Hollywood films and documentaries across the Atlantic," Jennifer Fay writes, "to tutor Germans in the gestures, speech, and affect of democratic sociality."[52] For this project, US state officials relied on ideas about "mimetic pedagogy," which had a longer genealogy and also rhymed with the "psychocultural" anthropological work that emerged in the 1940s, in particular to propose that democratic character structures could be modeled by film and imitated by spectators. The ideas were similar to those examined earlier in this book, which triggered pedagogical experiments with film—for example, the ones sponsored by the MPPDA about film and character education—but they were now constructed more broadly: media as a form of mimetic political pedagogy to transform a population. "Reeducation," Fay argues, "aimed at disposing Germany's general will toward democratic capitalism compatible with U.S. economic and political interests."[53] Similar practices also took place in Japan. The United States' occupying military collaborated closely with Hollywood to help foster the circulation of over six hundred films intended to democratize the country and, more importantly, to respond to the rise of communism in East Asia and facilitate "the integration of war-torn Japan into a new political, economic, and security system that increasingly revolved around the United States."[54] The continuation of ideas and practices about mimetic pedagogy and cinema now played a role in geopolitical practices and in the formation and orchestration of the liberal "free world." Related to this, after World War II ended, the United States also sought to redesign the media systems of the defeated countries of Italy, Germany, and Japan in the image of the commercial system in place in the United States.[55] (One sees something similar in post-2003 Iraq.)

The CIA got in on the act too. Or put another way, the central institution of the global US security state began to use culture, and film, to support its operational remit to roll back communism, export freedom, and secure property rights and the circulation of capital. The history of the broader investment of the CIA in culture, from the establishment of the Congress for Cultural Freedom in 1950 on, has been illuminated in recent work. It has shown, among other things, how the CIA sponsored modernist, nonrepresentational art—including abstract expressionism, what the president of the Museum of Modern Art, Nelson Rockefeller, called "free enterprise painting"—and European tours of black jazz musicians to highlight the freedom of the liberal capitalist system (give or take the reality of racial segregation).[56] In 1954, the CIA collaborated in the multiagency "Militant Liberty" Program, which aimed to embed "American-style democratic values in foreign cultures, especially in such new theaters of the Cold War as Central America, the Middle East, and Southeast Asia."[57] According to a secret report, the program was designed to "explain the true conditions existing under Communism in simple terms and to explain the principles upon which the Free World way of life is based," so as "to awaken free peoples to an understanding of the magnitude of the danger confronting the Free World; and to generate a motivation to combat that threat."[58] Cinema was particularly prized by the architects of the program because of "the common assumption of Cold War western propagandists that the moving image was the most appropriate medium for 'Third World' audiences."[59]

In 1955, representatives of the top echelons of the defense department held meetings in Hollywood with directors, including John Ford, Cecil B. DeMille, and other significant film industry players. The hope was that the theme of "freedom" could be inserted more clearly into Hollywood films. To monitor this, a CIA agent inside Hollywood read scripts and wrote secret reports about the film industry for the agency.[60] (The CIA did, in other words, what the FBI assumed communists were doing.) Recent research has suggested that the agent was Luigi Luraschi, a long-time executive of Paramount, the first of the corporate studios.[61] Luraschi was head of foreign and domestic censorship at the studio, working to regulate its output and enable it to circulate without political interference, while also being employed by the state to ensure that the films were politically useful to its goals to secure the free world. Taking this even further, the CIA itself became a film producer, when it spent three hundred thousand dollars to finance a feature-length animated version of George Orwell's satirical allegory of Stalinism, *Animal Farm*, which was released theatrically in 1955.[62]

Part of these efforts were propaganda, but they also mutated into the broader category of "psychological warfare," defined by the CIA as "the planned use by a nation of propaganda and activities other than combat which communicate ideas and information intended to influence the opinions, attitudes, emotions and behavior of foreign groups in ways that will support the achievements of national aims." Furthermore, "the most effective kind of propaganda" was that in which "the subject moves in the direction you desire for reasons which he believes to be his own."[63] Broadly speaking the distinction was drawn between propaganda as involving overt, visible efforts to influence and covert psychological warfare (what is sometimes called PSYOPS). The latter could also be used to intervene and directly shape events as they were happening. The CIA operated together here with the Psychological Strategy Board, established in 1951, which reported to the NSC.[64] Both worked on the basis of the ideas that subjects were malleable and mimetic and could be shaped by media. Both also were heirs to Bernays's theorizing of PR as a practice that works best when the subject is unaware of its existence. PR and PSYOPS share similar logics and cross-pollinated in intriguing ways in the Cold War period, when the state took on the enormous task of PR for global liberal capitalism.

The Psychological Strategy Board was officially dissolved in 1953 and its operations transferred to the Operations Coordinating Board and the United States Information Agency (USIA). The Operations Coordinating Board mostly took on the role of coordinating psychological warfare, working closely in this respect with the CIA and the NSC, whereas the USIA took on more of the overt and visible propaganda projects.[65] The USIA fostered the use of radio, such as Voice of America, which is broadcast in several languages across the globe; had a press and publications section; sponsored various local activities in the fields of culture and information; and operated a motion picture division that produced a number of newsreels and pedagogic films and also collaborated with Hollywood to help circulate the films globally to the frontlines of the Cold War.[66] The USIA's goal was "to persuade foreign peoples that it lies in their own interest to take actions which are also consistent with the national objectives of the United States":[67] Adam Smith writ large as geopolitical strategy. The history of this process in Southeast Asia is instructive, for the region was a crucial battleground amid Cold War fears that crumbling European empires were breeding grounds for the rise of communism. (In 1948–60, for example, the British were fighting a bitter guerilla conflict in Malaya, mostly against communist insurgents.) Projectors, power generators, and films were lent to schools, government agencies, and various other groups and organizations, so that by the mid-1950s posts in Bangkok, Jakarta, Kuala Lumpur, Manila, Saigon, and Singapore "each had dozens of projectors, film libraries with hundreds of movies and documentaries, specially assigned 'film officers,' and technicians."[68]

The USIA also used mobile film trucks to circulate its films across Indonesia, the Philippines, Thailand, and Vietnam (from 1950), extending its efforts to Cambodia and Laos shortly thereafter. This example joins others examined in this book that demonstrate the imperative to use cinema as a mobile communicative form to help shape political and economic realities, including the Bureau of Commercial Economics in the United States, from around 1913; Britain's Conservative Party, from 1925, the Empire Marketing Board, from 1928, and across the empire in the 1930s; and the USDA, from 1925. Some of these developments with the circulation of media mutated into "counterinsurgency" strategies, developed first by the British in Malaya as a campaign to "win hearts and minds" and utilized thereafter by the United States in Vietnam, Afghanistan, and Iraq. Media and state PR were often integral to these strategies. Coups, carpet-bombing, and state murder took over when those fail. Violence and media, hard and soft power, production and repression intertwine.

By the early 1950s, in the context of the orchestration of the security of the global liberal system, the question of the efficacy of media in influencing people became newly pressing. The NSC posed the question directly to the USIA in 1955, asking them to gauge who was influenced by the media they produced and circulated, who the agency's targets were, what the attitudes of these target audiences were, and how effective the propaganda and psychological operations were at influencing and changing those attitudes.[69] Taking its cue from the NSC, the USIA began to try and measure audiences and the effectiveness of their media in influencing them, turning in particular to the methods of public opinion polling that had started mostly in the 1930s—in the wake of Lippmann—and gathered pace thereafter. The efforts fed into the growth of communication studies in the 1950s. (Corporate philanthropic money contributed to that growth also.) In addition, this imperative to measure impact began to shape policy in ever-more expansive ways, particularly after the successful Soviet launch of the Sputnik satellite in 1956, after which the USIA began to counsel policy makers to consider the PR potential of developments in science and technology. "Global public opinion polling," writes James Schwoch, "was now a crucial component of national security," so that the reflection on PR and psychological impact was integrated into policy, which itself became a component of the Cold War.[70] It was in this context that USIA officials observed, in 1959, that a landing on the moon would have a better global psychological impact than other policy objectives. The classic stoner conversation about whether the United States really went to the moon or not gets at something more fundamental, that is, because the principal prize of the space policy was the global satellite–enabled broadcasting of images of technological advancement as PR for liberal capitalism.

Recent scholarship has suggested that the subsequent battles between the United States and the Soviet Union to establish primacy in the "space race" were simultaneously battles over global communications and its potential for surveillance.[71] The first US satellites in the early 1960s were developed in conjunction with Bell Labs and AT&T, as well as with RCA (just as radio and sync sound cinema had been previously), sparking another revolution in global communications and media.[72] The moment the satellite Telstar enabled global television in 1962 can be situated in a longer history, mined in part in this book, that encompasses the telegraph and telephone lines that stretched across the United States and under the Atlantic (1866 and 1926, respectively), radio, and other material infrastructures (railways, canals, roads): a complex entwining of communicative, semiotic, and material networks driven by the globalizing imperatives of capital. By the early 1950s, those imperatives were increasingly intertwined with the development and exploitation of new forms of technology that were—like satellites—frequently simultaneously media and military technologies. The computer and the Internet—the emergence of "the digital"—were part of that too, emerging initially from the Defense Department's Advanced Research Projects Agency, which in the 1970s created an early version of the Internet (ARPANET) that ran along AT&T lines, partly to transform point-to-point communication, to enable a system with various pathways to better withstand nuclear attack.[73] Key digital technologies and platforms were subsequently developed from complex alliances between the military/state and business. Google and various social media data-mining companies, for example, received early financing from the CIA's investment arm In-Q-Tel.[74] Today, data are used by the state to police "radicalism" and are sold by Google and others to data brokers and advertisers. Ever-more powerfully destructive weaponry has been and continues to be central to this complex also. Vast sums of money were spent on "defense" during the Cold War, and beyond, making technology corporations and the banks that finance them very wealthy and further solidifying the compact between the state, the technology industries, and finance capital.

But let me reiterate that this process did not begin with the Cold War, at least as commonly defined, but must be situated in a longer genealogy of the second-stage industrial revolution, of the rise of corporations with globalizing imperatives linked together with finance capital, and of the close ties between those imperatives and those of "imperialist" liberal states. Indeed, the "Cold War" in this context is properly understood as beginning in 1919, when a militantly liberal counter-offensive against labor groups and the possible reconfiguring of political economy motivated the establishment of new state powers to police its populations and *secure* the smooth functioning of liberal capitalism. The FBI's involvement in that process in 1919 mutated into the anticommunist witch hunts of the 1940s and 1950s, just as the production of media to facilitate liberal capitalism by corporations like Ford and by the state in the 1910s grew into the convergent media complex. The latter developed in the 1920s and was intensified in the context of the Depression in the 1930s and of the global Cold War beginning in the latter parts of the 1940s. The mediated projection of the freedom and happiness of liberal capitalism expanded thereafter with the use of the portable film technologies and television that arrived in the 1930s and spread widely in the 1950s in particular. Corporations continued to make films, and the sale of film projectors grew enormously.[75] Television also expanded and began to take over some of the roles hitherto carried out by film and radio to become what Anna McCarthy has called "a technology of liberal rule."[76] (Some of that continued directly from the earlier history outlined here, so for example the 1930s DuPont radio show *Cavalcade of America* transferred to NBC in 1952, and Ford had a television show following on from its CBS radio show beginning in the late 1940s.)[77] In short, then, the Cold War must be situated in a longer genealogy of the intertwined state/corporate/capital imperatives to foster the security of a globalizing liberal capitalism. For that project, media became integral in the early twentieth century in the various and complex ways I have sought to delineate.

"EXPLORE OUR BRANDS"

Carpet-bombing civilians in faraway lands to export freedom and democracy was (and is) an expensive business. By the latter years of the 1960s, the lengthy, costly war in Vietnam catalyzed with other economic crises that emerged when the "fix" established by the New Deal and by loosely Keynesian economic strategies began to unravel, resulting in enduring "stagflation" when rising inflation and unemployment combined with slowing economic growth. The period of "growth liberalism," from the point of military spending in the early 1940s and the public works expenditures of the 1950s—notably, the construction of the interstate freeway system first imagined in GM's immersive cinematic spectacle at the New York World's Fair—began to slow down from around 1964 onward.[78] Competition from the rebuilt economies of Germany and Japan, and from the cheaper labor regimes that were arising in the "developing world," also contributed to the slowdown of the postwar economic expansion. The oil crisis of the early 1970s played a role also, catalyzing with other developments to produce a sustained economic crisis that, for example, forced the United States off the gold standard—that relic of an earlier liberal era—in 1973 and forced Britain to accept an International Monetary Fund bailout in 1976. Various competing accounts of the causes of this failure of postwar liberalism have been articulated, split, broadly speaking, between those who argue the liberal compact could not resolve the fundamental contradictions of capital and neoliberals who contend, among other things, that governmental regulation of the market damaged its functioning.

The neoliberals prevailed. Adam Smith was resurrected, stripped of his concern for balancing ethics and economics, and pressed into service to proselytize for the eradication of state regulation and in turn the deracination of welfare systems. The history of this victory and the precepts of neoliberalism do not need extensive explication here.[79] Broadly speaking the logics connected to laissez-faire liberalism. The naming of this configuration as "neoliberalism," notably by Latin American observers and activists responding to the long history of US economic imperialism, made this connection clear. The militantly liberal counteroffensive that was first seen in the Depression intensified. The argument that markets could not be regulated, and ought to be left free to allocate resources appropriately was articulated forcefully in economist Friedrich Von Hayek's postwar work, which proved influential with economists, particularly those at the University of Chicago. In 1962, the leader of that group, Milton Friedman, wrote a book called *Capitalism and Freedom* that articulated the position so central to the corporate propaganda of the latter 1930s and state policy across the Cold War—that free trade and freedom are inextricable. The argument gained visibility when Friedman won a Nobel Prize in economics in 1976 and when his 1980 book *Free To Choose* was adapted for television in the United States at the dawn of the Reagan administration.

Von Hayek's ideas catalyzed also with the popular "philosophy" and literature of Ayn Rand, which became particularly well known after publication of her novels *The Fountainhead* (1943) and *Atlas Shrugged* (1956).[80] Rand's particular conception of a militantly liberal individualism was forged largely through the Hollywood films she watched in the 1920s after immigrating to the United States from Soviet Russia. In the late 1920s, she worked as a screenwriter for Cecil B. DeMille and in the costume department at RKO, before Warner Bros. brought out a film adaptation of *The Fountainhead* in 1949. How appropriate that the liberalism of a corporate form financed, by Rand's arrival, by banks – RKO was, through GE/RCA, directly tied to significant banks – would influence the articulation of a philosophy of individualism that became widely popular and influential, including among significant economic and policy elites. (Economist Alan Greenspan, for example, was part of a close-knit group surrounding Rand, ironically called "the collective." In his role as chairman of the Federal Reserve from 1987 to 2006, he presided over the disastrous deregulation of the economy, including the dissolution of the New Deal division of commercial and investment banks, which had a direct impact on the global financial crisis of 2008.)[81] To cut a longer story short, the articulation of a newly militant liberalism began in scattered ways in the late 1930s and was expanded through significant and visible economic and cultural work from the postwar years through the 1970s, becoming the operating logic of state policy and the capitalist world system.

By the 1970s, the International Monetary Fund and the World Bank had become newly militant institutions, largely controlled by the United States, and were using their leverage with "Third World" borrowers, who frequently had been devastated by the legacies of imperialism, to force acceptance of structural adjustment programs and loans. These programs and loans forced the borrowing countries to give priority to external debt; to adopt austerity programs; and to cultivate agricultural crops for export to pay debts, rather than to feed their own populations. They also pushed for privatization, which enabled transnational banks and corporations to own substantial resources.[82] Economic and liberal imperialism was exported across the global system, enabling newly productive sites of investment for the pools of industrial and finance capital formed in the United States and the Global North, at the same time further integrating "peripheral" states into a global market system.

GATT had mutated into the World Trade Organization (WTO) in 1995 and had further mandated the lowering of protectionist measures to enable the "free flow" of materials and capital. (But not people: in 2014, to give just one example, thirty-five hundred people died in the Mediterranean Sea while trying to reach Europe.)[83] The *free* movement of media was integral to this global liberal order, and GATT played, and the WTO now plays, a central role in enabling corporate media to circulate liberally.[84] Close ties between state and corporate objectives in this regard are readily visible. *Wikileaks,* for example, recently released caches of secretive state materials that show in precise detail how diplomats and other state officials work to help smooth the movement of US corporate media across the world.[85] The efforts resemble those initiated by the State and Commerce Departments in the 1920s. Indeed, the connections between corporate media institutions and state actions also continue in this regard. The institutional descendant of the old Hays Office, the Motion Picture Association of America, now plays a central role in policing Intellectual Property (IP) and "piracy" across the world, while also lobbying for the reduction of protectionist tariffs. It does so in partnership with state officials. The expansive protection of property rights—like that seen in Guatemala and elsewhere—mutated in this respect to the protection of IP, particularly noticeable when GATT transformed into the WTO and when the 1994 North American Free Trade Agreement succeeded in establishing detailed protections for intellectual property rights.[86] Policing IP is now a central objective of state policy and its global articulation through institutions like the WTO, and it is enfolded into transnational trade agreements, including the recently signed Trans-Pacific Partnership, that simultaneously support the objectives of corporate media institutions and the state.

The increasing centrality of media as "property" in this expanded sense in these relatively recent global trade agreements also responds to and exemplifies the growing centrality of media and culture to the so-called post-industrial, or service, economy. Capital itself has mutated in complex ways. Between 1980 and 1998, for example, "annual world exchange of electronic culture" grew from $95 to $388 billion, and it is estimated that copyright and patents are now worth $360 billion a year in the United States, more than the aerospace, automobile, and agricultural industries.[87] Policy decisions in that same period had enormous impact on the growth of very large media, communications, and tech corporations, which now wield significant influence and control vast swathes of "convergent" media and communications in the digital era. The neoliberalization of media began first in the Reagan administration, when the antitrust regulation of vertical integration was overturned, and was further enshrined in the 1996 Telecommunications Act signed by Bill Clinton.[88] Clinton's intervention accelerated the relaxed rules regarding vertical integration in the Reagan years and further enabled cross media ownership, fostering a wave of mergers that led to the formation of a small number of very large corporations with significant holdings in film, television, cable, newspapers, magazines, the Internet, and more.

Zukor, Fox, and other media moguls from the first era of corporate mass media would have been envious indeed. News Corporation, for example, has operations in the United States, South America, Europe, Asia, and Australia and owns the former Fox film studios, part of a global portfolio of important newspapers (eg, the *Wall Street Journal* in the United States, the *Times* in the United Kingdom), TV networks and satellite stations (eg, Fox, Sky), and other ancillary and "synergized" endeavors (eg, Fox Music and Twentieth Century Fox Licensing and Merchandising, HarperCollins, Dow Jones business news).[89] Controlling IP and expanding profits across sectors is crucial to these convergent endeavors. GE, to take another example of a corporation that has flitted in and out of this history, bought NBC in 1986 (sixty years after first establishing it in 1926) and Universal Studios in 2004, thus tying together one of the largest tech corporations in the world with an expansive media portfolio.[90] (The "Explore Our Brands" section of their website takes a lot of clicking; in 2008, the company had revenues in excess of $183 billion.)[91] The corporation established by Edison and the House of Morgan, which employed Ronald Reagan as part of its television PR in the 1950s, now creates movies, television, and online media, as well as advanced military technology, including drones.[92]

Democracy is badly damaged by this neoliberal concentration of media. Lippmann's dream, in the early 1920s, that a technocratic elite would organize society has been realized, though now principally by the market economy, which neoliberals believe to be the most efficient allocator of resources. The unrelenting expansion of the market system has mostly left behind the kinds of didactic media I began this book with. For media is now more fully, militantly, liberal, and these values are carried through a relentlessly banal media culture suffused by individualist and consumerist logics that are incapable of picturing the kinds of collective actions necessary to realize humane transformation.

The drone is a fitting endpoint for this history. Marking the concrete and material enmeshing of state/military/corporate use of media technologies—mobile cameras synced with remote real-time visual communications and loaded with missiles—they further the goals of a still-expanding liberal capitalism that began most clearly across the period when GE was created by mergers enabled by finance capital (1892), and in turn created RCA (1919), NBC (1926), and RKO (1928). Nowadays that expansive liberalism uses drone cameras, computer networks, and remote missiles to export freedom by killing people in other states in direct contravention of the liberal rule of law. Drones are also increasingly used by tax-dodging, worker-exploiting companies like Amazon to speed up the circulation of consumer objects. The drone in this respect plays the role I argue media has long undertaken: to expand global liberalism and a consumer economy. Quite clearly this effort has grown more intense and pervasive in our current era of permanent war, through an expanded digital media reliant on the kinds of expensive, quickly obsolescent technology—developed in corporate and university research labs; built by exploited workers with minerals dug up in mostly in "post"-imperial states; and largely financed through advertising and, in its social variant, the selling of data to advertisers, allowing them to more precisely *target* consumers.

DISCIPLINE AND PUBLISH

The brutal escalating violence of this liberal global system is readily visible in multiple ways, and since 2008, it has been clearly accelerating with the "austerity" enforced by liberal states to bail out finance capital. Take, for example, the devastating facts about global poverty and climate change: 1 in 2 children in the world lives in poverty, causing the deaths of 22,000 children each day and 3.1 million each year; around 2.1 billion people must try to survive on less than $3.10 per day; and the catastrophic effects of industrialization and consumer culture on climate, environment, and food supplies are escalating rapidly.[93] Quite obviously, then, a clear understanding of media's role in the orchestration of this profoundly unequal, murderous, and damaging global system is a pressing, urgent need.

Unfortunately, the disciplines that emerged to examine film, and then radio, television, and communications, were shaped by particular exigencies that have limited their potential to be useful to progressive transformation. The corporate lobbying and trade group the MPPDA, for example, sponsored disciplinary research that deemphasized questions of ownership and political economy (see chapter 10). From that point on, the study of film was fostered in the humanities largely in dialogue with institutions formed to promote the study of what is still inexplicably called "English" literature.[94] Partly this produced a liberal study and appreciation that mutated into forms of banal aesthetic and representational analysis. Communication and media studies, in contrast, was fostered within the social sciences, often with money from philanthropic foundations—the Ford Foundation was the most significant—to foster the study of the limited effects and utility of media for the liberal political and economic system. Cold War exigencies were significant here, and money from the state sluiced through higher education institutions to foster research and teaching to sustain liberal capitalist "democracy." The balkanization of the study of media has blunted its collective potential. Nowadays the disciplines do not talk to each other but only to themselves; they are often rooted in specialized languages that do not communicate widely; and the work that has flourished is disparate and frequently divorced from the urgent necessity to transform a media system integral to the way power functions. Even the muted examination of media is marginal in the academy: the discipline of history, for example, mostly mistakenly ignores the history of the media systems that frame our understanding of the world.

What is to be done? I have drawn some simple conclusions for myself from the history articulated in this book, and the evident reality of our deeply unequal world, and I shall list some of them here. But with the significant caveat articulated at the beginning of this book in the acknowledgments that the positions I take are ones taught to me by other scholars; by students; by media-makers; and by the people I live, talk, and sofa with. They are *but* my views; but they are not *just* mine: 1) scholarship should focus on questions of power and the intersecting axes of oppression as a matter of urgency and reflect carefully on their utility for actual progressive transformation (for example, film studies folk, perhaps we do not need too many more essays with titles like "this thing" *in* "this film"?); 2) these imperatives to study power and foster progressive transformation ought to be central to the disciplines that explore media, and "film" ought to be enfolded within a more expansive but militant discipline; 3) scholarship should be accompanied by a pedagogy that is radical in form and content; 4) scholarship and pedagogy alone are not enough, and this radical praxis should extend as far as it can. Quite clearly this media praxis needs to be a collective project across outdated disciplinary divisions, as well as those that separate the academy from the world. One must think also carefully about whether the institutions that have fostered the study of media mostly for economic gain—universities—can enable the kind of work and practices that is urgently needed. No doubt many more conclusions can be drawn and more questions asked. But here I end, looping back to where I began, just as the narratives of so many films of the corporate studio era did in the first iteration of the collision of media with globalizing liberal capital in the period under my immediate purview in the preceding pages.

CHAPTER 1

1. Here I principally follow economic historian Martin Sklar, who argues that "corporate liberalism" emerged as a prevalent praxis in the United States around the turn of the century, among government, judicial, and industrial and financial organizations, "to transact the corporate reconstruction of the political-economic order on the basis of the mutual adaptation of corporate capitalism and the American liberal tradition." Sklar, *Corporate Reconstruction*, 34.

2. The history of the 1927 Radio Act and the subsequent 1934 Communications Act, which restated its principal logic, is explicated best by McChesney, *Telecommunications*.

3. Kuhn, Loeb, an investment bank based in Chicago that had earlier played significant roles in financing railways, commissioned a report on the studio that came to be called Paramount. H. D. H. Connick, "Survey of the Motion Picture Industry with Particular Reference to the Famous Players—Lasky Corporation," docketed case files, 1915–43, 835, commission exhibits 446, box 428, Federal Trade Commission, auxiliary case files 1915–1936, record group 122, National Archives and Records Administration II at College Park, MD (NARA). Hereafter NARA materials from state bureaus and departments will be referenced by their record group number (RG), along with a corresponding box number, date, and page number if available.

4. Chandler, *Visible Hand*, 79–187.

5. Marx, *Capital*, 1:257. Money (M) transforming into commodity capital (C) to generate more money (M′) is, Marx writes, "the general formula for capital, in the form in which it appears directly in the sphere of circulation."

6. GE was formed from a merger of Edison General Electric with the Thomson-Houston Company in 1892. The board of directors of GE at its outset was "dominated by Morgan banking interests." Reich, *Making of American Industrial Research*, 46–48.

7. Hunter, Dulin and Co., *Golden Harvest*.

8. I rely here on the distinctions between "core" and "periphery" proposed principally by Immanuel Wallerstein. Wallerstein argues the capitalist world system that emerged in the fifteenth century in Europe, and expanded thereafter, ultimately divided the world into core, semiperipheral, and peripheral zones, creating an exploitative international division of labor. The core economic zones developed manufacturing and industry, banking and financial management, capital accumulation and bourgeois class formation, in addition to strong state organization. The periphery contained highly exploitative and labor-intensive economies of mining, planting, peasant farming, and landlord rentierism. Wallerstein, *Capitalist World Economy;* Wallerstein, *Politics*.

9. I use language here drawn from Robert McChesney's important *Rich Media, Poor Democracy* and from traditions of radical work on political economy and media, including notably Herman and Chomsky, *Manufacturing Consent*.

10. In this book, I mostly use "state" rather than "government" to signal the persistence of state structures—such as the civil service, the military, the police, and the legal system—that have greater continuity than governments placed in temporary control of the state. In this I follow a relatively common usage of state as genus to government as species, as well as the traditions of political philosophy (particularly Marxist) that theorize state as an apparatus, as a national and international legal system, and as both an autonomous and constrained structure. I tend in what follows to focus on the practices of government, rather than on the "nature" of the state, with a loose working model that sees the state as "relatively autonomous" but also substantively constrained by the imperatives to generate and protect capital and elite interests. I am grateful to Priya Jaikumar for guidance here.

11. Freyer, "Business Law," in Engerman and Gallman, *Cambridge Economic History*, 462–70.

12. "Trade Follows the Motion Picture," *Commerce Reports*, January 22, 1923, 191. Edward Lowry, the European representative from the Hollywood trade and public relations organization, the Motion Pictures Producers and Distributors of America (MPPDA) articulated this argument publicly in his "Trade Follows the Film," *Saturday Evening Post*, November 7, 1925, 12.

13. Vasey, *World According to Hollywood*, 43; Grazia, *Irresistible Empire*, 299; Miller et al., *Global Hollywood*, 60–67.

14. *Departments of State, Justice, Commerce, and Labor Appropriations Bill, 1926: Hearings before the Subcommittee of the Committee on Appropriations*, U.S. Senate, 68th Cong., 2nd sess. on H.R. 11753 (Washington, 1926), 44. (Statement of Herbert Hoover, commerce secretary of the United States). The bureau supplied information about foreign censorship regulations, tariffs, copyright, and taxation laws; published lists of producers, distributors, and exhibitors in foreign markets; and kept track of theater capacity and construction. North, "Our Foreign Trade," 100–108.

15. Hays, "Supervision from Within," in Kennedy, *Story of the Films*, 37–38.

16. Hays, *Memoirs of Will H. Hays*, 333–34.

17. Luce, "American Century," 20–23.

18. H. M. Government, *Report of the Imperial Conference, 1926*, Cmd. 2768 (London: HMSO, 1926). The position of the Federation of British Industries (hereafter in notes FBI)

is articulated in "Minutes of a Conference on the Subject of British Film Production, Held at the Offices of the Federation of British Industries, on Wednesday, May 6, 1925," MSS200/F/1/1/159, 2, Modern Records Centre, University of Warwick; "FBI Report of Its Overseas Committee," *Kinematograph Weekly,* April 22, 1926, 42; and statements by its senior officials (e.g., those in the *Times,* January 21, 1927, 10).

19. Lister in Her Majesty's Stationery Office, 53.

20. Quoted in Dickinson and Street, *Cinema and State,* 19.

21. Tallents, *Projection of England.*

22. Cinematograph Films Bill, HC Deb, March 16, 1927, vol. 203, cc2039–112.

23. Williamson, *National Crisis,* 43–54; Eichengreen, "British Economy," in Floud and Johnson, *Cambridge Economic History,* 71–100.

24. Cinematograph Films Bill, HC Deb, March 16, 1927, vol. 203, cc2039–112.

25. Grieveson, *Policing Cinema.*

26. Quoted in Higson and Maltby, introduction, in Higson and Maltby, *"Film Europe,"* 9.

27. I use *biopolitical,* following the philosopher and historian Michel Foucault, to mean the practice of the modern liberal state in regulating bodies and populations to ensure its continuity. Foucault, "Security, Territory, and Population," 67; Foucault, "Subject and Power."

28. Foucault, "Liberalism," 27–50. See in particular the definitions on pp. 20–21.

29. Quoted in Foucault, "Liberalism," 28.

30. Foucault, "Governmentality," 87–104. The shift from mercantilism to liberal economic ordering is outlined in Arrighi, *Long Twentieth Century,* 47–58; Frieden, *Global Capitalism,* 1–6.

31. A. Smith, *Wealth of Nations,* 399.

32. Marx, *Capital,* in particular 1:736–38. See, for example, Poovey, *History,* 214–18.

33. Macpherson, *Political Theory.*

34. Macpherson, *Life and Times,* 23–76.

35. Macpherson, "Human Rights," 76–85.

36. Macpherson, *Life and Times,* 23–44.

37. Hobsbawm, *Age of Revolution,* 46, 184–89; E. Thompson, *Making of the English.*

38. McChesney, *Telecommunications,* 15–26.

39. On these connections see, for example, Semmel, *Liberal Ideal;* Metha, *Liberalism and Empire;* and N. Smith, *Endgame,* 28–52.

40. Harvey, *New Imperialism,* 26.

41. Bryan, *Gold Standard,* 17–32.

42. Polanyi, *Great Transformation,* 139. New state bureaucracies emerged to implement this, making clear that this was not a self-regulating system but one constructed for the benefits of capital (33–219).

43. Eichengreen and Marc Flandreau, introduction to Eichengreen and Flandreau, *Gold Standard,* 6–7.

44. Angevine, *Railroad and the State,* 165–93; Fishlow, "Internal Transportation," in Engerman and Gallman, *Cambridge Economic History,* in particular 572–94.

45. White, *Railroaded,* in particular 59–62.

46. Zinn, *People's History*, 249.

47. Livingston, *Pragmatism*, 36. See also Lamoreaux, "Entrepreneurship," in Engerman and Gallman, *Cambridge Economic History*, 418–22.

48. Chandler, *Visible Hand*, 79–187.

49. Wilkins, "Multinational Enterprise," in Chandler and Mazlish, *Leviathans*, 45–80.

50. Lamoreaux, "Partnerships," in Lipartito and Sicilia, *Constructing Corporate America*, 32–35.

51. Freyer, "Business Law," in Engerman and Gallman, *Cambridge Economic History*, 462–70. The *Santa Clara County v. Southern Pacific Railroad* (1886) decision held that corporations possessed a constitutional status that for jurisdictional and litigation purposes was like a real person.

52. Banner, *American Property*, 71.

53. Sklar, *Corporate Reconstruction*, 51.

54. Bureau of Mines, Department of Interior, "Descriptive List of Motion Picture Films and Plan of Distribution," November 1924, NARA, RG70, Bureau of Mines, general classified files, box 75, 1925.

55. Gramsci, "Fordism and Americanism," in *Gramsci Reader*.

56. League of Nations, International Educational Cinematographic Institute, *Report to the Council on the Third Session of the Governing Body of the Institute*, January 2, 1931, C.694 M.291, League of Nations Archives, Geneva.

57. I borrow the phrase "manufacturing consent" from three interlinked sources: Lippman, *Public Opinion*, 158; Bernays, "Engineering of Consent," 113–20; Herman and Chomsky, *Manufacturing Consent*.

58. Halsey, Stuart and Co., *Motion Picture Industry*, 4.

CHAPTER 2

1. 38 Stat., 63rd Cong., 76, June 23, 1913, 76, 77. The statute appointed a Government Exhibit Board, which made funds available for the production and exhibition of films, mostly at the government pavilion at the exposition in 1915. $500,000 were initially set aside.

2. B. T. Galloway to W. O. Thompson, March 9, 1914, 2, RG16, Records of the Office of the Secretary of Agriculture, General Correspondence of the Office of the Secretary, 1906–1970, box no. 151, 1914, NARA.

3. Arthur Edwin Krows makes the same claim in "Motion Pictures," part 33, 14.

4. *Report to the Secretary of Agriculture on the Work of the Committee on Motion Picture Activities*, November 30, 1914, RG16, box 151, 1914, NARA; Folsom, "Use," 592; C. W. Puglsey to C. B. Smith, March 14, 1923, RG16, box 998, NARA; N. Greene, *1000 and One*, 127; US Department of Agriculture, *Motion Pictures*.

5. I draw this brief account of the agricultural policies of the United States from various sources, including Carpenter, *Forging*, 179–254, 290–325; Daniel, *Breaking the Land*, 3–22, 237–89; Eisner, *From Warfare State*, 181–221; and Sanders, *Roots of Reform*, in particular 217–66.

6. Act to establish a Department of Agriculture , Pub. L. No. 387, 12 Stat. (1862), cited in Rasmussen, *Readings*, 105–6. Also in 1862, the Morrill Land Grant Act mandated the donation of public land "owned" by the federal government to the states. This land could be sold

for settlement and the receipts used to endow, support, and maintain colleges of "agriculture and the mechanic arts" (Rasmussen, *Readings,* 109–10; Sanders, *Roots of Reform,* 315.) On the expanded legislative powers of the US government from the Civil War moment onward, see Bensel, *Yankee Leviathan.*

7. Knobloch, *Culture of Wilderness,* in particular 3–7. This is one aspect of what political scientist James C. Scott calls the "high modernist ideology" of the liberal capitalist state. J. Scott, *Seeing Like a State,* 4.

8. On the broad delineation of this development, see Carpenter, *Forging,* 14–36; on the USDA, see 179–254, and 290–325.

9. Sanders, *Roots of Reform,* 314–39; R. Scott, *Reluctant Farmer.*

10. Ingersent and Rayner, *Agricultural Policy,* 1–8; Paarlberg and Paarlberg, "Agricultural Policy," 136–61.

11. Pollock, *Humane Economy,* 1–11; 57–84.

12. Federico, *Feeding the World,* 187–201.

13. Zunz, *Why the American Century?,* 47–114.

14. Smith-Lever Act, Pub. L. No. 372, 38 Stat (1914).

15. Otter, "Making Liberal Objects," 570–90.

16. The testing and development of this mobile technology can be traced in *Report to the Secretary of Agriculture on the Work of the Committee on Motion Picture Activities,* November 30, 1914, RG16, box 151, 6; George Wharton, chairman of the Committee on Motion Picture Activities, Memorandum to Chiefs of Bureaus, Independent Offices, and to the Committee on Motion Picture Activities, March 3, 1917, RG16, box 415, 1; John L. Cobbs Jr., "Memorandum for the Secretary," April 29, 1921, RG16, box 837, 4, all NARA.

17. *When Wages Stop or, Safety First in the Petroleum Industry* (1923), for example, was made in cooperation with a group of California oil companies that included Standard Oil.

18. David K. Niles, *Reel and Slide,* December 1918, 18. Niles is listed as "Chief, Motion Picture Section," Bureau of Naturalization, US Department of Labor.

19. Letter, Office of Indian Affairs, Department of the Interior, to Dr. Tigert, February 16, 1923, RG12, Records of the Office of Education, Records of the Office of the Commissioner, Historical Files, 1870–1950, box 17, 1, NARA. Between 1908 and 1920, the Bureau of Indian Affairs collaborated with the Rodman Wanamaker Expeditions, including on the 1913 "Expedition of Citizenship," which produced films showing Native Americans being "invited" to declare allegiance to the US flag. *The Rodman Wanamaker Expedition of Citizenship to the North American Indian: Carrying the Flag and a Message of Hope to a Vanishing Race* (Bureau of Indian Affairs/Rodman Wanamaker, 1913). The bureau distributed a film made by the religious Harmon Foundation called *Government Service and Its Problems* (Harmon Foundation, c. 1933) that aimed "to show the effort of the federal government in handling our Indian problem." "Government Service and Its Problems," the Religious Motion Picture Foundation, [1933?], RG200HF, Records of the Harmon Foundation Gift Collection, Motion Picture Files, box 4, 1, NARA. The Harmon films were used in reservation schools as part of the governmental effort to educate Native Americans in what the commissioner of the Office of Indian Affairs called "responsibility" and "self government." Collier, *Indians of the Americas,* 264.

20. *Fit to Win* (US Public Health Service, 1919), for example, taught men about the dangers of venereal disease, while *The Science of Life* series, produced by the US Public Health

Service and Bray Studios, consisted of twelve short films that emphasized how proper diet and exercise enabled healthy development and produced "well-born" children. Ostherr, *Cinematic Prophylaxis*, 4–11.

21. *Highways of Friendship* (Highway Education Board, 1924), *Roads for All America* (Highway Education Board, 1924), and *Wheels of Progress* (US Bureau of Public Roads, 1926) were all made as part of a project led by the United States to construct a Pan-American highway. I discuss this further in chapter 7.

22. Bureau of Education, Department of the Interior, "The Federal Executive Departments as Sources of Information for Libraries," *Bulletin*, no. 74 (Washington, DC: Government Printing Office, 1919), 135, 136; "Visual Instruction: Division of Educational Extension," [1919], RG12, Records of the Bureau of Education, Records of the Office of the Commissioner, Historical Files, 1870–1950, box 42, 1–5, NARA; US Department of the Interior, *Visual Education*.

23. Freeman, *Visual Instruction*; McClusky, *Visual Instruction*; Hoban and Zisman, *Visualizing the Curriculum*.

24. Zunz, *Why the American Century?*, xi.

25. *Hearings before the Subcommittee of the Committee on Appropriations, U.S. Senate, 1926*, 44 (statement of Herbert Hoover, commerce secretary of the United States).

26. Hounshell, *From the American System*, 217–62.

27. Braverman, *Labor and Monopoly Capital*.

28. Seiler, *Republic of Drivers*.

29. Luger, *Corporate Power*.

30. Meyer, *Five Dollar Day*, in particular 123–48.

31. Watts, *People's Tycoon*, 178–98.

32. David Lewis suggests the motion picture unit at Ford had a massive annual budget of $600,000. D. Lewis, *Public Image*, 115. This is considerably higher than, for example, the USDA's budget in 1923, which was $13,000. I have not been able to verify Lewis's figure, but for some information on budgets, see "Information Regarding Materials Used by the Photographic Department," September 30, 1919, accession 75, box 10, misc. correspondence, 1919–1927, Benson Ford Research Center, Henry Ford Museum and Greenfield Village (hereafter RCHFM). Ford's films were widely seen. The company distributed them through its own dealers and for a time gave them away free to cinemas. In 1920, the company claimed a minimum of four thousand theaters and coverage of one seventh of the weekly motion picture audience in the United States; by 1924, *Ford News* asserted that the films had been seen by sixty million people worldwide. "Factory Facts from Ford," accession 951, box 11, RCHFM; *Ford News*, October 1, 1924, 1.

33. *Ford News*, February 1, 1922, 6.

34. For example, *How Henry Ford Makes 1000 Cars a Day* (1914); *Ford Plant, Tractors, and Workers* (1917); *Where and How Fords Are Made* (1919); *Industrial Working Conditions* (1921).

35. Ford's Highland Park Factory was equipped to show moving pictures, and the famous River Rouge factory also included a movie-screening space, which seated two hundred. *Ford News*, June 15, 1923, 7.

36. *Ford News*, January 1, 1922, 1; *Reel and Slide*, March 1918, 31; *Ford News*, February 1, 1922, 3; *Ford News*, February 15, 1922, 6.

37. *Moving Picture Age* (January 1, 1920), 7.

38. Bodnar, *Remaking America,* 171–75.

39. In 1914, for example, 71 percent of the workforce at Ford's main auto assembly factory was foreign born. Of these workers, 53 percent came from Russia, Romania, Italy, and Austria-Hungary. Meyer, "Adapting the Immigrant," 74.

40. Between October 1912 and October 1914, Ford hired fifty-four thousand workers to maintain an average workforce of thirteen thousand—an annual turnover rate of 416%. Montgomery, *Fall,* 233–38.

41. "The Story of the Bureau of Commercial Economics" (Washington DC: Bureau of Commercial Economics, 1920), no pagination. Francis Holley and Anna Maris Boggs established the bureau in 1913. Its early history can be traced in US Senate, Speech by the Hon. Robert Owen, February 26, 1923, 67th Cong., Sess. 4, reprinted and distributed by the Bureau of Commercial Economics (Washington DC: Bureau of Commercial Economics, 1923), 3; Krows, "Motion Pictures," part 42, 387, 404; S. Savage, "Eye Beholds," 29–30; S. Savage, "Unravelling," 62–77.

42. Bureau of Commercial Economics, n.d., included in correspondence between the bureau and the USDA, RG16, box 214, 1915, NARA.

43. *New York Times,* September 5, 1919, 10, reported that the bureau would show its films about "social, economic, and industrial problems . . . free from trucks which will be sent all over the State."

44. The USDA came to a similar conclusion about the corporate basis of the bureau's work. George Wharton, the chair of the USDA's Committee on Motion Picture Activities, responded to the bureau's request for USDA films by observing that the bureau's work was "largely devoted to the exposition of the work of corporations," and the films purchased and exhibited by the bureau "suggest not only their utilization along high-class advertising lines but also their utilization to present matters relating to the public aspects of certain lines of business, from the standpoint of the corporations involved." George Wharton, "Memorandum for the Secretary," February 17, 1915, RG16, box 214, 1915, 1, NARA. Publicity material lists an impressive array of sponsoring organizations, including transport and infrastructure companies, electrical and communication companies, banks, chemical and agricultural machinery organizations, and mineral and oil extraction companies. Bureau of Commercial Economics, Inc., n.d., included in correspondence between the bureau and the USDA, RG16, box 214, 1915; Francis Holley, letter to Carl Vrooman, assistant secretary, Department of Agriculture, February 8, 1915, RG16, box 214, 1915, 2–3, both NARA; Holley, "Industrial Information."

45. Bureau of Commercial Economics, "Publicity with Motion Pictures."

46. *Weekly Film Review,* May 30, 1915, 1.

47. Francis Holley, "Industrial Education and the Uses of the Cinematograph in Public Instruction," address delivered to the Second Pan American Scientific Congress, Washington, DC, January 4, 1916, 15, RG16, box 299, 1916, 14–15, NARA.

48. Bureau of Commercial Economics, "Story of the Bureau," 1920, no pagination.

49. Bureau of Commercial Economics, "Publicity with Motion Pictures," no pagination.

50. Francis Holley, letter, 1924, dossier no. 37604, classement 13.c, document no. 38613, League of Nations Archives, Geneva.

51. Rosenberg, *Spreading the American Dream.*

52. *Washington Post,* April 14, 1916, 4; *Washington Post,* May 31, 1916, 12.

53. K. Savage, "Self Made Monument," 5–32.

54. Congressional activity orchestrating the exposition was extensive. See, for example, 38 Stat., 63rd Cong., 76, Sess. 1, ch. 3, 1913; Sess. 1, chs. 3, 4, 1913; Sess. 2, ch. 223, 1914.

55. W. L. Stern, "Motion Pictures at the Exposition," *Moving Picture World,* March 13, 1915, 1595; "Pictures at World's Fair," *Billboard,* April 10, 1915, 47; "Exposition Pays Tribute to Motion Picture Art," *New York Dramatic Mirror,* 73, July 7, 1915, 22–23.

56. On Ford and the exposition, see Lewis, *Public Image,* 118; *Vintage Ford,* September–October 1994, cited in *Model T Forum,* www.mtfca.com/discus/messages/80257/90734.html?1255871963.

57. Watts, *People's Tycoon,* 147, D. Lewis, "Henry Ford," 17; Wik, *Henry Ford,* 37.

58. Waller, "Nontheatrical Theaters."

59. The economic consequences of the Panama Canal are outlined in Maurer, *What Roosevelt Took.* Two expositions celebrated the completion of the canal: the Panama-Pacific International Exposition held in San Francisco between February and December 1915, and the Panama-California Exposition held in San Diego between March 1915 and January 1917. Rydell, *All the World's a Fair,* 208–33.

60. Frederic Haskin, *Panama Canal* (New York: Doubleday, Page, 1914), quoted in Adas, *Dominance by Design,* 198.

61. Colombia had refused to accept an American offer of ten million dollars for the right to build a canal across the Isthmus of Panama, which was then Colombia's northern-most province. In November 1903, with the US warship *Nashville* in place to keep Colombian troops from interfering, rebels in Panama declared their independence. Soon after, they leased the canal zone to the United States. Work on the canal began the following year. The actions of the United States were consistent with a broader Latin American foreign policy that sought to position the United States as hemispheric policeman—as it also had in Cuba, the Dominican Republic, Haiti, and Nicaragua—to sustain geopolitical "security" and establish economic patterns that would support US industry and finance capital. An aggressive foreign policy supported economic imperialism. Major, *Prize Possession,* 34–63.

62. In 1902, Congress had authorized President Theodore Roosevelt to pay forty million dollars to France to buy its uncompleted assets in the Isthmus of Panama for the construction of the canal. J. P. Morgan Sr. carried out the financing for what was then probably the largest real estate transaction in history. Chernow, *House of Morgan,* 111.

63. "Gold" workers were a privileged minority of white Americans, while "silver" workers were a subjugated majority of mostly West Indian laborers. The latter died at four times the rate of the former. J. Greene, *Canal Builders,* 123–58.

64. M. Mann, "Autonomous Power," 109–36; Harvey, *New Imperialism,* 98. Mann refers to infrastructural power as the positive capacity of the state to "penetrate civil society" and implement policies throughout a given territory.

65. Salvatore, "Imperial Mechanics," 663–91.

66. Eckes and Zeiler, *Globalization,* 26.

67. For example, the Morgan financial house had investments in Mexico, in the Caribbean, and in the sugar plantations in Cuba. Dawley, "Abortive Rule," in Fraser and Gerstle, *Ruling America,* 159–60.

68. K. Thompson, *Exporting Entertainment,* 41.

69. Obermayer and Obermaier, *Panama Papers*.

70. Ed Vulliamy, "How a US President and JP Morgan Created the State of Panama—and Turned It into a Tax Haven," *Observer*, April 10, 2016, 6–7.

71. "US Corporations Have $1.4tn Hidden in Tax Havens, Claims Oxfam Report," *Guardian*, April 14, 2016. Estimates are that GE has $119 billion in assets held offshore, while Apple, so central to the digital ecosystem, has $181 billion.

CHAPTER 3

1. Gallagher and Robinson, "Imperialism of Free Trade."

2. Arrighi, *Long Twentieth Century*, 47–57, 159–324. The broad sweep of these developments is explicated in Eric Hobsbawm's multivolume history: *Age of Revolution, 1789–1848; Age of Capital, 1848–1875; Age of Empire, 1875–1914; Age of Extremes, 1914–1991*.

3. Hobsbawm, *Age of Empire*, 34–55.

4. I have drawn, in doing so, principally on the work of Immanuel Wallerstein. See, for example, Wallerstein, *World-Systems*.

5. Lippmann, *Public Opinion*, 158.

6. A. Smith, *Wealth of Nations*, 399.

7. Ibid., 277.

8. Ibid., 300.

9. Adam Smith (*Wealth of Nations*, 277) defines "political economy" as a "branch of the science of a statesmen or legislator." Foucault discerns three principal meanings for the term *political economy* from its inception in the eighteenth century: 1) an analysis of the production and circulation of wealth; 2) a reference to methods of government that can procure the state's prosperity; and 3) a "general reflection on the organization, distribution, and limitation of powers in a society." Foucault, *Birth of Biopolitics*, 13. I am principally interested in the two latter uses of the term, both to understand the way liberal states orchestrate economy and how power functions and reproduces itself.

10. Adam Smith's famous example of the advantages of greater specialization and division of labor focused on pin-making. The principles of this led to a growing international division of labor. London banker David Ricardo pursued this latter question by exploring the comparative cost of goods within and across countries. See the account in Irwin, *Against the Tide*, 75–98. Economists call this the law of comparative advantage, and its logic militated toward free trade and a global market.

11. Wilhelm von Humboldt, *The Limits of State Action*, ed. J. W. Burrow, 1792, cited in Manent, *Intellectual History*, 65–66.

12. Hartz, *Liberal Tradition;* Appleby, *Capitalism;* Appleby, *Liberalism and Republicanism*. Christopher Tomlins and William Novak both show how conceptions of police and ideas of the common good shaped American legal traditions and legislative practices in the nineteenth century, producing a complex mix of republican and liberal traditions. Tomlins, *Law, Labor, and Ideology;* Novak, *People's Welfare*.

13. A. Smith, *Theory of Moral Sentiments*.

14. The "new liberalism" of J. S. Mill in this sense is visible in *On Liberty*, 1858, and *Representative Government*, 1861 (Mill, *Three Essays*). Mill is discussed widely, but see Macpherson, *Life and Times*, 50–63; and Arblaster, *Rise and Decline*, 277–83, for a useful account of

Mill's revisionism. The broader transformations of liberalism in Britain in the latter parts of the nineteenth century are discussed in Biagini, *Liberty*. Scholarship on "progressivism" in the United States is voluminous. For representative examples, see Wiebe, *Search for Order;* Boyer, *Urban Masses;* and, extending into the 1930s, Dawley, *Struggles for Justice*. Global interchange between British liberalism and American progressivism is discussed in Rodgers, *Atlantic Crossings*.

15. Macpherson, *Life and Times,* 23–69. Property ownership was frequently taken as essential to the exercise of "democratic" rights. Macpherson, *Democratic Theory,* 25–30, 120–32.

16. I discuss the emergence of the New Deal in the United States in more detail in chapter 12. Its parameters in the context of a longer history of liberalism are addressed in, for example, Dawley, *Struggles for Justice,* 295–408; Plotke, *Building;* and Gerstle, "Protean Character," 1043–73.

17. Amartya Sen argues that neoliberal economists have emphasized only parts of Smith's account of liberal political economy and exaggerated the role and efficacy of the market. Sen, "Uses and Abuses," 257–71. Giovanni Arrighi similarly argues that Smith's thought has been misunderstood, from the nineteenth century onward, and reframed as a dogmatic belief in minimalist government and self-regulating markets. Arrighi, *Adam Smith in Beijing,* 42–44, passim.

18. Fraser and Gerstle, *Rise and Fall;* Harvey, *Brief History,* in particular 1–86.

19. Arblaster, *Rise and Decline,* 15.

20. Thomas Hobbes, in his 1651 book *Leviathan,* reconceived the individual as existing outside of monarchical or religious hierarchies and as driven by desire that must in part be renounced to form social contracts.

21. Macpherson, *Political Theory;* Macpherson, *Life and Times,* 23–76.

22. Arblaster, *Rise and Decline,* 166. Locke defined property in individualistic terms in *The Second Treatise of Government* (*Two Treatises,* 287–88). Locke's chapter on property is extracted also in Macpherson, *Property,* 15–28.

23. Macpherson, *Rise and Fall,* 76–85; Macpherson, *Life and Times,* 23–44.

24. Blackstone, *Commentaries,* 139.

25. "Lived hegemony is always a process," Raymond Williams observes. "It has to be continually renewed, recreated, defended and modified." Williams, *Marxism and Literature,* 112–13.

26. Hobsbawm, *Age of Revolution,* 46, 184–89.

27. Harvey, *Spaces of Global Capitalism,* 69–116.

28. Marx, *Capital,* 1:875; Foucault, *Discipline and Punish,* 85.

29. Polanyi, *Great Transformation,* 163.

30. Hobsbawm, *Age of Revolution,* 202–3; Polanyi, *Great Transformation,* 82.

31. Foucault, *Discipline and Punish;* Burchell, Gordon, and Miller, *Foucault Effect;* Dean, *Constitution of Poverty*.

32. Polanyi, *Great Transformation,* 140.

33. Here I summarize (and necessarily simplify) the central argument of Polyani's *Great Transformation,* particularly part two, "Rise and Fall," 33–219.

34. Hobsbawm, *Industry and Empire*. If I may be permitted a minor digression, this elaboration of a free trade economy was the context that led to the building of free trade

halls, most famously the one built between 1853 and 1856 in industrial Manchester. It was built on the site of the Peterloo Massacre, which took place in 1819, when cavalry charged into crowds of people protesting about parliamentary representation. I recently returned to Manchester, the city of my youth, with my family to watch some of the Olympic games and noticed that the Free Trade Hall is now a Radisson hotel, where "stylish spaces create a mood of understated luxury in the city centre." It was a dizzying history lesson. Manchester was close to the center of the industrial revolution. But it is now predominantly a postindustrial city, with the economy retooled around consumerism, tourism, and the "creative industries," exemplified by corporately funded public relations events like the Olympics. Manchester now mostly thrives on this postindustrial economy and includes the so-called MediaCity, where large parts of the British Broadcasting Company were recently relocated, and stadiums for local football teams buttressed by money from deregulated media and consequently from the United States (Manchester United) and the Middle East (Manchester City). I saw The Smiths play live at the Free Trade Hall as a teenager, in 1986, in the midst of a neoliberal regime in the process of destroying union rights and the working-class industrial communities that had been so central to the globally dominant regime of British imperial capitalism—"Manchester, so much to answer for." One can now, incidentally, take degrees in those "creative industries," as higher education institutions like King's College, London, have turned themselves into commercial and market-orientated entities. It is another irony of this history that this mostly involves targeting students from overseas, in particular East Asia.

35. Hobsbawm, *Age of Revolution,* 200–201.

36. Beckert, "Emancipation and Empire," 1405–38.

37. Washbrook, "South Asia," 489–90.

38. For example, Harvey, *New Imperialism;* Arrighi, *Long Twentieth Century;* Callinicos, *Imperialism.*

39. Arrighi, *Adam Smith,* 231.

40. Hobsbawm, *Age of Empire,* 51. The importance of finance capital to British imperialism is explicated in Cain and Hopkins, *British Imperialism,* in particular 114–50. Likewise, Lance E. Davis and Robert A. Huttenback estimate that the capital invested in Europe in 1910–14 ranged between 9 and 12 percent, while over the same period in the empire, the figure was 39–40 percent. Davis and Huttenback, *Mammon,* 40–46.

41. Bryan, *Gold Standard,* 17–32.

42. Polanyi, *Great Transformation,* 14.

43. Constantine, *Making.*

44. Prakash, *Another Reason;* Stoler, *Race.*

45. MacCabe, "'To take ship,'" in Grieveson and MacCabe, *Empire and Film,* 7.

46. Knobloch, *Culture of Wilderness,* 19.

47. White, *"It's Your Misfortune,"* 85–91, 125–26.

48. Tomlins, "Supreme Sovereignty," in Dubber and Valverde, *Police,* 52.

49. White, *"It's Your Misfortune,"* 115, 135.

50. Jones, "History"; Adas, "From Settler Colony," 1692–1720; Hoxie, "Retrieving the Red Continent," 1153–67.

51. Livingston, *Pragmatism,* 32. Livingston (26–28) suggests this complex begins with the mechanization of prairie farming in the 1840s and 1850s, which stimulated demand for

capital goods and thus industrial capitalism. White estimates that over a hundred million acres of Native American lands were sold to the railroads. White, *"It's Your Misfortune,"* 145.

52. Beckert, "Emancipation and Empire," 1435; Hobsbawm, *Age of Capital,* 171–72; Williams, *Roots,* 185–93.

53. Beckert, *Monied Metropolis,* 145–71.

54. Dawley, *Struggles for Justice,* 123. See also M. Sklar, *United States,* 1–77.

55. Carpenter, *Forging of Bureaucratic Autonomy.*

56. I am guided here by William J. Novak's account of the emergence of a newly expanded federal state power in the 1860s and of its mutation into an expansive conception of state police power, marked in particular by a radical expansion of the ideas of regulation, public management, administration, and "new policies and practices of socialization, social police, and social control." Novak, "Police Power," in Dubber and Valverde, *Police,* 54–73 (quotation, 54). After the Civil War, Novak argues, there emerged a new emphasis on the constitutional rights of individual citizens, which replaced previous common-law norms. This is one example of the growing dominance of liberal conceptions of individuality and citizenship. Novak, "Legal Transformation," in Jacobs, Novak, and Zelizer, *Democratic Experiment;* Novak, "Legal Origins," in Sarat, Garth, and Kagan, *Looking Back.*

57. Bensel, *Yankee Leviathan;* Bensel, *Political Economy.*

58. Rodgers, *Atlantic Crossings,* 152.

59. P. Anderson, "Imperium," 5–111.

60. Carpenter, *Forging,* 212–54; Scott, *Seeing Like a State.*

61. Barrow, *Universities,* 53–54.

62. Rasmussen, *Readings,* 109–10; Sanders, *Roots of Reform,* 315.

63. Spring, *Education.*

64. Barrow, *Universities;* Bowles and Gintis, *Schooling in Capitalist America;* Zunz, *Why the American Century?* (in particular the definition of a "new institutional matrix," xi–ii).

65. Noble, *America by Design.*

66. Livingston, *Pragmatism,* 36.

67. Fishlow, "Internal Transportation," in Engerman and Gallman, *Cambridge Economic History,* in particular 572–94. Land grants accounted for somewhere between ten thousand and twelve thousand miles of new track in 1868–73.

68. Marx, *Grundrisse,* 524–39. See also Kern, *Culture of Time.*

69. Berman, *All That Is Solid.*

70. Stannage, *Victorian Internet;* B. Anderson, *Imagined Communities;* Henkin, *Postal Age.*

71. Zinn, *People's History,* 249.

72. M. Sklar, *Corporate Reconstruction,* 4, passim.

73. Chandler, *Visible Hand,* 79–187.

74. Freyer, "Business Law," in Engerman and Gallman, *Cambridge Economic History,* 462–70.

75. M. Sklar, *Corporate Reconstruction,* 51.

76. M. Sklar, *Corporate Reconstruction,* 34. The term is defined on pages ix–x, and the broad parameters of Sklar's analysis of the accommodation of liberal government to corporate form is sketched out in pages 20–40. The term *corporate liberalism* has been widely debated and has been used as a way of exploring the transformation of liberalism in the

United States in the latter years of the nineteenth century, as well as the emergence of a form that transcends classical liberal laissez-faire but precedes the partial emergence of a welfare statism starting from the early 1930s. One development within this is an emphasis on the emergence of organized private associations, headed by elites, which become instruments through which the state works. See, for example, Hawley, "Discovery and Study," 309–20; McQuaid, "Corporate Liberalism," 342–68. The term is used and developed, with some differences in emphasis, by, for example, Lustig, *Corporate Liberalism*; Barrow, *Universities*, in particular 12–30; Dawley, *Struggles for Justice*, 297–333; Zunz, *Making America Corporate*; and Himmelberg, *Business-Government Cooperation*.

77. Freyer, "Business Law," in Engerman and Gallman, *Cambridge Economic History*, 475–76; Cain and Hopkins, *British Imperialism*, 125–34.

78. Chandler, *Visible Hand*, 285.

79. Lamoreaux, *Great Merger Movement*; M. Sklar, *Corporate Reconstruction*, 44–46.

80. Chandler, *Visible Hand*, 9; Barrow, *Universities*, 14–24. On US Steel, see Misa, *Nation of Steel*, 164–71.

81. Zinn, *People's History*, 252.

82. The process of concentration was initiated and directed by investment financiers, and this led to the formation of distinct financial groups connected by stock ownership, interlocking corporate board membership, related expertise, and the underwriting of particular companies or industries. Financial groups in this sense were the "dominant forces in the American economy during the opening decades of the twentieth century." See Barrow, *Universities*, 19. Barrow (17–24) gives a number of examples, including the financial group led by the investment bank J. P. Morgan, which was supported in its capital generation by several commercial banks and insurance companies and was closely tied, by stock ownership and membership of boards, to massive railroad companies (including the Northern and Western Pacific) accounting for 26 percent of rail miles in the country; utility companies (including, American Telephone and Telegraph and GE), which generated around 37 percent of the electrical capacity in the United States; and natural resources (including US Steel and Continental Oil).

83. Engerman and Sokoloff, "Technology and Industrialization," in Engerman and Gallman, *Cambridge Economic History*, 395–98.

84. Buroway, *Manufacturing Consent*.

85. Dawley, *Struggles for Justice*, 48–55. On the accompanying economic debates, see M. Sklar, *Corporate Reconstruction*, 53–85.

86. Steigerwalt, *National Association*.

87. Werking, "Bureaucrats," 322.

88. Rosenberg, *Spreading the American Dream*, 66–70.

89. See in particular Schoonover, *Uncle Sam's War*.

90. Cited in Hobsbawm, *Age of Empire, 1875–1914*, 45.

91. McCormick, *China Market*; LeFeber, *American Search for Opportunity*; Schoonover, *Uncle Sam's War*.

92. Koistinen, *Mobilizing for Modern War*. See also Saldin, *War*, 12–13, 32–33.

93. Musser, *Emergence of Cinema*, 225–61. The films are discussed also in Whissel, *Picturing American Modernity*, 58–60, 216–19

94. On the related role of the tabloid press, see, for example, Spencer, *Yellow Journalism*, 123–52.

95. Nearing and Freeman, *Dollar Diplomacy*; Veeser, *World Safe for Capitalism*.

96. Rosenberg, *Spreading the American Dream*, 59. The banking House of Morgan was one of the primary instruments for this dollar diplomacy. "The new alliance was mutually advantageous," Ron Chernow writes, "Washington wanted to harness the new financial power to coerce foreign governments into opening their markets to American goods or adopting pro-American policies. The banks, in turn, needed levers to force debt repayment and welcomed the government's police powers in distant places." Chernow, *House of Morgan*, 131.

97. Nearing and Freeman, *Dollar Diplomacy*; Rosenberg, *Financial Missionaries*, 1–30.

98. Grandin, "Liberal Traditions," 87–88; Rosenberg, *Spreading the American Dream*, 130–31.

99. The Bureau of Foreign and Domestic Commerce became "one of the Commerce Department's major divisions, quintupling its staff to 2,500" in the 1920s, when the Department of Commerce became dominant "in most matters of foreign economic affairs." Rosenberg, *Spreading the American Dream*, 140. Years earlier, incidentally, Hoover had worked as a publicist for the Panama-Pacific International Exposition. Brown, "Science Fiction," in Kaplan and Pease, *Cultures*, 141.

100. M. Sklar, *Corporate Reconstruction*, 423; Livingston, *Origins*, 215–34. Sklar argues that the passage of banking, tariff, and taxation legislation all in that consequential year of 1913 "signified the triumph of the emergent corporate-capitalist order" and, combined with other legislation in the 1913–1916 period, "represented the culmination of corporate liberalism in its emergent phase of ascendancy." Sklar, *Corporate Reconstruction*, 422–23, 422.

101. Hawley, "Herbert Hoover," 116–40. See also Noble, *America by Design*, 76–83.

102. M. Sklar, *Corporate Reconstruction*, 86–332.

103. Chandler, *Visible Hand*, 12.

104. McCraw, "Government," in Chandler, Amatori, and Hikino, *Big Business*, 526–27.

105. Zinn, *People's History*, 254.

106. Lamoreaux, "Partnerships," 48–50.

107. M. Sklar, *Corporate Reconstruction*, 168–73.

108. Goodwyn, *Democratic Promise*.

109. Frieden, *Global Capitalism*, 35.

110. Frieden, *Global Capitalism*, 34–35. On the House of Morgan's extensive ties with the Roosevelt and Taft administrations in the early years of the twentieth century, see Wiebe, "House of Morgan," 49–60.

111. Chernow, *House of Morgan*, 76.

112. Postel, *Populist Vision*; Eichengreen and Flandreau, *Gold Standard*, 19.

113. J. P. Morgan Sr., for example, entertained Mark Hanna, a former Ohio banker and chairman of the Republican National Committee, on his expensive boat to lobby for a gold standard plank in the Republican Party platform. Chernow, *House of Morgan*, 77.

114. Livingston, *Origins*, 96–104.

115. Musser, *Emergence of Cinema*, 150–54.

116. Auerbach, "McKinley at Home," 803.

117. Pollock, *Humane Economy*, 166.

118. Quoted in Whissel, *Picturing American Modernity*, 150.

119. Ibid., 149.

120. Rydell, *All the World's a Fair*, 126–53.

121. Musser, *Emergence of Cinema,* 305–08.

122. Metzger, *Blood and Volts,* 111.

123. Misa, *Nation of Steel,* 266–68.

124. Dawley, *Struggles for Justice,* 151–53.

125. Montgomery, *Workers' Control in America.* The formation and destruction of the Industrial Workers of the World is examined in Dubofsky, *We Shall Be All.*

126. Ewen, *PR!,* 74–79.

127. For example, on Bahrain's and Israel's use of PR firms to justify brutally repressive actions, see *Guardian* journalist Brian Whitaker's blog at http://al-bab.com/; and *Peace, Propaganda, and the Promised Land,* directed by Sut Jhally and Bathseba Ratzkoff (2004).

128. Simmon, *"American in the Making,"* 122.

129. Noble, *America by Design,* 125.

130. Bureau of Mines, Department of the Interior, *Descriptive List of Motion Picture Films and Plan of Distribution,* November 1924, RG70 Bureau of Mines, General Classified Files, box 75, 1925, NARA. Krows clarifies that the films were distributed from the Bureau of Mines Experiment Station in Pittsburgh and from fourteen regional subcenters. Krows, "Motion Pictures," part 33, 16.

131. Hawley, *Great War,* 6–9.

132. The broad outline of this shift is charted in Foucault, "Governmentality," 73–87. See also Gordon, "Governmental Rationality," 1–52. The detailed examination of the emergence of liberalism, and its mutation into neoliberalism, is explicated in Foucault, *Birth of Biopolitics.*

133. Writes Foucault, "This emergence of an internal limitation of governmental reason could be located roughly around the middle of the eighteenth century. What permitted its emergence? . . . What is it, starting from the middle of the eighteenth century? Obviously, it is political economy." Foucault, lecture 10, January 1979, *Birth of Biopolitics,* 13.

134. Foucault, "Security," 67.

135. Ian Hacking, "How Should We Do?," in Burchell, Gordon, and Miller, *Foucault Effect,* 181–96.

136. Wallerstein, *Modern World System,* 218–22; Rose, *Psychological Complex.*

137. For example, Foucault, "Subject and Power," 208–26; Rose, "Expertise and the Government," 359–97.

138. Galston, "Civic Education."

139. For example, Foucault, lecture 24, January 1979, in *Birth of Biopolitics,* 65–73; Dean, *Constitution of Poverty.*

140. Foucault, *History of Sexuality,* 143, 142.

141. "A Brief Account of the Educational Work of the Ford Motor Company," Detroit 1916, 3, accession 951, box 3, RCHFM, 3.

142. Ford, *My Life and Work,* 128.

143. "A Brief Account of the Educational Work of the Ford Motor Company," Detroit 1916, 6.

144. The *Annals of the American Academy of Political and Social Science* ran two special issues in 1915 (vol. 59, September) and 1916 (vol. 65, May) on what Meyer Bloomfield called "the problem of handling men." Bloomfield, "New Profession," 122.

145. Marquis, "Ford Idea," 915.

146. Joyce, *Rule of Freedom,* 15.

147. Hobbes, *Leviathan*, 72.
148. Foucault, "Technologies of the Self," 19.
149. Foucault, lecture 24, January 1979, in *Birth of Biopolitics*, 64–65.
150. Foucault, *Discipline and Punish*, 200.
151. Ibid., 201.
152. Ibid., 203.
153. Prakash, *Another Reason*; Stoler, *Race*.
154. I am glossing over some significant conceptual distinctions between the structure and logic of my argument about liberal political *economy* and the work on liberal governing rationality and practice. I do so because I am less interested here in metatheoretical debate and more invested in optimizing a conceptual framework that enables, first, the description and analysis of the principal dynamics of liberal political economy across a particular *history*, and second, an understanding of the roles that media and culture came to play in the enactment of this governmental rationality. Even so, it behooves me to say something about the distinction between my interest in economy and, in particular, governing rationales and practices. I have proposed that liberalism emerged as the political corollary to the expansion of a capitalist market economy and liberalism in theory and practice prioritized the establishment of a self-regulating market economy. The tendency of this process rendered the social as an addendum to the market and produced the conditions that led to the growth of economic concentration—with the ability of powerful economic entities to frame and direct the political process—and the expansion of a capitalist system around the globe. I have thus far proposed that states and corporations had particular objectives in fostering wealth, and that these were frequently—increasingly—isomorphic across the long nineteenth century. Foucault, however, purposively deemphasized the role of the state and had little to say, at least directly or substantively, about the place of economy in the practices of liberal governmentality. Indeed, the logic of his argument was that power exceeds the state and a whole series of nonstate innovations is equally significant in the elaboration of the pervasive logics and practices of liberal governance. Foucault talks in this respect of a "'governmentalization' of the state," characterized for example by the emergence of new forms of regulation and discipline outside the state, which are often eventually incorporated within it. (Foucault, "Governmentality," 103.) Foucault's arguments were consistent with his critique of Marxism, and what he saw as its overreliance on a totalizing conception of the state and corresponding ideas about the centralized enactment of power as either ideological or coercive. The conceptual arsenal of Marxism, Foucault's work suggested, does not permit one to go beyond the mode of production to make intelligible the forms of domination that emerge at other points in social space, or to regard these forms of domination as conceptually distinct from the relations of production. (The clearest articulation of this distinction is probably in Foucault, "Truth and Power," 109–33.) I am not alone in using the insights of both traditions of scholarship. One finds much reflection on Foucault and Marx (sometimes by way of Gramsci) in cultural studies, for example. (One useful example is Bennett, *Culture*, 60–84.) Foucault himself made a few remarks here and there about how discipline and bio-power connect to the logics of capitalism. In *Discipline and Punish* he notes in passing that surveillance becomes integral to new capitalist practices of factory production (and quotes Marx on this). And he later writes, "The growth of a capitalist economy gave rise to the specific modality of disciplinary power, whose general formulas, techniques of submit-

ting forces and bodies, in short, 'political anatomy,' could be operated in the most diverse political regimes, apparatuses or institutions." Foucault, *Discipline and Punish*, 175, 221. Likewise, in the first volume of *The History of Sexuality* he writes, "This bio-power was without question an indispensable element in the development of capitalism; the latter would not have been possible without the controlled insertion of bodies into the machinery of production and the adjustment of the phenomena of population to economic processes" (140–41). Foucault's specific genealogy of liberalism in lectures and writing in the late 1970s began also as a response to the contemporary emergence of neoliberalism and its intensification of ideas about free markets and the limited role of the state. In any case, I have adopted a loose pragmatic working assumption that prioritizes the structuring influence of economy, and indeed of the expanded power of economic entities beginning in the latter parts of the nineteenth century. In this I am sympathetic to the arguments about the form and function of a capitalist market economy, which have animated traditions of Marxist scholarship. I am, however, also interested in the political rationalities of liberalism, in particular their transmutation into media forms and policies. In this I am receptive to the argument that liberalism innovates new forms of governmental order, in particular new practices of self-regulation and security that are frequently connected to economic objectives—but not invariably and not always straightforwardly. I hope that what this model lacks in conceptual purity is made up for by its *usefulness* in helping describe and explain what I take to be the principal dynamics of liberal political and economic power and the ways in which film, media, and culture supplemented and facilitated its enactment across a contingent history and evolving world system.

155. Grieveson, *Policing Cinema*, 11–36.

156. Mill, *Principles of Political Economy*, bk. 4, ch. 7, sects. 1 and 2, in *Collected Works*, 761.

157. *Mutual Film Corporation v. Industrial Commission of Ohio*, 236 U.S. 230 (1915), 244. Grieveson, "Not Harmless Entertainment," in Stamp and Keil, *American Cinema's Transitional Era*.

158. Grieveson, *Policing Cinema*, 32–36, 193–216.

159. Uricchio and Pearson, *Reframing Culture*.

160. Grieveson, *Policing Cinema*, 78–120. Frykholm, *Lost Tycoon*.

161. R. Greene, "Y Movies," 20–36; Greene, "Pastoral Exhibition," in Acland and Wasson, *Useful Cinema*, 205–29.

162. Grieveson, *Policing Cinema*, 67–70.

163. Arnold, *Culture and Anarchy*, 6, 56.

164. I take this to be one of the central arguments of Nancy Armstrong's fascinating history of the novel, *How Novels Think*.

165. Hunter, *Culture and Government*.

166. Bennett, *Birth of the Museum*.

167. Andrew Carnegie, cited in Uricchio and Pearson, *Reframing Culture*, 23.

168. On the broad currency of ideas of mimesis in psychology, sociology and psychoanalysis, see Sarbin, "Attempts to Understand," 759–67; Allport, "Historical Background"; Leys, "Mead's Voices," 277–307; Borch-Jacobsen, *Freudian Subject*, and *Emotional Tie*.

169. Baldwin, *Mental Development*, 24.

170. Ibid., 487–88.

171. Tarde, *Laws of Imitation,* 68.

172. E. Ross, *Social Control.*

173. S. Barrows, *Distorting Mirrors*; Leys, "Mead's Voices," 278–79; Bramson, *Political Context,* 57–72; Leach, "Mastering the Crowd," 99–115.

174. Addams, *Spirit of Youth,* 86.

175. I draw here on Eric Hobsbawm's account of the causes of the war, in both *Age of Empire,* 302–27, and *Age of Extremes,* 21–31.

CHAPTER 4

1. The "state of exception" elaborated during wartime enabled the extension of military authority into the civil sphere and radically transformed existing conceptions of the liberal state. Constitutional and liberal norms protecting individual liberties, for example, were suspended, and the distinctions among legislative, executive, and judicial powers were loosened. In the early 1920s, and more fully in the face of the collapse of European democracies in the 1930s, jurists and political theorists began to explore the proposed importance of these exceptional state practices to the very maintenance of constitutional security. I draw here specifically on Giorgio Agamben's analysis of these shifting practices of governance in his book *State of Exception* (see especially 1–33). By this now rather familiar logic, the state might need to act in ways outside of the legal system in order to sustain security and the fusion of geopolitical and economic interests, which began most clearly with the compact among the state, transnational corporations, and globalizing capital forged in the latter parts of the nineteenth century and manifested acutely in the practices of economic imperialism and warfare throughout the twentieth century.

2. Winkler, *Nexus,* 5–7.

3. The insulating material for submarine cable technology was made from gutta-percha, sourced mostly from Southeast Asian plantations, in particular from Malaysia. Britain also controlled the extrusion patent for gutta-percha. Hills, *Struggle for Control,* 16, 23. Cables themselves were mostly made from copper, most likely sourced from Chile and from the "copper belt" region of Central Africa, in what are now Zambia (formerly Northern Rhodesia) and the Democratic Republic of Congo.

4. Winkler, *Nexus,* 5–6.

5. Ibid., in particular 44–60. Winkler cites Wilson's remarks at the first Pan American Financial Conference in May 1915, where he called for expanded cable and shipping connections to enable "true commercial relations" (55).

6. Headrick, *Invisible Weapon.*

7. Douglas, *Inventing American Broadcasting,* 102–43.

8. Ibid., 241. AT&T's interest in radio patents was initially a defensive measure to prevent wireless telephony competing with its monopoly over wired networks.

9. Ibid., 268–79.

10. Chernow, *House of Morgan,* 307–8.

11. The final articulation of this is included in the *Defense of the Realm Manual,* 6th ed., accessed November 6, 2013, https://archive.org/stream/realmdefenseoogrearich#page/no /mode/2up). See Hutcheson, "Defense," 341–42.

12. Thurlow, *Secret State,* 15–73.

13. Peterson, *Propaganda for War,* 16–17.

14. Ibid., 12–70.

15. Monger, *Patriotism and Propaganda.*

16. P. M. Taylor, "British Official Attitudes," in Pronay and Spring, *Propaganda,* 26–27; Sproule, *Propaganda and Democracy,* 7–8. Goebbels and Hitler cited this as evidence of the need to create a significant Nazi propaganda machine in the early 1930s.

17. Capozzola, "World War 1," in Kazin, *Princeton Encyclopedia,* 911–14.

18. Messinger, *Battle for the Mind,* 26.

19. Ibid., 26. The Zimmerman telegraph was included in the widely circulated government publication *How the War Came to America,* Red, White and Blue Series, no. 1, Washington, DC, 1917.

20. The billion-dollar figure is cited in Frieden, *Global Capitalism,* 130. J.P. Morgan Sr.'s partner Thomas W. Lamont said, "We wanted the Allies to win, from the outset of the war. We were pro-Ally by inheritance, by instinct, by opinion." Lamont, cited in Higgs, "World Wars," in Fishback et al., *Government,* 431–32. "By late 1916," Emily Rosenberg writes, "the American stake in Allied successes had become so great that the Treasury Department and the Federal Reserve Board grew alarmed. The loans . . . stimulated American industry, but made continued prosperity dependent on an allied victory." Rosenberg, *Spreading the American Dream,* 67.

21. Petersen, *Propaganda for War,* 108.

22. Arrighi, *Long Twentieth Century,* 270–71.

23. The quotation that serves as the heading for this section comes from *Reel and Slide,* July 1918, 8. The most complete history of the CPI is Vaughn, *Holding Fast the Inner Lines.* The CPI's import for new practices of state propaganda is suggestively sketched by Chomsky in, for example, *Media Control,* notably 11–21; and is explored by Ewen, *PR!,* 108–25; Messinger, *Battle for the Mind,* 15–37.

24. Vaughn, *Holding Fast,* 5–7.

25. Ibid., 6.

26. Ewen, *Pr!,* 104–10.

27. Creel, *How We Advertised America,* 17.

28. Rosenberg, "War," 63.

29. Creel, *How We Advertised America,* 89. See also Ewen, *Pr!,* 103–4. Creel claimed later that there were seventy-four thousand four-minute men, who delivered 7,555,190 speeches to audiences estimated at 134,454,514. Creel, *How We Advertised America,* 85.

30. Mastrangelo, "World War I," 609.

31. The list of bulletins produced for the four-minute men is reproduced in Creel, *How We Advertised America,* 86–87.

32. US Committee on Public Information, "Where Did You Get Your Facts?," *Four Minute Man Bulletin* 35 (August 26, 1918), cited in Ewen *PR!,* 103.

33. D. M. Kennedy, *Over Here,* 72.

34. Ewen, *Pr!,* 3; Sharrett, "9/11," 125–31.

35. Ewen, *Pr!,* 115.

36. Creel, *How We Advertised America,* 119–23.

37. Ibid., 274.

38. Ibid., 273.

39. Dwight Eisenhower, cited in James Kurth, "Military-Industrial Complex," in Chambers, *Oxford Companion*, 440–42.

40. Creel, *How We Advertised America*, 126.

41. Vaughn, *Holding Fast*, 205; Creel, *How We Advertised America*, 123.

42. Creel, *How We Advertised America*, 127; Hilderbrand, *Power and the People*, 163.

43. Hoover to Arthur Friend (Famous Players Lasky), August 9, 1917, United States Food Administration Collection, cited in DeBauche, *Reel Patriotism*, 111.

44. Parts of that history are traced in Colwell, *"End of the Road"*; and Lord, "Models of Masculinity."

45. Creel, *How We Advertised America*, 273.

46. Ibid., 276.

47. Creel, *Rebel at Large*, 169.

48. Creel, *How We Advertised America*, 278–81.

49. Ibid., 276.

50. Vasey, *World According to Hollywood*, 14.

51. Krows, "Motion Pictures," part 6, *Educational Screen* (February 1939), 52.

52. *Exhibitor's Trade Review*, June 23, 1917, 173. On the bond campaigns, see Kimble, *Mobilizing the Home Front*.

53. DeBauche, *Reel Patriotism*, 118–19.

54. *Motography*, June 16, 1917, 1247.

55. Liberty Loans Committee to Charles F. Horner, Treasury Department, October 21 1918, RG16, box 693, NARA; NAMPI advertisement, *Variety*, October 12, 1917, 36–37; *Moving Picture World*, October 19, 1918, 351–52.

56. Gilbert, *American Financing*, 140; Ott, *When Wall Street Met Main Street*, 2, 34, 55, 57.

57. Ott, *When Wall Street Met Main Street*, 9–35.

58. Ibid., 59, 60.

59. Ott, "When Wall Street Met Main Street," 2008, 625.

60. Woodrow Wilson, *Exhibitor's Trade Review*, July 1918, cited in DeBauche, *Reel Patriotism*, 109.

61. Espionage Act, June 15 1917, c. 30, 40 Stat. 219. For more on the Espionage and Sedition Acts and subsequent legal responses, see Rabban, *Free Speech*, 248–98.

62. Debs, "The Canton, Ohio, Speech," June 16, 1918, accessed August 10, 2016, www.marxists.org/archive/debs/works/1918/canton.htm.

63. Sterling, "In Defense of Debs," 20–22.

64. Sedition Act, May 16, 1918, c. 75, 40 Stat. 553.

65. Ibid.

66. Ibid., 554.

67. McCartin, *Labor's Great War*, 68–69.

68. Dawley, *Struggles for Justice*, 188.

69. Gary, *Nervous Liberals*, 22.

70. Rosenberg, "Economic Interest," 38–39.

71. Kohn, *American Political Prisoners*, 14–19.

72. *Moving Picture World*, December 22, 1917, 1786; *Moving Picture World*, December 29, 1917, 1947; Wood, *Film and Propaganda*, 296.

73. P. Anderson, "Imperium," 30.

74. *Schenck v. United States 249 U.S. 47.* See also *Debs v. United States* 249 U.S. 211 (1919).

75. For material on the 1917 Immigration Act, the 1918 Alien Anarchist Act, Americanization campaigns, and the corporate counteroffensive in 1919 against union membership, see, for example, Higham, *Strangers in the Land,* 200–203; Capozzola, *Uncle Sam Wants You,* 202–4; Dawley, *Struggles for Justice,* 259–60.

76. Higham, *Strangers in the Land,* 230–32.

77. In 1922, deputy head of the bureau, J. Edgar Hoover, ordered that Chaplin be watched closely as a suspected communist sympathizer. Bureau agents reported that Chaplin was part of a Communist plot to use movies to make a "propagandist appeal for the cause of the labor movement and the revolution." "Report of Special Agent A. A. Hopkins," August 15, 1922, Los Angeles, cited in S. J. Ross, *Hollywood Left,* 11.

78. Franklin K. Lane, to secretary of war, January 23 1919, RG12, box 42, Records of the Bureau of Education, Records of the Office of the Commission, Historical Files, 1870–1950; J. J. Cotter, Administrative Assistant, Department of the Interior, Memorandum for Dr. Pettijohn, June 6, 1919, Visual Instruction Section, Division of Educational Extension, "Purpose of Section. Re-stated from Various Reports Submitted to the Director since January 1, 1919," RG12, box 16, 1; "Memorandum from Mr. Pettijohn to Dr. Claxton," undated, RG12, 1. All documents from NARA.

79. "In Charge of the Work of Visual Instruction," Division of Educational Extension, to Mr. J. F. Abel, February 3, 1919, RG12, box 42, 1, NARA.

80. C. H. Moore, "Future of the Screen in Education and Industrials," *Reel and Slide,* August 1919, 10.

81. Krows, "Motion Pictures," part 8, *Educational Screen* (April 1939), 123.

CHAPTER 5

1. McCartin, *Labor's Great War,* 147–72; Dawley, *Struggles for Justice,* 234–50.

2. Thurlow, *Secret State,* 110–25; Philips, *General Strike.*

3. Shideler, *Farm Crisis.*

4. Hobsbawm, *Industry and Empire,* 176–77. Trade union membership increased from four million in 1913 to eight million in 1919. Eichengreen, "British Economy," in Floud and Johnson, *Cambridge Economic History.*

5. The 1918 Representation of the People Act in Britain widened suffrage by abolishing practically all property qualifications for men and enfranchising women over thirty who met some property qualifications. The latter restrictions were lifted with the Representation of the People (Equal Franchise) Act of 1928.

6. Thurlow, *Secret State,* 119.

7. Ibid., 49, 119.

8. Higham, *Strangers in the Land,* 202.

9. Capozzola, *Uncle Sam Wants You,* 202.

10. Gerstle, *American Crucible,* 92; Boyer, *Urban Masses,* 191–202.

11. For example, the American Protective League was founded in 1917; the American Legion was founded in 1919; and the Ku Klux Klan became a national movement in the 1920s. Higham, *Strangers in the Land,* 255–56.

12. Ford, *My Life*, 128.

13. Upton Sinclair, *Boston*, vol. 2 (New York, 1928), cited in Dawley, *Struggles for Justice*, 290.

14. The Society for the Extension of University Teaching was established in 1890, by which point university extension work was being carried out in twenty-eight states. Peters, "'Every Farmer,'" 196–97.

15. Bureau of Education, Department of the Interior, "The Federal Executive Departments as Sources of Information for Libraries," *Bulletin*, no. 74 (Washington: Government Printing Office, 1919), 135, 136.

16. Barrow, *Universities*, 95–123.

17. Carpenter, *Forging*, 212.

18. Rasmussen, *Readings*, 143.

19. D. Hamilton, "Building the Associative State," 213.

20. J. Scott, *Seeing Like a State*.

21. Sanders, *Roots of Reform*, 391–92; Carpenter, *Forging*, 219–20; Wiser, "Public Policy," 24–30.

22. D. Hamilton, "Building the Associative State," 210.

23. *Science* 18 (November 13, 1903), 463, cited in Giesen, *Boll Weevil Blues*, vii.

24. Olmstead and Rhode, *Creating Abundance*, 139–54.

25. R. Scott, *Reluctant Farmer*, 210–313.

26. Giesen suggests that the "boll weevil's invasion" presented USDA officials with "an unmatched opportunity to rethink the agricultural systems of . . . the entire South." Giesen, *Boll Weevil Blues*, 2.

27. Carpenter, *Forging*, 230–31.

28. Kirby, *Rural Worlds Lost*, 20.

29. Sanders, *Roots of Reform*, 323.

30. Rockefeller's philanthropic activities extended beyond the GEB and at times involved the use of film in pedagogic projects. Rockefeller funded the International Health Board to counter, in particular, health problems like hookworm, which were common in agricultural regions of the South. E. Brown, "Public Health in Imperialism," 897–903. Brown argues that Rockefeller's philanthropic goals were underscored by the practical benefits of increasing Southern productivity. The International Health Board later worked in cooperation with the British state to produce a film on the hookworm problem, which also flourished in tropical regions encompassed by the British Empire. Burns, "American Philanthropy," in Grieveson and MacCabe, *Empire and Film*, 55–68.

31. R. Scott, *Reluctant Farmer*, 237–53; Beerlage, "Organizing the Farm," 424–25.

32. US House, Committee on Agriculture, *Cooperative Agricultural Extension Work*, 63rd Cong., 2nd sess., 1914, cited in Sanders, *Roots of Reform*, 335. The act is discussed further in Ferleger, "Arming American Agriculture," 211–26.

33. Finegold and Skocpol, *State and Party*, 59.

34. Bowles and Gintis, *Schooling in Capitalist America*, 194.

35. Ingersent and Rayner, *Agricultural Policy*, 1–8; Federico, *Feeding the World*.

36. My argument here about the governmental logics of agricultural reform draws on the work of scholars across various disciplines, but it also differs in emphasis from the work of some significant political scientists. Elisabeth Sanders, for example, reads the establish-

ment of an extension service as led by the demands of farmers, who thus helped to shape a new interventionist state. Sanders, *Roots of Reform*. Sanders is undoubtedly right to direct attention toward the agency of farmers, and it is clear that farmers fought for and welcomed aspects of the extension service and other state interventions. But at the point of application, these policies were compromise formations that unequally balanced the needs of farmers with the more heavily weighted and valued needs of the economy and the state. Hence farming problems were consistently defined in scientific terms and not, say, as problems of an inequitable system of property rights and land ownership.

37. Sanders, *Roots of Reform*, 391.

38. The system of property rights put in place in the latter years of the nineteenth century to support the growth of farming favored the establishment of large corporate-style farms, particularly in the use of auctions enabling rich businessmen to buy large expanses of land and sell or rent it for profit. Kirby, *Rural Worlds Lost*, 1–22; Danbom, *Born in the Country*, 120–30.

39. Fitzgerland, *Every Farm a Factory*, 10–32, 106–28.

40. Ngai, *Impossible Subjects*, 91–166.

41. McDean, "Professionalism," 64–82.

42. *Report to the Secretary of Agriculture on the Work of the Committee on Motion Picture Activities*, November 30, 1914, RG16, box 151, NARA; John L. Cobbs, "Memorandum to the Secretary," April 29, 1921, RG16, box 837, NARA.

43. *Report to the Secretary of Agriculture on the Work of the Committee on Motion Picture Activities*, November 30, 1914, RG16, box 151, NARA.

44. John L. Cobbs, "Memorandum to the Secretary," April 29 1921, RG15, box 837, NARA.

45. For example, "Memorandum from Motion Picture Committee to Mr. G. W. Wharton," February 14, 1914; "Memorandum from the Chairman of the Motion Picture Committee to Dr. B. T. Galloway," May 5, 1914; *Report to the Secretary of Agriculture on the Work of the Committee on Motion Picture Activities*, November 30, 1914; and "To Chiefs of Bureaus and Independent Offices, and to the Committee on Motion Picture Activities: Demonstration of Current-Generating and Motion-Picture Projecting Apparatus Mounted on a Trailer," March 3, 1917. All RG16, box 151, NARA.

46. *Report to the Secretary of Agriculture on the Work of the Committee on Motion Picture Activities*, November 30, 1914, RG16, box 151, NARA.

47. Ibid.

48. "Memorandum from the Chairman of the Motion Picture Committee to Dr. B. T. Galloway," May 5, 1914, RG16, box 151, NARA. (Forty USDA films were shown at the exposition in 1915. Krows, "Motion Pictures," part 33 [January 1942], 14.)

49. Ibid.

50. *Report to the Secretary of Agriculture on the Work of the Committee on Motion Picture Activities*, November 30, 1914, RG16, box 151, NARA; Letter from United States Secretary of Agriculture David Houston to Wm. H Bloomer, May 28, 1914, RG16, box 151, 2, NARA.

51. The screening took place in October 1913 at the University of North Carolina at Chapel Hill. The department official who ran the screening wrote a letter afterward: "I wish you had been present, for I cannot convey to you the enthusiasm and interest of the

audience." "Mr. Davis to Thomas N. Carver," October 26, 1913, cited in Zwarich, "Bureaucratic Activist," 31–33.

52. *Report to the Secretary of Agriculture on the Work of the Committee on Motion Picture Activities,* November 30, 1914, 9, RG16, box 151, NARA.

53. Scattered departmental records show that $10,000 was given over to the motion picture department in 1918, and that this was increased to $13,000 in 1921. *Informal Report of Motion Picture Work,* February 21, 1918, RG16, box 578; John L. Cobbs Jr., "Memorandum for the Secretary," April 29, 1921, RG16, box 837, 2, 3, both NARA.

54. "Memorandum for the Secretary," April 29, 1921, RG16, box 837, 3, NARA.

55. "Motion Picture Policies of the US Department of Agriculture," January 31, 1923, RG16, box 998, 1–2, NARA.

56. Krows, "Motion Pictures," part 33 (January 1942), 14; *Annual Report of the Office of Motion Pictures,* 1923, RG16, box 998, NARA.

57. Strom, "Texas Fever," 49–74.

58. Ibid., 51–53.

59. Ibid., 54.

60. The particular form of cattle immunization developed by the USDA was, Strom argues, "aimed at capital-intensive, commercial farming. . . . This bias in favor of large-scale farmers on the part of the USDA . . . became more pronounced with the increasing stress on tick eradication." Ibid., 59.

61. B. T. Galloway to W. O. Thompson, March 9, 1914, RG16, box 151, 2, NARA (emphasis added).

62. *Report to the Secretary of Agriculture on the Work of the Committee on Motion Picture Activities,* November 30, 1914, RG16, box 151, 9, NARA.

63. *Report on Motion Picture Activities,* October 6, 1915, RG16, box 214, 7, NARA.

64. Ibid.

65. Ibid.

66. Knapp was greatly concerned that the first demonstration farm in Terrel, TX, was two miles outside of town because he feared this would discourage farmers from visiting it. Giesen, *Boll Weevil Blues,* 18–19.

67. *Report to the Secretary of Agriculture on the Work of the Committee on Motion Picture Activities,* November 30, 1914, RG16, box 151, 6, NARA.

68. Ibid., 6–7.

69. George Wharton, chairman of the Committee on Motion Picture Activities, "Memorandum to Chiefs of Bureaus, Independent Offices, and to the Committee on Motion Picture Activities," March 3, 1917, RG16, box 415, 1, NARA.

70. *Report on Extension of the Use of the Motion Picture Films of the U.S. Department of Agriculture,* RG16, box 415, 1917, 4, 10, NARA.

71. John L. Cobbs Jr., "Memorandum for the Secretary," April 29, 1921, RG16, box 837, 4, NARA.

72. US Department of Agriculture, *Motion Pictures,* 1922, 9.

73. "Questionnaire on Use of Motion Pictures," January 1922, RG16, box 915, 1, NARA.

74. "To Extension Directors," August 17, 1922, RG16, box 915, 1, NARA.

75. Fred Pickering to Chief of the Bureau of Animal Industry, August 25, 1922, RG16, box 915, 1, NARA.

76. Ibid., 2.

77. *Report on Extension of the Use of Motion Picture Films of the U.S. Department of Agriculture*, 1917, RG16, box 415, 2, 4, 9, NARA. See also "Preliminary Working Plans and Organization for Motion Picture Activities," March 11, 1918, RG16, box 578, 2, NARA.

78. Jonas Howard, "The Wisconsin Idea; How It Operates," *Reel and Slide* 1, no. 7 (September 1918), 9.

79. C. H. Moore to W. D. McGuire, January 27, 1919, box 46, National Board of Review of Motion Pictures Collections, Rare Books and Manuscripts Division, New York Public Library, hereafter NBR.

80. "Memorandum for the Secretary," April 29, 1921, RG16, box 837, 3, NARA.

81. *Report on Extension of the Use of Motion Picture Films of the U.S. Department of Agriculture*, 1917, RG16, box 415, 3, NARA.

82. Ibid., 4.

83. Ibid., 4.

84. Ibid., 2.

85. W. C. Henderson, "Memorandum for the Secretary," July 7 1917, RG16, box 415, 1–5, NARA; Don Carlos Ellis to Orrin G. Cocks, January 14, 1919, box 46, NBR.

86. The Bureau of Animal Industry was established in 1884 after Germany banned the importation of American pork. "Its major impetus," Gabriel Kolko writes, "was to fight European restrictions, not to aid the American consumer, and in doing so it effectively represented the interests of the major American packers who had the most to gain from the Department's success." Kolko, *Triumph of Conservatism*, 100, 98–112. Bureau films supported this goal too. *Behind the Breakfast Plate* (Bureau of Animal Industry, c. 1923), for example, showed "modern methods of pork production" in the United States and was "designed to encourage foreign market for American pork." US Department of Agriculture, *Motion Pictures*, 1923, 13.

87. US Department of Agriculture, *Motion Pictures*, 1923, 5.

88. Ibid., 6.

89. Ibid., 10.

90. The script guidelines for what came to be called *Helping Negros*, available at the National Archives II, call here for a "close up, in a characteristic pose." "Cooperative Extension Work in Agriculture and Home Economics, State of Alabama," Records of the Federal Extension Service, RG33, box 1, 1, NARA.

91. Winn, "Documenting Racism," 36–37.

92. Ibid., 39–40.

93. "Motion Picture Policies of the U.S. Department of Agriculture," October 31, 1923, RG16, box 998, 4, NARA.

94. C. W. Pugsley, Assistant Secretary, to Members of the Motion Picture Theatre Owners of America, April 30, 1923, RG16, box 915, NARA.

95. The script outline of this film, dated January 27, 1922, is in RG33, box 1, NARA.

96. Zwarich, "Bureaucratic Activist," 40.

97. US Department of Agriculture, *Motion Pictures*, 1923, 9.

98. F. Taylor, *Principles of Scientific Management*, 1911. Taylor's ideas filtered also into home economics as a rationalization of domestic practices.

99. "'Poor Mrs Jones' Finds She Is Rich," August 14, 1925, RG33, Records of the Federal Extension Service, box 2, 1, NARA.

100. Franklin K. Lane, to Secretary of War, January 23, 1919, Records of the Bureau of Education, Records of the Office of the Commission, Historical Files, 1870–1950, RG12, box 42, NARA; J. J. Cotter, administrative assistant, Department of the Interior, "Memorandum for Dr. Pettijohn," June 6, 1919, Visual Instruction Section, Division of Educational Extension, "Purpose of Section. Re-stated from Various Reports Submitted to the Director since January 1, 1919," RG12, box 16, 1, NARA. The draft bill for the creation of a motion picture laboratory in the Bureau of Education allocated twenty thousand dollars for its establishment. "A Bill to Create a Moving Picture Laboratory in the Bureau of Education," [1919?], Records of the Office of the Commissioner, RG12, box 94, NARA.

101. "In Charge of the Work of Visual Instruction," Division of Educational Extension, to Mr. J. F. Abel, February 3, 1919, RG12, box 42, 1, NARA.

102. C. H. Moore, "Future of the Screen in Education and Industrials," *Reel and Slide* (August 1919), 10.

103. Gerstle, *American Crucible*, 91.

104. Extension Leaflet, no. 1, December 1919; J. J. Cotter, Administrative Assistant, Department of the Interior, "Memorandum for Dr. Pettijohn," June 6, 1919, Visual Instruction Section, Division of Educational Extension, "Purpose of Section. Re-stated from Various Reports Submitted to the Director since January 1, 1919," RG12, box 16, 1, 2, 3, NARA. See also "Visual Instruction: Division of Educational Extension," [early 1919?], RG12, box 42, 1–5, NARA. This breaks the immediate work of the Visual Instruction Service into four areas: "inventory of available materials," establishing "relationship with Departments," examining the "machinery of distribution," and completing a "plan for permanent service in Visual Instruction," 1–2.

105. R. F. Egner, "A Suggestion for a National Educational Film Service for Educational Institutions," [1919?], RG12, box 42; J. J. Pettijohn, director of the Division of Educational Extension, Bureau of Education, to Hon. P. P. Claxton, United States Commissioner of Education, August 18, 1919, RG12, box 42, NARA. Extension Leaflet no. 1, for example, contained a list of "Educational Institutions Equipped with Motion-Picture Projection Machines," and a bulletin in 1924 listed all "Visual Education Departments in Educational Institutions." Bureau of Education, Department of Interior, Extension Leaflet, no. 1 (1919); A. P. Hollis, Bureau of Education, Department of Interior, *Bulletin*, no. 8 (1924), both in Records of the Office of the Commissioner, RG12, box 94, NARA.

106. Saettler, *Evolution*, 111; "The Wisconsin Idea: How It Operates," *Reel and Slide*, September 1918, 9; Orgeron, Orgeron, and Streible, "History," in Orgeron, Orgeron, and Streible, *Learning*, 18.

107. *Annual Report of the Visual Instruction Section, Bureau of Education, Department of the Interior, for the Fiscal Year Ending June 30, 1920*, RG12, box 16, 3, NARA.

108. For secondary accounts of the field, see Saettler, *Evolution*, 123–77; Cuban, *Teachers and Teaching*, in particular 9–26; Slide, *Before Video*, 64–66; and Wiatr, "Between Word," 333–51.

109. The history of the National Academy of Visual Instruction is recounted by George Kleine, in a manuscript in "Subject Correspondence, 1886–1946," George Kleine Papers, box 41, Library of Congress (hereafter GKLOC). *Moving Picture Age* grew out of *Reel and Slide*, the first journal, started in 1918, devoted to visual instruction. It became the official organ of the National Academy of Visual Instruction.

110. Program, First Annual Conference of the National Academy of Visual Instruction, July 14–17, 1920, Madison, Wisconsin, "Subject Correspondence," 41, GKLOC.

111. Saettler, *Evolution*, 144–45.

112. US Department of the Interior, Bureau of Education, *Visual Education Departments in Educational Institutions* (Washington, DC: Government Printing Office, 1924).

113. The Emergency Quota Act limited the annual number of immigrants from any country to 3 percent of the number of persons from that country living in the United States, according to the 1910 census. Even more restrictively, the 1924 Johnson-Reed Act reduced migrant numbers to a quota system based on 2 percent of each migrant group's population, according to the 1890 census. Roediger, *Working toward Whiteness*, 139–56.

114. Dawley, *Struggles for Justice*, 249.

115. US Senate Commission on Education and Labor. *Hearing on S17: Americanization Bill*. Ed 66th Cong. 1st Sess., 1919, cited in Cabán, "Subjects and Immigrants," 31.

116. New York Legislature, *Revolutionary Radicalism* (Albany, 1920), cited in Dawley, *Struggles for Justice*, 259.

117. McClymer, "Americanization Movement," 98.

118. Capozzola, *Uncle Sam Wants You*, 211. The legion's subsequent use of film is explicated by Tom Rice in "War in Peace," in Wasson and Grieveson, *Cinema's Military Industrial Complex*.

119. Higham, *Strangers in the Land*, 244; Carlson, "Americanization," 452; McCartin, "'An American Feeling,'" in Lichtenstein and Harris, *Industrial Democracy in America*.

120. W. A. Ryan, "History of the Americanism Committee of the Motion Picture Industry of the United States," [1919?], box 27, NBR, n.p.

121. "Prospectus of The National Visual Education Association," June 1920, RG12, box 16, NARA (emphasis added).

122. See, for example, Weber, *Comparative Effectiveness*, 1922; Freeman, *Visual Instruction*, 1924.

123. Reese, "Origins of Progressive Education," 1–24.

124. Alfred H. Saunders, "National Alliance of Pedagogical Cinematography," 1921, "Subject Correspondence," 41, GKLOC.

125. Locke, *Some Thoughts concerning Education*, 1693; Rousseau, *Emile*, 1762.

126. Habermas, *Structural Transformation*, 129–40.

127. Welter, *Popular Education*.

128. Galston, "Civic Education," 90.

129. McClymer, "Americanization Movement."

130. Ibid., 99–100.

131. Higham, *Strangers in the Land*, 241–42. The division was financed in part by railroad magnates and bankers.

132. Reese, *History*, 79–94.

133. Claxton, *Report of the Commissioner of Education*, 1917, RG12, 16, NARA.

134. Baldwin, *Mental Development*, 24.

135. Krows, "Motion Pictures," part 20 (October 1940), 334.

136. "Memorandum to the Advisory Commission of the Council of National Defense concerning the Committee for Immigrants in America, National Americanization Committee and Affiliated Organizations," 1917, Historical Files, 1870–1950, RG12, box 1, 13,

NARA. I take this to be the National Americanization Committee, directed by Frances Kellor. In 1917, this committee created the Immigration Committee of the US Chamber of Commerce, the board of which featured prominent individuals such as Thomas Edison; commissioner of education, Philander P. Claxton; and financial elites like Mrs. Vincent Astor, Mrs. Cornelius Vanderbilt, Elbert H. Gary (cofounder of US Steel), and department store magnate Rodman Wanamaker.

137. David K. Niles, *Reel and Slide,* December 1918, 18.

138. *Los Angeles Times,* January 3, 1920, cited in S. Ross, *Working-Class Hollywood,* 129; W. A. Ryan, "History of the Americanism Committee of the Motion Picture Industry of the United States,"[1919?], box 27, NBR, n.p.

139. S. Ross, *Working-Class Hollywood,* 141.

140. University of California, Bulletin of the University Extension Division, Department of Visual Instruction, Supplementary Announcement and Catalogue of Motion Pictures and Slides (Berkeley: University of California, 1922), 4.

141. Ibid., 5.

142. *Moving Picture Age,* January 1922, 24. The Society for Visual Education began film production in 1920 and made a series of films aimed at schools, "comprising nine subjects covering the foundation and settlement of the United States of America; six on the economic history of the same; four on civics; nine representing regional geography; three on nature study, and two dealing with hygiene and sanitation. Each reel was accompanied by a teacher's syllabus." Krows, "Motion Pictures," part 20 (October 1940), 334–35.

143. N. Greene, *1000 and One,* 57, 28.

144. *Moving Picture Age,* January 1922, 24.

145. The establishment of the Bureau of Mines is a further example of the state's efforts to orchestrate research to benefit large industry. In 1913, a new act enlarged the scope of the bureau to include "such fundamental inquiries and investigations as will lead to increasing safety, efficiency, and economy in the mining industry." A. Hunter Dupree, *Science in the Federal Government* (Cambridge, MA: Harvard University Press, 1957), cited in Noble, *America by Design,* 125.

146. *The Miners Lesson,* Records of the Bureau of Mines, Information Division, 1913–58, RG70, box 1, NARA.

147. *Safety Lessons in Metal Mining,* Records of the Bureau of Mines, Information Division, 1913–1958, RG70, box 1, NARA.

148. Zinn, *People's History,* 320.

149. Ibid., 345.

150. Bureau of Mines, Department of Interior, *Descriptive List of Motion Picture Films and Plan of Distribution,* November 1924, General Classified Files, RG70, box 75, 1925, NARA. Krows tells us that the films were distributed from the Bureau of Mines Experiment Station in Pittsburgh and from fourteen regional subcenters. "The circulation, however, has always been exceedingly wide, the excellent safety lessons making the reels especially valuable in regular schools and in centers devoted to adult education." Krows, "Motion Pictures," part 33 (January 1942), 16.

151. Records of the Bureau of Mines, Information Division, 1913–1958, RG70, box 2, NARA.

152. Bureau of Mines, Department of the Interior, *Descriptive List of Motion Picture Films and Plan of Distribution,* November 1924, General Classified Files, RG70, box 75, 1925,

21; *When Wages Stop*, title and scene content, Records of the Bureau of Mines, Information Division, 1913–1958, RG70, box 1, NARA (my emphasis).

153. There is a script outline for this film in the records of the Bureau of Mines, Information Division, 1913–1958, RG70, box 1, NARA. The film was revised and rereleased in 1928.

154. The longer list is in "List of Films, July 1924," Bureau of Mines General Classified Files, 1925, RG70, box 75, NARA.

155. I quote here from the brief descriptions of the films in the University of Arizona University Extension Division, *Educational Moving Pictures and Slides* (Tucson: University of Arizona, 1926), 14–15. The Yale films are discussed in more detail in Tyrrell, *Historians in Public*, 78–82; and Pearson, "White Man's Country," 23–41.

156. Yale Chronicles of America Photoplays, 3, 22.

157. Ibid., 5.

158. Balibar, "Nation Form," in Balibar and Wallerstein, *Race, Nation, Class*, 96.

159. Wallerstein, "Construction of Peoplehood," in Balibar and Wallerstein, *Race, Nation, Class*, 78.

160. The history of the Ku Klux Klan's use of cinema is well told by Tom Rice in *White Robes, Silver Screens*.

161. Tyrrell, *Transnational Nation*, 130.

162. Ibid., 131.

163. Schulman, "Governing Nature," 376.

164. Krows, "Motion Pictures," part 33 (January 1942), 16.

165. "The Moving Picture a Big Asset in Work of Y.M.C.A. Organizations," *Moving Picture Age*, August 1920, 15.

166. R. Greene, "Pastoral Exhibition," in Acland and Wasson, *Useful Cinema*, 212.

167. The Bureau of Motion Pictures and Exhibits, Industrial Department, International Committee, YMCA, "Use of Industrial and Educational Motion Pictures in the Y.M.C.A. Practical Program," New York, 1919, 3.

168. Musser, *Emergence of Cinema*, 359–60.

CHAPTER 6

1. *Ford Times*, October 1912, cited in Williams, Haslam, and Williams, "Ford versus 'Fordism,'" 525.

2. "Information Regarding Materials Used by the Photographic Department," September 30, 1919, accession 75, box 10, Misc. Correspondence, 1919–27, RCHFM. Time-motion study was started at Ford in 1907 and organized into a department in 1913. Gartman, *Auto Slavery*, 50. Frank and Lillian Gilbreth carried out was what probably the most significant use of film by time-motion experts. Frank Gilbreth's 1911 book *Motion Study* used film as a tool for the study and improvement of the worker's physical movements. See Curtis, "Images of Efficiency," in Hediger and Vonderau, *Films That Work*, 85–100.

3. Williams, Haslam, and Williams, "Ford versus 'Fordism,'" 521–22. The literature on the establishment of the moving assembly line is very large, testament to its status as one of the most significant industrial developments of the twentieth century. See Hounshell, *From the American System*, 217–62; Meyer, *Five Dollar Day*, 9–36; Gartman, *Auto Slavery*, 83–101; Watts, *People's Tycoon*, 141–47.

4. Braverman, *Labor and Monopoly Capital*, 127–62.

5. Marx, *Selected Writings*, 379.

6. Arnold and Faurote, *Ford Methods*, 360.

7. The head of the photographic department at Ford, A. B. Jewett, wrote an article in the trade journal *Reel and Slide* that told of how the Ford "branches act as 'exchanges', and through them our films are distributed to between five and six thousand exhibitors each week and to an audience of between five and six million." *Reel and Slide*, March 1, 1918, 31. In a letter to Henry Ford, Irving R. Bacon, the official photographer and painter at Ford, claimed a high point of seven thousand "contacts" before the company started charging for the films in 1918. Bacon to Ford, Feb. 11, 1921, accession 1, box 172, folder 19, RCHFM.

8. "Ford Film Collection Documents Americana," *Film World and A-V News Magazine*, 20, no.1 (January 1964). From 1918 on, the Ford films were distributed by the Goldwyn Film Distributing Company, which superseded the extant alternative distribution system internal to the Ford Company. "Information Regarding Materials Used by the Photographic Department," September 30, 1919, accession 75, box 10, Misc. Correspondence, 1919–27, 2, RCHFM.

9. Lewis, *Public Image*, 115. Lewis claims that by 1918 Ford was "the largest motion picture distributor on earth." The figure of six hundred thousand dollars annually represented a very significant investment in cinema. For comparison, Hollywood film producer William Fox wrote in 1919 that three Tom Mix feature films averaged forty-two thousand dollars to produce. Fox was notoriously cheap, but Mix was a big star. See Semenov and Winter, *William Fox*, 101.

10. *Ford News*, January 1, 1922, 1.

11. The Ford films, making up 1,500,000 feet of motion pictures, were donated to the National Archives in 1963. See National Archives publication no. 70–6, Mayfield Bray, *Guide to the Ford Film Collection in the National Archives* (1970), also available at https://archive.org/details/guidetofordfilmcoobrayrich, though the list of individual film titles is far from complete.

12. *Ford Times*, February 1917, 302.

13. *Reel and Slide*, March 1918, 31.

14. "Factory Facts from Ford," accession 951, box 11, RCHFM.

15. *Ford News*, October 1, 1924, 1.

16. Fuller, *At the Picture Show*, 83.

17. *Ford Times*, July 1916, 534–40.

18. *Ford News*, January 1, 1922, 1; *Ford News*, February 1 1922, 3; *Ford News*, February 15, 1922, 6; *Ford News*, June 15, 1923, 7.

19. Watts, *People's Tycoon*, xii

20. Ford, *My Life*, 1922.

21. Watts, *People's Tycoon*, xi; Michael Dobbs, "Ford and GM Scrutinized for Alleged Nazi Collaboration," *Washington Post*, November 30, 1998, A1, 4. Hitler in turn cited Ford's anti-Semitic stance on the alleged Jewish control of financial markets approvingly in his book *Mein Kampf*. Hitler wrote, "Every year makes them [Jews] more and more the controlling masters of the producers in a nation of one hundred and twenty millions; only a single great man, Ford, to their fury still maintains full independence." Adolph Hitler, *Mein Kampf* (New York: Hurst and Blackett, 1939), cited in Lee, *Henry Ford*, 59.

22. Lucic, *Charles Sheeler*, 89–90.

23. Meyer, *Five Dollar Day*; Gartman, *Auto Slavery*, in particular 84–99.

24. Buroway, *Manufacturing Consent*, 113.

25. *Los Angeles Times*, June 22, 1913, cited in Watts, *People's Tycoon*, 140; Lewis, "Henry Ford—Movie Producer," 17. Other contemporary news accounts suggest that Ford was influenced by conversations with Thomas Edison. See, for example, *New York Times*, January 11, 1914, 10.

26. Ford, cited in Lewis, "Henry Ford—Movie Producer," 44.

27. *Ford Times*, July 1916, 536.

28. Ibid., 536, 537.

29. Ibid., 535, 536, 538, 539.

30. Harris, *Humbug*, 75–89; Segal, *Technological Utopianism*; D. Nye, *American Technological Sublime*.

31. "Not until the narrator begins to follow a particular character," Rick Altman writes, "will the text be recognized as narrative. Or, to put it more accurately, not until a particular character is followed will we sense the activity of a narrator, thereby defining the text as narrative." Altman, *Theory of Narrative*, 16.

32. Grierson, "First Principles of Documentary," in Macdonald and Cousins, *Imagining Reality*.

33. The script has two titles. "The Power Farm" is crossed out and "An All Year Friend" is handwritten in. The extant film is titled *Farm Progress*, and this is how it is catalogued in the National Archives. The script and the extant film vary a little, but have several scenes and intertitles in common.

34. *Ford News*, March 15, 1924, 1.

35. Ling, *America and the Automobile*, in particular 37–63. Morton Keller argues that the Federal Highway Act of 1916 "began a commitment that became one of the most consequential government policies of the century." Keller, *Regulating a New Economy*, 71.

36. Seely, *Building*, 66–99.

37. Luger, *Corporate Power*, 12.

38. Montgomery, *Fall*, 233–38. Between October 1912 and October 1914, Ford had to hire fifty-four thousand workers to maintain an average workforce of thirteen thousand. This marked an annual turnover of workers of 416 percent.

39. Tone, *Business of Benevolence*.

40. Meyer, *Five Dollar Day*, 108. On the new wage policy, see also Watts, *People's Tycoon*, 178–98.

41. James Couzens, cited in Watts, *People's Tycoon*, 190. Couzens later became mayor of Detroit.

42. For a related argument about automobility, see Seiler, *Republic of Drivers*, in particular 1–17.

43. Gramsci, "Fordism and Americanism," in *The Gramsci Reader*.

44. Ford, *My Life*, 128.

45. On the sociological department, see, for example, Meyer, *Five Dollar Day*, 114–19.

46. Ford, *My Life*, 128.

47. "A Brief Account of the Educational Work of the Ford Motor Company," Detroit 1916, 3, accession 951, box 3, 3, RCHFM.

48. Ibid., 6.

49. Henry Ford, cited in Abel, "Making of Men," 39.

50. Marquis, "Ford Idea," 915.

51. I refer to Hugo Münsterberg, whose book *The Photoplay: A Psychological Study,* was published in 1916. Münsterberg's 1913 book *Psychology and Industrial Efficiency* is often read as the foundational text of industrial psychology. See Hale, *Human Science.*

52. Meyer, "Adapting the Immigrant," 74.

53. Meyer, *Five Dollar Day,* in particular 156–62.

54. Marquis, cited in Watts, *People's Tycoon,* 217.

55. "A Brief Account of the Educational Work of the Ford Motor Company," Detroit 1916, 3, accession 951, box 3, 12, RCHFM.

56. The National Archives research catalog gives two possible dates for the film prints of *Democracy in Education* in the Ford Collection: c. 1919 and 1922 (FC-190a and FC-486). Clearly the film was produced in 1919 and repackaged as part of the Ford Educational Library in 1922. Ford films were regularly altered and re-released for the library series. While both versions use identical title cards, each saying "Ford Educational Library" at the bottom of the frame, the second version also has a copyright notice identifying the film as from 1922. It runs for six and a quarter minutes, as opposed to the five minutes of the 1919 version. The 1922 version is longer because it has the following additional titles and footage:

1) An intertitle and shot, after the shot of a draft of the Declaration of Independence—"and established a democracy in which life, liberty and the pursuit of happiness are guaranteed to all"—followed by a sequence of a crowd of children walking toward the camera and smiling.

2) Two shots after the intertitle—"In 1916, there were many who thought that the crowded condition and manifold temptations of city life"—showing a city street and then a tenement building with washing hanging out to dry.

3) One shot after the title ending—"had completely destroyed those ideals so firmly established by our forefathers. But at the challenge of autocracy"—of a ship slowly sinking.

4) A title about cooperation. After calling for "SELF CONTROL—the ability to conduct one's own business with the respect for the rights of others," there is an additional title demanding "CO-OPERATION—the ability to work with and through other people in the achievement of social purposes." This is followed by footage of a number of people building a wooden trailer.

5) Title and shot in the concluding sequence. In surveying the benefits of education, including government and science, the 1922 version also includes "Art," followed by a shot of a statue. Ford also produced a booklet—*Ford Educational Library, Civics and Citizenship of the U.S.: Democracy in Education* (February 25, 1922)—guiding teachers in how to describe and explain the film for students. This follows exactly the 1922 version.

The digital movie files available at NARA are identical to those hosted by the Internet archive (archive.org). My thanks to Dan Streible for guidance here.

57. Detroit Public Schools, *Course of Study in Visual Education* (Detroit, 1926), 65.

58. *Ford News,* February 1, 1921, 4.

59. Sklar, *Corporate Reconstruction,* 34.

60. "Ford Educational Library, Civics and Citizenship (11) Democracy in Education," 1922, n.p. The title of Dewey's book is erroneously listed as "Democracy in America."

61. Dewey, *Democracy and Education*, 32.

62. Dewey, *School and Society*, 29.

63. Lichtenstein and Harris, introduction to Lichtenstein and Harris, *Industrial Democracy in America*, 4.

64. McCartin, "'An American Feeling,'" in Lichtenstein and Harris, *Industrial Democracy in America*, 69.

65. Meyer, *Five Dollar Day*, 175–86.

66. Ibid., 183.

67. "Ford Educational Library, Civics and Citizenship (11) Democracy in Education," 1922, n.p.

68. Norwood, "Ford's Brass Knuckles," 365–91.

69. Meyer, *Five Dollar Day*, 91.

70. *Ford News*, February 15, 1926, 4.

71. A pamphlet produced by Ford, entitled "The World in Pictures," outlined the scheme: schools had to amass 322 subscriptions to the *Dearborn Independent*, at $1.50 each. Accession 951, box 55, RCHFM.

72. *Moving Picture Age* 4, no. 2 (February 1921), 30.

73. "The Ford Educational Library," 1922, accession 951, box 14, RCHFM.

74. *Ford News*, March 1, 1922, 5.

75. The Judd committee, as it was called, was financially supported by the Motion Pictures Producers and Distributors of America after its president Will Hays had appeared at the National Education Association summer meeting in 1922. See Saettler, *Evolution*, 145–47. The MPPDA was seeking ways to turn a profit from the emerging educational market, while also ensuring this did not impinge on the profits of theatrical motion pictures. The committee also suited their public relations goals to deflect critical regulatory attention away from commercial cinema.

76. Lewis, *Public Image*, 117; "Ford Film Collection Documents Americana," *Film World and A-V News Magazine*, 20, no.1 (January 1964), 9.

77. The exposes in the *Dearborn Independent* ran for two years, and the articles were reprinted as four volumes of *The International Jew*, selling ten million copies in the United States. The volume was translated into sixteen languages. Lee, *Henry Ford*, 14.

78. *The Protocols of the Learned Elders of Zion* was purported to be a document written by Jewish leaders, who had ratified a plan for world domination. Watts, *People's Tycoon*, 376–97.

79. *Dearborn Independent*, November 26, 1921, 12; *Dearborn Independent*, cited in Lee, *Henry Ford*, 30.

80. For example, "Pomona Cleans Up Movies—Restores Sunday," and "A New Type of Producer," *Dearborn Independent*, April 23, 1921, 2, 12; "Salvaging the Wreck of the Movie Film," *Dearborn Independent*, August 23, 1924, 13; "It's Spring—and He's 'Cleaning'—the Movies," *Dearborn Independent*, May 21, 1921, 15.

81. *Ford News*, February 1, 1922, 6.

82. Woeste, "Insecure Equality."

83. Sinclair, *Flivver King*, 59.

84. GM had overtaken Ford as the most successful car producer by 1929. Chandler, *Giant Enterprise*, 3–4.

85. Kuhn, *GM Passes Ford*; Freeland, *Struggle for Control*.

86. McQuaid, "Corporate Liberalism," 346–47.

87. McCraw and Tedlow, "Henry Ford," in McCraw, *Creating Modern Capitalism*, 283–84.

88. Meyer, "Persistence of Fordism," in Lichtenstein and Meyer, *On the Line*.

89. On Ford's opposition to the New Deal, see Watts, *People's Tycoon*, 436–43.

90. *New York Times*, cited in Segal, *Recasting the Machine Age*, 76.

91. Raushenbush, *Fordism*, 23, 39.

92. Norwood, "Ford's Brass Knuckles," 365–391.

93. Lucic, *Charles Sheeler*, 89–102.

94. See Guillén, *Taylorized Beauty*, in particular 6–7, 28–29.

95. On the radio show, see Wik, *Henry Ford*, 55; and Watts, *People's Tycoon*, 492–98. Ford's displays at the Century of Progress Fair in 1933–34 are outlined in a pamphlet the company produced for the fair. Accessed February 25, 2014, http://century.lib.uchicago.edu/images/century0329.pdf.

96. Arnove, *Philanthropy and Cultural Imperialism*.

97. Ouellette and Hay, *Better Living*, 26; McCarthy, *Citizen Machine*, 4, 18, 63, 120–21.

98. Wamsley, *American Ingenuity*, 15.

99. Segal, *Recasting the Machine Age*. On the Muscle Shoals Project, see 24–26.

100. Rosen, *Change Mummified*, 95.

101. Batchelor, *Henry Ford*, 11; Watts, *People's Tycoon*, 412.

102. Wallace, "Visiting the Past," in Benson, Brier, and Rosenzweig, *Presenting the Past*, 137–61.

103. Batchelor, *Henry Ford*, 33.

104. I refer here to Andre Bazin's famous description of cinema as "change mummified." Bazin, *What Is Cinema?*, 15.

CHAPTER 7

1. Ling, *America and the Automobile*, 37–63.

2. Guldi, *Roads to Power*, 4, *passim*; Shideler, *Farm Crisis*, 46–75.

3. Seely, *Building*, 66–99.

4. Strother, "Panama-Pacific," 353; Popp, "Machine-Age Communication," 459–84; Castells, *Rise of Network Society*.

5. *The Pan American Confederation for Highway Education* (Washington, DC: Pan American Confederation for Highway Education, 1925), 13; *Highways of Friendship* (Washington, DC: Highway Education Board, 1924), 22. I am grateful to my colleague Stephanie Schwartz for kindly sharing some of this material with me.

6. Grazia, *Irresistible Empire*, 140, 145.

7. S. Hamilton, *Trucking Country*, 7, 9.

8. Rosenberg, *Spreading the American Dream*, 66–67; Gilderhus, *Pan American Visions*.

9. Nearing and Freeman, *Dollar Diplomacy*.

10. Grandin, "Liberal Traditions," 87–88.

11. Rosenberg, *Spreading the American Dream,* 131, 149.

12. Rosenberg, *Spreading the American Dream,* 130–31; Bucheli, "Major Trends," 339–62.

13. Rosenberg, *Spreading the American Dream,* 38–62.

14. Rosenberg, *Spreading the American Dream,* 70–71; Grazia, *Irresistible Empire,* 213 (Grazia mistakenly identifies the year of the Webb-Pomerene Act as 1919); Miller et al., *Global Hollywood 2,* 61.

15. Arrighi, *Long Twentieth Century,* 269–99; Rosenberg, *Spreading the American Dream,* 7–15.

16. Department of Agriculture, *Report on Motion Picture Activities,* October 6, 1915, General Correspondence of the Office of the Secretary, 1906–70, RG16, box 214, 4, NARA.

17. Ibid., 3.

18. Ibid., 5.

19. Seely, *Building,* 11–23.

20. I. Holley, "Blacktop," 703–33.

21. Seely, *Building,* 27.

22. Ibid., 14–15, 27.

23. *Motion Pictures of the United States Department of Agriculture,* 1935, Records of the Extension Service, RG33, box 1, 33 (emphasis added), NARA.

24. These films are listed in the 1935 catalogue. An internal 1917 memorandum listed the following films having been completed by 1917, all of which appear to follow the OPR's technical use of film to support road-building programs: *Testing Rock to Determine Its Value for Road Building, Road Tests with Traction Dynamometer, Cement and Concrete Tests, Gravel Road Construction in Virginia, Macadam Road Construction in Maryland, Concrete Road Construction (Ohio Post Road), Bituminous Macadam Road Construction (Maine Road).* "List of Motion Pictures," General Correspondence of the Office of the Secretary, 1907–70, RG16, box 415, 1917, NARA.

25. Seely, *Building,* 46–65.

26. Seely, *Building,* 53. Firestone sourced much of its rubber in Liberia. The company loaned large sums to the Liberian government after receiving guarantees from the US government that it would support the security of its investment. Writes Rosenberg, "Firestone Rubber, for all practical purposes, ran Liberia's economy." Rosenberg, *Spreading the American Dream,* 134.

27. Seely, *Building,* 63.

28. Ibid., 71–88. These maps were supplemented by the so-called Pershing Map in 1922, created by the bureau in consultation with the War Plans Division of the US Army to plot military strategic routes. General of the Armies John Pershing presented this plan to Congress in 1922, and most of the seventy-eight thousand miles of roads requested were built, with many of them becoming interstate highways. McNichol, *Roads That Built America,* 62.

29. Seely, *Building,* 73.

30. W. Wells, "Fueling the Boom," 72, 73.

31. C. W. Warburton, Memorandum for Mr. W. A. Jump, April 2, 1924, RG16, box 1070, NARA.

32. Rosenberg, *Spreading the American Dream,* 138–60.

33. See also *Ford News,* March 15, 1924, 1; C. W. Warburton, Memorandum for Mr. W. A. Jump, April 2, 1924, RG16, box 1070, NARA. Bureau of Public Roads Chief Thomas Harris

MacDonald set up the Highway Education Board as a public relations arm, which produced material for schools, held nationwide contests, and had a speaker's bureau.

34. Press Service, Bureau of Public Roads, "'Road to Happiness,' New Motion Picture Showing Value of Highways to Community," March 10, 1924, RG16, box 1070, 1924, NARA. The press service distributed information about the film to "Farm Papers; Farm Editions of Daily Papers; Daily Newspapers (One in a city—all cities); Sunday Editions of Dailies; Washington Correspondents and Free Lance Writers; County Seat Papers; Trade Papers as Follows: Highway Publications; Motion Picture List; Auto Journals." Press Service, Memorandum to Mr. Perkins, Motion Pictures, March 11, 1924, RG16, box 1070, 1924, NARA.

35. *Motion Pictures of the United States Department of Agriculture,* 1935, Records of the Extension Service, RG33, box 1, 33, NARA.

36. Salvatore, "Early American Visions," 59–63.

37. Downes, "Autos over Rails," 565.

38. Pyke Johnson to Francis White, Latin American Div., US Department of State, December 8, 1923, cited in Downes, "Autos over Rails," 565.

39. *Highways of Friendship* (Washington, DC: Highway Education Board, 1924), 50.

40. Calvin Coolidge, cited in *Highways of Friendship* (Washington, DC: Highway Education Board, 1924), 1.

41. Charles Evans Hughes, cited in *Highways of Friendship* (Washington, DC: Highway Education Board, 1924), 3.

42. Ibid.

43. Ibid., 10.

44. For a fascinating account of Ford's jungle rubber plant, see Grandin, *Fordlandia.*

45. Downes, "Autos over Rails," 570, 579–80.

46. *Highways of Friendship* (Washington, DC: Highway Education Board, 1924), 53.

47. Ibid., 29, 28.

48. *The Pan American Confederation for Highway Education* (Washington, DC: Pan American Confederation for Highway Education, 1925), 12, 5.

49. Ibid., 13.

50. Department of Agriculture, *Report on Motion Picture Activities,* October 6, 1915, General Correspondence of the Office of the Secretary, 1906–70, RG16, box 214, 3, NARA.

51. Klein, "What Are Motion Pictures?," 83.

52. Salvatore, "Imperial Mechanics," 677.

53. Josephson, *Empire of the Air.*

54. Rosenberg, *Spreading the American Dream,* in particular 122–37.

55. The American-led transpacific cable was first laid in 1902. See Hills, *Struggle for Control,* 136–47. The development of All American Cable, with financial backing from J. P. Morgan Sr., in the 1880s, and its challenge to British cable interests in South America thereafter, is outlined in Rosenberg, *Spreading the American Dream,* 89–92.

56. Coolidge, cited in *Highways of Friendship* (Washington, DC: Highway Education Board, 1924), 1.

57. "A Brief Account of the Educational Work of the Ford Motor Company," Detroit 1916, 3, accession 951, box 3, 3, RCHFM, 12.

58. *Commerce Reports,* April 24, 1922, 191.

59. Rosenberg, *Spreading the American Dream,* 101; Miller et al., *Global Hollywood* 2, in particular 65–71.

60. Hawley, *Great War,* 101–4; Rosenberg, *Spreading the American Dream,* 140–41.

61. Departments of State, Justice, Commerce, and Labor Appropriations Bill, 1926, *Hearings before the Subcommittee of the Committee on Appropriations, U.S. Senate,* 68th Cong., 2nd sess. on H.R. 11753 (Washington, DC: Government Printing Office, 1925), 44.

62. Vasey, *World According to Hollywood,* 43; Grazia, *Irresistible Empire,* 299.

63. Bjork, "U.S. Commerce Department," 585.

64. Hays, *Memoirs of Will Hays,* 508.

65. North, "Our Foreign Trade," 100–108.

66. C. J. North to Bettina Gunczy, National Board of Review, January 13, 1928, box 95, NBR.

67. Klein, "What Are Motion Pictures?," 83.

68. *Commerce Reports,* January 22, 1923, 91, cited in Bjork, "U.S. Commerce Department," 577.

69. North, "Our Foreign Trade," 105.

70. Klein, "What Are Motion Pictures?," 79.

CHAPTER 8

1. Harvey, *New Imperialism,* 180. Capitalist imperialism is a "contradictory function," Harvey proposes, of two logics of power, one concerned primarily with command over and use of capital, the other primarily with command over and use of the human and natural resources specific to a territory or territories (26).

2. But see the very useful accounts in Stollery, *Alternative Empires,* 140–202; and Jaikumar, *Cinema,* 13–64.

3. Williamson, *National Crisis,* 43–54; Tomlinson, "Imperialism and After"; Eichengreen, "British Economy," in Floud and Johnson, *Cambridge Economic History.* The Conservative Party had in the early years of the twentieth century unsuccessfully proposed a tariff system in response to the increasingly protectionist economic policies of other major industrialized nations. Green, *Crisis of Conservatism.*

4. Gallagher and Robinson, "Imperialism of Free Trade."

5. Drummond, *Imperial Economic Policy,* 28–29.

6. Rooth, *British Protectionism,* 71–100; Cain and Hopkins, *British Imperialism,* 464–71; Hobsbawm, *Age of Extremes,* 106–7.

7. Schivelbusch, *Three New Deals,* 1–48; Hobsbawm, *Age of Extremes,* 93–97.

8. In their influential book *British Imperialism, 1688–2000,* P. J. Cain and A. G. Hopkins emphasize the import of finance capital, and the drive to create an international trading system centered in London and mediated by sterling, to British imperialism. World trade, they show, was to be provided through loans to foreign governments, and subsequently through direct investment, and was to be controlled by the city and the Treasury. This would all be tied together by a regime of free trade, and the resulting expansion of global commerce would be handled, transported, and insured by British firms. Lance E. Davis and Robert A. Huttenback estimate that the capital invested in Europe in 1910–14 ranged from 9 to 12 percent. Over the same period in the empire, the figure was from 39 to 40 percent. Davis and Huttenback, *Mammon,* 40–41, 46.

9. Rooth, *British Protectionism*, 37–38.

10. Hobsbawm, *Industry and Empire*, 180–84; Cain and Hopkins, *British Imperialism*, 415.

11. On the political logics of early twentieth-century conservatism, see, for example, Green, *Crisis of Conservatism*, in particular 59–119 and 223–41.

12. McKibbin, *Ideologies of Class*, 259–93; Jarvis, "British Conservatism," 59–84.

13. Eichengreen, "British Economy."

14. Philips, *General Strike*.

15. Leopold Amery *My Political Life*, vol. 1 (London: 1953), 253, cited in Constantine, "'Bringing the Empire Alive,'" in Mackenzie, *Imperialism and Popular Culture*, 196. Amery was secretary of the state for the colonies between 1924 and 1929 and for Dominion affairs between 1925 and 1929.

16. Drummond, *Imperial Economic Policy*, 32–35, 43–85; Middlemas, *Politics in Industrial Society*, 174–214.

17. Frank, *Capitalism and Underdevelopment*; Wallerstein, *Capitalist World-Economy*. On the impact of these strategies on colonial economies see, for example, Rodney, "Colonial Economy," 153–61.

18. Rooth, *British Protectionism*, 30–31; Constantine, *Making*.

19. Butler, *Britain and Empire*, 5–6.

20. The settlement empire of Canada, Australia, New Zealand, and South Africa had become increasingly economically important to Britain, largely because their economies could sustain the purchase of imports and because they were dependent on British finance capital for infrastructural development. These countries provided 50 percent of empire imports between 1909 and 1913 and received 54.6 percent of exports to the empire. By 1934, empire trade provided 35.3 percent of British imports and received 43.9 percent of exports. A. R. Dilley, "Economics of Empire," 103.

21. "By accepting the constitutional equality and autonomy of the Dominions," Philip Williamson writes, "the Conservative government had intended to outflank secessionist movements and under the new guise of 'Commonwealth' enable the white Empire to be maintained through ties of sentiment, defense needs, and economic interest." Williamson, *National Crisis*, 80. On the effects of economic depression in the early 1930s on anti-imperialist activity, see Hobsbawm, *Age of Extremes*, 106–7.

22. Hawley, *Great War*, 111–12; Hobsbawm, *Age of Extremes*, 98; Kaufman, *Efficiency and Expansion*, 259–60.

23. When Britain left the gold standard in 1931, it established a "sterling area" and "encouraged" the white settler Dominions to peg their currencies to sterling (the formal empire had no choice), and this aimed specifically to reduce the dollar gap caused by trade and postwar debt to the United States. The British had lost about a quarter of their global investments during the war, mainly those in the United States, which they had to sell to buy war supplies. Drummond, *Floating Pound*; Cain and Hopkins, *British Imperialism*, 449–53.

24. P. Taylor, "British Official Attitudes," 28.

25. Marjorie Grant Cook in collaboration with Frank Fox, *The British Empire Exhibition 1924: Official Guide* (London: Fleetway Press, 1924), cited in Rice, "Exhibiting Africa," in Grieveson and MacCabe, *Empire and Film*, 116. See also Mackenzie, *Propaganda and Empire*, 96–120.

26. Scannell and Cardiff, *Social History,* 3–22; LeMahieu, *Culture for Democracy,* 141–50; Potter, *Broadcasting Empire.* John Reith's manifesto for constructing the BBC as a public utility cited George V's opening address at the Empire Exhibition as a crucial example of the way media could form collective identities.

27. Pronay, "Political Censorship of Films, 113. On the British council, see also Taylor, *British Propaganda,* 76–78. On the development of cultural institutions between the wars, see Minihan, *Nationalization of Culture,* 172–215.

28. "The Cinema in Education," *Times,* June 4, 1923, 7.

29. Low, *History,* 53.

30. Edward Davson, "Empire Films," *Times,* October 10, 1923, 11.

31. Ibid.

32. Ronald McNeill (financial secretary to the Treasury), *Hansard* 189 (December 8, 1925) cc238–39.

33. James Marchant, "Scope for Imperial Films," *Times,* June 11, 1924, 8.

34. Rice, "Exhibiting Africa," 120.

35. Timothy Hollins offers the only substantive engagement with this development. See his "Presentation of Politics" and "Conservative Party," 359–69.

36. "Propaganda by Cinema," *Times,* April 8, 1926, 9.

37. Hollins, "Conservative Party," 363.

38. Richards, "Patriotism with Profit," 25–41.

39. "Political Propaganda Experiment," *Times,* April 13, 1926, 12.

40. J. C. C. Davidson, *Memoirs of a Conservative. J.C.C Davidson's Memoirs and Papers 1910–1937* (London, 1969), 337, cited in Cockett, "Party," in Seldon and Ball, *Conservative Century,* 548.

41. Cockett, "Party," 548.

42. Joseph Ball, cited in S. Jones, *British Labour Movement,* 19. Joseph Ball was appointed director of publicity, a newly created post, in 1927.

43. Tom Rice, "*West Africa Calling,*" www.colonialfilm.org.uk/node/1329, has an account of the film, alongside a digital viewing copy of it. British Instructional Films produced the film for the Conservative Party.

44. Larkin, *Signal and Noise,* 39.

45. There was, for example, a similar structure in a serial feature in Conservative Party newspapers, whereby the fictional character Mrs. Maggs talks to her younger colleague, Betty the Maid, about the issues of the day. See Jarvis, "Mrs Maggs and Betty," 129–52.

46. On this film, see Tom Rice, "*Empire Trade,*" www.colonialfilm.org.uk/node/1312.

47. "Political Propaganda Experiment," *Times,* April 13, 1926, 12. In the 1931 election season, the cinema vans visited seventy-nine towns; during the 1935 election, an estimated 1.5 million people watched films from the vans. Nicholas, "Construction," in Francis and Zweiniger-Bargielowska, *Conservatives and British Society,* 134.

48. The financial organization of the film unit is visible in part in the records held in the Conservative Party Archives at the Bodleian Library in Oxford. See in particular CC04/1/34 and F/N 47–48. There were twelve van operators in 1929; in 1935 the weekly cost of running eleven vans was £263. The Conservative and Unionist Film Association's budget in 1934 was triple that of the whole budget for the Conservative Publicity Department. Cockett, "Party," 560.

49. Ramsden, "Baldwin and Film," 133.

50. "Propaganda by Cinema," *Times,* April 8, 1926, 9.

51. Hollins, "Conservative Party," 361.

52. On this practice, see Larkin, *Signal and Noise,* 73–122; and Charles Ambler, "Projecting," in Grieveson and MacCabe eds., *Film and the End of Empire,* 199–224.

53. Edward G. Lowry, "Certain Factors and Considerations Affecting the European Market," Internal MPPDA memorandum, October 25, 1928, reproduced in Higson and Maltby, *"Film Europe,"* 353.

54. *Kinematograph Weekly,* August 6, 1925, 30–31.

55. Ibid., 31.

56. Minutes of a conference on the subject of British Film Production, held at the Offices of the Federation of British Industries, on Wednesday, May 6, 1925, MSS200/F/1/1/159, 2, Modern Records Centre, University of Warwick.

57. Max Muspratt, *Times,* January 21, 1927, 10.

58. Ibid.

59. Philip Cunliffe-Lister, president of the Board of Trade, memorandum, "The British Film Industry," February 6, 1926, 1, War Cabinet and Cabinet: Memoranda, Public Records Office, National Archives, UK, CAB 24/178/70. Hereafter archival papers from the Public Records Office of the National Archives, UK, are cited by the referencing system used in the archive. In this case, for example, the identifier is CAB 24/178/70.

60. Sir Philip Cunliffe-Lister, *HC Deb,* March 16, 1927, vol. 203, cc2039–112.

61. Cunliffe-Lister, "British Film Industry," 2.

62. When the talks between the different sectors of the industry broke down, the leading trade journal *Kinematograph Weekly* noted dryly, "the General Strike intervened." *Kinematograph Weekly,* August 5, 1926, 31.

63. Minutes of a conference on the subject of British Film Production, held at the Offices of the Federation of British Industries on Wednesday May 6, 1925, MSS200/F/1/1/159, Modern Records Centre, University of Warwick, 3.

64. "False Values," *Times,* March 22, 1927, 15.

65. G. A. Atkinson, column, *Daily Express,* March 18, 1927, 6.

66. *Morning Post,* cited in Higson and Maltby, "'Film Europe,'" in Higson and Maltby, *"Film Europe,"* 9.

67. FBI, "Report of Its Overseas Committee," *Kinematograph Weekly,* April 22, 1926, 42.

68. Low, *History,* 96.

69. 1926 Imperial Economic Conference report, cited in Lowry memo, in Higson and Maltby, *"Film Europe,"* 354–55.

70. Dickinson and Street, *Cinema and State,* 27.

71. *HC Deb,* March 16, 1927, vol. 203, cc2039–112.

72. Ibid. The bill emerged from committee in July 1927 and passed its third reading in Parliament in November. It was debated in the Lords in December and became law. The Cinematograph Films Act provided that in the first year the distributors quota should be 7.5 percent and the exhibitors 5 percent. Both quotas were to increase by stages to 20 percent in 1936 and remain at that level until 1938, when the act expired.

73. *HC Deb,* November 14, 1927, vol. 210, cc691.

74. "The Films Bill. Mr. Snowden's Objections," *Times,* March 23, 1927, 8.

75. "The Film Bill," *Times*, March 14, 1927, 15.
76. Higson, "Polyglot Films," in Higson and Maltby, *"Film Europe,"* 275.
77. *HC Deb*, March 16, 1927, vol. 203, cc2039–112.
78. Ibid.
79. Ibid.
80. Sir Heskith Bell, *Minority Report in the Colonial Films Committee Report, 1930*, cited in Commission on Educational and Cultural Films, *Film in National Life*, 133.
81. See, for example, Christie, "'Captains and the Kings,'" in Grieveson and MacCabe, *Empire and Film*, 21–33.
82. *Film in National Life*, 126.
83. Sinha, "'Lowering Our Prestige,'" 305.
84. Pronay, "Political Censorship," 104.
85. W. Ormsby Gore, for the Secretary of State for the Colonies, Letter to All Colonies and Protectorates (except Malta, Palestine, and Tanganykia), October 1, 1927, Public Records Office, Colonial Office (CO) records 323/990/1.
86. "Memorandum Prepared in the Colonial Office, Colonial Film Conference, 1927: Cinematograph Films," CO 323/990/1, 12.
87. Enclosure no. 4, in circular dispatch dated October 1, 1927, "Travelling Cinemas," CO 323/990/1.
88. *Report of the Colonial Films Committee*, CO 323/109/10.
89. Pronay, "Political Censorship," 112.
90. S. Jones, *British Labour Movement*, 105; "Propaganda by Film," editorial, *Times*, June 16, 1930, 11. Now and again there was some crossover between the regulation of Soviet film and film traversing the empire, for it was feared that the Soviet Union was using film propaganda to foment colonial nationalism in South Asia. ("Film exhibitions in Malaya and elsewhere in the East," a Colonial Office memorandum in 1927 noted, were "a factor in the spread of communist doctrines.") "Memorandum Prepared in the Colonial Office, Colonial Film Conference, 1927: Cinematograph Films," CO 323/990/1, 1.
91. Imperial Economic Committee, cited in Meredith, "Imperial Images," 31.
92. Self, "Treasury Control," 160.
93. *Report of the Imperial Economic Committee*, cited in "The Work of the Empire Marketing Board, Report no. 1," July 1926, 1, CO 323/962/7, 1.
94. Amery, *My Political Life*, 352.
95. *Report of the Imperial Economic Committee*, cited in "The Work of the Empire Marketing Board, Report no. 1," July 1926, 1, CO 323/962/7, 2.
96. See the details in Constantine, "'Bringing the Empire Alive,'" in Mackenzie, *Imperialism and Popular Culture*, 203–4. The advertising executive William Crawford was appointed as vice chairman of the board. Crawford's thinking on the power of advertising and its connections to education was influential on the board. "The real power of advertising," Crawford wrote, "is not to sell goods, but to form habits of thinking." Crawford, cited in LeMahieu, *Culture for Democracy*, 163–64. This logic connected to Amery's conception of the board as a way of "selling the idea of Empire."
97. See Amery, *My Political Life*, 347; Williamson, *Stanley Baldwin*, 83–87; Ramsden, "Baldwin and Film," in Pronay *Politics, Propaganda and Film*, 133.
98. Tallents, *Projection of England*, 11.

99. Tallents, *Projection of England,* cited in Hoare, "Educational Cinematography," 9.

100. Tallents, *Projection of England,* 12.

101. Ibid., 24.

102. Ibid., 19.

103. Constantine, *Buy and Build.*

104. "Note on a Proposal for the Preparation of a Film under the Auspices of the Empire Marketing Board," January 28, 1927, CO 760/37 EMB/C/1, 1–3.

105. "Minutes of the 1st Meeting of the Film Conference held at the Board's Offices," February 1, 1927, 1, CO 760/37.

106. "The collaboration of Mister Kipling," the EMB's memorandum recorded, "would, it was felt, prove of the greatest value to the film as a commercial asset." First Meeting of the EMB Film Committee Conference, February 1, 1927, CO 760/37.

107. Tallents, "Birth of British Documentary," part 1, 17.

108. The most complete account of Grierson's intellectual and aesthetic formation is Aitken, *Film and Reform,* 16–89.

109. John Grierson, "Notes for English Producers," Public Records Office, Board of Trade (BT) 64/86 6880, April 1927, 1.

110. John Grierson, "Notes for English Producers," BT 64/86 6880, April 1927, 17.

111. Ibid., 18. (On Grierson's extensive writings about Soviet cinema, see Stollery, *Alternative Empires,* 147–49.)

112. John Grierson, "Notes for English Producers," BT 64/86 6880, April 1927, 20.

113. Ibid., 17.

114. Cunliffe-Lister, letter to Leopold Amery, May 10, 1927, BT 64/86 I.M.5511, cited in Swann, *British Documentary Film Movement,* 13.

115. "Exhibition of Films at the Imperial Institute Theatre, Film Conference, Empire Marketing Board," September 12, 1927, 1. The EMB gave a grant of six thousand pounds to the Imperial Institute to convert a room into a cinema hall and a thousand pounds for the running of the cinema. "The Cinema in Education," *Times,* October 31, 1927, 8.

116. "Cinema as Aid to Agriculture," *Times,* October 24, 1927, 18.

117. John Grierson, "Further Notes on Cinema Production," July 18, 1927, CO 760/37 EMB/C/4, 8.

118. Ibid., 9.

119. John Grierson, "Film Propaganda," 1930, CO 323/1102/2, 7.

120. Empire Marketing Board, Film Committee, Minutes of the Seventh Meeting, November 13, 1928, CO 758/89/3, 2.

121. John Grierson, "Government Cinema Activities in the United States," EMB/c/15, 12/9/1928, 2.

122. John Grierson proposed establishing a film library at the Imperial Institute in a memorandum in March 1928. "The Empire Marketing Board and the Cinema," CO 760/37 EMB/C/9.

123. *Film in National Life,* 126.

124. "Colonial Office Conference, 1927: Cinematograph Films: Memorandum on British Films, prepared by The Federation of British Industries," annex 2, CO 323/974/1.

125. Julian Huxley, *Africa View* (London: Chatto), 1, cited in Sanogo, "Colonialism," in Grieveson and MacCabe, *Empire and Film,* 231.

126. Tom Rice, "Bekefilm," Colonial Film: Moving Images of the British Empire, www.colonialfilm.org.uk/production-company/bekefilm; Smyth, "Development," 437–50

127. Notcutt and Latham, *African and the Cinema*, 24

128. Ibid., 25

129. Windel, "Bantu Educational Kinema Experiment," in Grieveson and MacCabe, *Empire and Film*, 207–11.

130. Later, the Colonial Film Unit set up in 1939 to centralize this use of cinema to educate the colonized in Africa sent a Post Office Savings Bank van alongside its cinema van and encouraged local populations to watch the films and then sign up for a new bank account. See the details in "The Mobile Cinema Van in the Villages," *Colonial Cinema*, March 1945, 11–14.

131. Sanogo, "Colonialism," 237–38.

132. James Burns, "American Philanthropy," 56. The film and an astute analysis of its context and form by Tom Rice are available at www.colonialfilm.org.uk/node/735.

133. See Tom Rice, "Colonial Film Unit," www.colonialfilm.org.uk/production-company/colonial-film-unit; and "Anti-plague Operations, Lagos," www.colonialfilm.org.uk/node/1526.

134. Reynolds, "Bantu Educational Kinema Experiment," 61.

135. James Burns, *Flickering Shadows*, 27.

136. Notcutt and Latham, *African and the Cinema*, 75.

137. Ibid., 98.

138. Reynolds, "Bantu Educational Kinema Experiment," 64.

139. See also Reynolds, "Image and Empire," 90–108.

140. Burns, "American Philanthropy," 55–69.

141. D. Trotter, "Representing Connection," in Grieveson and MacCabe, *Empire and Film*, 152.

142. Hardy, *John Grierson*, 58.

143. The film is available on the Colonial Film website, alongside an article by Tom Rice. www.colonialfilm.org.uk/node/40.

144. Empire Marketing Board, Film Committee, Minutes of the Sixth Meeting of the Film Committee, May 7, 1928, CO 758/89/3, 1–2.

145. Hardy, *John Grierson*, 63.

146. Empire Marketing Board, Film Committee, Minutes of the Sixteenth Meeting, January 8, 1931, CO 758/89/3, 47.

147. Empire Marketing Board, Film Committee, Minutes of the 21st (Special) Meeting, May 6, 1931, CO 758/89/3, 62.

148. Ibid.

149. On the dissolution of the EMB, see Constantine, "'Bringing the Empire Alive,'" 218–20.

150. See Anthony, "Imperialism and Internationalism," in Grieveson and MacCabe, *Empire and Film*, 138–42.

151. Stollery, *Alternative Empires*, 167–68.

152. Gary Evans, *John Grierson and the National Film Board: The Politics of Wartime Propaganda* (Toronto: Toronto University Press, 1984), 49, cited in Nelson, *Colonized Eye*, 43.

153. Ibid.

154. See the accounts in Nelson, *Colonized Eye,* 43–60; and Druick, *Projecting Canada.*

155. Jaikumar, *Cinema,* in particular 41–64.

156. Arrighi, "Hegemony Unravelling—2," 101–4. Cordell Hull, US secretary of state, described the Ottawa Agreement as "the greatest injury in a commercial way that has been inflicted on this country since I have been in public life." Cited in Callinicos, *Imperialism,* 168.

157. Bazin, *What Is Cinema?,* 15.

158. Dupin, "Postwar Transformation," 443–44.

159. Gilroy, "Great Games," in Grieveson and MacCabe, *Film and the End of Empire,* 14.

CHAPTER 9

1. The League of Nations was founded in January 1920, after ratification of the Treaty of Versailles, specifically to develop new patterns of diplomacy, to provide a forum for collective security, and to help reform a liberal, capitalist world system. The league covenant enshrined within the Treaty of Versailles as its first twenty-six articles called for an organization that would function through two major organs, an assembly made up of all members and a council consisting of the major powers as permanent members and four smaller nations chosen by the assembly. The hierarchical organization of the league was at odds with ideals of national equality. This was likewise the case for the establishment of a system of mandates, whereby territories, "which are inhabited by peoples not yet able to stand by themselves under the strenuous conditions of the modern world," were placed under the tutelage of "advanced nations" (which, as Eric Hobsbawm wryly noted, "would not dream of exploiting them for any other purpose"). Wallerstein, *Geopolitics and Geoculture,* 151; Hobsbawm, *Age of Extremes,* 34. Britain was given mandate power over Iraq and Palestine and France over, among other countries, Syria. I have not heard much about those countries in the news recently, so I do not know how that turned out.

2. League of Nations, International Educational Cinematographic Institute, *Report to the Council on the Third Session of the Governing Body of the Institute,* January 2, 1931, C.694 M.291, League of Nations Archives, Geneva. Hereafter materials from this archive are referenced by their classification numbers.

3. The broad outline of those developments, and the contradictory dynamics that both produced a supranational political apparatus and simultaneously extended new principles of national self-determination, can be found in Hobsbawm, *Age of Extremes,* in particular 54–141; Steiner, *Lights That Failed,* 40–46, 349–86. On the roles of the Versailles settlement and the league in establishing new forms of nationalism, see Mazower, *Dark Continent,* 40–76. Even though the initial design of the league was mapped out in large part by Woodrow Wilson, the US Senate refused to sign on to the Treaty of Versailles, largely to avoid entanglement in future European conflicts. On this refusal, see, for example, Hawley, *Great War,* 43–45.

4. Zoë Druik's pioneering work on the league's use of cinema has traced the ways in which it presaged the United Nation's media policies and strategies. Druik, "'Reaching the Multimillions,'" 66–92. Overall, more than two hundred employees of the league's Permanent Secretariat entered the service of the United Nations. Mazower, *Governing the World,* 153.

5. Antony Anghie, for example, has argued that the mandates system of the league, which gave Britain and France control over German colonial territories, marked the moment and mechanism through which direct imperial control gave way to control exercised by international organizations. Anghie, *Imperialism,* in particular 262–65.

6. Louis Pauly has identified the two main bodies of the economic and financial organization of the league, the Economic Committee and the Financial Committee, as forerunners of the General Agreement on Trade and Tariff and the International Monetary Fund. Pauly, "League of Nations," 1–52.

7. Indeed, the league started its own radio station, Radio Nations, in 1926, at the same time that it was working to make cinema useful for liberal internationalism. League of Nations, Organisation for Communications and Transit, "Systematic Survey of Communications of Importance to the Workings of the League of Nations at Times of Emergency," August 15, 1934, 99, C.348, M. 161.

8. Malcolm W. Davis, "The League of Minds," in *Pioneers in World Order,* edited by Harriet Eager Davis (New York: Columbia University Press, 1944), 242, cited in Druik, "International Educational Cinematographic Institute," 81.

9. Lippmann, *Public Opinion.*

10. Julien Luchaire, "Relations of the Cinematograph to Intellectual Life," memorandum submitted to the International Committee for Intellectual Co-operations, July 28, 1924. Reprinted in Seabury, *Motion Picture Problems,* 237.

11. Ibid., 237, 239.

12. Ibid., 259–60.

13. I am indebted in this paragraph to Richard Maltby's discussion of Seabury in "Cinema," in Higson and Maltby, *"Film Europe,"* in particular 83–87.

14. Seabury, *Public,* vii.

15. Ibid., ix–x.

16. Ibid., 181–274.

17. The history of these investigations is outlined in "Request for Collaboration in Regard to Cinematograph Questions by the Child Welfare Committee of the League," Intellectual Co-operation Organisation, Temporary Expert Committee of Representatives of the Film Industry, I.C.E/P.F. 2, Geneva, June 27, 1933.

18. Seabury, *Motion Picture Problems,* 152.

19. Higson, "Cultural Policy," in Higson and Maltby, *"Film Europe,"* 124.

20. Woodrow Wilson, "Fourteen Points," January 8, 1918, accessed August 29, 2014, http://avalon.law.yale.edu/20th_century/wilson14.asp.

21. Wilson and the United States were not alone in formulating plans for a supranational political organization at this moment. Certainly Wilson's position significantly shaped the way the league was formed. But we can see a longer genealogy of the league in other transnational political and economic organizations—to take two examples from this book alone, the Pan-American Union and the British Commonwealth—and the British in particular had developed plans for a postwar league during the course of World War I. Close ties between Anglo-American political elites made the League Covenant "very much the product of . . . Anglo-American partnership." Steiner, *Lights That Failed,* 41. When the United States failed to ratify the Versailles Treaty, the operations of the league were largely governed by Britain and France, which had their own particular agendas for maintaining

imperial order and (for France in particular) preventing a resurgent Germany. See, for example, Steiner, *Lights That Failed*, 40–46; Mazower, *Governing the World*, in particular 128–41.

22. Wilson in effect sought to use the Paris peace settlement "to institutionalize a transnational liberal capitalist order around the League of Nations." Callinicos, *Imperialism*, 166.

23. Lenin, "Socialist Revolution"; Ingeborg Plettenberg, "The Soviet Union and the League of Nations," in *The League of Nations in Retrospect* (Berlin, 1980), cited in Steiner, *Lights That Failed*, 353; Jane Degras, ed., *The Communist International, 1919–1943: Documents*, vol. 2 (London: Oxford University Press, 1956–65), 35, cited in Mazower, *Governing the World*, 177. See also Hobsbawm, *Age of Extremes*, 31–32, 63–64; Arrighi, *Long Twentieth Century*, 66.

24. Hogan, *Informal Entente*, 13–37. "Wilson's Fourteen Points," Perry Anderson has recently observed, "were distinguished mainly by their call for an Open Door." Anderson, "Imperium," 10.

25. Frieden, *Global Capitalism*, 133. Lamont, alongside Wilson's assistant secretary to the Treasury, Norman Davis (who had made millions from investments in Cuba), accordingly wrote a memorandum on Wilson's suggestion, which attributed "American prosperity in the last decade" to the "growth of its export trade" with Europe. Economic instability in Europe, the memo continued, would therefore cause "serious business and industrial depression" in the United States. Thus the government, working as a (junior) partner to private finance capital, should do all it could to help with the reconstruction of the European economy. Lamont, letter to Wilson, May 15, 1919, enclosing "Observations upon the European Situation: Possible Measures to Be Taken," cited in Hogan, *Informal Entente*, 29.

26. Gelfand, *Inquiry*. On the influential House, and on his curiously prophetic anonymous 1912 novel *Philip Dru: Administrator*, see Lasch, *New Radicalism*, 225–50.

27. Lippmann's work for the *Inquiry* is outlined in Steel, *Walter Lippmann*, 128–40.

28. "The hierarchies of Wilson liberal internationalism," G. John Ikenberry writes, were "manifest in notions of racial and civilizational superiority." Ikenberry, "Liberal Internationalism 3.0," 75. Hence while membership in the league was "attractive to former territories of the Austro-Hungarian Empire, or to dominions and colonies of Britain, because it provided access to a language of national rights and privileges," there was a de facto color line in operation, meaning "Africa surfaced largely as a subject of interest for the Council and the secretariat at the behest of Western powers—an object of the League, not an actor in its own right." Clavin, *Securing the World Economy*, 6–7.

29. One of the outcomes of the secretive inquiry was the establishment of a think tank and lobbying group that would henceforth play a significant role in helping shape US foreign policy—the Council on Foreign Relations. The council is now a powerful elite organization, counting among its members senior politicians, media owners and journalists, industrialists, and bankers. Its website locates its beginnings in the *Inquiry*. Accessed September 1, 2014, www.cfr.org/about/history/.

30. Both Susan Pedersen and Mark Mazower emphasize aspects of the league's progressive interventions in, for example, the regulation of trafficking in women and children, the management of epidemic disease, and the humane treatment of refugees. Pedersen, "Back to the League," 1091–117; Mazower, *Governing the World*, 143–48.

31. Clavin, *Securing the World Economy*, 1.

32. Clavin writes, "J. P. Morgan's perspective was crucial, because its participation, secured in May 1923, brought in other European investors, notably from France and Italy, who were sufficiently reassured by the American interest to buy themselves." Clavin, *Securing the World Economy*, 28. Morgan and other banks were extensively involved in the reconstruction of postwar Europe, working largely on the premises outlined by Lamont's memorandum to Wilson. This extensive private investment in European reconstruction effectively took on roles abrogated by the US state, when it failed to ratify the Versailles Treaty. "Contrary to myth," Alex Callinicos writes, "the debacle of the Versailles Treaty did not lead to an American retreat into isolation. On the contrary, the Republican administrations that held office in Washington between 1921 and 1933 consistently pursued a strategy based on close collaboration with a network of central and investment bankers (including notably the Federal Reserve Bank of New York, J. P. Morgan, and the Bank of England), the aim of which was to restabilize and reconstruct European capitalism by using the leverage that Washington had gained when it emerged from the Great War as the world's main creditor." Callinicos, *Imperialism*, 166.

33. Clavin, *Securing the World Economy*, 15–22.

34. Frieden, *Global Capitalism*, 137.

35. Clavin, *Securing the World Economy*, in particular 33–46.

36. Ibid., 42.

37. See the discussion in Clavin, *Securing the World Economy*, 83–123.

38. Maltby, "Cinema," 88–90.

39. Ibid., 95.

40. Higson, "Cultural Policy," 125.

41. International Educational Cinematographic Institute, *Report to the Council on the First Session of the Governing Body of the Institute*, November 5–9, 1928, C. 573 (revised), 2.

42. The budget for the establishment and early operations of the institute is outlined in International Educational Cinematographic Institute, *Report to the Council on the Third Session of the Governing Body of the Institute*, October 8–10, 1930, C. 694 M. 291, 3–4.

43. Druik, "International Educational Cinematograph Institute," 83.

44. On LUCE, see, for example, Hay, *Popular Film Cultures*, 201–32.

45. Druik, "International Educational Cinematograph Institute," 84.

46. On the connections between LUCE and the Soviets, see Salazkina, "Moscow-Rome-Havana," 99–100.

47. I draw here on various documents relaying and discussing the work of the institute, including International Institute of Educational Cinematography, Governing Body, First Session, I.C.E/C.A./1, Geneva, October 23, 1928; International Educational Cinematographic Institute, Governing Body, I.C.E/C.A./5, Geneva, July 31, 1929; International Educational Cinematographic Institute, *Report of the Permanent Executive Committee to the Governing Body*, I.C.E./C.A./10, Geneva, September 30, 1930. The connections between the league's investment in using cinema to develop new agricultural practices and those of the USDA were specifically examined in "The Use of Educational Motion Pictures by the United States Department of Agriculture," *International Review of Educational Cinematography* 1, no. 5 (November 1929): 591–95. On the work of the institute, see also "The Role and the Purpose of

the International Educational Cinematographic Institute," *International Review of Educational Cinematography* 1 (July 1929): 12–25; Wilke, "Cinematography," in particular 340–46.

48. L'IICE sponsored the *International Review of Educational Cinematography* (1929–35), followed by *Intercine* (1935). Both journals were published in English, French, German, Italian, and Spanish.

49. Maltby, "Cinema," 98.

50. Frederick Herron to Earl Bright, July 22, 1929, Motion Picture Association of America Archives, New York, Reel 7, 1929, League of Nations File, cited in Maltby, "Cinema," 98.

51. Maltby, "Cinema," 98.

52. Ibid., in particular 99–104.

53. International Educational Cinematography Institute, *Report to the Council on the Second Session of the Governing Body*, held in Rome, October 2–4, 1929, C.3, M.1 (1930), 8.

54. "The Cinema at the Service of the Scientific Organisation of Labour," *International Review of Educational Cinematography* 1, no. 1 (July 1929): 90.

55. "The Film in the Service of Scientific Management," *International Review of Educational Cinematography* 2, no. 1 (January 1930): 71.

56. Coutrot, "Cinema and Scientific Management," 840–41.

57. "The Federation of British Industries," *International Review of Educational Cinematography* noted in early 1930, "is preparing to publish a series of films illustrating the several branches of national production in the industrial field and the methods used in marketing the commodities." "Industry and the Film," *International Review of Educational Cinematography* 2, no. 1 (January 1930): 74.

58. "The Cinema as an Auxiliary to the Scientific Organisation of Labour," *International Review of Educational Cinematography* 2, no. 6 (June 1930): 717. See also Druik, "'Reaching the Multimillions,'" 76.

59. Letter from British League of Nations Union, dated April 26, 1932, 6A. 33439. Steiner describes the British League of Nations Union as "one of the most influential and largest pressure groups of the 1920s." Steiner, *Lights That Failed*, 359.

60. Letter from the secretary of the Organisation of Intellectual Cooperation to the British League of Nations Union, dated April 16, 1932, 6A. 33439/32641; International Educational Cinematographic Institute, *Report to the Council on the Fifth Session of the Governing Body of the Institute*, held October 26–27, 1932, C. 33 M. 12 1933, 5.

61. Anghie, *Imperialism*, in particular 262–65. The Mandates system, Mazower writes, "extended imperial control in a less overt form." Mazower, *Governing the World*, 166.

62. Intellectual Cooperation Organisation, *Report by Professor A. Rocco, Chairman of the Governing Body of the International Educational Cinematographic Institute, on the Institute's Activities*, Geneva, June 27, 1933, C.I.C.I. 323, 9.

63. The British report on the Bantu Educational Kinema Experiment was shared with the league and a copy, with the classification mark B.17580. 2745 and a stamp saying "received 8 July 1935," can be found in the league's archives.

64. The first draft of the convention was circulated from early 1930. International Educational Cinematographic Institute, "Preliminary Draft International Convention for the Abolition of Customs Barriers against Educational Films," I.C.E/C.E.P./5, Geneva, January 30, 1930.

65. *Convention for Facilitating the International Circulation of Films of an Educational Character* (1933; repr. London: His Majesty's Stationery Office, 1935), 2.

66. The MPPDA could accordingly happily support that latter imperative and was consistently supportive of the league's efforts to foster economic circulation. Even so, it worked to influence the convention to make sure that the "educational" in "educational cinema" was narrowly defined to avoid European producers, including "entertainment films with pedagogic elements." See the account in Maltby, "Cinema," 98–99.

67. The 1926 congress in Paris, for example, had similarly "recommended" that "Western films shall portray in a simple, romantic, ethical and entertaining matter the history, culture, science, and powerful industrial developments of the Western nations—the heritage of humanity—and that the film should likewise serve to reveal the ancient culture, and all the wonders of the East." Cited in Seabury, *Motion Picture Problems,* 361. Druik remarks on this passage that "This fundamentally orientalist framework reflected the League's conceptualization of film as an instrument of colonization and promotion of European culture." Druik, "'Reaching the Multimillions,'" 73.

68. See the account in International Educational Cinematographic Institute, *Report to the Council of the League of Nations of the Seventh Session of the Governing Body of the Institute,* Stresa, June 24, 1934, C.350.M.163, 1934.

69. Mazower, *Dark Continent,* 72. "Mussolini and Hitler accepted the basic geopolitical tenets of nineteenth-century imperialism," Mazower observes, "while jettisoning its liberalism" (72).

70. Hobsbawm, *Age of Extremes,* 37. The Japanese had proposed a clause declaring the principle of racial equality to the covenant of the league in 1919, but this was dismissed because it was straightforwardly inconsistent with the ideas of racial and civilizational hierarchy integral to segregationist policies in the United States and to European imperialism. See Mazower, *Governing the World,* 162–64.

71. Mazower, *Governing the World,* 183.

72. Hawley, "Herbert Hoover," 116–40.

73. Hilmes, *Hollywood and Broadcasting,* 26–77.

74. Headrick, *Invisible Weapon.*

75. Douglas, *Inventing American Broadcasting,* 102–43, 266–67.

76. Ibid., 268–79.

77. *Annual Report of the Secretary of the Navy,* 1918, cited in Douglas, *Inventing American Broadcasting,* 280.

78. Sobel, *RCA,* 37.

79. RCA served as the independent marketing arm of the patents pool. GE and Westinghouse thus manufactured RCA receivers and parts, with 60 percent of production assigned to GE and 40 percent to Westinghouse. AT&T made and sold transmitters and controlled both wired and wireless telephony. All of the companies owned RCA stock and had representatives on the RCA board of directors. Smulyan, *Selling Radio,* 43.

80. The chairman of the RCA board was General James G. Harbord, who worked for Morgan's Bankers Trust Co. Fellow board members, Douglas Gomery observes, included Newton D. Baker, director of seven other companies including Mutual Life Insurance Company, Cleveland Trust Company, the Baltimore and Ohio Railroad, and the Goodyear Tire

and Rubber Company. "In other words," Gomery concludes, "RCA was fully integrated into corporate America." Gomery, *History of Broadcasting,* 23.

81. Douglas, *Inventing American Broadcasting,* 288.

82. Ibid., 290.

83. Smulyan, *Selling Radio,* 53–55.

84. One hundred and sixty-six broadcast licenses were issued to colleges and universities between 1921 and 1925, and almost as many broadcasters were affiliated with other types of nonprofit organizations. McChesney, *Telecommunications,* 14.

85. Smulyan, *Selling Radio,* 22. See also Wik, "Radio in Rural America."

86. Douglas, *Inventing American Broadcasting,* 309.

87. Hoover's stance was consistent with his corporate, liberal, probusiness agenda and with his interest in establishing cooperative associational groups encompassing business and government. In interviews and private correspondence, he asserted his belief in the superiority of a broadcasting system "in the hands of private enterprise," and that "those directly engaged in radio, particularly in broadcasting, should be able, to a very large extent, to regulate and govern themselves." Herbert Hoover, interview, *Cleveland Plain Dealer,* Summer 1925; Herbert Hoover to Karl Broadley, November 24, 1925, both cited in McChesney, *Telecommunications,* 13.

88. Douglas, *Inventing American Broadcasting,* 316.

89. Hilmes, *Hollywood and Broadcasting,* 17.

90. RCA, *Why America Leads in Radio* (New York, 1924), cited in Boddy, "Rhetoric," 40.

91. "First Car Radios—History and Development of Early Car Radios," Radio Museum, accessed November 7, 2014, www.radiomuseum.org/forum/first_car_radios_history_and_development_of_early_car_radios.html.

92. Hilmes, *Hollywood and Broadcasting,* 18–19.

93. Gomery, *History of American Broadcasting,* 18.

94. Complaints by citizens and other broadcasters had reached the point, Michele Hilmes argues, "that it behooved RCA/NBC to be able to point to the existence of at least one viable competitor in order to head off antimonopoly legislation." Hilmes, *Hollywood and Broadcasting,* 20.

95. Gomery, *History of American Broadcasting,* 23–28. See also Hilmes, *Hollywood and Broadcasting,* 43–45.

96. Marchand, *Advertising the American Dream,* 94.

97. Gomery, *History of American Broadcasting,* 38–47.

98. McChesney, *Telecommunications,* 15–18.

99. Ibid., 18–29.

100. Ibid., 28, 66.

101. McChesney, *Telecommunications,* 38–91; McChesney, *Rich Media, Poor Democracy,* in particular 193–213.

102. Bernays, *Biography of an Idea,* 432.

103. McChesney, *Rich Media, Poor Democracy,* 218.

104. See also Streeter, *Selling the Air.* This brings to mind the joke of a friend of mine, Mark Betz, which is this: self-regulation.

105. Chomsky and Herman, *Manufacturing Consent;* McChesney, *Rich Media, Poor Democracy.*

CHAPTER 10

1. Lasswell, *Propaganda,* 222. Stuart Ewen quotes this same passage in his brilliant history of public relations. Ewen, *Pr!,* 175. Ewen appears also in Adam Curtis's remarkable documentary series *The Century of the Self* (BBC, 2002). I draw on both for my understanding of the history of PR in particular.

2. E. Ross, *Social Control;* Lippmann, *Public Opinion,* 158.

3. Gerstle, "Protean Character," 1043–73; Agamben, *State of Exception,* 86–88.

4. Bernays, "This Business of Propaganda," 198.

5. Bernays, "Engineering of Consent"; McGovern, "Consumption and Citizenship," in Strasser, McGovern, and Judt, *Getting and Spending.*

6. On wealth disparity in the 1920s, see, for example, Dawley, *Struggles for Justice,* 337–39. On growing contemporary inequalities, see, for example, Piketty, *Capital.*

7. Press agents were first noticed in the presidential primary in 1912. Turner, "Manufacturing Public Opinion," 322. Bernays, who had been a theatrical press agent, invented the term *Counsel on Public Relations* after the war to escape the stigma that was starting to be associated with propaganda. See the account of this in Bernays, *Biography of an Idea,* 287–97. The Library of Congress has digitized some material relating to Coolidge's presidency and the period. Included is a typewritten definition of the term *public relations,* written by Bernays in 1927. The Counsel on Public Relations "interprets the client to the public and the public to his client" and is a "creator of events" and "crystallizer of public opinion." Bernays, "Counsel on Public Relations: A Definition," January 26, 1927, *Prosperity and Thrift: The Coolidge Era and the Consumer Economy, 1921–1929,* Library of Congress.

8. Lippmann, *Public Opinion,* 18. I use the typescript manuscript written about this event by Bernays, "Breakfast with Coolidge," which is included in the *Prosperity and Thrift* material at the Library of Congress. It is dated February 8, 1962; the corresponding chapter in Bernays's memoirs is on pages 339–42. Bernays also mentions this event briefly in an interview in Curtis, *The Century of the Self* (episode 1, "Happiness Machines").

9. Bernays, "Breakfast with Coolidge," 4, 11 (emphasis added).

10. Bernays, "Putting Politics," 472.

11. Dawley, *Struggles for Justice,* 297–333.

12. Freud, *Group Psychology.*

13. On this shift see, for example, Fink, *Progressive Intellectuals,* 13–51.

14. Freud, *Civilization and Its Discontents.*

15. In his memoirs Bernays recalled a dinner at his home in New York in 1933: "Karl von Wiegand, foreign correspondent of the Hearst newspapers, an old hand at interpreting Europe and just returned from Germany, was telling us about Goebbels and his propaganda plans to consolidate Nazi power. Goebbels had shown Wiegand his propaganda library, the best Wiegand had ever seen. Goebbels, said Wiegand, was using my book *Crystallizing Public Opinion* as a basis for his destructive campaign against the Jews of Germany. This shocked me. . . . Obviously the attack on the Jews of Germany was no emotional outburst of the Nazis, but a deliberate, planned campaign." Bernays, *Biography of an Idea,* 652.

16. Addams, *Spirit of Youth,* 93.

17. The broad outline of that shift is delineated in D. Ross, *Origins,* in particular 53–97.

18. On the broad currency of ideas of mimesis for subject formation, see the essays collected in Borch-Jacobsen, *Emotional Tie;* for the central place ideas of mimesis occupied in social thought in America in the early twentieth century, see Leys, "Mead's Voices," 277–307. On the import of this mimetic paradigm on Freud and psychoanalysis, see Borch-Jacobsen, *Freudian Subject*; and on psychology and social psychology, see Allport, "Historical Background."

19. Sarbin, "Attempts to Understand," 759–67.

20. Bernheim, *Suggestive Therapeutics*, 125, 15 (emphasis added).

21. Bernheim, *Suggestive Therapeutics*, 164. On Bernheim and hypnosis, see Gauld, *History of Hypnotism*, 334–40.

22. Freud, "Preface," in Freud, *Standard Edition*. Freud wrote this after visiting with Bernheim on the way to the International Congress for Experimental and Therapeutic Hypnosis in Paris in 1889. See Ellenberger, *Discovery of the Unconscious*, 762.

23. Andriopoulos, *Possessed*.

24. Scipio Sighele, *Le Crime à Deux*; Le Bon, *Crowd;* Tarde, *Laws of Imitation;* Sidis, *Psychology of Suggestion;* Park, *Crowd and the Public*.

25. Tarde, *Laws of Imitation*, 68.

26. R. Nye, *Origins of Crowd Psychology*, 59–190; Barrows, *Distorting Mirrors*, 7–42, 73–92.

27. Le Bon, *Crowd*, 34.

28. Ibid., 21.

29. Ibid., 108, 71.

30. McDougall, *Introduction to Social Psychology;* Wallas, *Human Natures in Politics;* W. Trotter, *Instincts of the Herd*. See also Allett, "Crowd Psychology," 213–27.

31. Le Bon, *Crowd*, 26.

32. Tarde, *Laws of Imitation*, xiv (emphasis added).

33. Howard, "Social Psychology," 36.

34. Leys, "Mead's Voices," 278–79. Ewen reports that *"The Crowd* had a resounding impact on an entire generation of social thought." Ewen, *PR!,* 64. The broad configuration of American social thought in the period is surveyed and examined in Bramson, *Political Context of Sociology*; and D. Ross, *Origins*. On the human sciences and the university, see Veysey, *Emergence*, 73–78.

35. Baldwin, *Mental Development*, 336–38 (emphasis added).

36. Ibid., 487–88.

37. Veysey, *Emergence*, 73–78, 117–18; D. Ross, "Development," in Oleson and Voss, *Organization of Knowledge*.

38. Bramson, *Political Context of Sociology*, in particular 11–46.

39. On Tarde's influence on Edward Ross, see Bramson, *Political Context of Sociology*, 58; on Tarde's influence in the United States more generally, see Clark, *Gabriel Tarde*, 65–66.

40. E. Ross, *Social Control*. On Ross's influential work, see also Weinberg, *Edward Alsworth Ross*.

41. Dewey, "Need for Social Psychology," 272.

42. Park and Burgess, *Introduction*, 785, 42.

43. RM. Williams, "Sociology in America," in Bonjean, Schneider, and Lineberry, *Social Science in America*, 83.

44. E. Ross, *Social Psychology;* E. Ross, "Nature and Scope," 577–83.

45. E. Ross, *Social Psychology,* 87.

46. Crowd psychology and related work on suggestion and imitation tended in the United States to focus more clearly on media than actual physical assemblies. John Durham Peters makes a similar observation in "Satan and Savior," 258.

47. Addams, *Spirit of Youth,* 86.

48. Grieveson, *Policing Cinema,* 11–22, 58–66; Grieveson, "Cinema Studies," in Grieveson and Wasson, *Inventing Film Studies,* 3–37.

49. John Collier, "The Problem of Motion Pictures," reprinted by the National Board of Censorship from the proceedings of the child welfare conference, Clark University, June 1910, in box 74, NBR (emphasis added).

50. William A. McKeever, *Good Housekeeping,* August 1910, 184, 186.

51. Jump, "Social Influence," n.p.

52. Howard, "Social Psychology," 40.

53. Healy, *Individual Delinquent,* 307.

54. Ibid., 340.

55. Münsterberg, *Photoplay,* 97. On Münsterberg and industrial psychology, see Hale, *Human Science.* For Münsterberg's use of hypnosis, see Moskowitz, "Hugo Münsterberg," 834–38.

56. *Mutual Film Corporation v. Industrial Commission of Ohio,* 236 U.S. 230 (1915).

57. Vaughn, *Holding Fast,* 5–6.

58. Creel, *How We Advertised America.*

59. Charles A. Beard and Mary R. Beard, *The Rise of American Civilization* (New York, 1927), cited in Ewen, *PR!,* 119.

60. Dodge, "Psychology of Propaganda," 838.

61. Wallas, *Human Nature in Politics,* 18.

62. Lasswell, *Propaganda Technique,* 9.

63. McPherson, *Psychology of Persuasion;* Pierce, *Our Unconscious Mind;* Lipsky, *Man the Puppet.*

64. Lippmann, *Liberty and the News,* 1920; Lippmann, *Public Opinion,* 1922; Lippmann, *Phantom Public,* 1925.

65. J. Carey, *Communication as Culture,* 75.

66. Steel, *Walter Lippmann,* 172. Steel discusses Wallas's impact on Lippmann (27–28) and Lippmann's work in Europe (141–54).

67. Lippmann, *Public Opinion,* 23.

68. Ibid., 18.

69. Ibid., 50.

70. Ibid.

71. Ibid., 21.

72. Ibid., 96.

73. Ibid., 24.

74. Ibid., 29.

75. Ibid.

76. Ibid., 97.

77. Taylor Patterson, *Cinema Craftsmanship,* quoted in Lippmann, *Public Opinion,* 97; Lippmann, *Public Opinion,* 97.

78. Lippmann, *Public Opinion*, 96.

79. Lippmann, *Drift and Mastery*. Lippmann's work helping draft the text that became Wilson's Fourteen Points declaration, which mutated into the liberal lobbying organization the Council on Foreign Relations, is outlined in Steele, *Walter Lippmann*, 128–40.

80. Dewey made this argument about Lippmann forcefully in his 1927 book *The Public and Its Problems*.

81. Macpherson, *Life and Times*.

82. Lasswell, *Propaganda Technique;* Lasswell, "Propaganda," 521–27; Lasswell and Blumenstock, *World Revolutionary Propaganda*. "Lasswell's early career," J. Michael Sproule observes, "provides the clearest marker of academe's drift away from concerns about a manipulated public to an interest in a public measured and managed." Sproule, *Propaganda and Democracy*, 71.

83. A. Carey, *Taking the Risk;* Chomsky, *Necessary Illusions*.

84. Mark Crispin Miller, introduction to Bernays, *Propaganda*, 17.

85. Dewey, review of *Public Opinion* (originally published in the *New Republic*, 1922), cited in Fink, *Progressive Intellectuals*, 31.

86. Horkheimer and Adorno, *Dialectic of Enlightenment*.

87. Ewen writes, "To put it simply, Bernays's career—more than that of any other individual—roughed out what have become the strategies and practices of public relations in the United States." Ewen, *PR!*, 4. See also, John and Lamme, "Evolution of an Idea," 223–35.

88. Bernays, *Propaganda*, 54.

89. Bernays, *Biography of an Idea*, 157.

90. Bernays, *Biography of an Idea*, 157; Bernays, "Publicity in International Trade," 3.

91. Bernays, "Publicity in International Trade," 3.

92. Bernays, *Propaganda*, 27.

93. Ibid., 290–91.

94. Bernays, *Crystallizing Public Opinion*, 19.

95. Ibid., 9.

96. Bernays, *Propaganda*.

97. Bernays, *Biography of an Idea*, 291. See also Ewen, *PR!*, 159.

98. Bernays, *Biography of an Idea*, 49–61.

99. The strategies of the various producers of a cycle of white slave films from 1913, and the ensuing regulatory and legal consequences, are discussed in Grieveson, *Policing Cinema*, 151–91; on the PR strategies of exploitation filmmakers, see Schaefer, *Bold! Daring! Shocking! True!*, 96–135.

100. Bernays, *Propaganda*.

101. Ibid.

102. Bernays, *Biography of an Idea*, 149.

103. Ibid., 131.

104. Ibid., 316, 314, 318, 280.

105. Ibid., 406, 407.

106. Bernays, *Biography of an Idea*, 432. The biographer of Paley confirms this account, crediting Bernays with scripting the statement Paley made to Congress. S. Smith, *In All His Glory*, 132–35.

107. "I recognized the power of the processes I was working with," Bernays wrote elsewhere in his autobiography, "in each case an example of coincidence of interest between the public and the private interest." Bernays, *Biography of an Idea,* 208.

108. Ibid., 386.

109. Larry Tye has a fuller account of Bernays' work for American Tobacco that makes use also of Bernays's papers from the Library of Congress. Tye, *Father of Spin,* 23–50.

110. I draw on the following works in particular for my understanding of the history of communication studies: Hardt, *Critical Communication Studies*; Carey, *Communication as Culture*; Delia, "Communication Research," 20–98; Peters, "Democracy"; Gary, *Nervous Liberals,* in particular 85–130.

111. Chicago Motion Picture Commission Hearings, *Report,* 46.

112. Ibid., 134.

113. Watson and Lashley, *Report* (1920), 152.

114. Ibid., 152.

115. Watson and Lashley, *Report* (1921), 112. Erethitic in this context meant overly excitable.

116. I examine some aspects of that redefinition in Grieveson, *Policing Cinema,* 193–216.

117. Geiger, "Effects," 78, 80, 81.

118. Thrasher, *Gang,* 107, 108, 111.

119. The studies were all published in 1933 by Macmillan and included the following: P. W. Holaday and George G. Stoddard, *Getting Ideas from the Movies;* Ruth C. Peterson and L. L. Thurston, *Motion Pictures and the Social Attitudes of Children;* Frank K. Shuttleworth and Mark A. May, *The Social Conduct and Attitudes of Movie Fans;* W. S. Dysinger and Christian A Ruckmick, *The Emotional Response of Children to the Motion Picture Situation;* Charles C. Peters, *Motion Pictures and Standards of Morality;* Samuel Renshaw, Vernon L. Miller, and Dorothy Marquis, *Children's Sleep;* Herbert Blumer, *Movies and Conduct;* Herbert Blumer and Philip Hauser, *Movies, Delinquency and Crime.* The volume on film aesthetics, *How to Appreciate Motion Pictures,* was authored by Edgar Dale, and W. W. Charters' overview of the PFS was entitled *Motion Pictures and Youth: A Summary.* Two additional studies were published in 1935, both by Edgar Dale: *The Content of Motion Pictures* and *Children's Attendance at Motion Pictures.* The eleventh study, *Boys, Movies, and City Streets,* by Frederick M. Thrasher and Paul G. Cressey, never appeared.

120. Frances Payne Bingham Bolton was born to a wealthy industrialist family, and she used a large inheritance from her uncle, Oliver Hazard Payne, to finance philanthropic activities related in particular to children. He had made an enormous fortune after becoming associated with the formation of US Steel, with J. P. Morgan; after becoming affiliated with Rockefeller's Standard Oil; and as the organizer of the American Tobacco Trust.

121. For the most complete account of the establishment of the Payne Fund Studies, see Jowett, Jarvie, and Fuller, *Children and the Movies,* 17–56.

122. Short, *Generation of Motion Pictures,* 33.

123. On the import and influence of Addams's work for the development of sociology at the University of Chicago, see D. Ross, *Origins,* 226–27.

124. Jowett, Jarvie, and Fuller, *Children and the Movies,* 60–61.

125. On the import of the program at Chicago, see Mathews, *Quest,* in particular 85–157. The other institutions included Ohio State, the University of Iowa, New York University, and Yale University.

126. Jowett, Jarvie, and Fuller, *Children and the Movies,* 64.

127. W. W. Charters, "Chairman's Preface," in Dysinger and Ruckmick, *Emotional Responses of Children,* viii.

128. Ibid.

129. Dysinger and Ruckmick, *Emotional Responses of Children,* 117–18; Ruckmick, "How?," 210. See also Malin, "Mediating Emotion," 366–90.

130. Peterson and Thurstone, *Motion Pictures.*

131. M. Anderson, "Taking Liberties," in Grieveson and Wasson, *Inventing Film Studies,* 43, 49.

132. Park, *Crowd and the Public.* On Park, see Odum, *American Sociology,* 131–35; D. Ross, *Origins,* in particular 306–08.

133. On collective behavior, see Park and Burgess, *Introduction,* 865–933 (for Le Bon specifically, see 887–92, 905–9); on social control, see Park and Burgess, 27–42, 785–853. On Park's work on crowds, cities, and social control, see also R. Turner, *Robert E. Park.*

134. Robert Park, "Suggestions for a Study of the Influence of Moving Pictures on Juvenile Delinquency" (1928), cited in Jowett, Jarvie, and Fuller, *Children and the Movies,* 71.

135. On Park's reluctant exit from the project, see Jowett, Jarvie, and Fuller, *Children and the Movies,* 71. On symbolic interactionism, and Blumer's work therein, see for example, Denzin, *Symbolic Interactionism,* 106–14.

136. Blumer and Hauser, *Movies, Delinquency, and Crime.*

137. Ibid., 30, 201, 35, 79.

138. Ibid., 198, 202.

139. Blumer, *Movies and Conduct,* 74. Richard Butsch makes this connection also in his essay "Class and Audience Effects," 114 . Blumer draws explicitly on work on mass behavior in his account of the effects of cinema in "Moulding," 115–27.

140. Blumer, *Movies and Conduct,* 198.

141. Ibid., 126.

142. Jowett, Jarvie, and Fuller, *Children and the Movies,* 115. Cressey's unfinished and unpublished study is included in this book (133–216).

143. See DeFleur and Ball-Rokeach, *Theories of Mass Communication,* 168–201.

144. M. Anderson, "Taking Liberties," 45.

145. Press releases from autumn 1932 proclaimed the studies had found evidence of the deleterious effects of the movies. Jowett, Jarvie, and Fuller, *Children and the Movies,* 94. Forman also published three articles in the popular women's magazine *McCall's:* Henry James Forman, "To the Movies—But Not to Sleep!," *McCall's,* September 1932, 12–13; Forman, "Movie Madness," *McCall's,* October 1932, 14–15; Forman, "Molded by Movies," *McCall's,* November 1932, 17.

146. Forman, *Our Movie Made Children,* 4.

147. Ibid.

148. "Child's Reactions to Movies Is Shown," *New York Times,* May 28, 1933. On Short's press offensive, see Jowett, Jarvie, and Fuller, *Children and the Movies,* in particular 95–101.

149. Jowett, Jarvie, and Fuller, *Children and the Movies,* 111.

150. "A Code to Maintain Social and Community Values in the Production of Silent, Synchronized and Talking Motion Pictures," March 31, 1930, in "Documents on the Genesis of the Production Code," ed. Richard Maltby, *Quarterly Review of Film and Video* 15, no. 4 (1995): 61.

151. See Garth Jowett, "Politics and the Payne Fund," accessed July 21, 2014, www.case. edu/artsci/wrss/documents/Jowett_001.pdf. The paper has no publication details with it. Jowett writes, "Mr. and Mrs. Bolton, an important part of the Republican political organization in Ohio, were not eager to run head-on into Will Hays and the motion picture industry. For that reason the work of the National Committee was kept relatively quiet with little public fanfare of their early achievements" (53).

152. Adler, *Art and Prudence,* in particular 147–212. Jarvie suggests that Adler was "directly encouraged" in his research by the MPPDA. Jowett, Jarvie, and Fuller, *Children and the Movies,* 116, 366n91.

153. Maltby, "Production Code."

154. Moley, *Are We Movie Made?*

155. For details, see L. Jacobs, "Reformers and Spectators," 36–40.

156. L. Jacobs, "Reformers and Spectators." In *Movies and Conduct,* Blumer had also suggested that instruction could produce emotional distance, thus counteracting the processes of emotional possession. "The more effective and so desirable form of control comes," he wrote, "through instruction and through frank discussion" (140).

157. I. Hunter, *Culture and Government.*

158. I examine some of that history, including some of the developments beginning in the 1930s and continuing in the postwar period, in Grieveson, "Discipline and Publish," 168–75.

159. Wasson, *Museum Movies.*

160. See McChesney, "Payne Fund," in Jowett, Jarvie, and Fuller, *Children and the Movies,* 303–35.

161. Gary, *Nervous Liberals,* 86.

162. Lasswell, "Structure and Function," in Bryson, *Communication of Ideas,* 37. In *Nervous Liberals,* Gary writes, "Normally attributed solely to Lasswell, the 'who said what to whom and with what effect?' paradigm was actually the product of months and months of paper exchanges, meetings, and oral and written dialogue among seminar members" (88).

163. Gary, *Nervous Liberals,* 88, 91.

164. I draw for this brief outline of the American Film Center from Gary, *Nervous Liberals,* 109–14.

165. Kracauer, *From Caligari to Hitler.* See Wasson, *Museum Movies,* 125, 145.

166. See, for example, DeFleur and Ball-Rokeach, *Theories of Mass Communication,* 188–95.

167. Hardt, *Critical Communication Studies,* 132–44.

168. J. Carey, "Communications and the Progressives," 265.

169. Seabury to Short, December 13, 1927, cited in Jowett, Jarvie, and Fuller, *Children and the Movies,* 41.

CHAPTER 11

1. Hunter, Dulin and Co, *Golden Harvest*; Halsey, Stuart and Co, *Motion Picture Industry*.

2. Hunter, Dulin and Co, *Golden Harvest*, 17; Halsey, Stuart and Co, *Motion Picture Industry*, 4. Hunter, Dulin, for example, suggested nickelodeons came into existence in the 1890s, rather than in 1905, and *The Birth of a Nation* was released in 1913 rather than in 1915. Hunter, Dulin and Co, *Golden Harvest*, 8, 9. Janet Wasko's invaluable history of finance and Hollywood speculates that Halsey, Stuart based their report in large part on Hunter, Dulin's. Wasko, *Movies and Money*, 32. The figure of $1.5 billion was repeated, also in 1927, by Attilio H. Giannini, the president of the Bowery and East River National Bank. Giannini, "Financial Aspects," in J. Kennedy, *Story of the Films*, 91.

3. Hunter, Dulin and Co, *Golden Harvest*, 28. "Real estate, in the form of substantial theatres and office blocks bulks large in the typical balance sheet ... the motion picture concerns bid fair to become among the most extensive chain owners of business locations in the whole country." Halsey, Stuart and Co, *Motion Picture Industry*, 4. *Barron's* wrote the following: "Importance of the vast real estate holdings of these two companies [Paramount and Loews] is not sufficiently realized. It can be safely said that Famous Players and Loews are among the greatest owners of high grade real estate chain property in the world." *Barron's*, May 7, 1926, 18.

4. Hunter, Dulin and Co, *Golden Harvest*, 8. The figures reflect the rise in investments from 1925, the second stage of investment in Hollywood after that initiated immediately at the end of the war. Halsey, Stuart, for example, report that two hundred million dollars in securities were issued in 1925. Halsey, Stuart and Co, *Motion Picture Industry*, 22.

5. Halsey, Stuart and Co, *Motion Picture Industry*, 4.

6. Ibid., 3.

7. Halsey, Stuart and Co, *Motion Picture Industry*, 3; Hunter, Dulin and Co, *Golden Harvest*, 10 (emphasis added).

8. Halsey, Stuart and Co, *Motion Picture Industry*, 10; Hunter, Dulin and Co, *Golden Harvest*, 7.

9. Halsey, Stuart and Co, *Motion Picture Industry*, 20.

10. Halsey, Stuart and Co, *Motion Picture Industry*, 22. Halsey, Stuart was itself a significant investment bank, working in particular on public utility bonds as well as distributing South American securities. It grew "in size and prestige" between 1916 and 1930, by which point it ranked third among investment banks "in total volume of issues managed in the boom period of 1927–1931." Carosso, *Investment Banking in America*, 260. The company was, in 1928, "one of the very first investment houses to use radio advertising"—an interesting conjuncture of finance capital and corporate media in the immediate wake of the 1927 Radio Act. Carosso, *Investment Banking in America*, 260.

11. Nielsen, "Towards a Workers' History," in Alvarado and Thompson eds., *Media Reader*, 166–80.

12. Marx, *Capital*, 3:599; Hunter, Dulin and Co, *Golden Harvest*, 31.

13. Hunter, Dulin and Co, *Golden Harvest*, 12; Halsey, Stuart and Co, *Motion Picture Industry*, 28. A quick, simple economics lesson, for those like me with no background in economics (and no money): a bond promises to pay back money at a specified date and is

used by companies to raise finances through debt. This model of debt financing was massively expanded after the war. Debt financing does not involve ownership rights. Equity financing, which also became significant in the film industry beginning in the 1910s, includes the issuing of preferred and common stock by investment and (before 1933) commercial banking firms. Common and preferred stock represents ownership rights in a corporation and pays out dividends after payment of debt plus interest. The issuance of stocks and bonds usually happens through an investment bank or investment division of a commercial bank. These banks indirectly supply capital by acting as wholesalers or retailers of corporate bond and stock issues. Most often investment banks sell them on to other banks, either investment or commercial, or to large institutional investors (eg, pension or insurance funds). Commercial banks began to develop securities divisions after 1900, largely because this was becoming an increasingly significant way of generating capital, but the 1933 Glass-Steagall Act limited banks to either investment or commercial functions. Carosso, *Investment Banking in America,* in particular 79–109.

14. Marx, *Capital,* 1:248; Arrighi, *Long Twentieth Century,* 5–6, 8–9, *passim.*

15. Bond campaigns during the war had discovered and constructed a new market for securities. Bankers estimated the bond market in 1917 at 350,000 individuals, but the first Liberty Loan was subscribed to by over 4,000,000, and the subsequent issues reached 9.4, 18.4, 22.8, and 11.8 million subscriptions. "War bonds provided millions of Americans with their first experience in owning intangible property." Carosso, *Investment Banking in America,* 226. New investment bank and investment affiliates of commercial banks grew from this point, adding common and preferred stocks to their bond issues in the 1920s (Carosso, 273). Bond issues raised more new capital for corporations than stock issues until 1928, but that began to change in the "speculative fever" of 1928 and 1929 that preceded the stock market crash. Overall, new corporate securities issues increased from nearly $3 billion in 1920 to over $9 billion in 1929. Kotz, *Bank Control,* 43–44.

16. The report on Paramount for Kuhn, Loeb was written by H. D. H. Connick, vice president of the American International Corporation (AIC). The report is usefully summarized by Howard T. Lewis in his book *Cases on the Motion Picture Industry* (61–79), under the fictitious name Gilmore, Field, and Co. A copy of the actual report was also introduced in evidence in the Federal Trade Commission's (FTC) investigation into Paramount's business practices, which was initiated in 1921. Mark Lynn Anderson uncovered this in his research at the National Archives in Washington, DC, and, with characteristic generosity, shared a copy of the report with me. H. D. H. Connick, "Survey of the Motion Picture Industry with Particular Reference to the Famous Players—Lasky Corporation," Docketed Case Files, 1915–43, 835, Commission Exhibits 446, box 428, Auxiliary Case Files 1915–1936, Federal Trade Commission (hereafter Connick, "Survey"). I examine the report further below and, where possible, make reference to the appropriate pages in Lewis's book.

17. Carosso, *Investment Banking in America,* 219–20. In February and June 1915, Kuhn, Loeb bought two of the Pennsylvania Railroad bond issues, the first for fifty million dollars and the second for sixty-five million. The two issues were each paid with a single check, "the largest check up to that time ever drawn in the United States" (220).

18. For example, note the banal observation in Kristin Thompson and David Bordwell's textbook *Film History* that "increasing vertical integration" was "one of the main trends in the industry during the 1920s" and, despite the "rampant rise of racism" in that decade, the

"film industry, however, benefitted from the high level of capital available during this period, and its films reflected the fast pace of life in the 'Jazz Age'" (70, 156). Elsewhere, Adolph Zukor had his name changed to Adolf, probably a somewhat uncomfortable transformation for a Jewish émigré from central Europe (157). The neutral description of these developments, and the *benefits* capital brought to the industry, speak to a profound misreading of the ways this corporate form emerged in sync with expanding forms of finance capital and to the varied functions this had for the global expansion of capital. Orthodox economic accounts of Hollywood, where they exist, tend also to affirm the decisions that led to "vertical integration." For example, in their account of Warner Bros.' strategies in the 1920s, Michael Pokorny and John Sedgwick explore how they "led to a series of heroic corporate decisions in the direction of vertical integration" ("Warner Bros.", 180). I tend not to think of the control and commodification of media, culture, and the public sphere as a heroic achievement.

19. I paraphrase Frederic Jameson here, who in an essay on the cultures of globalization talks of "the becoming cultural of the economic, and the becoming economic of the cultural." Jameson, "Notes on Globalization," 60. Elsewhere, Jameson usefully reminds us that "mass cultural production and consumption itself are as profoundly economic as the other productive areas of late capitalism and as fully a part of the latter's generalized commodity system" ("Culture and Finance Capital," 252).

20. *Federal Trade Commission v. Famous Players-Lasky et al.*, Complaint No. 835 (1921).

21. Wasko estimates that nearly 20 percent of the boards of directors of the six largest film corporations in the late 1920s were bankers. Wasko, *Movies and Money*, 47.

22. Kotz's *Bank Control of Large Corporations in the United States* is particularly helpful in this context. But see also Thomas Guback's useful foreword to Wasko's *Movies and Money*, xii–iii. The question of control is empirical and conceptual. In brief, early work on finance capital in the 1910s suggested that banks played the most significant roles in the development of monopoly capitalism and that these financial interests began to dominate the operations of corporations. This sense of the power of "financial groups" and "trusts" to control industries was widely articulated also in the Progressive Era United States. Yet other scholars began to argue that large transnational corporations became independent of financial groups and so were the primary units of advanced capitalism (eg, Baron and Sweezy, *Monopoly Capitalism*). Kotz provides a useful summary of the back and forth between the managerialist and financial control positions (see in particular 1–13) and sides mostly with the latter position. Congressional and other governmental studies undertaken in the 1930s, Kotz argues, "documented many cases of financial control over nonfinancial corporations during the 1920s," so that the "evidence suggests that through the 1920s financial control remained a major form of control, and probably the most prevalent type of control, over large manufacturing, railroad, and power utility corporations" (49). I propose to be as precise and empirical as possible with the specific example of film studios, which frequently manifested a complex mix of owner, managerial, and financial control across the period of the interwar years.

23. I refer to this corporation by the name Paramount here for the sake of simplicity. It is rooted in the company Famous Players, established by Adolph Zukor in 1912. Zukor made an agreement in 1914 with the distribution company Paramount, and in 1916 he took over Paramount and also merged it with Jesse L. Lasky's Feature Play Company to form Famous

Players-Lasky. In 1925 Famous Players—Lasky merged with Balaban and Katz, a Chicago-based theater chain that owned many important first-run theaters in the Midwest. The firm as a whole came to be called Paramount—Publix. For a succinct history, see Gomery, *Hollywood Studio System*, 11–26.

24. H. Lewis, *Cases*, vii. Kennedy's involvement in the film industry is explored in Beauchamp, *Joseph Kennedy*.

25. H. Lewis, *Cases*, 61–62. See also Zukor, "Origin and Growth," in J. Kennedy, *Story of the Films*, 73.

26. H. Lewis, *Cases* 62. It seems possible that the 1919 in-house publication called *The Story of the Famous Players-Lasky Corporation*, uncovered by Mark Lynn Anderson in his research on (among other things) early histories of Hollywood, is the report initially produced by the studio for Kuhn, Loeb. Mark generously shared the publication with me. It is part detailed account of the history and operations of the studio, complete with financial information, and public relations guff. Even if it were not directly written for the bank, some of the details in it reappear directly in Connick's report, suggesting that he at least saw the publication as he was investigating the corporation. (For example, the list of national and global distribution offices is the same across both texts.) Anderson describes the publication as "a business history of the studio" that includes materials on its capital stock, its history, details of corporate structure and infrastructure, personnel, and budgets. *Story* emphasizes the enormity of the reach of Paramount—the "corporation encircles the globe"—and the mechanization of its operations. Anderson, "Historian Is Paramount," 14; Famous Players Lasky Corporation, *Story*, 5. Written for, or at least certainly used by, an investment bank, the report makes clear both the influence of Taylorist and Fordist practices on film production, as well as the way the studio presented itself to the holders of capital as a modern and technologically efficient business enterprise.

27. The organization of AIC appears to have been led by the National City Bank, which had particular interests in Latin America. See Frank Moore Colby and Talcott Williams, *The New International Encyclopaedia*, vol. 23 (January 1917), 399. Wasko suggests the company was organized by Frank Vanderlip, president of the National City Bank, to exploit foreign trade and to profit from the war and its weakening effect on Europe. Wasko, *Movies and Money*, 42n4. In this sense the organization was straightforwardly a motor of the process that shifted global economic power from Europe to the United States.

28. Vice President Connick wrote the report, and when he later testified before the Federal Trade Commission about his role in Paramount, he noted that he had been the "director of works of the Panama Pacific Exposition." *New York Telegraph*, April 23, 1923.

29. See Carosso, *Investment Banking in America*, 19, 81–82. Clyde Barrow suggests the Kuhn, Loeb financial group was allied with the Bank of Manhattan, with several significant railroads (including the Pennsylvania, Union Pacific, Chicago, and Northwestern), and with Western Union Telegraph Co. Barrow, *Universities*, 22.

30. The figures reported were 15,000 cinemas in the United States in 1919, with an aggregate seating capacity of over 8 million, which produced an estimated total annual income for theaters of $675 million for the theatrical year ending August 31, 1918. The export of film from the United States increased in value from just over $200 million in 1913 to nearly $600 million in the first six months of 1919. Paramount estimated there were 17,240 theaters "in foreign countries." Weekly sales of positive film stock increased from 3 million feet in 1913

to 10 million in 1919. The sale of Simplex projection machines increased from 1,000 in 1912 to 5,000 in 1920. In 1919, fan magazines had a circulation of 950,000. Connick, "Survey," 6–8; H. Lewis, *Cases,* 62–67.

31. For example, John E. Barber, of the First National Bank of Los Angeles and the Los Angeles Trust and Savings, wrote an article in the financial paper *Barron's* entitled "The Appeal of Motion Pictures to Capital," which described "the distribution of the product [as] the most important division of the industry to anyone with a financial interest in pictures." *Barron's,* April 24, 1922, 11. See also John E. Barber, "The Bankers and the Motion Picture Industry," *Coast Banker,* June 1921, 664–65; and Flint, "Financing the Motion Pictures," in Photoplay Research Society of Los Angeles, *Opportunities,* 112–13.

32. Connick, "Survey," 18–19; H. Lewis, *Cases,* 67.

33. Connick, "Survey," 32.

34. H. Lewis, *Cases,* 76.

35. Connick, "Survey," 3.

36. H. Lewis, *Cases,* 78–79.

37. Conant, *Antitrust,* 25.

38. Chandler, *Visible Hand,* 285.

39. Connick, "Survey," 41; H. Lewis, *Cases,* 76. Connick's comment referred back to his observation that the executives had not had "corporate training" ("Survey," 40).

40. H. Lewis, *Cases,* 73.

41. *Wall Street Journal,* December 11, 1919, 15. Later the *Wall Street Journal* reported that F. G. Lee resigned his position at Irving National Bank "to accept active chairmanship of [the] finance committee of Famous Players-Lasky Corp." Zukor said, "'He was the first banker in the United States . . . to make a study of the motion picture business and to recognize its investment qualities. He is particularly valuable to Famous Players—Lasky Corp. and to the entire industry since he knows both the picture business and finance.'" (*Wall Street Journal,* December 14, 1921, 7).

42. The final part of Connick's report explored, approvingly, Zukor's plans to buy and construct new cinemas and so vertically integrate his company to tap the profits accruing from exhibition, or, in Connick's language, "Mr Zukor's plan to sell his product direct to the people." Connick, "Survey," 43, 43–48.

43. "Famous Players-Lasky Corp. Offers 25,000 Shares Stock," *Wall Street Journal,* June 26, 1919, 9.

44. Connick, "Survey," 21.

45. Zukor, "Origins and Growth," in J. Kennedy, *Story of the Films,* 59.

46. Zukor, "Origins and Growth," in J. Kennedy, *Story of the Films,* 61. On the earlier establishment of a theatrical star system, see McArthur, *Actors and American Culture.*

47. See here also Musser, "Conversions and Convergences," 154–74.

48. Economic historian Gerben Bakker has shown how "feature films were disproportionally and increasingly profitable" in this transitional period "and that therefore an escalation of outlays on sunk costs on feature film production could be a profitable strategy." Bakker, *Entertainment Industrialised,* 214.

49. Zukor, "Origins and Growth," in J. Kennedy, *Story of the Films,* 64. I emphasize "personality" here in light of Warren Susman's well-known and significant argument about

the shift from a culture of "character" to one of "personality" in the early twentieth century. Susman argues the transformation was one from a culture that validated character as duty, reputation, and moral rectitude toward one that "insisted on 'personality,' which emphasized being liked and admired." The validation of personality dovetailed with the new culture of abundance and consumption, marked by new technologies, institutions, and cultural forms (electricity, photography, department stories, comics, cinema, dime novels, etc), which emerged in the early twentieth century. Susman suggests the crucial staging ground for this shift was the 1920s and 1930s. Susman, *Culture as History,* 271–85.

50. Zukor, "Origins and Growth," 65.

51. Pickford started off at Famous Players in 1914 on twenty thousand dollars a year, which quickly became a thousand dollars a week. In 1915, the contract was renegotiated to two thousand dollars a week and half of the profits of her productions. In June 1916, a separate production unit called the Pickford Film Corporation was set up, so that in essence Pickford became an independent producer and partner to what was then Famous Players-Lasky. Pickford was to gain numerous bonuses—further control over the filmmaking process, ten thousand dollars a week, and 50 percent of the profits. Hampton, *History of the Movies,* 194; Balio, "Stars in Business," in Balio, *American Film Industry,* 157–63.

52. Bowser, *Transformation of Cinema,* 227.

53. Adolph Zukor, "Famous Players in Famous Plays," *Moving Picture World,* July 1914, 186 (my emphasis).

54. *In the Matter of Famous Players-Lasky Corp.,* 11 F.T.C. 187 (1927).

55. Two of the other significant production companies were Bosworth, Inc., and the Lasky Feature Play Company, organized by a former vaudeville producer working closely with the playwright and stage manager Cecil B. DeMille. The number of films needed to supply cinemas that changed programs twice per week was 104. Before Paramount, the distribution system for the new feature films either proceeded through selling the film rights territory-by-territory to buyers, who rented them out for a flat fee (the so-called states rights method) and through film exhibitions arranged by the producers themselves, the approach Zukor used for *Queen Elizabeth* and others. *Motion Picture World,* July 27, 1912, 311. Paramount was significant then because unlike the states rights system, it distributed on a percentage basis, which allowed producers to share in the success of their films. The shift enabled distributors and producers, that is, to control rental value. Long runs also made possible more sustained efforts to advertise films.

56. Hampton, *History of the Movies,* 154–61; Dick, *Engulfed,* 10–12.

57. *In the Matter of Famous Players-Lasky Corp.,* 11 F.T.C., 187 (1927). The precise timeline of these events is laid out in the FTC decision, which gives May 20, 1916 as the date Zukor and Lasky acquired 50 percent of the capital stock of Paramount and July 19, 1916 as the date the "Famous Players–Lasky Corporation" was "incorporated" (11 FTC, 202). Connick's report for AIC and Kuhn, Loeb likewise gave the date of the "incorporation" of the company as July 1916. H. Lewis, *Cases,* 68.

58. Dick, *Engulfed,* 11.

59. The FTC investigation of and decision on Famous Players–Lasky listed contracts between the company and S. A. Lynch Enterprises, a southern exhibition chain, signed in April 1917, and the acquisition of stock and interests in other significant theaters and theater

chains, beginning notably in early 1919. *In the Matter of Famous Players-Lasky Corp.,* 11 F.T.C. 187, 208–09 (1927). What this reveals was that Zukor's strategy of merging production, distribution, and exhibition was ongoing when he approached Kuhn, Loeb.

60. Huetting, *Economic Control.*

61. H. Lewis, *Motion Picture Industry,* 15–18. First National had some financial connections to the Bank of Italy. Puttnam, *Movies and Money,* 94.

62. Balio, "Stars in Business," in Balio, *American Film Industry,* 162.

63. Later, in 1923, First National constructed studios and began producing its own films; and later still, in 1928, First National was taken over by Warner Bros. H. Lewis, *Motion Picture Industry,* 17–18; *Wall Street Journal,* September 27, 1928, 3.

64. Indeed, as Mark Lynn Anderson astutely notes, Paramount itself told this history of First National in a similar way, in documents submitted to the FTC investigators, portraying "vertical integration as a necessary and even sensible defense against First National's backward integration into production … Here, FPL's enormity was no longer justified through discourses of efficiency and quality but through an argument about the necessity of vertical integration to preserve industrial competition." Anderson, "Historian Is Paramount," 17. Yet the history of the company's alliances with regional theater chains from 1917 onward makes it clear that the strategy to vertically integrate the industry began before the start of First National.

65. Connick's report for AIC had observed that a "theater with a larger seating capacity was at a financial advantage because the larger items of operating expense—management, film rental, and orchestra—did not increase proportionally with the number of seats." H. Lewis, *Cases,* 65; Connick, "Survey," 15–16.

66. The varied strategies of "coercion" and "intimidation" used by Paramount in this struggle are listed in the FTC decision and include threats to build competing theaters, to interfere with the supply of film, and to reduce prices in controlled theaters to destroy the business of others. *In the Matter of Famous Players-Lasky Corp.,* 11 F.T.C., 187, 193–94 (1927).

67. *In the Matter of Famous Players-Lasky Corp.,* 11 F.T.C., 204 (1927); Koszarski, *An Evening's Entertainment,* 75; Balio, *American Film Industry,* 223.

68. S. Ross, *Working-Class Hollywood.*

69. On distribution and the economics of the mainstream film industry, see, for example, Wasko, *How Hollywood Works,* 59–103.

70. Tedlow, *New and Improved.*

71. Marchand, *Advertising the American Dream,* 218, 221.

72. Ohmann, *Selling Culture.* The company's 1919 corporate history claimed it "was the *first* company to advertize *to the public* through the medium of national magazines." Famous Players-Lasky Corporation, *Story,* 51 (emphasis in original).

73. Hays, "Supervision from Within," in J. Kennedy, *Story of the Films,* 38.

74. Kent, "Distributing the Product," in J. Kennedy, *Story of the Films,* 204–5. The 1919 report for Kuhn, Loeb had noted twenty-seven film exchanges, suggesting some considerable growth in Paramount's distribution network between then and Kent's account in 1927. H. Lewis, *Cases,* 71.

75. Kent, "Distributing the Product," in J. Kennedy, *Story of the Films,* 211.

76. *The Story of the Famous Players—Lasky Corporation,* which was the publication used or at least read by Connick, listed a sales force of 1,241 people backed up by a

central office in New York of 300 people (27). The publication is littered with photographs of exchange offices and the people working in them, providing a photographic record of probably the least-visualized aspect of cinema history—the crucial networks of distribution.

77. Famous Players-Lasky Corporation, *Story*, 27.

78. Ibid., 44.

79. Ibid., 6. The corporation's elaborate "supervision" of these infrastructural processes made it necessary for a "salesman" to be "made to feel that the sleepless eye of the home office is always upon him" (30). The celebration of this rational efficiency in this publication suggests again that it was at least partly designed to impress investment bankers.

80. Ibid., 27.

81. Kent, "Distributing the Product," 222.

82. Famous Players-Lasky Corporation, *Story*, 71; cited also in M. Anderson, "Historian Is Paramount," 14.

83. See the description of the zone protection process in H. Lewis, *Motion Picture Industry*, 201–29.

84. The complex debates about accounting practices in the industry that one sees in the bank reports on Hollywood also revolved around this question of temporality and value. These were ultimately resolved by—as Mark Garrett Cooper has astutely observed—relocating "value in relationship to the habits of consumption" rather than in relationship to the cost of production. Cooper, *Love Rules*, 137. Paramount did this by writing off value as 80 percent in the first year, by writing off value as 20 percent in the second year, and by carrying the negative "on our books at one dollar" after the second year. Kent, "Distributing the Product," 222–23.

85. Kent, "Distributing the Product," 226.

86. The most complete accounts of this process are in Musser, *Emergence of Cinema*; and Bordwell, Staiger, and Thompson, *Classical Hollywood Cinema*, 155–240.

87. Tom Gunning, "D. W. Griffith and the Narrator System: Narrative Structure and Industry Organization in Biograph Films, 1908–1909" (PhD diss., New York University, 1986), 59, cited in Uricchio and Pearson, *Reframing Culture*, 47.

88. The articulation of this in the "transitional" years 1907–13 is best outlined in Keil, *Early American Cinema*.

89. Connick suggested fan magazines had a circulation of 950,000 by 1919. "Survey," 8. The emergence, form, and function of fan magazines are examined in Fuller, *At the Picture Show*, in particular 115–68. The increasing interest in the private lives of stars is explored by deCordova in *Picture Personalities*.

90. Connick, "Survey," 27 (my emphasis). See also H. Lewis, *Cases*, 68.

91. Halsey, Stuart and Co, *Motion Picture Industry*, 11.

92. Bernays, "Breakfast with Coolidge," 4; H. Lewis, *Motion Picture Industry*, 119.

93. R. Dale, "Visible Nation."

94. Writing in the business magazine entitled *System*, Zukor had observed as early as 1918 that "a star who is popular in Maine will be equally so not only in Arizona but also in England, China, and the Argentine" and that the "whole world likes Mary Pickford." Zukor, "Pleasing Most of the People Most of the Time," *System* 34, no. 4 (1918), 481, cited in Cooper, *Love Rules*, 140.

95. For a useful examination of some aspects of these commercial tie-ins between film, stars, and commodities, in the context of the rise of a consumer culture, see Eckert, "Carole Lombard"; Higashi, *Cecil B. DeMille.*

96. This is not a randomly chosen example. Reagan's work as spokesman and presenter for GE between 1954 and 1962 was significant to his conversion to conservatism and set the terms for his procorporate presidency in the 1980s. Evans, *Education of Ronald Reagan.*

97. Paramount devoted twelve pages to extolling the success of its "exploitation" of films, and of its extensive advertising and public relations departments, in Famous Players-Lasky Corporation, *Story,* 51–62.

98. Daly, *Literature, Technology, and Modernity,* 79.

99. It is a common misconception to label studio-era films simply "classical." Yes, certainly, linear narrative was integral to the pleasures they offered, but film was a commercial form that drew on traditions of melodrama to intersperse narrative with spectacle and other forms of pleasure, which maximized its audience reach. One sees this clearly in a film like *The Covered Wagon,* which had an overall linear construction telling the story of a wagon train from Kansas to the West Coast but intertwined and interspersed this with a romance plot and with various bits of spectacle and hokum (dance scenes, attacks by "Indians," races to the rescue, and so on). The idea that a Hollywood financed by banks, with investment bankers on the boards of studios, would prioritize only a particular kind of narrative form is absurd. Likewise, the idea that spectacle (or what too often gets called "attractions" in the field of early cinema studies) is simply distinct from narrative seems to me mistaken. Commercial film entertainment hybridizes narrative and other forms of spectacle in ways quite clearly influenced by melodrama in particular, joining together the pleasures of narrative with that of spectacle to maximize audience reach. On the import of melodrama for this form, see Altman, "Dickens," in Gaines, *Classical Hollywood,* 9–48; and L. Williams, "Melodrama Revised," in Browne, *Refiguring American Film Genres,* 42–88. The hybridization of linear narrative forms adopted in some respects from the novel and from melodrama derived largely from the stage is particularly visible in the early Paramount features, such as *The Prisoner of Zenda* (1914) and *Tess of the D'Urbervilles* (1914), which used stories drawn from well-known nineteenth-century novels but were based on the stage adaptations of those novels.

100. Harvey, *Seventeen Contradictions,* 59. Harvey is describing the general tendencies of capital to privately appropriate property and wealth. I am arguing that stories produced by central actors in this process—corporations, banks—have played a significant role in enabling and sustaining the fictions of capital.

101. For example, *Wall Street Journal,* May 6, 1920, 8 (on the formation of a company with three million dollars in capital for production and distribution in India); *Wall Street Journal,* January 20, 1920, 6 (on the construction of "a chain of large motion picture theaters from coast to coast"); and *Wall Street Journal,* July 10, 1922, 6.

102. Hunter, Dulin and Co, *Golden Harvest,* 7.

103. Perkins, *Wall Street,* 95–98. The US assets of the company were valued at about seven million dollars. Edmund Lynch became chair of the board of directors and de facto CEO, and the company concentrated initially on distribution. When Congress passed a protective tariff on imports of raw film stock, Lynch used a patent controlled by Pathé and

allied with DuPont Chemicals to produce raw film stock. DuPont was diversifying from armaments, and film stock was a lucrative business.

104. Conant, *Antitrust*, 25.

105. Bakker, *Entertainment Industrialised*, 218, 220.

106. See M. Anderson, *Twilight of the Idols*.

107. M. Anderson, "Historian Is Paramount," 29. Zukor's scandal, and the fallout in particular from the Taylor scandal, is explored also by William Mann in his historical novel *Tinseltown*.

108. *Wall Street Journal*, January 24, 1921, 8.

109. The letter is reproduced in Ramsaye, *Million and One Nights*, 816 (emphasis added).

110. Hays was to be paid $100,000 a year for three years. When his contract ended, it was increased to $150,000 a year, with an expense allowance of $100,000 a year, which did not need to be accounted for. (A quick Internet calculation suggests the salary would equal about $1.5 million today.) Trumpbour, *Selling Hollywood*, 293n19. The Hays Office was said to cost $2 million a year. H. Lewis, *Motion Picture Industry*, 218.

111. Hays, *Memoirs*, 325.

112. *Wall Street Journal*, March 15, 1922, 9. The full articles of incorporation are available in the online archive of MPPDA materials, organized by Richard Maltby and Ruth Vasey and housed at Flinders University. The precise URL for this record, no. 54, is http://mppda.flinders.edu.au/records/54. In 1924 a West Coast branch of the MPPDA, called the Association of Motion Picture Producers, was established. It was legally separated from the MPPDA to avoid antitrust litigation. Hawley, "Three Facets," 117. The fact there were New York and Hollywood branches indicates, as Ian Jarvie surmises, that the MPPDA was principally "the trade association of the major New York distributors." Jarvie, *Hollywood's Overseas Campaign*, 303.

113. "The first year," Hays wrote in his *Memoirs*, "we attacked four chief distribution problems: unethical practices of exhibitors, by which distributors were robbed of legitimate income; film thefts; an improved Railway Express plan for transportation of films; and regional boards of trade to assist in common problems of selling and distributing" (355).

114. Jarvie, *Hollywood's Overseas Campaign*, 303; Maltby, "Production Code," in Balio, *Grand Design*, 42.

115. Maltby, "Production Code," in Balio, *Grand Design*, 42.

116. Maltby, *Harmless Entertainment*, 97.

117. Hays, *Memoirs*, in particular 153–77, 246–51.

118. Ibid., 277.

119. Hawley, "Three Facets," 95–123.

120. Hays expressed the ideals of corporate liberalism precisely in his *Memoirs* in this way: "In a democratic commonwealth each business, each industry, and each art has as much right to, and as much duty towards self-regulation as the general citizenry to self-government" (327).

121. Perhaps the simplest apposite corresponding example is when Bernays, working on the assumption that this would both confer prestige and that the "masses" will "usually . . . follow the example of a trusted leader," invited various members of the medical and cultural elites of New York to attend the risqué play *Damaged Goods*. Bernays, *Propaganda*, 73.

122. Vasey, *World According to Hollywood*, 33–34.

123. Cited in Inglis, *Freedom of the Movies*, 5.

124. Hays, *Memoirs*, 337–38.

125. J. Horner Platten to D. W. Griffith, October 12, 1923, D. W. Griffith Collection, Museum of Modern Art, cited in Wasko, *Movies and Money*, 23.

126. J. Horner Platten, "Motion Pictures—A New Public Utility?," *Bankers Magazine*, October 1926, cited in Wasko, *Movies and Money*, 23.

127. *Wall Street Journal*, June 7, 1922, 7. The description of the Bond Club comes from their website. Accessed September 4, 2015, http://thebondclub.com/.

128. John E. Barber, "The Appeal of Motion Pictures to Capital," *Barron's*, April 24, 1922, 11.

129. Platten, "Motion Pictures," 458, cited in Wasko, *Movies and Money*, 23.

130. Hunter, Dulin and Co, *Golden Harvest*, 10–11.

131. Maltby, "Standard Exhibition Contract," 145.

132. Vasey, *World According to Hollywood*, 43.

133. Jarvie, *Hollywood's Overseas Campaign*, 313, 315–16, and more generally 302–35.

134. Hays, *Memoirs*, 365, 404.

135. Ibid., 504.

136. See here Cowen, *Deadly Life of Logistics*.

137. Julius Klein to F. H. Elliot, August 30, 1921, RG151, Bureau of Foreign and Domestic Commerce, General—Motion Pictures, NARA.

138. Klein to Hays, January 29, 1923, RG151, NARA.

139. Hays, *Memoirs*, 398.

140. Hays, *Memoirs*, 334. On this and its post–World War II expansion, see also Lee, "'Little State Department,'" 371–97.

141. Volume II, brief, Federal Trade Commission, cited in H. Lewis, *Cases*, 248.

142. *Federal Trade Commission v. Famous Players-Lasky Corporation, et al.*, Record of testimony, 17393, cited in H. Lewis, *Cases*, 234.

143. *In the Matter of Famous Players-Lasky Corp.*, 11 F.T.C. 187 (1927).

144. Ibid., 205–6.

145. H. Lewis, *Cases*, 256; *Annual Report of Federal Trade Commission*, June 30, 1928, 6–7.

146. Vasey, *World According to Hollywood*, 47–48.

147. Part of Paramount's response is cited in H. Lewis, *Cases*, 259–60.

148. *Federal Trade Comm. V. Paramount Famous Lasky Corp.*, 57 F. (2d) 152, 155 (C.C.A. 2d, 1932). See also "The Motion Picture Industry and the Anti-Trust Laws," *Columbia Law Review* 36 no. 4 (April 1936), 647–48.

149. The lawyers listed in the FTC decision for Paramount, Lasky, and Zukor were the firm Cravath, Henderson and DeGersdorff, as well as Gilbert Montague in New York City and Joseph Folk in Washington, DC. In her book *Gentlemen Bankers*, Susie Pak notes the "Cravath firm was actually Kuhn, Loeb & Co's counsel," and was occasionally used also by the House of Morgan (280n16). Montague's procorporate legal practices are examined in W. Wells, "Counterpoint to Reform," 423–50. Wells describes Montague as "one of the country's leading corporate lawyers" (423) and examines his work against antitrust regulation in support of forms of oligopoly that Montague regarded as more effectively "efficient" than open markets.

150. Lewis, *Motion Picture Industry*, 180.

151. Davis, "Transformation," 437–55.

152. Gomery, *Coming of Sound*, 35–36.

153. *Barron's*, May 17, 1926, 18.

154. Wasko, *Movies and Money*, 70–76.

155. The material in this paragraph draws in particular from Gomery, *Coming of Sound*, 35–46.

156. Melnick, *American Showman*, 245–47.

157. Hays, *Memoirs*, 390–91.

158. The material in this paragraph draws in particular from Gomery, *Coming of Sound*, 47–54.

159. Melnick, *American Showman*, 285. When he returned, Lindbergh was presented with the Distinguished Flying Cross by President Coolidge, and the ceremony was broadcast on the newly established NBC radio network.

160. Adas, *Dominance by Design*, 206.

161. Reich, *Making*, 133–34.

162. Chandler, *Visible Hand*, 201.

163. Ibid., 201.

164. Reich, *Making*, 139.

165. Chandler, *Visible Hand*, 201–2.

166. Reich, *Making*, 151–53.

167. Wu, *Master Switch*, 54.

168. Reich, *Making*, 179.

169. Ibid., 4.

170. Noble, *America by Design*.

171. US Federal Communications Commission, *Proposed Report Telephone Investigation* (Washington, DC: Government Printing Office, 1938), 235–36, cited in Wurtzler, *Electric Sounds*, 27.

172. Noble, *America by Design*, 93.

173. Coombe, *Cultural Life*, 6–7.

174. Gomery, *Coming of Sound*, 31–32.

175. Wurtzler, *Electric Sounds*, 83.

176. Western Electric had secured licensing agreements in 1925 with Victor and Columbia, the two largest US phonograph corporations. Wurtzler, *Electric Sounds*, 42–43. GE bought Victor in 1929, and the company effectively became a subsidiary of GE's subsidiary, RCA (46).

177. I follow Castells here in defining technology as material culture. Castells, *Rise of Network Society*, 29.

178. Gomery, *Coming of Sound*, 41–43.

179. Ibid., 33.

180. Reich outlines the development of research at GE in *Making*, in particular 42–128.

181. Gomery, *Coming of Sound*, 63–76.

182. Bancamaerican-Blair and Lehman Brothers had representatives on the board. Wasko, *Movies and Money*, 80–82.

183. Gomery, *Coming of Sound*, 79, 154.

184. Dick, *Engulfed*, 18–19.

185. Ibid., 21.

186. Sinclair, *Upton Sinclair*, 1933.

CHAPTER 12

1. See Watts, *People's Tycoon*, 401–26. Ford had worked for the Edison Illuminating Company as a young man (34–36).

2. Bernays recalled in his memoirs that "Hearst Metrotone News and Fox Movietone News covered the event for the newsreels." Bernays, *Biography of an Idea*, 456. Fox, as we have seen, used sound newsreels as part of a strategy of expansion in the second half of the 1920s, which saw it briefly become the largest vertically integrated film studio.

3. Freeberg, *Age of Edison*, 306; Watts, *People's Tycoon*, 401–2.

4. Young's career exemplified this meshing of corporate and state interests: he had served as general counsel for GE before establishing RCA with state encouragement and support; coauthored the Dawes Plan in 1924, which reduced German reparations (with financial support from Morgan); authored the Young Plan in 1929, which further stream-lined reparations; and sat on Hoover's President's Commission on Recent Economic Changes in 1922–29. Frieden, *Global Capitalism*, 176–77; Dawley, *Struggles for Justice*, 337.

5. Freeberg, *Age of Edison*, 308; GE, "Transformation Timeline," accessed June 22, 2017, www.ge.com/about-us/history/1913–1924.

6. Gruening, *Public Pays;* Mark Crispin Miller, introduction to Bernays, *Propaganda*, 27; Doob, *Propaganda*, 50.

7. Monticone, "'Useful Cinema,'" 74–99.

8. Zinn, *People's History*, 375; Finegold and Skocpol, *State and Party*, 190. The three highest taxpayers in the United States at this point—John D. Rockefeller, Ford, and Mellon—were all in the room together. (I assume Morgan had "better" tax lawyers.)

9. GE's strategies are explicated in D. Nye, *Image Worlds*, in particular 9–30.

10. Marchand, *Creating the Corporate Soul*, 130–34, 148–63.

11. D. Nye, *Electrifying America*, 16.

12. D. M. Diggs, "The Entering Wedge," *General Electric Digest* 2 (July–August 1922): 9, cited in D. Nye, *Image Worlds*, 20.

13. D. Nye, *Image Worlds*, 22–24.

14. The "caveats" from 1888—a description of an invention to be developed further before applying for a patent—are reprinted in Hendricks, *Edison Motion Picture Myth*, 158. See the discussion in Krämer, "Lure," 13–19.

15. Lamont to Hoover, October 19, 1929, cited in Ferguson, "From Normalcy to New Deal," 41.

16. D. Nye, *Electrifying America*, 215.

17. Eichengreen, *Hall of Mirrors*, 3–4, 18–33.

18. Baran and Sweezy, *Monopoly Capital*, 225.

19. The boom on Wall Street at the end of the 1920s had started diverting funds from foreign lending to domestic speculation, and this weakened the economies in Europe in particular. Perhaps some of the capital sluicing through the film and technology industries was part of this. The net export of capital from the United States—which had risen from less

than two hundred million dollars in 1926 to over a billion in 1928—plunged to two hundred million dollars in 1929. Arrighi, *Long Twentieth Century*, 274.

20. Hobsbawm, *Age of Extremes*, 100–101.

21. Dowd, *Twisted Dream*, 103.

22. Zinn, *People's History*, 378.

23. Frieden, *Global Capitalism*, 178.

24. Ewen, *PR!*, 233.

25. Frieden, *Global Capitalism*, 173–228.

26. The "final destruction," Arrighi comments, "of the single web of world commercial and financial transactions on which the fortunes of the City of London were based." Arrighi, *Long Twentieth Century*, 274.

27. Mellon, cited in Eichengreen, *Golden Fetters*, 251.

28. Zinn, *People's History*, 381–82. The War Department "was nervous enough to dust off its counterrevolutionary war plans." Dawley, *Struggles for Justice*, 354.

29. Zinn, *People's History*, 386–91; Dawley, *Struggles for Justice*, 373–74.

30. Roosevelt, cited in Frieden, *Global Capitalism*, 189.

31. Hobsbawm, *Age of Extremes*, 87.

32. Roosevelt, cited in Ewen, *PR!*, 237.

33. Schivelbusch, *Three New Deals*, 1–17.

34. P. Anderson, "Homeland," 7.

35. Eisner, *From Warfare State*, 332–40.

36. Kennedy wrote in 1936, "It can certainly be said without exaggeration, that the Chief Executive has been at pains to protect the invested wealth of the nation ... At no time has he failed to assert or imply his belief in the essential capitalistic economy under which America and the American system have developed." Joseph P. Kennedy, *I'm for Roosevelt* (New York: Reynal and Hitchcock, 1936), cited in Finegold and Skocpol, *State and Party*, 176.

37. Roosevelt's inaugural address asked Congress "for broad Executive power to wage a war against the enemy, as great as the power that would be given to me if we were in fact invaded by a foreign foe." Roosevelt, cited in Eisner, *From Warfare State*, 304. The analogy with war significantly enabled the *extension* of state power, thereafter delegated also to corporate and financial institutions.

38. Dawley, *Struggles for Justice*, 414.

39. Ferguson, "From Normalcy to New Deal," 42; Frieden, *Global Capitalism*, 245; Eisner, *From Warfare State*, 299–322; Finegold and Skocpol, *State and Party*, in particular 66–114.

40. Ferguson, "From Normalcy to New Deal," 47, 93; Ferguson, "Industrial Conflict," in Fraser and Gerstle, *Rise and Fall*. See also Perry Anderson, "Imperium," 20. In the election of 1936, Anderson notes, FDR had the support of globalizing institutions like Chase Manhattan (controlled by John D. Rockefeller), Goldman Sachs, Standard Oil, General Electric, International Harvest, IBB, ITT, United Fruit, and Pan Am. Capital-intensive companies like GE were more able to support measures that increased wage costs than labor-intensive industries—such as, say, clothing—and were willing to support state welfare provisions as long as the burden was shared out across business.

41. Ferguson, "From Normalcy to New Deal," 93.

42. For example, Von Hayek, *Road to Serfdom*.

43. Friedman and Schwartz, *Monetary History*.

44. Sen, "Uses and Abuses," 257–71.

45. Thorpe, *American Warfare State*.

46. This act dealt a fatal blow to the House of Morgan's domination of US financial markets. "By separating investment from commercial banking, this measure destroyed the unity of the two functions whose combination had been the basis of Morgan hegemony in American finance." Ferguson, "From Normalcy to New Deal," 83. Ferguson contends that Roosevelt was supported by non–Morgan-affiliated banks, in particular the John D. Rockefeller–controlled Chase National Bank.

47. Gordon, *New Deals*; Dawley, *Struggles for Justice*, 359–68.

48. Eisner, *From Warfare State*, in particular 299–348; Brinkley, *End of Reform*, 35–36. See also Hart, "Herbert Hoover's Last Laugh," 419–44.

49. Eisner, *From Warfare State*, in particular 57–59.

50. Ferguson, "From Normalcy to New Deal," 80

51. Dawley, *Struggles for Justice*, 362–63; Finegold and Skocpol, *State and Party*, 168, 198.

52. Skocpol, "Political Response," in Dubrofsky, *New Deal*, 76.

53. Bellush, *Failure of the N.R.A.*

54. Finegold and Skocpol, *State and Party*, 198; Bledstein, "New Deal," in Dubrofsky, *New Deal*, 7–8.

55. Gomery, "Hollywood," in Kindem, *American Movie Industry*, 204–14; Muscio, *Hollywood's New Deal*, 117–26.

56. Muscio, *Hollywood's New Deal*, 125.

57. R. Sklar, *Movie-Made America*, 168–69.

58. National Recovery Review Board, cited in Eisner, *From Warfare State*, 316.

59. National Recovery Review Board, cited in Dawley, *Struggles for Justice*, 369.

60. Eisner, *From Warfare State*, 322–32.

61. Dawley, *Struggles for Justice*, 345–47, 366–67; Finegold and Skocpol, *State and Party*, 23, 173, 192.

62. Katz, "American Welfare State," 512–13.

63. Frieden, *Global Capitalism*, 245.

64. Dawley, *Struggles for Justice*, 383; Gordon, *New Deals*, 257.

65. Brinkley, *Liberalism and Its Discontents*, 10.

66. Fraser, "'Labor Question,'" in Fraser and Gerstle, *Rise and Fall*, 68. Brinkley accounts for the New Deal efforts to stimulate consumption in *End of Reform*, 65–85.

67. J. Smith, "New Deal Order," 524.

68. Schivelbusch, *Three New Deals*, 138–84.

69. J. Smith, *Building New Deal Liberalism*, 206–8.

70. Jordan A. Schwarz, *The New Dealers: Power Politics in the Age of Roosevelt* (New York, 1993), xi, cited in Smith, *Building New Deal Liberalism*, 15.

71. P. Anderson, "Imperium," 24–39.

72. Smith, *Building New Deal Liberalism*, 232–57. On the mutation of the New Deal into the Cold War, see, for example, Gerstle and Fraser, introduction to Gerstle and Fraser, *Rise and Fall*, ix–xxv; Brinkley, *End of Reform*, 265–72.

73. Saunders, *Who Paid the Piper?*, 1–6, 279–301.

74. Hanson, "Official Propaganda," 176–77.

75. Winfield, *FDR,* 53–102.

76. Craig, *Fireside Politics,* 140–66.

77. Steele, *Propaganda,* 8–9.

78. Winfield, *FDR,* 83–86. Early worked as a press reporter and as the Washington editor of the Paramount Newsreel Company between 1927 and 1932. McIntyre worked in the CPI, and then as a representative of newsreel companies in Washington, before moving to work specifically with the influential Pathé newsreel.

79. Muscio, *Hollywood's New Deal,* 33–34; Leuchtenburg, *Franklin D. Roosevelt,* 169.

80. Ewen, *PR!,* 245.

81. See, for example, Craig, *Fireside Politics;* Starr, *Creation of the Media,* 374–76; Schivelbusch, *Three New Deals,* 73–80.

82. Horten, *Radio Goes to War,* 17.

83. Ibid., 18–19.

84. See, for example, Daniel, Foresta, Strange, and Stein, *Official Images;* Trachtenberg, "FSA File," in Trachtenberg, *Lincoln's Smile;* Finnegan, *Picturing Poverty;* Shivelbusch, *Three New Deals,* in particular 73–184.

85. Tagg, *Disciplinary Frame.*

86. J. Scott, *Seeing Like a State.*

87. Schivelbusch, *Three New Deals,* 167.

88. Ibid., 167, 160.

89. Jack Ellis and Betsy McLane write, "The only negative criticism, leveled at it frequently, is that following its moving evocation of the history of this big country, its people, and its natural resources, it adds a commercial. The last six minutes on the TVA are much weaker; even the photographic quality drops. . . . The sponsor's message seems tacked on." Ellis and McLane, *New History,* 84–85.

90. Lorentz's previous (and first) film, *The Plow That Broke the Plains* (1937), does something similar. In its original form, the film showed the historical origins of the problem of the Dust Bowl and its current magnitude, ending with a sequence showing the building of "beltville communities" supported by the Resettlement Administration. That particular policy was never realized, and this sequence was deleted from the film—but its triadic structure resembles *The River,* showing again that a resolution is brought about by the actions of government.

91. For example, Ellis and McLane state simply, "Documentary in the institutional or Griersonian sense—engaging and educating citizens in the affairs of the nation—began in June 1935, in Washington, D.C.," when Pare Lorentz "convinced" politicians "what was needed was a new kind of dramatic/informational/persuasive movie," which would be exemplified, they argue, by *The Plow That Broke the Plains* and *The River.* Ellis and McLane, *New History,* 81–82.

92. F. A. Gutheim, "T.V.A.: A New Phase in Architecture," *Magazine of Art* 33 (September 1940): 527, cited in Schivelbusch, *Three New Deals,* 159.

93. For more on rural electrification in the New Deal, see Tobey, *Technology as Freedom.*

94. Inspection Report, *You Can't Get Away with It,* RG65, September 8, 1937, 2, NARA.

95. C. Potter, *War on Crime.*

96. Munby, *Public Enemies,* 108–18.

97. On the history of the United States Film Service, see MacCann, *People's Films*, 87–117; Kahana, *Intelligence Work*, 118–22.

98. FDR, letter to Lowell Mellet, August 13, 1939, cited in Snyder, *Pare Lorentz*, 204.

99. MacCann, *People's Films*, 104–14. Conservative opposition to New Deal media frequently argued that it constituted propaganda. See for example Herring, "Official Publicity."

100. Hays had good reason to dislike Lorentz, who had previously coauthored a book with Morris L. Ernst called *Censored: The Private Life of the Movie*, which had mocked the workings of the Hays office. When Lorentz needed stock footage of World War I battle scenes for *The Plow That Broke the Plains*, Hays specifically instructed the major studios to refuse him. The story gets told, usually in documentary histories, as evidence of Lorentz's chutzpa—he managed to get the footage with the help of his friend the filmmaker King Vidor—but what it shows better is both the considerable power that Hays's organization the MPPDA possessed to police the social function of cinema and the political stakes of this regulation.

101. Rabinovitz, *They Must Be Represented*, 90–91.

102. The history of the expansion of small gauges and portable projection systems is mapped out in Wasson, "Suitcase Cinema," 148–52.

103. Tedlow, "National Association of Manufacturers," 45.

104. Workman, "Manufacturing Power," 287.

105. Walker and Sklar, "Business Finds Its Voice," 317.

106. Wolfskill, *Revolt of the Conservatives*, 19–26; Dawley, *Struggles for Justice*, 369.

107. Jouett Shouse, president of the Liberty League, cited in Wolfskill, *Revolt of the Conservatives*, 67.

108. Fones-Wolf, "Creating," 230–32.

109. Ibid., 226.

110. Marchand, *Creating the Corporate Soul*, 218–23.

111. Ewen, *PR!*, 309–10.

112. NAM, *What Is Your American System All About?*, 1936, cited in Ewen, *PR!*, 305.

113. National Association of Manufacturers, "The Role of the NAM Information Program," 1937, cited in St. John and Arnett, "National Association," 104.

114. Ibid., 104.

115. Workman, "Manufacturing Power," 288.

116. Wasson, "Other Small Screen," 99.

117. Walker and Sklar, "Business Finds Its Voice," 318.

118. Ibid., 325.

119. Ibid., 320–21.

120. Ibid., 320–25.

121. Pierre S. du Pont had invested in GM in 1914 and was elected president of the company in 1920. Marchand, *Creating the Corporate Soul*, 131–33; see 229–48 on GM's public relations in this period.

122. *New York Times*, December 5, 1935, cited in Marchand, *Creating the Corporate Soul*, 203.

123. Ewen, *PR!*, 299.

124. For example, the NAM campaign, closely allied with the Liberty League, was also supplemented by the work of the National Industrial Information Committee, a front

organization founded by GM's Alfred Sloan, which was directly controlled by NAM. The committee also sponsored radio programs and produced motion pictures. Workman, "Manufacturing Power," 288.

125. Walker and Sklar, "Business Finds Its Voice," 322–23.

126. See also Prelinger, "Eccentricity," in Hediger and Vonderau, *Films That Work*, 211–20; Prelinger, "Smoothing the Contours," in Orgeron, Orgeron, and Streible, *Learning*, 338–55; Bird, "Enterprise and Meaning," 24–30.

127. NAM claimed the film reached an audience of 6.5 million. NAM, "Motion picture Showings of Your Town by States," n.d., cited in St. John and Arnett, "National Association," 110.

128. "New EPA Rule Will Threaten Manufacturers' Competitive Advantage," press release, June 2, 2014, NAM, accessed March 28, 2016, www.nam.org/Communications/Articles/2014/05/New-EPA-Rule-Will-Threaten.aspx.

129. The Center for Media and Democracy, "National Association of Manufacturers," accessed March 28th 2016, www.sourcewatch.org/index.php/National_Association_of_Manufacturer. The legislation was seen as violating the principles of free speech because it "compelled speech" to elucidate where the minerals were from. Amnesty has challenged NAM over this—so far unsuccessfully—and the case details can be found at the following link, accessed March 28, 2016, www.citizen.org/litigation/forms/cases/getlinkforcase.cfm?cID = 787).

CHAPTER 13

1. Bernays, *Biography of an Idea*, 623–27.

2. Lichtenberg, "Business Backs New York," 314.

3. D. Nye, *American Technological Sublime*, 223.

4. Ewen, *PR!*, 336.

5. Flickers, "Presenting."

6. Wasson, "Other Small Screen," 86–99.

7. Marchand, "Designers," 23–40.

8. Norman Bel Geddes, *Magic Motorways* (New York: Radom House, 1941), 289, cited in Fotsch, "Building of a Superhighway," 79.

9. GM press release, April 15–16, 1939, cited in Marchand, *Creating the Corporate Soul*, 304.

10. GM, *Press Guide*, 1940, cited in Marchand, *Creating the Corporate Soul*, 306.

11. Frank Hartig of the GM public relations department wrote the script. "Futurama," *World's Fair: Enter the World of Tomorrow*, New York Public Library, http://exhibitions.nypl.org/biblion.

12. Marchand, *Creating the Corporate Soul*, 303.

13. Zunz, *Why the American Century?*, 94–96.

14. Ford Motor Company, *Ford Exposition*, 6.

15. Wasson, "Other Small Screen," 87.

16. Elizabeth Ram, "The Electric Kitchen," *World's Fair*, New York Public Library.

17. David Sarnoff, cited in Ron Simon, "Introducing Television at the Fair," *World's Fair*, New York Public Library.

18. Flickers, "Presenting," 302.

19. Krämer, "Lure," 31–32.

20. Cotter, *1939–1940*, 42–43.

21. Wagner, "'Particularly Effective Argument,'" 10.

22. Levavy, "Land of Liberty," 442–43.

23. Palmer, "Cecil B. DeMille," 47. The affiliate was called Teaching Film Custodians. It traces its genesis back to 1934, when Hays asked Mark May, who had participated in the Payne Fund studies, to explore the possibilities of excerpting theatrical films for schools. Saettler, *Evolution*, 113.

24. Wasson, "Other Small Screen," 87.

25. P. Anderson, "Imperium," 42.

26. Kurth, "Military-Industrial Complex," 440–42.

27. Castells, *Rise of Network Society*, 1:40–47.

28. Arrighi, *Long Twentieth Century*, 274–76.

29. N. Smith, *Endgame of Globalization*, 114. Nine hundred thousand people had already been killed by conventional bombs. P. Anderson, "Consilium," 115.

30. Sbardellati, *J. Edgar Hoover*.

31. Ceplair and Englund, *Inquisition in Hollywood*. "Cultural front" is Michael Denning's term for the surge in working-class and democratic culture in the 1930s and 1940s. Denning, *Cultural Front*.

32. Grieveson, *Policing Cinema*, 136–42; *The Black Panthers*, directed by Stanley Nelson (2015).

33. J. Lewis, "'We Do Not Ask,'" 3–30.

34. "Eric A. Johnston," *Variety*, September 26, 1945, 3.

35. Gomery, *Hollywood Studio System*, 178–83.

36. J. Lewis, "'We Do Not Ask,'" 18.

37. Just a few weeks after the infamous Waldorf statement that announced the blacklist, Johnston said, "There will be no more *Grapes of Wrath*, we'll have no more *Tobacco Roads*." J. Lewis, "'We Do Not Ask,'" 11.

38. P. Anderson, "Imperium," 30.

39. The detailed empirical history of this, in all its remarkable craziness, is told in Weiner, *Legacy of Ashes*.

40. Brendan Fischer, "A Banana Republic Once Again?," *Center for Media and Democracy's PR Watch*, December 27, 2010.

41. Tye, *Father of Spin*, 160–78.

42. For the details, see Cullather, *Operation PBSUCCESS*.

43. N. Smith, *The Endgame of Globalization*, 120.

44. A 1954 NSC statement on US policy toward Latin America that same year explicitly said the United States supports governments that "base their economies on a system of private enterprise and, as essential thereto . . . create a political and economic climate conducive to private investment." National Security Council, "United States Objectives and Course of Action with Respect to Latin America," cited in Herman and McChesney, *Global Media*, 150.

45. Arrighi, *Long Twentieth Century*, 68–69, 278–79.

46. Herman and McChesney, *Global Media*, 17.

47. Ambrose and Brinkley, *Rise to Globalism*, 75–94.

48. Frieden, *Global Capitalism,* 287–90.

49. Hobsbawm, *Age of Extremes,* 241.

50. N. Smith, *Endgame of Globalization,* 114.

51. Steil, *Battle of Bretton Woods.*

52. Fay, *Theaters of Occupation,* xiii.

53. Ibid., xviii.

54. Kitamura, *Screening Enlightenment,* xii

55. Herman and McChesney, *Global Media,* 17.

56. Saunders, *Who Paid the Piper?*; Wilford, *Mighty Wurlitzer.* Rockefeller is quoted in Saunders, *Who Paid the Piper?,* 258.

57. Wilford, *Mighty Wurlitzer,* 117.

58. Joint Chiefs of Staff, "Presentation of 'Militant Liberty' to Chief of Naval Operations," December 16, 1955, cited in Saunders, *Who Paid the Piper?,* 284.

59. Wilford, *Mighty Wurlitzer,* 117.

60. Saunders, *Who Paid the Piper?,* 290–93; Wilford, *Mighty Wurlitzer,* 120–21.

61. Eldridge, "'Dear Owen.'"

62. Leab, *Orwell Subverted.*

63. National Security Council Directive, July 10, cited in Saunders, *Who Paid the Piper?,* 4.

64. Schwoch, *Global TV,* 44–45.

65. Ibid., 45–49.

66. Belmonte, *Selling the American Way,* 63–83; Cull, *Cold War.*

67. Minutes of the 337th meeting of the Operations Coordinating Board, August 8, 1955, cited in Frey, "Tools of Empire," 544.

68. Frey, "Tools of Empire," 553.

69. I draw here on Schwoch's terrific research in *Global TV,* in particular 48–67.

70. Ibid., 53.

71. Schwoch, *Global TV;* Parks, *Cultures in Orbit.*

72. Schwoch, *Global TV,* 118–38.

73. Wu, *Master Switch,* 168–75.

74. Nafeez Ahmed, "How the CIA Made Google," *Insurge Intelligence,* January 22, 2015; Lee Fang, "The CIA Is Investing in Firms That Mine Your Tweets and Instagram Photos," *Intercept,* April 14, 2016.

75. Wasson, "Suitcase Cinema"; Fones-Wolf, *Selling Free Enterprise;* Heffelfinger, "*Home Town Story.*"

76. McCarthy, *Citizen Machine,* 7.

77. Ibid., 37–42.

78. Brenner, "Structure vs Conjuncture," 41–44.

79. The scholarship on neoliberalism is now voluminous, befitting the centrality of the ideology to the contemporary ordering of the world. For a useful overview, see Harvey, *Brief History.*

80. For a terrific introduction to Rand, see the first episode of Adam Curtis's *All Watched Over by Machines of Loving Grace* (BBC, 2011). See also Jennifer Burns, *Goddess of the Market.*

81. Christopher Hitchens, "Greenspan Shrugged," *Vanity Fair,* December 2000.

82. See, for example, M. Davis, *Planet of Slums,* especially 151–73.

83. Melissa Fleming, "Crossings of Mediterranean Sea Exceed 300,000," UN Refugee Agency, August 28, 2015.

84. Miller et al., *Global Hollywood,* 84–90.

85. See in particular the Public Library of US Diplomacy, https://search.wikileaks.org /plusd/.

86. Herman and McChesney, *Global Media,* 29.

87. Miller and Maxwell, "'For a Better Deal!,'" in Kapur and Wagner, *Neoliberalism and Global Cinema.*

88. See, for example, Holt, *Empires of Entertainment.*

89. Meehan, "Legacy of Neoliberalism," in Kapur and Wagner, *Neoliberalism and Global Cinema.*

90. Kunz, *Culture Conglomerates,* 33–40.

91. NBC Universal website, accessed May 4, 2016, www.nbcuniversal.com/.

92. Josh Constine, "Airware's Drone Operating System Gets Strategic Investment, Tech, Clients from GE Ventures," *TechCrunch,* November 19, 2014.

93. UNICEF, "The State of the World's Children," 2009, accessed April 18, 2016, www. unicef.org/rightsite/sowc/fullreport.php; "Series on Maternal and Child Nutrition," *Lancet,* 2013, accessed June 3, 2016, www.thelancet.com/series/maternal-and-child-nutrition; The World Bank, "Poverty," accessed April 18, 2016, www.worldbank.org/en/topic/poverty /overview. In early 2014, the Intergovernmental Panel on Climate Change of the United Nations issued its fifth assessment report, which stated that climate change is happening more rapidly and profoundly than predicted. Accessed April 8, 2014, www.ipcc.ch/.

94. Grieveson, "Discipline and Publish."

BIBLIOGRAPHY

ARCHIVES AND COLLECTIONS

Baker Library and Special Collections, Bloomberg Center, Harvard Business School, Harvard University, US.

Benson Ford Research Center, Henry Ford Museum and Greenfield Village (RCHFM), Dearborn, MI, US.

The British Film Institute National Archive, London, UK.

Colonial Film: Moving Images of the British Empire, www.colonialfilm.org.uk/home.

Conservative Party Archive, Bodleian Libraries, University of Oxford, UK.

Imperial War Museum Film and Video Archive, London, UK.

League of Nations Archives, Geneva, Switzerland. Materials from this archive are referenced by their classification numbers.

The Library of Congress, Washington, DC, US. This includes the George Kleine Papers, 1886–1946 (GKLOC in the notes) and online materials curated by the library, notably "Prosperity and Thrift: the Coolidge Era and the Consumer Economy," https://memory. loc.gov/ammem/coolhtml/coolhome.html; and "The Spanish American War in Motion Pictures," www.loc.gov/collections/spanish-american-war-in-motion-pictures/about-this-collection/.

Margaret Herrick Library, Academy of Motion Picture Arts and Sciences, Los Angeles, CA, US.

Media History Digital Library, http://mediahistoryproject.org/.

The Modern Records Centre, University of Warwick, UK.

Motion Picture Films and Sound and Video Recordings, National Archives at College Park, MD, US.

Motion Picture Producers and Distributors of America, Inc., 1922–1939, Digital Archive, Flinders University, Australia, http://mppda.flinders.edu.au/.

Moving Image Research Center, Motion Picture, Broadcasting and Recorded Sound, Library of Congress, Washington, DC, US.

The National Archives, College Park, MD, US. NARA records from state bureaus and departments are referenced by their record group (RG) number, with a corresponding box number, date, and page number when available.

The National Archives, Kew, UK. Citations from the Public Records Office at the National Archives indicate the specific department or office of origin—for example, Colonial Office Records—followed by the identifier used in the archive's referencing system.

The National Archives, Washington, DC, US.

National Board of Review of Motion Pictures Collection (NBR), Rare Books and Manuscripts Division, New York Public Library, US. NBR records are referenced by box number, date, and page number when available.

New York Public Library for the Performing Arts (NYPL), Dorothy and Lewis B. Cullman Center, New York, US.

Prelinger Archives, https://archive.org/details/prelinger.

Wikileaks, Public Library of US Diplomacy, https://search.wikileaks.org/plusd/.

PUBLISHED WORKS

Abel, O. J. "The Making of Men, Motor Cars and Profits." *Iron Age* 95 (January 7, 1915): 33–41.

Acland, Charles, and Haidee Wasson, eds. *Useful Cinema* (Durham, NC: Duke University Press, 2011).

Adas, Michael. *Dominance by Design: Technological Imperatives and America's Civilizing Mission* (Cambridge, MA: Harvard University Press, 2006).

———. "From Settler Colony to Global Hegemon: Integrating the Exceptionalist Narrative of the American Experience into World History." *American Historical Review* 106, no. 5 (December 2001): 1692–1720.

Addams, Jane. *The Spirit of Youth and the City Streets* (New York: Macmillan, 1909).

Adler, Mortimer. *Art and Prudence* (New York: Longmans Green, 1937).

Agamben, Giorgio. *State of Exception.* Translated by Kevin Attell (Chicago: University of Chicago Press, 2005).

Aitken, Ian. *Film and Reform: John Grierson and the Documentary Film Movement* (London: Routledge, 1990).

Allett, John. "Crowd Psychology and the Theory of Democratic Elitism: The Contribution of William McDougall." *Political Psychology* 17, no. 2 (June 1996): 213–27.

Allport, Gordon W. "The Historical Background of Modern Social Psychology." In vol. 1 of *Handbook of Psychology,* edited by Gardner Lindzey and Elliot Aronson. 2nd ed. (Reading, PA: Addison-Wesley, 1968).

Altman, Rick. "Dickens, Griffith, and Film Theory Today." In Gaines, *Classical Hollywood,* 9–48.

———. *A Theory of Narrative* (New York: Columbia University Press, 2008).

Alvarado, Manuel, and John O. Thompson, eds. *The Media Reader* (London: British Film Institute, 1990).

Ambler, Charles. "Projecting the Modern Colonial State: The Mobile Cinema in Kenya." In Grieveson and MacCabe, *Film and the End of Empire,* 199–224.

Ambrose, Stephen, and Douglas Brinkley. *Rise to Globalism: American Foreign Policy since 1938* (New York: Penguin, 1997).

Amery, Leopold. *My Political Life* (London: Hutchinson, 1953).

Anderson, Benedict. *Imagined Communities: Reflections on the Origins and Spread of Nationalism* (London: Verso, 1983).

Anderson, Mark Lynn. "The Historian Is Paramount." *Film History* 26, no. 2 (2014): 1–30.

———. "Taking Liberties: The Payne Fund Studies and the Creation of the Media Expert." In Grieveson and Wasson, *Inventing Film Studies*, 38–65.

———. *Twilight of the Idols: Hollywood and the Human Sciences in the 1920s* (Berkeley: University of California Press, 2011).

Anderson, Perry. "Consilium." *New Left Review* 83 (September–October 2013): 113–67.

———. "Homeland." *New Left Review* 81 (May–June 2013): 5–32.

———. "Imperium." *New Left Review* 83 (September–October 2013): 5–111.

Andriopoulos, Stefan. *Possessed: Hypnotic Crimes, Corporate Fictions, and the Invention of Cinema* (Chicago: University of Chicago Press, 2008).

Angevine, Robert G. *The Railroad and the State: War, Politics, and Technology in Nineteenth-Century America* (Stanford, CA: Stanford University Press, 2004).

Anghie, Antony. *Imperialism, Sovereignty and the Making of International Law* (Cambridge: Cambridge University Press, 2004).

Anthony, Scott. "Imperialism and Internationalism: The British Documentary Movement and the Legacy of the Empire Marketing Board." In Grieveson and MacCabe, *Empire and Film*, 135–48.

Appleby, Joyce. *Capitalism and a New Social Order: The Republican Vision of the 1790s* (New York: New York University Press, 1984).

———. *Liberalism and Republicanism in the Historical Imagination* (Cambridge, MA: Harvard University Press, 1992).

Arblaster, Anthony. *The Rise and Decline of Western Liberalism* (Oxford: Basil Blackwell, 1984).

Armstrong, Nancy. *How Novels Think: The Limits of British Individualism from 1719–1900* (New York: Columbia University Press, 2005).

Arnold, Horace I., and Fay I. Faurote. *Ford Methods and Ford Shops* (New York: Engineering Magazine Company, 1915).

Arnold, Matthew. *Culture and Anarchy: An Essay in Political and Social Criticism* (New York: Bobbs-Merrill, 1971). First published 1869.

Arnove, Robert, ed. *Philanthropy and Cultural Imperialism: The Foundations at Home and Abroad* (Bloomington: Indiana University Press, 1982).

Arrighi, Giovanni. *Adam Smith in Beijing* (London: Verso, 2007).

———. "Hegemony Unravelling—2." *New Left Review* 33 (May–June 2005): 83–116.

———. *The Long Twentieth Century: Money, Power, and the Origins of Our Times* (London: Verso, 1994).

Auerbach, Jonathan. "McKinley at Home: How Early American Cinema Made News." *American Quarterly* 51, no. 4 (1999): 792–832.

Bakker, Gerben. *Entertainment Industrialised: The Emergence of the International Film Industry, 1890–1940* (Cambridge: Cambridge University Press, 2008).

Baldwin, James Mark. *Mental Development in the Child and in the Race* (New York: Macmillan, 1895).

Balibar, Etienne. "The Nation Form: History and Ideology." In Balibar and Wallerstein, *Race, Nation, Class*, 86–106.

Balibar, Etienne, and Immanuel Wallerstein. *Race, Nation, Class: Ambiguous Identities* (London: Verso, 1991).

Balio, Tino, ed. *The American Film Industry* (Madison: University of Wisconsin Press, 1985).

———. "Stars in Business: The Founding of United Artists." In Balio, *American Film Industry*, 157–63.

Banner, Stuart. *American Property: A History of How, Why, and What We Own* (Cambridge, MA: Harvard University Press, 2011).

Baran, Paul, and Paul Sweezy. *Monopoly Capitalism* (New York: Modern Reader Paperbacks, 1966).

Barrow, Clyde. *Universities and the Capitalist State: Corporate Liberalism and the Reconstruction of American Higher Education* (Madison: University of Wisconsin Press, 1990).

Barrows, Susanna. *Distorting Mirrors: Visions of the Crowd in Late Nineteenth-Century France* (New Haven, CT: Yale University Press, 1981).

Batchelor, Ray. *Henry Ford: Mass Production, Modernism and Design* (Manchester, UK: Manchester University Press, 1994).

Bazin, Andre. *What Is Cinema?* Translated by Hugh Gray. Vol. 1 (Berkeley: University of California Press, 1967).

Beauchamp, Cari. *Joseph Kennedy Presents His Hollywood Years* (New York: Vintage Books, 2009).

Beckert, Sven. "Emancipation and Empire: Reconstructing the Worldwide Web of Cotton Production in the Age of the American Civil War." *American Historical Review* (December 2004): 1405–38.

———. *The Monied Metropolis: New York City and the Consolidation of the American Bourgeoisie, 1850–1896* (Cambridge: Cambridge University Press, 2001).

Beerlage, Nancy K. "Organizing the Farm Bureau: Family, Community, and Professionals, 1914–1928." *Agricultural History* 75, no. 4 (Autumn 2001): 406–37.

Beller, Jonathan. *The Cinematic Mode of Production: Attention Economy and the Society of the Spectacle* (Lebanon, NH: Dartmouth University Press, 2006).

Bellush, Bernard. *The Failure of the N.R.A.* (New York: W. W. Norton, 1976).

Belmonte, Laura A. *Selling the American Way: U.S. Propaganda and the Cold War* (Philadelphia: University of Pennsylvania Press, 2008).

Bennett, Tony. *The Birth of the Museum: History, Theory, Politics* (London: Routledge, 1995).

———. *Culture: A Reformer's Science* (London: Sage, 1998).

Bensel, Richard Franklin. *The Political Economy of American Industrialization, 1877–1900* (Cambridge: Cambridge University Press, 2000).

———. *Yankee Leviathan: The Origins of Central State Authority, 1859–1877* (Cambridge: Cambridge University Press, 1990).

Benson, Susan Porter, Stephen Brier, and Roy Rosenzweig, eds. *Presenting the Past: Essays on History and the Public* (Philadelphia: Temple University Press, 1986).

Berman, Marshall. *All That Is Solid Melts into Air: The Experience of Modernity* (London: Verso, 1983).

Bernays, Edward L. *Biography of an Idea: Memoirs of Public Relations Counsel Edward L. Bernays* (New York: Simon and Schuster, 1965).

———. *Crystallizing Public Opinion* (New York: Liveright, 1961). First published 1923.

———. "Engineering of Consent." *Annals of the American Academy of Political and Social Science* 250 (March 1947): 113–20.

———. *Propaganda* (Brooklyn: Ig, 2005). First published 1928.

———. "Publicity in International Trade: How Public Opinion Abroad Was Influenced by the United States Government during the War." *Association News* 1, no. 24 (1920): 1–5.

———. "Putting Politics on the Market." *Independent*, May 19, 1928, 470–72.

———. "This Business of Propaganda." *Independent*, September 1, 1928, 198–99.

Bernheim, Hippolyte. *Suggestive Therapeutics: A Treatise on the Nature and Uses of Hypnotism.* Translated by Christian A. Herber (New York: G. P. Putnam's Sons, 1889).

Biagini, Eugenio. *Liberty, Retrenchment and Reform: Popular Liberalism in the Age of Gladstone, 1860–1880* (Cambridge: Cambridge University Press, 1992).

Bird, William. "Enterprise and Meaning: Sponsored Film, 1939–1949." *History Today* 39, no. 12 (December 1989): 24–30.

Bjork, Ulf Jonas. "The U.S. Commerce Department Aids Hollywood Exports, 1921–1933." *Historian* 62, no. 3 (March 2000): 575–88.

Blackstone, William. *Commentaries on the Laws of England, in Four Books.* Vol. 1, *1765* (London: A Strahan, 1800).

Bledstein, Barton J. "The New Deal: The Conservative Achievements of Liberal Reform." In Dubrofsky, *New Deal.*

Bloomfield, Meyer. "The New Profession of Handling Men." *Annals of the American Academy of Political and Social Science* 59 (September 1915), 121–126.

Blumer, Herbert. "Moulding of Mass Behavior through the Motion Picture." *Publications of the American Sociological Society* 29, no. 3 (August 1933): 115–27.

———. *Movies and Conduct* (New York: Macmillan, 1933).

Blumer, Herbert, and Philip Hauser, *Movies, Delinquency, and Crime* (New York: Macmillan, 1933).

Boddy, William. "The Rhetoric and the Economic Roots of the American Broadcasting Industry." *Ciné-Tracts* 2, no. 2 (Spring 1979): 37–54.

Bodnar, John. *Remaking America: Public Memory, Commemoration, and Patriotism in the Twentieth Century* (Princeton, NJ: Princeton University Press, 1992).

Bogle, Lori Lyn. *The Pentagon's Battle for the American Mind: The Early Cold War.* Texas A&M Military History (State College: Texas A&M University Press, 2004).

Bonjean, Charles M., Louis Schneider, and Robert L. Lineberry, eds. *Social Science in America* (Austin: University of Texas Press, 1976).

Borch-Jacobsen, Mikkel. *The Emotional Tie: Psychoanalysis, Mimesis, and Affect.* Translated by Douglas Brick and Others (Stanford, CA: Stanford University Press, 1993).

———. *The Freudian Subject.* Translated by Catherine Porter (Basingstoke, UK: Macmillan, 1989).

Bordwell, David, Janet Staiger, and Kristin Thompson. *The Classical Hollywood Cinema: Film Style and Mode of Production to 1960* (London: Routledge, 1985).

Bowles, Samuel, and Herbert Gintis. *Schooling in Capitalist America: Educational Reform and the Contradictions of Economic Life* (London: Routledge and Kegan Paul, 1976).

Bowser, Eileen. *The Transformation of Cinema, 1907–1915* (Berkeley: University of California Press, 1990).

Boyer, Paul. *Urban Masses and Moral Order in America, 1820–1920* (Cambridge, MA: Harvard University Press, 1978).

Bramson, Leon. *The Political Context of Sociology* (Princeton, NJ: Princeton University Press, 1961).

Braverman, Harry. *Labor and Monopoly Capital: The Degradation of Work in the Twentieth Century* (New York: Monthly Review Press, 1998). First Published 1974.

Brenner, Robert. "Structure vs Conjuncture." *New Left Review* 43 (January–February 2007): 33–59.

Brinkley, Alan. *The End of Reform: New Deal Liberalism in Recession and War* (New York: Vintage, 1995).

———. *Liberalism and Its Discontents* (Cambridge, MA: Harvard University Press, 2000).

Brown, Bill. "Science Fiction, the World's Fair, and the Prosthetics of Empire, 1910–1915." In Kaplan and Pease, *Cultures of United States Imperialism*, 129–63.

Browne, Nick, ed. *Refiguring American Film Genres* (Berkeley: University of California Press, 1998).

Brown, E. R. "Public Health in Imperialism: Early Rockefeller Programs at Home and Abroad." *American Journal of Public Health* 66, no. 9 (September 1976): 897–903.

Brown, Judith, and William Roger Louis, eds. *The Oxford History of the British Empire*. Vol. 4, *The Twentieth Century* (Oxford: Oxford University Press, 1999).

Bryan, Steve. *The Gold Standard at the Turn of the Twentieth Century: Rising Powers, Global Money, and the Age of Empire* (New York: Columbia University Press, 2010).

Bryson, Lymon, ed., *The Communication of Ideas* (New York: Harper and Brothers, 1948).

Bucheli, Marcelo. "Major Trends in the Historiography of the Latin American Oil Industry." *Business History Review* 84 (Summer 2010): 339–62.

Burchell, Graham, Colin Gordon, and Peter Miller, eds. *The Foucault Effect: Studies in Governmentality* (London: Harvester Wheatsheaf, 1991).

Bureau of Commercial Economics. *Publicity with Motion Pictures* (Washington DC: Bureau of Commercial Economics, 1920).

Burns, James. "American Philanthropy and Colonial Filmmaking—the Rockefeller Foundation, the Carnegie Corporation, and the Birth of Colonial Cinema." In Grieveson and MacCabe, *Empire and Film*, 55–68.

———. *Flickering Shadows: Cinema and Identity in Colonial Zimbabwe*. Ohio University Research in International Studies (Athens: Ohio University Press, 2002).

Burns, Jennifer. *Goddess of the Market: Ayn Rand and the American Right* (Oxford: Oxford University Press, 2009).

Buroway, Michael. *Manufacturing Consent: Changes in the Labor Process under Monopoly Capitalism* (Chicago: University of Chicago Press, 1979).

Butler, L. J. *Britain and Empire: Adjusting to a Post-imperial World* (London: I. B. Tauris, 2002).

Butsch, Richard. "Class and Audience Effects: A History of Research on Movies, Radio, and Television." *Journal of Popular Film and Television* 29, no. 3 (Fall 2001): 112–20.

Cabán, Pedro. "Subjects and Immigrants during the Progressive Era." *Discourse* 23, no. 3 (2001): 24–51.

Cain, P. J., and A. G. Hopkins. *British Imperialism, 1688–2000*. 2nd ed. (New York: Longman, 2002).

Callinicos, Alex. *Imperialism and Global Political Economy* (London: Polity, 2009).

Capozzola, Christopher. *Uncle Sam Wants You: World War I and the Making of the Modern American Citizen* (Oxford: Oxford University Press, 2008).

———. "World War 1." In Kazin, *Princeton Encyclopedia of American Political History*, Vol. 2, 911–18.

Carey, Alex. *Taking the Risk Out of Democracy: Corporate Propaganda versus Freedom and Liberty.* Edited by Andrew Lohrey (Urbana: University of Illinois Press, 1995).

Carey, James W. *Communication as Culture: Essays on Media and Society* (Winchester, UK: Unwin Hyman, 1989).

———. "Communications and the Progressives," *Critical Studies in Mass Communication* 6 (1989): 264–82.

Carlson, Robert A. "Americanization as an Early Twentieth-Century Adult Education Movement." *History of Educational Quarterly* 10, no. 4 (Winter 1970): 440–64.

Carosso, Vincent P. *Investment Banking in America: A History* (Cambridge, MA: Harvard University Press, 1970).

Carpenter, Daniel P. *The Forging of Bureaucratic Autonomy: Reputations, Networks, and Policy Innovation in Executive Agencies, 1862–1928* (Princeton, NJ: Princeton University Press, 2001).

Castells, Manuel. *The Rise of Network Society.* 3 vols. 2nd ed. (Oxford: Blackwell, 2000).

Ceplair, Larry, and Steve Englund. *The Inquisition in Hollywood: Politics in the Film Community, 1930–1960* (Urbana: University of Illinois Press, 2003).

Chambers, John Whiteclay II, ed. *The Oxford Companion to American Military History* (Oxford: Oxford University Press, 1999).

Chandler, Alfred Jr. *Giant Enterprise: Ford, General Motors, and the Automobile Industry* (New York: Harcourt, 1964).

———. *The Visible Hand: The Managerial Revolution in American Business* (Cambridge, MA: Harvard University Press, 1977).

Chandler, Alfred, Franco Amatori, and Takashi Hikino, eds. *Big Business and the Wealth of Nations* (Cambridge: Cambridge University Press, 1997).

Chandler, Alfred, and Bruce Mazlish, eds. *Leviathans: Multinational Corporations and the New Global History* (Cambridge: Cambridge University Press, 2005).

Charters, W. W. *Motion Pictures and Youth: A Summary* (New York: Macmillan, 1933).

Chernow, Ron. *The House of Morgan: An American Banking Dynasty and the Rise of Modern Finance* (New York: Atlantic Monthly Press, 1990).

Chicago Motion Picture Commission Hearings. *Report* (Chicago: Chicago Historical Society, 1920).

Chomsky, Noam. *Media Control: The Spectacular Achievements of Propaganda* (New York: Seven Stories, 2002).

———. *Necessary Illusions: Thought Control in Democratic Societies* (London: Pluto Press, 1999).

———. *Profits over People: Neoliberalism and Global Order* (New York: Seven Sisters Press, 1999).

Christie, Ian. "'The Captains and the Kings Depart': Imperial Departure and Arrival in Early Cinema." In Grieveson and MacCabe, *Empire and Film,* 21–33.

Clark, Terry N., ed. *Gabriel Tarde: On Communication and Social Influence* (Chicago: University of Chicago Press, 1969).

Clavin, Patricia. *Securing the World Economy: The Reinvention of the League of Nations, 1920–1946* (Oxford: Oxford University Press, 2013).

Cockett, Richard. "The Party, Publicity, and the Media." In Seldon and Ball, *Conservative Century*, 547–78.

Collier, John. *The Indians of the Americas* (New York: W. W. Norton, 1947).

Columbia Law Review, "The Motion Picture Industry and the Anti-Trust Laws," *Columbia Law Review* 36 no. 4 (April 1936): 635–52.

Colwell, Stacie. "*The End of the Road:* Gender, the Dissemination of Knowledge, and the American Campaign against Venereal Disease during World War I." *Camera Obscura* 29 (May 1992): 91–129.

Commission on Educational and Cultural Films, *The Film in National Life* (London: George Allen and Unwin, 1933).

Conant, Michael. *Antitrust in the Motion Picture Industry* (Berkeley: University of California Press, 1960).

Constantine, Stephen. "'Bringing the Empire Alive': The Empire Marketing Board and Imperial Propaganda, 1926–1933," in Mackenzie, *Imperialism and Popular Culture*, 192–231.

———. *Buy and Build: The Advertising Posters of the Empire Marketing Board* (London: HMSO, 1986).

———. *The Making of British Colonial Development Policy, 1914–1940* (London: Frank Cass, 1984).

Coombe, Rosemary J. *The Cultural Life of Intellectual Properties: Authorship, Appropriation, and the Law* (Durham, NC: Duke University Press, 1998).

Cooper, Mark Garrett. *Love Rules: Silent Hollywood and the Rise of the Managerial Class* (Minneapolis: University of Minnesota Press, 2003).

Cotter, Bill. *The 1939–1940 New York World's Fair* (Chicago: Arcadia, 2009).

Coutrot, Jean. "The Cinema and Scientific Management." *International Review of Educational Cinematography* 2 (July–August 1930).

Cowen, Deborah. *The Deadly Life of Logistics: Mapping Violence in Global Trade* (Minneapolis: University of Minnesota Press, 2014).

Craig, Douglas B. *Fireside Politics: Radio and Political Culture in the United States, 1920–1940* (Baltimore: John Hopkins University Press, 2000).

Crawford, Susan P. *Captive Audience: The Telecom Industry and Monopoly Power in the New Gilded Age* (New Haven, CT: Yale University Press, 2013).

Creel, George. *How We Advertised America: The First Telling of the Amazing Story of the Committee on Public Information That Carried the Gospel of Americanism to Every Corner of the Globe* (New York: Harper and Brothers, 1920).

———. *Rebel at Large: Recollections of Fifty Crowded Years* (New York: G. P. Putnam's Sons, 1947).

Cuban, Larry. *Teachers and Teaching: The Classroom Use of Technology since 1920* (New York: Teachers College Press, 1986).

Cullather, Nicholas. *Operation PBSUCCESS: The United States and Guatemala, 1952–1954* (Washington, DC: Center for the Study of Intelligence, 1994).

Cull, Nicholas. *The Cold War and the United States Information Agency: American Propaganda and Public Diplomacy, 1945–1989* (Cambridge: Cambridge University Press, 2008).

Curtis, Scott. "Images of Efficiency: The Films of Frank B. Gilbreth." In Hediger and Vonderau, *Films That Work*, 85–100.

Dale, Edgar. *Children's Attendance at Motion Pictures* (New York: Macmillan, 1933).

———. *The Content of Motion Pictures* (New York: Macmillan, 1933).

———. *How to Appreciate Motion Pictures* (New York: Macmillan, 1933).

Dale, Rachel Kapelke. "Visible Nations: Hollywood's Commodification of 'European' Female Stars, 1929–1939." PhD diss., University College London, 2015.

Daly, Nicholas. *Literature, Technology, and Modernity, 1860–2000* (Cambridge: Cambridge University Press, 2004).

Danbom, David. *Born in the Country: A History of Rural America*. 2nd ed. (Baltimore: John Hopkins University Press, 2006).

Daniel, Pete. *Breaking the Land: The Transformation of Cotton, Tobacco, and Rice Cultures since 1880* (Urbana: University of Illinois Press, 1985).

Daniel, Pete, Merry Foresta, Maren Strange, and Sally Stein, eds. *Official Images: New Deal Photography* (Washington, DC: Smithsonian Institution Press, 1987).

Davis, G. Cullom. "The Transformation of the Federal Trade Commission, 1914–1929" *Mississippi Valley Historical Review* 49, no. 3 (December 1962): 437–55.

Davis, Lance, and Robert Huttenback. *Mammon and the Pursuit of Empire: The Political Economy of British Imperialism, 1860–1912* (New York: Cambridge University Press, 1986).

Davis, Mike. *Planet of Slums* (London: Verso, 2006).

Dawley, Alan. "The Abortive Rule of Big Money." In Fraser and Gerstle, *Ruling America*, 149–80.

———. *Struggles for Justice: Social Responsibility and the Liberal State* (Cambridge, MA: Harvard University Press, 1991).

Dean, Mitchell. *The Constitution of Poverty: Towards a Genealogy of Liberal Governance* (London: Routledge, 1991).

Debauche, Leslie Midkiff. *Reel Patriotism: The Movies and World War I* (Madison: University of Wisconsin Press, 1997).

DeCordova, Richard. *Picture Personalities: The Emergence of the Star System in America* (Urbana: University of Illinois Press, 1990).

DeFleur, Melvin L., and Sandra J. Ball-Rokeach. *Theories of Mass Communication*. 5th ed. (New York: Longman, 1989).

Delia, Jesse G. "Communication Research: A History." In *Handbook of Communication Sciences*, edited by Charles Berger and Steven H. Chafee (Newbury Park, CA: Sage, 1987), 20–98.

Denning, Michael. *The Cultural Front* (London: Verso, 1996).

Denzin, Norman K., *Symbolic Interactionism and Cultural Studies: The Politics of Interpretation* (Oxford: Blackwell, 1992).

Dewey, John. *Democracy and Education: An Introduction to the Philosophy of Education* (New York: Macmillan, 1950). First Published 1916.

———. "The Need for Social Psychology." *Psychological Review* 24 (July 1917): 266–77.

———. *The Public and Its Problems* (New York: Holt, 1927).

———. *School and Society* (Chicago: University of Chicago Press, 1971). First published 1915.

Dick, Bernard F. *Engulfed: The Death of Paramount Pictures and the Birth of Corporate Hollywood* (Lexington: University Press of Kentucky, 2001).

Dickinson, Margaret, and Sarah Street. *Cinema and State: The Film Industry and Government, 1927–84* (London: BFI, 1985).

Dilley, A. R. "The Economics of Empire." In Stockwell, *The British Empire*, 101–30.

Dodge, Raymond. "The Psychology of Propaganda." *Religious Education* 15 (1920). In Park and Burgess, *Introduction to the Science of Sociology*, 837–40.

Doob, Leonard. *Propaganda: Its Psychology and Technique* (New York: H. Holt, 1935).

Douglas, Susan J. *Inventing American Broadcasting, 1899–1922* (Baltimore: John Hopkins University Press, 1987).

Dowd, Douglas F. *The Twisted Dream: Capitalist Development in the U.S. since 1776* (Cambridge, MA: Winthrop, 1977).

Downes, Richard. "Autos over Rails: How US Business Supplanted the British in Brazil, 1910–28." *Journal of Latin American Studies* 24, no. 3 (October 1992): 551–83.

Dreyfus, Herbert, and Paul Rabinov, eds. *Michel Foucault: Beyond Structuralism and Hermeneutics* (Brighton: Harvester, 1982).

Druick, Zoë. "The International Educational Cinematographic Institute, Reactionary Modernism, and the Formation of Film Studies." *Canadian Journal of Film Studies* 16, no. 1 (Spring 2007): 80–97.

———. *Projecting Canada: Government Policy and Documentary Film at the National Board of Canada* (Montreal: McGill-Queen's University Press, 2007).

———. "'Reaching the Multimillions': Liberal Internationalism and the Establishment of Documentary Film." In Grieveson and Wasson, *Inventing Film Studies*, 66–92.

Drummond, Ian M. *The Floating Pound and the Sterling Area, 1931–1939* (Cambridge: Cambridge University Press, 1981).

———. *Imperial Economic Policy 1917–1939: Studies in Expansion and Protection* (London: George Allen and Unwin, 1974).

Dubber, Markus D., and Mariana Valverde, eds. *Police and the Liberal State* (Stanford, CA: Standard University Press, 2008).

Dubofsky, Melvyn, ed., *The New Deal: Conflicting Interpretations and Shifting Perspectives* (New York: Garland, 1992).

———. *We Shall Be All: A History of the Industrial Workers of the World* (Chicago: Quadrangle Books, 1969).

Dupin, Christopher. "The Postwar Transformation of the British Film Institute and Its Impact on the Development of a National Film Culture in Britain." *Screen* 47, no. 4 (Winter 2006): 443–51.

Dysinger, Wendell S., and Christian A. Ruckmick. *The Emotional Responses of Children to the Motion Picture Situation* (New York: Macmillan, 1933).

Eckert, Charles. "The Carole Lombard in Macy's Window." *Quarterly Review of Film Studies* 3, no. 1 (1978): 1–21.

Eckes, Alfred E. Jr., and Thomas W. Zeiler. *Globalization and the American Century* (Cambridge: Cambridge University Press, 2003).

Eichengreen, Barry. "The British Economy between the Wars." In Engerman and Gallman, *Cambridge Economic History*, 71–100.

———. *Golden Fetters: The Gold Standard and the Great Depression, 1919–1939* (New York: Oxford University Press, 1992).

———. *Hall of Mirrors: The Great Depression, the Great Recession, and the Uses—and Misuses—of History* (Oxford: Oxford University Press, 2015).

Eichengreen, Barry, and Marc Flandreau, eds. *The Gold Standard in Theory and History.* 2nd ed. (New York: Routledge, 1997).

Eisner, Marc Allen. *From Warfare State to Welfare State: World War I, Compensatory State Building, and the Limits of Modern Order* (University Park: Pennsylvania State University Press, 2000).

Eldridge, David. "'Dear Owen': The CIA, Luigi Luraschi, and Hollywood, 1953." *Historical Journal of Film, Radio, and Television* 20, no. 2 (2000): 149–96.

Ellenberger, Henri. *The Discovery of the Unconscious: The History and Evolution of Dynamic Psychiatry* (New York: Basic Books, 1970).

Ellis, Jack, and Betsy McLane, *A New History of Documentary Film* (New York: Continuum, 2006).

Engerman, Stanley L., and Robert E. Gallman, eds. *The Cambridge Economic History of the United States.* Vol. 2, *The Long Nineteenth Century* (Cambridge: Cambridge University Press, 2000).

Engerman, Stanley L., and Kenneth Sokoloff. "Technology and Industrialization, 1790–1914." In Engerman and Gallman, *Cambridge Economic History*, 367–402.

Evans, Thomas. *The Education of Ronald Reagan: The General Electric Years* (New York: Columbia University Press, 2006).

Ewen, Stuart. *PR! A Social History of Spin* (New York: Basic Books, 1996).

Famous Players-Lasky Corporation. *The Story of the Famous Players-Lasky Corporation* (New York: Famous Players-Lasky Corporation, 1919).

Fay, Jennifer. *Theaters of Occupation: Hollywood and the Reeducation of Postwar Germany* (Minneapolis: University of Minnesota Press, 2008).

Federico, Giovanni. *Feeding the World: An Economic History of Agriculture, 1800–2000* (Princeton, NJ: Princeton University Press, 2005).

Ferguson, Thomas. "From Normalcy to New Deal: Industrial Structure, Party Competition, and American Public Policy in the Great Depression." *International Organization* 38, no. 1 (Winter 1984): 41–94.

———. "Industrial Conflict and the Coming of the New Deal: The Triumph of Multinational Liberalism in America." In Fraser and Gerstle, *Rise and Fall*, 3–31.

Ferleger, Louis. "Arming American Agriculture for the Twentieth Century: How the USDA's Top Managers Promoted Agricultural Development." *Agricultural History* 74, no. 2 (Spring 2000): 211–26.

Finegold, Kenneth, and Theda Skocpol. *State and Party in America's New Deal* (Madison: University of Wisconsin Press, 1995).

Fink, Leon. *Progressive Intellectuals and the Dilemmas of Democratic Commitment* (Cambridge, MA: Harvard University Press, 1997).

Finnegan, Cara. *Picturing Poverty: Print Culture and FSA Photographs* (Washington, DC: Smithsonian Institution Press, 2003).

Fishback, Price, et al., eds. *Government and the American Economy: A New History* (Chicago: University of Chicago Press, 2007).

Fishlow, Albert. "Internal Transportation in the Nineteenth and Early Twentieth Centuries." In Engerman and Gallman, *Cambridge Economic History*, 543–642.

Fitzgerland, Deborah. *Every Farm a Factory: The Industrial Ideal in American Agriculture* (New Haven, CT: Yale University Press, 2003).

Flickers, Andreas. "Presenting the 'Window on the World' to the World: Competing Narratives of the Presentation of Television at the World's Fairs in Paris (1937) and New York (1939)." *Historical Journal of Film, Radio and Television* 28, no. 3 (August 2008): 291–310.

Flint, Motley H. "Financing the Motion Pictures." In Photoplay Research Society of Los Angeles, *Opportunities*.

Floud, Roderick, and Paul Johnson, eds. *The Cambridge Economic History of Modern Britain.* Vol. 2, *Economic Maturity, 1860–1939* (Cambridge: Cambridge University Press, 2004).

Folsom, Josiah C. "The Use of Educational Motion Pictures by the United States Department of Agriculture," *International Review of Educational Cinematography* (November 1929): 591–94.

Fones-Wolf, Elizabeth. "Creating a Favorable Business Climate: Corporations and Radio Broadcasting, 1934 to 1954." *Business History Review* 73, no.2 (Summer 1999): 221–55.

———. *Selling Free Enterprise: The Business Assault on Labor and Liberalism, 1945–60* (Champaign: University of Illinois Press, 1994).

Ford, Henry. *My Life and Work* (London: William Heinemann, 1924).

Ford Motor Company, *The Ford Exposition: World's Fair* (Michigan: Ford Motor Company, 1939).

Forman, Henry. *Our Movie Made Children* (New York: Macmillan, 1933).

Fotsch, Paul Mason. "The Building of a Superhighway Future at the New York World's Fair." *Cultural Critique* 48 (Spring 2001): 65–97.

Foucault, Michel. *The Birth of Biopolitics: Lectures at the College de France, 1978–1979.* Edited by Michel Senellart. Translated by Graham Burchell (London: Palgrave Macmillan, 2008).

———. *Discipline and Punish: The Birth of the Prison.* Translated by Alan Sheridan (New York: Vintage Books, 1995).

———. *Essential Works of Foucault, 1954–1984.* Edited by Paul Rabinov. Vol. 1, *Ethics* (London: Penguin, 2000).

———. "Governmentality." In Burchell, Gordon, and Miller, *Foucault Effect,* 87–104.

———. *The History of Sexuality.* Vol. 1, *An Introduction.* Translated by Robert Hurley (London: Penguin, 1990). First published 1976.

———. "Liberalism and the Implementation of a New Art of Government in the Eighteenth Century." In *The Birth of Biopolitics: Lectures at the College de France, 1978–1979,* edited by Michel Senellart and translated by Graham Burchell, 27–50 (London: Palgrave Macmillan, 2008).

———. "Security, Territory, and Population." In *Michel Foucault: Essential Works of Foucault, 1954–1984,* edited by Paul Rabinov, 67–72. Vol. 1, *Ethics* (London: Penguin, 2000).

———. "The Subject and Power." In *Michel Foucault: Beyond Structuralism and Hermeneutics,* edited by Herbert Dreyfus and Paul Rabinov, 208–26 (Brighton: Harvester, 1982).

———. "Technologies of the Self." In *Technologies of the Self: A Seminar with Michel Foucault,* edited by Luther Martin, Huck Gutman, and Patrick Hutton, 16–49. (London: Tavistock Publications, 1989).

——. "Truth and Power." In *Power/Knowledge: Selected Interviews and Other Writings, 1972–1977,* edited by Colin Gordon (New York: Pantheon, 1980).

Francis, Martin, and Ina Zweiniger-Bargielowska, eds. *The Conservatives and British Society, 1880–1990* (Cardiff: University of Wales Press, 1996).

Frank, Andre Gunder. *Capitalism and Underdevelopment in Latin America* (New York: Monthly Review Press, 1969).

Fraser, Steve. "The 'Labor Question.'" In Fraser and Gerstle, *Rise and Fall,* 55–84.

Fraser, Steve, and Gary Gerstle, eds. *The Rise and Fall of the New Deal Order, 1930–1980* (Princeton, NJ: Princeton University Press, 1989).

——. *Ruling America: A History of Wealth and Power in a Democracy* (Cambridge, MA: Harvard University Press, 2005).

Freeberg, Ernest. *The Age of Edison: Electric Light and the Invention of Modern America* (New York: Penguin Books, 2013).

Freeland, Robert F. *The Struggle for Control of the Modern Corporation: Organizational Change at General Motors, 1924–1970* (New York: Cambridge University Press, 2001).

Freeman, Frank, ed. *Visual Instruction: A Comparative Study of Motion Pictures and Other Methods of Instruction* (Chicago: University of Chicago Press, 1924).

Freud, Sigmund. *Civilization and Its Discontents.* Translated by James Strachey (New York: W. W. Norton, 1962). First published 1930.

——. *Group Psychology and the Analysis of the Ego.* Translated by James Strachey (London: Hogarth Press, 1959). First published 1922.

——"Preface to the Translation of Bernheim's *Suggestion.*" In Freud, *Standard Edition,* 75–85.

——. *The Standard Edition of the Complete Psychological Works of Sigmund Freud.* Edited by James Strachey. Vol. 1 (London: Vintage, 2001).

Freyer, Tony A. "Business Law and American Economic History." In Engerman and Gallman, *Cambridge Economic History,* 462–70.

Frey, Marc. "Tools of Empire: Persuasion and the United States Modernizing Mission in Southeast Asia." *Diplomatic History* 27, no. 4 (September 2003): 543–68.

Frieden, Jeffry A. *Global Capitalism: Its Fall and Rise in the Twentieth Century* (New York: W. W. Norton, 2006).

Friedman, Milton, and Anna J. Schwartz. *A Monetary History of the United States, 1867–1960* (Princeton, NJ: Princeton University Press, 1963).

Frykholm, Joel. *The Lost Tycoon: George Kleine and American Cinema, 1890–1930* (London: British Film Institute, 2016).

Fuller, Kathy. *At the Picture Show: Small-Town Audiences and the Creation of Movie Fan Culture* (Washington DC: Smithsonian Institution Press, 1996).

Gaines Jane, ed. *Classical Hollywood: The Paradigm Wars* (Durham, NC: Duke University Press, 1992).

Gallagher, John, and Ronald Robinson. "The Imperialism of Free Trade." *Economic History Review* 6, no. 1 (1953): 1–15.

Galston, William. "Civic Education in the Liberal State." In *Liberalism and Moral Life,* edited by Nancy L. Rosenblum, 89–102 (Cambridge: Harvard University Press, 1989).

Gartman, David. *Auto Slavery: The Labor Process in the American Automobile Industry, 1897–1950* (New Brunswick, NJ: Rutgers University Press, 1986).

Gary, Brett. *The Nervous Liberals: Propaganda Anxieties from World War I to the Cold War* (New York: Columbia University Press, 1999).

Gauld, Alan. *A History of Hypnotism* (Cambridge: Cambridge University Press, 1992).

Geiger, Joseph Roy. "The Effects of the Motion Picture on the Mind and Morals of the Young." *International Journal of Ethics* 34, no. 1 (October 1923): 69–83.

Gelfand, Lawrence. *The Inquiry: The American Preparations for Peace, 1917–1919* (New Haven, CT: Yale University Press, 1963).

Gerstle, Gary. *American Crucible: Race and Nation in the Twentieth Century* (Princeton, NJ: Princeton University Press, 2001).

———. "The Protean Character of American Liberalism." *American Historical Review* 99, no. 4 (October 1994): 1043–73.

Giannini, Attilio H. "Financial Aspects." In J. Kennedy *Story of the Films*, 77–98.

Giesen, James. *Boll Weevil Blues: Cotton, Myth, and Power in the American South* (Chicago: University of Chicago Press, 2011).

Gilbert, Charles. *American Financing of World War I* (Westport, CT: Greenwood Press, 1970).

Gilbreth, Frank Bunker. *Motion Study: A Method for Increasing the Efficiency of the Workman* (New York: D. Van Nostrand, 1911).

Gilderhus, Mark T. *Pan American Visions: Woodrow Wilson in the Western Hemisphere* (Tucson: University of Arizona Press, 1986).

Gilroy, Paul. "Great Games: Film, History and Working-through Britain's Colonial Legacy." In Grieveson and MacCabe, *Film and the End of Empire*, 13–32.

Gomery, Douglas. *The Coming of Sound* (New York: Routledge, 2005).

———. *A History of Broadcasting in the United States* (Oxford: Blackwell, 2008).

———. "Hollywood, the National Recovery Administration, and the Question of Monopoly Power." In Kindem, *American Movie Industry*, 204–14.

———. *The Hollywood Studio System: A History* (London: British Film Institute, 2005).

Goodwyn, Lawrence. *Democratic Promise: The Populist Movement in America* (New York: Oxford University Press, 1976).

Gordon, Colin. "Governmental Rationality: An Introduction." In Burchell, Gordon, and Miller, *Foucault Effect*, 1–52.

Gordon, Colin. *New Deals: Business, Labor, and Politics in America, 1920–1935* (Cambridge: Cambridge University Press, 1994).

Gramsci, Antonio. *The Gramsci Reader: Selected Writings, 1916–1935.* Edited by David Forgacs (New York: New York University Press, 2000).

Grandin, Greg. *Fordlandia: The Rise and Fall of Henry Ford's Forgotten Jungle City* (New York: Metropolitan Books, 2009).

———. "The Liberal Traditions in the Americas: Rights, Sovereignty, and the Origins of Liberal Multilateralism." *American Historical Review* 117, no. 1 (February 2012): 68–91.

Grant, Mariel. *Propaganda and the Role of the State in Inter-war Britain* (Oxford: Clarendon Press, 1994).

Grazia, Victoria de. *Irresistible Empire: America's Advance through Twentieth-Century Europe* (Cambridge, MA: Harvard University press, 2005).

Green, E. H. *The Crisis of Conservatism: The Politics, Economics and Ideology of the British Conservative Party, 1880–1914* (London: Routledge, 1995).

Greene, Julia. *The Canal Builders: Making America's Empire at the Panama Canal* (New York: Penguin Press, 2009).

Greene, Nelson Lewis. *1000 and One: The Blue Book of Non-theatrical Films*. 10th ed. (Chicago: Educational Screen, 1934).

Greene, Ronald Walter. "Pastoral Exhibition: The YMCA Motion Picture Bureau and the Transition to 16mm, 1928–1939." In Acland and Wasson, *Useful Cinema*, 205–29.

———. "Y Movies: Film and the Modernization of Pastoral Power." *Communication and Critical/Cultural Studies* 2, no. 1 (March 2005): 20–36.

Greenwald, Glenn. *No Place to Hide: Edward Snowden, the NSA, and the U.S. Surveillance State* (New York: Metropolitan Books, 2014).

Grierson, John. "First Principles of Documentary." In *Imagining Reality: The Faber Book of Documentary,* edited by Kevin Macdonald and Mark Cousins, 97–101 (London: Faber and Faber, 1996).

Grieveson, Lee. "Cinema Studies and the Conduct of Conduct." In Grieveson and Wasson, *Inventing Film Studies,* 3–37.

———. "Discipline and Publish: The Birth of Cinematology." *Cinema Journal* 49, no. 1 (Fall 2009): 168–76.

———. "Not Harmless Entertainment: Local and State Censorship in the United States in the 1910s." In Stamp and Keil, *American Cinema's Transitional Era,* 268–84.

———. *Policing Cinema: Movies and Censorship in Early Twentieth-Century America* (Berkeley: University of California Press, 2004).

Grieveson, Lee, and Colin MacCabe, eds. *Empire and Film* (London: British Film Institute, 2011).

———. *Film and the End of Empire* (London: British Film Institute, 2011).

Grieveson, Lee, and Haidee Wasson, eds. *Inventing Film Studies* (Durham, NC: Duke University Press, 2008).

Gruening, Ernest. *The Public Pays: A Study of Power Propaganda* (New York: Vanguard Press, 1931).

Guillén, Mauro F. *The Taylorized Beauty of the Mechanical: Scientific Management and the Rise of Modernist Architecture* (Princeton, NJ: Princeton University Press, 2006).

Guldi, Jo. *Roads to Power: Britain Invents the Infrastructure State* (Cambridge, MA: Harvard University Press, 2012)

Habermas, Jürgen. *The Structural Transformation of the Public Sphere.* Translated by Thomas Burger (Cambridge, MA: MIT Press, 1989).

Hacking, Ian. "How Should We Do the History of Statistics?" In Burchell, Gordon, and Miller, *Foucault Effect,* 181–96.

Hale, Mathew Jr. *Human Science and Social Order: Hugo Münsterberg and the Origins of Applied Psychology* (Philadelphia: Temple University Press, 1980).

Halsey, Stuart and Co. *The Motion Picture Industry as a Basis for Bond Financing* (Chicago: Halsey, Stuart, 1927).

Hamilton, David E. "Building the Associative State: The Department of Agriculture and American State-Building." *Agricultural History* 64, no. 2 (1990): 207–18.

Hamilton, Shane. *Trucking Country: The Road to America's Wal-Mart Economy* (Princeton, NJ: Princeton University Press, 2008).

Hampton, Benjamin. *A History of the Movies* (New York: Covici Friede 1931).

Hanson, Elisah. "Official Propaganda and the New Deal." *American Academy of Political and Social Science* 179 (May 1935): 176–86.

Hardt, Hanno. *Critical Communication Studies: Communication, History and Theory in America* (London: Routledge, 1992).

Hardy, Forsyth. *John Grierson: A Documentary Biography* (London: Faber and Faber, 1979).

Harris, Neil. *Humbug: The Art of P. T. Barnum* (Boston: Little, Brown, 1973).

Hart, David M., "Herbert Hoover's Last Laugh: The Enduring Significance of the 'Associative State' in the United States." *Journal of Policy History* 10, no. 4 (October 1998): 419–44.

Hartz, Louis. *The Liberal Tradition in America: An Interpretation of American Political Thought since the Revolution* (New York: Harcourt Brace, 1955).

Harvey, David. *A Brief History of Neo-liberalism* (Oxford: Oxford University Press, 2005).

———. *The New Imperialism* (Oxford: Oxford University Press, 2003).

———. *Seventeen Contradictions and the End of Capitalism* (Oxford: Oxford University Press, 2014).

———. *Spaces of Global Capitalism: Towards a Theory of Uneven Capitalist Development* (London: Verso, 2006).

Hawley, Ellis. "The Discovery and Study of a 'Corporate Liberalism,'" *Business History Review* 52, no. 3 (Autumn 1978): 309–20.

———. *The Great War and the Search for a Modern Order: A History of the American People and Their Institutions, 1917–1933* (New York: St Martin's Press, 1979).

———. "Herbert Hoover, the Commerce Secretariat, and the Vision of an 'Associative State,' 1921–1928." *Journal of American History* 61, no. 1 (June 1974): 116–40.

———. "Three Facets of Hooverian Associationalism: Lumber, Aviation, and Movies, 1921–1930." In *Regulation in Perspective: Historical Essays,* edited by Thomas McCraw, 108–15 (Cambridge, MA: Harvard University Press, 1981).

Hayek, Friedrich Von. *The Road to Serfdom* (London: Routledge, 1944).

Hay, James. *Popular Film Cultures in Fascist Italy: The Passing of the Rex* (Bloomington: Indiana University Press, 1987).

Hays, Will. *The Memoirs of Will H. Hays* (Garden City, NJ: Doubleday, 1955).

———. "Supervision from Within." In J. Kennedy, *Story of the Films,* 29–54.

Headrick, Daniel R. *The Invisible Weapon: Telecommunications and International Politics 1851–1945* (New York: Oxford University Press, 1991).

Healy, William. *The Individual Delinquent* (Boston: Little, Brown, 1915).

Hediger, Vinzenz, and Patrick Vonderau eds. *Films That Work: Industrial Film and the Productivity of Media* (Amsterdam: Amsterdam University Press, 2009).

Heffelfinger, Elizabeth. "*Home Town Story*: General Motors, Marilyn Monroe, and the Production of Economic Citizenship." *Journal of Popular Film and Television* 37, no. 3 (2009): 126–36.

Hendricks, Gordon. *The Edison Motion Picture Myth* (Berkeley: University of California Press, 1961).

Henkin, David M. *The Postal Age: The Emergence of Modern Communications in Nineteenth-Century America* (Chicago: The University of Chicago Press, 2006).

Her Majesty's Stationery Office. *Imperial Conference, 1926: Summary of Proceedings* (London: HMSO, 1926).

Herman, Edward, and Noam Chomsky. *Manufacturing Consent: The Political Economy of the Mass Media* (London: Vintage Books, 1994).

Herman, Edward, and Robert McChesney, *The Global Media: The New Missionaries of Corporate Capitalism* (London: Continuum, 2004).

Herring, E. Pendleton. "Official Publicity under the New Deal." *Annals of the American Academy of Political and Social Science* 179 (May 1933): 167–75.

Higashi, Sumiko. *Cecil B. DeMille and American Culture: The Silent Era* (Berkeley: University of California Press, 1994).

Higgs, Robert. "The World Wars." In Fishback et al., *Government and the American Economy*, 431–55.

Higham, John. *Strangers in the Land: Patterns of American Nativism, 1860–1925*. 2nd ed. (New Brunswick, NJ: Rutgers University Press, 1992).

Higson, Andrew. "Cultural Policy and Industrial Practice: Film Europe and the International Film Congresses of the 1920s." In Higson and Maltby, *"Film Europe,"* 117–31.

———. "Polyglot Films for an International Market: E. A. Dupont, the British Film Industry, and the Idea of a European Cinema, 1926–1930," in Higson and Maltby, *"Film Europe,"* 274–301.

Higson, Andrew, and Richard Maltby, eds. *"Film Europe" and "Film America": Cinema, Commerce and Cultural Exchange 1920–1939* (Exeter, UK: University of Exeter Press, 1999).

———. "'Film Europe' and 'Film America': An Introduction." In Higson and Maltby, *"Film Europe,"* 1–31.

Hilderbrand, Robert C. *Power and the People: Executive Management of Public Opinion in Foreign Affairs, 1897–1921* (Chapel Hill: University of North Carolina Press, 1981).

Hills, Jill. *The Struggle for Control of Global Communication: The Formative Century* (Urbana: University of Illinois Press, 2002).

Hilmes, Michele. *Hollywood and Broadcasting: From Radio to Cable* (Urbana: University of Illinois Press, 1990).

Himmelberg, Robert F., ed. *Business-Government Cooperation, 1917–1932* (New York: Garland, 1994).

Hoare, F. A. "Educational Cinematography." In *Films and Education* (London: Commission on Educational and Cultural Films, 1932).

Hoban, Charles F., and Samuel B. Zisman. *Visualizing the Curriculum* (New York: Cordon, 1937).

Hobbes, Thomas. *Leviathan.* (New York: Cosimo, 2009). First published 1651.

Hobsbawm, Eric. *The Age of Capital, 1848–1875* (1975; repr. London: Abacus, 1999).

———. *The Age of Empire, 1875–1914* (1989; repr. London: Abacus, 2010).

———. *The Age of Extremes, 1914–1991* (London: Abacus, 1994).

———. *The Age of Revolution, 1789–1848* (1962; repr. London: Abacus, 2011).

———. *Industry and Empire: An Economic History of Britain since 1750* (London: Weidenfeld and Nicolson, 1969).

Hogan, Michael J. *Informal Entente: The Private Structure of Cooperation in Anglo-American Economic Diplomacy, 1918–1928* (Chicago: Imprint, 1991).

Holaday, P. W., and George G. Stoddard, *Getting Ideas from the Movies* (New York: Macmillan, 1933).

Holley, Francis. "Industrial Information by Motography" (Philadelphia: Bureau of Commercial Economics, 1915).

Holley, Irving Brinton. "Blacktop: How Asphalt Paving Came to the Urban United States." *Technology and Culture* 44, no. 4 (October 2003): 703–33.

Hollins, Timothy. "The Conservative Party and Film Propaganda between the Wars." *English Historical Review* 96, no. 379 (April 1981): 359–69.

———. "The Presentation of Politics: The Place of Party Publicity, Broadcasting and Film in British Politics, 1918–1939." PhD diss., University of Leeds, 1981.

Holt, Jennifer. *Empires of Entertainment: Media Industries and the Politics of Deregulation, 1980–1996* (New Brunswick, NJ: Rutgers University Press, 2011).

Horkheimer, Max, and Theodor Adorno. *Dialectic of Enlightenment* (London: Verso, 1997). First published 1944.

Horten, Gerd. *Radio Goes to War: The Cultural Politics of Propaganda during World War II* (Berkeley: University of California Press, 2003).

Hounshell, David A. *From the American System to Mass Production, 1800–1932* (Baltimore: John Hopkins University Press, 1984).

Howard, George Elliot. "Social Psychology of the Spectator." *American Journal of Sociology* 18, no. 1 (July 1912): 33–50.

Hoxie, Frederick E. "Retrieving the Red Continent: Settler Colonialism and the History of American Indians in the U.S." *Ethnic and Racial Studies* 31, no. 6 (2008): 1153–67.

Huetting, Mae D. *Economic Control of the Motion Picture Industry* (Philadelphia: University of Pennsylvania press, 1944).

Hunter, Dulin and Co. *The Golden Harvest of the Silver Screen* (California: Hunter, Dulin, 1927).

Hunter, Ian. *Culture and Government: The Emergence of Literary Education* (London: Macmillan, 1988).

Hutcheson, John A. Jr. "Defense of the Realm Act." In *The Encyclopedia of World War I: A Political, Social, and Military History,* edited by Spencer C. Tucker. Vol. 1 (Santa Barbara: ABC-CLIO, 2005).

Ikenberry, G. John. "Liberal Internationalism 3.0: America and the Dilemmas of Liberal World Order." *Perspectives on Politics* 7, no. 1 (March 2009): 71–87.

Ingersent, Ken A., and A. J. Rayner. *Agricultural Policy in Western Europe and the United States* (Cheltenham, UK: Edward Elgar, 1999).

Inglis, Ruth. *Freedom of the Movies: A Report on Self-Regulation from the Commission on the Freedom of the Press* (Chicago: University of Chicago Press, 1947).

Irwin, Douglas. *Against the Tide: An Intellectual History of Free Trade* (Princeton, NJ: Princeton University Press, 1996).

Jacobs, Lea. "Reformers and Spectators: The Film Education Movement in the Thirties." *Camera Obscura* 8, no. 1:22 (January 1990): 28–49.

Jacobs, Meg, William Novak, and Julian E. Zelizer, eds. *The Democratic Experiment: New Directions in American Political History* (Princeton, NJ: Princeton University Press, 2003).

Jaikumar, Priya. *Cinema at the End of Empire: A Politics of Transition in Britain and India* (Durham, NC: Duke University Press, 2006).

Jameson, Frederic. "Culture and Finance Capital." *Critical Inquiry* 24, no. 1 (Autumn, 1997): 246–65.

———. "Notes on Globalization as a Philosophical Issue." In *The Cultures of Globalization,* edited by Frederic Jameson and Masao Miyoshi, 54–77 (Durham, NC: Duke University Press, 1998).

Jarvie, Ian. *Hollywood's Overseas Campaign: The North Atlantic Movie Trade, 1920–1950* (Cambridge: Cambridge University Press, 1992).

Jarvis, David. "British Conservatism and Class Politics in the 1920s." *English Historical Review* 111, no. 440 (February 1996): 59–84.

———. "Mrs Maggs and Betty: The Conservative Appeal to Women Voters in the 1920s." *Twentieth Century British History* 5, no. 2 (1994): 129–52.

Jones, Gareth Stedman. "The History of U.S. Imperialism." In *Ideology in Social Science,* edited by Robin Blackburn (New York: Vintage, 1972).

Jones, Stephen G. *The British Labour Movement and Film, 1918–1939* (London: Routledge and Kegan Paul, 1987).

Josephson, Matthew. *Empire of the Air: Juan Trippe and the Struggle for World Airways* (New York: Harcourt Brace, 1944).

Jowett, Garth, Ian C. Jarvie, and Kathryn H. Fuller. *Children and the Movies: Media Influence and the Payne Fund Controversy* (Cambridge: Cambridge University Press, 1996).

Joyce, Patrick. *The Rule of Freedom: Liberalism and the Modern City* (London: Verso, 2003).

Jump, Rev. H. A. *The Social Influence of the Moving Picture* (New York: Playground and Recreation Association of America, 1911).

Kahana, Jonathan. *Intelligence Work: The Politics of American Documentary* (New York: Columbia University Press, 2008).

Kaplan, Amy, and Donald E. Pease. *Cultures of United States Imperialism* (Durham, NC: Duke University Press, 1993).

Kapur, Jyotsna, and Keith B. Wagner, eds. *Neoliberalism and Global Cinema: Capital, Culture, and Marxist Critique* (London: Routledge, 2013).

Katz, Michael B. "The American Welfare State and Social Contract in Hard Times." *Journal of Policy History* 22, no. 4 (2010): 508–29.

Kaufman, Burton. *Efficiency and Expansion: Foreign Trade Organization in the Wilson Administration, 1913–1921* (Westport, CT: Greenwood Press, 1974).

Kazin, Michael, ed. *The Princeton Encyclopedia of American Political History.* Rebecca Edwards and Adam Rothman, associate editors (Princeton, NJ: Princeton University Press, 2010).

Keil, Charlie. *Early American Cinema in Transition: Story, Style, and Filmmaking, 1907–1913* (Madison: University of Wisconsin Press, 2001).

Keller, Morton. *Regulating a New Economy: Public Policy and Economic Change in America, 1900–1933* (Cambridge, MA: Harvard University Press, 1990).

Kennedy, David M. *Over Here: The First World War and American Society* (New York: Oxford University Press, 1980).

Kennedy, Joseph P., ed. *The Story of the Films as Told by Leaders of the Industry to the Students of the Graduate School of Business Administration George F. Baker Foundation Harvard University* (Chicago: A. W. Shaw, 1927).

Kent, Sidney R. "Distributing the Product." In J. Kennedy, *Story of the Films,* 203–32.

Kern, Stephen. *The Culture of Time and Space* (Cambridge, MA: Harvard University Press, 1983).

Kimble, James J. *Mobilizing the Home Front: War Bonds and Domestic Propaganda* (College Station: Texas A&M University Press, 2006).

Kindem, Gorham, ed. *The American Movie Industry* (Carbondale: Southern Illinois University Press, 1982).

Kirby, Jack Temple. *Rural Worlds Lost: The American South 1920–1960* (Baton Rouge: Louisiana State University Press, 1987).

Kitamura, Hiroshi. *Screening Enlightenment: Hollywood and the Cultural Reconstruction of Defeated Japan* (Ithaca, NY: Cornell University Press, 2010).

Klein, Julius. "What Are Motion Pictures Doing for Industry?" *Annals of the American Academy of Political and Social Science* 128 (November 1926): 79–83.

Klein, Naomi. *The Shock Doctrine: The Rise of Disaster Capitalism* (London: Penguin, 2007).

Knobloch, Frieda. *The Culture of Wilderness: Agriculture as Colonization in the American West* (Chapel Hill: University of North Carolina Press, 1996).

Kohn, Stephen M. *American Political Prisoners: Prosecutions under the Espionage and Sedition Acts* (Westport, CT: Praeger, 1994).

Koistinen, Paul A. C. *Mobilizing for Modern War: The Political Economy of American Warfare, 1865–1919* (Lawrence: University Press of Kansas, 1997).

Kolko, Gabriel. *The Triumph of Conservatism: A Reinterpretation of American History, 1900–1916* (New York: Free Press, 1963).

Koszarski, Richard. *An Evening's Entertainment: The Age of The Silent Feature Picture, 1915–1928* (Berkeley, CA.: University of California Press, 1990).

Kotz, David M. *Bank Control of Large Corporations in the United States* (Berkeley: University of California Press, 1978).

Kracauer, Siegfried. *From Caligari to Hitler: A Psychological History of the German Film* (Princeton, NJ: Princeton University Press, 1947).

Kramer, Paul A. "Power and Connection: Imperial Histories of the United States in the World." *American Historical Review* 116, no. 5 (December 2011): 1348–91.

Krämer, Peter. "The Lure of the Big Picture: Film, Television and Hollywood." In *Big Picture, Small Screen: The Relations between Film and Television,* edited by John Hill and Martin McLoone (Luton, UK: John Libbey, 1996).

Krows, Arthur Edwin. "Motion Pictures—Not for Theatres," *Educational Screen* (September 1938–June 1944): 58 installments.

Kuhn, Arthur J. *GM Passes Ford, 1918–1939: Designing the General Motors Performance-Control System* (University Park: Pennsylvania State University Press, 1986).

Kunz, William. *Culture Conglomerates: Consolidation in the Motion Picture and Television Industries* (Lanham, MD: Rowman and Littlefield, 2006).

Kurth, James. "Military-Industrial Complex. In Chambers, *Oxford Companion to American Military History,* 438–40.

Lamoreaux, Naomi R. "Entrepreneurship, Business Organization, and Economic Concentration." In Engerman and Gallman, *Cambridge Economic History,* 403–34.

———. *The Great Merger Movement in American Business, 1895–1904* (Cambridge: Cambridge University Press, 1985).

———. "Partnerships, Corporations, and the Limits on Contractual Freedom in U.S. History: An Essay in Economics, Law, and Culture." In Lipartito and Sicilia, *Constructing Corporate America*, 29–65.

Larkin, Brian. "Circulating Empires: Colonial Authority and the Immoral, Subversive Problem of American Film." In *Globalizing American Studies,* edited by Brian T. Edwards and Dilip Parameshwar Gaonkar (Chicago: University of Chicago Press, 2010), 155–83.

———. *Signal and Noise: Media, Infrastructure, and Urban Culture in Nigeria* (Durham, NC: Duke University Press, 2008).

Lasch, Christopher. *The New Radicalism in America, 1889–1963: The Intellectual as a Social Type* (New York: W. W. Norton, 1965).

Lasswell, Harold. "Propaganda." In Vol. 2 of *Encyclopedia of the Social Sciences,* edited by Edwin R. A. Seligman, 527–38 (New York: Macmillan, 1934).

———. *Propaganda Technique in World War I* (Cambridge, MA: MIT Press, 1971). First published 1927 as *Propaganda Technique in the World War.*

———. "The Structure and Function of Communication in Society." In Bryson, *Communication of Ideas,* 84–99.

Lasswell, Harold, and Dorothy Blumenstock. *World Revolutionary Propaganda* (New York: Alfred A. Knopf, 1939).

Leab, Daniel. *Orwell Subverted: The CIA and the Filming of* Animal Farm (Philadelphia: Penn State University Press, 2007).

Leach, Eugene E. "Mastering the Crowd: Collective Behavior and Mass Society in American Social Thought, 1917–1939." *American Studies* 27, no. 1 (1986): 99–114.

Le Bon, Gustave. *The Crowd: A Study of the Popular Mind* (London: T. Fisher, 1897).

Lee, Albert. *Henry Ford and the Jews* (New York: Stein and Day, 1980).

Lee, Kevin. "'The Little State Department': Hollywood and the MPAA's Influence on U.S. Trade Relations." *Northwestern Journal of International Law and Business* 28, no. 2 (Winter 2008): 371–97.

LeFeber, Walter. *The American Search for Opportunity, 1865–1913,* Vol. 2 of *The Cambridge History of American Foreign Relations.* (Cambridge: Cambridge University Press, 1993).

LeMahieu, D. L. *A Culture for Democracy: Mass Communication and the Cultivated Mind in Britain between the Wars* (Oxford: Clarendon Press, 1988).

Lenin, V. I. "The Socialist Revolution and the Right of Nations to Self-Determination: Theses." In *National Liberation, Socialism and Imperialism* (New York: International Publications, 1968). First published 1916.

Leuchtenburg, William. *Franklin D. Roosevelt and the New Deal, 1932–1940* (New York: Harper, 2009).

Levavy, Sara Beth. "Land of Liberty in the World of Tomorrow." *Film History* 18, no. 4 (2006): 440–58.

Lewis, David. "Henry Ford—Movie Producer." *Ford Life* (January–February 1971): 17–19.

———. *The Public Image of Henry Ford: An American Folk Hero and His Company* (Detroit: Wayne State University, 1976).

Lewis, Howard T. *Cases on the Motion Picture Industry* (New York: McGraw Hill, 1930).

———. *The Motion Picture Industry* (New York: D. Van Nostrand, 1933).

Lewis, Jon. *Hollywood v. Hardcore: How the Struggle Over Censorship Created the Modern Film Industry* (New York: New York University Press, 2002).

———. "'We Do Not Ask You to Condone This': How the Blacklist Saved Hollywood." *Cinema Journal* 39, no. 2 (Winter 2000): 3–30.

Leys, Ruth. "Mead's Voices: Imitation as Foundation, or, the Struggle against Mimesis." *Critical Inquiry* 19, no. 2 (Winter 1993): 277–307.

Lichtenberg, Bernard. "Business Backs New York World Fair to Meet the New Deal Propaganda." *Public Opinion Quarterly* 2 (April 1938): 314–20.

Lichtenstein, Nelson, and Howell John Harris, eds. *Industrial Democracy in America: The Ambiguous Promise* (Cambridge: Cambridge University Press, 1993).

Ling, Peter J. *America and the Automobile: Technology, Reform, and Social Change* (Manchester, UK: Manchester University Press, 1990).

Lipartito, Kenneth, and David B. Sicilia, eds. *Constructing Corporate America: History, Politics, Culture* (Oxford: Oxford University Press, 2004).

Lippmann, Walter. *Drift and Mastery: An Attempt to Diagnose the Current Unrest* (New York: Mitchell Kennerly, 1914).

———. *Liberty and the News* (New York: Harcourt, Brace and Howe, 1920).

———. *The Phantom Public* (New York: Harcourt Brace, 1925).

———. *Public Opinion* (New York: Free Press, 1997). First published 1922.

Lipsky, Adam. *Man the Puppet: The Art of Controlling Minds* (New York: Frank Maurice, 1925).

Livingston, James. *Origins of the Federal Reserve System: Money, Class, and Corporate Capitalism, 1890–1913* (Ithaca, NY: Cornell University Press, 1986).

———. *Pragmatism and the Political Economy of Cultural Revolution, 1850–1940* (Chapel Hill: University of North Carolina Press, 1994).

Locke, John. *Collected Works.* Edited by John M. Robson (London: Routledge and Kegan Paul, 1965).

———. *Some Thoughts concerning Education* (London: A. and J. Churchill, 1693).

———. *Two Treatises of Government.* Edited by Peter Laslett (Cambridge: Cambridge University Press, 1991).

Lord, Alexandra M. "Models of Masculinity: Sex Education, the United States Public Health Service, and the YMCA, 1919–1924." *Journal of the History of Medicine and Allied Sciences* 58, no. 2 (2003): 123–52.

Lorentz, Pare, and Morris L. Ernst. *Censored: The Private Life of the Movie* (New York: Jonathan Cape, 1930).

Low, Rachel. *The History of the British Film, 1918–1929* (London: George Allen and Unwin, 1971).

Luce, Henry. "The American Century." *Life,* February 17, 1941, 61–65.

Lucic, Karen. *Charles Sheeler and the Cult of the Machine* (Cambridge, MA: Harvard University Press, 1991).

Luger, Stan. *Corporate Power, American Democracy, and the Automobile Industry* (Cambridge: Cambridge University Press, 2000).

Lustig, Jeffrey R. *Corporate Liberalism: The Origins of Modern American Political Theory, 1890–1920* (Berkeley: University of California Press, 1982).

MacCabe, Colin. "'To Take Ship to India and See a Naked Man Spearing Fish in Blue Water': Watching Films to Mourn the End of Empire." In Grieveson and MacCabe, *Empire and Film,* 1–17.

MacCann, Richard. *The People's Films: A Political History of U.S. Government Motion Pictures* (New York: Hastings House, 1973).

Mackenzie, John M., ed. *Imperialism and Popular Culture* (Manchester, UK: Manchester University Press, 1986).

———. *Propaganda and Empire* (Manchester, UK: Manchester University Press, 1986).

Macpherson, C. B. *Democratic Theory: Essays in Retrieval* (Oxford: Clarendon Press, 1973).

———. "Human Rights as Property Rights." In *The Rise and Fall of Economic Justice and Other Papers* (Oxford: Oxford University Press, 1985), 76–85.

———. *The Life and Times of Liberal Democracy* (Oxford: Oxford University Press, 1977).

———. *The Political Theory of Possessive Individualism: Hobbes to Locke* (Oxford: Clarendon Press, 1962).

———, ed. *Property: Mainstream and Critical Positions* (Oxford: Basil Blackwell, 1978).

———. *The Rise and Fall of Economic Justice and Other Papers* (Oxford: Oxford University Press, 1985).

Major, John. *Prize Possession: The United States and the Panama Canal 1903–1979* (Cambridge: Cambridge University Press, 1993).

Malin, Brenton J. "Mediating Emotion: Technology, Social Science, and Emotion in the Payne Fund Motion-Picture Studies." *Technology and Culture* 50, no. 2 (April 2009): 366–90.

Maltby, Richard. "The Cinema and the League of Nations." In Higson and Maltby, *"Film Europe" and "Film America,"* 82–116.

———. *Harmless Entertainment: Hollywood and the Ideology of Consensus* (Metuchen, NJ: Scarecrow Press, 1983).

———. "The Production Code and the Hays Office." In *Grand Design: Hollywood as a Modern Business Enterprise, 1930–1939*, edited by Tino Balio, 37–72 (New York: Charles Scribner's Sons, 1993).

———. "The Standard Exhibition Contract and the Unwritten History of the Classical Hollywood Cinema." *Film History* 25, nos. 1–2 (2013): 138–53.

Manent, Pierre. *An Intellectual History of Liberalism.* Translated by Rebecca Balinski (Princeton, NJ: Princeton University Press, 1995).

Mann, Michael. "The Autonomous Power of the State: Its Origins, Mechanisms, and Results." In *States in History,* edited by John A. Hall (Oxford: Oxford University Press, 1986).

Mann, William. *Tinseltown: Murder, Morphine, and Madness at the Dawn of Hollywood* (New York: Harper Collins, 2014).

Marchand, Roland. *Advertising the American Dream: Making Way for Modernity, 1920–1940* (Berkeley: University of California Press, 1985).

———. *Creating the Corporate Soul: The Rise of Public Relations and Corporate Imagery in American Big Business* (Berkeley: University of California Press, 1998).

———. "The Designers Go to the Fair, II: Normal Bel Geddes, the General Motors 'Futurama,' and the Visit to the Factory Transformed." *Design Issues* 8, no. 2 (Spring 1992): 22–40.

Marquis, Samuel. "The Ford Idea in Education." *National Educational Association of the U.S. Addresses and Proceedings,* 1916

Marx, Karl. *Capital: A Critique of Political Economy.* Vol. 1 (London: Penguin, 1990). First published 1867.

———. *Capital: A Critique of Political Economy.* Vol. 2 (London: Penguin, 1992). First published 1885.

———. *Capital: A Critique of Political Economy.* Vol. 3 (London: Penguin, 1991). First published 1884.

———. *Grundrisse* (London: Penguin, 1973). First published 1861.

———. *Selected Writings.* Edited by David McLellan (New York: Oxford University Press, 1977).

Mastrangelo, Lisa. "World War I, Public Intellectuals, and the Four Minute Men: Convergent Ideals of Public Speaking and Civic Participation." *Rhetoric and Public Affairs* 12, no. 4 (2009): 607–33.

Mathews, F. H. *Quest for an American Sociology* (Montreal: McGill-Queen's University Press, 1977).

Maurer, Noel. *What Roosevelt Took: The Economic Impact of the Panama Canal, 1903–1929* (Boston: Harvard Business School, 2006).

May, Lary. *The Big Tomorrow: Hollywood and the Politics of the American Way* (Chicago: University of Chicago Press, 2000).

Mazower, Mark. *Dark Continent: Europe's Twentieth Century* (London: Penguin, 1998).

———. *Governing the World: The History of an Idea* (London: Penguin, 2012).

McArthur, Benjamin. *Actors and American Culture, 1880–1920* (Philadelphia: Temple University Press, 1984).

McCarthy, Anna. *The Citizen Machine: Governing by Television in 1950s America* (New York: New Press, 2010).

McCartin, Joseph A. "'An American Feeling': Workers, Managers, and the Struggle for Industrial Democracy in the World War I Era." In Lichtenstein and Harris, *Industrial Democracy in America*, 67–86.

———. *Labor's Great War: The Struggle for Industrial Democracy and the Origins of Modern American Labor Relations, 1912–1921* (Chapel Hill: University of North Carolina Press, 1997).

McChesney, Robert. *Corporate Media and the Threat to Democracy* (New York: Seven Stories Press, 1997).

———. *Digital Disconnect: How Capitalism Is Turning the Internet against Democracy* (New York: New Press, 2013).

———. "The Payne Fund and Radio Broadcasting, 1928–1935." In Jowett, Jarvie, and Fuller, *Children and the Movies*, 303–35.

———. *Rich Media, Poor Democracy: Communication Politics in Dubious Times* (New York: New Press, 1999).

———. *Telecommunications, Mass Media, and Democracy: The Battle for the Control of U.S. Broadcasting, 1928–1935* (New York: Oxford University Press, 1993).

McClusky, F. Dean. *Visual Instruction: Its Value and Its Needs. A Report* (New York: Mancall, 1932).

McClymer, John F. "The Americanization Movement and the Education of the Foreign-Born Adult, 1914–25." In *American Education and the European Immigrant: 1840–1940*, edited by Bernard J. Weiss, 96–116 (Urbana: University of Illinois Press, 1982).

McCormick, Thomas J. *China Market: America's Quest for Informal Empire, 1893–1901* (Chicago: Quadrangle books, 1967).

McCraw, Thomas, ed. *Creating Modern Capitalism* (Cambridge, MA: Harvard University Press, 1997).

———. "Government, Big Business, and the Wealth of Nations." In Chandler, Amatori, and Hikino, *Big Business and the Wealth of Nations*, 522–45.

McCraw, Thomas K., and Richard S. Tedlow. "Henry Ford, Alfred Sloan, and the Three Phases of Marketing." in McCraw, *Creating Modern Capitalism*, 264–300.

McDean, Harry. "Professionalism, Policy, and Farm Economists in the Early Bureau of Agricultural Economics." *Agricultural History* 57, no. 1 (Jan. 1983): 64–82.

McDougall, William. *An Introduction to Social Psychology* (London: Methuen, 1960). First published 1908.

McGovern, Charles. "Consumption and Citizenship in the United States, 1900–1940." In Strasser, McGovern, and Judt, *Getting and Spending*, 37–58.

McKibbin, Ross. *The Ideologies of Class* (Oxford: Oxford University Press, 1991).

McNichol, Dan. *The Roads That Built America: The Incredible Story of the U.S. Interstate System* (New York: Sterling, 2006).

McPherson, William. *The Psychology of Persuasion* (New York: E. P. Dutton, 1920).

McQuaid, Kim. "Corporate Liberalism in the American Business Community, 1920–1940." *Business History Review* 52, no. 3 (Autumn 1978): 342–68.

Meehan, Eileen R. "A Legacy of Neoliberalism: Patterns in Media Conglomeration." In Kapur and Wagner, *Neoliberalism and Global Cinema*, 38–58.

Melnick, Ross. *American Showman: Samuel 'Roxy' Rothafel and the Birth of the Entertainment Industry* (New York: Columbia University Press, 2012).

Meredith, David. "Imperial Images: The Empire Marketing Board, 1926–1932." *History Today* 37, no. 1 (January 1987): 30–36.

Messinger, Gary S. *The Battle for the Mind: War and Peace in the Era of Mass Communication* (Amherst: University of Massachusetts Press, 2011).

Metha, Uday Singh. *Liberalism and Empire: A Study in Nineteenth-Century British Liberal Thought* (Chicago: University of Chicago Press, 1999).

Metzger, Th. *Blood and Volts: Edison, Tesla and the Electric Chair* (New York: Autonomedia, 1996).

Meyer, Stephen III. "Adapting the Immigrant to the Line: Americanization in the Ford Factory, 1914–1921," 14, no. 1, *Journal of Social History* 14 (Fall 1980): 67–82.

———. *The Five Dollar Day: Labor Management and Social Control in the Ford Motor Company, 1908–1921* (Albany: State University of New York, 1981).

———. "The Persistence of Fordism," In *On the Line: Essays in the History of Auto Work*, edited by Nelson Lichtenstein and Stephen Meyer, 73–99 (Urbana: University of Illinois Press, 1989).

Middlemas, Keith. *Politics in Industrial Society: The Experience of the British System since 1911* (London: André Deutsch, 1979).

Miller, Toby, Nitin Govil, John McMurria, Richard Maxwell, and Ting Wang. *Global Hollywood*. 2nd ed. (London: British Film Institute, 2005).

Miller, Toby, and Richard Maxwell. "'For a Better Deal, Harass Your Governor!': Neoliberalism and Hollywood." In Kapur and Wager, *Neoliberalism and Global Cinema*, 19–37.

Mill, John Stuart. *The Collected Works of John Stuart Mill, Volume III – Principles of Political Economy Part 11* (1848), ed., John M. Robson (Toronto: University of Toronto Press, 1965).

——. *Three Essays: On Liberty, Representative Government, the Subjection of Women* (Oxford: Oxford University Press, 1975).

Minihan, Janet. *The Nationalization of Culture: The Development of State Subsidies to the Arts in Great Britain* (New York: New York University press, 1977).

Misa, Thomas J. *A Nation of Steel: The Making of Modern America, 1865–1925* (Baltimore: John Hopkins University Press, 1995).

Moley, Raymond A. *Are We Movie Made?* (New York: Macy-Masius, 1938).

Monger, David. *Patriotism and Propaganda in First World War Britain* (Liverpool: Liverpool University Press, 2012).

Montgomery, David. *The Fall of the House of Labor: The Workplace, The State, and American Labor Activism, 1865–1925* (Cambridge: Cambridge University Press, 1987).

——. *Workers' Control in America: Studies in the History of Work, Technology, and Labor Struggles* (Cambridge: Cambridge University Press, 1980).

Monticone, Paul. "'Useful Cinema,' of What Use? Assessing the Role of Motion Pictures in the Largest Public Relations Campaign of the 1920s." *Cinema Journal* 54, no. 4 (Summer 2015): 74–99.

Moskowitz, Merle J. "Hugo Münsterberg: A Study in the History of Applied Psychology." *American Psychologist* 32, no. 10 (October 1977): 824–42.

Munby, Jonathan. *Public Enemies, Public Heroes: Screening the Gangster from Little Caesar to Touch of Evil* (Chicago: University of Chicago Press, 1999).

Münsterberg, Hugo. *The Photoplay: A Psychological Study* (1916). In *Hugo Munsterberg on Film: The Photoplay: A Psychological Study and Other Writings,* edited by Allan Langdale (New York: Routledge, 2002).

——. *Psychology and Industrial Efficiency* (Boston: Houghton Mifflin, 1913).

Muscio, Giuliana. *Hollywood's New Deal* (Philadelphia: Temple University Press, 1997).

Musser, Charles. "Conversions and Convergences: Sarah Bernhardt in the Era of Technological Reproducibility." *Film History* 25, nos. 1–2 (2013): 154–74.

——. *The Emergence of Cinema: The American Screen to 1907* (New York: Scribner's, 1990).

Nearing, Scott, and Joseph Freeman. *Dollar Diplomacy: A Study in American Imperialism* (New York: Allen and Unwin, 1925).

Nelson, Joyce. *The Colonized Eye: Rethinking the Grierson Legend* (Toronto: Between the Lines, 1988).

Ngai, Mae M. *Impossible Subjects: Illegal Aliens and the Making of Modern America* (Princeton, NJ: Princeton University Press, 2004).

Nicholas, Siân. "The Construction of a National Identity: Stanley Baldwin, 'Englishness' and the Mass Media in Inter-War Britain." In Francis and Zweiniger-Bargielowska, *Conservatives and British Society*, 127–46.

Nielsen, Michael. "Towards a Workers' History of the US Film Industry." In Alvarado and Thompson, *Media Reader*, 166–80.

Noble, David. *America by Design: Science, Technology, and the Rise of Corporate Capitalism* (Oxford: Oxford University Press, 1977).

North, C. J. "Our Foreign Trade in Motion Pictures." *Annals of the American Academy of Political and Social Science* 128 (November 1926): 100–108.

Norwood, Stephen. "Ford's Brass Knuckles: Harry Bennett, the Cult of Muscularity, and Anti-labor Terror, 1920–1945." *Labor History* 37, no. 3 (1996): 365–91.

Notcutt, L. A., and G. C. Latham. *The African and the Cinema: An Account of the Bantu Educational Kinema Experiment during the Period March 1935 to May 1937* (London: Edinburgh House Press, 1937).

Novak, William J. "The Legal Origins of the Modern American State." In Sarat, Garth, and Kagan, *Looking Back at Law's Century*, 249–83.

———. "Legal Transformation of Citizenship in Nineteenth-Century America." In Jacobs, Novak, and Zelizer, *Democratic Experiment*, 85–119.

———. *The People's Welfare: Law and Regulation in Nineteenth-Century America* (Chapel Hill: University of North Carolina Press, 1996).

———. "Police Power and the Hidden Transformation of the American State." In Dubber and Valverde, *Police and the Liberal State*, 54–73.

Nye, David. *American Technological Sublime* (Cambridge, MA: MIT Press, 1994).

———. *Electrifying America: Social Meanings of a New Technology* (Cambridge, MA: MIT Press, 1997).

———. *Image Worlds: Corporate Identities at General Electric* (Cambridge, MA: Harvard University Press, 1985).

Nye, Russell. *The Origins of Crowd Psychology: Gustave Le Bon and the Crisis of Mass Democracy in the Third Republic* (London: Sage, 1975).

Obermayer, Bastian, and Frederik Obermaier. *The Panama Papers: Breaking the Story of How the Rich & Powerful Hide Their Money* (London: Oneworld, 2017).

Odum, Howard W. *American Sociology: The Story of Sociology in the United States through 1950* (New York: Longmans, Green, 1951).

Ohmann, Richard. *Selling Culture: Magazines, Markets, and Class at the Turn of the Century* (London: Verso, 1996).

Oleson, Alexandra, and John Voss, eds. *The Organization of Knowledge in Modern America, 1860–1920* (Baltimore: John Hopkins University Press, 1979).

Olmstead, Alan L., and Paul W. Rhode. *Creating Abundance: Biological Innovation and American Agricultural Development* (Cambridge: Cambridge University Press, 2008).

Orgeron, Devon, Marsha Orgeron, and Dan Streible. "A History of Learning with the Lights Off." In Orgeron, Orgeron, and Streible, *Learning with the Lights Off*, 15–66.

———, eds. *Learning with the Lights Off: Educational Film in the United States* (Oxford: Oxford University Press, 2012).

Ostherr, Kirsten. *Cinematic Prophylaxis: Globalization and Contagion in the Discourse of World Health* (Durham, NC: Duke University Press, 2005).

Otter, Chris. "Making Liberal Objects: British Techno-social Relations 1800–1900." *Cultural Studies* 21, no. 4–5 (July/September 2007): 570–90.

Ott, Julia Cathleen. *When Wall Street Met Main Street: The Quest for an Investors' Democracy* (Cambridge, MA: Harvard University Press, 2011).

———. "When Wall Street Met Main Street: The Quest for an Investors' Democracy and the Emergence of the Retail Investor in the United States, 1890–1930." *Enterprise and Society* 9, no. 4 (December 2008): 619–30.

Ouellette, Laurie, and James Hay. *Better Living through Reality TV: Television and Post-welfare Citizenship* (London: Blackwell, 2008).

Paarlberg, Robert, and Dan Paarlberg. "Agricultural Policy in the Twentieth Century." *Agricultural History* 74, no. 2 (Spring 2000): 136–61.

Pak, Susie. *Gentlemen Bankers: The World of J. P. Morgan* (Cambridge, MA: Harvard University Press, 2013).

Palmer, Allen. "Cecil B. DeMille Writes America's History for the 1939 World's Fair." *Film History* 5, no. 1 (March 1993): 36–48.

Park, Robert. *The Crowd and the Public and Other Essays.* Edited by Henry Elsner Jr. Translated by Charlotte Elsner (Chicago: University of Chicago Press, 1972). First published 1904 as *Masse und Publikum.*

Park, Robert E., and Ernest W. Burgess, *Introduction to the Science of Sociology* (Chicago: University of Chicago Press, 1969). First published 1921.

Parks, Lisa. *Cultures in Orbit: Satellites and the Televisual* (Durham, NC: Duke University Press, 2005).

Pauly, Louis W. "The League of Nations and the Foreshadowing of the International Monetary Fund." *Princeton Essays in International Finance* 201 (December 1996): 1–52.

Pearson, Roberta. "A White Man's Country: Yale's *Chronicles of America.*" In *Memory and Popular Film,* edited by Paul Grainge, 23–41 (Manchester, UK: Manchester University Press, 2003).

Pedersen, Susan. "Back to the League of Nations." *American Historical Review,* October 2007: 1091–1117.

Perkins, Edwin J. *Wall Street to Main Street: Charles Merrill and Middle-Class Investors* (Cambridge: Cambridge University Press, 2006).

Peters, Charles C. *Motion Pictures and Standards of Morality* (New York: Macmillan, 1933).

Petersen, H. C. *Propaganda for War: The Campaign against American Neutrality, 1914–1917* (Norman: University of Oklahoma Press, 1939).

Peters, John Durham. "Democracy and American Mass Communication Theory: Dewey, Lippmann, Lazarsfeld." *Communication* 11, no. 3 (1989): 199–220.

———. "Satan and Savior: Mass Communication in Progressive Thought." *Critical Studies in Mass Communication* 6, no. 3 (1989): 247–63.

Peterson, Ruth C., and L. L. Thurstone. *Motion Pictures and the Social Attitudes of Children* (New York: Macmillan, 1933).

Peters, Scott J. "'Every Farmer Should be Awakened': Liberty Hyde Bailey's Vision of Agricultural Extension Work." *Agricultural History* 80 no. 2 (Spring 2006): 190–219.

Philips, Gordon Ashton. *The General Strike: The Politics of Industrial Conflict* (London: Weidenfeld and Nicolson, 1976).

Photoplay Research Society of Los Angeles. *Opportunities in the Motion Picture Industry: And How to Qualify for Positions in Its Many Branches* (New York: Arno Press, 1970). First published 1922.

Picketty, Thomas. *Capital in the Twenty-First Century* (Cambridge, MA: Harvard University Press, 2014).

Pierce, Frederick. *Our Unconscious Mind and How to Use It* (New York: E. P. Dutton, 1922).

Plotke, David. *Building a Democratic Political Order: Reshaping American Liberalism in the 1930s and 1940s* (Cambridge: Cambridge University Press, 1996).

Pokorny, Michael, and John Sedgwick. "Warner Bros. in the Inter-war Years: Strategic Responses to the Risk Environment of Filmmaking." In Sedgwick and Pokorny, *An Economic History of Film,* 151–85.

Polanyi, Karl. *The Great Transformation: The Political and Economic Origins of Our Times* (Boston: Beacon Press, 1957).

Pollock, Norman. *The Humane Economy: Populism, Capitalism, and Democracy* (New Brunswick, NJ: Rutgers University Press, 1990).

Poovey, Mary. *A History of the Modern Fact: Problems of Knowledge in the Sciences of Wealth and Society* (Chicago: University of Chicago Press, 1998).

Popp, Richard. "Machine-Age Communication: Media, Transportation, and Contact in the Interwar United States." *Technology and Culture* 52 (July 2011): 459–84.

Postel, Charles. *The Populist Vision* (Oxford: Oxford University Press, 2007).

Potter, Claire. *War on Crime: Bandits, G-Men, and the Politics of Mass Culture* (New Brunswick, NJ: Rutgers University Press, 1998).

Potter, Simon. *Broadcasting Empire: The BBC and the British World, 1922–1970* (Oxford: Oxford University Press, 2012).

Prakash, Gyan. *Another Reason: Science and the Imagination of Modern India* (Princeton, NJ: Princeton University Press, 1999).

Prelinger, Rick. "Eccentricity, Education and the Evolution of Corporate Speech: Jam Handy and His Organization." In Hediger and Vonderau, *Films That Work*, 211–20.

———. "Smoothing the Contours of Didacticism: Jam Handy and His Organization." In Orgeron, Orgeron, and Streible, *Learning with the Lights Off*, 338–55.

Pronay, Nicholas. "The Political Censorship of Films in Britain Between the Wars." In Pronay and Spring, *Propaganda, Politics and Film*, 98–125.

Pronay, Nicholas, and D. W. Spring, eds. *Propaganda, Politics and Film, 1918–1945* (London: Macmillan, 1982).

Puttnam, David. *Movies and Money*. With Neil Watson (New York: Alfred A. Knopf, 1998).

Rabban, David. *Free Speech in Its Forgotten Years* (Cambridge: Cambridge University Press, 1997).

Rabinovitz, Paula. *They Must Be Represented: The Politics of Documentary* (London: Verso, 1994).

Ramsaye, Terry. *A Million and One Nights: A History of the Motion Picture* (New York: Simon and Schuster, 1926).

Ramsden, J. A. "Baldwin and Film." In Pronay and Spring, *Propaganda, Politics and Film*, 126–43.

Rasmussen, Wayne D. *Readings in the History of American Agriculture* (Urbana: University of Illinois Press, 1960).

Raushenbush, Carl. *Fordism* (New York: League for Industrial Democracy, 1937).

Reese, William J. *History, Education, and the Schools* (London: Palgrave, 2007).

———. "The Origins of Progressive Education." *History of Education Quarterly* 41, no. 1 (Spring 2001): 1–24.

Reich, Leonard S. *The Making of American Industrial Research: Science and Business at GE and Bell, 1876–1926* (Cambridge: Cambridge University Press, 1985).

Renshaw, Samuel, Vernon L. Miller, and Dorothy Marquis. *Children's Sleep* (New York: Macmillan 1933).

Reynolds, Glenn. "The Bantu Educational Kinema Experiment and the Struggle for Hegemony in British East and Central Africa, 1935–1937." *Historical Journal of Film, Radio and Television* 29, no. 1 (March 2009): 57–78.

———. "Image and Empire: Anglo-American Cinematic Interventions in Sub-Saharan Africa, 1921–1937." *South African Historical Journal* 48 (May 2003): 90–108.

Rice, Tom. "Exhibiting Africa: British Instructional Films and the Empire Series (1925–1928)." In Grieveson and MacCabe, *Empire and Film*, 115–34.

———. "War in Peace: The American Legion and the Continuing Service of Film." In Wasson and Grieveson, *Cinema's Military Industrial Complex.*

———. *White Robes, Silver Screens: Movies and the Making of the Ku Klux Klan* (Bloomington: Indiana University Press, 2016).

Richards, Jeffrey. "Patriotism with Profit: British Imperial Cinema in the 1930s." In *British Cinema History,* edited by James Curran and Vincent Porter (London: Weidenfeld and Nicholson, 1983), 245–56.

Rodgers, Daniel. *Atlantic Crossings: Social Politics in a Progressive Age* (Cambridge, MA: Harvard University Press, 1998).

Rodney, W. "The Colonial Economy." In *General History of Africa,* edited by A. Adu Boahen, 332–50. Vol. 7, *Africa under Colonial Domination 1880–1935* (Paris: UNESCO, 1990).

Roediger, David. *Working toward Whiteness: How America's Immigrants Became White* (New York: Basic Books, 2005).

Rooth, Tim. *British Protectionism and the International Economy: Overseas Commercial Policy in the 1930s* (Cambridge: Cambridge University Press, 1992).

Rosenberg, Emily S. "Economic Interest and United States Foreign Policy." In *American Foreign Relations Reconsidered, 1890–1993,* edited by Gordon Martel (London: Routledge, 1994).

———. *Financial Missionaries to the World: The Politics and Culture of Dollar Diplomacy, 1900–1930* (Cambridge, MA: Harvard University Press, 1999).

———. *Spreading the American Dream: American Economic and Cultural Expansion, 1890–1945* (New York: Hill and Wang, 1982).

———. "War and the Health of the State: The U.S. Government and the Communications Revolution during World War I." In *Selling War in a Media Age: The Presidency and Public Opinion in the American Century,* edited by Kenneth Osgood and Andrew K. Frank (Gainesville: University Press of Florida, 2010).

Rose, Nikolas. "Expertise and the Government of Conduct." *Studies in Law, Politics and Society* 14 (1994): 359–97.

———. *The Psychological Complex: Psychology, Politics, and Society, 1869–1939* (London: Routledge and Kegan Paul, 1986).

Rosen, Philip. *Change Mummified: Cinema, Historicity, Theory* (Minneapolis: University of Minnesota Press, 2001).

Ross, Dorothy. "The Development of the Social Sciences." In Oleson and Voss, *Organization of Knowledge,* 107–38.

———. *The Origins of American Social Science* (Cambridge: Cambridge University Press, 1991).

Ross, Edward A. "The Nature and Scope of Social Psychology." *American Journal of Sociology* 18, no. 5 (March 1908): 577–83.

———. *Social Control: A Survey of the Foundations of Order* (New York: Macmillan, 1901).

———. *Social Psychology* (New York: Macmillan, 1908).

Ross, Steven J. *Hollywood Left and Right: How Movie Stars Shaped American Politics* (New York: Oxford University Press, 2011).

———. *Working-Class Hollywood: Silent Film and the Shaping of Class in America* (Princeton, NJ: Princeton University Press, 1998).

Rousseau, Jean-Jacques. *Emile: Or, On Education.* Translated by Allan Bloom (New York: Basic Books, 1979). First published 1762.

Ruckmick, Christian A. "How Do Motion Pictures Affect the Attitudes and Emotions of Children? The Galvanic Technique Applied to the Motion Picture Situation." *Journal of Educational Sociology* 6, no. 4 (December 1932): 210–19.

Rydell, Robert W. *All the World's a Fair: Visions of Empire at American International Expositions, 1876–1916* (Chicago: University of Chicago Press, 1984).

Saettler, Paul. *The Evolution of American Educational Technology* (Englewood, NJ: Libraries Unlimited, 1990).

Salazkina, Masha. "Moscow-Rome-Havana: A Film-Theory Road Map." *October* 139 (Winter 2012): 97–116.

Saldin, Robert P. *War, the American State, and Politics since 1898* (Cambridge: Cambridge University Press, 2011).

Salvatore, Ricardo D. "Early American Visions of a Hemispheric Market in South America." In *Trans-national America: The Fading of Borders in the Western Hemisphere,* edited by Berndt Ostendorf, 45–64 (Heidelberg: C. Winter, 2002).

———. "Imperial Mechanics: South America's Hemispheric Integration in the Machine Age." *American Quarterly* 58, no. 3 (September 2006): 663–91.

Sanders, Elisabeth. *Roots of Reform: Farmers, Workers, and the American State, 1877–1917* (Chicago: University of Chicago Press, 1999).

Sanogo, Aboubakar. "Colonialism, Visuality and the Cinema: Revisiting the Bantu Educational Kinema Experiment." In Grieveson and MacCabe, *Empire and Film,* 227–46.

Sarat, Austin, Bryant Garth, and Robert A. Kagan, eds. *Looking Back at Law's Century* (Ithaca, NY: Cornell University Press, 2002).

Sarbin, Theodore R. "Attempts to Understand Hypnotic Phenomena." In *Psychology in the Making: Histories of Selected Research Problems,* edited by Leo Postman (New York: Alfred A. Knopf, 1964).

Saunders, Frances Stonor. *Who Paid the Piper? The CIA and the Cultural Cold War* (London: Granta, 1999).

Savage, Kirk. "The Self Made Monument: George Washington and the Fight to Erect a National Memorial." In *Critical Issues in Public Art: Content, Context, and Controversy,* edited by Harriet F. Senie and Sally Webster, 5–32 (Washington, DC: Smithsonian Institution Press, 1992).

Savage, Sean. "The Eye Beholds: Silent Era Industrial Film and the Bureau of Commercial Economics." MA thesis, New York University, 2007.

———. "Unravelling the *Madison News Reel:* An Unlikely Convergence of Collage, Industrial, and Local Film." *Moving Image* 8, no. 2 (Fall 2008): 61–77.

Sbardellati, John. *J. Edgar Hoover Goes to the Movies: The FBI and the Origins of Hollywood's Cold War* (Ithaca, NY: Cornell University Press, 2012).

Scannell, Paddy, and David Cardiff. *A Social History of British Broadcasting.* Vol. 1, *1922–1939* (London: Basil Blackwell, 1991).

Schaefer, Eric. *Bold! Daring! Shocking! True! A History of Exploitation Films, 1919–1959* (Durham, NC: Duke University Press, 1999).

Schivelbusch, Wolfgang. *Three New Deals: Reflections on Roosevelt's America, Mussolini's Italy, and Hitler's Germany, 1933–1939* (New York: Picador, 2006).

Schoonover, Thomas D. *Uncle Sam's War of 1898 and the Origins of Globalization* (Lexington: University Press of Kentucky, 2013).

———. *The United States in Central America, 1860–1911: Episodes of Social Imperialism and Imperial Rivalry in the World System* (Durham, NC: Duke University Press, 1991).

Schulman, Bruce J. "Governing Nature, Nurturing Government: Resource Management and the Development of the American State, 1900–1912." *Journal of Policy History* 17, no. 4 (2005): 375–403.

Schwoch, James. *Global TV: New Media and the Cold War, 1946–69* (Chicago: University of Illinois Press, 2009).

Scott, David. *Refashioning Futures* (Princeton, NJ: Princeton University Press, 1999).

Scott, James C. *Seeing Like a State: How Certain Schemes to Improve the Human Condition Have Failed* (New Haven, CT: Yale University Press, 1998).

Scott, Roy V. *The Reluctant Farmer: The Rise of Agricultural Extension to 1914* (Urbana: University of Illinois Press, 1970).

Seabury, William. *Motion Picture Problems: The Cinema and the League of Nations* (New York: Avondale Press, 1929).

———. *The Public and the Motion Picture Industry* (New York: Macmillan, 1926).

Sedgwick, John, and Michael Pokorny, eds. *An Economic History of Film* (London: Routledge, 2005).

Seely, Bruce E. *Building the American Highway System: Engineers as Policy Makers* (Philadelphia: Temple University Press, 1987).

Segal, Howard P. *Recasting the Machine Age: Henry Ford's Village Industries* (Amherst: University of Massachusetts Press, 2005).

———. *Technological Utopianism in American Culture* (Chicago: University of Chicago Press, 1985).

Seiler, Cotton. *Republic of Drivers: A Cultural History of Automobility in America* (Chicago: University of Chicago Press, 2008).

Seldon, Anthony, and Stuart Ball, eds. *Conservative Century: The Conservative Party since 1900* (Oxford: Oxford University Press, 1994).

Self, Robert. "Treasury Control and the Empire Marketing Board: The Rise and Fall of Nontariff Preference in Britain, 1924–1933." *Twentieth Century British History* 5, no. 2 (1994): 153–82.

Semenov, Lillian Wurtzel, and Carla Winter, eds. *William Fox, Sol. M. Wurtzel, and the Early Fox Film Corporation* (Jefferson, NC: McFarland, 2001).

Semmel, Bernard. *The Liberal Ideal and the Demons of Empire: Theories of Imperialism from Adam Smith to Lenin* (Baltimore: John Hopkins University Press, 1993).

Sen, Amartya. "Uses and Abuses of Adam Smith." *History of Political Economy* 43, no. 2 (2011): 257–71.

Sharrett, Christopher. "9/11, the Useful Incident, and the Legacy of the Creel Committee." *Cinema Journal* 43, no. 4 (Summer 2004): 125–31.

Shideler, James H. *Farm Crisis, 1919–1923* (Berkeley: University of California Press, 1957).

Short, William H. *A Generation of Motion Pictures, 1927* (New York: Garland, 1978).

Shuttleworth, Frank K., and Mark A. May. *The Social Conduct and Attitudes of Movie Fans* (New York: Macmillan, 1933).

Sidis, Boris. *The Psychology of Suggestion: A Research into the Subconscious Nature of Man and Society* (New York: Appleton, 1898).

Sighele, Scipio. *Le Crime à Deux* (Lyon: A. Deux, 1893).

Simmon, Scott. "*An American in the Making:* About the Film." In *Treasures III: Americans in the Making* (San Francisco: National Film Preservation Foundation, 2007).

Sinclair, Upton. *The Flivver King* (Detroit: United Automobile Workers of America, 1937).

———. *Upton Sinclair Presents William Fox* (New York: Arno Press, 1970). First published 1933.

Sinha, Babli. "'Lowering Our Prestige': American Cinema, Mass Consumerism, and Racial Anxiety in Colonial India." *Comparative Studies of South Asia, Africa and the Middle East* 29, no. 2 (2009): 291–305.

Sklar, Martin J. *The Corporate Reconstruction of American Capitalism, 1890–1916: The Market, the Law, and Politics* (Cambridge: Cambridge University Press, 1988).

———. *The United States as a Developing Country: Studies in U.S. History in the Progressive Era and the 1920s* (Cambridge: Cambridge University Press, 1992).

Sklar, Robert. *Movie-Made America: A Cultural History of American Movies* (New York: Vintage Books, 1994).

Skocpol, Theda. "Political Response to Capitalist Crisis: Neo-Marxist Theories of the State and the Case of the New Deal." In Dubofsky, *New Deal*, 238–84.

Slide, Anthony. *Before Video: A History of Non-theatrical Film* (New York: Greenwood Press, 1992).

Smith, Adam. *The Theory of Moral Sentiments*. Edited by Knud Haakonssen (Cambridge: Cambridge University Press, 2002). First published 1759.

———. *The Wealth of Nations* (New York: Barnes and Noble, 2004). First published 1776.

Smith, Jason Scott. *Building New Deal Liberalism: The Political Economy of Public Works, 1933–1956* (Cambridge: Cambridge University Press, 2006).

———. "The New Deal Order." *Enterprise and Society* 9, no. 3 (September 2008): 521–34.

Smith, Neil. *The Endgame of Globalization* (London: Routledge, 2005).

Smith, Sally Bedell. *In All His Glory* (New York: Simon and Schuster, 1990).

Smulyan, Susan. *Selling Radio: The Commercialization of American Broadcasting, 1920–1934* (Washington, DC: Smithsonian Institution Press, 1994).

Smyth, Rosaleen. "The Development of British Colonial Film Policy, 1927–1939 with Special Reference to East and Central Africa. *Journal of African History* 20, no. 3 (1979): 437–50.

Snyder, Robert. *Pare Lorentz and the Documentary Film* (Reno: University of Nevada Press, 1994).

Sobel, Robert. *RCA* (New York: Stein and Day, 1986).

Solanas, Fernando, and Octavio Getino. "Towards a Third Cinema: Notes and Experiences for the Development of Cinema of Liberation in the Third World." In *New Latin American Cinema*, edited by Michael T. Martin. Vol. 1, *Theory, Practices and Transcontinental Articulations* (Detroit: Wayne State University Press, 1997).

Spencer, David R. *The Yellow Journalism: The Press and America's Emergence as a World Power* (Chicago: Northwestern University Press, 2007).

Spring, Joel. *Education and the Rise of the Corporate State* (Boston: Beacon, 1972).

Sproule, J. Michael. *Propaganda and Democracy: The American Experience of Media and Mass Persuasion* (Cambridge: Cambridge University Press, 1997).

Stamp, Shelley, and Charlie Keil, eds. *American Cinema's Transitional Era: Audiences, Institutions, Practices* (Berkeley: University of California Press, 2004).

Stannage, Ton. *The Victorian Internet: The Remarkable Story of the Telegraph and the Nineteenth Century's Online Pioneers* (London: Bloomsbury, 1998).

Starr, Paul. *The Creation of the Media: Political Origins of Modern Communications* (New York: Basic Books, 2004).

Steele, Richard W. *Propaganda in an Open Society: The Roosevelt Administration and the Media, 1933–1941* (Westport, CT: Greenwood Press, 1985).

Steel, Ronald. *Walter Lippmann and the American Century* (Boston: Little, Brown and Company, 1980).

Steigerwalt, Albert K. *The National Association of Manufactures 1895–1914* (Ann Arbor: University of Michigan, 1964).

Steil, Benn. *The Battle of Bretton Woods: John Maynard Keynes, Harry Dexter White, and the Making of a New World Order* (Princeton, NJ: Princeton University Press, 2013).

Steiner, Zara. *The Lights That Failed: European International History, 1919–1933* (Oxford: Oxford University Press, 2005).

Sterling, David. "In Defense of Debs: The Lawyers and the Espionage Act Case." *Indiana Magazine of History* 83, no. 1 (March 1987): 17–42.

St. John, Burton III, and Robert Arnett. "The National Association of Manufacturers' Community Relations Short Film *Your Town*: Parable, Propaganda, and Big Individualism." *Journal of Public Relations Research* 26, no. 2 (2014): 103–16.

St. John, Burton III, and Margot Opdycke Lamme. "The Evolution of an Idea: Charting the Early Public Relations Ideology of Edward L. Bernays." *Journal of Communication Management* 15, no. 3 (2011): 223–35.

Stockwell, Sarah, ed. *The British Empire: Themes and Perspectives* (London: Blackwell, 2008).

Stoler, Ann Laura. *Race and the Education of Desire: Foucault's History of Sexuality and the Colonial Order of Things* (Durham, NC: Duke University Press, 1995).

Stollery, Martin. *Alternative Empires: European Modernist Cinemas and the Cultures of Imperialism* (Exeter, UK: University of Exeter Press, 2000).

Strasser, Susan, Charles McGovern, and Matthias Judt, eds. *Getting and Spending: European and American Consumer Societies in the Twentieth Century* (Cambridge: Cambridge University Press, 1998).

Streeter, Thomas. *Selling the Air: A Critique of the Politics of Commercial Broadcasting in the United States* (Chicago: University of Chicago Press, 1993).

Strom, Claire. "Texas Fever and the Dispossession of the Southern Yeoman Farmer." *Journal of Southern History* 66, no. 1 (Feb. 2000): 49–74.

Strother, French. "The Panama-Pacific International Exposition." *World's Work* 30, no. 3 (July 1915): 350–59.

Susman, Warren. *Culture as History: The Transformation of American Society in the Twentieth Century* (New York: Pantheon, 1984).

Swann, Paul. *The British Documentary Film Movement, 1926–1946* (Cambridge: Cambridge University Press, 1989.)

Tagg, John. *The Disciplinary Frame: Photographic Truths and the Capture of Meaning* (Minneapolis: University of Minnesota Press, 2009).

Tallents, Stephen. "The Birth of British Documentary." Parts 1 and 2. *Journal of the University Film Association* 20, no. 1 (1968): 1:15–21; Part 2, 20, no. 2 (1968): 2:27–32.

———. *The Projection of England*, 1932 (London: Olen Press, 1955).

Tarde, Gabriel. *The Laws of Imitation.* Translated by Elsie Clews Parsons (New York: Holt, 1903).

Taylor, Frederick Winslow. *The Principles of Scientific Management* (Norcross, GA: Engineering and Management, 1998). First published 1911.

Taylor, Philip M., "British Official Attitudes towards Propaganda Abroad, 1918–1939." In Pronay and Spring, *Propaganda, Politics and Film*, 23–49 .

———. *British Propaganda in the 20ᵗʰ Century: Selling Democracy* (Edinburgh: Edinburgh University Press, 1999).

Tedlow, Richard S. "The National Association of Manufacturers and Public Relations during the New Deal." *Business History Review* 50, no. 1 (Spring 1976): 25–45.

———. *New and Improved: The Story of Mass Marketing in America* (New York: Basic Books, 1990).

Thompson, E. P. *The Making of the English Working Class* (Harmondsworth, UK: Penguin, 1963).

Thompson, Kristin. *Exporting Entertainment: America in the World Film Market, 1907–1934* (London: British Film Institute, 1985).

Thompson, Kristin, and David Bordwell, *Film History: An Introduction* (New York: McGraw-Hill, 1994).

Thorpe, Rebecca U. *The American Warfare State: The Domestic Politics of Military Spending* (Chicago: University of Chicago Press, 2014).

Thrasher, Frederick. *The Gang: A Study of 1,313 Gangs in Chicago* (Chicago: University of Chicago Press, 1927).

Thurlow, Richard. *The Secret State: British Internal Security in the Twentieth Century* (Oxford: Blackwell, 1994).

Tobey, Roland C. *Technology as Freedom: The New Deal and the Electrical Modernization of the American Home* (Berkeley: University of California Press, 1996).

Tomlins, Christopher L. *Law, Labor, and Ideology in the Early American Republic* (Cambridge: Cambridge University Press, 1993).

———. "The Supreme Sovereignty of the State: A Genealogy of Police in American Constitutional Law, from the Founding Era to Lochner." In Dubber and Valverde, *Police and the Liberal State*, 33–53.

Tomlinson, B. R. "Imperialism and After: The Economy of the Empire on the Periphery." In Brown and Louis, *The Oxford History of the British Empire*, 357–78.

Tone, Andrea. *The Business of Benevolence* (Ithaca, NY: Cornell University Press, 1997).

Trachtenberg, Alan. "The FSA File: From Image to Story." In Trachtenberg, *Lincoln's Smile*, 265–98.

———. *Lincoln's Smile and Other Enigmas* (New York: Hill and Wang, 2007).

Trotter, David. "Representing Connection: A Multimedia Approach to Colonial Film, 1918–1939." In Grieveson and MacCabe, *Empire and Film*, 151–66.

Trotter, Wilfred. *Instincts of the Herd in Peace and War* (London: T. Fisher Unwin, 1916).

Trumpbour, John. *Selling Hollywood to the World: U.S. and European Struggles for Mastery of the Global Film Industry, 1920–1950* (Cambridge: Cambridge University Press, 2002).

Turner, George Kibbe. "Manufacturing Public Opinion: The New Art of Making Presidents by Press Bureau." *McClure's Magazine* 39 (July 1912).

Turner, Ralph H., ed. *Robert E. Park on Social Control and Collective Behavior* (Chicago: University of Chicago Press, 1967).

Turow, Joseph. *The Daily You: How the New Advertising Industry Is Defining Your Identity and Your Worth* (New Haven, CT: Yale University Press, 2012).

Tye, Larry. *The Father of Spin: Edward L. Bernays and the Birth of Public Relations* (New York: Henry Holt and Company, 1998).

Tyrrell, Ian. *Historians in Public: The Practice of American History, 1890–1970* (Chicago: University of Chicago Press, 2005).

———. *Transnational Nation: United States History in Global Perspective since 1789* (London: Palgrave Macmillan, 2007).

Uricchio, William, and Roberta Pearson. *Reframing Culture: The Case of the Vitagraph Quality Films* (Princeton, NJ: Princeton University Press, 1993).

US Department of Agriculture. *Motion Pictures of the United States Department of Agriculture* (Washington, DC: Government Printing Office, 1923).

———. *Motion Pictures of the United States Department of Agriculture* (Washington, DC: Government Printing Office, 1935).

———. *Motion Pictures of the US Department of Agriculture: A List of Films and Their Uses* (Washington, DC: USDA Division of Publications, 1922).

US Department of the Interior. *Visual Education Departments in Educational Institutions* (Washington, DC: Government Printing Office, 1924)

Vasey, Ruth. *The World According to Hollywood, 1918–1939* (Madison: University of Wisconsin Press, 1997).

Vaughn, Stephen. *Holding Fast the Inner Lines: Democracy, Nationalism, and the Committee on Public information* (Chapel Hill: University of North Carolina Press, 1980).

Veeser, Cyrus. *A World Safe for Capitalism: Dollar Diplomacy and America's Rise to Global Power* (New York: Columbia University Press, 2002).

Veysey, Lawrence. *The Emergence of the American University* (Chicago: University of Chicago Press, 1970).

Wagner, Phil. "'A Particularly Effective Argument': *Land of Liberty* (1939) and the Hollywood Image (Crisis)." *Film and History* 41, no. 1 (Spring 2011): 7–25.

Walker, S. H., and Paul Sklar. "Business Finds Its Voice. Part II: Motion Pictures and Combined Efforts." *Harpers Monthly Magazine*, December 1, 1937.

Wallace, Michael. "Visiting the Past: History Museums in the United States." In Benson, Brier, and Rosenzweig, *Presenting the Past*, 137–61.

Wallas, Graham. *Human Natures in Politics* (London: Macmillan, 1908).

Waller, Gregory. "Nontheatrical Theaters: The Panama-Pacific International Exposition (1915)." Paper Presented at the Society for Cinema and Media Studies Conference, Boston, 2012.

Wallerstein, Immanuel. *The Capitalist World Economy* (Cambridge: Cambridge University Press, 1979).

———. "The Construction of Peoplehood: Racism, Nationalism, Ethnicity." In Balibar and Wallerstein, *Race, Nation, Class*, 71–85.

———. *Geopolitics and Geoculture: Essays on the Changing World-System* (Cambridge: Cambridge University Press, 1991).

———. *The Modern World System IV: Centrist Liberalism Triumphant, 1789–1914* (Berkeley: University of California Press, 2011).

———. *The Politics of the World Economy* (Cambridge: Cambridge University Press, 1984).

———. *World-Systems Analysis: An Introduction* (Durham, NC: Duke University Press, 2004).

Wamsley, James S. *American Ingenuity: Henry Ford Museum and Greenfield Village* (New York: Harry N. Abrams, 1985).

Washbrook, David. "South Asia, the World System, and World Capitalism." *Journal of Asian Studies* 49, no. 3 (August 1990): 479–508.

Wasko, Janet. *How Hollywood Works* (London: Sage, 2003).

———. *Movies and Money: Financing the American Film Industry* (Norwood, NJ: Ablex, 1982).

Wasson, Haidee. *Museum Movies: The Museum of Modern Art and the Birth of Art Cinema* (Berkeley: University of California Press, 2005).

———. "The Other Small Screen: Moving Images at New York's World Fair, 1939." *Canadian Journal of Film Studies* 21, no. 1 (Spring 2012): 81–103.

———. "Suitcase Cinema." *Cinema Journal* 51, no. 2 (Winter 2012): 148–52.

Wasson, Haidee, and Lee Grieveson, eds. *Cinema's Military Industrial Complex* (Berkeley: University of California Press, 2018).

Watson, John B., and Karl S. Lashley. *Report of the United States Interdepartmental Social Hygiene Board* (Washington, DC: Government Printing Office, 1920).

———. *Report of the United States Interdepartmental Social Hygiene Board* (Washington, DC: Government Printing Office, 1921).

Watts, Steven. *The People's Tycoon: Henry Ford and the American Century* (New York: Alfred A. Knopf, 2005).

Wayne, Mike, ed. *Understanding Film: Marxist Perspectives* (London: Pluto Press, 2005).

Weber, J. J. *Comparative Effectiveness of Some Visual Aids in Seventh Grade Instruction* (Chicago: Educational Screen, 1922).

Weinberg, Julius. *Edward Alsworth Ross and the Sociology of Progressivism* (Madison: State Historical Society of Wisconsin, 1972).

Weiner, Tim. *Legacy of Ashes: The History of the CIA* (London: Penguin, 2008).

Wells, Christopher W. "Fueling the Boom: Gasoline Taxes, Invisibility, and the Growth of the American Highway Infrastructure, 1919–1956." *Journal of American History*, 99, no. 1 (June 2012): 72–81.

Wells, Wyatt. "Counterpoint to Reform: Gilbert H. Montague and the Business of Regulation." *Business History Review* 78, no. 3 (Autumn 2004): 423–50.

Welter, Rush. *Popular Education and Democratic Thought in America* (New York: Columbia University Press, 1962).

Werking, Richard Hume. "Bureaucrats, Businessmen, and Foreign Trade: The Origins of the United States Chamber of Commerce." *Business History Review* 52, no. 3 (Autumn 1978): 321–41.

Westad, Odd Arne. *The Global Cold War and the Making of Our Times* (New York: Cambridge University Press, 2005).

Whissel, Kristen. *Picturing American Modernity: Traffic, Technology, and the Silent Cinema* (Durham, NC: Duke University press, 2008).

White, Richard. *"It's Your Misfortune and None of My Own": A New History of the American West* (Norman: University of Oklahoma Press, 1991).

———. *Railroaded: The Transcontinentals and the Making of Modern America* (New York: W. W. Norton, 2011).

Wiatr, Elizabeth. "Between Word, Image, and the Machine: Visual Education and Films of Industrial Process." *Historical Journal of Film, Radio, and Television* 22, no. 3 (2002): 333–51.

Wiebe, Robert H. "The House of Morgan and the Executive, 1905–1913." *American Historical Review* 65, no. 1 (Oct. 1959), 49–60.

———. *The Search for Order, 1877–1920* (New York: Hill and Wang, 1967).

Wik, Reynold M. *Henry Ford and Grass-Roots America* (Ann Arbor: University of Michigan Press, 1973).

———. "The Radio in Rural America during the 1920s." *Agricultural History* 55 (October 1981): 339–50.

Wilford, Hugh. *The Mighty Wurlitzer: How the CIA Played America* (Cambridge, MA: Harvard University Press, 2008).

Wilke, Jürgen. "Cinematography as a Medium of Communication: The Promotion of Research by the League of Nations and the Role of Rudolph Arnheim." *European Journal of Communication* 6, no. 3 (September 1991): 337–53.

Wilkins, Mira. "Multinational Enterprise to 1930: Discontinuities and Continuities." In Chandler and Mazlish, *Leviathans,* 45–80

Williams, Karel, Colin Haslam, and John Williams. "Ford versus 'Fordism': The Beginnings of Mass Production?" *Work, Employment and Society* 6, no. 4 (December 1992): 517–55.

Williams, Linda. "Melodrama Revised." In Browne, *Refiguring American Film Genres,* 42–88.

Williamson, Philip. *National Crisis and National Government: British Politics, the Economy and Empire, 1926–1932* (Cambridge: Cambridge University Press, 1992).

———. *Stanley Baldwin: Conservative Leadership and National Values* (Cambridge: Cambridge University Press, 1999).

Williams, Raymond. *Marxism and Literature* (Oxford: Oxford University Press, 1977).

Williams, Robin M. Jr. "Sociology in America." In Bonjean, Schneider, and Lineberry, *Social Science in America,* 77–111.

Williams, William A. *The Roots of Modern American Empire: A Study of the Growth and Shaping of Social Consciousness in a Marketplace Society* (New York: Random House, 1969).

Windel, Aaron. "The Bantu Educational Kinema Experiment and the Political Economy of Community Development." In Grieveson and MacCabe, *Empire and Film,* 207–66.

Winfield, Betty Houchin. *FDR and the News Media* (New York: Columbia University Press, 1994).

Winkler, Jonathan Reed. *Nexus: Strategic Communications and American Security in World War I* (Cambridge, MA: Harvard University Press, 2008).

Winn, J. Emmett. "Documenting Racism in an Agricultural Extension Film." *Film and History* 38, no. 1 (Spring 2008): 33–43.

Wiser, Vivian. "Public Policy and USDA Science, 1897–1913." *Agricultural History* 64, no. 2 (1990): 24–30.

Woeste, Victoria Saker. "Insecure Equality: Louis Marshall, Henry Ford, and the Problem of Defamatory Antisemitism, 1920–1929." *Journal of American History* 91, no. 3 (December 2004): 877–905.

Wolfskill, George. *The Revolt of the Conservatives: A History of the American Liberty League, 1934–1940* (Boston: Houghton Mifflin, 1962).

Wood, Richard, ed. *Film and Propaganda in America: A Documentary History.* Vol. I, *World War I* (Westport, CT: Greenwood Press, 1990).

Workman, Andrew A. "Manufacturing Power: The Organizational Revival of the National Association of Manufacturers, 1941–1945." *Business History Review* 72, no. 2 (Summer 1998): 279–317.

Wurtzler, Steve J. *Electric Sounds: Technological Change and the Rise of Corporate Mass Media* (New York: Columbia University Press, 2007).

Wu, Tim. *The Master Switch: The Rise and Fall of Information Empires* (New York: Alfred A. Knopf, 2010).

Yale Chronicles of America Photoplays (New Haven: Yale University Press, c. 1925).

Zinn, Howard. *A People's History of the United States From 1492 to the Present.* 2nd ed. (London: Longman, 1996).

Zukor, Adolph. "Origin and Growth of the Industry." In J. Kennedy, *Story of the Films*, 55–76.

Zunz, Oliver. *Making America Corporate, 1870–1920* (Chicago: University of Chicago Press, 1990).

———. *Why the American Century?* (Chicago: University of Chicago Press, 1998).

Zwarich, Jennifer. "The Bureaucratic Activist: Federal Filmmakers and Social Change in the U.S. Department of Agriculture's Tick Eradication Campaign." *Moving Image* 9, no. 1 (Spring 2009): 19–53.

INDEX